BRITAIN
1995
AN OFFICIAL HANDBOOK

Prepared by the Central Office of Information
London: HMSO

© Crown Copyright 1994
Applications for reproduction should be made to HMSO
First published 1994

ISBN 0 11 701859 7

Contents

List of Illustrations

Photographs

Acknowledgments for the use of photographs appear on p. 530.

Foreword

Britain 1995 is the 46th in the series of Handbooks prepared by the Central Office of Information (COI). Drawing on a wide range of official and other authoritative sources, it provides a factual overview of Government policy and developments in Britain.

Handbook is widely recognised as an established work of reference, not only in Britain but overseas, where it is an important element of the information service provided by British diplomatic posts. It is sold by HMSO and its agents throughout the world.

New Features

The text has, of course, been fully updated and revised. There are more pages, more charts, tables and graphs, and more colour pictures.

In addition, for the first time in *Handbook*'s history, we have asked a well-known commentator on British affairs—the BBC radio journalist John Humphrys—to write an introduction giving his impressions on how Britain has changed in the fifty years since World War II. We hope this will be the first of several such 'guest' contributions.

Coverage

Every effort is made to ensure that the information given in *Handbook* is accurate at the time of going to press. The text, generally, is based on information available up to September 1994.

As far as possible, *Handbook* presents information that applies to Britain as a whole. However, this is not always possible. Care should be taken when using Handbook to note whether the information given refers to:

- Britain, formally the United Kingdom of Great Britain and Northern Ireland;
- Great Britain, which comprises England, Wales and Scotland;
- England and Wales, which are grouped together for many administrative and other purposes; or, in some instances,
- England alone.

Aspects of Britain

COI also produces the Aspects of Britain series of paperbacks, which cover in depth Britain's political, economic and social structure, and its place in the international community. Appropriate titles are given in the list of further reading at the end of most chapters. For further information please write to COI Reference Services or phone 0171 261 8310.

Acknowledgments

Britain 1995 has been compiled with the co-operation of around 250 organisations, including other government departments and agencies. The editor would like to thank all those who have contributed their comments.

Readers' Comments

We welcome readers' comments and suggestions on *Handbook*. These should be sent to:

The Editor
Britain: An Official Handbook
Reference Services
Central Office of Information
Hercules Road
London SEI 7DU

Britain: 50 Years of Change

by John Humphrys

I am writing what follows on an ICL personal computer. When I have finished and the spell-checker has automatically corrected my many typing mistakes I shall use the external modem to E-mail my copy to another computer many miles away.

If that strikes you as an odd way to begin an introduction to this, the fiftieth anniversary edition of the official *Handbook*,[1] consider what it would have meant to a reader of the first *Handbook*: nothing—it would have been utter nonsense. Personal computers did not exist and neither did any of the other amazing gadgets that are making my life as a journalist so much easier.

The history of the last fifty years coincides almost exactly with the history of the computer. Never (to misquote the man who still occupied 10 Downing Street when *Handbook's* ancestor was first published) has so much been owed by so many to something so insignificant: the tiny microchip.

Did I say 'owed'? True, journalists like me have been liberated from the tyranny of the correcting fluid. But what of the typist who used to make a living retyping my messy manuscript or the postman who delivered my completed document, or even the manufacturer of the envelope in which I sent it? The microchip means less work for all of them.

The sliver of silicon, with its unfathomable tattoo of soldered metal that gives my computer its brain power, has had a greater influence on this country in the past fifty years than all the massive steam hammers and roaring furnaces of the previous fifty. The silicon chip has proved to be the ultimate weapon of the technological revolution, just as the musket or the Gatling gun . was of earlier revolutions. It is an infinitely more powerful force than the sans-culottes in 18th-century France or the Bolsheviks in 20th-century Russia. Its influence has been all-pervasive: on industry and transport, commerce and culture. It is hard to think of a single aspect of our national life that has not been affected in one way or another by this technology.

From Coal to Gas

When *Handbook* was first published, almost half the population of Great Britain worked in the manufacturing industries. In the tip-scarred valleys of South Wales and the great coalfields of Nottinghamshire the winding gear of the deep mines turned endlessly, 24 hours a day, seven days a week, producing coal to warm homes or fuel steel mills and factories.

Now the only collieries left in the Rhondda are museums. Miners, with coal dust still in their lungs, but none under their fingernails, sell tickets to tourists and serve the heritage industry instead of the smokestack industries. In the whole of Britain today only 17 deep mines survive, compared with 850 nearly fifty years ago.

Coal was, quite simply, no longer king. Technology had stolen its throne. First, nuclear power stations began to feed electricity into the national grid. (Predictions that nuclear technology would meet all our energy needs proved wide of the mark, but it does supply a fifth.) Then the engineers and scientists turned to the computer to help them discover and evaluate vast reservoirs of oil and natural gas under the North Sea.

---

[1]Although the title *Britain Handbook* was not used until the 1949–50 edition, COI Reference Services produced books entitled *Post-War Britain* in 1946 and 1948. The first handbook, entitled *Post-War Reconstruction in Britain January 1941–November 1944* and produced by COI's predecessor, the Ministry of Information, was issued in 1945.

The effect of North Sea development on the British economy was profound: billions of pounds pumped into the national coffers in precious foreign earnings, and vast amounts saved on the national fuel bill. Many a Chancellor of the Exchequer must have offered a silent prayer of thanks to those great platforms in the North Sea as he studied the figures for the balance of payments. But if we sold most of the oil, we kept most of the gas, and that too affected our way of life. For generations, prosperity has marched hand in hand with pollution. No one living in a big British city for the past fifty years could have escaped the terrible smog produced by a million coal fires. Technology changed all that, with central heating in virtually every home and gas the most popular fuel—no more pea-soupers.[2]

UK Consumption of Fuels for Energy Use (million tonnes oil equivalent)

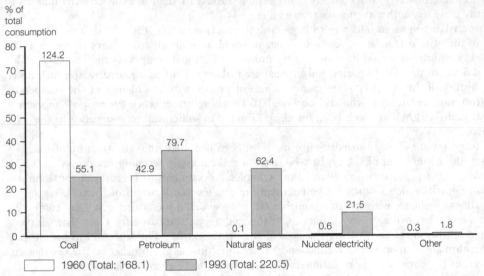

% of total consumption

1960 (Total: 168.1)   1993 (Total: 220.5)

Source: *Digest of United Kingdom Energy Statistics 1994*

But we were rapidly developing a different kind of pollution, and for that too we had technology to thank. When the war ended only the wealthy and the aspiring middle classes had motor cars. In 1952 there were just over 2 million cars on Britain's roads. By 1980 there were 14.6 million. Now there are more than 20 million. Fifty years ago Britain had no motorways. When the first short stretch of the Ml opened north of Watford in 1963, we drove miles to see it and wonder at it—oh, days of innocence! How we yearn for those relatively car-free days now as we sit on that same stretch of motorway on a Friday evening, heading north out of London at the speed of an arthritic snail.

Fifty years ago the car was associated with freedom: now Britain, like most other industrialised nations, has begun to question the great car economy and is wondering where it will all end. It has proved to be one of the enduring conundrums of the past fifty years: more and better roads have meant more and bigger traffic jams. And now we have a different, a more insidious, form of pollution that happens not on the dark days of winter when coal fires blaze, but on the hot days of July and August, when the sun reacts with car exhaust fumes. Technology saved us from one form of pollution. Towards the end of the decade we were asking whether it could save us—with catalytic converters and the like— from another.

---

[2] The popular name given to thick fogs that were common in British cities until the Clean Air Acts of 1956 and 1968.

Fifty years ago factory chimneys spewed their waste into the skies above Britain. Today there are fewer chimneys—and fewer factories. The very same microchip which revolutionised British industry created new industries in countries on the other side of the world. They ceased to be our customers and became our competitors. Many 'Third World' countries became 'developing countries' and then 'newly industrialised nations'. Exploiting the latest technology and lower labour costs in brand new factories, the Pacific Rim countries produced steel at a far more competitive price than could an established mill in Scotland. From the yards of South Korea came the great ships whose keels were once laid on the Tyne or the Clyde. The decline of the British motor cycle industry, which once built the fastest and finest machines in the world, became a metaphor for British industry, driven to extinction by the Japanese, the venerable BSA giving way to the Kawasaki.

So it was with cars. The cars that now clog our roads no longer bear proudly the names of British manufacturers: Austin of England, Morris Oxford, Hillman Minx. One after another they fell victim to international competition and either disappeared altogether or were swallowed whole. The last great British mass manufacturer, Rover Group, was sold to the German company BMW in 1994.

The effect of all this on unemployment was dramatic. During the 1950s about a third of a million people were out of work. By the end of the 1960s the figure had passed half a million; it peaked at just over 3 million in 1986.

Tourism and Toyotas

Yet it was not all gloom on the jobs front; new service and high technology manufacturing industries were beginning to replace the old smokestack industries. Britain was changing its role in the world, from that of a country which made things and sold them abroad, to one which offered more and more services. The financial sector was a prime example. The City of London, already an established financial centre, grew rapidly and contributed vast amounts to the national balance sheet. By the 1980s tourism had become the second biggest industry in Britain. Only five countries in the world earned more from tourism than Britain—imagine what we'd have done if the sun shone regularly! In 1950 service industries provided about half our gross domestic product; by 1993 that had increased to more than two-thirds. The manufacturing industries had produced more than a third; by 1993 it was less than a quarter.

But the technology which had worked against us could also work in our favour. The Japanese companies who had proved such stern competitors for our indigenous electronic and motor manufacturing industries were now beginning to assemble or build television sets and cars in Europe. Many of them came to Britain, bringing their technology with them, and discovering a workforce that was more than willing and able to exploit it. From the mining valleys of South Wales to the industrial wastelands of north-east England, the Japanese had arrived.

Crucial to this new relationship between worker and boss was the transformation in labour relations wrought during the years when Margaret Thatcher, Britain's first woman prime minister, dominated the political scene like no leader since Winston Churchill more than half a century earlier. New employment laws played their part in persuading workers and unions to adapt to more flexible working practices, but increasing unemployment and the demands of the new industries were at least as important.

In 1979 the unions were at the peak of their power—trade union membership stood at 13.3 million and in that year 29.5 million days were lost in strikes. Striking was universally known as the 'British disease'.

Now membership of trade unions has fallen to around 9 million (it is still falling) and the number of days lost to industrial action to below 700,000 a year, among the lowest in Europe. The old mistrust between the TUC and a Conservative government had given way to a working relationship that even allowed for a Conservative employment minister to address the TUC on its home turf.

Once again, technology had played a key role. The pattern of employment which existed in the 1940s and 1950s had changed beyond recognition fifty years later. During the war millions of women had left hearth and home, cast aside their patterned pinafores, donned overalls and worked to keep the wheels of industry turning. Instead of producing scones, they produced shells. Instead of waiting for their menfolk to hand over their weekly housekeeping allowance on Friday evenings, they were earning their own money. They were independent for the first time in their lives, and many of them liked it that way. When the men came home and the women were once again consigned to the kitchen, many rebelled, and they were to keep rebelling for the next fifty years. At the start of the 1950s, there were fewer than 7 million women working in Britain. By the 1990s there were more than 11 million.

For the unions, women were far more difficult to recruit and to organise than their husbands. Most of them were in part-time work. Many were perfectly happy to accept wages lower than the traditional going rate for the job because their income supplemented their husbands'. It wasn't vital to keep body and soul together, but it helped pay for a new washing machine or a fortnight in Spain or an evening out. They were, in today's jargon, 'flexible'.

Employment by Sector 1948 and 1994

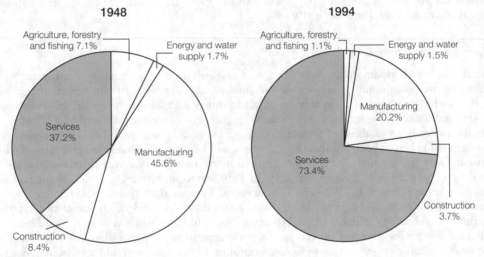

Sources: *Britain 1949-50*, Department of Employment statistics

The labour market was changing in other ways too. In the 1950s, '60s and '70s most men— certainly skilled manual workers and white collar workers—believed they had a right to a job for life. They might not expect to stay with the same company from school or university to retirement, but neither did they expect to move around very much.

The classic example was banking. Get a job with a bank, and your problems were over. You might—just possibly—move to another bank, but only if you were terribly ambitious and weren't being promoted quickly enough. You certainly didn't expect to be sacked, not unless you'd run off with the day's takings. The young lad leaving school clutching his School Certificate who was lucky enough to become a junior clerk in his local Barclays or Lloyds could reasonably expect to be an assistant manager or better when the time came for his retirement party 45 years later.

By the mid-1990s that same lad would have much more trouble landing the job in the first place (his local bank branch might well have been closed down) and if he did, he could expect to have many more retirement parties. From 1990 to 1994 the big High Street banks had, between them, reduced their workforce by a staggering 100,000. The concept of a job for life had ceased to exist.

Chips with Everything

Once again, technology was the driving force behind the change. You had only to compare a bank clerk in the 1950s with his Victorian counterpart to understand why. True, he'd have had a Parker fountain pen instead of the quill employed by Bob Cratchit,[3] but much, if not most, of his time was spent patiently adding up columns of figures and transferring them to thick, leather-bound ledgers—not really so different from Cratchit. Fifty years later, the young clerk needed to be barely more numerate than a rubber band and could almost manage without a pen. The computer did it for him. The computer also composed and calculated our statements, and if we wanted to go even further into the red made it so much easier by thrusting money at us through a hole in the wall. Then it calculated the interest we now owed and sent out the warning letters. Who needed bank clerks?

And so it was in building societies, insurance companies, social security offices and even the great departments of state. A curious thing happened to us, the customers, during all this. We had begun this new age thinking we loved computers. What fun, a calculator that did more than add up and multiply! You could play games with it and the children could learn so much so quickly. Then we might receive a bank statement informing us that we owed the bank a sum approximating to the National Debt, and a bill from the electricity board telling us that we had used enough electricity in our suburban semi during the past quarter to light the city of Birmingham for a year, and we began to have second thoughts.

In much the same way as we had discussed the weather—or food rationing after the war—we talked about how good life had been BC: Before the Computer. After a really bad experience we would blame all our ills on the blasted computer. Managers complained too. They had been promised miracles by computer salesmen. 'Install this very latest mainframe,' they were told, 'and your problems will be over.' Just like cowboys buying magical potions from snake-oil salesmen in the Wild West, they should have read the label rather more carefully. They thought they'd instantly be able to produce twice as much with half the workforce and discovered they couldn't. They needed whole new departments to handle what they'd begun to call 'information technology'.

But that period of transition was relatively short. Now we all take the computer for granted, even though some parents may curse the inventor of the games of which their children have become so fond. Oddly enough, we are prepared to stand in the rain outside banks queueing at the hole in the wall rather than wait in the dry to be served by a real human being. By and large the bills are accurate and if the statement says you owe more than you thought, you probably do. And managers *could* start reducing the workforce. The recession at the end of the 1980s, after a period of unprecedented growth, encouraged them to lose their awe of their IT departments.

That recession brought in its train another fundamental change to the pattern of employment in Britain. It was made possible because of the growing realisation that the real power of computers lay not only in their ability to make billions of calculations a second, but in their ability to store and deliver unimaginable amounts of information at the touch of a key.

What computerised robots were beginning to do to the man on the assembly line and the bank clerk, the massive data banks and the terminals which delivered instant access to their contents were poised to do to their managers. Analysts had already begun to recognise that the old rule of recession (when it's over all the jobs will return) could no longer be taken for granted. And the recession had affected jobs very differently than in earlier slumps: the middle class—middle managers—were among the victims too, not just in Britain but in most other industrialised nations. Information technology, deregulation and a much more competitive, ruthless approach by senior management took a scythe to their ranks. In 1993 the *Sunday Times* commissioned an opinion poll which discovered that more than a third of the middle-class men

---

[3] Bob Cratchit was the downtrodden clerk in Charles Dickens's *A Christmas Carol*.

questioned were worried about losing their jobs over the next 12 months. One in five middle-class families had had recent experience of unemployment.

But who exactly *were* the 'middle class' and what was happening to the whole class structure of our society? At the end of the war, it was pretty straightforward. There was a tiny upper class, a larger middle class and a huge working class. That was how the pollsters (a new breed of expert) saw it, and that was largely how we saw ourselves. A generation later, the ranks of the middle classes had swollen and accounted for a third of the nation. Today almost half of us are categorised as middle class and very, very few of us call ourselves working class—or upper class.

Every social historian has his own theory to explain this phenomenon, but you need to be neither a sociologist nor a pollster to spot some of the causes: in particular, increasing prosperity and a massive growth in higher education have led to more and more people challenging the class system in all its manifestations and refusing to accept the status quo.

Personal Disposable Income and Consumers' Expenditure 1948–92 (at 1990 prices)

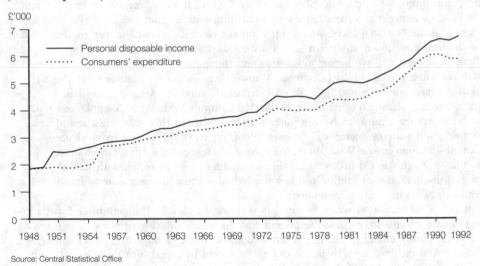

Source: Central Statistical Office

Again, technology and the revolution in communications have played their part. Rich or poor, duke or dustman, we all watch television, probably the greatest leveller any society has ever created. So let us step back 50 years—*before* every home had one—and spend a Saturday evening with a middle class family who would have considered themselves quintessential middle class.

The Good Old Days?

Mr and Mrs Green and their three children are sitting in front of the coal fire in their largeish suburban home, Mr Green sucking on a pipe, Mrs Green puffing rather more delicately on a cigarette. The smallest of their children has just finished listening to Children's Hour on their enormous wireless set with its glowing glass valves. Mrs Green is worrying about whether to let Elizabeth go to the dance at the Town Hall. Well, she is only just eighteen and the dance goes on until midnight. Perhaps it will be all right if Father promises to pick her up promptly after the last waltz. She wonders, idly, if she herself might ever learn to drive. Probably not. Well, women don't, do they? And anyway, where could she possibly find the time, what with the bridge club and the church and Father does get so cross if she's not at home when he returns from the office.

Life is so much more difficult since the maid left to go and work in the local biscuit factory. Mrs Green can't imagine why she's done it. Surely it is so much more pleasant to work as a maid in a nice middle-class family than in that noisy factory with all those rather vulgar women.

Mr Green ponders on young Charles, their elder son; he's just done well in the Matric and might yet make it to university. It would be expensive, but no real problem. After all, he has a good pension to look forward to and Elizabeth's bringing in a few pounds a week. Pays for her keep. Just as well he'd knocked on the head that nonsense of *her* going to university. Waste of a good education. She'll only go off and get married and who needs a degree for that!

A typical middle class family? Well, perhaps not. More a case of bundling several caricatures together, but it does illustrate how much things have changed in a relatively short time.

Elizabeth would surely not allow her parents to force her to give up her dream of university because she's a mere girl. In post-war Britain only a handful of students were women. Today more than half of them are and employers discriminate at their peril.

The modern Mrs Green wouldn't even dream about a maid. She might have a daily help, a nanny or an au pair, but she might equally allow her dishwasher and washing machine to take the strain—she might even be at work herself! By 1990 nine homes out of ten had a washing machine.

Nor, in all likelihood, would she expect an eighteen year-old daughter to trot home at a specified time on Saturday night. She would have lived through 1960s Britain and the so-called sexual revolution, and she wouldn't be at all surprised to discover that Elizabeth was on the pill. Nor would she be surprised by the number of single mothers, the tolerance of homosexuality or many other aspects of modern society that would have appalled the Mrs Green of the 1940s.

Would she still be going to church? Probably not. Church membership has declined steadily from the end of the war. If she did, however, she might well expect guitars and a woman priest. The Church of England is not what it was in 1950.

She would certainly drive, if only to take the youngsters to school. In the past 25 years the numbers of seven- and eight-year-olds going to school on their own has fallen from 80 per cent to 9 per cent. Parents' fear of traffic is one reason, but some may also fear something more sinister. The Green children would have played in the street or in the woods nearby without their parents giving a thought to it. Mrs Green would have walked home from church on a Sunday night through the dark streets of her suburb by herself with scarcely a backward glance. Today she would be more likely to keep the doors locked in her car and activate the burglar alarm after she'd got home.

Crime in Britain—burglaries and violent crime particularly—increased steadily throughout the latter half of the century, just as it did in the United States and every other western European country. And, as with so many other countries, a growing amount of crime is linked with drugs. If Mrs Green had talked about drugs she'd have meant aspirins.

Europe and Beyond

Fifty years ago Mr Green's attitude towards Europe might well have been 'We don't need you; we can look after ourselves. We won the war, after all.' The odds are that by the mid-80s his company would have been involved in business all over Europe.

Britain first shunned membership of the Common Market, then tried and failed to become a member and finally succeeded. By the start of the 1990s the Greens might even have described themselves as 'Europeans'. They would almost certainly have stopped taking their holidays in Bournemouth or Bognor and joined the rest of Britain in Spain or France or Italy. By the end of the 1980s the old joke headline 'Fog in Channel: Continent isolated' had lost its point. We are all Europeans now—even if we still resolutely refuse to speak any language other than our own.

Britain has been at peace for most of the past fifty years. There have been exceptions—the Suez Crisis, which finally put paid to Britain's notion of herself as one of the 'great powers', the victory in the Falklands and the Gulf War—but they have been relatively brief episodes and the general population has been largely uninvolved. The battle against the IRA has been different. British troops were sent to Northern Ireland in 1969 to defend the Catholic minority against the Protestant majority, and ended up as targets of the IRA. In the years that followed scarcely a man, women or child has been unaffected by the activities of that tiny group of terrorists. Some have had loved ones maimed or killed by indiscriminate bombs or bullets; all of us have had our lives altered to some extent by the security precautions which have flowed from the bombings, even if only by a tube train cancelled on the London Underground because of a bomb warning.

Mr Green would have been astonished at the extent to which Britain has become a multi-racial society. From 1955 to 1962 about half a million Commonwealth citizens settled in Britain. Many of them were followed by their dependants. In the early 1960s some feared that terrible social conflict would follow mass immigration. Today there are just over 3 million people of ethnic minority origin in Britain. There has been some racial tension—there still is—but popular fears were never realised.

Mr Green would, doubtless, find much else to criticise if he were still with us. He would certainly not have approved of our growing intolerance of the habit which finally killed him off: smoking. What would he make of those sad little groups who huddle outside office buildings, condemned to indulge their nicotine habit outside their 'smoke-free environment'? As a staunch disciplinarian he might deplore the fact that headmasters no longer beat their pupils as he was beaten at school—and that the birch and the hangman's rope have become museum pieces.

He would approve of the fact that Britain is still a nation of inventors, even if not every invention is as successful as the computer and the hovercraft, nor every design as enduring as the mini—the car *and* the skirt. He would disapprove of the welfare state on the basis that it encouraged layabouts to expect something for nothing, and he would have rejoiced in saying 'I told you so !' as politicians struggle to grapple with a growing social security budget. But even *he* would be forced to admit that people are vastly better off than they were in his day.

When the social scientists seek to define poverty today they do so in terms of whether a child has to share a bedroom or regularly has a holiday away from home, not whether he goes to bed on an empty stomach or has a decent pair of shoes. The definition is always being adjusted—upwards.

The National Health Service was still in its embryonic state when Mr Green was puffing on his pipe in front of his fire. It, too, is now under enormous pressures, and for much the same reason as the welfare state: growing demands on finite resources. We spend three times as much in real terms today as we did in Mr Green's day, and still there are enormous problems. But if you are going to be ill and you do not have a huge bank balance, then Britain is still the place to be.

Mr Green would proudly assert traditional values and insist that all the old traditions are being eroded. He would be wrong. The monarchy may have lost some of its mystique and mass appeal—television and a succession of unsuccessful marriages saw to that—but it endures and the majority want it to continue. Parliament still goes its eccentric way but, though politicians in opposition may argue for change, the unwritten constitution is still the envy of many a less confident democracy which has safeguards written into every clause and sub-paragraph.

Mr and Mrs Green had few doubts about their place in society or Britain's place in the world. They were, if anything, rather smug and self-satisfied. They would probably not be at ease in the Britain of fifty years later. Modern Britain is more questioning, less sure of itself. It is an infinitely more liberal society, infinitely more tolerant. People are less respectful of authority, less polite to their neighbours. But there is one characteristic the Greens would certainly have shared with the generations who succeeded them. They would have complained. A great deal. All the time. Greens past and present would almost certainly have agreed on this at least: Britain is the worst country in the world to live in—except, of course, for all the others.

Britain and its People

1   Introduction

Britain comprises Great Britain (England, Wales and Scotland) and Northern Ireland, and is one of the member states of the European Union (EU). Its full name is the United Kingdom of Great Britain and Northern Ireland.

Physical Features

Britain constitutes the greater part of the British Isles. The largest of the islands is Great Britain. The next largest comprises Northern Ireland and the Irish Republic. Western Scotland is fringed by the large island chain known as the Hebrides and to the north east of the Scottish mainland are the Orkney and Shetland Islands. All these have administrative ties with the mainland, but the Isle of Man in the Irish Sea and the Channel Islands between Great Britain and France are largely self-governing, and are not part of the United Kingdom.

With an area of about 242,000 sq km (93,000 sq miles), Britain is just under 1,000 km (about 600 miles) from the south coast to the extreme north of Scotland and just under 500 km (around 300 miles) across in the widest part.

The climate is generally mild and temperate. Prevailing winds are south-westerly and the weather from day to day is mainly influenced by depressions moving eastwards across the Atlantic. The weather is subject to frequent changes. In general, there are few extremes of temperature, which rarely rises above 32°C (90°F) or falls below -10°C (14°F).

Average annual rainfall is more than 1,600 mm (over 60 inches) in the mountainous areas of the west and north but less than 800 mm (30 inches) over central and eastern parts. Rain is fairly well distributed throughout the year, but, on average, March to June are the driest months and September to January the wettest. During May, June and July (the months of longest daylight) the mean daily duration of sunshine varies from five hours in northern Scotland to eight hours in the Isle of Wight; during the months of shortest daylight (November, December and January) sunshine is at a minimum, with an average of an hour a day in northern Scotland and two hours a day on the south coast of England.

> ## Weather Records in Britain
>
> - Highest air temperature: 37.1°C (98.8°F) at Cheltenham (Gloucestershire), 3 August 1990
> - Lowest air temperature: -27°C (-17°F) at Braemar (Grampian), 11 February 1895 and 10 January 1982
> - Highest annual rainfall: 6,527 mm (257 inches) at Sprinkling Tarn (Cumbria) in 1954
> - Lowest annual rainfall: 236 mm (9 inches) at Margate (Kent) in 1921
> - Highest rainfall in a day: 280 mm (11 inches) at Martinstown (Dorset), 18 July 1955
> - Strongest gust of wind: 278 km/h (173 mph), at Cairngorm (Highland), 20 March 1986
>
> Source: Meteorological Office.

Historical Outline

The name 'Britain' derives from Greek and Latin names probably stemming from a Celtic original. Although in the prehistoric timescale the Celts were relatively late arrivals in the British Isles, only with them does Britain emerge into recorded history. The term 'Celtic' is often used rather generally to distinguish the early inhabitants of the British Isles from the later Anglo-Saxon invaders.

Britain

SCOTLAND

Shetland Islands

Orkney Islands

SCOTLAND

Hebrides

Western Isles

Outer Hebrides

Inner Hebrides

Highland

Grampian

Tayside

Fife

Central

Edinburgh

Lothian

Strathclyde

Borders

Atlantic Ocean

Dumfries and Galloway

Northumberland

Tyne and Wear

NORTHERN IRELAND

Belfast

Cumbria

Durham

Cleveland

North Sea

North Yorkshire

ENGLAND

Isle of Man

Irish Sea

Lancashire

West Yorkshire

Humberside

IRISH REPUBLIC

Merseyside

1

South Yorkshire

Lincolnshire

Cheshire

Derbyshire

2

Clwyd

Gwynedd

Staffordshire

3

Leicester

Norfolk

WALES

Powys

4

Cambridge

Suffolk

Hereford and Worcester

5

6

Dyfed

9

7

Gwent

Gloucestershire

8

Essex

11

12

Oxford

Cardiff

13

Avon

Berkshire

10

London

Wiltshire

Surrey

Kent

Somerset

Hampshire

West Sussex

East Sussex

Devon

Dorset

Isle of Wight

Strait of Dover

BELG

Cornwall

English Channel

FRANCE

Isles of Scilly

Channel Islands

International boundaries

Country boundaries

County boundaries (regional boundaries in Scotland)

| 0 | 50 | 100 | 150 km |
| 0 | | 50 | 100 miles |

1. Greater Manchester
2. Nottinghamshire
3. Shropshire
4. West Midlands
5. Warwickshire
6. Northamptonshire
7. Bedfordshire
8. Hertfordshire
9. Buckinghamshire
10. Greater London
11. West Glamorgan
12. Mid Glamorgan
13. South Glamorgan

Note: The structure of local government is being reviewed, which may alter certain of the county boundaries.

After two expeditions by Julius Caesar in 55 and 54 BC, contact between Britain and the Roman world grew, culminating in the Roman invasion of AD 43. Roman rule was gradually extended from south-east England to include Wales and, for a time, the lowlands of Scotland. The final Roman withdrawal in 409 followed a period of increasing disorder during which the island began to be raided by Angles, Saxons and Jutes from northern Europe. It is from the Angles that the name 'England' derives. The raids turned into settlement and a number of small English kingdoms were established. The Britons maintained an independent existence in the areas now known as Wales and Cornwall. Among these kingdoms more powerful ones emerged, claiming overlordship over the whole country, first in the north (Northumbria), then in the midlands (Mercia) and finally in the south (Wessex). However, further raids and settlement by the Vikings from Scandinavia occurred, although in the 10th century the Wessex dynasty defeated the invading Danes and established a wide-ranging authority in England.

Dates of some of the main events in Britain's history are given on p. 6. The early histories of England, Wales, Scotland and Northern Ireland are included in Chapters 2 to 5, which also deal with the main aspects of their social, economic and political life. Additional material is included on the political situation in Northern Ireland. Table 1.1 gives a selection of some of the main statistics for each of the four lands.

Channel Islands and Isle of Man

Although the Channel Islands and the Isle of Man are not part of the United Kingdom, they have a special relationship with it. The Channel Islands were part of the Duchy of Normandy in the 10th and 11th centuries and remained subject to the English Crown after the loss of Normandy to the French. The Isle of Man was under the nominal sovereignty of Norway until 1266, and eventually came under the direct administration of the British Crown in 1765. Today the territories have their own legislative assemblies and systems of law. The British Government is responsible for their international relations and external defence.

Table 1.1: General Statistics

	England	Wales	Scotland	Northern Ireland	United Kingdom
Population (mid-1992) ('000)	48,378	2,899	5,111	1,610	57,998
Area (sq km)[a]	130,423	20,766	77,080	13,483	241,752
Population density (persons per sq km)	371	140	66	119	240
Gross domestic product (£ per head, 1992)	8,908	7,545	8,616	7,185	8,766
Employees in employment ('000, June 1993)	18,068	958	1,984	544	21,554
Percentage of employees (June 1993) in:					
services	73.2	70.1	72.2	73.0	73.0
manufacturing	20.5	21.9	18.3	18.2	20.3
construction	3.7	4.1	5.4	4.0	3.9
energy and water supply	1.5	2.0	2.7	1.3	1.6
agriculture, forestry and fishing	1.2	1.9	1.4	3.5	1.3
Unemployment rate (per cent, seasonally adjusted, June 1994)	9.3	9.6	9.2	13.2	9.4

Sources: *Regional Trends*, Office of Population Censuses and Surveys, Department of Employment
[a]Figures for area are not on a strictly comparable basis; those for England and Wales include inland water, while those for Scotland and Northern Ireland are for the land area only.

Significant Dates

55 and 54 BC: Julius Caesar's expeditions to Britain

AD 43: Roman conquest begins under Claudius

122–38: Hadrian's Wall built

c409: Roman army withdraws from Britain

450s onwards: foundation of the Anglo-Saxon kingdoms

597: arrival of St Augustine to preach Christianity to the Anglo-Saxons

664: Synod of Whitby opts for Roman Catholic rather than Celtic church

789–95: first Viking raids

832–60: Scots and Picts merge under Kenneth Macalpin to form what is to become the kingdom of Scotia

860s: Danes overrun East Anglia, Northumbria and eastern Mercia

871–99: reign of Alfred the Great in Wessex

1066: William the Conqueror defeats Harold Godwinson at Hastings and takes the throne

1215: King John signs Magna Carta to protect feudal rights against royal abuse

1301: Edward of Caernarvon (later Edward II) created Prince of Wales

1314: battle of Bannockburn ensures survival of separate Scottish kingdom

1337: Hundred Years War between England and France begins

1348–49: Black Death (bubonic plague) wipes out a third of England's population

1381: Peasants' Revolt in England

1455–87: Wars of the Roses between Yorkists and Lancastrians

1477: first book to be printed in England, by William Caxton

1534–40: English Reformation; Henry VIII breaks with the Papacy

1536–42: Acts of Union integrate England and Wales administratively and legally and give Wales representation in Parliament

1547–53: Protestantism becomes official religion in England under Edward VI

1553–58: Catholic reaction under Mary I

1558: loss of Calais, last English possession in France

1558–1603: reign of Elizabeth I; moderate Protestantism established

1588: defeat of Spanish Armada

c1590–c1613: plays of Shakespeare written

1603: union of the two crowns under James VI of Scotland

1642–51: Civil Wars between King and Parliament

1649: execution of Charles I

1653–58: Oliver Cromwell rules as Lord Protector

1660: monarchy restored under Charles II

1688: Glorious Revolution; accession of William and Mary

1707: Act of Union unites England and Scotland

c1760s–c1830s: Industrial Revolution

1761: opening of the Bridgewater Canal ushers in Canal Age

1775–83: American War of Independence leads to loss of the Thirteen Colonies

1793–1815: Revolutionary and Napoleonic Wars

1801: Act of Union unites Great Britain and Ireland

1825: opening of the Stockton and Darlington Railway, the world's first passenger railway

1829: Catholic emancipation

1832: First Reform Act extends the franchise

1914–18: First World War

1921: Anglo-Irish Treaty establishes the Irish Free State; Northern Ireland remains part of the United Kingdom

1939–45: Second World War

1952: accession of Elizabeth II

1973: Britain enters European Community (now the European Union)

2   England

England is predominantly a lowland country, although there are upland regions in the north (the Pennine Chain, the Cumbrian mountains and the Yorkshire moorlands) and in the south west, in Cornwall, Devon and Somerset. The greatest concentrations of population (see Table 2.1) are in London and the South East, the West Yorkshire and north-west industrial cities, the Midlands conurbation around Birmingham, the north-east conurbations on the rivers Tyne and Tees, and along the Channel coast.

Early History

In 1066 the last successful invasion of England took place. Duke William of Normandy defeated the English at the Battle of Hastings. Normans and others from France came to settle. French became the language of the nobility for the next three centuries and the legal and social structures were influenced by those prevailing across the Channel.

With the final loss of the English Crown's possessions in France during the late Middle Ages, and the union of England and Scotland in 1707, England's position as the most populous part of the British nation state was established.

Government

England has no government minister or department exclusively responsible for its central administration, in contrast to Wales, Scotland and Northern Ireland. Instead, there are a number of government departments, whose responsibilities in some cases also cover aspects of affairs in Wales and Scotland (see Appendices).

There are currently 524 English parliamentary constituencies represented in the House of Commons. The provisional recommendations of the current boundary review (see p. 51) would increase this to 529 after the next general election. In September 1994 England had 316 Conservative Members of Parliament, 194 Labour, 13 Liberal Democrat and the Speaker of the House of Commons. Conservative support tends to be strongest in suburban and rural areas, and the Conservatives have a large majority of the parliamentary seats in the southern half of England and in East Anglia. The Labour Party derives its main support from urban industrialised areas. Liberal Democrat support in England is particularly strong in the South West, where the party holds seven of its 13 English seats.

Local government is mainly administered through a two-tier system of counties (see map, p. 4) subdivided into districts. However, there are some single-tier authorities. The Local Government Commission is reviewing the structure of local government in England (see p. 75).

The English legal system comprises on the

7

Table 2.1: Population and Population Density Mid-1992

	Population	People per sq km		Population	People per sq km
North	**3,102,300**	**201**	**Greater London**	**6,933,000**	**4,393**
Cleveland	559,500	938	Hampshire	1,593,700	422
Cumbria	490,200	72	Hertfordshire	999,700	610
Durham	607,500	250	Isle of Wight	124,800	328
Northumberland	307,200	61	Kent	1,539,700	412
Tyne and Wear	1,137,900	2,106	Oxfordshire	585,800	225
			Surrey	1,037,900	619
Yorkshire and Humberside	**5,014,100**	**325**	West Sussex	717,700	361
Humberside	884,400	252			
North Yorkshire	721,800	87	**South West**	**4,768,000**	**200**
South Yorkshire	1,306,200	838	Avon	973,300	730
West Yorkshire	2,101,600	1,033	Cornwall and Isles of Scilly	477,000	134
			Devon	1,049,200	157
East Midlands	**4,082,900**	**261**	Dorset	667,500	252
Derbyshire	950,900	362	Gloucestershire	543,900	205
Leicestershire	910,300	357	Somerset	474,100	137
Lincolnshire	601,400	102	Wiltshire	583,000	168
Northamptonshire	591,900	250	**West Midlands**	**5,289,700**	**407**
Nottinghamshire	1,028,400	476	Hereford and Worcester	694,800	177
			Shropshire	413,900	119
East Anglia	**2,093,900**	**167**	Staffordshire	1,053,600	388
Cambridgeshire	682,600	201	Warwickshire	493,600	249
Norfolk	765,100	142	West Midlands (Metropolitan County)	2,633,700	2,930
Suffolk	646,200	170			
South East	**17,769,400**	**653**	**North West**	**6,412,400**	**873**
Bedfordshire	539,400	437	Cheshire	971,900	417
Berkshire	763,700	607	Greater Manchester	2,578,900	2,006
Buckinghamshire	651,700	347	Lancashire	1,420,700	463
East Sussex	722,200	402	Merseyside	1,440,900	2,199
Essex	1,560,300	425			
			England	**48,532,700**	**372**

Source: Office of Population Censuses and Surveys

one hand a historic body of conventions known as 'common law' and 'equity', and, on the other, parliamentary and European Community (EC) legislation. In the formulation of common law since the Norman Conquest, great reliance has been placed on precedent. Equity law derives from the practice of petitioning the King's Chancellor in cases not covered by common law.

The Church of England, which was separated from the Roman Catholic Church at the time of the Reformation, is the Established Church; the Sovereign must always be a member of the Church and appoints its two archbishops and 42 other diocesan bishops.

The Economy

Considerable changes in the economy of England have occurred during the 20th century. In the second half of the century, jobs in service industries have grown and now account for nearly three-quarters of employees in employment, with expansion having been particularly noticeable in financial and business services. Services account for over three-quarters of gross domestic product (GDP) in London and the South East, and over 20 per cent of employees in Greater London work in financial services. London is one of the world's leading centres of banking, insurance and other financial services.

Manufacturing, although declining as a proportion of the employment base, remains important in a number of areas. In terms of GDP, it is most significant in the West Midlands (where manufacturing accounted for 30 per cent of the region's GDP in 1992) and the North. The region with the highest proportion of employment in manufacturing is the West Midlands again, followed by the East Midlands, Yorkshire and Humberside and the North.

East Anglia has been the fastest-growing English region in terms of both population and employment since the 1960s, although in the recession of the early 1990s the unemployment rate rose faster here than in most other regions. Once largely agricultural, high-technology industry has in recent years developed in the region.

In agriculture, dairying is most common in the west of England; sheep and cattle are reared in the hilly and moorland areas of the North and South West. Arable farming, pig and poultry farming and horticulture are concentrated in the east and south.

Tourism and leisure now form one of England's biggest industries, worth some £16,600 million in 1992 and contributing 4 per cent of gross national product. Tourism and leisure also provide many jobs.

Transport

The motorway network comprises four long-distance routes linking London and the cities of the Midlands, the North and North

Table 2.2: Percentage Change in Population, Employment and Housing Stock

	Population 1981–92	Employment[a] 1981–93	Dwelling stock 1981–92
North	−0.6	−0.9	6.6
Yorkshire and Humberside	1.7	2.5	7.6
East Midlands	5.4	5.4	11.9
East Anglia	10.3	20.3	16.6
South East	4.1	−0.2	12.4
South West	8.3	11.8	15.7
West Midlands	1.7	0.6	8.3
North West	−0.9	−2.9	5.7
England	**3.3**	**2.0**	**10.6**

Source: *Regional Trends*
[a]Employees in employment plus self-employed.

West, and the South West; the London orbital
route (M25); and over 30 shorter motorways.
In all, there are about 2,700 km (1,700 miles)
of motorway in England, plus about 7,900 km
(4,900 miles) of other trunk roads.

On the railways a major development was
the official opening in May 1994 of the
Channel Tunnel, which links Britain with the
European rail system.

Table 2.3: Attendances at English Tourist Attractions, 1993

		millions
Blackpool Pleasure Beach	F	6.7*
British Museum	F	5.8
National Gallery	F	3.9
Palace Pier, Brighton	F	3.5*
Alton Towers	P	2.6
Westminster Abbey	F	2.5*
Madame Tussaud's	P	2.4
Pleasure Beach, Great Yarmouth	F	2.4*
Tower of London	P	2.3
York Minster	F	2.2*
Canterbury Cathedral	F	2.2*
Pleasureland, Southport	F	2.0*
St Paul's Cathedral	P	1.9
Tate Gallery	F	1.8
Natural History Museum	P	1.7

Source: British Tourist Authority
F Free admission
P Paid-for admission
* Estimated visitor numbers

Cultural and Social Affairs

London has a wealth of cultural centres,
including four major art galleries and
many renowned museums, together with
theatres, ballet and opera houses and
concert halls. Other major cities and
towns also have a broad range of cultural
interests. Many theatres outside London
are used for touring by the national
theatre, dance and opera companies.
Numerous regions and towns have
associations with great English writers and
artists, such as William Shakespeare
(Stratford-upon-Avon), William Wordsworth
(Lake District), Arnold Bennett (Stoke-on-
Trent), the Brontë sisters (Yorkshire),
Thomas Hardy (Dorset) and John Constable
(Essex and Suffolk).

Despite the relatively high population
density and degree of urbanisation, there
are still many unspoilt rural and coastal
areas There are seven National Parks, six
forest parks, 36 designated 'areas of
outstanding natural beauty', 22
environmentally sensitive areas, almost
200 country parks approved by the
Countryside Commission, 800 km (500 miles)
of designated heritage coastline, and about
2,000 historic buildings and some
3,600 gardens open to the public. There are
also safari, wildlife and theme parks, all
offering family activities and entertainment.

Further Reading

Regional Trends, annual report. HMSO.

3   Northern Ireland

About half of the 1.5 million people in Northern Ireland are settled on the eastern coastal region, the centre of which is Belfast, with a population of some 287,100. Most industry is situated in this eastern part of the province.

According to the 1991 Census 50.6 per cent of the people regarded themselves as Protestants and 38.4 per cent Roman Catholics. Most of the Protestants are descendants of Scots or English settlers who crossed to north-eastern Ireland; they are British by culture and tradition and committed to maintaining the constitutional link with the British Crown. The Roman Catholic population is mainly Irish by culture and history, and the majority of them favour a united Ireland.

Geography

Northern Ireland is at its nearest point only 21 km (13 miles) from Scotland. It has a 488-km (303-mile) border in the south and west with the Irish Republic. At its centre lies Lough Neagh, Britains largest freshwater lake (381 sq km, 147 sq miles). Many of the principal towns lie in valleys leading from the Lough, including the capital, Belfast, which stands at the mouth of the river Lagan. The Mourne Mountains, rising sharply in the south-east, include Slieve Donard, Northern Ireland's highest peak (852 m, 2,796 ft).

History

During the tenth century Ireland was dominated by the Vikings. In 1169 Henry II of England launched an invasion of Ireland. He had been granted its overlordship by the English Pope Adrian IV, who was anxious to bring the Irish church into full obedience to Rome. Although a large part of the country came under the control of Anglo-Norman magnates, little direct authority was exercised from England during the Middle Ages.

The Tudor monarchs showed a much greater tendency to intervene in Ireland. During the reign of Elizabeth I, a series of campaigns was waged against Irish insurgents. The main focus of resistance was the northern province of Ulster. With the collapse of this resistance and the flight of its leaders in 1607, Ulster was settled by immigrants from Scotland and England.

The English civil wars (1642-51) led to further risings in Ireland and these were crushed by Cromwell. There was more fighting after the overthrow of James II, a Roman Catholic, in 1688. During this, the Protestant forces besieged in Derry were rescued by those of William of Orange, who became the British king.

Throughout most of the 18th century there was an uneasy peace. In 1782 the Irish

11

Parliament (dating from medieval times) was given legislative independence; the only constitutional tie with Great Britain was the Crown. The Parliament only represented the privileged Anglo-Irish minority and Catholics were excluded from it. An abortive rebellion led by Wolfe Tone's United Irishmen movement took place in 1798, and in 1801 Ireland was unified with Great Britain. As a result of this Union, Ireland was represented in the British Parliament in London.

The Irish question was one of the major issues of British politics during the 19th century and after. In 1886 the Liberal Government introduced a Home Rule Bill designed to give an Irish Parliament authority over most internal matters while reserving control over external affairs to Britain. This led to a split in the Liberal Party and the failure of the Bill. In 1893 a second Home Rule Bill was approved by the House of Commons but was rejected by the House of Lords.

The question returned to the political agenda in 1910 because Asquith's Liberal Government was dependent on support from the Irish Parliamentary Party, which favoured Home Rule. The controversy intensified as Unionists and Nationalists formed private armies in Ireland. In 1914 Home Rule was enacted by the Government of Ireland Act. However, implementation was prevented by the threat of armed resistance on the part of the Protestant Unionist majority in Ulster and by the outbreak of the First World War.

A nationalist rising in Dublin in 1916 was suppressed and its leaders executed. Two years later the nationalist Sinn Fein party won a large majority of the Irish seats in elections to the Westminster Parliament. Its members refused to attend the House of Commons and, instead, formed the Dail Eireann in Dublin. A nationalist guerrilla force known as the Irish Republican Army (IRA) began operations against the British administration in 1919.

The Government of Ireland Act 1920 provided for the establishment of two Home Rule parliaments, one in Dublin and the other in Belfast. The Act was implemented in 1921 in Northern Ireland, when six of the nine counties of the province of Ulster received their own Parliament and remained represented in, and subject to the supreme authority of, the British Parliament.

In the South the IRA continued to fight for independence from the British administration. After the signature of a truce in June 1921, the Anglo-Irish Treaty of December 1921 established the Irish Free State, which became a republic in 1949.

For 50 years from 1921 Northern Ireland had its own devolved Parliament, in which the mainly Protestant Unionists consistently formed the majority and therefore constituted the Government after successive elections. Nationalists resented this domination and their effective exclusion from political office.

An active and articulate civil rights movement emerged during the late 1960s. Although reforms were made in response (see p. 14), sectarian disturbances developed and this required the introduction of British Army troops in 1969 to support the police in keeping order. Subsequently, sectarian divisions were exploited by the actions of terrorists from both sides, but most notably by the Provisional Irish Republican Army, who claimed to be protecting the Roman Catholic minority.

Despite the reform programme, the inter-communal violence continued, leading to a decision by the British Government to take over responsibility for law and order in 1972. The Northern Ireland Government resigned in protest against this decision and direct rule from London began.

Government

Under the system of direct rule, the United Kingdom Parliament approves all laws and Northern Ireland's government departments are directed and controlled by the Secretary of State, who is a Cabinet minister (see p. 66).

Northern Ireland elects 17 members to the House of Commons. In the most recent general election in April 1992 the Ulster Unionists won 9 seats, the Democratic Unionists 3, the Ulster Popular Unionists 1 and the nationalist Social Democratic and Labour Party (SDLP) 4. The Alliance Party, set up to offer an alternative to unionist and nationalist parties, did not obtain a seat.

Sinn Fein also fought the election but lost its only seat to the SDLP.

Three members of the European Parliament are elected in Northern Ireland (see p. 112).

Efforts to Achieve Devolved Government

Legislation passed in 1973 provided for a measure of devolved government in Northern Ireland. This was implemented in January 1974 following agreement between political parties there to form a power-sharing Executive. The Executive, however, collapsed in May 1974 as a result of a protest strike by unionist 'loyalists'.

Attempts have been made by successive British governments to find a means of restoring a widely acceptable form of devolved administration. A 78-member Assembly was elected by proportional representation in 1982 in order to make proposals for the resumption of devolved government and to monitor the work of the government departments. The Assembly was dissolved four years later following its failure to discharge these responsibilities.

The British Government remains committed to the principle of a locally accountable administration acceptable to, and enjoying the support of, Unionists and Nationalists. In 1991 and 1992 the four main constitutional parties—the Ulster Unionists, Democratic Unionists, Alliance Party and Social Democratic and Labour Party—held a series of talks to see whether they could reach an agreement taking into account three sets of relationships relevant to the Northern Ireland problem—those within Northern Ireland, within the island of Ireland, and between the British and Irish governments. The talks ended in November 1992 without full agreement.

Since September 1993 the British Government has been engaged in a series of bilateral discussions with three of the four Northern Ireland parties (the Democratic Unionist Party have declined to take part) to explore the basis upon which they might come together for further dialogue. Over the same period the Government has also been engaged in intensive discussions with the Irish Government on a framework document.

The aim is to produce a shared assessment of the elements of a settlement which is likely to have the best prospects of attracting widespread agreement right across the community in Northern Ireland. It is hoped that this will facilitate the resumption of multilateral talks with the aim of achieving agreement in an overall political settlement.

Relations with the Irish Republic

The British and Irish governments have for many years recognised the importance of working to bring peace to Northern Ireland. The 1985 Anglo-Irish Agreement created an Inter-governmental Conference in which both governments can discuss issues such as cross border co-operation and security. The Agreement provides for the Irish Government to put forward views and proposals on matters related to Northern Ireland provided that these are not the responsibility of a devolved administration in Northern Ireland. Each government retains full sovereign responsibility for decisions and administration within its own jurisdiction.

Security co-operation with the Irish Republic has improved significantly since 1985. Progress has been made in a number of areas, including improved communications, technical co-operation and joint assessments of threats from terrorists.

The Downing Street Declaration

The Downing Street Declaration, signed on 15 December 1993 by the British Prime Minister, John Major, and his Irish counterpart, Albert Reynolds, is a statement of fundamental principles which complements other political talks (see above) in the search for a settlement in Northern Ireland. It does not envisage, nor advocate, any particular outcome. It does, however, make clear that the consent of a majority of the people in Northern Ireland is required before any constitutional change can come about.

The text reaffirms that the British Government will uphold the democratic wish of the majority of the people in Northern Ireland on the issue of whether they prefer to support the Union or a sovereign united

Ireland. On this basis the British Government reiterates that it has no selfish strategic or economic interest in Northern Ireland, and that, were a majority in Northern Ireland to wish it, the Government would introduce legislation to bring about a united Ireland. For its part the Irish Government accepts that it would be wrong to attempt to impose a united Ireland without the freely given consent of a majority of the people of Northern Ireland.

The Irish Government also confirms that, in the event of an overall settlement, it will put forward and support proposals for change in the Irish Constitution which would fully reflect the principle of consent in Northern Ireland.

The British and Irish Governments agreed in the Declaration that only democratically mandated parties with an established commitment to exclusively peaceful methods would be free to participate in future dialogue. In the event of a permanent cessation of violence by the Provisional IRA, Sinn Fein could join that process.

In August 1994 the Provisional IRA announced a complete cessation of its military operations. Welcoming this news, the British Government stressed the need for the IRA to make clear that this cessation was permanent before any discussions with Sinn Fein could take place.

In September 1994 the Prime Minister said that the outcome of any talks between the Northern Ireland political parties would be put to the people there in a referendum. In addition, he lifted the broadcasting restrictions on Sinn Fein and other organisations.

Another step towards lasting peace was taken in mid-October 1994 as 'loyalist' paramilitaries responded to calls by the Government and by leading figures in Northern Ireland to give up violence with the announcement of a ceasefire. The Government said that it would look to the 'loyalists' to match deeds to words.

On 21 October the Prime Minister announced that he was prepared to make a working assumption that the IRA ceasefire was intended to be permanent. He added that the Government could move carefully towards the beginning of dialogue with Sinn Fein.

Human Rights

Economic and social deprivation exist on both sides of the Northern Ireland community, but, on all major social and economic indicators, Catholics experience significantly greater levels of disadvantage than Protestants, which sustains feelings of discrimination and alienation; these in turn influence attitudes to political and security issues. The Government is fully committed to tackling discrimination and ensuring that all the people of Northern Ireland have equal opportunities in employment and housing, in education and in the expression of their political and cultural identity.

Reforms introduced over the period of direct rule include legislation against discrimination, the creation of independent and impartial authorities to manage public services and investigate complaints, and a series of measures to safeguard civil liberties.

The aim is to encourage a more pluralistic and tolerant society with parity of esteem for both traditions. The goal of the Royal Ulster Constabulary, for example, is to provide a high-quality effective police service to all the people, in partnership with the community and in co-operation with other agencies. There is an Independent Commission for Police Complaints (see p. 85). The Standing Advisory Commission on Human Rights advises the Secretary of State on the effectiveness of anti-discrimination laws.

An independent Chief Electoral Officer maintains the accuracy of the electoral register. Electoral boundaries for parliamentary constituencies are determined by impartial statutory procedures conducted by the Boundary Commission for Northern Ireland. The Northern Ireland Ombudsman and Commissioner for Complaints deal with complaints against government departments and local authorities.

Direct or indirect discrimination in employment on grounds of religious belief or political opinion is unlawful. Legislation requires registration by employers with the Fair Employment Commission, compulsory monitoring of the religious composition of workforces, review of recruitment, training and promotion procedures, and affirmative action if fair employment is not provided. There are criminal penalties and economic sanctions for defaulting employers and the Fair Employment Tribunal deals with individual complaints of discrimination.

Security Policy

Terrorism is rejected by the overwhelming majority of the people in Northern Ireland. Although the overall level of violence is now far lower than in the early 1970s, over 3,120 people have been killed and over 36,000 injured since 1969.

Certain temporary emergency powers are in force which require annual renewal by Parliament; they are also reviewed each year by an independent observer appointed by the Government. They include special powers of arrest of those suspected of certain serious crimes, non-jury courts to try terrorist offences (see pp. 90-1), and the banning of terrorist organisations (see p. 82). Suspected terrorists are tried for criminal offences, not for their political beliefs.

If members of the security forces break the law, they can and will be prosecuted like any other citizen. An independent commission supervises police investigations into the more serious complaints against police officers and, at its discretion, the investigation of others. Northern Ireland's legal system is broadly similar to that in England and Wales (see Chapter 8).

An independent Commissioner observes and reports on the conditions under which terrorist suspects are detained by the security forces in holding centres. The Commissioner submits an annual report to the Secretary of State, which is made public.

Draft codes of practice have been published, for public consultation, on the detention, treatment, questioning and identification of suspects. Breach of any of the codes' provisions by a police officer will be a disciplinary offence.

Although an accused is not obliged to say anything, courts are able to draw inferences from his or her refusal to explain, for example, marks on clothing or presence at a certain place.

The Economy

Northern Ireland had a gross domestic product of some £11,475 million in 1992 and a workforce of some 736,000 in June 1993. Trends in output and employment tend to reflect overall trends in Britain. Almost half of manufacturing output is sold to the rest of Britain and a quarter is sold locally.

Unemployment is higher than in the rest of Britain and reached 13 per cent in August 1994, compared with 9.2 per cent in the United Kingdom as a whole.

Industrial development policy is carried out by five agencies associated with the Department of Economic Development:

- the Industrial Development Board deals with companies with more than 50 employees and with inward investment;
- the Local Enterprise Development Unit promotes enterprise and the development of small businesses employing up to 50 employees;
- the Training and Employment Agency is responsible for training the workforce;
- the Northern Ireland Tourist Board promotes tourism; and
- the Industrial Research and Technology Unit provides advice and assistance to encourage research and development and technology transfer.

Nearly 180 of the IDB's 490 client companies come from outside Northern Ireland, mainly from Europe, North America and Asia.

> One of the most recent investments is a £36.6 million plant in County Londonderry by a Hong Kong company making plastic containers for compact discs; it will create 314 jobs.

In 1993–94 two Korean companies, one making car stereos and the other manufacturing printed circuit boards, announced their intention to invest in Northern Ireland, as has an Indonesian fabric manufacturing company. These three investments will mean a total of about 1,250 new jobs. Various incentives are available from the Industrial Development Board.

Considerable public expenditure is devoted to urban renewal in Belfast and Londonderry, and to a rural development programme. The Making Belfast Work programme encourages growth in jobs and small businesses, improves training, and makes improvements to the environment and living conditions. In addition, a government and private sector scheme is redeveloping the banks of the river Lagan in the heart of the city. In Londonderry there is a town centre development programme as well as community action to create more jobs.

Northern Ireland has parity with England, Scotland and Wales on taxation and services. The British Government makes a contribution of over £3,000 million a year to maintain social services at the level of those in Great Britain, to meet the cost of security measures and to compensate for the natural disadvantages of geography and lack of resources. Resources are focused on those suffering the highest level of social and economic disadvantage.

In 1986 the British and Irish governments established the International Fund for Ireland. Some three-quarters is spent in Northern Ireland, the rest going to border areas in the Republic. Programmes cover business enterprise, tourism, community relations, urban development, agriculture and rural development. Donors include the United States, the European Union, Canada and New Zealand.

Cultural and Social Affairs

Northern Ireland's heritage is preserved and portrayed by the Ulster Museum in Belfast,

the Ulster Folk and Transport Museum in County Down, and a number of smaller museums and interpretative centres. The Ulster-American Folk Park in Omagh specialises in the history of Irish emigration to America; it has an extensive computer database on emigrants which is available for use by the public.

Local arts festivals are an important feature of the arts calendar, the highlight being the Belfast Festival, based at Queens University. The Ulster Orchestra has a notable reputation. Government support for the arts is channelled through the Arts Council for Northern Ireland, which gives financial help and advice to opera and drama companies, orchestras and festivals, arts centres, galleries, theatres, writers and artistic groups.

Local district councils provide leisure facilities, including leisure centres and swimming pools. The Government finances the Sports Council for Northern Ireland, which promotes sport and physical recreation.

Health and personal social services correspond fairly closely to those in the rest of Britain.

Although publicly maintained schools must be open to children from all religions, in practice Roman Catholic and Protestant children are mainly educated in separate schools. There are 21 integrated schools providing education for some 4,000 Protestant and Roman Catholic children and this process is being encouraged by the Government (see p. 412).

Owner occupation of housing has increased from 54 per cent in 1981 to 68 per cent in 1993. The Housing Executive is the sole public housing authority and allocates homes to those in greatest need.

Local television and radio programmes are broadcast and there is a local press (see p. 478). National television and radio broadcasts are also received and the national press is sold widely.

Further Reading

Bardon, Jonathon. *A History of Ulster.* Blackstaff Press, 1992.

Northern Ireland. Aspects of Britain series, HMSO, 1992.

Northern Ireland Expenditure Plans and Priorities: The Government's Expenditure Plans 1994–45 to 1996–97. HMSO, 1994.

4 Scotland

Three-quarters of the population of Scotland and most of the industrial towns are in the central lowlands. The chief cities are Edinburgh (the capital), Glasgow, Aberdeen and Dundee. Just over half of Scotland consists of the sparsely populated highlands and islands in the north.

Scotland contains large areas of unspoilt and wild landscape, and the majority of Britain's highest mountains—nearly 300 peaks over 913 m (3,000 ft). The Grampians in the central highlands contain Ben Nevis (1,343 m, 4,406 ft), the highest peak in Britain.

Table 4.1: Population, June 1993

	Population	Population density (people per sq km)
Regions:		
Borders	105,300	23
Central	272,900	104
Dumfries and Galloway	147,900	23
Fife	351,200	269
Grampian	528,100	61
Highland	206,900	8
Lothian	753,900	429
Strathclyde	2,286,800	169
Tayside	395,200	53
Islands:		
Orkney Islands	19,760	20
Shetland Islands	22,830	16
Western Isles	29,410	10
Scotland	5,120,200	66

Source: General Register Office for Scotland.

Early History

At the time of the Roman invasion of Britain, what is now Scotland was mainly inhabited by the Picts. Despite a long campaign, Roman rule was never permanently extended to most of Scotland. In the sixth century, the Scots from Ireland settled in what is now Argyll, giving their name to the present-day Scotland. Lothian was populated by the Angles, while Britons moved north to Strathclyde. In the ninth century parts of Scotland were subject to raids by the Vikings; a united Scottish kingdom was established at this time.

The powerful English monarchy threatened Scottish independence in the Middle Ages, particularly under Edward I, and war between the two kingdoms was frequent. There were also, however, strong links with England; several Scottish kings held land and titles in England and there was intermarriage between the Scottish and English royal families. Cultural influences on Scotland were also strong. Despite reverses such as the defeat of William Wallace's uprising in 1298, Robert the Bruce's victory over Edward II of England at Bannockburn ensured the survival of a separate kingdom of Scotland.

The two crowns were eventually united when Elizabeth I of England was succeeded in 1603 by James VI of Scotland (James I of England), who was her nearest heir. Even so, England and Scotland remained separate political entities during the 17th century, apart from an enforced period of unification under Oliver Cromwell in the 1650s. The religions of the two kingdoms had also developed in different directions, with England retaining an Episcopalian church (governed by bishops) and Scotland embracing a Presbyterian system (see p. 435). In 1707 both countries, realising the benefits of closer political and economic union, agreed on a single parliament for Great Britain. Scotland retained its own system of law and church settlement.

Government

There are special arrangements for the conduct of Scottish affairs within the British system of government and separate Acts of Parliament are passed for Scotland where appropriate. There are 72 Scottish seats in the House of Commons. The General Election in April 1992 resulted in the election of 49 Labour Members of Parliament, 11 Conservative, 9 Liberal Democrat and 3 Scottish Nationalist.

Scottish administration is the responsibility of the Secretary of State for Scotland, a member of the Cabinet, working through The Scottish Office, which has its headquarters in Edinburgh and an office in London.

Review of Scottish Government

In 1993 the Government issued a White Paper, *Scotland in the Union: A Partnership for Good*, following a wide-ranging examination of Scotland's place in Britain and the role of Parliament in Scottish affairs. A series of initiatives is being taken to improve the parliamentary arrangements for handling Scottish business. This involves the widening of the range of business handled by the Scottish Grand Committee (which consists of all 72 Scottish MPs); meeting in Scotland as well as at Westminster; improved scrutiny of Scottish legislation through special standing committees; and greater accountability of Scottish Office ministers through parliamentary question time (see p. 59).

Certain functions are being transferred from Whitehall departments to The Scottish Office. For example, responsibility for the Scottish Arts Council was transferred from the Department of National Heritage in April 1994. To make The Scottish Office more accessible, a central enquiry unit and information points are being established in many towns.

Local Government Reform

Local government currently operates on a two-tier basis broadly similar to that in England and Wales. The three islands councils (for the Orkney, the Shetland and the Western Isles) are single-tier authorities.

Major changes are planned for local government. Provisions are contained in the Local Government etc. (Scotland) Bill now being considered by Parliament. This would create a single-tier structure of 32 councils. Existing regional and district councils would be replaced by 29 new councils, while the three islands councils would be unchanged. Edinburgh, Glasgow, Dundee and Aberdeen would each have its own single-tier council. The new councils would be required to devise plans to increase the involvement of local people in council activities. It is envisaged that the new authorities would assume full control in April 1996.

Legal System

The principles and procedures of the Scottish legal system differ in many respects from those of England and Wales. These differences stem, in part, from the adoption of elements from other European legal systems, based on Roman law, during the 16th century. One difference is in the verdicts which a jury may give—in Scotland a jury can give a verdict of 'not proven' when, as with a 'not guilty' verdict, the accused is acquitted.

The Economy

Scotland has experienced the same pressure on its traditional industries as Wales and the north of England. However, since 1987 economic growth in Scotland has on average been greater than in Britain as a whole and it was less affected by the recession in the early 1990s than were other areas.

The most significant development has been the discovery in the early 1970s of oil and gas under the North Sea. Up to about 100,000 jobs are estimated to have arisen directly or indirectly as a result of North Sea activities.

Industry

As traditional industries such as coal, steel and shipbuilding have declined, there has been growth in high technology industries such as chemicals, electronic engineering and lighter forms of mechanical and instrument engineering. The electronics industry, which includes many of the world's leading companies in this field (such as IBM and Motorola), provides nearly 13 per cent of jobs in manufacturing and about 19 per cent of manufacturing output and 17 per cent of manufacturing investment. By 1993 over 190 plants were employing about 41,500 workers, one of the biggest concentrations of the electronics industry in Western Europe.

Some traditional industries, such as high-quality tweeds and other textiles, and food and drink products, remain important. There are over 100 whisky distilleries, mostly in the north-east. Whisky exports, valued at £1,958 million in 1992, represent about one-fifth of Scotland's manufacturing exports.

Industrial Development

Government measures have helped to attract firms to Scotland, and investment by overseas companies has helped to make a significant contribution to the growth of modern technologically based industries. In 1992 about 82,200 people were employed in overseas-owned manufacturing units, representing a quarter of manufacturing employment in Scotland.

Government support for enterprise and training is channelled through Scottish Enterprise and Highlands and Islands Enterprise, which both have general functions in economic development, training and environmental improvement in the Scottish lowlands and the Highlands and Islands respectively. They contract with 22 Local Enterprise Companies (led by the private sector), which arrange the provision of training and business support.

Services

A marked expansion has occurred in services, which now employ over 70 per cent of the workforce. Financial and business services are of growing importance, and over 200,000 people are employed in the sector. There are four Scottish-based clearing banks and they have limited rights to issue their own banknotes. About one-third of investment funds in Britain are managed from Scotland, which is also a base for a large number of insurance companies.

Tourism and leisure also make a

significant contribution to the economy, directly providing over 180,000 jobs. In 1993, 10.9 million visitors spent about £2,000 million in Scotland.

Agriculture, Forestry and Fishing

About 75 per cent of the land area of Scotland is devoted to agriculture. Much of this is rough grazing (including common grazing) for cattle and sheep. Scotland's cattle industry has a worldwide reputation, both for the quality of meat and for pedigree breeds. Arable farms are highly productive, and the principal crop is barley, which is used in the making of whisky and beer.

Scotland accounts for nearly half of Britain's forest area and for over one-third of timber production. The bulk of new planting in Britain takes place in Scotland, mostly in the upland and mountain areas.

Fishing remains an important activity, particularly in the north-east and the islands. Scotland accounts for over 70 per cent by weight and over 60 per cent by value of the fish landed in Britain by British vessels.

Energy and Water Resources

Nuclear and hydro-electric generation supply a higher proportion of energy than in any other part of Britain. Over 40 per cent of Scotland's electricity comes from nuclear power, with hydro-power and other renewables contributing more than 10 per cent.

With abundant rainfall, there is an extensive supply of water from upland sources. Water supply is currently the responsibility of the regional and islands councils, although under the plans for local government reform these responsibilities would pass to three public water authorities, which would own and operate the water and sewerage services. They would be able to attract private capital to help to fund major investment projects.

Transport

Communications, both domestic and international, have improved in many parts of Scotland. The electrification scheme of the Edinburgh to London railway was completed in 1991. The A74 road linking Glasgow and Carlisle is being upgraded to provide a northward extension of the M6 motorway, while the Central Scotland motorway network is to be completed. Proposals to improve public and private transport services around the Firth of Forth are being considered, including investment of about £380 million in a second Forth Road Bridge and associated road links.

Environment

Scotland's countryside contains a rich variety of wildlife, with some species not found elsewhere in Britain. There are 71 national nature reserves and over 1,370 Sites of Special Scientific Interest; 33 Special Protection Areas have been designated under the European Community directive on wild birds. Four regional parks and 40 national scenic areas have been designated, covering 13 per cent of the land surface. Four of the 11 forest parks in Great Britain are in Scotland, and a fifth spans the border between Scotland and England.

Housing and Urban Regeneration

The tenure pattern is somewhat different from that in the rest of Britain. Home ownership is increasing but, at 55 per cent, is still lower than in other areas of Britain. About 35 per cent of housing is rented from the public sector, compared with 20 per cent for Britain as a whole. Projects to tackle the problems in inner city areas and some peripheral housing estates include a series of partnerships between The Scottish Office and other groups, such as local communities and the private sector.

Health

In certain diseases—for example, lung cancer and heart disease—the health record in Scotland is not as good as elsewhere in Britain. In 1992 the Government issued a policy statement with a range of initiatives to improve health in Scotland. Targets were set for the year 2000 and progress is already being made in reducing mortality rates from cancer and coronary heart disease, and in lowering the levels of cigarette smoking.

Education

The concept of universal education was accepted in Scotland as early as the 16th century. The Scottish education system has a number of distinctive features, for example, in examinations (see p. 419). There are 12 universities, of which four—St Andrews, Glasgow, Aberdeen and Edinburgh—were established in the 15th century and four in the 1960s, with four being accorded university status in 1992–93.

Cultural and Social Affairs

Gaelic, a language of ancient Celtic origin, is spoken by some 80,000 people; the greatest concentration of Gaelic speakers is in the islands of the Hebrides. The Government is encouraging people to learn more about the Gaelic language and culture. Government support for Gaelic—which amounted to £12 million in 1993–94—covers three main areas: education, Gaelic organisations and television broadcasting.

The annual Edinburgh International Festival is one of the world's leading cultural events. Held in August and September, it is the largest of its kind in the world. Since 1982 Glasgow has also held its own international arts festival, the Mayfest, which is now the second largest festival in Britain. Scotland possesses a number of major collections of the fine and applied arts such as the Burrell Collection in Glasgow. A new Museum of Scotland is to be built in Edinburgh to house the National Museums' Scottish collection. Many Scots have achieved eminence in arts and sciences.

The predominant Church of Scotland is a Protestant church which is Presbyterian in form; it is governed by a hierarchy of church courts, each of which includes lay people.

The sport of golf originated in Scotland, and there are over 400 golf courses, including St Andrews, Gleneagles, Turnberry, Muirfield, Troon and Prestwick, which are internationally renowned. A wide range of outdoor activities, such as mountaineering, hill walking and fishing, are also pursued. Winter sports are becoming increasingly popular in the Cairngorm Mountains, Glencoe and a number of other areas.

Further Reading

Scotland. Aspects of Britain series, HMSO, 1993.

Scotland in the Union: A Partnership for Good. Cm 2225. HMSO, 1993.

Serving Scotland's Needs: The Government's Expenditure Plans 1994–95 to 1996–97. Departments of the Secretary of State for Scotland and the Forestry Commission. Cm 2514. HMSO, 1994.

5 Wales

Two-thirds of the population of Wales live in the southern valleys and the lower-lying coastal areas. The chief urban centres are Cardiff (with a population of nearly 300,000), Swansea, Newport and Wrexham. However, much of Wales is hilly or mountainous. The highest mountains are in Snowdonia and the tallest peak is Snowdon (1,085 m, 3,560 ft).

Wales is a principality; Prince Charles, the heir to the throne, was invested by the Queen with the title of Prince of Wales at Caernarfon Castle in 1969, when he was 20. The Welsh name of the country is Cymru.

Early History

After the collapse of Roman rule in Britain (see p. 3), Wales remained a Celtic stronghold, although often within the English sphere of influence. For much of the period, it was divided into a number of separate principalities, and unity was achieved only sporadically. In 1267 Llywelyn ap Gruffudd, who had achieved control over a large portion of Wales, was recognised as Prince of Wales by the English. However, on his death in 1282, Edward I launched a successful campaign to bring Wales under English rule. The series of great castles that he had built in north Wales remain among Britain's finest historic monuments (see p. 354). Edward I's eldest son—later Edward II—was born at Caernarfon in 1284 and was given the title Prince of Wales, which continues to be borne by the eldest son of the reigning monarch to this day.

Continued strong Welsh national feeling was indicated by the rising led by Owain Glyndŵr at the beginning of the 15th century. The Tudor dynasty, which ruled England from 1485 to 1603, was of Welsh ancestry. The Acts of Union of 1536 and 1542 united England and Wales administratively, politically and legally.

Language

At the 1991 census Welsh speakers made up 19 per cent of the population. In the rural north and west, Welsh remains the first language of most of the population; in recent decades the language has experienced a revival in the largely anglicised areas of south-east and north-east Wales.

The Government has reaffirmed its commitment to enhancing Welsh culture and developing greater use of the Welsh language. Bilingual education in schools is encouraged (see p. 418), and there has been an extended use of Welsh for official purposes and in broadcasting. There are now many more bilingual publications and most road signs are bilingual. Expenditure of £6.8 million in support of the language is planned in 1994–95. The Welsh Language Act 1993 establishes the principle that, in the context of business of public sector bodies and the administration of justice in Wales, Welsh and English should be treated on an equal basis. The Act also set up the Welsh Language Board (formerly an advisory body) on a statutory basis. Its aim is to promote and facilitate the use of the Welsh language. One of its first tasks is to prepare guidelines on the form and content of Welsh language schemes.

Government

The country returns 38 Members of Parliament to the House of Commons. For the last 60 years the industrial communities have tended to support the Labour Party in elections, ensuring a Labour majority of seats. Following the 1992 General Election, Wales has 27 Labour Members of Parliament, 6 Conservative, 4 Plaid Cymru (Welsh Nationalist) and 1 Liberal Democrat. Special arrangements exist for the discussion of Welsh affairs in the Welsh Grand Committee, whose function is to consider matters relating exclusively to Wales; Bills are referred to it for consideration as to whether they should be given a second reading (see p. 58).

The Secretary of State for Wales, who is a member of the Cabinet, has wide-ranging responsibilities relating to the economy, education, welfare services and the provision of amenities. The headquarters of the administration is the Welsh Office, in Cardiff;

it also has an office in London. The legal system is identical to the English one.

A major change in the structure of local government is planned. Under the Local Government (Wales) Act 1994, the existing eight county councils and 37 district councils will be replaced by 22 unitary authorities from April 1996.

The Economy

Recent decades have seen fundamental changes in the basis of the Welsh economy. The most notable features have been expansion in service industries and the development of a more diverse range of manufacturing industries, including many at the forefront of technology. For example, Wales is now an important centre for electronics, information technology, automotive components, chemicals and materials. The traditional industry of steelmaking remains important, and Wales accounts for about a third of steel production in Britain. Coalmining, though, as elsewhere in Britain, has declined substantially. Only one deep mine of significance is now in operation, although there are also a number of smaller mines and opencast sites.

In services the most marked growth has been in financial and business services, and leisure services. Annual earnings from tourism, for example, are estimated at about £1,300 million and the industry employs about 95,000 people. The Wales Tourist Board seeks to develop tourism in ways

Table 5.1: Population Mid-1993

	Population	Population density (people per sq km)
Clwyd	415,900	171
Dyfed	351,500	61
Gwent	450,300	327
Gwynedd	240,200	62
Mid Glamorgan	544,300	535
Powys	119,900	24
South Glamorgan	413,200	993
West Glamorgan	371,200	453
Wales	**2,906,500**	**140**

Source: *Regional Trends*

which will yield the optimum economic benefit for the people of Wales.

Although south Wales remains the principal industrial area, new industries and firms have been introduced in north-east Wales and light industry attracted to the towns in the rural areas of mid- and north Wales.

Inward Investment

Wales has been particularly successful in attracting investment from overseas companies. In recent years it has obtained about 20 per cent of overseas inward investment into Britain. In total, 169 new projects were secured from abroad and the rest of Britain in 1993–94; these are expected to lead to around 14,000 new jobs and £765 million of capital investment.

Economic Development

The economic programmes of the Welsh Office are complemented by the work of the Welsh Development Agency and the Development Board for Rural Wales, which have wide powers to promote industrial, environmental and social change. Planned expenditure by these bodies in 1994–95 totals £165 million and £27 million respectively. One of the main areas of activity is providing accommodation for business, increasingly in partnership with the private sector. The Agency has also undertaken the largest land reclamation programme in Europe, and all the significant remaining industrial dereliction in Wales is expected to have been removed by the end of the 1990s.

The south Wales valleys is one of the main areas to have been affected by the decline in traditional industries. The Programme for the Valleys was the most extensive programme of economic and urban regeneration undertaken in Wales. Its achievements included additional private sector investment of nearly £700 million, involving 24,000 jobs; 240,000 sq m (2.6 million sq ft) of new industrial floorspace; and the improvement of over 7,000 homes.

In 1993 this was succeeded by a new five-year Programme for the Valleys. The emphasis of the new programme is moving away from centralised initiatives towards local partnerships, and greater emphasis is being placed on links with Europe.

A development corporation has been set up to stimulate the regeneration of the Cardiff Bay area and its proposals include a new barrage across the harbour mouth. The regeneration is expected to attract £1,200 million of private investment and to support about 23,000 new jobs.

Agriculture and Forestry

Agriculture occupies over 80 per cent of the land area. The main activities are sheep and cattle rearing in the hill regions and dairy farming in the lowlands. About 12 per cent of Wales is covered by woodland.

Transport

Improvements to road and rail links, such as the upgrading of the north Wales coast road, have helped the Welsh economy in recent years. In the south there are motorway links across the Severn Bridge to southern England and the Midlands, and high-speed rail services to a number of destinations in England. A second major motorway crossing of the Severn is under construction, with completion planned in 1996. Work on motorway links to the new bridge started in 1993.

Environment

About one-quarter of Wales is designated as a National Park or Area of Outstanding Natural Beauty (see p. 350). As well as the three National Parks—Snowdonia, the Brecon Beacons and the Pembrokeshire Coast—and the five Areas of Outstanding Natural Beauty, there are two national trails, 31 country parks and large stretches of heritage coast. There are about 50 National Nature Reserves and about 870 Sites of Special Scientific Interest. Nearly all of the rivers and canals are classified as having water of good or fair quality, and a significant improvement has been achieved in the quality of bathing waters.

Cultural and Social Affairs

Welsh literature is one of the oldest and richest in Europe, and there is a national library. The Welsh people also have strong musical traditions; the country is well known for its choral singing and the Welsh National Opera has an international reputation. Special festivals, known as eisteddfodau, encourage Welsh literature and music. The largest is the annual Royal National Eisteddfod, consisting of competitions in music, singing, prose and poetry entirely in Welsh. Artists from all over the world come to the town of Llangollen for the annual International Musical Eisteddfod.

A £21 million expansion scheme at the National Museum of Wales, in Cardiff, has been completed. New galleries and a permanent Evolution of Wales exhibition were opened in 1993. Visitor numbers to the Museum have increased, and totalled some 923,000 in 1993–94. Work on a third building at the National Library of Wales, costing some £11 million, started in summer 1994.

There is no established church, the Anglican church in Wales having been disestablished in 1920 following decades of pressure from adherents of the Methodist and Baptist churches. Methodism in particular spread rapidly in Wales in the 18th century, assuming the nature of a popular movement among Welsh speakers and finding strong support later in industrial communities.

An active local press includes a number of Welsh language publications. The fourth television channel, Sianel Pedwar Cymru (S4C), broadcasts most of its programmes in Welsh during peak viewing hours and is required to see that a significant proportion of programmes are in Welsh.

The education system is similar to that in England. Welsh and English are both used as media of instruction in a number of schools. Most Welsh-medium schools are situated in the traditionally Welsh-speaking, largely rural, areas. There are also designated bilingual schools in the anglicised, mainly industrial areas to cater for children whose parents want them to be educated through the medium of both languages. Welsh is a core subject in Welsh-speaking schools and a foundation subject elsewhere under the National Curriculum (see p. 418). The collegiate University of Wales, founded in 1893, comprises six member institutions.

Among many sporting activities, there is particular interest in rugby union football, which has come to be regarded as the Welsh national game. The provision of sports facilities, such as indoor sports halls and swimming pools, has increased in recent years.

Further Reading

The Government's Expenditure Plans 1994–95 to 1996–97. A Report by the Welsh Office and the Office of Her Majesty's Chief Inspector of Schools in Wales. Cm 2515. HMSO, 1994.

Wales. Aspects of Britain series, HMSO, 1993.

6 The Social Framework

Among the main social changes during the second half of the 20th century are longer life expectancy and a lower birth rate, reflected in a growing proportion of elderly people; a higher divorce rate; wider educational opportunities; technological progress and a higher standard of living.

POPULATION

According to mid-1993 estimates, Britain's population is 58 million, the 17th largest in the world. Statistics are derived from the census (taken every ten years), with allowance made for subsequent births and deaths (obtained from compulsory registration), and migration.

The population has been growing slowly since the early 1980s. On mid-1992-based projections, the population in Britain is forecast to rise to 59.8 million in 2001 and 61.3 million in 2011.

Birth Rates

In 1993 there were 762,000 live births, slightly fewer than in 1992, compared with 634,200 deaths in 1992. The total period fertility rate (an indication of average family size) remains below 2.1, the level leading to the long-term replacement of the population, although it is estimated that it will increase from 1.8 in 1992 to 1.9 for women born in or after 1980.

Contributory factors to the relatively low birth rate in recent years (13.5 live births per 1,000 population in 1992) include:

- the trends towards later marriage and towards postponing births, which have led to an increase in the average age of women having children—27.9 years in England and Wales in 1992 compared with 26.8 in 1981;
- the current preference for smaller families than in the past, which has led to a significant decline in the proportion of families with four or more children;[1] and
- more widespread and effective contraception, making it easier to plan families, and the greater prevalence of voluntary sterilisation for both men and women.

Mortality

At birth the expectation of life for a man is about 73 years and for a woman 78 years, compared with 49 years for men and 52 years for women in 1901. There has, however, been only a small increase in life expectancy in the older age groups.

---

[1] In 1991, 66 per cent of families consisted of a married couple with one or two dependent children, compared with 15 per cent of families consisting of a married couple with three or more dependent children.

The general death rate was 11 per 1,000 population in 1992. There has been a decline in mortality at most ages, particularly among children. The infant mortality rate (deaths of infants under one year old per 1,000 live births) was 6.6 in 1993; neonatal mortality (deaths of infants under four weeks old per 1,000 live births) was 4.3; and maternal mortality is about 0.07 per 1,000 total births. The decline in mortality reflects better nutrition, rising standards of living, the advance of medical science, the growth of medical facilities, improved health measures, better working conditions, education in personal hygiene and the smaller size of families.

Deaths caused by circulatory diseases (including heart attacks and strokes) now account for nearly half of all deaths, and mortality from heart disease in England and Wales remains high compared with that of other developed countries. The next largest cause of death is cancer, which is responsible for nearly one-quarter of deaths.

Cigarette smoking is the greatest preventable cause of illness and death in Britain. However, there has been a significant decline in the prevalence of smoking, with 29 per cent of adult males and 28 per cent of adult females smoking cigarettes in 1992, as against 52 and 41 per cent respectively in 1972. In 1992 the Government set out strategies in England and Scotland for continuing the overall improvement in health, emphasising disease prevention and health promotion.

The Government is pursuing a comprehensive strategy against drug misuse in Britain. Initiatives are aimed at reducing both the supply of, and demand for, drugs. A number of government priorities, aimed at supporting the overall goals of improving the country's health and providing high-quality care for those who need it, have been listed (see p. 372).

Marriage and Divorce

Britain has one of the highest marriage and divorce rates in the European Union. In 1992 there were 311,500 marriages in Great Britain, of which 38.5 per cent were remarriages of one or both parties. Some 36.3 per cent of marriages were remarriages where one or both parties had been divorced. Of the population aged 16 or over in England and Wales in 1992, 57 per cent were married, 27 per cent single, 9 per cent widowed and 7 per cent divorced. The average age for first marriages in England and Wales is now about 27.9 for men and 25.9 for women.

In 1992 there were about 13.6 divorces for every 1,000 married couples in England and Wales. The rates are lower in Scotland and Northern Ireland. In 1992, 160,400 divorces were granted in England and Wales. The average age of people at the time of divorce in England and Wales is now about 38.9 for men and 36.3 for women.

Another feature, common to many other Western European countries, has been an increase in cohabitation, and 18 per cent of non-married men and women aged 16–59 in Great Britain were cohabiting in 1992. Between 1979 and 1992 the proportion of non-married women aged 18–49 who were cohabiting rose from 11 to 21 per cent. Cohabitation is particularly high (28 per cent) among divorced women, but recently the largest increase has been for single women.

There is some evidence of a growing number of stable non-married relationships. Roughly half of all births outside marriage (which accounted for 31 per cent of live births in Britain in 1992) are registered by both parents giving a single address as their place of residence.

Age and Sex Structure

The most significant changes in the age structure of the population have been the growing numbers of elderly people and the decline in the proportion of young people. The proportion of young people aged under 16 fell from 25.5 per cent in 1971 to 20.6 per cent in 1993. During the same period the proportion of elderly people (those aged 65 and over) increased from 13.2 to 15.8 per cent, while 18.3 per cent of the population were over the normal retirement ages (65 for men and 60 for women), compared with 16.3 per cent in 1971.

There is a ratio of about 104 females to every 100 males. There are about 3 per cent more male than female births every year. Because of the higher mortality of men at all ages, there is a turning point, at about 50 years of age, beyond which the number of women exceeds the number of men. This imbalance increases with age so that there are many more women among the elderly.

Distribution of Population

The population density is about 241 inhabitants per sq km, which is well above the EU average of about 153 per sq km. Of the four lands, England is the most densely populated, with 372 people per sq km. Scotland is the least densely populated, with 66 people per sq km. Wales and Northern Ireland have 140 and 121 people per sq km respectively.

Since the 19th century there has been a trend, especially in London, for people to move away from congested urban centres into the suburbs. Between 1981 and 1991 all metropolitan counties (with the exception of West Yorkshire) experienced small decreases in population, the largest being in Merseyside (5 per cent). There has also been a geographical redistribution of the population, away from Scotland and the northern regions of England. The regions with the highest rates of increase in population between 1981 and 1991 were East Anglia (10 per cent) and the South West (8 per cent). Retirement migration is also a feature of population movement, the main recipient areas (where in some towns the retired constitute over one-quarter of the population) being the south coast of England and East Anglia.

Migration

From 1988 to 1992 some 1.1 million people left Britain (excluding the Channel Islands and the Isle of Man) to live abroad and about 1.2 million came from overseas to live in Britain, so that net immigration increased the population by about 75,500. (These figures exclude migration to and from the Irish Republic.)

In 1992 the total inflow of people intending to stay in Britain was 215,900, some 19 per cent less than in 1991. The outflow of people leaving to live abroad, at 227,000, was 5 per cent lower than in 1991.

Of the 227,000 departing residents in 1993:
- 25 per cent left for other EU countries;
- 19 per cent for Australia, Canada or New Zealand;
- 16 per cent for the United States;
- 13 per cent for other Commonwealth countries;
- 6 per cent for the Middle East; and
- 2 per cent for South Africa.

Of the 215,900 new residents in 1993:
- 32 per cent from other EU countries;
- 16 per cent came from Australia, Canada or New Zealand;
- 22 per cent from other Commonwealth countries;
- 8 per cent from the United States;
- 3 per cent from the Middle East; and
- 3 per cent from South Africa.

Nationality

Under the British Nationality Act 1981 there are three main forms of citizenship:
- British citizenship for people closely connected with Britain;
- British Dependent Territories citizenship for people connected with the dependent territories (see p. 114); and
- British Overseas citizenship for those citizens of the United Kingdom and Colonies who did not acquire either of the other citizenships when the 1981 Act came into force.

British citizenship is acquired automatically at birth by a child born in Britain if his or her mother or father is a British citizen or is settled in Britain. A child adopted in Britain by a British citizen is a British citizen. A child born abroad to a British citizen born, adopted, naturalised or registered in Britain is generally a British citizen by descent. The Act safeguards the citizenship of a child born abroad to a British citizen in Crown service, certain related services, or in service under a European Union institution.

British citizenship may also be acquired:

- by registration for certain children, including those born in Britain who do not automatically acquire such citizenship at birth or who have been born abroad to a parent who is a citizen by descent;

- by registration for British Dependent Territories citizens, British Overseas citizens, British subjects under the Act, British Nationals (Overseas) and British protected persons after five years' residence in Britain, except for people from Gibraltar, who may be registered without residence;

- by registration for stateless people and those who have previously renounced British nationality; and

- by naturalisation for all other adults aged 18 or over.

Naturalisation is at the Home Secretary's discretion. Requirements include five years' residence, or three years if the applicant's spouse is a British citizen. Those who are not married to a British citizen are also required to have a sufficient knowledge of English, Welsh or Scottish Gaelic; they must also intend to have their main home in Britain or be employed by the Crown, by an international organisation of which Britain is a member, or by a company or association established in Britain.

Legislation passed in 1983 conferred British citizenship on Falkland Islanders who did not acquire it under the 1981 Act. Special arrangements covering the status of British Dependent Territories citizens connected with Hong Kong when the territory returns to the People's Republic of China in 1997 are made by the Hong Kong (British Nationality) Order 1986. Under this, such citizens are entitled, before 1997, to acquire a status known as British National (Overseas) and to hold a passport in that status. In addition, the British Nationality (Hong Kong) Act 1990 made provision for the registration as British citizens before

30 June 1997 of up to 50,000 people who are able to meet certain criteria and who are recommended by the Governor, together with their spouses and children who are still minors.

In 1993 about 45,000 people acquired British citizenship by naturalisation or registration in Britain.

Immigration

Immigration into Britain is controlled under the Immigration Rules, and the Asylum and Immigration Appeals Act 1993. These set out the requirements to be met by those, excluding British citizens, who seek entry to or leave to remain in Britain. British citizens and those Commonwealth citizens who had the right of abode before 1 January 1983 maintain the right of abode and are not subject to immigration control.

Under the Immigration Rules nationals of certain specified countries or territorial entities must obtain a visa before they can enter Britain. Other nationals subject to immigration control require entry clearance when coming to work or settle in Britain. Visas and other entry clearances are normally obtained from the nearest or other specified British diplomatic post in the applicant's home country.

Nationals of European Economic Area (EEA) countries—EU member states plus Austria, Finland, Iceland, Norway and Sweden (see p. 118)—are not subject to substantive immigration control. They may work in Britain without restriction. Provided that they are working or able to support themselves financially, EEA nationals have a right to reside in Britain. Britain respects its obligations under the United Nations Convention and Protocol relating to the Status of Refugees. These provide that refugees lawfully resident in a contracting state should enjoy treatment at least as favourable as that accorded to other foreign nationals in similar circumstances.

In 1993, nearly 10 million foreign and Commonwealth nationals (excluding EU nationals) were admitted to Britain. About 55,600 people were accepted for settlement.

LANGUAGE

English is the main language spoken in
Britain, and is also one of the most widely
used in the world.[2] Recent estimates suggest
that 310 million people speak it as their first
language, with a similar number speaking it as
a second language. It is an official language in
a large number of overseas countries, and is
widely used as the main language for
purposes such as air traffic control and
academic gatherings.

Modern English derives primarily from
one of the dialects of Anglo-Saxon. However,
it has been very greatly influenced by other
languages, particularly, following the Norman
conquest, by French. French was the
language of the nobility and the law courts
for many years after 1066. The re-emergence
of English as the universal language of
England was signified by such events as the
Statute of Pleadings in 1362, which laid down
that English was to be used in court. The
14th century also saw the first major English
literature since Anglo-Saxon days, with the
writing of works such as *Piers Plowman* by
William Langland and *The Canterbury
Tales* by Geoffrey Chaucer. However, there
remained great regional variations in
the language, and spellings were not
always standardised.

---

[2] For Welsh language see p. 22; for Gaelic see p. 21.

The 16th and early 17th centuries saw a
considerable flowering of English literature,
with writers such as William Shakespeare,
Edmund Spenser and Christopher Marlowe.
Cranmer's prayerbook and the Authorised
('King James') Version of the Bible, which
have had a profound effect on literature down
to modern times, also date from this period.
The work of lexicographers, of whom the
most famous was Samuel Johnson (1709–84),
also led to greater standardisation in matters
such as spelling.

ETHNIC AND NATIONAL MINORITIES

For centuries people from overseas have
settled in Britain, either to escape political or
religious persecution or in search of better
economic opportunities.

The Irish have long formed a large section
of the population. Jewish refugees who came
to Britain towards the end of the 19th
century and in the 1930s were followed by
other European refugees after 1945.
Substantial immigration from the Caribbean
and the South Asian sub-continent dates
principally from the 1950s and 1960s. In
recent years, the number of people coming
from the South Asian sub-continent has
remained roughly stable, but there has been a
rise in immigration from some African
countries, such as Ghana and Nigeria
(see Table 6.1).

The 1991 census included for the first

Table 6.1: Acceptances for Settlement 1983–1993

	1983	1993	% change
Pakistan	6,440	6,650	3.3
India	5,380	4,890	−9.1
United States	3,940	4,060	3.0
Nigeria	360	2,750	663.9
Bangladesh	4,870	2,550	−47.6
Sri Lanka	920	1,940	110.9
Japan	1,010	1,810	79.2
Australia	2,680	1,680	−37.3
Hong Kong	1,050	1,510	43.8
Ghana	560	1,350	141.1
Jamaica	310	1,270	309.7
Philippines	680	1,200	76.5
Iran	1,980	1,070	−46.0

Source: Home Office.

time a question on ethnic grouping. This found that 94.5 per cent of the population belonged to the 'white' group, while just over 3 million people (5.5 per cent) described themselves as belonging to another ethnic group (see Table 6.2). Members of other ethnic groups were heavily concentrated in industrial and urban areas, and over half lived in the South East. The highest proportion was in the London borough of Brent: nearly 45 per cent of the population. Ethnic minority groups also accounted for over a third of the population in the London boroughs of Newham, Tower Hamlets and Hackney.

Outside London the main concentrations were in Leicester, Slough, Luton, Bradford, the West Midlands and the Pennine conurbation. Regional concentrations varied among the ethnic groups. About three-fifths of people from black ethnic groups lived in London, compared with about two-fifths of Indians and 18 per cent of Pakistanis, who were concentrated in other metropolitan areas such as West Yorkshire.

Overall, 47 per cent of the ethnic minority population were born in Britain. A higher proportion is under 16 than for the white group (33 per cent and 19 per cent respectively), but a much lower proportion is over pensionable age (3 per cent and about 17 per cent respectively).

According to the Labour Force Survey, economic activity rates for men of working age in Great Britain tend to be similar to those for the white groups. In autumn 1993 they were 77 per cent for the black group, 76 per cent for the Indian group, and 73 per cent for both the white and Pakistani/Bangladeshi populations. The variations are much greater for women: 61 per cent of those from the black ethnic group were economically active, compared with 59 per cent in the Indian group, 53 per cent in the white group and only 26 per cent in the Pakistani/Bangladeshi group.

Alleviating Racial Disadvantage

Although many members of the black and Asian communities are concentrated in the inner cities, where there are problems of deprivation and social stress, progress has been made over the last 20 years in tackling racial disadvantage in Britain.

Many individuals have achieved distinction in their careers and in public life, and the proportion of ethnic minority members occupying professional and managerial positions is increasing. There are at present six ethnic minority Members of Parliament, and the number of ethnic minority councillors in local government is growing. There has also been an expansion of commercial enterprise, and numerous self-help projects in ethnic minority communities have been established. Black competitors have represented Britain in a range of sporting activities (such as athletics and football), and ethnic minority talents in the arts and in entertainment have increasingly been recognised.

The principal means of combating disadvantage is through the economic, environmental, educational and health programmes of central government and local authorities. There are also special allocations, mainly through Home Office and Department of the Environment grants, which channel extra resources into projects of specific benefit to ethnic minorities. These include, for example, the provision of specialist teachers for children needing English language tuition. Cultural and recreational schemes and the health and personal social services also take account of the particular needs of ethnic minorities.

Table 6.2: Population by Ethnic Group, 1991, Great Britain

	Number of People *(000s)*	Per cent
White	51,874	94.5
Other groups	3,015	5.5
of whom:		
Black	891	1.6
Indian	840	1.5
Pakistani	477	0.9
Bangladeshi	163	0.3
Chinese	157	0.3
Other	488	0.9

Source: Office of Population Censuses and Surveys

The Government is promoting equal opportunities for ethnic minorities through training programmes, including greater provision for unemployed people who need training in English as a second language.

In recognition of the tensions that can arise between the police and ethnic minorities, there is statutory consultation between the police and the community. Liaison work is also undertaken with children in schools.

Race Relations Legislation

The Race Relations Act 1976 strengthened previous legislation passed in the 1960s. It makes discrimination unlawful on grounds of colour, race, nationality or ethnic or national origin in the provision of goods, facilities and services, in employment, in housing, in education and in advertising. The 1976 Act also gave complainants direct access to civil courts and, for employment complaints, to industrial tribunals. It is a criminal offence to incite racial hatred under the provisions of the Public Order Act 1986.

Commission for Racial Equality

The Commission for Racial Equality was established by the 1976 Act. It has power to investigate unlawful discriminatory practices and to issue non-discrimination notices, requiring such practices to cease. It has an important educational role and has issued codes of practice in employment, education, health care and housing. It also provides advice to the general public about the Race Relations Act and has discretion to assist individuals with their complaints about racial discrimination. In 1993 the Commission registered 1,630 applications for assistance and handled successfully 210 litigation cases. It can also undertake or fund research.

The Commission supports the work of over 90 racial equality councils. These are autonomous voluntary bodies set up in most areas with a significant ethnic minority population to promote equality of opportunity and good relations at the local level. The Commission helps pay the salaries of the racial equality officers employed by the councils, most of whom also receive funds from their local authorities. It also gives grants to ethnic minority self-help groups and to other projects run by or for the benefit of the minority communities.

THE ECONOMIC AND SOCIAL PATTERN

Marked improvements in the standard of living have taken place during the 20th century. According to a United Nations report on human development published in 1994, Britain ranked tenth out of 173 countries on a human development index that combines life expectancy, education levels and basic purchasing power.

Britain has also performed well economically. Growth between 1980 and 1990 was higher than in all other major EU countries except Spain. Subsequently, following the recession of the early 1990s, Britain has been one of the first countries to experience recovery. Gross domestic product in Britain grew by 1.9 per cent in 1993, with an increase in manufacturing output and growth in retail sales. Inflation has recently been around 2 per cent a year, with the underlying level of inflation in 1993 and 1994 the lowest since 1967.

Income and Wealth

Earnings from employment remain the main source of household income for most people, although the proportion of household income (57 per cent in 1992, compared with 68 per cent in 1971) has been declining. Sources which have become more important include private pensions and annuities (11 per cent, up from 5 per cent in 1971) as the number of people who have made such provision has grown. By 1992, disposable income—the amount of money people have available to spend after the deduction of income tax, National Insurance contributions and contributions to pension schemes—is now at its highest ever level. Disposable income in 1992 was nearly 80 per cent higher than in 1971 after allowing for inflation.

The proportion of household income paid

in income tax has remained steady in recent years and stood at 13 per cent in 1992. The top 20 per cent of households by income received 41 per cent of income in 1990–91. Wealth is less evenly distributed, with the richest 10 per cent of the population having 50 per cent of marketable wealth in 1991. The inclusion of 'non-marketable' rights in occupational and state pension schemes reduces this share substantially, to 36 per cent. Since the mid-1970s there has been little change in the distribution of marketable wealth.

A large proportion of personal wealth—33 per cent in 1992—is in dwellings, down quite sharply from the level of immediately preceding years as house prices have fallen. The proportion of net wealth held in shares declined up to 1984, but has since increased. The Government's privatisation programme has contributed to the growth in share ownership. In 1993 about 10 million people—

22 per cent of the adult population in Great Britain—owned shares, compared with 7 per cent in 1979.

Eating and Drinking Habits

The general level of nutrition remains high. There has been a significant shift in eating patterns over the last decade, reflecting greater emphasis on health, frozen and convenience foods. Changes in household consumption of selected foods between 1983 and 1993 are shown in the diagram below. Consumption of several items, such as packet sugar, eggs, fresh potatoes and fresh green vegetables, has declined substantially. Other changes include:
- a decline in consumption of beef, lamb and pork—this has been partly offset by a continuing increase in poultry consumption, which is now at a record level;

Changes in Average Household Food Consumption 1983–1993

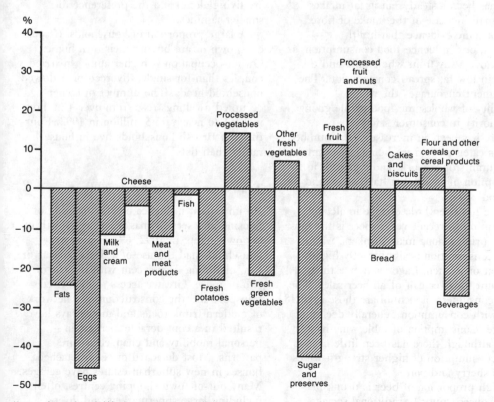

Note: Average household food consumption may be affected by the decline in household size as well as changes in eating habits.

Source: *National Food Survey*, MAFF.

- an increase in purchases of semi-skimmed milk, with skimmed milk now constituting more than half of the total household consumption of liquid milk;

- a decline in the total consumption of cooking and spreading fats, with large falls in butter and lard usage being partly offset by rapid rises in the consumption of vegetable and salad oils and reduced fat spreads;

- a trend away from consumption of some fresh green vegetables such as cabbages and beans towards leafy salads and cauliflowers;

- a large increase in purchases of fruit juice; and

- a switch in fish consumption away from fresh white fish towards canned fish and shellfish.

Average mineral and nutrient intakes are generally above the daily amounts recommended by the Department of Health. There has been a steady fall in fat intakes, and a small increase in the intake of fibre. There is some evidence that health considerations influence food consumption, as in the move away from whole milk and the growth in low fat spread consumption. The Government encourages the widest availability of wholesome food, while giving high priority to consumer safety.

There has been an increase in the number of meals eaten away from home, for example, in restaurants or at work, and a growth in the consumption of food from 'take-away' and 'fast-food' shops.

There has been little change in alcohol consumption in recent years. Beer is the most popular drink among male drinkers, whose overall consumption is significantly higher than that of women. Lager is now estimated to account for over half of all beer sales. The largest consumers of alcohol are those aged 18 to 24, with consumption generally declining with age. Consumption of table wine has grown, although there has been little change in the consumption of higher strength wines such as sherry and port.

A high proportion of beer is drunk in public houses ('pubs'), traditional social centres for many people, and in clubs. The Licensing Act 1988 relaxed restrictions on the opening hours of public houses, but this has not resulted in a significant increase in consumption. There are signs that they are becoming more popular with families: more meals are being served and the consumption of non-alcoholic drinks is increasing. Under proposals in the Deregulation and Contracting Out Bill (see p. 197), pubs would be able to apply for a children's certificate. This would allow children under 14 into designated areas if accompanied by an adult.

Households

The average size of households in Great Britain has fallen from over four people in 1911 to three in 1961 and 2.4 in 1992. The fall reflects a greater number of people living on their own (14 per cent of adults in 1992), or in one-parent families, the increasing number of old people (more of whom are living alone) and the preference for smaller families.

A large proportion of households, 67 per cent, own or are buying their own homes. Owner-occupation is higher among married couples than for single, divorced or widowed household heads. The number of owner-occupied dwellings rose from over 4 million in 1951 to nearly 15.5 million in 1992. Four-fifths of British households live in houses rather than flats.

Transport and the Environment

An important influence on the planning of housing and services has been the growth of car ownership; in 1992, 69 per cent of households had the use of at least one car or van, including 24 per cent with the use of two or more. Greater access to motorised transport and the construction of a network of modern trunk roads and motorways have resulted in a considerable increase in personal mobility and changed leisure patterns. Most detached or semi-detached houses in new suburban estates have garages. Many out-of-town shopping centres, often including large supermarkets and do-it-yourself stores, have been built with the motorist in mind.

Although the growth in car ownership has brought benefits, there have been a number of problems, notably increased congestion, noise and air pollution arising from motor vehicle emissions. Cars, taxis and motor cycles accounted for 87 per cent of all passenger transport in Great Britain in 1992, compared with 55 per cent in 1961. To relieve road congestion, the Government regards carefully targeted improvements to the road system as essential. The Government is also seeking to use the planning system (see p. 343) to reduce people's need to travel without inhibiting their freedom to do so. To help meet the British target for reducing carbon dioxide emissions (see p.362), it is increasing fuel duty by 5 per cent a year in real terms.

Women

The economic and domestic lives of women have been transformed in the 20th century. These changes are due partly to the removal of much of sex discrimination in political and legal rights. A major feature has been the rise in the number of women, especially married women, at work. With the decline in family size, more women are now combining raising a family with paid employment. Women now make up more than two-fifths of the workforce. The growth of part-time and flexible working patterns, and training and retraining schemes, allows more women to take advantage of employment opportunities. More than 740,000 women now run their own businesses—nearly double the number who did so in 1980.

Availability of Certain Durable Goods

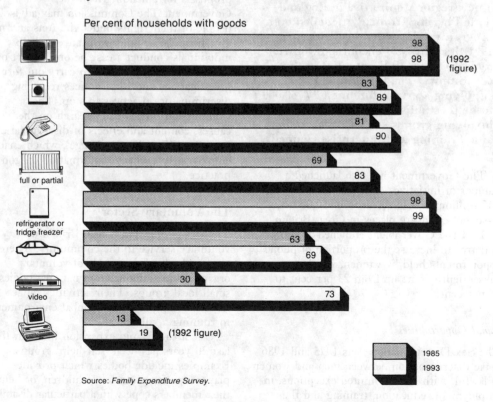

Per cent of households with goods

	1985	1993
(television)	98	98 (1992 figure)
(washing machine)	83	89
(telephone)	81	90
central heating full or partial	69	83
refrigerator or fridge freezer	98	99
(car)	63	69
video	30	73
(home computer)	13	19 (1992 figure)

Source: *Family Expenditure Survey.*

In 1992 the Department of Employment assumed responsibility for co-ordinating policy and strategy on women's issues. The Secretary of State set up a working group to advise on practical measures to extend equal opportunities for women in the workplace and elsewhere. The Women's National Commission, an official advisory committee, represents the views of women to the Government and other public bodies. About 50 of the main national women's organisations are represented on the Commission.

The Government supports the 'Opportunity 2000' campaign, an employer-led initiative to increase the quantity and quality of women's participation in the workforce. Membership stands at some 200 employers, with organisations employing nearly a quarter of the workforce being committed to the campaign.

> In April 1994 the Department of Employment and the Equal Opportunities Commission announced a new regional initiative in England— 'Fair Play for Women', modelled on a programme launched in Wales in 1991. Its aim is to encourage women to realise their full potential in the community. The Government is supplying start-up funding of £750,000 to help establish regional consortia involving groups such as trade unions and Training and Enterprise Councils.

The Government has also launched a number of initiatives. It is spending £45 million to help set up over 50,000 out-of-school childcare places in Great Britain. In 1991 the Government launched an initiative to increase the proportion of public appointments held by women, which has subsequently gone up from 23 per cent to 28 per cent.

Equal Opportunities

The Sex Discrimination Acts 1975 and 1986 make discrimination between men and women unlawful, with certain limited exceptions, in employment, education, training and the provision of housing, goods, facilities and services. Discriminatory job recruitment advertisements are also unlawful. Complaints of discrimination concerning employment are dealt with by industrial tribunals; other complaints are taken before county courts in England and Wales or the Sheriff Court in Scotland. Under the Equal Pay Act 1970, as amended in 1984, women in Great Britain are entitled to equal pay with men when doing work that is the same or broadly similar, or work which is rated as equivalent or work which is of equal value. Parallel legislation on sex discrimination and equal pay is in operation in Northern Ireland.

The Equal Opportunities Commission, set up in 1975 (1976 in Northern Ireland under separate laws), has powers to enforce some parts of the Sex Discrimination and Equal Pay Acts. Its statutory duties are to work towards the elimination of sex discrimination, to promote equality of opportunity, and to keep legislation on sex discrimination and equal pay under review, submitting proposals for amending it to the Government The Commission may advise people of their rights under the Acts and may give financial or other assistance to help individuals conduct a case before a court or tribunal. It is empowered to carry out formal investigations and issue notices requiring discriminatory practices to stop. The Commission carries out research on the causes, content and effects of discrimination. It runs an 'Equality Exchange', which enables employers to exchange information on good practice.

The Voluntary Sector

There is a long tradition in Britain of voluntary service to the community. There are hundreds of thousands of voluntary organisations, ranging from national bodies to small local groups. Their activities range from helping protect the global environment to running a village hall.

One area of rapid expansion in about the last 20 years has been 'self-help' groups. Examples include bodies which provide playgroups for pre-school children, or help their members cope with a particular disability.

Voluntary organisations may be staffed by professional workers, but all rely on the efforts of volunteers at some level. It has been estimated that up to half of all adults take part in some form of organised voluntary activity in the course of the year. Many volunteers are involved in work which improves the quality of life in their local communities or, more widely, give their time to help organise events and groups in areas as diverse as social welfare, education, sport and the arts. A very large number are also involved in activities to protect or improve the environment, for example, the National Trust (see p. 348), which has over 2 million members.

The Government greatly values the voluntary sector's contribution to society and, as a result, is keen to encourage productive partnerships between the statutory and voluntary sectors. For example, voluntary organisations are important providers of government-supported employment and training services for unemployed people.

The Home Office Voluntary Services Unit is responsible for co-ordinating government policy towards the voluntary sector throughout Britain. It also aims to support a healthy and cost-effective voluntary sector and to promote volunteering. In connection with this, the 'Make a Difference' initiative was launched in March 1994, bringing the business, voluntary and public sectors together to develop effective local voluntary action. As one aspect of the initiative, the Government is giving grants to partnerships of people from business, the public and voluntary sectors who come forward with the most innovative ideas for encouraging volunteering.

Funding

Voluntary organisations receive income from several sources, including contributions from individuals, businesses and trusts; central and local government grants; and earnings from commercial activities and investments. They also receive fees (from central and local government) for those services which are provided on a contractual basis. In 1992–93 direct grants to voluntary organisations from government amounted to £563 million.

Tax changes in recent budgets have helped the voluntary sector secure more funds from industry and individuals. The Gift Aid scheme provides tax relief on single cash donations to charity of more than £250. By June 1994 charities had received donations of more than £730 million under the scheme and had claimed tax repayments of £244 million on them. Employees can also make tax-free donations to charity from their earnings. The Payroll Giving scheme provides tax relief on donations of up to £900 a year.

Table 6.3: Income of the Top Fund-raising Charities 1992–3

Charity	£ million total income	Voluntary income[a]
National Trust	132.4	70.4
Save the Children Fund	99.6	65.2
Barnardo's	75.5	34.5
Oxfam	73.3	53.3
Salvation Army	64.5	31.4
Royal National Lifeboat Institution	62.3	55.8
British Red Cross Society	60.7	28.0
Spastics Society	56.6	21.5
Imperial Cancer Research Fund	53.0	47.5
Royal National Institute for the Blind	47.0	24.9
Cancer Research Campaign	44.7	40.9
Christian Aid	42.1	26.4

Source: Charities Aid Foundation.
[a] Mostly donations but also includes other funds such as legacies and proceeds of charity shops.

Charities

In England and Wales there are over 171,000 charities registered with the Charity Commission. The Commission also gives advice to trustees of charities on their administration. Organisations are charities if they are established for exclusively charitable purposes such as the relief of poverty, the advancement of education or religion, or the promotion of certain other purposes of public benefit. These may include good community relations, the prevention of racial discrimination, the protection of health and the promotion of equal opportunity. The Charity Commission also has a statutory responsibility to ensure that charities make effective use of their resources. The Charities Act 1992 strengthened the Commissioners' power to investigate and supervise charities, thereby increasing their accountability.

The Charities Aid Foundation, an independent body, is one of the main organisations that aid the flow of funds to charity from individuals, companies and grant-making trusts.

Umbrella Organisations

The National Council for Voluntary Organisations is one of the main co-ordinating bodies in England, providing close links between voluntary organisations, government departments, local authorities, the European Commission and the private sector; around 625 national voluntary organisations are members. It also protects the interests and independence of voluntary agencies, and provides them with advice, information and other services. Councils in Scotland, Wales and Northern Ireland perform similar functions. The National Association of Councils for Voluntary Service is another umbrella organisation providing resources and advice, with over 230 local councils for voluntary service throughout England. Their role is to encourage the development of local voluntary action, mainly in urban areas. The rural equivalent is Action with Communities in Rural England, an organisation which represents 38 rural community councils.

Leisure Trends

About 14 per cent of total household expenditure went on leisure goods and services in 1993. The most common leisure activities are home-based, or social, such as visiting relatives or friends. Television viewing is by far the most popular leisure pastime, and nearly all households have a television set, with 96 per cent in 1992 having a colour set. Average viewing time is nearly 27 hours a week. Around 73 per cent of households now have at least one video recorder, compared with 30 per cent in 1985.

Listening to radio has been increasing, and averages over 10 hours a week. Purchases of compact discs have risen very rapidly, and in 1992 for the first time exceeded the sales of audio cassettes. The proportion of households with a compact disc player has grown considerably, from 15 per cent in 1989 to 39 per cent in 1993.

Other popular pursuits include: reading, do-it-yourself home improvements, gardening and going out for a meal, for a drink or to the cinema. About half of households have a pet, the most common being dogs and cats, with roughly 7 million of each in Britain.

Holidays

In 1993, 61 per cent of the adult population took at least one long holiday of four or more nights away from home. The number of long holidays taken by British residents was nearly 56 million, of which 33 million were taken in Britain. The most frequented free attraction was Blackpool Pleasure Beach (Lancashire), with 6.7 million visitors. The most popular destinations for summer holidays are the West Country, Scotland and Wales.

In 1993 the most popular destinations for overseas holidays by British residents were:

- Spain (25 per cent);
- France (11 per cent);
- the United States (9 per cent); and
- Greece (8 per cent).

In all, British residents took over 23 million holidays overseas in 1993, of which 58 per cent involved 'package' arrangements. About 74 per cent of all holidays abroad are taken in Europe, although more people are taking holidays further afield, such as to the United States. The proportion of adults taking two or more holidays a year was 16 per cent in 1993.

Further Reading

Immigration and Nationality. Aspects of Britain series, HMSO, 1992.

Annual Reports
Family Spending. HMSO.
General Household Survey. HMSO.
Social Trends. HMSO.
Women and Men in Britain. Equal Opportunities Commission.

Government and Administration

7　Government

The system of parliamentary government in Britain is not based on a written constitution, but is the result of gradual evolution over many centuries. The monarchy is the oldest institution of government, dating back to at least the ninth century. Parliament is one of the oldest representative assemblies in the world. In government among the most significant recent developments have been the steps taken to improve management. New management structures— such as the creation of executive agencies—have been developed; competition has been introduced or extended; and arrangements for pay are changing. The aim of all these changes is to safeguard and improve the standards of the public services.

Development of the British System of Government

The growth of political institutions in England can be traced back to the period of Saxon rule, which lasted from the fifth century AD until the Norman Conquest in 1066 (see p. 7). This period saw the origins of the institution of kingship, and of the idea that the king should seek the advice of a council of prominent men.

The period of Norman rule after 1066 saw a considerable strengthening of royal power. However, the monarchy eventually experienced difficulties in controlling the growing machinery of government. The actions of King John (1199–1216) led to opposition from the nobility and leading figures in the Church. In 1215 the barons forced the King to agree to a series of concessions embodied in a charter which became known as Magna Carta. The charter, which provided for the protection of the rights of freemen against the abuse of royal power, came to be regarded as the key expression of the rights of the community against the Crown.

The first known occurrence of the term 'Parliament' to describe the meetings of nobles to advise the king is in 1236; by the late 13th century representatives of counties and towns were also occasionally being summoned at the same time, usually to express political support, but increasingly to give consent to taxation. By the end of the 15th century Parliament existed in a form virtually recognisable today: as a body whose function was to agree to taxes and to legislate, and which consisted of two separate chambers—the House of Commons and the House of Lords.

Although the influence of government in Parliament was considerable, the body was always an area for political conflict; one such clash led to the outbreak of the Civil War in 1642 between Crown and Parliament. Following the defeat of the royalist armies and the execution of Charles I in 1649, the monarchy and the House of Lords were abolished and the country was proclaimed a republic. However, the republican experiment came to an end in 1660, two years after the death of the 'Lord Protector', Oliver Cromwell. Charles I's son was restored to the throne as Charles II.

Charles II's successor, James VII and II (1685–88), sought both to bypass Parliament and to make it more amenable. As a result, in 1688 a group of leading men invited William of Orange (a grandson of Charles I and the husband of Mary, James VII and II's eldest daughter) to 'secure the infringed liberties' of the country. James VII and II fled into exile. Following the success of the revolution of 1688, Parliament in 1689 passed the Bill of Rights, which defined the rights and privileges of Parliament.

Increasingly thereafter parliamentary control of national finance made it impracticable for the Sovereign to ignore the wishes of Parliament. Ministers were appointed by the Sovereign, but they had to have sufficient support in the House of Commons to enable them to persuade Parliament to pass legislation and vote for taxation. The development of 'party' during the 18th and 19th centuries provided them with the machinery for securing that support, while the personal involvement of the monarch in policy and the day-to-day business of administration declined, leaving government in the hands of the cabinet, presided over by a 'Prime' Minister.

Since the mid-19th century the Prime Minister has normally been the leader of the party with a majority in the House of Commons.

The Reform Act of 1832 altered the medieval system of parliamentary representation and standardised the qualifications for the right to vote. Subsequent reforms gave the vote to virtually all adults—women were finally enfranchised in 1918, but not on the same terms as men until 1928.

The British Constitution

The British constitution is to a large extent a product of the historical events described above. Unlike the constitutions of most other countries, it is not set out in any single document. Instead it is made up of statute law, common law and conventions. (Conventions are rules and practices which are not legally enforceable but which are regarded as indispensable to the working of government.)

The constitution can be altered by Act of Parliament, or by general agreement, and is thus adaptable to changing political conditions.

The organs of government overlap but can be clearly distinguished. Parliament is the legislature and the supreme authority. The executive consists of:

- the Government—the Cabinet and other ministers responsible for national policies;

- government departments, responsible for national administration;

- local authorities, responsible for many local services; and

- public corporations, responsible for operating particular nationalised industries or other bodies, subject to ministerial control.

The judiciary (see Chapter 8) determines common law and interprets statutes.

The Monarchy

The monarchy is the oldest institution of government, going back to at least the 9th century. Queen Elizabeth II is herself directly descended from King Egbert, who united England under his rule in 829. The only interruption in the history of the monarchy was the republic, which lasted from 1649 to 1660 (see above).

The Royal Family from the Reign of Queen Victoria to August 1994

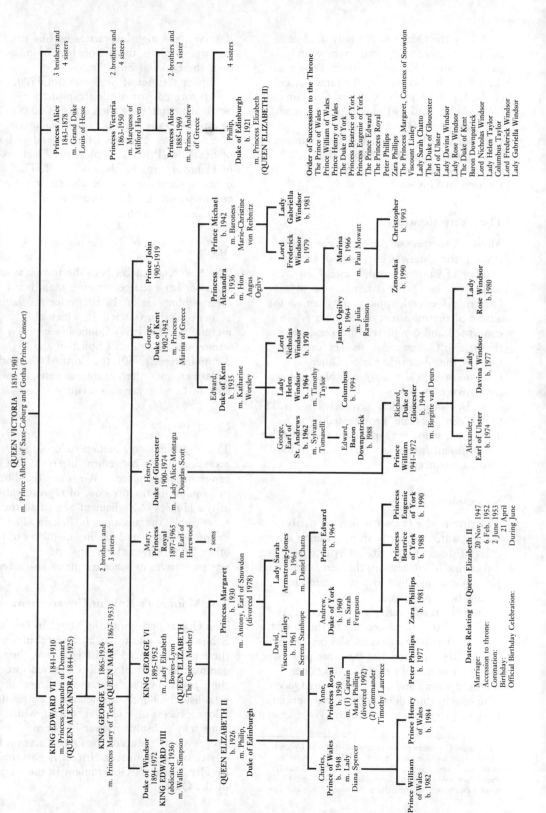

Today the Queen is not only head of State, but also an important symbol of national unity. The royal title in Britain is: 'Elizabeth the Second, by the Grace of God of the United Kingdom of Great Britain and Northern Ireland and of Her other Realms and Territories Queen, Head of the Commonwealth, Defender of the Faith'.

In the Channel Islands and the Isle of Man the Queen is represented by a Lieutenant-Governor.

The Commonwealth

Although the seat of the monarchy is in Britain, the Queen is also head of state of a number of Commonwealth states.[1] In each such state the Queen is represented by a Governor-General, appointed by her on the advice of the ministers of the country concerned and completely independent of the British Government. In each case the form of the royal title varies. Other Commonwealth states are republics or have their own monarchies.

In British dependent territories (see p. 114) the Queen is usually represented by governors, who are responsible to the British Government for the administration of the countries concerned.

Succession

The title to the Crown is derived partly from statute and partly from common law rules of descent. Despite interruptions in the direct line of succession, the hereditary principle upon which it was founded has always been preserved.

Sons of the Sovereign have precedence over daughters in succeeding to the throne. When a daughter succeeds, she becomes Queen Regnant, and has the same powers as a king. The consort of a king takes her husband's rank and style, becoming Queen. The constitution does not give any special rank or privileges to the husband of a Queen

Regnant, although in practice he fills an important role in the life of the nation, as does the Duke of Edinburgh.

Under the Act of Settlement of 1700, which formed part of the Revolution Settlement following the events of 1688 (see p. 44), only Protestant descendants of a granddaughter of James I of England and VI of Scotland (Princess Sophia, the Electress of Hanover) are eligible to succeed. The order of succession can be altered only by common consent of the countries of the Commonwealth.

Accession

The Sovereign succeeds to the throne as soon as his or her predecessor dies: there is no interregnum. He or she is at once proclaimed at an Accession Council, to which all members of the Privy Council (see p. 63) are summoned. The Lords Spiritual and Temporal (see p. 50), the Lord Mayor and Aldermen and other leading citizens of the City of London are also invited.

Coronation

The Sovereign's coronation follows the accession after a convenient interval. The ceremony takes place at Westminster Abbey in London, in the presence of representatives of the Houses of Parliament and of all the great public organisations in Britain. The Prime Ministers and leading members of the other Commonwealth nations and representatives of other countries also attend.

The Monarch's Role in Government

The Queen personifies the State. In law, she is head of the executive, an integral part of the legislature, head of the judiciary, the commander-in-chief of all the armed forces of the Crown and the 'supreme governor' of the established Church of England. As a result of a long process of evolution, during which the monarchy's absolute power has been progressively reduced, the Queen acts on the advice of her ministers. Britain is governed by Her Majesty's Government in the name of the Queen.

---

[1] The other Commonwealth countries of which the Queen is head of state are: Antigua and Barbuda, Australia, Bahamas, Barbados, Belize, Canada, Grenada, Jamaica, New Zealand, Papua New Guinea, Saint Christopher and Nevis, Saint Lucia, Saint Vincent and the Grenadines, Solomon Islands and Tuvalu.

Within this framework, and in spite of a trend during the past hundred years towards giving powers directly to ministers, the Queen still takes part in some important acts of government. These include summoning, proroguing (discontinuing until the next session without dissolution) and dissolving Parliament; and giving Royal Assent to Bills passed by Parliament. The Queen also formally appoints many important office holders, including government ministers, judges, officers in the armed forces, governors, diplomats, bishops and some other senior clergy of the Church of England. She is also involved in pardoning people convicted of crimes; and in conferring peerages, knighthoods and other honours.[2] An important function is appointing the Prime Minister (see p. 61). In international affairs the Queen, as head of State, has the power to declare war and make peace, to recognise foreign states and governments, to conclude treaties and to annex or cede territory.

With rare exceptions (such as appointing the Prime Minister), acts involving the use of 'royal prerogative' powers are now performed by government ministers, who are responsible to Parliament and can be questioned about particular policies. Parliamentary authority is not required for the exercise of these prerogative powers, although Parliament may restrict or abolish such rights.

The Queen continues to play a role in the working of government. She holds Privy Council meetings, gives audiences to her ministers and officials in Britain and overseas, receives accounts of Cabinet decisions, reads dispatches and signs state papers. She must be consulted on every aspect of national life, and must show complete impartiality.

Provision has been made to appoint a regent to perform these royal functions should the Queen be totally incapacitated. The regent would be the Queen's eldest son, the Prince of Wales, then those, in order of succession to the throne, aged 18 or over.

In the event of her partial incapacity or absence abroad, the Queen may delegate certain royal functions to the Counsellors of State (the Duke of Edinburgh, the four adults next in line of succession, and the Queen Mother). However, Counsellors of State may not, for instance, dissolve Parliament (except on the Queen's instructions), nor create peers.

Ceremonial and Royal Visits

Ceremonial has always been associated with the British monarchy, and, in spite of changes in the outlook of both the Sovereign and the people, many traditional ceremonies continue to take place. Royal marriages and royal funerals are marked by public ceremony, and the Sovereign's birthday is officially celebrated in June by Trooping the Colour on Horse Guards Parade. State banquets take place when a foreign monarch or head of State visits Britain; investitures are held at Buckingham Palace and the Palace of Holyroodhouse in Scotland to bestow honours; and royal processions add significance to such occasions as the state opening of Parliament.

Each year the Queen and other members of the royal family visit many parts of Britain. They are also closely involved in the work of many charities. For example, the Prince of Wales is actively involved in the Youth Business Trust set up to encourage small firms and self employment in inner cities, while the Princess Royal is President of the Save the Children Fund and takes an active interest in third world development issues. The Queen pays state visits to foreign governments, accompanied by the Duke of Edinburgh. She also tours the other countries of the Commonwealth. Other members of the royal family pay official visits overseas, occasionally representing the Queen.

Royal Income and Expenditure

Until 1760 the Sovereign had to provide for payment of all government expenses, including the salaries of officials and the expenses of the royal palaces and households. These were met from hereditary revenues,

[2] Although most honours are conferred by the Queen on the advice of the Prime Minister, a few are granted by her personally—the Order of the Garter, the Order of the Thistle, the Order of Merit and the Royal Victorian Order.

mainly income from Crown lands, and income from some other sources granted to the monarch by Parliament. The income from these sources eventually proved inadequate and in 1760 George III turned over to the Government most of the hereditary revenue. In return he received an annual grant (Civil List) from which he continued to pay royal expenditure of a personal character, the salaries of government officials, the costs of royal palaces, and certain pensions. The latter charges were removed from the Civil List in 1830.

Present Arrangements

Today the expenditure incurred by the Queen in carrying out her public duties is financed from the Civil List and from government departments (which meet the cost of, for example, the Royal Yacht and the aircraft of the Queen's Flight). All such expenditure is approved by Parliament. In 1991 Civil List payments were fixed at £7.9 million a year for ten years. About three-quarters of the Queen's Civil List provision is required to meet the cost of staff They deal with, among other things, state papers and correspondence and the organisation of state occasions, visits and other public engagements undertaken by the Queen in Britain and overseas. The Queen's private expenditure as Sovereign is met from the Privy Purse, which is financed mainly from the revenue of the Duchy of Lancaster;[3] her expenditure as a private individual is met from her own personal resources.

Since April 1993 the Queen has voluntarily paid income tax on all her personal income and on that part of the Privy Purse income which is used for private purposes. The Queen also pays tax on any realised capital gains on her private investments and on the private proportion of assets in the Privy Purse. Inheritance tax will not, however, apply to transfers from one sovereign to his or her successor, although any personal bequests other than to the

successor will be subject to inheritance tax. In line with these changes the Prince of Wales pays income tax on the income from the Duchy of Cornwall to the extent that it is used for private purposes.

Under the Civil List Acts, other members of the royal family also receive annual parliamentary allowances to enable them to carry out their public duties. The Prince of Wales, however, receives no such allowance, since as Duke of Cornwall he is entitled to the income of the estate of the Duchy of Cornwall. Each year the Queen refunds the Government for all annuities paid to members of the royal family except the Queen Mother and the Duke of Edinburgh.

Parliament

Origins of Parliament

The medieval kings were expected to meet all royal expenses, private and public, out of their own revenue. If extra resources were needed for an emergency, such as a war, the Sovereign would seek to persuade his barons, in the Great Council—a gathering of leading men which met several times a year—to grant aid. During the 13th century several kings found the private revenues and baronial aids insufficient to meet the expenses of government. They therefore summoned not only the great feudal magnates but also representatives of counties, cities and towns, primarily to get their assent to extraordinary taxation. In this way the Great Council came to include those who were summoned by name (those who, broadly speaking, were to form the House of Lords) and those who were representatives of communities—the commons. The two parts, together with the Sovereign, became known as 'Parliament' (the term originally meant a meeting for parley or discussion).

Over the course of time the commons began to realise the strength of their position. By the middle of the 14th century the formula had appeared which in substance was the same as that used nowadays in voting supplies to the Crown—that is, money to the Government—namely, 'by the Commons

---

[3] The Duchy of Lancaster is an inheritance which, since 1399, has always been enjoyed by the reigning Sovereign. It is kept quite apart from his or her other possessions and is separately administered by the Chancellor of the Duchy of Lancaster.

with the advice of the Lords Spiritual and Temporal'. In 1407 Henry IV pledged that henceforth all money grants should be approved by the House of Commons before being considered by the Lords.

A similar advance was made in the legislative field. Originally the King's legislation needed only the assent of his councillors. Starting with the right of individual commoners to present petitions, the Commons as a body gained the right to submit collective petitions. Later, during the 15th century, they gained the right to participate in giving their requests—their 'Bills'—the form of law.

The subsequent development of the power of the House of Commons was built upon these foundations. The constitutional developments of the 17th century (see p. 44) led to Parliament securing its position as the supreme legislative authority.

The Powers of Parliament

The three elements which make up Parliament—the Queen, the House of Lords and the elected House of Commons—are constituted on different principles. They meet together only on occasions of symbolic significance such as the state opening of Parliament, when the Commons are summoned by the Queen to the House of Lords. The agreement of all three elements is normally required for legislation, but that of the Queen is given as a matter of course.

Parliament can legislate for Britain as a whole, or for any part of the country. It can also legislate for the Channel Islands and the Isle of Man, which are Crown dependencies and not part of Britain. They have local legislatures which make laws on island affairs (see p. 5).

As there are no legal restraints imposed by a written constitution, Parliament may legislate as it pleases, subject to Britain's obligations as a member of the European Union. It can make or change any law, and overturn established conventions or turn them into law. It can even prolong its own life beyond the normal period without consulting the electorate.

In practice, however, Parliament does not assert its supremacy in this way. Its members bear in mind the common law and normally act in accordance with precedent. The House of Commons is directly responsible to the electorate, and in this century the House of Lords has recognised the supremacy of the elected chamber. The system of party government helps to ensure that Parliament legislates with its responsibility to the electorate in mind.

The European Union

As a member of the European Union, Britain recognises the various types of Community legislation and wider policies. It sends 81 elected members to the European Parliament (see p. 112).

The Functions of Parliament

The main functions of Parliament are:
- to pass laws;
- to provide, by voting for taxation, the means of carrying on the work of government;
- to scrutinise government policy and administration, including proposals for expenditure; and
- to debate the major issues of the day.

In carrying out these functions Parliament helps to bring the relevant facts and issues before the electorate. By custom, Parliament is also informed before all important international treaties and agreements are ratified. The making of treaties is, however, a royal prerogative exercised on the advice of the Government and is not subject to parliamentary approval.

The Meeting of Parliament

A Parliament has a maximum duration of five years, but in practice general elections are usually held before the end of this term. The maximum life has been prolonged by legislation in rare circumstances such as the two world wars. Parliament is dissolved and writs for a general election are ordered by the Queen on the advice of the Prime Minister.

The life of a Parliament is divided into sessions. Each usually lasts for one year—normally beginning and ending in October or November. There are 'adjournments' at night, at weekends, at Christmas, Easter and the late Spring Bank Holiday, and during a long summer break usually starting in late July. The average number of 'sitting' days in a session is about 160 in the House of Commons and about 145 in the House of Lords. At the start of each session the Queen's speech to Parliament outlines the Government's policies and proposed legislative programme. Each session is ended by prorogation. Parliament then 'stands prorogued' for about a week until the new session opens. Prorogation brings to an end nearly all parliamentary business: in particular, public Bills which have not been passed by the end of the session are lost.

The House of Lords

The House of Lords consists of the Lords Spiritual and the Lords Temporal. The Lords Spiritual are the Archbishops of Canterbury and York, the Bishops of London, Durham and Winchester, and the 21 next most senior diocesan bishops of the Church of England. The Lords Temporal consist of:

- all hereditary peers and peeresses of England, Scotland, Great Britain and the United Kingdom (but not peers of Ireland);

- life peers created to assist the House in its judicial duties (Lords of Appeal or 'law lords');[4] and

- all other life peers.

Hereditary peerages carry a right to sit in the House provided holders establish their claim and are aged 21 years or over. However, anyone succeeding to a peerage may, within 12 months of succession, disclaim that peerage for his or her lifetime. Disclaimants lose their right to sit in the House but gain the right to vote and stand as candidates at parliamentary elections. When a disclaimant dies, the peerage passes on down the family in the usual way.

Peerages, both hereditary and life, are created by the Sovereign on the advice of the Prime Minister. They are usually granted in recognition of service in politics or other walks of life or because one of the political parties wishes to have the recipient in the House of Lords. The House also provides a place in Parliament for people who offer useful advice, but do not wish to be involved in party politics.

Peers who attend the House (the average daily attendance is some 380) receive no

> The potential membership of the House of Lords is about 1,200, but this number is reduced by about 80 by a scheme which allows peers who do not wish to attend to apply for leave of absence for the duration of a Parliament. In addition some hereditary peers do not establish their claim to succeed and so do not receive a writ of summons entitling them to sit in the House; there were around 90 such peers in early 1994.

salary for their parliamentary work, but can claim for expenses incurred in attending the House (for which there are maximum daily rates) and certain travelling expenses.

Officers of the House of Lords

The House is presided over by the Lord Chancellor, who takes his place on the woolsack[5] as ex-officio Speaker of the House. In his absence his place is taken by a deputy. The first of the deputy speakers is the Chairman of Committees, who is appointed at the beginning of each session and normally chairs Committees of the Whole House and some domestic committees. The Chairman and the Principal Deputy Chairman of Committees are the only Lords who receive salaries as officers of the House.

---

[4] The House of Lords is the final court of appeal for civil cases in Britain and for criminal cases in England, Wales, and Northern Ireland.

[5] The woolsack is a seat in the form of a large cushion stuffed with wool from several Commonwealth countries; it is a tradition dating from the medieval period, when wool was the chief source of the country's wealth.

In mid-1994 there were 1,198 members of the House of Lords, including the two archbishops and 24 bishops. The Lords Temporal consisted of 758 hereditary peers who had succeeded to their titles, 15 hereditary peers who had had their titles conferred on them (including the Prince of Wales), and 399 life peers, of whom 21 were 'law lords'.

The Clerk of the Parliaments is responsible for the records of proceedings of the House of Lords and for the text of Acts of Parliament. He is the accounting officer for the cost of the House, and is in charge of the administrative staff of the House, known as the Parliament Office. The Gentleman Usher of the Black Rod, usually known as 'Black Rod', is responsible for security, accommodation and services in the House of Lords' part of the Palace of Westminster.

The House of Commons

The House of Commons is elected by universal adult suffrage (see below) and consists of 651 Members of Parliament (MPs). In mid-1994 there 60 women, three Asian and three black MPs. Of the 651 seats, 524 are for England, 38 for Wales, 72 for Scotland, and 17 for Northern Ireland.

General elections are held after a Parliament has been dissolved and a new one summoned by the Queen. When an MP dies or resigns,[6] or is given a peerage, a by-election takes place. Members are paid an annual salary of £31,687 and an office costs allowance of up to £41,308. There are also a number of other allowances, including travel allowances, a supplement for London members and, for provincial members, subsistence allowances and allowances for second homes. (For ministers' salaries see p. 62.)

Officers of the House of Commons

The chief officer of the House of Commons is the Speaker, elected by MPs to preside over the House. Other officers include the

Chairman of Ways and Means and two deputy chairmen, who act as Deputy Speakers. They are elected by the House on the nomination of the Government but are drawn from the Opposition as well as the government party. They, like the Speaker, neither speak nor vote other than in their official capacity. Responsibility for the administration of the House rests with the House of Commons Commission, a statutory body chaired by the Speaker.

Permanent officers (who are not MPs) include the Clerk of the House of Commons, who is the principal adviser to the Speaker on its privileges and procedures. The Clerk's departmental responsibilities relate to the conduct of the business of the House and its committees. The Clerk is also accounting officer for the House. The Serjeant-at-Arms, who waits upon the Speaker, carries out certain orders of the House. He is also the official housekeeper of the Commons' part of the building, and is responsible for security. Other officers serve the House in the Library, the Department of the Official Report (*Hansard*), the Finance and Administration Department and the Refreshment Department.

Parliamentary Electoral System

For electoral purposes Britain is divided into constituencies, each of which returns one member to the House of Commons. To ensure that constituency electorates are kept roughly equal, four permanent Parliamentary Boundary Commissions, one each for England, Wales, Scotland and Northern Ireland, keep constituencies under review. They recommend any adjustment of seats that may seem necessary in the light of population movements or other changes. Reviews are conducted every 8 to 12 years. Elections are by secret ballot.

Voters

British citizens, together with citizens of other Commonwealth countries and citizens of the Irish Republic resident in Britain, may vote provided they are:
- aged 18 or over;

---

[6] An MP who wishes to resign from the House can only do so by applying for an office under the Crown as Crown Steward or Bailiff of the Chiltern Hundreds, or Steward of the Manor of Northstead.

- included in the annual register of electors for the constituency; and
- not subject to any disqualification.

People not entitled to vote include members of the House of Lords, patients detained under mental health legislation, sentenced prisoners and people convicted within the previous five years of corrupt or illegal election practices. Members of the armed forces, Crown servants and staff of the British Council employed overseas (together with their wives or husbands if accompanying them) may be registered for an address in the constituency where they would live but for their service. British citizens living abroad may apply to register as electors for a period of 20 years after they have left Britain.

Voting Procedures

Each elector may cast one vote, normally in person at a polling station. Electors whose circumstances on polling day are such that they cannot reasonably be expected to vote in person at their local polling station—for example, electors away on holiday—may apply for an absent vote at a particular election. Electors who are physically incapacitated or unable to vote in person because of the nature of their work or because they have moved to a new area may apply for an indefinite absent vote. People entitled to an absent vote may vote by post or by proxy, although postal ballot papers cannot be sent to addresses outside Britain.

Voting is not compulsory; 76.9 per cent of a total electorate of 43.3 million people voted in the general election in April 1992. The simple majority system of voting is used. Candidates are elected if they have more votes than any of the other candidates (although not necessarily an absolute majority over all other candidates).

Candidates

British citizens and citizens of other Commonwealth countries, together with citizens of the Irish Republic, may stand for election as MPs provided they are aged 21 or over and are not disqualified. Those disqualified include undischarged bankrupts; people sentenced to more than one year's imprisonment; clergy of the Church of England, Church of Scotland, Church of Ireland and Roman Catholic Church; peers; and holders of certain offices listed in the House of Commons Disqualification Act 1975. A candidate's nomination for election must be proposed and seconded by two electors registered as voters in the constituency and signed by eight other electors.

Candidates do not have to be backed by a political party. A candidate must also deposit £500, which is returned if he or she receives 5 per cent or more of the votes cast.

The maximum sum a candidate may spend on a general election campaign is £4,642 plus 3.9 pence for each elector in a borough constituency, or 5.2 pence for each elector in a county constituency. Higher limits have been set for by-elections in order to reflect the fact that they are often regarded as tests of national opinion in the period between general elections. The maximum sum is £18,572 plus 15.8 pence for each elector in borough seats, and 20.8 pence for each elector in county seats. A candidate may post an election communication to each elector in the constituency, free of charge. All election expenses, apart from the candidate's personal expenses, are subject to the statutory limit.

The Political Party System

The party system, which has existed in one form or another since the 18th century, is an essential element in the working of the constitution. The present system depends upon the existence of organised political parties, each of which presents its policies to the electorate for approval. The parties are not registered nor formally recognised in law, but in practice most candidates in elections, and almost all winning candidates, belong to one of the main parties.

For the last 150 years a predominantly two-party system has existed. Since 1945 either the Conservative Party, the origins of which go back to the 18th century, or the Labour Party, which emerged in the last decade of the 19th century, has held power.

A new party—the Liberal Democrats—was formed in 1988 when the Liberal Party, which traced its origins to the 18th century, merged with the Social Democratic Party, formed in 1981. Other parties include two nationalist parties, Plaid Cymru (founded in Wales in 1925) and the Scottish National Party (founded in 1934). In Northern Ireland there are a number of parties. They include the Ulster Unionist Party, formed in the early part of this century; the Democratic Unionist Party, founded in 1971 by a group which broke away from the Ulster Unionists; and the Social Democratic and Labour Party, founded in 1970.

Since 1945 eight general elections have been won by the Conservative Party and six by the Labour Party; the great majority of members of the House of Commons have belonged to one of these two parties. The results of the general election of April 1992 are shown in Table 7.1.

The party which wins most seats (although not necessarily the most votes) at a general election, or which has the support of a majority of members in the House of Commons, usually forms the Government. By tradition, the leader of the majority party is asked by the Sovereign to form a government. About 100 of its members in the House of Commons and the House of Lords receive ministerial appointments (including appointment to the Cabinet—see p. 62) on the advice of the Prime Minister. The largest minority party becomes the official Opposition, with its own leader and 'shadow cabinet'.

The Party System in Parliament

Leaders of the Government and Opposition sit on the front benches of the Commons with their supporters (the backbenchers) sitting behind them.

Similar arrangements for the parties also apply to the House of Lords; however, Lords who do not wish to be associated with any political party may sit on the 'cross-benches'.

The effectiveness of the party system in Parliament rests largely on the relationship between the Government and the opposition parties. Depending on the relative strengths of the parties in the House of Commons, the Opposition may seek to overthrow the Government by defeating it in a vote on a 'matter of confidence'. In general, however, its aims are to contribute to the formulation of policy and legislation by constructive criticism; to oppose government proposals it considers objectionable; to seek amendments to government Bills; and to put forward its own policies in order to improve its chances of winning the next general election.

The detailed arrangements of government business are settled, under the direction of the Prime Minister and the Leaders of the two Houses, by the Government Chief Whip in consultation with the Opposition Chief Whip. The Chief Whips together constitute the 'usual channels' often referred to when

Table 7.1: Results of the April 1992 General Election

Party	Members elected	Number of votes cast	% of votes cast
Conservative	336	14,094,116	41.9
Labour	271	11,557,134	34.4
Liberal Democrats	20	5,998,446	17.8
Plaid Cymru (Welsh Nationalist)	4		
Scottish National	3		
Ulster Unionist (Northern Ireland)	9		
Ulster Democratic Unionist (Northern Ireland)	3	1,960,703	5.9[a]
Ulster Popular Unionist (Northern Ireland)	1		
Social Democratic and Labour (Northern Ireland)	4		
Total	651	33,610,399	100.0

[a]These figures include votes for other parties whose candidates were unsuccessful.

the question of finding time for a particular item of business is discussed. The Leaders of the two Houses are responsible for enabling the Houses to debate matters about which they are concerned.

Outside Parliament, party control is exercised by the national and local organisations. Inside, it is exercised by the Chief Whips and their assistants, who are chosen within the party. Their duties include keeping members informed of forthcoming parliamentary business, maintaining the party's voting strength by ensuring members attend important debates, and passing on to the party leadership the opinions of backbench members. Party discipline tends to be less strong in the Lords than in the Commons, since Lords have less hope of high office and no need of party support in elections.

The formal title of the Government Chief Whip in the Commons is Parliamentary Secretary to the Treasury. Of the other Government Whips, three are officers of the Royal Household (one of these is Deputy Chief Whip), five hold titular posts as Lords Commissioners of the Treasury and five are Assistant Whips. The Opposition Chief Whips in both Houses and two of the Opposition Assistant Whips in the Commons receive salaries. The Government Whips in the Lords hold offices in the Royal Household; they also act as government spokesmen.

Financial Assistance to Parties

Annual assistance from public funds helps opposition parties carry out parliamentary work at Westminster. It is limited to parties which had at least two members elected at the previous general election or one member elected and a minimum of 150,000 votes cast. The amount is £3,442.50 for every seat won at the previous general election, plus £6.89 for every 200 votes.

Parliamentary Procedure

Parliamentary procedure is based on custom and precedent, partly codified by each House in its Standing Orders. The system of debate is similar in both Houses. Every subject starts off as a proposal or 'motion' by a member. After debate, in which each member may speak only once, the motion may be withdrawn: if it is not, the Speaker or Chairman 'puts the question' whether to agree with the motion or not. The question may be decided without voting, or by a simple majority vote. The main difference of procedure between the two Houses is that the Speaker or Chairman in the Lords has no powers of order; instead such matters are decided by the general feeling of the House.

In the Commons the Speaker has full authority to enforce the rules of the House and must guard against the abuse of procedure and protect minority rights. The Speaker has discretion on whether to allow a motion to end discussion so that a matter may be put to the vote and has powers to put a stop to irrelevance and repetition in debate, and to save time in other ways. In cases of grave disorder the Speaker can adjourn or suspend the sitting. The Speaker may order members who have broken the rules of behaviour of the House to leave the Chamber or can initiate their suspension for a period of days.

The Speaker supervises voting in the Commons and announces the final result. In a tied vote the Speaker gives a casting vote, without expressing an opinion on the merits of the question. The voting procedure in the House of Lords is broadly similar, although the Lord Chancellor does not have a casting vote.

Financial Interests

The Commons has a public register of MPs' financial interests. Members with a financial interest in a debate in the House must declare it when speaking. If the interest is direct, immediate and personal, the member cannot vote on the issue. In other proceedings of the House or in dealings with other members, ministers or civil servants, MPs must also disclose any relevant financial interest.

There is no register of financial interests in the Lords, but Lords speaking in a debate in which they have a direct interest are expected to declare it.

Public Access to Parliamentary Proceedings

Proceedings of both Houses are normally public. The minutes and speeches (transcribed verbatim in *Hansard*, the official report) are published daily.

The records of the Lords from 1497 and of the Commons from 1547, together with the parliamentary and political papers of a number of former members of both Houses, are available to the public through the House of Lords Record Office.

The proceedings of both Houses of Parliament may be broadcast on television and radio, either live or, more usually, in recorded or edited form. Complete coverage is available on cable television.

The Law-making Process

Statute law consists of Acts of Parliament and delegated legislation made by Ministers under powers given to them by Act (see p. 57). While the law undergoes constant refinement in the courts, changes to statute law are made by Parliament.

Draft laws take the form of parliamentary Bills. Proposals for legislation affecting the powers of particular bodies (such as local authorities) or the rights of individuals (such as certain proposals relating to railways, roads and harbours) are known as Private Bills, and are subject to a special form of parliamentary procedure. Bills which change the general law and which constitute the significant part of the parliamentary legislative process are Public Bills.

Public Bills can be introduced into either House, by a government minister or by an ordinary ('private' or 'backbench') member. Most Public Bills that become Acts of Parliament are introduced by a government Minister and are known as 'Government Bills'. Bills introduced by other members of Parliament are known as 'Private Members' Bills.'

The main Bills which constitute the Government's legislative programme are announced in the Queen's Speech at the State opening of Parliament, which usually takes place in November, and the Bills themselves are introduced into one or other of the Houses over the succeeding weeks.

Before a government Bill is drafted, there may be consultation with professional bodies, voluntary organisations and other agencies interested in the subject, and interest and pressure groups which seek to promote specific causes. Proposals for legislative changes are sometimes set out in government 'White Papers', which may be debated in Parliament before a Bill is introduced. From time to time consultation papers, sometimes called 'Green Papers', set out government proposals which are still taking shape and seek comments from the public.

Private Members' Bills

Early in each session backbench Members of the Commons hold a ballot (draw lots) for the opportunity to introduce a Bill on one of the Fridays during the session on which such Bills have precedence over government business. The first 20 Members whose names are drawn win this privilege, but it does not guarantee that their Bills will pass into law. Members may also present a Bill on any day without debate, and on most Tuesdays and Wednesdays on which the Commons is sitting there is also an opportunity to seek leave to present a Bill under the 'ten minute rule', which provides an opportunity for a brief speech by the Member proposing the Bill (and by one who opposes it). Few of these Bills make further progress or receive any debate, but in most sessions a few do become law. Recent examples include the Osteopaths Act 1993, the Noise and Statutory Nuisance Act 1993 and the Race Relations (Remedies) Act 1994. Private Members' Bills do not often call for the expenditure of public money; but if they do they cannot proceed to committee stage unless the Government decides to provide the necessary money resolution. Peers may introduce Private Members' Bills in the House of Lords at any time. A Private Members' Bill passed by either House will not proceed in the other House unless it is taken up by a Member of that House.

Passage of Public Bills

Public Bills must normally be passed by both Houses. Bills relating mainly to financial matters are almost invariably introduced in the Commons. Under the provisions of the Parliament Acts, the powers of the Lords in relation to 'money Bills' are very restricted. The Parliament Acts also provide for a Bill to be passed by the Commons without the consent of the Lords in certain (very rare) circumstances.

The process of passing a public Bill is similar in each House. On presentation the Bill is considered, without debate, to have been read a first time and is printed (although a substantial number of Private Members' Bills are never printed). After an interval, which may be between one day and several weeks, a Government Bill will receive its second reading debate, during which the general principles of the Bill are discussed. If it obtains a second reading in the Commons, a Bill will normally be committed to a standing committee (see p. 57) for detailed examination and amendment. In the Lords, the committee stage usually takes place on the floor of the House, and this procedure may also be followed in the Commons if that House so decides (usually in cases where there is a need to pass the Bill quickly or where it raises matters of constitutional importance). The Commons may also decide to divide the committee stage of a Bill between a standing committee and a committee of the whole House (which is commonly the case with the annual Finance Bill).

The committee stage is followed by the report stage ('consideration') on the floor of the House, during which further amendments may be made. In the Commons, this is usually followed immediately by the third reading debate, where the Bill is reviewed in its final form. In the Lords, a Bill may be further amended at third reading.

After passing its third reading in one House a Bill is sent to the other House, where it passes through all the stages once more, and where it is, more often than not, further amended. Amendments made by the second House must be agreed by the first, or a compromise agreement reached, before a Bill can go for Royal Assent.

In the Commons, the House may vote to limit the time available for consideration of a Bill. This is done by passing a 'timetable' motion proposed by the Government, commonly referred to as a 'guillotine'.

There are special procedures for Public Bills which consolidate existing legislation or which enact private legislation relating to Scotland.

Royal Assent

When a Bill has passed through all its parliamentary stages, it is sent to the Queen for Royal Assent, after which it is part of the law of the land and known as an Act of Parliament. Royal Assent takes the form of an announcement rather than any signature or mark on a copy of the Bill. The Royal Assent has not been refused since 1707. A list of the main public Bills receiving Royal Assent since autumn 1993 is given on p. 515.

Limitations on the Power of the Lords

Most government Bills introduced and passed in the Lords pass through the Commons without difficulty, but a Lords Bill which was unacceptable to the Commons would not become law. The Lords, on the other hand, do not generally prevent Bills insisted upon by the Commons from becoming law, though they will often amend them and return them for further consideration by the Commons. By convention the Lords pass Bills authorising taxation or national expenditure without amendment. Under the Parliament Acts 1911 and 1949, a Bill that deals only with taxation or expenditure must become law within one month of being sent to the Lords, whether or not they agree to it, unless the Commons directs otherwise. If no agreement is reached between the two Houses on a non-financial Commons Bill the Lords can delay the Bill for a period which, in practice, amounts to at least 13 months. Following this the Bill may be submitted to the Queen for Royal Assent, provided it has been passed a second time by the Commons. The Parliament Acts make one important exception: any Bill to lengthen the life of a Parliament requires the full assent of both Houses in the normal way.

The limits to the power of the Lords, contained in the Parliament Acts, are based on the belief that nowadays the main legislative function of the non-elected House is to act as a chamber of revision, complementing but not rivalling the elected House.

Delegated Legislation

In order to reduce unnecessary pressure on parliamentary time, primary legislation often gives ministers or other authorities the power to regulate administrative details by means of 'delegated' or secondary legislation. To minimise any risk that delegating powers to the executive might undermine the authority of Parliament, such powers are normally only delegated to authorities directly accountable to Parliament. Moreover, the Acts of Parliament concerned usually provide for some measure of direct parliamentary control over proposed delegated legislation, by giving Parliament the opportunity to affirm or annul it. Certain Acts also require that organisations affected must be consulted before rules and orders can be made.

A joint committee of both Houses reports on the technical propriety of these 'statutory instruments'. In order to save time on the floor of the House, the Commons uses standing committees to debate the merits of instruments; actual decisions are taken by the House. The House of Lords has also appointed a delegated powers scrutiny committee which examines the appropriateness of the powers to make secondary legislation in Bills as they come before that House.

Private Legislation

Private Bills are promoted by people or organisations outside Parliament (often local authorities) to give them special legal powers. They go through a similar procedure to public Bills, but most of the work is done in committee, where procedures follow a semi-judicial pattern. The promoter must prove the need for the powers sought and the objections of opposing interests are heard. Both sides may be legally represented. Hybrid Bills are public Bills which may affect private rights. As with private Bills, the passage of hybrid Bills through Parliament is governed by special procedures which allow those affected to put their case.

Parliamentary Committees

Committees of the Whole House

Either House may pass a resolution setting itself up as a committee of the whole House to consider Bills in detail after their second reading. This permits unrestricted discussion: the general rule that an MP or Lord may speak only once on each motion does not apply in committee.

Standing Committees

House of Commons standing committees debate and consider public Bills at the committee stage. The committee considers the Bill clause by clause, and may amend it before reporting it back to the House. The standing committees include two Scottish standing committees, and the Scottish, Welsh and Northern Ireland Grand Committees. Ordinary standing committees do not have names but are referred to simply as Standing Committee A, B, C, and so on; a new set of members is appointed to them to consider each Bill. Each committee has between 16 and 50 members, with a party balance reflecting as far as possible that in the House as a whole.

The Scottish Grand Committee comprises all 72 Scottish members (and may be convened anywhere in Scotland as well as Westminster). It may consider the principles of Scottish Bills referred to it at second reading stage. It also debates Scottish public expenditure estimates and other matters concerning Scotland only which may be referred to it.

The Welsh Grand Committee, with all 38 Welsh members and up to five others, considers Bills referred to it at second reading stage, and matters concerning Wales only. Similarly, the Northern Ireland Grand Committee debates matters relating specifically to Northern Ireland. It includes all 17 Northern Ireland members and up to 25 others.

There are also standing committees to

debate proposed European legislation, and to scrutinise statutory instruments made by the Government.

The Lords' equivalent to a standing committee, a Public Bill Committee, is rarely used; instead the committee stage of a Bill is taken by the House as a whole.

Select Committees

Select committees are appointed for a particular task, generally one of enquiry, investigation and scrutiny. They report their conclusions and recommendations to the House as a whole; in many cases their recommendations invite a response from the Government, which is also reported to the House. A select committee may be appointed for a Parliament, or for a session, or for as long as it takes to complete its task. To help Parliament with the control of the executive by examining aspects of public policy, expenditure and administration, 17 committees have been established by the House of Commons to examine the work of the main government departments and their associated public bodies. The Foreign Affairs Select Committee, for example, 'shadows' the work of the Foreign & Commonwealth Office. The committees are constituted on a basis which is in approximate proportion to party strength in the House.

Other regular Commons select committees include those on Public Accounts, European Legislation, Members' Interests, and the Parliamentary Commissioner for Administration (the 'Parliamentary Ombudsman'—see p. 60). 'Domestic' select committees also cover the internal workings of Parliament.

In their examination of government policies, expenditure and administration, committees may question ministers, civil servants and interested bodies and individuals. Through hearings and published reports, they bring before Parliament and the public an extensive body of fact and informed opinion on many issues, and build up considerable expertise in their subjects of inquiry.

In the House of Lords, besides the Appeal and Appellate Committees, in which

the bulk of the House's judicial work is transacted, there are two major select committees (along with several sub-committees), on the European Community and on Science and Technology.

Joint Committees

Joint committees, with a membership drawn from both Houses, are appointed in each session to deal with Consolidation Bills and delegated legislation. The two Houses may also agree to set up joint select committees on other subjects.

Party Committees

In addition to the official committees of the two Houses there are several unofficial party organisations or committees. The Conservative and Unionist Members' Committee (the 1922 Committee) consists of the backbench membership of the party in the House of Commons. When the Conservative Party is in office, ministers attend its meetings by invitation and not by right. When the party is in opposition, the whole membership of the party may attend meetings. The then leader appoints a consultative committee, which acts as the party's 'shadow cabinet'.

The Parliamentary Labour Party comprises all members of the party in both Houses. When the Labour Party is in office, a parliamentary committee, half of whose members are elected and half of whom are government representatives, acts as a channel of communication between the Government and its backbenchers in both Houses. When the party is in opposition, the Parliamentary Labour Party is organised under the direction of an elected parliamentary committee, which acts as the 'shadow cabinet'.

Other Forms of Parliamentary Control

House of Commons

In addition to the system of scrutiny by select committees, the House of Commons offers a number of opportunities for the examination of government policy by both the Opposition and the Government's own backbenchers. These include:

1. Question time, when for 55 minutes on Monday, Tuesday, Wednesday and Thursday, ministers answer MPs' questions. The Prime Minister's question time is every Tuesday and Thursday when the House is sitting. Parliamentary questions are one means of seeking information about the Government's intentions. They are also a way of raising grievances brought to MPs' notice by constituents. MPs may also put questions to ministers for written answer; the questions and answers are published in *Hansard*. There are some 50,000 questions every year.

2. Adjournment debates, when MPs use motions for the adjournment of the House to raise constituency cases or matters of public concern. There is a half-hour adjournment period at the end of the business of the day, while immediately before the adjournment for each recess (Parliament's Christmas, Easter, Whitsun and summer breaks) a full day is spent discussing issues raised by private members. There are also adjournment debates following the passage, three times a year, of Consolidated Fund[7] or Appropriation Bills.[8]

In addition, an MP wishing to discuss a 'specific and important matter that should have urgent consideration' may, at the end of question time, seek leave to move the adjournment of the House. On the very few occasions when leave is obtained, the matter is debated for three hours in what is known as an emergency debate, usually on the following day.

3. Early day motions (EDMs) provide a further opportunity for backbench MPs to express their views on particular issues. A number of EDMs are tabled each sitting day; they are very rarely debated but can be useful in gauging the degree of support for the issue by the number of signatures of other MPs which the motion attracts.

4. The 20 Opposition days each session, when the Opposition can choose subjects for debate. Of these days, 17 are at the disposal of the Leader of the Opposition and three at the disposal of the second largest opposition party.

5. Debates on three days in each session on details of proposed government expenditure, chosen by the Liaison Committee.

Procedural opportunities for criticism of the Government also arise during the debate on the Queen's speech at the beginning of each session; during debates on motions of censure for which the Government provides time; and during debates on the Government's legislative and other proposals.

House of Lords

Similar opportunities for criticism and examination of government policy are provided in the House of Lords at daily question time and during debates.

Control of Finances

The main responsibilities of Parliament, and more particularly of the House of Commons, in overseeing the revenue of the State and public expenditure, are to authorise the raising of taxes and duties, and the various objects of expenditure and the sum to be spent on each. It also has to satisfy itself that the sums granted are spent only for the purposes which Parliament intended. No payment out of the central government's public funds can be made and no taxation or loans authorised, except by Act of Parliament. However, limited interim payments can be made from the Contingencies Fund.

The Finance Act is the most important of the annual statutes, and authorises the raising of revenue. The legislation is based on the Chancellor of the Exchequer's Budget statement. It includes a review of the public finances of the previous year, and proposals for future expenditure (see p. 155).

---

[7]At least two Consolidated Fund Acts are passed each session authorising the Treasury to make certain sums of money available for the public service.
[8]The annual Appropriation Act fixes the sums of public money provided for particular items of expenditure.

Scrutiny of public expenditure is carried out by House of Commons select committees (see p. 58).

European Union Affairs

To keep the two Houses informed of EU developments, and to enable them to scrutinise and debate Union policies and proposals, there is a select committee in each House (see p. 58) and two Commons standing committees debate specific European legislative proposals. Ministers also make regular statements about Union business.

The Commons' Ability to Force the Government to Resign

The final control is the ability of the House of Commons to force the Government to resign by passing a resolution of 'no confidence'. The Government must also resign if the House rejects a proposal which the Government considers so vital to its policy that it has declared it a 'matter of confidence' or if the House refuses to vote the money required for the public service.

Parliamentary Commissioner for Administration

The post of Parliamentary Commissioner for Administration (the 'Parliamentary Ombudsman') was established under the Parliamentary Commissioner Act 1967. The Ombudsman is independent of government and reports to a Select Committee of the House of Commons. He investigates complaints from members of the public (referred through MPs) alleging that they have suffered injustice arising from maladministration. The Ombudsman's jurisdiction covers central government departments and a large number of non-departmental public bodies. He cannot investigate complaints about government policy, the content of legislation or relations with other countries. In making his investigations, the Commissioner has access to all departmental papers, and has powers to summon those from whom he wishes to take evidence. When an investigation is completed, he sends a report with his findings to the MP who referred the complaint. In reports of justified cases, the Ombudsman normally recommends that the department provides redress (which can include a financial remedy for the complainant in appropriate cases). His recommendations are almost always put into practice. He submits an annual report to Parliament, and also publishes selected cases three times a year.

> A complaint to the Ombudsman: A man complained that an Employment Service Jobcentre had wrongly advised him that he was not eligible for a grant when starting a business. The Ombudsman found the complaint justified, and on his recommendation the Employment Service paid the complainant, ex gratia, £2,080—the amount of grant he would have received.

In 1993 the Ombudsman completed 208 investigations; of these he found 61 per cent wholly justified; 35 per cent partly justified; and 4 per cent unjustified.

The Parliamentary Ombudsman also monitors the 1994 Code of Practice on Open Government. He investigates complaints, referred through MPs, that government departments or bodies have refused access to official information. If he finds a complaint justified, he can recommend that the information is released.

Parliamentary Privilege

Each House of Parliament has certain rights and immunities to protect it from obstruction in carrying out its duties. The rights apply collectively to each House and to its staff and individually to each member.

For the Commons the Speaker formally claims from the Queen 'their ancient and undoubted rights and privileges' at the beginning of each Parliament. These include freedom of speech; first call on the attendance of its members, who are therefore free from arrest in civil actions and exempt from serving on juries, or being compelled to attend court as witnesses; and the right of access to the Crown, which is a collective privilege of the House. Further privileges include the rights of the House to control its own proceedings (so that it is able, for instance, to exclude 'strangers'[9] if it wishes); to decide upon legal disqualifications for membership and to declare a seat vacant on such grounds; and to punish for breach of its privileges and for contempt. Parliament has the right to punish anybody, inside or outside the House, who commits a breach of privilege—that is, offends against the rights of the House.

The privileges of the House of Lords are broadly similar to those of the House of Commons.

Her Majesty's Government

Her Majesty's Government is the body of ministers responsible for the conduct of national affairs. The Prime Minister is appointed by the Queen, and all other ministers are appointed by the Queen on the recommendation of the Prime Minister. Most ministers are members of the Commons, although the Government is also fully represented by ministers in the Lords. The Lord Chancellor is always a member of the House of Lords.

The composition of governments can vary both in the number of ministers and in the titles of some offices. New ministerial offices may be created, others may be abolished, and functions may be transferred from one minister to another.

Prime Minister

The Prime Minister is also, by tradition, First Lord of the Treasury and Minister for the Civil Service. The Prime Minister's unique position of authority derives from majority support in the House of Commons and from the power to appoint and dismiss ministers. By modern convention, the Prime Minister always sits in the House of Commons.

The Prime Minister presides over the Cabinet, is responsible for the allocation of

functions among ministers and informs the Queen at regular meetings of the general business of the Government.

The Prime Minister's other responsibilities include recommending a number of appointments to the Queen. These include:

- Church of England archbishops, bishops and deans and some 200 other clergy in Crown 'livings';
- senior judges, such as the Lord Chief Justice;
- Privy Counsellors; and
- Lord-Lieutenants.

They also include certain civil appointments, such as Lord High Commissioner to the General Assembly of the Church of Scotland, Poet Laureate, Constable of the Tower, and some university posts; and appointments to various public boards and institutions, such as the BBC (British Broadcasting Corporation), as well as various royal and statutory commissions. Recommendations are likewise made for the award of many civil honours and distinctions and of Civil List pensions (to people who have achieved eminence in science or the arts and are in financial need). The Prime Minister also selects the trustees of certain national museums and institutions.

The Prime Minister's Office at 10 Downing Street (the official residence in London) has a staff of civil servants who assist the Prime Minister. The Prime Minister may also appoint special advisers to the Office to assist in the formation of policies.

Departmental Ministers

Ministers in charge of government departments are usually in the Cabinet; they are known as 'Secretary of State' or 'Minister', or may have a special title, as in the case of the Chancellor of the Exchequer.

Non-departmental Ministers

The holders of various traditional offices, namely the Lord President of the Council, the Chancellor of the Duchy of Lancaster, the Lord Privy Seal, the Paymaster General and, from time to time, Ministers without

[9] All those who are not members or officials of either House.

Portfolio, may have few or no departmental duties. They are thus available to perform any duties the Prime Minister may wish to give them. In the present administration, for example, the Lord President of the Council is Leader of the House of Commons and the Chancellor of the Duchy of Lancaster is Minister for Public Service and Science.

Lord Chancellor and Law Officers

The Lord Chancellor holds a special position, as both a minister with departmental functions and the head of the judiciary (see p. 104). The four Law Officers of the Crown are: for England and Wales, the Attorney General and the Solicitor General; and for Scotland, the Lord Advocate and the Solicitor General for Scotland.

Ministers of State and Junior Ministers

Ministers of State usually work with ministers in charge of departments. They normally have specific responsibilities, and are sometimes given titles which reflect these functions. More than one may work in a department. A Minister of State may be given a seat in the Cabinet and be paid accordingly.

Junior ministers (generally Parliamentary Under-Secretaries of State or, where the senior minister is not a Secretary of State, simply Parliamentary Secretaries) share in parliamentary and departmental duties. They may also be given responsibility, directly under the departmental minister, for specific aspects of the department's work.

Ministerial Salaries

The salaries of ministers in the House of Commons range from £45,815 a year for junior ministers to £64,749 for Cabinet ministers. In the House of Lords salaries range from £38,894 for junior ministers to £52,260 for Cabinet ministers. The Prime Minister receives £78,292 and the Lord Chancellor £120,179. (The Leader of the Opposition receives £61,349 a year; two Opposition whips in the Commons and the Opposition Leader and Chief Whip in the Lords also receive salaries.)

The Cabinet

The Cabinet is composed of about 20 ministers (the number can vary) chosen by the Prime Minister and may include departmental and non-departmental ministers.

The functions of the Cabinet are to initiate and decide on policy, the supreme control of government and the co-ordination of government departments. The exercise of these functions is vitally affected by the fact that the Cabinet is a group of party representatives, depending upon majority support in the House of Commons.

Cabinet Meetings

The Cabinet meets in private and its proceedings are confidential. Its members are bound by their oath as Privy Counsellors not to disclose information about its proceedings, although after 30 years Cabinet papers may be made available for inspection in the Public Record Office at Kew, Surrey.

Normally the Cabinet meets for a few hours each week during parliamentary sittings, and rather less often when Parliament is not sitting. To keep its workload within manageable limits, a great deal of work is carried on through the committee system. This involves referring issues either to a standing Cabinet committee or to an *ad hoc* committee composed of the ministers directly concerned. The committee then considers the matter in detail and either disposes of it or reports upon it to the Cabinet with recommendations for action.

The membership and terms of reference of all ministerial Cabinet committees are published by the Cabinet Office. Where appropriate, the Secretary of the Cabinet and other senior officials of the Cabinet Office attend meetings of the Cabinet and its committees.

Diaries published by several former ministers have given the public insight into Cabinet procedures in recent times.

The Cabinet Office

The Cabinet Office is headed by the Secretary of the Cabinet (a civil servant who is also Head of the Home Civil Service) under the direction of the Prime Minister. It comprises the Cabinet Secretariat and the Office of Public Service and Science (OPSS).

The Cabinet Secretariat serves ministers collectively in the conduct of Cabinet business, and in the co-ordination of policy at the highest level.

The Chancellor of the Duchy of Lancaster is in charge of the Office of Public Service and Science and is a member of the Cabinet. The OPSS is responsible for:

- raising the standard of public services across the public sector through the Citizen's Charter (see p. 66);

- promoting openness in government;

- improving the effectiveness and efficiency of central government, through, among other things, the establishment of executive agencies and the market testing programme (see p. 69); and

- advice—through its Office of Science and Technology—on science and technology policy, expenditure and the allocation of resources to the research councils.

The Historical and Records Section is responsible for Official Histories and managing Cabinet Office records.

Ministerial Responsibility

'Ministerial responsibility' refers both to the collective responsibility for government policy and actions, which ministers share, and to ministers' individual responsibility for their departments' work.

The doctrine of collective responsibility means that the Cabinet acts unanimously even when Cabinet ministers do not all agree on a subject. The policy of departmental ministers must be consistent with the policy of the Government as a whole. Once the Government's policy on a matter has been decided, each minister is expected to support it or resign. On rare occasions, ministers have been allowed free votes in Parliament on government policies involving important issues of principle. In February 1994, for example, free votes were allowed on lowering the age of consent to homosexual sex from 21 to 18.

The individual responsibility of ministers for the work of their departments means that they are answerable to Parliament for all their departments' activities. They bear the consequences of any failure in administration, any injustice to an individual or any aspect of policy which may be criticised in Parliament, whether personally responsible or not. Since most ministers are members of the House of Commons, they must answer questions and defend themselves against criticism in person. Departmental ministers in the House of Lords are represented in the Commons by someone qualified to speak on their behalf, usually a junior minister.

Departmental ministers normally decide all matters within their responsibility. However, on important political matters they usually consult their colleagues collectively, either through the Cabinet or through a Cabinet committee. A decision by a departmental minister binds the Government as a whole.

On assuming office ministers must resign directorships in private and public companies, and must ensure that there is no conflict between their public duties and private interests.

The Privy Council

The Privy Council was formerly the chief source of executive power in the State; its origins can be traced back to the King's Court, which assisted the Norman monarchs in running the government. As the system of Cabinet government developed in the 18th century, however, much of the role of the Privy Council was assumed by the Cabinet, although the Council retained certain executive functions. Some government departments originated as committees of the Privy Council.

Nowadays the main function of the Privy Council is to advise the Queen on the approval of Orders in Council, including those made under prerogative powers, such as Orders approving the grant of royal charters of incorporation and those made under statutory powers. Responsibility for each Order, however, rests with the minister answerable for the policy concerned, regardless of whether he or she is present at the meeting where approval is given.

The Privy Council also advises the Sovereign on the issue of royal proclamations, such as those summoning or dissolving Parliament. The Council's own statutory responsibilities, which are independent of the powers of the Sovereign in Council, include supervising the registration authorities of the medical and allied professions.

Membership of the Council (retained for life, except for very occasional removals) is accorded by the Sovereign on the recommendation of the Prime Minister (or occasionally, Prime Ministers of Commonwealth countries) to people eminent in public life—mainly politicians and judges—in Britain and the independent monarchies of the Commonwealth. Cabinet Ministers must be Privy Counsellors and, if not already members, are admitted to membership before taking their oath of office at a meeting of the Council. There are about 400 Privy Counsellors. A full Council is summoned only on the accession of a new Sovereign or when the Sovereign announces his or her intention to marry.

Committees of the Privy Council

There are a number of Privy Council committees. These include prerogative committees, such as those dealing with legislation from the Channel Islands and the Isle of Man, and with applications for charters of incorporation. Committees may also be provided for by statute, such as those for the universities of Oxford and Cambridge and the Scottish universities. Membership of such committees is confined to members of the current administration. The only exceptions are the members of the Judicial Committee and the members of any committee for which specific provision authorises a wider membership.

Administrative work is carried out in the Privy Council Office under the Lord President of the Council, a Cabinet minister.

The Judicial Committee of the Privy Council is the final court of appeal for certain independent members of the Commonwealth, the British dependent territories, the Channel

Islands and the Isle of Man. It also hears appeals from the disciplinary committees of the medical and allied professions and certain ecclesiastical appeals.

Government Departments

Government departments and their agencies, staffed by politically neutral civil servants, are the main instruments for implementing government policy when Parliament has passed the necessary legislation, and for advising ministers. They often work alongside local authorities, statutory boards, and government-sponsored organisations operating under various degrees of government control.

A change of government does not necessarily affect the number or general functions of government departments, although major changes in policy may be accompanied by organisational changes.

The work of some departments (for instance, the Ministry of Defence) covers Britain as a whole. Other departments, such as the Department of Employment, cover England, Wales and Scotland, but not Northern Ireland. Others, such as the Department of the Environment, are mainly concerned with affairs in England. Some departments, such as the Department of Trade and Industry, maintain a regional organisation, and some which have direct contact with the public throughout the country (for example, the Department of Employment) also have local offices.

Departments are usually headed by ministers. In some departments the head is a permanent official, and ministers with other duties are responsible for them to Parliament. For instance, ministers in the Treasury are responsible for HM Customs and Excise, the Inland Revenue, the National Investment and Loans Office and a number of other departments as well as executive agencies such as the Royal Mint. Departments generally receive their funds directly out of money provided by Parliament and are staffed by members of the Civil Service.

The functions of the main government departments are set out on pp. 507–14.

Non-departmental Public Bodies

There are bodies which have a role in the process of national government, but are not government departments nor parts of a department (in April 1993 there were 1,389). There are three kinds of non-departmental public bodies: executive bodies, advisory bodies and tribunals. The last of these are a specialised group of bodies whose functions are essentially judicial (see p. 103).

Executive Bodies

Executive bodies normally employ their own staff and have their own budget. They are public organisations whose duties include executive, administrative, regulatory or commercial functions. They normally operate within broad policy guidelines set by departmental ministers but are in varying degrees independent of government in carrying out their day-to-day responsibilities. Examples include the Legal Aid Board, the Police Complaints Authority, the Countryside Commission and the Human Fertilisation and Embryology Authority.

Advisory Bodies

Many government departments are assisted by advisory councils or committees which undertake research and collect information, mainly to give ministers access to informed opinion before they come to a decision involving a legislative or executive act. In some cases a minister must consult a standing committee, but advisory bodies are usually appointed at the discretion of the minister. Examples include the British Overseas Trade Board and the Theatres Trust.

The membership of advisory councils and committees varies according to the nature of the work involved, but normally includes representatives of the relevant interests and professions.

In addition to standing advisory bodies, there are committees set up by the Government to examine specific matters and make recommendations. For certain important inquiries, Royal Commissions, whose members are chosen for their wide experience, may be appointed. Royal Commissions examine evidence from government departments, interested organisations and individuals, and submit recommendations; some prepare regular reports. Examples include the standing Royal Commission on Environmental Pollution, set up in 1970, and the Royal Commission on Criminal Justice, which issued its report in 1993 (see Chapter 8). Inquiries may also be undertaken by departmental committees.

Government Information Services

Each of the main government departments has its own information division, public relations branch or news department. These are normally staffed by professional information officers responsible for communicating their department's activities to the news media and the public (sometimes using publicity services provided by the Central Office of Information—see p. 512). They also advise their departments on the public's reaction.

The Lobby

As press adviser to the Prime Minister, the Prime Minister's Press Secretary and other staff in the Prime Minister's Press Office have direct contact with the parliamentary press through regular meetings with the Lobby correspondents. The Lobby correspondents are a group of political correspondents who have the special privilege of access to the Lobby of the House of Commons, where they can talk privately to government ministers and other members of the House. The Prime Minister's Press Office is the accepted channel through which information about parliamentary business is passed to the media.

Administration of Scottish, Welsh and Northern Ireland Affairs

Scotland

Scotland has its own system of law and wide administrative autonomy. The Secretary of State for Scotland, a Cabinet minister, has responsibility in Scotland (with some exceptions) for a wide range of policy matters (see p. 513). Following an examination of Scotland's place in Britain which began after the general election in April 1992, a number of changes to the responsibilities of The Scottish Office have been made. These make it responsible for more areas of policy.

The distinctive conditions and needs of Scotland and its people are also reflected in separate Scottish legislation on many domestic matters. Special provisions applying to Scotland alone are also inserted in Acts which otherwise apply to Britain generally.

British government departments with significant Scottish responsibilities have offices in Scotland and work closely with The Scottish Office.

Wales

Since 1964 there has been a separate Secretary of State for Wales, who is a member of the Cabinet and is responsible for many aspects of Welsh affairs. (For further details see p. 514.)

Northern Ireland

Since the British Government's assumption of direct responsibility for Northern Ireland in 1972 (see p.12), the Secretary of State for Northern Ireland has been the Cabinet minister responsible for Northern Ireland affairs. Through the Northern Ireland Office the Secretary of State has direct responsibility for constitutional developments, law and order, security, and electoral matters. The work of the Northern Ireland departments is also subject to the direction and control of the Secretary of State (see p. 513).

Citizen's Charter

The Citizen's Charter was launched by the Prime Minister in 1991. The Charter's aim is to raise the standard of public services and make them more responsive to their users. It is closely linked to other reforms, including the Next Steps programme, efficiency measures and the Government's contracting out and market

testing programmes (see p. 69). The Citizen's Charter is a ten-year programme which is intended to be at the heart of the Government's policy-making throughout the 1990s.

The Charter applies to all public services, at both national and local levels, and the privatised utilities. Most major public services have now published separate charters (by mid-1994 39 had been issued). In many cases separate charters have been published for services in Northern Ireland, Scotland and Wales. (Details of many of the charters can be found in the relevant chapters; a full list, together with information on how to obtain them, appears on p. 518.)

The Principles of Public Service

The Charter sets out a number of key principles which users of public services are entitled to expect:

Standards

Setting, monitoring and publishing explicit standards for the services that individual users can reasonably expect. Publication of actual performance against these standards.

Information and Openness

Full and accurate information should be readily available in plain language about how public services are run, their cost and performance, and who is in charge.

Choice and Consultation

There should be regular and systematic consultation with those who use services. Users' views about services, and their priorities for improving them, should be taken into account in final decisions about standards.

Courtesy and Helpfulness

Courteous and helpful service from public servants who will normally wear name badges Services available equally to all who are entitled to them and run to suit their convenience.

The dormouse is now an endangered species in Britain.
In an attempt to increase its numbers, English Nature
launched a National Dormouse Week in 1994.
Mice bred in captivity were released into the wild,
and the public were asked to monitor local woods for
signs of dormouse presence, such as opened hazelnuts.

Seeds from all over the world are stored
at the Royal Botanic Gardens Seed Bank at
Wakehurst Place, Sussex. They are cleaned,
dried, and kept at sub-zero temperatures;
it is thought that in this way they may be
able to survive for hundreds of years, saving
many species from possible extinction.

MULTI-CULTURAL BRITAIN

The Chinese New Year — the Year of the Dog — celebrated at London's Commonwealth Institute. The festival of music, martial arts, dance and drama was attended by adults and children from many London schools.

Members of the Jatra Opera Group rehearse at Spitalfields Market in East London. They took part in a four-day festival celebrating Bangladeshi culture and lifestyle.

Highland Games take place in various centres throughout Scotland during the summer, and attract large numbers of spectators from around the world. Scottish dancing is one of the competitions at the annual games held in Braemar.

London's Notting Hill Carnival, held in August each year, is the largest event of its kind in Europe, with hundreds of thousands of visitors coming to enjoy its mixture of arts, entertainment, music and spectacle.

Ironbridge Gorge, near Telford, Shropshire, is often described as the birthplace of industry. It is there that iron was first smelted from coke, and the world's first cast iron bridge was erected (seen here), from which the town gets its name. Some 250 years later Ironbridge is one of Britain's biggest museums, and its valley is designated a World Heritage Site.

At the Big Pit Mining Museum, Blaenavon, Wales, visitors can ride down the 90 m (300 ft) shaft to the pit bottom, as well as seeing the workshops, engines and forge, and an exhibition of photographs and artefacts describing the history of the pit, which stopped coal production in 1980.

Putting Things Right

If things go wrong, an apology, a full explanation and a swift and effective remedy should be given. Well publicised and easy to use complaints procedures with independent review wherever possible should be available.

Value for Money

Efficient and economical delivery of public services within the resources the nation can afford, and independent validation of performance against standards.

Implementing the Charter

A Cabinet minister, the Chancellor of the Duchy of Lancaster, is responsible for the Charter programme. The Chancellor of the Duchy is supported by the Citizen's Charter Unit within the OPSS (see p. 63). The Prime Minister also receives advice on the Charter from a Panel drawn from business, consumer affairs and education. The Panel works with the Citizen's Charter Unit and officials in all the departments to implement and develop the Citizen's Charter programme. The Prime Minister holds regular Citizen's Charter seminars with Advisory Panel members and Cabinet ministers to report on progress and plan further action.

Executive agencies (see p. 69) are expected to comply fully with the principles of the Citizen's Charter, and the pay of agency chief executives is normally directly related to their agency's performance. Performance-related pay is being introduced throughout the public service.

The mechanisms for implementing the Charter cover:

- more privatisation;
- wider competition;
- further contracting-out of service provision to private sector organisations;
- setting standards of service delivery;
- comprehensive publication of information on standards achieved;
- published performance targets, both local and national;
- more effective complaints procedures;
- tougher and more independent inspectorates; and
- better redress for the citizen if things go wrong.

Progress on the Charter

Projects to ensure that the Charter becomes an integral part of all public services and that members of the public are aware of the standards of service to which they are entitled include:

Charter Mark Awards

The Charter Mark Scheme has been introduced to reward excellence in delivering public services: winners are judged by the Prime Minister's Citizen's Charter Advisory Panel. Applicants have to demonstrate that they have achieved measurable improvements in the quality of services over the previous two years, and that their customers are satisfied with their services.

In 1993 awards were made to 93 of over 400 public service organisations and privatised utilities which had applied. Winners ranged from schools, local authority services and executive agencies, such as the Driver and Vehicle Licensing Agency, to British Gas. Award winners can use the Charter Mark on their products and equipment, and on stationery, vehicles and promotional material for up to three years.

Complaints Task Force

In June 1993 a task force was set up to review and recommend improvements to public service complaints procedures.

Charter Forums and Quality Networks

A programme of Charter Forums has been held around the country, providing an opportunity for local service providers to exchange information about best practice in implementing the Citizen's Charter. Following this, a series of Citizen's Charter Quality Networks was announced in July 1994. These would offer public service managers the opportunity to discuss lessons of good practice on a regular basis.

Open Government

In line with Citizen's Charter principles, the Government has a general policy of increasing the openness and accountability of public administration. In April 1994 it introduced a code of practice on access to government information. This commits the Government to release certain information as a matter of course and also to respond to requests for other factual information which it holds. The code will be policed by the Parliamentary Ombudsman. Similar codes of practice have been proposed to cover the health service and local authorities.

As part of the same openness, the Government is also to propose legislation to provide rights of access to health and safety information and personal records. These rights would add to a number of existing rights of access to information in specific areas such as environmental information.

The Civil Service

The Civil Service is concerned with the conduct of the whole range of government activities as they affect the community. These range from policy formulation to carrying out the day-to-day duties of public administration.

Civil servants are servants of the Crown. For all practical purposes the Crown in this context means, and is represented by, the Government of the day. In most circumstances the executive powers of the Crown are exercised by, and on the advice of, Her Majesty's Ministers, who are in turn answerable to Parliament. The Civil Service as such has no constitutional personality or responsibility separate from that of the Government of the day. The duty of the individual civil servant is first and foremost to the Minister of the Crown who is in charge of the Department in which he or she is serving. A change of minister, for whatever

reason, does not involve a change of staff. Ministers sometimes appoint special advisers from outside the Civil Service. The advisers are normally paid from public funds, but their appointments come to an end when the Government's term of office finishes, or when the Minister concerned leaves the Government or moves to another appointment.

The number of civil servants fell from 732,000 in April 1979 to 541,800 in January 1994, reflecting the Government's policy of controlling the cost of the Civil Service and of improving its efficiency.

About half of all civil servants are engaged in the provision of public services. These include paying sickness benefits and pensions, collecting taxes and contributions, running employment services, staffing prisons, and providing services to industry and agriculture. A quarter are employed in the Ministry of Defence. The rest are divided between central administrative and policy duties; support services; and largely financially self-supporting services, for instance, those provided by the Department for National Savings and the Royal Mint. The total includes about 48,000 'industrial' civil servants, mainly manual workers in government industrial establishments. Four-fifths of civil servants work outside London.

Equality of Opportunity

The Government is committed to achieving equality of opportunity for all its staff. In support of this commitment, the Civil Service, which recruits and promotes on the basis of merit, is actively pursuing policies to develop career opportunities for women, ethnic minorities and people with disabilities:

- women now represent 51.2 per cent of all non-industrial civil servants, and between 1992 and 1993 the proportion of women in the management grades of the service increased by 2 per cent to 31.9 per cent;
- representation of ethnic minority staff among non-industrial civil servants has increased from 4.2 per cent in 1989 to 5.2 per cent in 1993 and compares well with 4.9 per cent, which is the ethnic minority representation in the working population.

● 1.5 per cent of civil servants are registered as disabled, which is just above the proportion of registered disabled people in the workforce as a whole and twice the proportion employed in the private sector.

Progress is monitored and reported on regularly by the Cabinet Office (OPSS).

Management Reforms

Civil Service reforms are being implemented to ensure improved management performance, in particular through the increased accountability of individual managers, based on clear objectives and responsibilities. These reforms include performance-related pay schemes and other incentives.

Executive Agencies: Next Steps Programme

The Next Steps Programme, launched in 1988, aims to deliver government services more efficiently and effectively within available resources for the benefit of taxpayers, customers and staff. This has involved setting up, as far as is practicable, separate units or agencies to perform the executive functions of government. Agencies remain part of the Civil Service but under the terms of individual framework documents they enjoy greater delegation of financial, pay and personnel matters. Agencies are headed by chief executives who are accountable to ministers but who are personally responsible for the day-to-day operations of the agency.

No agency can be established until the 'prior options' of abolition, privatisation and contracting out have been considered and ruled out. These 'prior options' are reconsidered when agencies are reviewed after three to three-and-a-half years of operation.

By April 1994 96 agencies had been set up, together with 31 Executive Units of Customs and Excise and 31 Executive Offices of the Inland Revenue. Over 348,000 civil servants—60 per cent of the total—work in organisations run on Next Steps lines. In April 1994 a further 57 agency candidates—employing over 94,000 staff—had been identified as suitable for agency status.

In 1992–93 agencies met around 77 per cent of their key performance targets—a small improvement on the previous year because, in general, targets will have been made progressively tougher.

Competing for Quality

In 1991 the Government announced further proposals to extend competition and choice in the provision of public services. Value for money improvements in public expenditure are being sought through a range of techniques including market testing the in-house operation against external competition and, where appropriate, contracting out. By December 1993, £1,100 million worth of services had been market tested or otherwise examined, and annual savings of at least £135 million had been achieved.

Central Management and Structure

Responsibility for central co-ordination and management of the Civil Service is divided between the Treasury and the Cabinet Office (OPSS). In addition to its other functions, the Treasury is responsible for the structure of the Civil Service, for recruitment policy and for controlling staffing, pay, pensions and allowances. The OPSS, which is under the control of the Prime Minister, as Minister for the Civil Service, oversees the organisation, non-financial aspects of personnel management and overall efficiency of the Service. The function of official Head of the Home Civil Service is combined with that of Secretary to the Cabinet.

At the senior levels, where management forms a major part of most jobs, there are common grades throughout the Civil Service. These unified grades 1 to 7 are known as the Open Structure and cover grades from Permanent Secretary level to Principal level. Within the unified grades each post is filled by the person best qualified, regardless of the occupational group to which he or she previously belonged.

Below this the structure of the non-industrial Civil Service is based on a system of occupational groups. These groups assist the recruitment and matching of skills to posts and offer career paths in which specialist skills can be developed. Departments and agencies are being encouraged to develop their own pay and grading arrangements. They are expected to produce value-for-money benefits which are greater than those available through centrally controlled negotiation.

The Diplomatic Service

Staff in the 4,500 strong Diplomatic Service are those working in the Foreign & Commonwealth Office (see p. 109) and at British diplomatic missions abroad who are not in Home Civil Service grades and are not locally engaged.

The Service has its own grade structure, linked to that of the Home Civil Service. Terms and conditions of service are comparable, but take into account the special demands of the Service, particularly the requirement to serve abroad. Home civil servants, members of the armed forces and individuals from the private sector may also serve in the Foreign & Commonwealth Office and at overseas posts on loan or attachment.

Civil Service Recruitment

Recruitment is based on the principle of selection on merit by fair and open competition. Independent Civil Service Commissioners are responsible for approving the selection of people for appointment to the higher levels and to the fast-stream entry to the Home Civil Service and the Diplomatic Service. Recruitment of middle-ranking and junior staff is the responsibility of departments and executive agencies; it is monitored by the Commissioners. Departments and agencies can choose whether to undertake this recruitment work themselves, to employ a private sector recruitment agency or to use the Recruitment and Assessment Services Agency to recruit on their behalf.

People from outside the Civil Service may be recruited directly to all levels, particularly to posts requiring skills and experience more readily found in the private sector. The exchange of staff between the Civil Service and industry is also encouraged.

Training

Individual government departments and agencies are responsible for the performance of their own staff. They provide training and development to meet their business needs, to improve performance, and to help staff respond effectively to changing demands. Most training and development takes place within departments and agencies. In addition, the Civil Service College provides high-quality management and professional training, mainly for those who occupy, or hope to occupy, relatively senior positions. Considerable use is made of other providers in the private and public sectors.

Civil servants aged under 18 may continue their general education by attending courses, usually for one day a week ('day release' schemes). All staff may be entitled to financial support to continue their education, mainly in their own time. There are also opportunities for civil servants to undertake research and study in areas of interest to them and to their department or agency.

Promotion

Departments are responsible for promotion up to and including Grade 4. Promotion or appointment to Grades 1 and 2 and all transfers between departments at these levels are approved by the Prime Minister, who is advised by the Head of the Home Civil Service. Promotions and appointments to Grade 3 are approved by the Cabinet Office.

Political and Private Activities

Civil servants are required to perform loyally the duties assigned to them by the Government of the day, whatever its political persuasion. It is essential that ministers and the public should have confidence that the personal views of civil servants do not influence the performance of their official duties, given the role of the Civil Service in serving successive governments formed by different parties. The aim of the rules which govern political activities by civil servants is to allow them, subject to these fundamental principles, the greatest possible freedom to participate in public affairs consistent with their rights and duties as citizens. The rules are therefore concerned with activities liable to give public expression to political views rather than with privately held beliefs and opinions.

The Civil Service is divided into three groups for the purposes of deciding the extent to which individuals may take part in political activities:

- those in the 'politically free' group, consisting of industrial staff and non-office grades, are free to engage in any political activity outside official time, including adoption as a prospective candidate for the British or the European Parliament (although they would have to resign from the Service before giving their consent to nomination).

- those in the 'politically restricted' group, which comprises staff in Grade 7 and above as well as Administration Trainees and Higher Executive Officers (D), may not take part in national political activities but may apply for permission to take part in local political activities; and

- the 'intermediate' group, which comprises all other civil servants, may apply for permission to take part in national or local political activity, apart from candidature for the British or the European Parliament.

Where required, permission is granted to the maximum extent consistent with the Civil Service's reputation for political impartiality and the avoidance of any conflict with official duties. A code of discretion requires moderation and the avoidance of embarrassment to ministers.

Generally, there are no restrictions on the private activities of civil servants, provided that these do not bring discredit on the Civil Service, and that there is no possibility of conflict with official duties. For instance, a civil servant must comply with any departmental instruction on the need to seek authority before taking part in any outside activity which involves official experience.

Security

Each department is responsible for its own internal security. As a general rule the privately-held political views of civil servants are not a matter of official concern. However, no one may be employed on work which is vital to the security of the State who is, or has been involved in, or associated with, activities threatening national security. Certain posts are not open to people who fall into this category, or to anyone whose reliability may be in doubt for any other reason.

The Security Commission may investigate breaches of security in the public service and advise on changes in security procedure if requested to do so by the Prime Minister after consultation with the Leader of the Opposition.

Local Government

Although the origins of local government in England can be traced back to Saxon times, the first comprehensive system of local councils was established in the late 19th century.

Local Government Reform

A major reform of local government took place in 1974 in England and Wales and in 1975 in Scotland. This created two main tiers of local authority throughout England and Wales: counties and the smaller districts. Local government in London had been reorganised along the same lines in 1965. In Scotland functions were allocated to regions and districts on the mainland; single-tier authorities were introduced for the three Islands areas. In Northern Ireland changes were made in 1973 which left local authorities with fewer functions than in the rest of Britain.

The Local Government Act 1985 abolished the Greater London Council and the six metropolitan county councils in England. Most of their functions were transferred to the London boroughs and metropolitan district councils respectively in 1986 (see below).

Local Government Commission

The Local Government Act 1992 made provision for the establishment of a Local Government Commission to review the structure, boundaries and electoral arrangements of local government in England. The Commission, set up in 1992, is reviewing the structure of local government in all the shire counties of England, and is due to complete this work by the end of 1994. The first changes, on the Isle of Wight, will be implemented in April 1995. The reviews are considering whether the two-tier structure should be replaced by unitary or single-tier authorities in each area. The Government intends to direct the Commission to look at the boundaries of metropolitan areas once the review of the English shires is complete. The Government is also looking at ways of improving the internal management of local authorities.

The Local Government Commission's first progress report was published in December 1993. As well as conducting detailed opinion surveys in every review area, the Commission had received 155,000 letters and other communications directly from residents. The general pattern of response showed that people tended to identify most strongly with quite small, local communities; there was widespread support for a change to a unitary structure, with most support for change among those most knowledgeable about the review; and there was only limited support for unitary authorities to be based on existing district boundaries.

Scotland and Wales

The Local Government etc. (Scotland) Bill, which is under consideration in Parliament, would create 32 single-tier councils to replace the present system of regional and district councils. The three islands councils would remain. In Wales, the Government proposes to set up 22 unitary authorities to replace the existing eight county councils and 37 district councils. Legislation for this was enacted during 1994. The reform takes effect from 1 April 1996.

Local Authorities' Powers

Local authorities derive their power from legislation. Although local authorities are responsible for administering certain services, ministers have powers in some areas to secure a degree of uniformity in standards to safeguard public health or to protect the rights of individual citizens.

Relations with Central Government

The main link between local authorities and central government in England is the Department of the Environment. However, other departments such as the Department for Education and the Home Office are also concerned with various local government functions. In the rest of Britain the local authorities deal with the Scottish or Welsh Offices or the Department of the Environment for Northern Ireland, as appropriate.

Principal Types of Local Authority

At present England and Wales (outside Greater London) are divided into 53 counties, sub-divided into 369 districts. All the districts and 47 of the counties—the 'non-metropolitan' counties—have locally elected councils with separate functions. County councils provide large-scale services, while district councils are responsible for the more local ones (see p. 74).

Greater London is divided into 32 boroughs and the City of London, each of which has a council responsible for local government in its area. In the six metropolitan counties there are 36 district councils; there are no county councils. A number of services, however, require a statutory authority over areas wider than the individual boroughs and districts. These are:

● waste regulation and disposal (in certain areas);
● the fire services, including civil defence; and

● (outside London) public transport. These are run by joint authorities composed of elected councillors nominated by the borough or district councils. Local councils also provide many of the members of the police authorities (see p. 83).

In addition to the two-tier local authority system in England, over 8,000 parish councils or meetings provide and manage local facilities such as allotments and village halls and act as agents for other district council functions. They also provide a forum for discussion of local issues. In Wales over 700 community councils have similar functions.

On the mainland of Scotland local government is at present on a two-tier basis: nine regions are divided into 53 districts, each of which has an elected council. There are three virtually all-purpose authorities for the Orkneys, the Shetlands and the Western Isles. Provision is also made for local community councils.

The boundaries and electoral arrangements of local authorities in Wales and Scotland are kept under review by the Local Government Boundary Commissions for Wales and Scotland respectively. In 1992 the responsibilities of the former Local Government Boundary Commission for England passed to the Local Government Commission (see p. 72).

In Northern Ireland 26 district councils are responsible for local environmental and certain other services. Statutory bodies, such as the Northern Ireland Housing Executive and area boards, are responsible to central government departments for administering other major services (see p. 513).

Election of Councils

Local councils consist of elected councillors. Councillors are paid a basic allowance but may also be entitled to additional allowances and expenses for attending meetings or taking on special responsibilities. Parish and community councillors cannot claim allowances for duties undertaken within their own council areas. In Scotland community councillors are not eligible for any form of allowance.

In England and Wales each council elects its presiding officer annually. Some districts have the ceremonial title of borough, or city, both granted by royal authority. In boroughs and cities the presiding officer is normally known as the Mayor. In the City of London and certain other large cities, he or she is known as the Lord Mayor. In Scotland the presiding officer of the district council of each of the four cities is called the Lord Provost. In other councils he or she is known as a convenor or provost. District councils in Northern Ireland are presided over by mayors.

Councillors are elected for four years. All county councils in England and Wales, London borough councils, and about two-thirds of non-metropolitan district councils are elected in their entirety every four years. In the remaining districts (including all metropolitan districts) one-third of the councillors are elected in each of the three years between county council elections. In Scotland local elections are held every two years, alternately for districts and for regions and islands authorities. Each election covers the whole council.

Voters

Anyone may vote at a local government election in Britain provided he or she is:

● aged 18 years or over;

● a citizen of Britain or another Commonwealth country, or a citizen of the Irish Republic;

● not legally disqualified; and

● on the electoral register.

To qualify for registration a person must be resident in the council area on the qualifying date. In Northern Ireland there are slightly different requirements.

Citizens of the European Union will be able to register to vote and stand for election at local government elections by the end of 1995.

Candidates

Most candidates at local government elections stand as representatives of a national political party, although some stand as independents. Candidates must be British citizens, other Commonwealth citizens or citizens of the

Irish Republic, and aged 21 or over. In addition, they must either:

- be registered as local electors in the area of the relevant local authority; or
- have occupied (as owner or tenant) land or premises in that area during the whole of the preceding 12 months; or
- have had their main place of work in the area throughout this 12-month period.

No one may be elected to a council of which he or she is an employee, and there are some other disqualifications. All candidates for district council elections in Northern Ireland are required to make a declaration against terrorism.

Electoral Divisions and Procedure

Counties in England and Wales are divided into electoral divisions, each returning one councillor. Districts in England, Wales and Northern Ireland are divided into wards, returning one councillor or more. In Scotland the electoral areas in the regions and islands areas are called electoral divisions, each returning a single member; the districts are divided into wards, similarly returning a single member. Parishes (in England) and communities (in Wales) may be divided into wards. Wards return at least one councillor. The minimum parish/community council size is five councillors.

The procedure for local government voting in Great Britain is broadly similar to that for parliamentary elections. In Northern Ireland local government elections are held by proportional representation, and electoral wards are grouped into district electoral areas.

Council Functions and Services

At present in England county councils are responsible for strategic planning, transport planning, highways, traffic regulation, education,[10] consumer protection, refuse disposal, police,[11] the fire service, libraries

and the personal social services. District councils are responsible for services such as environmental health, housing, decisions on most local planning applications, and refuse collection. Both tiers of local authority have powers to provide facilities such as museums, art galleries and parks; arrangements depend on local agreement.

In the metropolitan counties the district councils are responsible for all services apart from the police, the fire service and public transport and, in some areas, waste regulation and disposal (see p. 358). In Greater London the boroughs and the Corporation of the City of London have similar functions, but London's metropolitan police force is responsible to the Home Secretary. Responsibility for public transport lies with London Transport (see p. 290).

In Wales the division of functions between county and district councils is much the same as that between county and district councils in non-metropolitan areas of England, except that Welsh district councils are responsible for refuse disposal and a few are also responsible for libraries.

In Scotland the functions of regional and district authorities are, at present, divided up in a similar way to the counties and districts in England and Wales. Because of their isolation from the mainland, the Orkneys, the Shetlands and the Western Isles have single, virtually all-purpose authorities; they take part in wider-scale administration for their police and fire services, however, and rely on the mainland for assistance in the more specialised aspects of education and social work.

In Northern Ireland local environmental and certain other services, such as leisure and the arts, are administered by the district councils. Responsibility for planning, roads, water supply and sewerage services is exercised in each district through a divisional office of the Department of the Environment for Northern Ireland. Area boards, responsible to central departments, administer education, public libraries and the health and personal social services locally. The Northern Ireland Housing Executive, responsible to the Department of the Environment for Northern Ireland, administers housing.

---

[10] Schools may, however, 'opt out' of local education authority control by obtaining grant-maintained status—see p. 411.

[11] In many areas, police forces cover more than one county, and in these cases a joint board is set up to act as police authority.

Changes in Local Government

There have been numerous changes in recent years in the way that local authorities approach their responsibilities. Many of these can be encapsulated under the term 'the enabling authority'. It is used to describe the general shift away from local authorities providing services directly and towards them arranging for services to be provided, or carrying out functions in partnership with other bodies. For example, councils often have nomination rights to housing association properties (see p. 330), so that they are acting not as provider but as 'gatekeeper'. Likewise, under the community care reforms, councils with social services responsibilities have to draw up care plans for those who need them (see p. 392), but the care will often be provided by the private or voluntary sectors funded by the council, rather than directly by the local authority itself.

Internal Organisation of Local Authorities

Local authorities have considerable freedom to make arrangements for carrying out their duties; these are set out in standing orders. Some decisions are made by the full council; many other matters are delegated to committees composed of members of the council. A council may delegate most functions to a committee or officer, although certain powers are legally reserved to the council as a whole. The powers and duties of local authority committees are usually laid down in the terms of reference. Parish and community councils in England and Wales are often able to do their work in full session, although they appoint committees from time to time as necessary.

In England and Wales committees generally have to reflect the political composition of the council (although the legislation governing this specifically excludes parish or community councils). In practice, this is often also the case in Scotland, although it is not enforced by legislation. People who are not members of the council may be co-opted onto decision-making committees and can speak and take part in debates; they cannot normally vote. Legislation also prevents senior officers and others in politically sensitive posts from being members of another local authority or undertaking public political activity. Some of these provisions have not been introduced in Northern Ireland.

Public Access

The public (including the press) are admitted to council, committee and sub-committee meetings, and have access to agendas, reports and minutes of meetings and certain background papers. Local authorities may exclude the public from meetings and withhold these papers only in limited circumstances.

Employees

Over 2 million people[12] are employed by local authorities in Great Britain. These include administrative, professional and technical staff, teachers, firefighters, those engaged in law and order services, and manual workers. Education is the largest service, employing some 40 per cent of all local government workers. Councils are individually responsible, within certain national legislative requirements, for deciding the structure of their workforces.

Senior staff appointments are usually made by the elected councillors. More junior appointments are made by heads of departments. Pay and conditions of service are usually a matter for each council, although there are scales recommended by national negotiating machinery between authorities and trade unions, and most authorities follow these.

Authorities differ in the degree to which they employ their own permanent staff to carry out certain functions or use private firms under contract. The Government's policy of promoting value for money is encouraging the use of private firms where savings can be made. Many local government functions, such as refuse collection and leisure management, must be put out to tender ('compulsory competitive tendering'—

---

[12] Full-time equivalents.

CCT), although the local authority's own workforce can put up an in-house bid. Between 1989 and 1992, CCT achieved average cost savings of 6 to 7 per cent. In November 1992 the Government announced proposals to extend CCT to local authorities' provision of a range of professional services.

Local Authority Finance

Local government expenditure accounts for about 25 per cent of public spending. The Government has sought to influence local government spending as part of a general policy of controlling the growth of public expenditure. Since 1984 the Government has had powers to limit or 'cap' local authority budgets (local authority taxation in Scotland) by setting a maximum amount for local authorities which have, in its view, set budgets which are excessive.

In 1993–94 expenditure by local authorities in Britain was about £70,200 million. Current expenditure amounted to £59,200 million, and capital expenditure, net of capital receipts, was £6,700 million and debt interest £4,400 million. Local government capital expenditure is financed primarily by borrowing and from capital receipts from the disposal of land and buildings.

Local authorities in Great Britain raise revenue through the council tax, which replaced the community charge system in April 1993 (see p. 162). They are also the beneficiaries of revenue from the national non-domestic rate, a property tax levied on businesses and other non-domestic properties.

Financial Safeguards

Local councils' annual accounts must be audited by independent auditors appointed by the Audit Commission in England and Wales, or by the Commission for Local Authority Accounts in Scotland. In Northern Ireland this role is exercised by a local government audit section appointed by the Department of the Environment for Northern Ireland.

Local Government Complaints System

Local authorities are encouraged to resolve complaints through internal mechanisms, and members of the public will often ask their own councillor for assistance in this. Local authorities must also appoint a monitoring officer whose duties include ensuring that the local authority acts lawfully in the conduct of its business.

Allegations of local government maladministration may be investigated by statutory independent Commissioners for Local Administration, often known as 'local government ombudsmen'. There are three of these in England, and one each in Wales and Scotland. A report is issued on each complaint investigated and, if injustice caused by maladministration is found, the local ombudsman normally suggests a remedy. The council must consider the report and reply to it.

In Northern Ireland a Commissioner for Complaints deals with complaints alleging injustices suffered as a result of maladministration by district councils and certain other public bodies.

Pressure Groups

Pressure groups are informal organisations which aim to influence Parliament and Government in the way decisions are made and carried out, to the benefit of their members and the causes they support. There is a huge range, covering politics, business, employment, consumer affairs, ethnic minorities, aid to developing countries, foreign relations, education, culture defence, religion, sport, transport, social welfare, animal welfare and the environment. Some have over a million members, others only a few dozen. Some exert pressure on a number of different issues; others are concerned with a single issue. Some have come to play a recognised role in the way Britain is governed; others seek influence through radical protest.

While political parties seek to win political power, pressure groups aim to influence those who are in power, rather than to exercise the responsibility of government and to legislate.

Pressure Groups and Policy

Pressure groups operating at a national level have a number of ways of influencing the way Britain is governed. Action by them may highlight a particular problem, which is then acknowledged by the Government. Groups whose scale of membership indicates that they are broadly representative in their field may then be consulted by a government department, or take part in Whitehall working groups or advisory councils. If the Government considers that legislation is necessary, then proposals are drafted, which are circulated to interested groups for their comments. Legislation is then put before Parliament, and at various times during the passage of a Bill—especially at the committee stage—pressure groups have opportunities to influence its content. If the Act includes delegated legislation (see p. 57), pressure groups may be consulted and have the opportunity to provide information and express their views.

Pressure Groups and Government

The principle of consultation to gain the consent and co-operation of as wide a range of organisations as possible, and ensure the smooth working of laws and regulations, plays an important part in the relationship between government departments and interested groups.

In some instances a department is under legal obligation to consult with interested groups. The Government has a duty to consult organised interests, providing the pressure groups involved have a broad enough membership for them to represent a majority view, and that they observe confidentiality about their discussions with the department. Members of pressure groups have direct expertise, and an awareness of what is practicable, and can give advice and information to civil servants engaged in preparing policy or legislation. In return, the pressure groups have the opportunity to express their opinions directly to the Government. The contacts between civil servants and pressure group representatives may be relatively informal—by letter or telephone—or more formal, through involvement in working parties or by giving evidence to committees of inquiry.

Administration by Pressure Groups

As well as providing information and opinions, pressure groups can also be involved in administering government policy. The Law Society—the representative body for solicitors—administered the Government's Legal Aid scheme until that function was taken over in 1989 by the Legal Aid Board (see p. 105). The Government also makes grants to pressure groups which, as well as speaking on behalf of their members or for an issue, also provide a service. Relate: National Marriage Guidance has received grants for the advice centres it runs, and government departments make grants to a number of pressure groups for research relating to public policy.

Pressure Groups and Parliament

Lobbying—the practice of approaching MPs or Lords, persuading them to act on behalf of a cause, and enabling them to do so by providing advice and information—is a form of pressure group activity which has substantially increased in recent years.

A common pressure group tactic is to ask members of the public to write to their MP about an issue—for example, the Sunday trading laws, or the plight of political prisoners in particular countries—in order to raise awareness and persuade the MP to support the cause.

Raising Issues in Parliament

Other ways through which pressure groups may exert influence include:
- suggesting to MPs or Lords subjects for private members' Bills (see p. 55); many pressure groups have ready-drafted legislation waiting to be sponsored;
- approaching MPs or Lords to ask parliamentary questions as a means of gaining information from the Government and of drawing public attention to an issue;
- suggesting to MPs subjects for Early Day Motions (see p. 59); and

- orchestrating public petitions as a form of protest against government policy, or to call for action. If the petition is to be presented in Parliament, it must be worded according to Commons or Lords rules, and be presented by an MP or Lord in his or her own House.

Sponsoring and Employing MPs

The trade unions sponsor a large number of Labour Party parliamentary candidates, by providing financial help with general election expenses, as well as making annual payments to the constituency parties of sponsored Labour MPs. Of the 269 Labour MPs elected at the 1992 general election, 165 were sponsored.

MPs may be employed as parliamentary advisers or consultants to pressure groups or companies. As a consultant, an MP might be expected to give information and advice about relevant parliamentary business, and speak on behalf of the interests concerned in

a debate. Any such employment must be registered in the published Register of Members' Interests (see p. 54), and must be declared in the course of any relevant speech in the House.

Parliamentary Lobbyists

Many pressure groups employ full-time parliamentary workers or liaison officers, whose job is to develop contacts with MPs and Lords sympathetic to their cause, and to brief them when issues affecting the group are raised in Parliament.

There are also public relations and political consultancy firms specialising in lobbying Parliament and Government. Such firms are employed by pressure groups—as well as by British and overseas companies and organisations—to monitor parliamentary business, and to promote their clients' interests where they are affected by legislation and debate.

Further Reading

The British System of Government. Aspects of Britain series, HMSO, 1994.

The Civil Service: Continuity and Change. Cm 2627, HMSO, 1994.

History and Function of Government Departments. Aspects of Britain series, HMSO, 1993.

Open Government. Cm 2290. HMSO, 1993.

Organisation of Political Parties. Aspects of Britain series, HMSO, 1994.

Parliament. Aspects of Britain series, HMSO, 1994.

Pressure Groups. Aspects of Britain series, HMSO, 1994.

Renewing Local Government in the English Shires. Local Government Commission. HMSO, £7.90

8 Justice and the Law

In response to increasing public concern about crime, the Government has toughened its law and order policy. This has been reflected in two major pieces of legislation—the Police and Magistrates' Courts Act and the Criminal Justice and Public Order Bill. The former is intended to improve police flexibility to tackle crime and to increase the efficiency of court administration. The latter includes new measures to combat crime and allows for the prompt enactment of some of the recommendations of the Royal Commission on Criminal Justice in England and Wales, which reported to the Government in July 1993.

England and Wales, Scotland, and Northern Ireland all have their own legal systems, with considerable differences in law, organisation and practice. All three have separate prosecution, prison and police services. Crime prevention policy and non-custodial treatment for offenders is very similar throughout Britain. There are different civil court and civil law systems in England and Wales and in Scotland; Northern Ireland's system is in many ways similar to the English and Welsh model.

Common Law and Statute Law

One of the main sources of law in England and Wales and in Northern Ireland is common law, which has evolved over centuries from judges' decisions. It forms the basis of the law except when superseded by legislation. In Scotland, too, the doctrine of legal precedent has been more strictly applied since the end of the 18th century.

Much of the law, particularly that relating to criminal justice, is statute law passed by Parliament. If a court reaches a decision which is contrary to the intentions of Parliament, then Parliament must either accept the decision or pass amending legislation. Some Acts create new law, while others are passed to draw together existing law on a given topic. Parliament can repeal a statute and replace it with another.

European Community Law

European Community law, deriving from Britain's membership of the European Union, is confined mainly to economic and social matters; in certain circumstances it takes precedence over domestic law. It is normally applied by the domestic courts, but the most authoritative rulings are given by the European Court of Justice (see p. 112).

Certain changes to United Kingdom law

have been made to bring it into line with rulings of Strasbourg's European Court of Human Rights.

Branches of the Law

There are two main branches of the law—criminal and civil. Criminal law is concerned with acts punishable by the State. Civil law covers:

- disputes between individuals about their rights, duties and obligations; and
- dealings between individuals and companies, and between one company and another.

Criminal Justice

Crime Statistics

Differences in the legal systems, police recording practices and statistical classifications make it impracticable to analyse in detail trends in crime for the country as a whole. Nevertheless, there has, as in Western Europe generally, been a substantial increase in crime since the early 1950s. Annual official statistics cover crime recorded by the police and can be affected by changes in unreported crime.

Recorded crimes in England and Wales in 1993 are detailed in Table 8.1. In the same year the Scottish police recorded 543,013 crimes, of which 186,212 were cleared up. In Northern Ireland, of the 66,228 recorded crimes about 24,088 were cleared up.

Most crime is committed by young males, is opportunist and is not planned by hardened professional criminals, although these do exist.

Crime tends to be concentrated in large cities and urban areas. About 94 per cent of offences recorded by the police in England and Wales are directed against property but only 5 per cent involve violence. Rising affluence has provided more opportunities for casual property crime. In 1957, for example, car crime was only one-tenth of total crime but this has risen to about 28 per cent. The demand for, and supply of, illegal drugs has been an increasing factor in the incidence of crime in recent years.

Regular crime surveys are undertaken in England and Wales, Scotland and in Northern Ireland. The 1992 survey in England and Wales asked respondents for information about how crime had affected them in 1991. It estimated a total of 15 million crimes in 1991, the majority of which were against property. Violent crime accounted for only 5 per cent of the total, while 36 per cent involved vehicles, 9 per cent were burglaries and 30 per cent other forms of theft. These surveys, the fifth of which is in progress, indicate that many crimes go unrecorded by the police, mainly because not all victims report them.

Crime Prevention

National publicity campaigns are a regular feature of the Government's programmes. The Home Office's Crime Prevention Centre

Table 8.1: Notifiable Crimes Recorded by the Police in England and Wales 1993

Offence Group	Recorded crimes	Crimes cleared up	Per cent
Violence against the person	205,416	156,636	76
Sexual offences	31,380	23,371	74
Burglary	1,369,998	266,420	19
Robbery	58,274	12,532	22
Theft and handling stolen goods	2,753,927	634,491	23
Fraud and forgery	163,132	82,956	51
Criminal damage[a]	697,841	113,494	16
Other	40,997	38,988	95
Total	5,320,965	1,328,888	25

Source: Home Office.
[a]Excludes criminal damage of £20 or under.

encourages local agencies to implement anti-crime measures and to assess the results.

Assisted by the police, local crime prevention panels (including mainly school-based youth panels) try to prevent crime through publicity, marking goods and equipment, and fund-raising to buy security devices. The police have also been closely involved in setting up 130,000 neighbourhood watch schemes in England and Wales. There are some 3,400 watch schemes in Scotland. Crime Concern, a national independent organisation, encourages local initiatives and business participation in crime prevention.

The Safer Cities programme tackles crime and the fear of crime in inner city and urban areas through joint action by local government, private businesses, the police and voluntary agencies. By March 1994, 20 projects had supported 3,600 crime prevention schemes with over £22 million of grant funds from central government. Although 16 of the projects under the first phase of the programme have closed, the programme is being expanded to up to 40 new projects in selected high-crime areas. Each project is led by a committee, drawn from local agencies and supported by a co-ordinator funded by the Home Office. There is a Safer Cities programme in Scotland and similar projects are being funded by the Government in Northern Ireland.

The National Board for Crime Prevention, set up in 1993, advises the Government about ways of involving all sections of the community in the development and delivery of crime prevention in England and Wales. The Scottish Crime Prevention Panel performs a similar function in Scotland.

Helping the Victim

There are some 370 victim support schemes —with some 10,000 volunteer visitors and covering 98 per cent of the population in England and Wales—providing practical help and emotional support to victims of crime. They are co-ordinated by a national organisation, Victim Support, which receives a government grant (over £10 million in 1994–95). Most of the grant goes to local schemes to meet either the salaries of co-ordinators or running costs.

Similar schemes operate in Scotland and Northern Ireland.

In England and Wales a witness service, organised by Victim Support with Home Office funding, provides support for victims and other witnesses attending Crown Courts. Some 40 witness schemes have been set up to help victims through the stress of giving evidence; these will be extended to all 76 main Crown Court centres by the end of 1995.

> The Government has accepted the 11 recommendations made by the Royal Commission on Criminal Justice on help for the victims of crime. Some reflect the standards of the *Victims' Charter*, published by the Government in 1990, and are already established practice. Others call for new procedures to be set up within and between the criminal justice agencies responsible for their delivery.

Blameless victims of violent crime in England, Wales and Scotland, including foreign nationals, may be eligible for compensation from public funds. In Northern Ireland there is statutory provision in certain circumstances for compensation to be paid from public funds for criminal injuries, and for malicious damage to property, including any resulting loss of profits. Britain is a party to a European Convention under which mutual arrangements for compensation apply to citizens of those countries in which the Convention is in force.

Strengthening the Law

Important measures to strengthen the criminal justice system have been taken in recent years. The courts, for instance, have powers to confiscate the proceeds of drug trafficking. A court can require an offender to pay an amount equal to the full value of the proceeds arising from the trafficking. Following a conviction, the onus is on the offender to prove that property does not represent the proceeds of trafficking. Restraint and confiscation orders made by courts can be enforced against assets held overseas, and vice versa, if a mutual enforcement agreement has been made between Britain and another state. A court, other than in Scotland, may also confiscate the proceeds of offences such as robbery, fraud, blackmail and insider dealing in shares.

New powers to clamp down on money launderers[1] came into force in February and April 1994, with heavy penalties for those who launder money gained from any sort of serious crime.

In 1992 Britain became the first country to ratify the 1990 Council of Europe convention which provides for international co-operation in the investigation, search, seizure and confiscation of the proceeds of all crimes.

There are strict legislative controls on firearms. The police license the possession of firearms and have powers to regulate their safe keeping and movement. The private ownership of certain highly dangerous types of weapon, such as machine guns, high-powered self-loading rifles and burst-fire weapons, is banned. Similar legislation applies in Northern Ireland.

It is unlawful to manufacture, sell or import certain weapons such as knuckledusters or to carry a knife in a public place without good reason.

The Criminal Justice Act 1991 made a number of reforms to the criminal law in England and Wales, mainly concerning sentencing and the system for early release of prisoners (see p. 97). Similar reforms in Scotland took effect from October 1993.

Legislation has been passed to improve the organisation and management of the police, so that they are better able to combat crime. A Bill before Parliament is designed to tilt the balance of the criminal justice system further against criminals and in favour of protecting law-abiding people.

Measures to Combat Terrorism

The Government has certain exceptional powers for dealing with and preventing

terrorist activities. These take account of the need to achieve a proper balance between the safety of the public and the rights of the individual.

Northern Ireland

The security forces in Northern Ireland have special powers to search, question and arrest. The police can hold a suspected terrorist on their own authority for up to 48 hours; detention for up to a further five days must be approved by the Northern Ireland Secretary. A person who is detained under emergency provisions is entitled to consult a solicitor privately.

Nobody may be imprisoned for political beliefs. All prisoners, except those awaiting trial, have been found guilty in court of criminal offences. The legislation is reviewed annually by an independent person whose reports are presented to Parliament, which has to renew the legislation each year.

Other Legislation

Other legislation applies throughout Britain and is renewable annually by Parliament. It provides for the exclusion from Great Britain, Northern Ireland or the United Kingdom of people involved in terrorism related to Northern Ireland affairs and for the banning of specified terrorist organisations in Great Britain. It also gives the police powers to arrest terrorist suspects without warrant and hold them for 48 hours. Ministerial approval may be given to extend detention for up to a further five days. This provision also applies to suspected international terrorists.

It is a criminal offence to finance terrorism or receive funds for use in the furtherance of terrorism. Police can apply for a court order to freeze a suspect's assets once he or she has been charged. Funds can be forfeited if a person is convicted. The legislation allows for reciprocal enforcement agreements with other countries.

The Government maintains that there should be no concessions to terrorist demands and that international co-operation is essential in tracking down terrorists and impeding their movement between countries.

---

[1] Money laundering is the process by which illegally obtained property—from drugs or arms trafficking, terrorist activities or other serious crimes—is given the appearance of having originated from a legitimate source.

THE POLICE SERVICE

Organisation

There are 52 police forces in Britain, mainly organised on a local basis: 43 in England and Wales, eight in Scotland and one (the Royal Ulster Constabulary) in Northern Ireland. The Metropolitan Police Force and the City of London force are responsible for policing London. The police service is financed by central and local government.

At the end of 1993 police strength in Britain was about 150,000, of which the Metropolitan Police numbered over 28,000. The establishment of the Royal Ulster Constabulary was around 8,500. Police strength in Scotland was just over 14,000. Each force has volunteer special constables who perform police duties in their spare time, without pay, acting in support of regular officers. The Government is planning to recruit a further 10,000 special constables by the end of 1996, so increasing the overall number by 50 per cent. In Northern Ireland there is a 5,000-strong part-time and full-time paid reserve.

Police forces are maintained in England and Wales by the local police authority; two-thirds of an authority's members are local councillors and one-third are magistrates. The Home Secretary is responsible for London's Metropolitan Police Force. The police authorities in Scotland are the regional and islands councils. In Northern Ireland the police force is responsible to a police authority appointed by the Government.

Chief constables run their police forces and are responsible for the appointment, promotion and discipline of all ranks below assistant chief constable. They are generally answerable to the police authorities, and must submit an annual report. The police authorities appoint the chief constable and other top officers. They also fix the maximum strength of the force, subject to approval by the Government, and provide buildings and equipment.

London's Metropolitan Police Commissioner and his immediate subordinates are appointed on the recommendation of the Home Secretary.

Central Authorities

The Home Secretary and the Scottish and Northern Ireland Secretaries approve the appointment of chief, deputy and assistant chief constables. Where necessary they can:

- approve a police authority's decision to retire a chief constable in the interests of efficiency;
- call for a report from a chief constable on matters relating to local policing; and
- institute a local inquiry.

These ministers can also make regulations covering:

- qualifications for appointment, promotion and retirement;
- discipline;
- hours of duty, leave, pay and allowances;
- uniform; and
- ranks.

Police forces are inspected by inspectors of constabulary, whose reports to central government are published. Lay inspectors, with a range of professional experience outside the police service, have been appointed for the first time.

Police officers are not allowed to join a trade union or to go on strike. All ranks, however, have their own staff associations.

Reform Programme

New legislation has been passed that is designed to change the relationship between central government, police authorities and chief constables, to improve the management of the police and to reduce cumbersome central controls. The main provisions of the Police and Magistrates' Courts Act include:

- setting key objectives for the police which give priority to fighting crime and protecting the public;
- placing a greater emphasis on community needs through local policing plans;
- strengthening the role of the Inspectorate of Constabulary, which will have a statutory responsibility to inspect the Metropolitan Police;

- ending detailed government controls on finance and manpower by giving chief constables new freedom to manage police and civilian staff and to determine staff numbers; and

- introducing fixed-term appointments for senior police officers and abolishing the ranks of deputy chief constable and chief superintendent.

The first two of these will not apply in Scotland, where the duties of the police have been set out in statute for many years.

New legislation provides for the appointment of independent members to police authorities in England and Wales outside London. The standard size of a police authority will be 17 members, comprising nine locally elected councillors, three magistrates and five independent members. The Home Secretary will be able to increase the size of a police authority beyond 17 if local circumstances make it desirable. The independent members will be chosen by the other members of the police authority, from a list of 10 names forwarded by the Home Secretary from a shortlist of 20 prepared by a local selection panel.

The Government has accepted all the recommendations of a 1993 report on reducing police paperwork in England and Wales. The report called for more effective use of information technology and better liaison between the police and the Crown Prosecution Service (see p. 88). Work is well advanced on implementing the recommendations.

Co-ordination of Police Operations

Certain police services are provided centrally either by the Government or through co-operation between forces. In England and Wales these include criminal intelligence, telecommunications, and research and development. In Scotland the main common services are centralised police training, the Scottish Crime Squad and the Scottish Criminal Record Office.

The National Criminal Intelligence Service, with a headquarters in London and five regional offices, provides police forces with information about major criminals and serious crime. Its Drugs Unit helps to co-ordinate police and Customs intelligence on drug trafficking. The Service also liaises with the International Criminal Police Organisation, which promotes international co-operation between police forces.

Britain has taken the lead in developing, with other European Union countries, a European police organisation designed to provide Union-wide intelligence about serious crime (see p. 127).

Almost all British police forces have specialist units to investigate company fraud.

Regional crime squads, co-ordinated at national level in England and Wales, deal with serious criminal activities, such as drug trafficking, which transcend individual force boundaries and may have national or international links.

The Police National Computer provides all British police forces with rapid 24-hour-a-day access to operationally essential information. Phoenix, formerly known as the National Criminal Records System, is being implemented on the Police National Computer in 1994, giving the police direct on-screen access to national records of arrests, bail decisions, and convictions. This will gradually replace the manual record-keeping service currently operated by the National Identification Bureau (NIB), which is located at Metropolitan Police headquarters but financed by all police forces. Phoenix will eventually provide information direct to other agencies such as the courts, the Prison Service and the Crown Prosecution Service. The Police National Network, providing integrated voice and data communications, should be fully operational by mid-1995.

Scottish criminal records are held on computer at the Scottish Criminal Record Office, which has an automatic national fingerprint record system; plans for a similar national system in England and Wales are on course for implementation during 1996–97.

The Police National Missing Persons Bureau, which comes under the NIB, was launched in March 1994. It is the first national database of vulnerable missing people, holding information which all forces and international agencies can share.

Forensic Science Service

The Forensic Science Service (FSS) provides scientific support primarily for forces in England and Wales. It has 600 staff, of whom about 400 are scientists. There are six operational laboratories and a research establishment. London's Metropolitan Police Force has its own forensic science laboratory, which is the largest in Europe.

As well as the 41 provincial police forces in England and Wales, other FSS customers include the Crown Prosecution Service, defence lawyers, coroners and civil litigants. In Scotland forensic science services are provided by forces' own laboratories. Northern Ireland has its own forensic science laboratory.

Police Discipline

A police officer may be prosecuted if suspected of a criminal offence. Officers are also subject to a disciplinary code designed to deal with abuse of police powers and maintain public confidence in police impartiality. If found guilty of breaching the code, an officer can be dismissed from the force.

New disciplinary procedures for the police in Great Britain, similar to those in operation elsewhere in the public service, were announced by the Government in September 1993. They include splitting the disciplinary system into two categories—unsatisfactory performance and misconduct. Guidance on operating the new procedures is being developed in consultation with police staff associations and police authority representatives. Its introduction awaits the coming into force of the Police and Magistrates' Courts Act. Similar reforms have been proposed in Northern Ireland.

Members of the public have the right to make complaints against police officers if they feel that they have been treated unfairly or improperly. In England and Wales the investigation and resolution of complaints is scrutinised by the independent Police Complaints Authority. In Scotland complaints against police officers involving allegations of any form of criminal conduct are referred to the procurator fiscal for investigation (see p. 89). The Police and Magistrates' Courts Act includes provisions to give the Scottish Inspectorate of Constabulary a new role regarding the handling of a complaint where the complainant is dissatisfied.

In Northern Ireland the Independent Commission for Police Complaints is required to supervise the investigation of a complaint regarding death or serious injury and has the power to supervise that of any other complaint. In certain circumstances, the Secretary of State may direct the Commission to supervise the investigation of matters that are not the subject of a formal complaint.

Community Relations

Police/community liaison consultative groups operate in every police authority; they consist of representatives from the police, local councillors and community groups.

Particular efforts are made to develop relations with young people through greater contact with schools. School governing bodies and head teachers have to describe in their annual reports the steps taken to strengthen their schools' links with the community, including the police.

The Government is committed to improving relations between the police and ethnic minorities. Central guidance recommends that all police officers should receive thorough training in community and race relations issues.

Several Home Office initiatives are designed to tackle racially motivated crime and to ensure that the issue is treated as a police priority. These include the issue of guidance to forces on their response to such crimes and the production of a booklet for victims. In addition, forces' arrangements for responding to racial incidents are monitored by the Inspectorate of Constabulary. Discriminatory behaviour by police officers, either to other officers or to members of the public, is an offence under the Police Discipline Code.

In October 1993 the Government launched the Parish Constables initiative in England and Wales, inviting police and parish councils (see p. 73) to set up pilot schemes to test new ideas on community policing. By April 1994, 46 schemes were in operation.

All police forces recognise the need to recruit women and members of the ethnic minorities in order to ensure that the police represent the community. At the end of 1993 there were 1,730 ethnic minority officers and 16,750 women police officers in England and Wales. Scottish police forces had 1,559 women officers. Every force has an equal opportunities policy.

Police Powers

Officers in Great Britain do not normally carry firearms, although in an emergency they can be issued on the authority of a senior officer. Officers in armoured response vehicles in London can wear their sidearms in holsters at all times. In Northern Ireland police officers are issued with firearms for personal protection and other firearms are available for duty purposes.

The Government can authorise interception of postal and telephone services by the police in order to:

● prevent and detect serious crime;

● protect national security; or

● safeguard Britain's economic well-being.

Any interception outside these procedures is a criminal offence.

A police officer in England and Wales has a general power of stop and search if he or she has reasonable grounds for suspecting that a person is carrying stolen goods, offensive weapons or implements that could be used for theft, burglary and other offences. The officer must, however, state and record the grounds for taking this action and what, if anything, was found.

Under new legislation before Parliament, police officers would be able to stop and search all people and vehicles for offensive weapons or knives if violence is likely to break out. This power would be linked to a specified time and area, and would require the authority of a superintendent or higher rank.

Arrest

In England and Wales the police have wide powers to arrest suspects with or without a warrant issued by a magistrate. For serious offences, known as 'arrestable offences', a suspect can be arrested without a warrant; this covers all offences for which a maximum period of five years' imprisonment can be imposed. Arrest without a warrant also applies to people suspected of committing serious 'arrestable offences' such as murder, rape and kidnapping. For lesser offences, arrest without warrant exists if it is not possible or appropriate to send out a summons to appear in court.

Detention, Treatment and Questioning

A government code of practice regulates detention, treatment and questioning of suspects by the police in England and Wales. A police officer can be disciplined if he or she fails to comply with the code. Evidence obtained in breach of the code may be ruled inadmissible in court.

An arrested person has a statutory right to consult a solicitor and to ask the police to notify a relative or other named person about the arrest. Where a person has been arrested in connection with a serious arrestable offence, but not yet charged, the police may delay for up to 36 hours the exercise of these rights if certain strict criteria are met.

The police must caution a suspect before any questions are put to him or her for the purpose of obtaining material which may be given in evidence in court. The caution informs the suspect that he or she is entitled to refuse to answer questions—the so-called 'right to silence'. In England and Wales this would be amended under the provisions of new legislation so that courts could draw an inference from a suspect's refusal to answer questions from police officers or during court proceedings. Such legislation is already in place in Northern Ireland.

Questions relating to an offence may not normally be put to a person after he or she has been charged or informed that he or she may be prosecuted.

The time a suspect is held in police custody before charge is strictly regulated. For lesser offences this may not exceed 24 hours. A person suspected of committing a serious arrestable offence, such as murder, rape, or kidnapping, can be detained for up to 96 hours without charge but only beyond 36 hours if a warrant is obtained from a magistrates' court. Reviews must be made of a person's detention at regular intervals—six hours after initial detention and thereafter every nine hours as a maximum—to check whether the criteria for detention are still satisfied. If they are not, the person must be released immediately.

Tape recording of interviews with suspected offenders takes place at police stations; a code of practice governing these tape recordings has been approved by Parliament.

A person who thinks that the grounds for their detention are unlawful may apply to the High Court for a writ of habeas corpus, requiring the person who detained them to appear before the court to justify the detention. Habeas corpus proceedings take precedence over others. Similar procedures apply in Northern Ireland and a similar remedy is available to anyone who is unlawfully detained in Scotland.

> Recognising that the use of DNA analysis has become a powerful tool in the investigation of crime, the Government is extending police powers to take body samples from suspects. New legislation would allow the police to take non-intimate samples without consent from anyone who is detained or convicted for a recordable offence, and to use the samples to search against existing records of convicted offenders or unsolved crimes. In time a national database would be built up.

Charging

Once there is sufficient evidence, the police have to decide whether to charge the person with the offence. As an alternative, they can, for example, decide to defer charging or to

take no further action and release the person with or without bail. They may also issue a formal caution (see p. 96), which may be taken into account if the person reoffends.

If charged, a person may be kept in custody if there is a risk that they might fail to appear in court or might interfere with the administration of justice. When no such considerations apply, the person must be released on or without bail. Where someone is detained after charge, they must be brought before a magistrates' court as soon as practicable. This is usually no later than the next working day.

Scotland

In Scotland the police have common law powers of arrest and may search an arrested person. A police officer may also search a person for stolen property if he or she has reasonable grounds for suspicion.

The police may detain and question a suspected person for up to six hours. After this period the person must either be released or charged. Tape recording of interviews with suspects is common practice. A court will only allow as evidence statements fairly obtained by the police. Anyone arrested must be brought before a court on the first working day after arrest. In less serious cases the police may release a person who gives a written undertaking to attend court.

Where the charges involve serious crime, the accused is brought before the sheriff in private, either to be committed for a period not exceeding eight days to allow further enquiries to be made or to be committed for trial.

Awaiting Trial

There are time limits on the period a defendant may be kept in custody awaiting trial in England and Wales. In cases tried before a magistrates' court these are 56 days from first appearance to trial or 70 days between first appearance to committal for trial (see p. 91) in the Crown Court. The limit in Crown Court cases is 112 days from committal to taking of the plea. When a time limit expires, the defendant is entitled to bail unless the court extends the limit; it can only do this if satisfied that there is a good and sufficient reason, and that the prosecution has acted expeditiously.

Bail

Most accused people are released on bail pending trial. They are not remanded in custody except where strictly necessary. In England and Wales, the court decides whether a defendant should be released on bail. Unconditional bail may only be withheld if the court believes that the accused would:

- abscond;
- commit an offence;
- interfere with witnesses; or
- otherwise obstruct the course of justice.

A court may also impose conditions before granting bail. If bail is refused, the defendant may apply to a High Court judge or to the Crown Court for bail. In certain circumstances the prosecution may appeal to a Crown Court judge against the granting of bail by magistrates. An application can also be made to the Crown Court for conditions imposed by a magistrates' court to be varied.

> It has been estimated that 50,000 offences in England and Wales are committed every year by people on bail. To curb this abuse, new legislation before Parliament would give the police powers of immediate arrest for breach of police bail and remove the presumption in favour of bail for people alleged to have offended while on bail. It would also restrict the right to bail for someone charged with murder, manslaughter or rape if previously convicted of the same offence.

In some cases a court may grant bail to a defendant on condition that he or she lives in an approved bail or probation/bail hostel.

The probation service's bail information schemes provide the Crown Prosecution Service with information about a defendant which assists it to decide whether to oppose bail and enables the courts to take an informed decision on whether to grant bail.

Scotland

Anyone accused of a crime, except murder or treason, is entitled to apply for release on bail. Even in murder cases, bail may exceptionally be granted at the discretion of the Lord Advocate or a quorum of the High Court. There is a right of appeal to the High Court by the accused person against the refusal of bail, or by the prosecutor against the granting of bail, or by either party against the conditions imposed.

If a person charged with a serious crime has been kept in custody pending trial, the trial must begin within 110 days of the date of full committal. Where the person is not in custody, the trial must begin within 12 months of first appearance before the sheriff. The trial of a person charged with a summary offence and held in custody must begin within 40 days of the date of first appearance in court.

Northern Ireland

In Northern Ireland bail may be granted by a resident magistrate except in cases dealt with under emergency provisions (see p. 14), where the decision is made by a judge of the High Court.

CRIMINAL COURTS

Prosecution

England and Wales

Once the police have instituted criminal proceedings against a person, the independent Crown Prosecution Service (CPS) takes control of the case, reviews the evidence and decides whether the case should be continued.

The CPS is divided into 13 regional areas, each of which is run by a locally based Chief Crown Prosecutor. CPS lawyers prosecute in the magistrates' courts, while barristers appear in the Crown Court.

A prosecution will only proceed if the prosecutor is satisfied that there is, on the evidence, a realistic prospect of conviction, and if so, that it is in the public interest for the prosecution to proceed. In nearly all cases the decision to prosecute is delegated to the lawyers in the area offices. However, some especially sensitive or complex cases, including terrorist offences and breaches of the Official Secrets Act, are dealt with by CPS headquarters.

Scotland

The Lord Advocate is responsible for prosecutions in the High Court of Justiciary, sheriff courts and district courts. There is no general right of private prosecution. The Lord Advocate is advised by the Crown Agent, who is head of the Procurator Fiscal Service and is assisted in the Crown Office by a staff of legally qualified civil servants.

Prosecutions in the High Court of Justiciary are prepared by procurators fiscal and Crown Office officials. They are conducted by the Lord Advocate, the Solicitor General for Scotland (the Lord Advocate's ministerial deputy) and advocate deputes, collectively known as Crown Counsel.

Crimes tried before the sheriff and district courts are prepared and prosecuted by procurators fiscal. The police and other law enforcement agencies investigate crimes and offences and report to the fiscal, who decides whether to prosecute, subject to the directions of Crown Counsel.

When dealing with minor crime, the fiscal can use alternatives to prosecution, such as formal warnings, diversion to social work and offers of fixed penalties. In the latter case, the offender does not have to accept such an offer; if he or she chooses to do so, proceedings are not brought and the payment does not count as a criminal conviction.

Northern Ireland

The Director of Public Prosecutions for Northern Ireland, appointed by the Attorney General, prosecutes all offences tried on indictment and may do so in other

(summary) cases. Most summary offences are prosecuted by the police.

Prosecutions for Fraud

The Serious Fraud Office prosecutes the most serious and complex cases of fraud in England, Wales and Northern Ireland. Investigations are conducted by teams of lawyers, accountants, police officers and other specialists. In Scotland the Crown Office Fraud Unit, which is part of the public prosecution service, directs the investigation and preparation for prosecution of serious and complex fraud cases.

Courts

England and Wales

Very serious offences such as murder, manslaughter, rape and robbery can only be tried on indictment in the Crown Court, where all contested trials are presided over by a judge sitting with a jury. Summary offences —the less serious offences and the vast majority of criminal cases—are tried by unpaid lay magistrates or, in a few areas, by paid stipendiary magistrates; both sit without a jury.

Offences in a third category—such as theft, the less serious cases of burglary and some assaults—are known as 'either way' offences. They can be tried either by magistrates or by jury in the Crown Court. Where magistrates consider an 'either way' case to be too serious for them to deal with, they may commit the accused to the Crown Court for trial. Even if magistrates consider the case suitable for summary trial, the accused has the right to choose trial by jury in the Crown Court.

All those charged with offences to be tried in the Crown Court must first appear before a magistrates' court, which decides whether to commit them to the Court for trial. However, under 1994 legislation, these committal proceedings will be abolished and replaced by a procedure allowing cases to be transferred administratively to the Crown Court. As recommended by the Royal Commission, the defence will still be able to argue that there is no case to answer in advance of trial at the Crown Court.

A magistrates' court, which is open to the public and the media, usually consists of three lay magistrates—known as justices of the peace—who are advised by a legally qualified clerk or a qualified assistant. There are about 29,400 lay magistrates. The 79 full-time, legally qualified stipendiary magistrates may sit alone and usually preside in courts where the workload is heavy.

Most cases involving people under 18 are heard in youth courts. These are specialist magistrates' courts which either sit apart from other courts or are held at a different time. Restrictions are placed on access by ordinary members of the public. Media reports must not identify a young person concerned in the proceedings, whether as defendant, victim or witness.

Where a young person under 18 is charged jointly with someone of 18 or over, the case is heard in an ordinary magistrates' court or the Crown Court. If the young person is found guilty, the court may transfer the case to a youth court for sentence.

An independent inspectorate has been set up to inspect the administration and management of magistrates' courts in order to improve performance and spread good practice. It does not comment on the judicial decisions of magistrates or their clerks in particular cases.

The Crown Court sits at 93 venues and is presided over by High Court judges, full-time Circuit Judges and part-time Recorders.

Courts Charter

A Courts Charter, setting out the standards of service which apply in the higher courts in England and Wales, came into operation in January 1993.

It outlines arrangements to help court users and ease the strains associated with court attendance. The procedure for dealing with complaints is displayed in all courts.

The Charter also covers the conduct of court business, and sets guideline time limits covering, among other things, the period between the start of proceedings and first appearance in court. It does not cover judicial decisions. Similar standards have been adopted by many magistrates' courts.

Scotland

The High Court of Justiciary tries the most serious crimes and has exclusive jurisdiction in cases involving murder, treason and rape. The sheriff court is concerned with less serious offences and the district court with minor offences.

Criminal cases in Scotland are heard under solemn or summary procedure. In solemn procedure, a defendant is tried by a judge sitting with a jury of 15 people. Details of the alleged offence are set out in a document called an indictment. In summary procedure the judge sits without a jury.

All cases in the High Court and the more serious ones in sheriff courts are tried by a judge and jury. Summary procedure is used in the less serious cases in the sheriff courts, and in all cases in the district courts. District court judges are lay justices of the peace. In Glasgow there are also stipendiary magistrates who are full-time lawyers with the same criminal jurisdiction in summary procedure as the sheriff.

Children under 16 who have committed an offence are normally dealt with by children's hearings (see p. 101).

The levels of service which citizens are entitled to expect from the main criminal justice agencies are set out in the Justice Charter for Scotland.

Northern Ireland

Cases involving minor summary offences are heard by magistrates' courts presided over by a full-time, legally qualified resident magistrate. Young offenders under 17 are dealt with by a juvenile court consisting of the resident magistrate and two specially qualified lay members, at least one of whom must be a woman.

The Crown Court deals with criminal trials on indictment. It is served by High Court and county court judges. Contested cases are heard by a judge and jury, although people charged with terrorist offences are tried by a judge sitting alone, because of the possibility of jurors being intimidated by terrorist organisations.

In non-jury Crown Court trials the onus remains on the prosecution to prove guilt beyond reasonable doubt and defendants have the right to be represented by a lawyer of their choice. The judge must set out in a written statement the reasons for convicting and there is an automatic right of appeal against conviction and sentence on points of fact as well as of law.

Trial

Criminal trials in Britain have two parties: the prosecution and the defence. The law presumes the innocence of an accused person until guilt has been proved by the prosecution. An accused person has the right to employ a legal adviser and may be granted legal aid from public funds (see p. 106). If remanded in custody, he or she may be visited by a legal adviser to ensure a properly prepared defence.

Disclosure to the Defence

In England and Wales, the prosecution in Crown Court cases must disclose to the defence all the statements from the witnesses on whom it proposes to rely. This must be done before any committal proceedings begin. This duty does not apply to offences tried in the magistrates' court, except when advance information is requested by the defence in 'either way' cases (see p. 89); in practice, however, the CPS adopts a more generous approach than is strictly required.

There is also a general duty to disclose to the defence evidence, documents and information which might have a bearing on the defence case. In circumstances where the material attracts public interest immunity or is otherwise subject to a duty of confidentiality, the prosecution is obliged to place it before the court for a ruling.

In Scottish solemn cases the prosecution must give the defence advance notice of the witnesses it intends to call and of the documents and other items on which it will rely. In summary cases this is usually done as a matter of practice, although there is no obligation on the Crown to do so.

Trial Procedure

Criminal trials normally take place in open court and rules of evidence, which are concerned with the proof of facts, are rigorously applied. If evidence is improperly admitted, or excluded, a conviction can be quashed on appeal.

During the trial the defendant has the right to hear and cross-examine prosecution witnesses. He or she can call his or her own witnesses who, if they will not attend voluntarily, may be legally compelled to do so. The defendant can also address the court in person or through a lawyer, the defence having the right to the last speech before the judge sums up. The defendant cannot be questioned without his or her consent. When a defendant does testify, he or she may be cross-examined about character or other conduct only in exceptional circumstances. Generally the prosecution may not introduce such evidence.

In Scotland cross-examination about the character or other conduct of the accused may be made in certain circumstances.

In Northern Ireland the judge can draw inferences from a refusal by a defendant to give evidence.

Child Witnesses

In England, Wales and Northern Ireland, child witnesses in cases involving offences of sex, violence or cruelty may give evidence in Crown Court proceedings from outside the courtroom by means of a live television link. In this way the child need not see his or her alleged attacker in court. In Scotland similar provisions apply. A child's sworn statement no longer has to be corroborated by other evidence for the court to hear it.

The Criminal Justice Act 1991 extended the availability of the live television link to youth court proceedings, and made further reforms to the law of evidence and procedure relating to child witnesses in England and Wales. Video-recorded interviews are admissible as the main evidence of a child witness, with any cross-examination taking place through the live television link.

In Scotland corroboration of the child's evidence is necessary to sustain a conviction.

Fraud Proceedings

In England, Wales and Northern Ireland the judge in complex fraud cases may order a preparatory open Crown Court hearing to determine questions regarding admissibility of evidence and any other questions of law. The judge also has the power to order the prosecution and the defence to serve certain statements on each other and to prepare the case in such a way that it is easier to understand.

Appeals may be made to the Court of Appeal from decisions of the judge in the preparatory hearings. The law on evidence has been changed to enable courts to have before them a wider range of written evidence in the form of business documents. Information technology is increasingly used in complex cases to present the material to the jury in a more comprehensible form.

The Jury

In jury trials the judge decides questions of law, sums up the evidence for the jury, and discharges or sentences the accused. The jury is responsible for deciding questions of fact. In England, Wales and Northern Ireland the verdict may be 'guilty' or 'not guilty', the latter resulting in acquittal. If the jury cannot reach a unanimous decision the judge may allow a majority verdict provided that, in the normal jury of 12 people, there are no more than two dissenters.

In Scotland the jury's verdict may be 'guilty', 'not guilty' or 'not proven'; the accused is acquitted if either of the last two verdicts is given. The jury consists of 15 people and a verdict of 'guilty' can only be reached if at least eight members are in favour. As a general rule no one may be convicted without corroborated evidence from at least two sources.

If the jury acquits the defendant, the prosecution has no right of appeal and the defendant cannot be tried again for the same offence.

A jury is independent of the judiciary. Any attempt to interfere with a jury is a criminal offence. Potential jurors are put on a panel before the start of the trial. In England and Wales the prosecution and the defence may challenge individual jurors on the panel, giving reasons for doing so. In Scotland the prosecution or defence may challenge up to three jurors without reason. In Northern Ireland each defendant has the right to challenge up to 12 potential jurors without giving a reason.

People between the ages of 18 and 70 (65 in Scotland) whose names appear on the electoral register, with certain exceptions, are liable for jury service and their names are chosen at random. Ineligible people include, for example, judges and people who have within the previous ten years been members of the legal profession or the police, prison or probation services. People convicted of certain offences within the previous ten years cannot serve on a jury. Anyone who has received a prison sentence of five years or more is disqualified for life.

Sentencing

If a person is convicted, the magistrate or judge (or their Scottish equivalent) decides on the most appropriate sentence, taking into account the facts of the offence, the circumstances of the offender, any previous convictions or sentences and any statutory limits on sentencing. The defence lawyer may make a speech in mitigation.

The Criminal Justice Act 1991 placed a requirement on the courts in England and Wales to obtain a 'pre-sentence' report from the probation service in all cases involving an offence triable either way before passing a custodial or more complex community sentence. However, to avoid unnecessary delays and costs, legislation before Parliament would give the courts discretion to dispense with this requirement where they are satisfied that they can properly sentence without one.

In Scottish cases where a custodial sentence may be imposed, it is mandatory for a court to obtain a pre-sentence report if the accused is under 21, has never served a custodial sentence or is a first offender. In other cases the judge decides whether to obtain such a report.

Appeals

England and Wales

A person convicted by a magistrates' court may appeal to the Crown Court against the sentence if he or she has pleaded guilty. An appeal may be made against both conviction and sentence, or sentence alone, if a 'not guilty' plea has been made. The High Court hears appeals on points of law and procedure —by either prosecution or defence—in cases originally dealt with by magistrates. If convicted by the Crown Court, a defendant can appeal to the Court of Appeal (Criminal Division) against both the conviction and the sentence imposed. The House of Lords is the final appeal court, but it will only consider cases that involve a point of law of general public importance and where leave to appeal is granted.

The Home Secretary may consider representations and intervene in cases tried on indictment where appeal rights have been exhausted. This is normally done only if there is new evidence or some other consideration of substance which was not before the original trial court. In such cases the Home Secretary refers the matter to the Court of Appeal.

> Following a Royal Commission recommendation, the Government has published a consultation paper on the establishment of a new independent Criminal Cases Review Authority, which would consider alleged miscarriages of justice and refer cases to the Court of Appeal.

The Attorney General may seek a ruling of the Court of Appeal on a point of law which has been material in a case where a person is tried on indictment. The Court of Appeal has power to refer the point to the House of Lords if necessary. The ruling will constitute a binding precedent, but an acquittal in the original case is not affected.

The Attorney General has the power to refer a case to the Court of Appeal if he or she considers that a sentence passed by the Crown Court for an offence triable only on indictment is unduly lenient. The Attorney General can also refer unduly lenient sentences for offences of indecent assault, making threats to kill, and of cruelty to, or neglect of, children; these offences can also be dealt with in magistrates' courts, but may only be referred if the defendant is sentenced in the Crown Court (see p. 89). The Court of Appeal may increase an unduly lenient sentence within the statutory maximum laid down by Parliament for the offence.

Scotland

All appeal cases are dealt with by the High Court of Justiciary and are heard by at least three judges. In both solemn and summary procedure, the accused may appeal against conviction, or sentence, or both. The Court may authorise a retrial if it sets aside a conviction. There is no further appeal to the House of Lords. In summary proceedings the prosecutor may appeal on a point of law against acquittal or sentence. The Lord Advocate may seek the opinion of the High Court on a point of law in a case where a person tried on indictment is acquitted. The acquittal in the original case is not affected.

Northern Ireland

In Northern Ireland, appeals from magistrates' courts against conviction or sentence are heard by the county court. An appeal on a point of law alone can be heard by the Northern Ireland Court of Appeal, which also hears appeals from the Crown Court against conviction or sentence. Procedures for a further appeal to the House of Lords are similar to those in England and Wales.

A person convicted of a terrorist offence in a non-jury court has an automatic right of appeal against conviction and sentence.

Coroners' Courts

In England and Wales, the coroner must hold an inquest if the deceased died a violent or unnatural death, a sudden death where the cause is unknown, or in prison or in other specified circumstances. In Northern Ireland in such circumstances the coroner investigates the matter to decide whether an inquest is necessary. The coroner's court establishes how, when and where the deceased died. A coroner may sit alone or, in certain circumstances, with a jury.

In Scotland the local procurator fiscal inquires privately into all sudden and suspicious deaths and may report the findings to the Crown Office. In a minority of cases a fatal accident inquiry may be held before the sheriff; this is mandatory in cases of death resulting from industrial accidents and of deaths in custody.

TREATMENT OF OFFENDERS

The Government considers that offenders who commit very serious crimes, particularly crimes of violence, should receive long custodial sentences, but that many other crimes can best be punished within the community through compensation and reparation.

Legislation sets the maximum penalties for offences, the sentence being entirely a matter for the courts, subject to these maxima. The Court of Appeal in England and Wales issues guidance to the lower courts on sentencing issues when points of principle have arisen on individual appeal cases.

The Royal Commission, noting that people pleading guilty in the Crown Court have usually been given a reduction of 25 per cent to 30 per cent in their sentence, recommended that there should be a more open system of sentence discounts, with earlier guilty pleas attracting higher discounts. Instituting a statutory basis for the court's action could help to achieve greater consistency in the application of discounts. Provision for this has been included in legislation before Parliament.

In Scotland, where many offences are not created by statute, the penalty for offences at common law range from absolute discharge to life imprisonment.

Custody

England and Wales

A custodial sentence is the most severe penalty ordinarily available to the courts. Under the Criminal Justice Act 1991, a custodial sentence can only be imposed where the offence is so serious that only such a sentence would be appropriate, or where there is a need to protect the public from a sexual or violent offender. A court is required to explain to the offender why it is passing a custodial sentence. The length of the sentence must reflect the seriousness of the offence.

A magistrates' court cannot impose a term of more than six months' imprisonment for an individual offence tried summarily. It can impose consecutive sentences for 'either way' offences (see p. 89), subject to an overall maximum of 12 months' imprisonment. If an offence carries a higher maximum penalty, the court may commit the offender for sentence at the Crown Court. The Crown Court may impose a custodial sentence for any term up to life, depending on the seriousness of the offence and the maximum penalty available.

If a court decides that an offence is sufficiently serious to justify an immediate custodial sentence of not more than two years, the sentence may be suspended for a period of at least one year and not more than two years if exceptional circumstances justify the suspension. If the offender commits another imprisonable offence during the period of suspension, the court may order the suspended sentence to be served in addition to any punishment imposed for the second offence. When passing a suspended sentence, the court must consider whether it would also be appropriate to impose a fine or make a compensation order. The court may also order supervision of the offender by a probation officer if the suspended sentence is for more than six months.

There is a mandatory sentence of life

---

imprisonment for murder throughout Britain. Life imprisonment is the maximum penalty for a number of serious offences such as robbery, rape, arson and manslaughter.

Scotland and Northern Ireland

In Scottish trials on indictment the High Court of Justiciary may impose a sentence of imprisonment for any term up to life, and the sheriff court any term up to three years. The latter may send any person to the High Court for sentence if the court considers its powers are insufficient. In summary cases, the sheriff or stipendiary magistrate may normally impose up to three months' imprisonment or six months' for some repeated offences. The district court can impose a maximum term of imprisonment of 60 days.

In Northern Ireland the position is generally the same as for England and Wales. A magistrates' court, however, cannot commit an offender for sentencing at the Crown Court if it has tried the case.

Non-custodial Treatment

Non-custodial sentences include:

- fines;
- compensation orders;
- probation and supervision orders;
- community service orders; and
- a combination order, which includes elements of probation and community service.

Fines

About 80 per cent of offenders are punished with a fine. There is no limit to the fine which the Crown Court (and High Court of Justiciary in Scotland) may impose on indictment. The maximum fine that can be imposed by a magistrates' court in England and Wales is £5,000, although many summary offences carry lower maxima. When fixing the amount of a fine, courts are required to reflect the seriousness of the offence and to take into account the financial circumstances of the offender.

Probation

The locally organised probation service in England and Wales supervises offenders in the community under direct court orders and after release from custody. It also provides offenders in custody with help and advice.

A court probation order can last between six months and three years; if the offender fails to comply with the order or commits another offence while on probation, he or she can be brought before the court again. A probation order can be combined with a community service order or a fine.

A probation order requires the offender to maintain regular contact with the probation officer. Special conditions attached to the order may require the offender to attend a day centre for up to 60 days. Probation is intended as a punishment, although the time spent by offenders under supervision in the community offers an opportunity for constructive work to reduce the likelihood of reoffending.

In England and Wales the probation service also administers supervision orders, the community service scheme and supervises those released from prison on parole.

The statutory Probation Inspectorate monitors the work of the voluntary and private sectors with the probation service in addition to its inspection and advisory duties.

In Scotland local authority social work departments supervise offenders on probation and supervision orders or on parole.

In Northern Ireland the service is administered by the government-funded Probation Board, whose membership is representative of the community.

Community Service

Offenders aged 16 or over convicted of imprisonable offences may, with their consent, be given community service orders. The court may order between 40 and 240 hours' unpaid service to be completed within 12 months. Examples of work done include decorating the houses of elderly or disabled people and building adventure playgrounds.

National standards for community service

orders ensure that all orders meet a common set of minimum requirements.

In England and Wales the court may make an order combining community service and probation. The maximum term for the probation element is the same as a probation order and the maximum period of community service is 100 hours.

Curfew Order

Legislation before Parliament would allow for the use of curfew orders with electronic monitoring in trial areas. Courts in the trial areas would be able to require offenders to remain at home for periods of between two and 12 hours a day. The order could be combined with probation or community service. A decision on whether to extend the order to courts throughout England and Wales would be taken in the light of the trials.

Compensation

The courts may order an offender to pay compensation for personal injury, loss or damage resulting from an offence. In England and Wales courts are required to give reasons for not awarding compensation to a victim. Compensation takes precedence over fines.

Other Measures

A court in England and Wales may discharge a person either absolutely or conditionally if it believes that it is not necessary to inflict punishment. If he or she is conditionally discharged, the offender remains liable to punishment for the offence if convicted of another offence within a period specified by the court (not more than three years).

Courts may also require an offender to keep the peace and/or be of good behaviour. If this requirement is not complied with, the offender is liable to forfeit a sum of money. Similar powers are available to courts in Northern Ireland.

Courts have the power to defer sentence, during which period the accused is required to be of good behaviour and to meet any other conditions stipulated by the court. The court may also warn the offender or grant an absolute discharge.

Police cautions are used particularly for young offenders; the caution is a form of warning and no court action is taken. New guidelines designed to stop the use of cautions for serious offences and to cut the number of repeated cautions were published by the Government in March 1994.

Prisons

The Prison Service in England and Wales and the Scottish Prison Service became executive agencies in April 1993. Government ministers remain accountable for policy but the Chief Executives are responsible for the delivery of services.

Prisoners are housed in accommodation ranging from open prisons to high security establishments. In England, Scotland and Wales sentenced prisoners are classified into groups for security purposes. There are separate prisons for women. There are no open prisons in Northern Ireland, where the majority of offenders are serving sentences for terrorist offences. People awaiting trial in custody are entitled to privileges not granted to convicted prisoners. Those under 21 are, where possible, separated from convicted prisoners.

There are about 130 prison establishments in England and Wales and some 20 in Scotland, many of which were built in the 19th century. Improvements are in progress to eliminate cells without access to integral sanitation, and a prison building programme is helping to alleviate overcrowding.

In Northern Ireland there are four prisons and a young offenders' centre. Four of these establishments have been built since 1972.

> The average prison population in 1993 was 44,566 in England and Wales, 1,933 in Northern Ireland, and 5,637 in Scotland.

A White Paper published in 1991 set out a programme of reforms for the prison service in England and Wales. The aim is to provide a better prison system, with more effective measures for security and control, more constructive relationships between prisoners and staff, and more stimulating and useful programmes for prisoners.

Private Sector Involvement

The Home Secretary is empowered to contract out the management of prisons in England and Wales to the private sector, as well as escort and guarding functions. A new privately-run remand centre—the Wolds in Humberside—came into use in April 1992. Blakenhurst local prison in Worcestershire, also under private management, opened in May 1993. Doncaster prison opened in June 1994.

In September 1993 the Government announced an increased role for the private sector in prison management. The intention is that about 10 per cent (12 prisons) should be managed by the private sector. The six new prisons that are planned will be designed, built, managed and financed by the private sector.

The court escort and custody services in the East Midlands and Humberside are run by a private security company and court work in London has begun to be contracted out. It is being phased in over 12 months. Education, health care and catering, and some other service functions are also being subjected to competitive processes.

Provision for the further contracting out of prisons and prisoner escort services in England and Wales—and, for the first time, in Scotland—is included in new legislation before Parliament. The legislation would also enable the prisoner escort service in Northern Ireland to be contracted out.

Early Release of Prisoners

The Criminal Justice Act 1991 has reformed the remission and parole systems in England and Wales, with new arrangements for the early release of prisoners and for their supervision and liabilities after release. The Parole Board continues to advise the Home Secretary on the early release or recall of long-term prisoners.

Prisoners serving terms of less than four years may be released once they have served half of their sentences in custody. Long-term prisoners (those serving more than four years) may be released once they have served two-thirds of their sentence; the Parole Board may release them on licence half-way through their sentence if they are serving between four and seven years. The Home Secretary has to give final consent to such parole if the prisoner is serving more than seven years. All prisoners sentenced to a year or more may be supervised on release until three-quarters of their sentence has passed. Certain sex offenders may be supervised to the end of their sentence.

If convicted of another offence punishable with imprisonment and committed before the end of the original sentence, a released prisoner may be liable to serve all or part of the original sentence outstanding at the time the fresh offence was committed. Similar changes have been adopted in Scotland.

Northern Ireland

In Northern Ireland prisoners serving a sentence of more than five days are eligible for remission of half their sentence. A prisoner serving a sentence of more than 12 months who is given remission is liable to be ordered to serve the remainder of this sentence if convicted of fresh imprisonable offences during this period.

Remission for those convicted of terrorist offences and serving sentences of five years or more is one-third. Any released prisoners convicted of another terrorist offence before the expiry of the original sentence must complete that sentence before serving any term for the second offence.

Life Sentence Prisoners

Arrangements for the early release of prisoners serving life sentences for offences other than murder are set out in the Criminal Justice Act 1991. The Home Secretary is required to release such prisoners after an initial period set by the trial judge if so directed by the Parole Board, which has to be satisfied that the protection of the public does not require

their further confinement. These
provisions conform with the requirements
of the European Convention on Human
Rights. Similar procedures have been
adopted in Scotland.

The release on licence of prisoners serving
mandatory life sentences for murder may
only be authorised by the Home Secretary on
the recommendation of the Parole Board. A
similar policy applies in Scotland.

On release, life sentence prisoners
remain on licence for the rest of their lives
and are subject to recall if their behaviour
suggests that they might again be a danger to
the public.

People serving life sentences for the
murder of police or prison officers, terrorist
murders, murder by firearms in the course
of robbery and the sexual or sadistic murder
of children are normally detained for at least
20 years.

In Northern Ireland the Secretary of
State reviews life sentence cases on the
recommendation of an internal review body.

At the end of 1993 there were about 3,150
prisoners serving life sentences in Prison
Service establishments in England and Wales,
of whom about 350 had been detained for
over 15 years.

Repatriation

Sentenced prisoners who are nationals of
countries which have ratified the Council of
Europe Convention on the Transfer of
Sentenced Persons or similar international
arrangements may apply to be returned to
their own country to serve the rest of their
sentence there.

Independent Oversight of the Prison System

Every prison establishment has a Board of
Visitors—a Visiting Committee in Scotland
—drawn from the local community. In order
to see that prisoners are being treated fairly,
members may go to any part of the prison
and interview any inmate at any time.

The independent Prisons Inspectorates
report on the treatment of prisoners and
prison conditions. Each establishment is
visited about every two years.

Prison Industries

Prison industries aim to give inmates work
experience which will assist them when
released and to secure a return which will
reduce the cost of the prison system. The
main industries are clothing and textile
manufacture, engineering, woodwork,
laundering, farming and horticulture. In
England and Wales most production caters
for internal needs and for other public
services, whereas in Scotland a greater
proportion is sold to the private sector. A few
prisoners are employed outside prison, some
in community service projects.

Prison Education

Full-time education of 15 hours a week is
compulsory for young offenders below school
leaving age. For older offenders it is
voluntary. Some prisoners study for public
examinations, including those of the Open
University. Competitive tendering for the
provision of education services in prisons in
England and Wales has taken place and
contracts have been awarded, many to further
and higher education establishments. In
England, Wales and Scotland, increased
emphasis is being placed on the development
and implementation of National Vocational
Qualifications (see p. 425) for inmates.

All new prisons have purpose-built
education units, and schemes to build new
education accommodation or enhance existing
facilities are also under way or planned at
many other establishments.

Physical education is voluntary for adult
offenders but compulsory for young
offenders. Practically all prisons have physical
education facilities, some of which are
purpose-built. Opportunities are given for
inmates to obtain sporting proficiency awards.
Inmates also compete against teams in the
local community.

Health Care

The Health Care Service for Prisoners in
England and Wales is responsible for the
physical and mental health of all those in
custody. A Health Advisory Committee

provides independent medical advice to government ministers, the Prison Service Chief Executive and the Director of Health Care.

A greater emphasis is being placed on 'buying in' health care services either from the National Health Service (NHS—see p. 369) or the private sector. The Prison Service is also committed to transferring mentally disordered offenders to the care and treatment of the NHS and social services where possible.

In Scotland psychiatric and psychological services are bought in from local Health Boards responsible for the National Health Service.

Privileges and Discipline

Prisoners may write and receive letters and be visited by relatives and friends, and those in all establishments in England and Wales may make telephone calls. Privileges include a personal radio; books, periodicals and newspapers; watching television; and the opportunity to make purchases from the prison shop with money earned in prison. Depending on facilities available, prisoners may be granted the further privileges of dining and recreation in association.

Breaches of discipline are dealt with by the prison governor. A Prisons Ombudsman for England and Wales has been appointed as a final appeal stage for prisoners' grievances.

The appointment of a Prisons' Complaints Adjudicator for Scotland is in hand and revised internal grievance procedures were implemented in February 1994.

Religion

Anglican, Church of Scotland, Roman Catholic and Methodist chaplains provide opportunities for worship and spiritual counselling, supported by visiting ministers of other denominations and faiths as required.

Preparation for Release

The Prison Service has a duty to prepare prisoners for release. Planning for safe release starts at the beginning of an offender's sentence and ties in with all the training, education and work experience provided. It is directed at equipping prisoners to fit back into society and to cope with life without reoffending. Risk assessment and confronting offending behaviour are essential elements of this process. Sentence planning is being extended progressively to all prisoners serving substantial sentences, in conjunction with extended arrangements for aftercare. Many medium- and long-term prisoners in the later parts of their sentences may be granted home leave for short periods.

The Pre-Release Employment Scheme in England and Wales and the Training for Freedom Scheme in Scotland enable selected long-term prisoners to spend their last six months before release in certain hostels attached to prisons in order to help them readapt to society. Hostellers work in the outside community and return to the hostel each evening. Frequent weekend leave allows hostellers to renew ties with their families.

In Northern Ireland prisoners serving fixed sentences may have short periods of leave near the end of their sentences and at Christmas. Life-sentence prisoners are given a nine-month pre-release programme which includes employment outside the prison.

Aftercare

Professional support is given to offenders following their release. All young offenders and all adult offenders in England and Wales sentenced to 12 months' imprisonment and over are supervised on release by the probation service—or, in the case of certain young offenders, by local authority social services departments. In Scotland, this support is provided by local authority social work services.

Young Offenders

England and Wales

Criminal proceedings cannot be brought against children below the age of 10 years.

Offenders between the ages of 10 and 18 fall within the jurisdiction of youth courts. Sixteen- and 17-year-olds may be given the same probation, curfew and community service orders as older offenders; also available to the court are the same supervision orders or attendance centre orders as are given to younger offenders.

Under a supervision order—which may remain in force for not more than three years—a child (10–13 years old) or young person (14–17 years old) normally lives at home under the supervision of a social worker or a probation officer. The order can be used to provide for remedial activities through a short residential course or, more usually, attendance at a day or evening centre.

Anyone under 21 years of age found guilty of an offence for which an adult may be imprisoned can be ordered to go to an attendance centre, as can an offender who refuses to comply with another order (for example, default in paying a fine or breach of a probation order). The maximum number of hours of attendance is 36 (or 24 if the offender is aged under 16) spread over a period; the minimum is 12 hours. The order aims to encourage offenders to make more constructive use of their leisure time.

Custodial sentences are available for juveniles from the age of 10 for murder or manslaughter, from the age of 14 for grave crimes and from the age of 15 for other imprisonable offences. Such a sentence can be given only if it can be justified by the seriousness of the offence or, in the case of violent or sexual offences, if it is necessary to protect the public.

In the case of a very serious crime committed by a young person aged 18 or under, detention in a place approved by the Home Secretary may be ordered, and must be ordered in the case of murder. Detention may be in a secure local authority residential unit, a centre managed by the Youth Treatment Service or a young offender institution.

The custodial sentence for those aged 18–20 is detention in a young offender institution. Alternatives include fines and compensation, attendance centre orders (for up to 36 hours) and community service orders (for between 40 and 240 hours).

In the area of parental responsibility, new legislation before Parliament would extend the powers given to the courts by the Criminal Justice Act 1991. The 1991 Act:

- strengthened courts' powers to make parents attend hearings in cases involving offenders up to the age of 18;

- strengthened the liability on parents to pay fines and compensation arising from the crimes committed by their children;

- contained greater power for courts to order parents to take proper care and control of their children if necessary to prevent further offences; and

- allowed such orders to be imposed for up to three years, or the offender's 18th birthday.

Where local authorities have assumed parental responsibility, the duty to attend court and pay any fines also applies.

Under the new legislation, courts would be able to order parents to ensure their children comply with community sentences. In every case when an offender aged between 10 and 15 years receives a community sentence, the court would be under a duty to consider such an order. Courts would have a power, as opposed to a duty, in the case of 16- and 17-year-olds. Courts would also be empowered to impose a secure training order on persistent offenders aged between 12 and 14. The order would mean a period of detention in a secure training centre followed by a period of supervision; it would be available for young offenders who have committed three or more imprisonable offences and who have failed to respond to punishment in the community. A further provision would double the maximum sentence for 15–17 year-olds in a young offender institution from one to two years. In addition, court powers to order long terms of detention for young offenders who commit serious crimes would be extended to include 10–13 year-olds.

Scotland

Criminal proceedings may be brought against any child aged 8 years or over, but the instructions of the Lord Advocate are necessary before anyone under 16 years of age is prosecuted.

Children under 16 who have committed an offence or are considered to be in need of care and protection may be brought before a children's panel. The panel, consisting of three lay people, determines in an informal setting whether compulsory measures of care are required and, if so, the form they should take. An official known as the reporter decides whether a child should come before a hearing. If the grounds for referral are not accepted by the child or parent, the case goes to the sheriff for proof. If he finds the grounds established, the sheriff remits the case to the reporter to arrange a hearing. The sheriff also decides appeals against a hearing's decision.

Young people aged between 16 and 21 serve custodial sentences in a young offender institution. Remission of part of the sentence for good behaviour, release on parole and supervision on release are available.

Northern Ireland

Those aged between 10 and 16 who are charged with a criminal offence are normally brought before a juvenile court. If found guilty of an offence punishable in the case of an adult by imprisonment, the court may order the offender to be placed in care, under supervision or on probation. The offender may also be required to attend a day attendance centre, be sent to a training school or committed to residence in a remand home. Non-custodial options are the same as in England and Wales.

Offenders aged between 16 and 24 who receive custodial sentences of less than three years serve them in a young offenders' centre.

Civil Justice

The Civil Law

The civil law of England, Wales and Northern Ireland covers business related to the family, property, contracts and torts (non-contractual wrongful acts suffered by one person at the hands of another). It also includes constitutional, administrative, industrial, maritime and ecclesiastical law. Scottish civil law has its own, broadly similar, branches.

CIVIL COURTS

England and Wales

Magistrates' courts have a concurrent jurisdiction with the county courts and the High Court in cases relating to children. The courts also have jurisdiction regarding, for example, appeals against local authority decisions and the recovery of unpaid local and central taxes.

The jurisdiction of the 270 county courts covers:

- actions founded upon contract and tort;
- trust and mortgage cases;
- actions for the recovery of land;
- cases involving disputes between landlords and tenants;
- complaints about race and sex discrimination;
- admiralty cases (maritime questions and offences) and patent cases; and
- divorce cases and other family matters.

Specialised work is concentrated in certain designated courts. In some types of cases, for example, admiralty cases, a county court is restricted to an upper financial limit. For small claims not exceeding £1,000, there are special arbitration facilities and simplified procedures. There are also special care centres and family hearing centres which deal with contested family matters involving children.

The High Court, which is divided into three, deals with the more complicated civil cases. Its jurisdiction covers mainly civil and some criminal cases; it also deals with appeals from tribunals and from magistrates' courts in both civil and criminal matters. The three divisions are:

- the Family Division, which is concerned with family law, including adoption and wills;

- the Chancery Division, which deals with corporate and personal insolvency; disputes in the running of companies, between landlords and tenants and in intellectual property matters; and the interpretation of trusts and contested wills; and

- the Queen's Bench Division, which is concerned with contract and tort cases, and deals with applications for judicial review. Maritime law and commercial law are the responsibility of the Division's admiralty and commercial courts.

In the event of overlapping jurisdiction between the High Court and the county courts, cases of exceptional importance, complexity or financial substance are reserved or transferred for trial in the High Court.

Appeals

Appeals in matrimonial, adoption, guardianship and child care proceedings heard by magistrates' courts go to the Family Division of the High Court. Appeals from the High Court and county courts are heard in the Court of Appeal (Civil Division), and may go on to the House of Lords.

The Law Lords deal with cases submitted to the House of Lords. They are professional judges who have been given life peerages. In addition, peers who have held high judicial office are qualified to sit as Lords appeal judges. A group of five judges usually deals with cases. The Lord Chancellor is president of the House in its judicial capacity.

Scotland

The civil courts are the Court of Session and the sheriff court, which have the same jurisdiction over most civil litigation, although cases with a value of less than £1,500 are dealt with only by the sheriff court. Appeals from the sheriff court may be made to the sheriff principal or directly to the Court of Session in ordinary actions.

In cases where the value of the claim is between £750 and £1,500, the case may be appealed to the sheriff principal on a point of law and to the Court of Session thereafter only if the sheriff principal certifies the case as suitable. In small claims cases where the value of the claim does not exceed £750 there may be an appeal to the sheriff principal on a point of law.

The Court of Session sits in Edinburgh, and in general has jurisdiction to deal with all kinds of action. It is divided into the Outer House (a court of first instance) and the Inner House (mainly an appeal court). Appeals to the Inner House may be made from the Outer House and from the sheriff court. From the Inner House an appeal may go to the House of Lords.

The Scottish Land Court deals exclusively with matters concerning agriculture. Its chairman has the status and tenure of a judge of the Court of Session and its other members are lay specialists.

Northern Ireland

Civil cases up to the value of £15,000 are dealt with in county courts. The magistrates' court in Northern Ireland also deals with certain limited classes of civil case. The superior civil law court is the High Court of Justice, from which an appeal may be made to the Court of Appeal. The House of Lords is the final civil appeal court. Appeals from county courts are dealt with by the High Court or the Court of Appeal.

Civil Proceedings

England and Wales

Civil proceedings are started by the aggrieved person. Actions in the High Court are usually begun by a writ served on the defendant by the plaintiff, stating the nature of the claim. Before the case is tried, documents (pleadings) setting out the scope of the dispute are filed with the court; the pleadings are also served on the parties. County court proceedings are initiated by a summons, usually served on the defendant by the court. Child care cases are initiated by an application in the magistrates' courts.

In order to encourage parties to confine the issues in dispute, the High Court and the county courts have power to order pre-trial exchange of witness statements. Courts may impose penalties in costs on parties who unreasonably refuse to admit facts or to disclose documents before trial.

Civil proceedings, as a private matter, can usually be abandoned or ended by settlement between the parties at any time. Actions brought to court are usually tried without a jury, except in defamation, false imprisonment or malicious prosecution cases or where fraud is alleged, when either party may apply for trial by jury. The jury decides questions of fact and determines the damages to be paid to the injured party; majority verdicts may be accepted. The Court of Appeal is able to increase or reduce damages awarded by a jury if it considers them inadequate or excessive.

A decree of divorce must be pronounced in open court, but a procedure for most undefended cases dispenses with the need to give evidence in court and permits written evidence to be considered by the county court district judge.

In civil cases heard by a magistrates' court, the court issues a summons to the defendant setting out details of the complaint and the date on which it will be heard. Parties and witnesses give their evidence at the court hearing. Family proceedings are normally heard by not more than three lay justices, including both men and women. Members of the public are not allowed to be present. The court may make orders concerning residence, contact and supervision of children, and in some cases maintenance payments for spouses and children.

Most judgments are for sums of money and may be enforced, in cases of non-payment, by seizure of the debtor's goods or by a court order requiring an employer to make periodic payments to the court by deduction from the debtor's earnings. Other court remedies may include an injunction restraining someone from performing an unlawful act. Refusal to obey a court order may result in imprisonment for contempt.

Normally the court orders the costs of an action to be paid by the party losing it, but, in the case of family law maintenance proceedings, a magistrates' court can order either party to pay the whole or part of the other's costs.

Scotland

Proceedings in the Court of Session or ordinary actions in the sheriff court are initiated by serving the defender with a summons—or, in sheriff court cases, an initial writ. A defender who intends to contest the action must inform the court; if he or she fails to do so, the court normally grants a decree in absence in favour of the pursuer. Where a case is contested, both parties must prepare written pleadings. Time is allowed for either party to adjust their pleadings in the light of what the other has said. At the end of this period a hearing will normally be arranged.

In cases involving sums between £750 and £1,500 in the sheriff court, a statement of claim is incorporated in the initial writ. The procedure is designed to enable most actions to be settled without the parties having to appear in court. Normally they, or their representatives, need appear only when an action is defended.

Northern Ireland

There are differences between proceedings in Northern Ireland and in England and Wales —for example, procedures in the county court start with the issue of a civil bill, which is served by the plaintiff on the defendant.

Tribunals

Tribunals exercise separate judicial functions. They are intended to be more accessible, less formal and less expensive than courts. They are normally set up under statutory powers, which also govern their constitution, functions and procedure. Tribunals often consist of lay people, but they are generally chaired by a legally qualified person.

Some tribunals settle disputes between private citizens. Industrial tribunals, for example, have a major role in employment disputes. Others, such as those concerned with social security, resolve claims by private citizens against public authorities. A further group, including tax tribunals, decide disputed claims by public authorities against private citizens. Tribunals usually consist of an uneven number of people so that a majority decision can be reached.

In the case of some tribunals a two-tier system operates, with an initial right of appeal to a lower tribunal and a further right of appeal, usually on a point of law, to a higher one, and in some cases to the Court of Appeal. Appeals from single tier tribunals can be made on a point of law only to the High Court in England and Wales, to the Court of Session in Scotland, and generally to the Court of Appeal in Northern Ireland.

The independent Council on Tribunals exercises general supervision over many tribunals. A Scottish Committee of the Council exercises the same function in Scotland.

Administration of the Law

GOVERNMENT RESPONSIBILITIES

England and Wales

The Lord Chancellor is the head of the judiciary and is responsible for the administration of all courts other than coroners' courts, and for a number of administrative tribunals. The highest judicial appointments are made by the Queen on the advice of the Prime Minister. The Lord Chancellor recommends all other judicial appointments to the Crown and appoints magistrates. He has general responsibility for the legal aid and advice schemes and for the administration of civil law reform.

The Home Secretary has overall responsibility for:

- criminal law;
- the police service;
- the prison system;
- the probation and after-care service; and

- advising the Queen on the exercise of the royal prerogative of mercy to pardon a person convicted of a crime or to remit all or part of a penalty imposed by a court.

The Attorney General and the Solicitor General are the Government's principal legal advisers and represent the Crown in appropriate domestic and international cases. They are senior barristers, elected members of the House of Commons and hold ministerial posts. The Attorney General is also Attorney General for Northern Ireland. As well as exercising various civil law functions, the Attorney General has final responsibility for enforcing the criminal law. The Solicitor General is the Attorney's deputy. As head of the Crown Prosecution Service, the Director of Public Prosecutions is subject to superintendence by the Attorney General, as are the Director of the Serious Fraud Office and the Director of Public Prosecutions for Northern Ireland.

Scotland

The Secretary of State recommends the appointment of all judges other than the most senior ones, appoints the staff of the High Court of Justiciary and the Court of Session, and is responsible for the administration and staffing of the sheriff courts. (The district and islands local authorities are responsible for the district courts.)

The Secretary of State is also responsible for Scottish criminal law, crime prevention, the police, the penal system and legal aid; he or she is advised on parole matters by the Parole Board for Scotland.

The Lord Advocate and the Solicitor General for Scotland are the chief legal advisers to the Government on Scottish questions and the principal representatives of the Crown for the purposes of Scottish litigation. Both are government ministers.

Northern Ireland

Court administration is the responsibility of the Lord Chancellor, while the Northern Ireland Office, under the Secretary of State, deals with policy and legislation concerning criminal law, the police and the penal system. The Lord Chancellor has general responsibility for legal aid, advice and assistance.

JUDGES AND LAWYERS

Judges are not subject to ministerial direction or control. They are normally appointed from practising barristers, advocates (in Scotland), or solicitors (see below). Lay magistrates in England and Wales and Scottish district court justices are trained to give them sufficient knowledge of the law, including the rules of evidence, and of the nature and purpose of sentencing.

In Northern Ireland members of a lay panel who serve in juvenile courts undertake training courses; resident magistrates are drawn from practising solicitors or barristers.

The Legal Profession

The legal profession has two branches: barristers (advocates in Scotland) and solicitors. Barristers and advocates advise on legal problems submitted through solicitors and present cases in all courts. Solicitors undertake legal business for individual and corporate clients; they can also, after appropriate training, present cases in all courts. Although people are free to conduct their own cases, most people prefer to be legally represented, especially in more serious cases.

Legislation in 1990 was designed to stimulate the development of good quality legal services for clients in Great Britain by lifting restrictions on who can provide these services, and by extending solicitors' rights of audience to the higher courts. In Scotland, solicitor-advocates were introduced to the higher courts in 1993. The first English solicitor-advocates appeared in the higher courts in February 1994.

The 1990 legislation also contains provisions which allow building societies, banks and other financial organisations to offer conveyancing and probate services under a scheme providing new safeguards to clients. People will also be able to negotiate a form of 'no win, no fee'

agreement with their legal advisers in certain types of case in due course. The implementation of these provisions is subject to parliamentary approval.

Similar proposals regarding the legal profession and legal services in Northern Ireland are being considered.

Complaints systems against solicitors, barristers and licensed conveyancers are backed up by the Legal Services Ombudsman for England and Wales, who conducts investigations into the way the professional bodies handle these complaints. There is a separate Ombudsman for Scotland.

LEGAL AID

A person needing legal advice or legal representation in court may qualify for help with the costs out of public funds, either free or with a contribution according to means.

Green Form Scheme

People whose income and capital are within certain limits are entitled to free advice from a solicitor on certain legal matters. In England and Wales the scheme provides for up to three hours' work for matrimonial cases where a petition is drafted and two hours' for other work. A similar scheme operates in Northern Ireland.

Legal Aid in Civil Proceedings

Civil legal aid, which covers representation before the court, may be available for most civil proceedings to those who satisfy the financial eligibility conditions. An applicant for legal aid must also show that he or she has reasonable grounds for taking, defending or being a party to proceedings. In England and Wales payments to lawyers are made through the Legal Aid Fund, administered by the Legal Aid Board. Scotland has a separate Legal Aid Fund, administered by the Scottish Legal Aid Board. Legal aid in Northern Ireland is administered by the Law Society for Northern Ireland.

In certain limited circumstances the successful unassisted opponent of a legally aided party may recover his or her costs in the case from the Legal Aid Board. Where the assisted person recovers or preserves money or property in the proceedings, the Legal Aid Fund will usually have a first charge on that money or property to recover money spent on the assisted person's behalf.

Legal Aid in Criminal Proceedings

In criminal proceedings in England, Wales and Northern Ireland legal aid may be granted by the court if it appears to be in the interests of justice and if a defendant is considered to require financial assistance. A legal aid certificate must be granted (subject to means) when a person is committed for trial on a murder charge or where the prosecutor appeals or applies for leave to appeal from the Court of Appeal to the House of Lords. In England and Wales a financial contribution may be payable. Where legal aid is granted for criminal cases in Northern Ireland it is free.

The Legal Aid Board in England and Wales makes arrangements for duty solicitors to assist unrepresented defendants in the magistrates' courts. Solicitors are available, on a 24-hour basis, to give advice and assistance to those being questioned by the police. The services of a solicitor at a police station and of the duty solicitor at court are free.

In Northern Ireland a voluntary duty solicitor scheme has been introduced at the main magistrates' court in Belfast.

Scotland

A duty solicitor is available to represent people in custody on their first appearance in the sheriff courts and the district courts without enquiry into the person's means. In other cases, a person seeking legal aid in summary criminal proceedings must apply to the Scottish Legal Aid Board, which must be satisfied that the costs of the case cannot be met by the applicant without undue hardship, and that it is in the interests of justice that legal aid is awarded.

In solemn proceedings the court decides on the availability of legal aid and must be satisfied that the accused cannot meet the costs of the defence without undue financial hardship. Where legal aid is granted to the accused in criminal proceedings, he or she is not required to pay any contribution towards expenses.

Free Representation Units

The Bar Council, the barristers' professional body, runs free representation units in England and Wales for clients at a variety of tribunals for which legal aid is not available. Most of the representation in London is carried out by Bar students supported and advised by full-time case workers. Elsewhere the work is carried out by barristers.

Law Centres

In some urban areas law centres provide free legal advice and representation. Financed from various sources, often including local government authorities, they usually employ full-time salaried lawyers and many have community workers. Much of their time is devoted to housing, employment, social security and immigration problems.

Free advice is also available in Citizens Advice Bureaux, consumer and housing advice centres and in specialist advice centres run by voluntary organisations.

Further Reading

Britain's Legal Systems. Aspects of Britain series, HMSO, 1993.
Criminal Justice. Aspects of Britain series, HMSO, forthcoming.
Home Office Annual Report. HMSO, 1994.
Report of the Royal Commission on Criminal Justice. HMSO, 1993.
Royal Commission on Criminal Justice. Interim Government Response. 1994.

External Affairs

9 Overseas Relations

Britain is a member of some 120 international organisations, including the United Nations (UN), North Atlantic Treaty Organisation (NATO) and the European Union (EU). Closer co-operation between member states of the EU is the central aim of the Maastricht Treaty on European Union, which came into effect in November 1993. Britain plays an active part in maintaining international peace and security and has been fully involved, for example, in efforts to bring about peace in former Yugoslavia. Britain also protects the interests of its dependent territories, which include Hong Kong, the Falkland Islands and Gibraltar.

ADMINISTRATION OF FOREIGN POLICY

Foreign & Commonwealth Office

The Foreign & Commonwealth Office (FCO) is in charge of overall foreign policy. The Foreign and Commonwealth Secretary is responsible for the work of the FCO and the Diplomatic Service. He is assisted by five ministers without Cabinet rank, one of whom is the Minister for Overseas Development responsible for the Overseas Development Administration (ODA). The FCO's Permanent Under-Secretary of State is head of the Diplomatic Service and provides advice to the Foreign and Commonwealth Secretary on all aspects of foreign policy.

About 2,500 FCO staff serve overseas, of whom 200 are seconded from other government departments and other public and private organisations. British diplomatic missions also employ about 7,100 locally-engaged staff.

About 26 per cent of frontline diplomatic staff are engaged on political/economic work, 18 per cent on commercial work, 20 per cent on entry clearance to Britain, 8 per cent on consular work, 5 per cent on aid administration, 3 per cent on information and 5 per cent on other activities, such as culture, science and technology. Heads of post account for the remaining 15 per cent, their time being divided between their embassy's various diplomatic tasks.

The FCO administers pre-entry control

overseas for people wishing to enter Britain. The first contact with Britain for many foreign nationals who wish to visit or settle is the visa section or consulate of a British mission, which deals with applications for entry clearance.

Britain remains committed to maintaining a worldwide diplomatic presence. Diplomatic or consular relations are maintained with 183 countries and there are missions at nine international organisations.

The FCO's only executive agency, Wilton Park Conference Centre, contributes to the solution of international problems by organising high-quality conferences in Britain, attracting top politicians, officials, business people, academics and other professionals from all over the world. Its home is the Wilton House Conference Centre in Sussex.

Other Departments

Other government departments, too, are concerned with overseas relations and foreign policy. The Ministry of Defence is responsible for British defence policy and for military liaison with Britain's allies and NATO; it also controls and administers the armed forces (see p. 133). The Department of Trade and Industry (DTI) has an important say on international trade policy and commercial relations with other countries, including EU member states. The FCO and the DTI have a joint export promotion organisation — Overseas Trade Services (see p. 172). The Treasury is involved in British international economic policy and is responsible for Britain's relations with the World Bank and other international financial institutions.

When other departments are involved the FCO decides policy in consultation with them. The department with the main interest usually takes the lead, particularly in EU matters and international economic policy. The FCO co-ordinates British EU policy through the Cabinet Office European Secretariat.

The British Council is responsible for British cultural relations with other countries (see p. 130).

INTERNATIONAL ORGANISATIONS

The United Nations

Britain is a member of the United Nations and one of the five permanent members of the Security Council along with France, the People's Republic of China, Russia and the United States. It is the sixth largest contributor to the UN budget. Britain is fully committed to the principles of the UN Charter and believes that all member states should ensure that the organisation maintains peace, assists developing countries effectively and protects human rights and fundamental freedoms. Under the UN Charter, member states are committed to:

● refrain from the threat or use of force against the territory or political independence of any state; and

● seek solutions to their disputes by peaceful means.

The Charter recognises and permits the right of individual or collective defence against armed attack and the existence of regional arrangements designed to maintain security.

The European Union

Britain is an active and committed member of the European Union (EU), which comprises the European Community (EC) and intergovernmental co-operation on foreign and security policy, and on justice and home affairs.

As one of the larger countries, Britain provides two of the 17 members of the European Commission, which puts forward policy proposals, executes decisions taken by the Council of the European Union and ensures that European Union rules are correctly observed. Britain is represented at each meeting of the Council, which is the main decision-making body. Each Council consists of government ministers from the 12 member states, representing national interests in the subjects under discussion — for example, trade, agriculture or transport. Each member state has a permanent representative at Union headquarters in Brussels.

The European Union

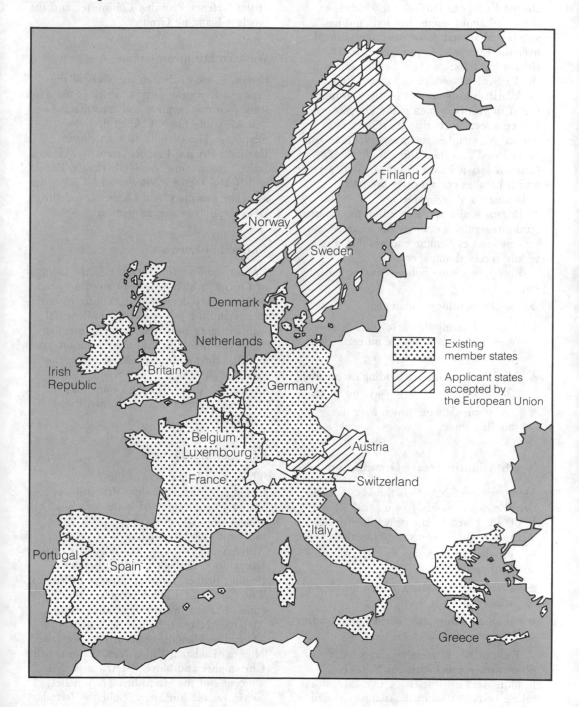

Existing member states

Applicant states accepted by the European Union

There are 567 members of the directly elected European Parliament, which is consulted about major decisions and has substantial shared power with the Council over the European Community budget. Britain has 87 seats. The fourth election to the Parliament took place in June 1994.

A British judge serves on the European Court of Justice, which is the Union's supreme legal authority. Its rulings must be applied by member states and sanctions can be imposed on those failing to do so. The Court is assisted by a Court of First Instance, which handles certain cases brought by individuals and companies.

Britain is also represented on the Court of Auditors, which examines Community revenue and expenditure to see that it is legally received and spent.

European Union policies are implemented by:

- legally binding regulations;
- legally binding directives, which allow member states to decide on methods of implementation;
- decisions, which are binding on member states, firms or individuals; and
- recommendations, which have no binding force.

North Atlantic Treaty Organisation

Membership of NATO is the keystone of British defence policy (see pp. 133–4). NATO is based on the principle of collective security and its core security functions are to:

- provide a foundation for security in Europe;
- deter aggression and defend member states against it; and
- provide a forum for allied transatlantic consultation.

Each of the 16 member states has a permanent representative at NATO headquarters in Brussels. The main decision-taking body is the North Atlantic Council, at which foreign ministers meet at least twice a year. Permanent representatives meet on a weekly basis at the other meetings of the Council. Defence ministers attend meetings of the Defence Planning Committee and the Nuclear Planning Group.

Western European Union

Britain is one of the ten members of the Western European Union, which is the main forum for co-operation and consultation on defence issues for NATO's European members. The current membership is Belgium, Britain, France, Germany, Greece, Italy, Luxembourg, the Netherlands, Portugal and Spain. Iceland, Norway and Turkey are associate members, and Denmark and the Irish Republic observer members.

Council of Europe

Britain is a founding member of the Council of Europe, which is open to any European parliamentary democracy accepting the rule of law and the protection of fundamental human rights and freedoms. The member states co-operate on culture, education, sport, health, crime and drug misuse prevention, youth affairs and the improvement of the environment. In 1950 the Council adopted its European Convention on Human Rights (see p. 125).

The Commonwealth

There are 51 members of the Commonwealth, including Britain. It is a voluntary association of states, nearly all of which were British territories to which independence was granted. The members are Antigua and Barbuda, Australia, Bahamas, Bangladesh, Barbados, Belize, Botswana, Britain, Brunei, Canada, Cyprus, Dominica, The Gambia, Ghana, Grenada, Guyana, India, Jamaica, Kenya, Kiribati, Lesotho, Malawi, Malaysia, Maldives, Malta, Mauritius, Namibia, Nauru, New Zealand, Nigeria, Pakistan, Papua New Guinea, Saint Christopher and Nevis, Saint Lucia, Saint Vincent and the Grenadines, Seychelles, Sierra Leone, Singapore, Solomon Islands, South Africa, Sri Lanka, Swaziland, Tanzania, Tonga, Trinidad and Tobago, Tuvalu, Uganda, Vanuatu, Western Samoa,

The Commonwealth

Zambia and Zimbabwe. Nauru and Tuvalu are special members, entitled to take part in all Commonwealth meetings and activities, with the exception of Commonwealth Heads of Government meetings. South Africa rejoined on 1 June 1994.

Consultation between member states takes place through:

- meetings of heads of government;
- specialised conferences of other ministers and officials;
- diplomatic representatives known as high commissioners; and
- non-governmental organisations.

The Queen is recognised as head of the Commonwealth and is head of state in Britain and 15 other member countries.

The Commonwealth Secretariat promotes consultation, disseminates information, and organises heads of Government meetings, ministerial meetings and other conferences. It administers co-operative programmes agreed at these meetings, including the Commonwealth Fund for Technical Co-operation, which provides expertise to Commonwealth developing countries.

Membership of the Commonwealth enables Britain to play a responsible part alongside other nations in aiding the development and stability of the Third World. Some two-thirds of British aid (see p. 127) goes to Commonwealth countries. The British Government participates fully in all Commonwealth activities and welcomes it as a means of consulting and co-operating with peoples of widely differing cultures.

Other International Bodies

Britain is a member of many other international bodies, including the International Monetary Fund, which regulates the international financial system and provides a source of credit for member countries facing balance-of-payments difficulties.

In addition, Britain, along with 24 other industrialised countries, belongs to the Organisation for Economic Co-operation and Development (OECD), which promotes economic growth, support for less developed countries and worldwide trade expansion.

Other organisations to which Britain belongs or extends support include the regional development banks in Africa, the Caribbean, Latin America and Asia.

BRITAIN'S DEPENDENT TERRITORIES

Britain's dependent territories have a combined population of about 6 million, of whom 5.8 million live in Hong Kong. Most territories have considerable self-government, with their own legislature. With the exception of the British Indian Ocean Territory, governors appointed by the Queen are responsible for external affairs, internal security (including the police) and the public service. Certain responsibilities are delegated to locally elected ministers but the ultimate responsibility for all government affairs rests with the Foreign and Commonwealth Secretary. The British Indian Ocean Territory has a Commissioner, not a Governor; the Commissioner is not responsible for external affairs. Britain seeks to provide the territories with security and political stability, ensure efficient and honest government and help them achieve economic and social development on a par with neighbouring countries.

The territories are:

- Anguilla;
- Bermuda;
- British Antarctic Territory;
- British Indian Ocean Territory;
- British Virgin Islands;
- Cayman Islands;
- Falkland Islands;
- Gibraltar;
- Hong Kong;
- Montserrat;
- Pitcairn, Ducie, Henderson and Oeno;
- St Helena and St Helena Dependencies (Ascension and Tristan da Cunha);
- South Georgia and the South Sandwich Islands; and
- Turks and Caicos Islands.

Few are rich in natural resources, and some are scattered groups of islands. There are no indigenous inhabitants in the British Antarctic Territory, British Indian Ocean Territory or South Georgia and the South Sandwich Islands.

Britain's policy is to help the inhabitants of the dependent territories to take independence if they want it and where it is practicable to do so. The reasonable needs of the dependent territories are a first call on the British aid programme.

Hong Kong

In 1984 Britain and the People's Republic of China signed the Sino-British Joint Declaration on Hong Kong, 92 per cent of which is leased from China until 1997. Under this agreement, Britain is responsible for the administration of Hong Kong until 30 June 1997. Hong Kong will then become a Special Administrative Region (SAR) of China, but its capitalist system and lifestyle will remain unchanged for at least 50 years. With the exception of foreign affairs and defence, the Hong Kong SAR will enjoy a high degree of autonomy and its government and legislature will be composed of Hong Kong people.

In September 1991 direct elections took place for the first time for 18 seats in the Legislative Council. Another 21 of the 60 seats were elected indirectly from functional constituencies. The remaining members are appointed.

The next Legislative Council elections will take place in September 1995. At these elections 20 members will be directly elected, 30 will be indirectly elected and the remaining 10 will be chosen by an election committee. In April 1993 the British and Chinese Governments began talks aimed at reaching agreement on arrangements for these elections and for elections to the municipal councils and district boards. Despite seven months of intensive negotiation, agreement was not reached. In June 1994 the Legislative Council passed the second of two bills covering electoral arrangements based on the Hong Kong Government's package of constitutional proposals announced in October 1992.

Falkland Islands

The Falkland Islands are the subject of a territorial claim by Argentina but the inhabitants wish to remain under British sovereignty. The Government does not accept the Argentine claim to sovereignty and is committed to defend the Islanders' right to live under a government of their own choosing. The Islanders' right of self-determination is set out in the 1985 Falkland Islands Constitution.

In 1982 Argentina invaded and occupied the Islands, but its forces were expelled as a result of British military action following Argentina's failure to abide by United Nations resolutions requesting its forces to withdraw. In recent years Britain and Argentina, while maintaining their respective positions on sovereignty, have restored diplomatic relations and continue to discuss their common interests in the South Atlantic, such as fisheries conservation and exploration for oil.

Gibraltar

Gibraltar is the subject of a territorial claim by Spain. Britain is committed to honouring the wishes of the people of Gibraltar on their future, as set out in the 1969 Gibraltar Constitution. Britain and Spain, while maintaining their respective positions on sovereignty, are pledged to increase practical co-operation between Gibraltar and Spain to the benefit of both peoples.

Caribbean Territories

The Dependent Territories Regional Secretariat in Barbados administers aspects of British Government policy towards the Caribbean territories. Jointly agreed country policy plans for each territory receiving British aid have been introduced.

An FCO minister chairs a ministerial group for the Caribbean territories, drawn from a number of Government departments and agencies, and benefiting from wider expertise than the FCO and ODA alone can offer. It meets two or three times a year.

EUROPEAN UNION POLICY

As a European power, Britain is concerned first of all with the prosperity and security of this area of the world.

The main instrument for achieving European prosperity is the European Union (EU), an association of 12 democratic nations — Belgium, Britain, Denmark, France, Germany, Greece, the Irish Republic, Italy, Luxembourg, the Netherlands, Portugal and Spain. Negotiations on an Accession Treaty for Austria, Finland, Norway and Sweden were completed in April 1994 and they signed the Treaty in June 1994 at the Corfu European Council meeting. Austria held a referendum on 12 June 1994, and voters supported accession. The other three countries will hold referendums in the autumn of 1994. Britain regards the Union as a means of strengthening democracy and reinforcing political stability in Europe, and of increasing the collective strength of member states in international negotiations. The Government wants Britain to be at the heart of a Union in which member states work effectively together by pooling their ideas and resources for shared purposes, provided that such objectives cannot be achieved by member states acting on their own.

The Union had its origins in the post-World War II resolve by Western European nations, particularly France and Germany, not to allow wars to break out again between themselves. The 1957 Rome Treaty, which established the European Community (EC—now part of the European Union), defined its aims as the harmonious development of economic activities, a continuous and balanced economic expansion and an accelerated rise in the standard of living. These objectives were to be achieved by the creation of a common internal market and progressive harmonisation of economic policies, involving:

- the elimination of customs duties between member states;

- free movement of goods, people, services and capital;

- a common commercial policy towards other countries;

- the elimination of distortions in competition within the common market;

- the creation of a Social Fund to improve job opportunities for workers and raise their standard of living;

- the adoption of common agricultural and transport policies; and

- the association of overseas developing countries with the Community in order to increase trade and promote economic and social development.

These objectives were confirmed and augmented by the Single European Act of 1986 and the 1992 Maastricht Treaty on European Union.

Maastricht Treaty

The Maastricht Treaty amends the Rome Treaty and makes other new commitments. It:

- introduces the concept of European Union citizenship as a supplement to national citizenship, provides some measure of institutional reform, and strengthens control of the Community's finances;

- provides on an intergovernmental basis for a common foreign and security policy and for greater co-operation on issues concerned with interior/justice policy;

- clarifies and codifies Union competences in areas such as regional strategy, consumer protection, education and vocational training, the environment and public health;

- provides for moves towards economic and monetary union; and

- embodies the principle of subsidiarity under which action is taken by the European Union only if its objectives cannot be achieved by member states acting alone.

Under an agreement reached in 1992 a subsidiarity test is applied to all European Commission proposals for action.

The Treaty was ratified by Britain and the other member states and came into force in November 1993.

Economic and Monetary Union

During the negotiations on economic and monetary union (EMU), the Government sought to ensure that:

- there would be no commitment by Britain to move to a single monetary policy or single currency;

- monetary matters would remain a national responsibility until the Union moved to a single currency and monetary policy;

- member states would retain primary responsibility for their economic policies; and

- there were clear and quantifiable convergence conditions which member states would have to satisfy before moving to a single currency.

The Maastricht Treaty provides for progress towards EMU in three stages: the first—completion of the single market—ended at the end of 1993. The second stage, which began on 1 January 1994, includes the establishment of a European Monetary Institute with a largely advisory and consultative role. Although the Institute will prepare for stage 3, monetary policy will still be a national responsibility. Member states will co-ordinate economic policies in the context of agreed non-binding policy guidelines. The British Government is participating in Stage 2.

Under the Treaty a single currency is envisaged by 1 January 1999, although member states will have to satisfy certain criteria on inflation rates, government deficit levels, currency fluctuation margins and interest rates. A special protocol recognises that Britain is not obliged or committed to move to this final stage of EMU without a separate decision to do so by the Government and Parliament at the appropriate time.

The Community Budget

The Community's revenue consists of:

- levies on agricultural imports;

- customs duties;

- the proceeds of a notional rate of value added tax of up to 1.4 per cent on a standard 'basket' of goods and services; and

- contributions from member states based on gross national product (GNP).

Overall revenue is limited by a ceiling of 1.2 per cent of Union GNP. Britain has an annual rebate worth some £2,000 million because of the fact that, without it, British net contributions would be far greater than that justified by its share of Union GNP.

An agreement on future finance was reached at the 1992 Edinburgh summit. Under this the revenue ceiling will remain at 1.2 per cent until 1995, when it will rise in steps, reaching 1.27 per cent of Union GNP in 1999. Agricultural spending will be less than half the budget by the end of the century, compared with 80 per cent in 1973 and 60 per cent at present. It was also agreed that more resources would be allocated to the poorer regions of the Union.

Single Market

The single market has been completed in several essential respects. It covers, among other things, the liberalisation of capital movements, the opening up of public procurement markets and the mutual recognition of professional qualifications. It is designed to reduce business costs, stimulate efficiency and encourage the creation of jobs and wealth. The British Government is supporting continuing work on extending the single market to important areas such as telecommunications and energy.

Transport

Britain fully supports the liberalisation of transport in the Union. Considerable progress has been made so far. Permits and quotas for international road haulage have been abolished. EU shipowners are entitled to operate on all international routes within the Union.

A single market has been established in civil aviation. Airlines of member states meeting established criteria, such as safety and financial fitness, are entitled to an operating licence allowing virtually unrestricted access to routes within the Union. They are free to set fares and rates acccording to commercial judgement. In 1993 a regulation came into effect regarding the allocation of take-off and landing slots at airports in order to back up the single market in aviation; it aims to protect the legitimate interests of established carriers while promoting competition by assisting new entrants.

With the opening of the Channel Tunnel in 1994 (see p. 293), there is a permanent rail link between Great Britain and continental Europe, allowing rail services to compete for international freight and passenger services.

Britain supports a number of initiatives designed to improve maritime safety and reduce the threat of pollution by shipping.

European Economic Area

The European Economic Area (EEA) Agreement entered into force on 1 January 1994. It extends most of the single market measures to Austria, Finland, Iceland, Norway and Sweden. It is hoped that Liechtenstein will join the EEA in the near future.

Trade

Britain is the world's fifth largest trading nation. EEA member states comprise the world's largest trading bloc, accounting for about a third of all trade.

The British Government fully supports an open world trading system, on which EU member states depend for future economic growth and jobs.

Under the Rome Treaty, the European Commission speaks on behalf of Britain and the other EU member states in international trade negotiations, such as the recently concluded GATT Uruguay Round. The Commission negotiates on a mandate agreed by the Council.

For further information on trade, see Chapter 12.

The Environment

European Union member states are at the forefront of many international measures on environmental issues, such as car exhaust pollution and the depletion of the ozone layer.

For further information, see p. 129.

Agriculture and Fisheries

The Common Agricultural Policy (CAP) is designed to secure food supplies and to stabilise markets. It has also, however, created overproduction and unwanted food surpluses, placing a burden on the Community's budget.

The Common Fisheries Policy is concerned with the rational conservation and management of fishery resources.

The operation of these policies, and Britain's advocacy of CAP reform, are described in Chapter 17.

Regional and Infrastructure Development

There are a number of Structural Funds designed to:

- promote economic development in poorer regions;
- improve regions seriously affected by industrial decline;
- combat long-term unemployment;
- train young people to find jobs; and
- promote development in rural areas.

Infrastructure projects and productive investments are financed by the European Regional Development Fund. The European Social Fund supports training and employment measures for the long-term unemployed and young people. The Guidance Section of the European Agricultural Guidance and Guarantee Fund supports agricultural restructuring and some rural development measures. A new fund to support restructuring in the fishing industry was created in 1993.

A new cohesion fund has been set up under the Maastricht Treaty to reduce disparities between levels of development in the poorer and richer member states.

Other programmes aim to assist the development of new economic activities in regions affected by the restructuring of traditional industries such as steel, coal and shipbuilding.

The European Investment Bank, a non-profit-making institution, lends at competitive interest rates to public and private capital projects. Lending is directed towards:

- less-favoured regions;

- transport infrastructure;

- protection of the environment;

- improving industrial competitiveness; and

- supporting loans to small and medium-sized enterprises.

The Bank also provides loans in support of the Community's policy of co-operation with the countries of the Mediterranean basin; Central and Eastern Europe; and the African, Caribbean and Pacific (ACP) states (see p. 171).

Employment and Social Affairs

In Britain's view, EC social policy should be primarily concerned with job creation and with maintaining a well-educated and trained workforce to ensure competitiveness in world markets. The Government supports:

- measures to safeguard health and safety at work, freedom of movement for workers, Union-wide recognition of professional and vocational qualifications, equal opportunities at work; and

- practical measures to increase jobs and cut unemployment which do not place more costs on employers.

At Maastricht the Government opposed the extension of Community social policy and qualified majority voting into new areas of social affairs on the grounds that the main responsibility for such policies should remain with individual member states. It negotiated the Social Protocol to the Maastricht Treaty, which allows other member states to agree social legislation in these areas which is not applicable in Britain.

Research and Development

Research collaboration among EU member states is promoted primarily through a series of framework programmes defining priorities and setting out the overall level of funding. The Fourth Framework Programme was adopted in April 1994. The British Government actively encourages British companies and organisations to participate in collaborative research and development (R & D) with European partners.

The Fourth Framework Programme gives priority to information and communications technology, industrial materials and technologies, the environment, biotechnology, agriculture, health and energy. There are also schemes for the exchange of researchers and for scientific collaboration with developing countries and the states of the former Soviet Union.

INTERNATIONAL PEACE AND SECURITY

Britain believes that states should not use, or threaten, force against other sovereign states and that they should resolve their disputes by peaceful means. The United Nations has the authority to seek to resolve disputes which threaten international peace and stability.

Peacekeeping

Britain is playing a full role in the expansion of UN peacekeeping and is one of the largest contributors of troops to UN operations. In addition, it pays its assessed share of nearly 6.4 per cent of the costs of UN peacekeeping.

Britain and France have taken a joint initiative to strengthen the UN's ability to conduct preventive diplomacy as a way of avoiding conflicts breaking out. Both countries have submitted a paper to the UN setting out the type of assistance they are prepared to provide and the range of military units available. Britain also seconds

military officers to the UN's Department for
Peacekeeping Operations. The British
Government has proposed that there should
be a UN general staff for peacekeeping.

> Nearly 4,000 British troops are serving
> on peacekeeping missions in Cyprus,
> Kuwait and former Yugoslavia.
> Their tasks include monitoring
> ceasefires, logistical support, relief
> convoy escort, naval monitoring and
> acting as unarmed military observers.
> In June 1994 Britain was the fourth
> largest contributor of troops to
> UN operations.

Former Yugoslavia

Britain is committed to supporting efforts to
establish a lasting and equitable peace in
former Yugoslavia and is deeply involved in
efforts to relieve suffering caused by the
fighting in Bosnia-Herzegovina and to
prevent it spreading.

Since the outbreak of inter-ethnic
hostilities in mid-1991 the European Union
and the UN have sought to bring peace to
the area. In September 1991 EU member
states established a peace conference to try
and obtain a ceasefire between Serbian and
Croatian forces. In February 1992 the UN
Protection Force (UNPROFOR) was set up
to monitor a ceasefire between Serbia
and Croatia.

Britain and the other EU member states
recognised Slovenia and Croatia in January
1992 and Bosnia-Herzegovina in April
1992. Serbia and Montenegro proclaimed
themselves the Federal Republic of
Yugoslavia, which has not achieved
international recognition. In December 1993
Britain and most of its EU partners decided
to establish diplomatic relations with the
former Yugoslav republic of Macedonia.

In April 1992 the conflict in Bosnia
between Serbs, Croats and Muslims
escalated. The UN imposed sanctions in
May on Serbia and Montenegro because of
their failure to take measures to cease
military intervention in Bosnia. In August
1992 Britain convened the London

Conference, co-chaired by the British Prime
Minister and the UN Secretary General,
which led to the creation of the International
Conference on the Former Yugoslavia
(ICFY). The main parties to the conflict
agreed to documents setting out clear
principles for a negotiated settlement.
Successive efforts by the co-chairmen of
ICFY to resolve the conflict on the basis of
these principles foundered because of the
Bosnian parties' failure to honour them. UN
and EU mediators continued their work to
see if a settlement could be reached. The
United States and Russia, too, sent envoys
to the area.

Following a British initiative, mediation
efforts have been placed in the hands of an
international contact group comprising
Britain, France, Germany, Russia and the
United States. The group has put forward a
plan under which the Muslim-Croat
federation would receive 51 per cent of the
land area of Bosnia-Herzegovina, the
remaining 49 per cent being allocated to the
Bosnian Serbs. The latter, however, rejected
the plan, while the Muslim-Croat federation
accepted it.

Fighting in Bosnia displaced many people
from their homes, and millions became
dependent on humanitarian relief. As at
September 1994 Britain had 3,350 troops in
UNPROFOR in the former Yugoslavia,
protecting aid convoys and supporting the
ceasefires in and around Sarajevo and in
central Bosnia. The British Government has
contributed over £170 million to the aid
effort and has made possible the delivery of
almost 300,000 tonnes of aid.

CENTRAL AND EASTERN EUROPE AND THE FORMER SOVIET UNION

With the disintegration of the Warsaw Pact
and the formation of democratically elected
governments in Eastern and Central Europe
and the former Soviet Union, the European
security situation has been transformed.

In November 1990 NATO Allies and
former Warsaw Pact states signed a joint
declaration in Paris saying that:
- they were no longer adversaries and
  would build new partnerships;

- they would maintain only enough military forces to prevent war and provide for effective defence; and
- they would form the North Atlantic Co-operation Council to foster co-operation and understanding.

In January 1994, a NATO summit meeting invited the non-NATO states in Eastern and Central Europe and the former Soviet Union to join a Partnership for Peace in order to:

- develop a practical working relationship; and

- enlist the Partners' assistance in peacekeeping operations and guide their armed forces towards compatibility with those of NATO countries.

The Partnership will also monitor things like the Partners' respect for international treaties, civilian control of the military and openness in defence budgeting.

Economic Help

Because of the vast economic problems following the fall of Communism, Britain and other Western countries took action to help deal with these and promote the development of market economies. Britain and other OECD countries set up the European Bank for Reconstruction and Development to channel investment to the region. The European Community's PHARE scheme is designed to assist the process of reform and development of infrastructure. Independent states of the former Soviet Union receive help through a separate Community programme (TACIS), which concentrates on financial services, transport, energy (including nuclear safety) and human resource development. Britain contributes about 16 per cent of both budgets.

Know How Fund and Other Schemes

The British Government's Know How Fund is designed to promote the transition to pluralist, democratic and market-based economies in Central Europe and the former Soviet Union. It covers 24 countries and

since 1989 has spent over £160 million on some 2,000 projects. The Know How Fund budget in 1994–5 is about £78 million.

The Fund concentrates its efforts in the former Soviet Union on energy, financial services (with a focus on privatisation and the creation of a strong commercial banking sector), food production and distribution, small business creation, health management and good government. The main emphasis in Central and Eastern Europe is on projects in banking, financial services, management of privatisation, management training and the development of small businesses. There are separate Know How Fund schemes covering environmental projects, voluntary organisations, support for local government and educational links.

Efforts are made to involve the British private sector in order to stimulate inward investment into the region. One scheme is designed to help firms appraise the commercial and financial viability of proposed investment operations, while another has been set up to help key local staff in new enterprises acquire management and business skills. A third scheme enables managers from the region to gain managerial experience during attachments of up to 5 weeks with British companies.

In addition, a scheme financed by the Treasury supports secondments in Britain for young and able financial managers from Russia.

Association Agreements

The European Community has strengthened relations with Bulgaria, the Czech Republic, Hungary, Poland, Romania and Slovakia by concluding Association Agreements with these countries. The agreements envisage European Union membership when these countries are able to assume the obligations of membership. Negotiations for similar agreements with the Baltic States will begin soon and are underway with Slovenia.

In 1992 the EC agreed to negotiate Partnership and Co-operation Agreements with all the states of the former Soviet Union. Agreements have been signed with Russia and Ukraine and concluded with

Kyrgyzstan and Kazakhstan. Negotiations with Belarus and Moldova are continuing.

Trade and Co-operation Agreements have been concluded with Albania and Slovenia and free trade agreements were negotiated with the three Baltic states in 1994.

The purpose of all these agreements is to reduce trade barriers, develop co-operation and increase political dialogue at all levels.

OTHER REGIONS

The Middle East

Middle East Peace Process

Britain warmly welcomed the breakthrough in the Middle East peace process in September 1993, when Israel and the Palestine Liberation Organisation (PLO) agreed to mutual recognition and signed a declaration of principles on interim self-government for the Palestinians in Israeli-held territories occupied in 1967. The first stage of the declaration was implemented in May 1994 when the Palestinians adopted self-government in the Gaza Strip and the Jericho area. Negotiations are continuing on increased transfer of responsibilities. Britain is also encouraging peace negotiations between Israel, Jordan, Syria and Lebanon. An agreement between Israel and Jordan was concluded in Washington in July 1994.

Britain, along with its other European Union partners, is supporting peace moves, politically and economically. Britain plans to spend £70 million on aid to the Palestinians and the peace process over the period from 1994 to 1996 through bilateral and multilateral channels. Many programmes are already under way and are designed to support Palestinian administration, police training, the Palestinian Monetary Authority, legal structures and the judiciary, water management, and health care. Assistance is also being provided for the planned Palestinian elections.

The Gulf Conflict

As a permanent member of the UN Security Council, Britain strongly condemned Iraq's invasion of Kuwait in August 1990 and supported all the Council's resolutions designed to force Iraqi withdrawal and restore international legality. Because of Iraq's failure to withdraw, its forces were expelled in February 1991 by an international coalition led by the United States, Britain, France and Saudi Arabia, acting under a UN mandate.

UN Security Council Resolution 687, adopted in April 1991, formalised the ceasefire in the Gulf War and stipulated conditions for Iraqi acceptance, including measures to prevent the development of weapons of mass destruction, recognition of the border with Kuwait and the payment of compensation to those who suffered as a result of the invasion of Kuwait. The resolution, fully supported by Britain, imposed sanctions on Iraq which remain in force until the Security Council is satisfied that Iraq is fully in compliance with it.

As part of the agreement ending hostilities, the Security Council authorised the creation of a Special Commission (UNSCOM) to supervise the elimination of Iraq's weapons of mass destruction. Britain has provided considerable support to UNSCOM and the International Atomic Energy Authority in the form of personnel, equipment and information since the first inspection in May 1991.

The Security Council approved a separate resolution (688) in response to continued oppression by the Iraqi regime of the civilian population in Northern Iraq and the marshes of Southern Iraq. 'No fly' zones operate over both areas to monitor Iraqi actions and to deter air attacks. Britain takes an active part in both operations.

Sub-Saharan Africa

For many years Britain has been concerned with the affairs of sub-Saharan Africa. Positive developments in the region since 1989 have included:

● a trend towards more accountable government (for example, multi-party elections in Kenya, Malawi and Zambia) and liberal economic policies, with countries committed to a greater degree of democracy; and

- the abolition of apartheid and the establishment of non-racial democracy in South Africa.

British policy towards South Africa has been to:

- encourage multi-party negotiations on the building of a new constitution; and

- help end political violence and intimidation.

The British Government maintains close relations with all the main parties associated with political reform in South Africa and welcomed the country's first non-racial elections in April 1994. Britain spent nearly £4 million on aid for the elections, of which £3 million was used to assist peacekeeping and £520,000 to train election officials and monitor policing of the elections. Observers were also sent as part of UN, European Union and Commonwealth missions.

The British Government is working with President Mandela and his Government of National Unity to prepare black South Africans to play their full part in the government and economy of their country. In addition to a £100 million aid package over the three years 1994–96, Britain is supporting South Africa's development through trade and investment, and with the backing of £1,000 million in official export credit guarantees.

Asia-Pacific Region

The dynamic growth of the East Asian economies has made the Asia-Pacific region more important for world affairs. There is also an encouraging trend towards political liberalisation. Britain has a long association with the region and is giving it an even higher priority in its foreign policy. Close relations are maintained with Japan, China, India and Pakistan, the ASEAN countries (Brunei, Thailand, Malaysia, the Phillipines and Singapore), Australia and New Zealand. Britain has defence links with some countries in the region. It is also contributing to the economic development of Vietnam.

The Indo-British Partnership Initiative, established in 1993, has done much to encourage commercial and investment links between the two countries.

Britain is stepping up political dialogue

with the countries of the region, developing British commercial activity through more trade and investment, and co-operating even more closely on international problem solving. Britain is keen to be associated with Asia-Pacific regional structures both bilaterally and through its membership of the European Union. It is also taking advantage of growing opportunities for English language teaching, co-operation in science and technology, and educational exchanges.

North and South America

Britain has long-established political, trade and cultural links with the United States. In particular, as founding members of NATO, both countries are closely involved in Western defence arrangements (see pp. 136–7) and, as permanent members of the UN Security Council, work together on all major international issues. Strong links are also maintained with Canada, with whom Britain shares membership of the Commonwealth, NATO and other key international organisations. All three countries are members of the Group of Seven who meet each year at the annual Economic Summit.

Important British connections with South America date from the participation of British volunteers in the wars of independence in the early 19th century. Britain has welcomed the fact that democratically elected governments are now the norm in the region; this, together with the trend towards free market economies, presents many opportunities for Britain to strengthen its relations with countries in the region.

There is a British post in every Latin American country and the programme of ministerial visits to the region has increased in recent years; notable examples have been the Prime Minister's visit to Columbia and Brazil in 1992 and the Foreign and Commonwealth Secretary's visits to Argentina and Chile in 1993, and Brazil in 1994.

ARMS CONTROL

Britain and the other members of NATO are pledged to pursue further progress in arms control and confidence-building measures. Under recent agreements nuclear forces in the former Soviet Union have been reduced and Russian forces have been withdrawn from Eastern Europe.

Nuclear Weapons

In July 1991 the United States and the former Soviet Union signed the first Strategic Arms Reduction Treaty (START), under which an equal limit of 6,000 nuclear warheads on both sides was agreed, with an equal sub-limit of 4,900 ballistic missile warheads. The Treaty required the parties to reduce their strategic missiles and warheads by about 35 per cent over 15 years, including a cut of up to 50 per cent in the most destabilising systems.

In January 1993 the United States and Russia signed a new treaty agreeing to reduce their strategic nuclear weapons by two-thirds within ten years. Both countries eliminated their intermediate range nuclear weapons under a separate treaty signed in 1987.

Nuclear Testing

Britain is committed to the successful outcome of the current negotiations on a comprehensive nuclear test ban treaty. It supports a treaty of indefinite duration, with effective verification and the widest possible adherence, in order to prevent the development of a sophisticated nuclear weapon by a would-be proliferator.

Given the possibility of an agreement on a nuclear test ban, British plans are based on the use of simulation and alternative technologies in order to ensure continued warhead safety and reliability in the long term.

Conventional Weapons

The Conventional Armed Forces in Europe (CFE) Treaty, signed in November 1990, commits the NATO allies and members of the former Warsaw Pact to reductions in five major classes of conventional weapons.

The ceilings for both groups of states in the area between the Atlantic and the Ural Mountains are 20,000 tanks, 30,000 armoured combat vehicles, 20,000 artillery pieces, 2,000 attack helicopters and 6,800 combat aircraft. No individual state may hold more than two thirds of the equipment the Treaty allows its group.

Weapons above the agreed ceilings must be destroyed or rendered permanently unfit for further military use. Intrusive arrangements to verify compliance are included in the Treaty.

In July 1992 a fresh agreement, to which Britain is a party, was concluded on permitted strengths of armed forces personnel within Europe.

Chemical Weapons

Britain took a leading part in the lengthy negotiations on a chemical weapons ban, having abandoned its own chemical weapons in the late 1950s. These negotiations were completed in June 1992 and 157 countries, including Britain, have signed a convention which enters into force 6 months after 65 states have ratified (but not before 13 January 1995).

The Chemical Weapons Convention will prohibit the production, stockpiling and use of chemical weapons. There is a system of challenge inspections to verify compliance and provisions for the monitoring of chemicals which can be used to make weapons.

Biological Weapons

The 1972 Biological and Toxin Weapons Convention prohibits the development, production and stockpiling of these weapons but currently lacks methods of verification. A 1991 review conference introduced confidence-building measures providing for exchange of information between the parties to the Convention and set up an expert group to identify and examine potential verification measures. This completed its work and its findings are being considered by a special conference of the parties to the Convention with a view to establishing arrangements for verification.

Non-Proliferation

Britain aims to:

- prevent the proliferation of nuclear weapons;
- ban the manufacture and possession of chemical and biological weapons;
- control the transfer of ballistic missiles and their components and technology; and
- prevent accumulations of conventional armaments which create regional instability.

Britain has signed a number of agreements designed to control the proliferation of weapons of mass destruction. These include the 1968 Non-Proliferation Treaty (NPT) on nuclear weapons, the 1972 Biological and Toxin Weapons Convention and the 1993 Chemical Weapons Convention (see p. 124). A review conference is to be held in 1995 to consider the extension of the NPT Treaty; Britain is seeking its unconditional and indefinite extension.

UN Register of Arms Transfers

Following a British initiative, the UN General Assembly voted to establish a universal and non-discriminatory register of conventional arms transfers. The register, covering seven categories of equipment, is designed to introduce greater openness and make it easier for the international community to monitor an excessive arms build-up in any one country. The register came into effect in January 1992. Britain is represented on a Panel of Government Experts which is considering whether the register's coverage should be expanded.

Confidence-Building Measures

Important confidence-building measures regarding military exercises and other activities in Europe are in force.

The Conference on Security and Co-operation in Europe (CSCE) provides a forum for dialogue on such matters as arms control. Participants include the republics of the former Soviet Union, the other European states and the United States and Canada.

Under the 1992 Vienna Document, CSCE participating states agreed on a number of further confidence-building measures, including:

- annual exchanges of information on military forces, equipment and budgets;
- prior notification of certain military activities; and
- challenge inspections and evaluation visits to military bases.

Open Skies Treaty

Britain played an important role in the negotiations leading to the signing in March 1992 of the Open Skies Treaty, which will allow flights over the entire territories of its participants by aircraft equipped with sensors, cameras and radar with the ability to detect military activity and equipment in all weathers, day and night. The Treaty has been signed by all NATO members, Belarus, Bulgaria, the Czech Republic, Georgia, Hungary, Kyrgyzstan, Poland, Romania, Russia, Slovakia and Ukraine.

The Treaty, which is of unlimited duration, will be phased in over three years; when fully in force, it will play a valuable stabilising role by allowing the major CSCE countries to check on military deployments.

HUMAN RIGHTS

The protection of human rights is an important part of British foreign policy. Universal respect for human rights is an obligation under the UN Charter, reinforced by human rights law in the form of UN and regional human rights treaties. The British Government played a key role at the 1993 Vienna UN World Conference on Human Rights, which reaffirmed that human rights are a legitimate concern of the international community. The expressions of concern about human rights do not, therefore, constitute interference in the internal affairs of another state.

The Universal Declaration of Human Rights was adopted by the UN General Assembly in 1948. Since this is not a legally binding document, the General Assembly adopted two international covenants in 1966, placing legal obligations on those states ratifying or acceding to them. The covenants came into force in 1976, Britain ratifying both in the same year. One covenant deals with economic, social and cultural rights and the other with civil and political rights. States which are parties to the covenants undertake to submit periodic reports detailing compliance with their terms. Each covenant has a UN treaty monitoring committee which examines these reports. Britain recognises the competence of these committees to receive and consider state-to-state complaints.

Other international conventions to which Britain is a party include those on:

- the elimination of racial discrimination;
- the elimination of all forms of discrimination against women;
- the rights of the child;
- torture and other cruel, inhuman or degrading treatment or punishment;
- prevention of genocide;
- the abolition of slavery; and
- the status of refugees.

The Council of Europe

Britain is bound by the Council of Europe's Convention for the Protection of Human Rights and Fundamental Freedoms, which covers:

- the right to life, liberty, security and a fair trial;
- respect for private and family life, home and correspondence;
- freedom of thought, conscience and religion;
- freedom of expression;
- freedom of peaceful assembly and association;
- the right to have a sentence reviewed by a higher tribunal; and
- the prohibition of torture and other inhuman or degrading treatment.

Complaints about violations of the Convention are made to the European Commission of Human Rights in Strasbourg. Although one state may lodge a complaint against another, most complaints are brought against states by individuals or groups. The Commission decides whether cases are admissible and, if so, examines the matter with the parties with a view to achieving a friendly settlement. If this fails, the Commission or the state concerned can refer the case to the European Court of Human Rights, which rules on whether the Convention has been breached. Britain accepts the Court's compulsory jurisdiction and the right of individual petition. Britain has signed, and is in the process of ratifying, the 11th Protocol to the Convention, which will replace the existing Commission and Court with a full-time Court.

Conference on Security and Co-operation in Europe

Britain is a signatory to the 1975 Helsinki Final Act, which established a framework for co-operation between CSCE states on European security, respect for human rights, economics, the environment and humanitarian issues. It was agreed that the Helsinki commitments should be reviewed at regular follow-up conferences. The Helsinki process contributed to the collapse of Communism, the reunification of Germany and the end of the Cold War.

The 1990 Charter of Paris committed CSCE participants to democracy, human rights and market economies. The CSCE has a Secretariat in Vienna, where Britain has a permanent delegation. Day-to-day business is conducted in the Permanent Committee. A Prague office organises the quarterly meetings of senior officials. The CSCE has 53 members, including virtually every country in Europe, the states of the former Soviet Union, and the United States and Canada. Yugoslavia was suspended in July 1992. All states participate on an equal basis, and decisions are taken by consensus.

The main areas of CSCE work are:

- early warning of potential conflict through preventive diplomacy missions and the CSCE High Commissioner on National Minorities;

- providing advice on human rights, democracy and law through the CSCE Office for Democratic Institutions, in Warsaw; and
- promoting security through arms control and military confidence building.

Westminster Foundation for Democracy

The Westminster Foundation for Democracy helps strengthen pluralistic democratic institutions in other countries.

The three main political parties (see p. 53) are represented on the Board of Governors, who are appointed by the Foreign and Commonwealth Secretary. There is also a representative of the smaller political parties, plus non-party figures drawn from business, trade unions, the academic world and other non-governmental organisations. The Foreign & Commonwealth Office has a non-voting advisory member. The Foundation is independent and the British Government cannot veto projects the Board chooses to support.

Advice is given by the Foundation on the development of:

- election systems, administration or monitoring;
- parliaments or other representative institutions;
- political parties;
- free media;
- trade unions; and
- human rights groups.

The Foundation is concentrating its efforts initially on Central and South-Eastern Europe, the former Soviet Union and on anglophone Africa. It does, however, consider sympathetically applications for projects elsewhere in the world.

INTERNATIONAL CRIME

The British Government attaches importance to action against international terrorism and to international co-operation against drug traffickers and organised crime. Britain and the other members of the European Union have agreed not to export arms or other military equipment to countries clearly implicated in supporting terrorist activity, and to take steps to prevent such material being diverted for terrorist purposes.

It is EU policy that:

- no concessions should be made to terrorists or their sponsors; and
- there should be solidarity between member states in the prevention of terrorism.

Britain participates actively in international forums on co-operation against illegal drug trafficking, maintains a substantial programme of overseas assistance in this field and stations drug liaison officers in a number of countries in order to liaise with the host authorities in the fight against drug trafficking. In recent years Britain has contributed over £20 million to the UN Drug Control Programme, which has the leading international role against the illegal drugs trade

In December 1991 EU member states agreed to set up a central European Police Office (EUROPOL) to provide Union-wide intelligence about serious crime. As a first step in this process, a EUROPOL Drugs Unit has been established. EU member states belong to the International Criminal Police Organisation (INTERPOL). British liaison with INTERPOL is provided by the National Criminal Intelligence Service (see p. 84).

Under the Maastricht Treaty, work in these areas is being intensified through increased intergovernmental co-operation.

DEVELOPMENT CO-OPERATION

The aim of Britain's overseas aid effort is to improve the quality of life and reduce poverty, suffering and deprivation in developing countries.

In 1992–93 British aid to developing countries was over £2,245 million. Of this, £1,278 million was allocated bilaterally and £903 million through international organisations such as the European Union (£412 million), the World Bank Group (nearly £250 million), the United Nations agencies (£173 million) and the regional development banks (£38 million). Some

£64 million was spent on aid administration. Assistance to former Communist countries in Europe totalled £146 million; bilateral technical assistance to these countries is given through the Know How Fund (see p. 121).

The British aid programme seeks to:

- promote economic reform;
- enhance productive capacity;
- promote good government;
- help developing countries reduce poverty;
- promote better education and health;
- improve the status of women in developing countries; and
- assist developing countries to tackle their environmental problems.

Economic Reform

Britain provides bilateral technical assistance, including advice on privatisation and the improvement of essential public services.

British multilateral aid supports the financing of reforms through contributions to the World Bank Group and the European Development Fund.

Most bilateral financial British support for reforms consists of technical assistance to eight low-income countries in the Special Programme of Assistance for Africa led by the World Bank.

The Private Sector

Help is given to encourage the private sector. The ODA's Small Enterprise Development Fund investigates and promotes new projects and activities. Private sector activity is supported by help to build up infrastructure.

The Commonwealth Development Corporation provides loans, equity funds and management services for financially viable investments in agriculture, fisheries, minerals, industry, public utilities, transport, communications and housing. By the end of 1993 it had investments and commitments worth £1,600 million in 341 projects.

Good Government

Respect for human rights, popular participation in decision-making and the rule of law are central concerns of the British aid programme because these are vital to successful development. In 1992–93, over £56 million was spent on public sector and civil service reform, strengthening police and judicial systems, improved accounting and audit procedures, and help to meet the cost of elections.

Reducing Poverty

Most direct or bilateral aid goes to the poorest countries. In India, Pakistan and Bangladesh—the major grant recipients in Asia—projects include rural development, urban slum upgrading and the provision of health, population and education services for poor people. Some of these are carried out in conjunction with non-governmental organisations; in 1992, for example, the ODA gave £7.8 million to the Bangladesh Rural Advancement Committee to support a special bank providing cheap credit to landless rural people.

Education

Assistance is given to education projects emphasising literacy and numeracy, and skills which build on these. British aid also helps education ministries to plan and manage their systems more efficiently and equitably.

> One of the most ambitious education projects supported by British aid is the provision of teacher training to 150,000 primary school teachers in 50,000 schools in Andhra Pradesh, India. Another is the provision of books for all primary schools in Zambia.

In 1992–93 some 13,000 training and scholarship awards were granted, most of which were taken up in British universities and further education colleges. Some training is provided in the trainee's own country or in other countries.

Assistance is given for the provision of books and journals. The Education Low-Priced Books Scheme provides textbooks for purchase by students at subsidised prices in about 86 developing countries.

Health

The ODA invests over £100 million a year on health care, water and sanitation, and population projects. The main aim is to help bring affordable health care services to the poorest and most vulnerable sections of the community. Assistance is targeted on a number of countries and special attention is given to:

- strengthening primary health care services, particularly for women and children;
- improving control of communicable diseases;
- helping to establish management systems to ensure the provision of good-quality care at an affordable cost; and
- improving access to reproductive health services.

Britain assists countries to improve the accessibility and quality of family planning services. No support is given for any such programme in which there is an element of coercion.

Over £33 million has been committed to the World Health Organisation's Global Programme on AIDS, which provides technical support and policy guidance to developing countries on national AIDS control programmes. In addition nearly £11 million has been allocated in direct support for 17 national AIDS programmes.

Status of Women

In 1992–93 some 8 per cent of bilateral aid was targeted on improving the status of women. Britain supports the promotion of female literacy and recognises the need to remove barriers to economic participation by women. The ODA funds projects aimed at providing women with additional skills, giving them access to credit and enabling them to develop small-scale business initiatives. Support is also given to training courses to help women overcome the barriers to advancement in public administration.

The Environment

British aid, in partnership with developing countries, promotes sustainable development to safeguard the world environment for current and future generations.

Britain is contributing £130 million to the Global Environment Facility (GEF) to help developing countries play their part in protecting the environment in the areas of climate change, biodiversity, depletion of the ozone layer and the pollution of international waters. It is the fifth largest contributor to the GEF.

Climate Change

Britain signed a convention on climate change at the 1992 Earth Summit and ratified it in December 1993. The aim of the Convention is to stabilise atmospheric concentrations of greenhouse gases at a level which will prevent dangerous climate change. It commits all parties to prepare national programmes identifying sources of such gases and steps to limit emissions. Britain has also financed country studies and the participation of developing countries in the work of the International Panel on Climate Change, which investigates and reports on climate change and on the responses which should be adopted.

Ozone Depletion

Britain is contributing $40 million towards the programme of the Montreal Protocol Multilateral Fund for its first six years of operation. The Protocol is a detailed agreement on restricting chemicals that contribute to ozone depletion. The Fund covers the extra costs faced by developing countries in complying with the Protocol as well as feasibility studies and technical assistance.

Biodiversity

Britain signed the Biodiversity Convention at the 1992 Earth Summit and ratified it on World Environment Day in June 1994. In addition to its contributions to the GEF, Britain is funding about £40 million worth of biodiversity projects through the bilateral aid programme. In Kenya, for example, the ODA is helping the National Museum to conserve the country's native flora; a British botanist is working with museum staff on a system to identify plant species at risk and to conserve them. The ODA also assists conservation of the world's genetic material in gene banks, botanic gardens and zoos.

Forestry

There are about 200 British aid projects under way or in preparation. These are designed to:
- help developing countries use their forests on a sustainable basis;
- limit deforestation by tackling its causes; and
- promote replanting on degraded land.

These programmes are worth some £152 million. In March 1994, £2.9 million was approved for the pilot phase of the Himachel Pradesh Forestry Project in India, which promotes the sustainable management of forest lands while maintaining and improving the livelihoods of local people dependent on the forests.

Urban Aid

Britain is financing a £68 million project to improve the living conditions of people in five Indian cities—Calcutta, Vijayawada, Hyderabad, Indore and Vishakhapatnam. This includes investment in roads and other essential services, health facilities and nursery schools.

Water

In 1992 British aid provided £39.7 million for water-related projects, including £16.8 million devoted to the provision of clean drinking water and/or sanitation in over 30 developing countries.
New projects committed in 1993 included:
- training in water resources management in Bangladesh, China and Chile;
- groundwater assessment studies in China and Mexico; and

- provision of rural drinking water supply and sanitation in Zimbabwe.

Renewable Natural Resources

Britain funds some £34 million of research each year in programmes covering agriculture, fisheries, forestry, livestock, land resources, pest control and post-harvest technology.

The Natural Resources Institute is the ODA's scientific arm and runs programmes focused on environmental concerns. These include:
- environmental monitoring and identification of areas for conservation; and
- improvement of pest control by minimising disturbance of wildlife habitats and relying less heavily on chemical pesticides.

Emergency Relief

The ODA's Disaster Unit co-ordinates the British Government's response to natural and man-made disasters worldwide; it also provides relief to refugees and displaced people.

As part of co-ordinated international responses, the ODA provides funds, supplies and trained personnel to direct the British effort on the ground.

In 1992 a joint British-German proposal led to the establishment of the UN's Department of Humanitarian Affairs, responsible for co-ordinating prompt responses to emergencies.

In 1992-93 British humanitarian assistance amounted to about £290 million. In addition, the British public sends substantial sums for emergency relief overseas through non-governmental organisations.

CULTURAL RELATIONS

British cultural relations are promoted by the British Council, which works in 228 towns and cities in 108 countries. The Council:
- helps people to study, train or make professional contacts in Britain;

ENVIRONMENTAL DESIGN

Woodley Primary School in Bordon,
Hampshire, which won the BBC Design
Award 1994. The architects, Nev Churcher
and Sally Daniels, aimed to integrate the
school into its woodland setting and to
provide an environment for the children
which was both practical and beautiful.

A demonstrator vehicle at
Ricardo Consulting Engineers,
winner of a Queen's Award for
Environmental Achievement for
its work in developing more
energy-efficient engines.

RURAL DEVELOPMENT

A dry stone waller at work in a village near the Mourne Mountains area of Northern Ireland. The local community had the idea of converting derelict cottages into self-catering tourist accommodation. They produced a business plan, and work went ahead with the help of funding from a government rural development scheme.

A knitwear exhibition at the Business Design Centre, London. The Rural Development Commission provides funding for small businesses to exhibit at trade exhibitions.

An oyster farm in a nature reserve in Lochinver, Scotland, set up with the help of a grant from Ross and Cromarty Enterprises. Pacific oysters, which can be eaten all year round, are sold to local hotels and restaurants.

Aberystwyth Science Park in Wales: all the units, which house organisations committed to scientific research and development, were built and funded by the Development Board for Rural Wales.

COMPUTER TECHNOLOGY

This virtual reality simulator developed by Denne Developments of Bournemouth, Dorset, responds to body movements, giving a realistic impression of surfing. The new technology has potential beyond leisure activities: among those who have already ordered a version of the simulator is NASA, which will use it with virtual reality headsets to train astronauts in the skills of spacewalking and its associated tasks.

Parallel processing uses a number of separate computers in co-operation, allowing data to be accessed and processed more quickly. Here, the director of the £1 million Parallel Computer Architectures Laboratory at Edinburgh University integrates geographical data from a variety of sources.

- enables British specialists to teach, advise or establish joint projects abroad;
- teaches English and promotes its use;
- provides library and information services; and
- makes British arts and literature more widely known.

The Council runs 185 libraries, resource centres and information centres, and 86 English language teaching centres. In 1993–94 about 8.2 million loans of books and other materials were made to 440,000 library members. Up to 100,000 people at any one time were taking part in the Council's English courses.

The Council is financed partly by a grant from the Foreign & Commonwealth Office. The training and education programmes organised by the Council as part of the British aid programme are another important source of income. About a quarter of the Council's income comes from other earnings.

Educational Exchanges

The British Council recruits teachers for work overseas, organises short overseas visits by British experts, encourages cultural exchange visits and organises academic interchange between British universities and colleges and those in other countries.

The ODA helps fund certain Council programmes such as:

- recruitment of staff for overseas universities;
- secondment of staff from British higher education establishments; and
- organisation of short-term teaching and advisory visits.

The Central Bureau for Educational Visits and Exchanges, which is now part of the British Council, administers teacher exchanges in Europe and the United States, short courses for language teachers and international study visits. Opportunities for young people include school and class links and English language summer camps. For the post-16 age group, there are work placements and English language assistants' posts as well as other exchange programmes.

Association of Commonwealth Universities

The Association of Commonwealth Universities promotes contact and co-operation between hundreds of member universities in Commonwealth countries or regions. It assists student and staff mobility by administering award schemes, and operates an academic appointments service. The Association publishes information about Commonwealth universities, courses and scholarships, and organises meetings in different parts of the world.

The arts

The British Council initiates or supports overseas tours by British theatre companies, orchestras, choirs, opera and dance companies and jazz, rock and folk groups, as well as visits by individual actors, musicians and artists. The Council also arranges for directors, designers, choreographers and conductors to work in other countries. In addition it organises and supports fine arts and other exhibitions as well as British participation in international exhibitions and film festivals.

Further Reading

Britain in the European Community. Aspects of Britain series, HMSO, 1992.

Britain, NATO and European Security. Aspects of Britain series, HMSO, 1994.

British Council Annual Report.

Departmental Report 1994: The Government's Expenditure Plans 1994–95 to 1997–98. Foreign & Commonwealth Office, including Overseas Development Administration.

European Union. Aspects of Britain series, HMSO 1994.

Statement on the Defence Estimates 1994. HMSO, 1994.

10 Defence

By April 1995, the strength of the armed forces will be around 120,000 in the Army, about 70,000 in the RAF and about 51,000 in the Royal Navy. Under plans outlined in the Defence Costs Study, there will be a net reduction of just under 19,000 defence jobs by the year 2000—2,200 in the Army, 7,500 in the RAF, 1,900 in the Royal Navy and 7,100 British-based civil servants.

INTRODUCTION

Britain's defence policy supports its wider security policy, which is to maintain the country's freedom and territorial integrity and that of its dependent territories, as well as its ability to pursue its legitimate interests at home and abroad.

With the removal of the strategic threat to Britain as a result of the end of the Cold War, progress is being made in security-building and co-operation with states in central and eastern Europe. However, the end of East–West confrontation has been followed by problems of instability, nationalism and extremism within Europe and beyond. These developments are the major factors shaping defence policy today. Britain and its allies in the North Atlantic Treaty Organisation (NATO) have responded to these changes by adapting their policies and the structure of their armed forces to meet the defence requirements of the future.

NATO remains the foundation of Britain's defence and security policies. In addition Britain works to increase security through its membership of the Western European Union (WEU), the European Union (EU), the Conference on Security and Co-operation in Europe (CSCE) and the United Nations (UN). These organisations have been involved in activities such as negotiating an end to conflicts, peacekeeping deployments and humanitarian missions.

The current fundamental restructuring of Britain's armed forces recognises the need for flexibility in the face of future uncertainty. The armed forces are, therefore, equipped to take part in integrated operations, ranging from small-scale peacekeeping or humanitarian missions to large-scale high intensity conflict. Britain's nuclear forces (see p. 137) provide the ultimate guarantee for its security.

The highest priority continues to be placed on maximising the cost effectiveness and military capabilities of the armed forces. Launched in December 1993, the Defence Costs Study (see p. 140) examined all areas of administration and support to the front line to ensure that the money spent contributes directly or indirectly to fighting capability.

THE NORTH ATLANTIC TREATY ORGANISATION

NATO has provided Britain's main means of defence against a major external threat for the past 45 years. It is the only security organisation with the military means to back up its security guarantees and has consequently undertaken action on behalf of the UN. NATO unites the interests of Europe and North America in the pursuit of peace, stability and well-being in the whole of Europe. All Britain's nuclear forces and most of its conventional forces are committed to NATO.

NATO is continuing the process of adaptation started with the 1991 Rome Declaration and the resulting new Strategic Concept to allow it to play a wider role in maintaining stability throughout Europe.

January 1994 NATO Summit

The January 1994 NATO Summit marked an important step in the Alliance's post-Cold War evolution. It launched a major initiative called Partnership for Peace, which seeks to deepen political and military ties between NATO and the central and eastern European countries in areas such as peacekeeping and humanitarian operations.

Partnership for Peace has been generally welcomed and supported. Over 20 states have already signed, including Russia, almost all the central and eastern European states, Sweden and Finland, and most of the central Asian and Trans-Caucasian states of the former Soviet Union.

In addition to its work within NATO on Partnership for Peace, Britain has signed formal Memoranda of Understanding on bilateral defence contacts with Albania, Bulgaria, the Czech Republic, Estonia, Hungary, Latvia, Lithuania, Poland, Romania, Russia, Slovakia and the Ukraine. Similar agreements have recently been reached with Belarus and Slovenia. The Memoranda are designed to promote stability in central and eastern Europe, exchange military information

and encourage co-operation on defence equipment. Britain provides advice on civil–military relations, including democratic control and accountability, and defence budgeting and management. These contacts are complementary to those within NATO.

The 1994 NATO Summit also:

- committed the Alliance to continued adaptation of its political and military structures in order to reflect all its roles and the development of the emerging European security and defence identity;

- endorsed the concept of joint task forces which will allow a flexible and effective response to a broad range of missions and for the inclusion of non-NATO forces and operations under WEU auspices;

- reaffirmed that the Alliance remains open to the membership of other European countries; and

- declared NATO's intentions to intensify its efforts against the proliferation of weapons of mass destruction.

NATO Force Structures

The size, availability and deployment of NATO forces continue to reflect the Alliance's defensive nature. Current NATO strategy involves:

- deployment in Europe of smaller and highly mobile forces;

- a move away from the concept of forward presence;

- a reduced reliance on nuclear weapons;

- the scaling back of the state of readiness of allied armed forces; and

- a reduction in training requirements and exercises.

NATO's Strategic Concept recognises that the far-reaching changes in the strategic setting, together with the growth of new risks to international order and stability, require an active response from the Alliance. While the primary role of Alliance military forces remains to guarantee the security and territorial integrity of its members, force levels are being reduced and restructured while missions are being broadened. Force structures comprising reaction, main defence and augmentation forces have been established and are intended to be mutually supporting.

NATO Command Structures

The NATO command structure has been adapted to the changing environment. At the highest level, the number of Commands has been cut back from three to two—Allied Command Europe and Allied Command Atlantic.

There have been considerable modifications in Allied Command Europe. Of importance to Britain is the formation of Allied Forces North West Europe, which incorporates the land mass of Britain and Norway, the United Kingdom air defence region and the North Sea; formed in July 1994, it is commanded from headquarters at RAF High Wycombe, in Buckinghamshire.

UNITED KINGDOM DEFENCE POLICY

Defence Roles and Military Tasks

British defence policy is defined in terms of overlapping Defence Roles One, Two and Three, which are to:

- ensure the protection and security of Britain and its dependent territories, even when there is no major external threat;
- insure against any major external threat to Britain and its allies; and
- contribute to promoting Britain's wider security interests through the maintenance of international peace and stability.

Within these three defence roles are 50 military tasks which define the military activities to be undertaken by the Ministry of Defence and the armed forces in order to give effect to defence and security policy.

Britain and Its Dependencies

The armed forces continue to have day-to-day responsibility for safeguarding Britain's territory, airspace and territorial waters. They also provide for the security and reinforcement, as necessary, of the dependent territories and, when required, support for the civil authority.

Maritime Defence

The Royal Navy ensures the integrity of British territorial waters and the protection of British rights and interests in the surrounding seas. The maintenance of a 24-hour-a-day, year-round presence in British waters provides considerable reassurance to merchant ships and other mariners. The Royal Air Force (RAF) also contributes to maritime requirements; the Nimrod MR2 force, in particular, provides invaluable surveillance of surface and sub-surface vessels.

Land Defence

By 1995 it is planned to have 24 regular infantry battalions earmarked for activities in Defence Role One. These will be augmented by the Territorial Army. Tasks include contributing to national and NATO nuclear forces and maintaining the security of the dependent territories.

Air Defence

Air defence of Britain and the surrounding seas is maintained by a system of layered defences. Continuous radar cover is provided by the Improved United Kingdom Air Defence Ground Environment (IUKADGE), supplemented by the NATO Airborne Early Warning Force, to which the RAF contributes six E–3D aircraft. The RAF also provides six squadrons of all-weather Tornado F3 air defence aircraft, supported by tanker aircraft and, in wartime, an additional F3 squadron and armed Hawk trainer aircraft. Royal Navy air defence destroyers are also linked to the IUKADGE, providing radar and electronic warfare coverage and surface-to-air missiles. Ground-launched Rapier missiles defend the main RAF bases. Naval aircraft also contribute to British air defence.

Overseas Garrisons

Britain maintains garrisons in Hong Kong, Gibraltar, the Sovereign Base Areas of Cyprus and the Falkland Islands. The Hong Kong garrison is being reduced in stages until 1997, when the territory will revert to Chinese sovereignty (see p. 115). Gibraltar provides headquarters and communications facilities for NATO in the western Mediterranean and Cyprus acts as a base for operations in the Middle East and North Africa.

British forces are stationed in the Falkland Islands to deter possible aggression from Argentina, which maintains its claim to the Islands (see p. 115).

Northern Ireland

The armed forces continue to provide support to the Royal Ulster Constabulary (RUC) in the fight against terrorism. There are currently 18 Army infantry units, including six battalions of the Home Service element of the Royal Irish Regiment. The Royal Navy patrols territorial waters around Northern Ireland and its inland waterways in order to deter and intercept the movement of terrorist weapons and personnel. The Royal Marines provide troops to meet Navy and Army commitments, while RAF helicopters provide support to ground forces.

The armed forces' operations meet requirements set by the RUC. The majority of operations are carried out jointly with the RUC, for example, setting up vehicle check points and providing escorts for police mobile patrols and foot patrols to guard police officers to enable them to carry out their duties in safety. The Army also provides specialist skills in bomb disposal, helicopter support and search.

Since the ceasefire announcement by the Provisional IRA on 31 August 1994 (see p. 14), the armed forces have continued their support for the RUC. Although the frequency of patrols has remained the same, the security forces have reduced their profile in line with the reduction in terrorist threat; for example, they wear berets instead of helmets and helicopter activity has declined.

Other Tasks

Other Defence Role One tasks include the provision of:

- military support to the machinery of government in war;
- military assistance to civil ministries, including assistance to maintain the essentials of life in the community and carrying out work of national importance;
- military aid to the civil community in emergencies and in routine situations;
- military search and rescue;
- military intelligence and surveillance;
- physical protection and security; and
- state ceremonial and routine public duties.

Britain and Its Allies

This second major defence role is discharged through Britain's membership of NATO.

Maritime Forces

Most Royal Navy ships are committed to NATO. Permanent contributions are made to NATO's standing naval forces in the Atlantic, the English Channel and the Mediterranean. The main components of the Fleet consist of:

- three aircraft carriers operating Sea Harrier aircraft and Sea King anti-submarine warfare helicopters;
- 35 destroyers and frigates;
- 12 nuclear-powered attack submarines; and
- amphibious forces, including two assault ships and a helicopter carrier which is currently under construction.

Land Forces

The multinational Allied Command Europe Rapid Reaction Corps (ARRC) is the key land component of NATO's rapid reaction forces and is scheduled to be fully operational by 1995. The Alliance invited Britain to be the lead nation of the Corps, recognising that its substantial professional forces, wide range of capabilities and recent operational experience made it well placed to assume this role.

> Modified RAF Tornado GR1 aircraft (designated GR1b), equipped with the Sea Eagle missile, have assumed the maritime attack role previously undertaken by Buccaneer aircraft. The introduction into service of the Tornado GR1b force will be completed in 1995. The RAF will continue to provide Nimrod maritime patrol aircraft and search and rescue helicopters.

Britain is providing the Corps headquarters and an armoured division based in Germany in peacetime. In addition, it is providing a second, more lightly armoured division, based in Britain and comprising two mechanised brigades and an airborne brigade. An airmobile brigade, also based in Britain, will join one of the two multinational divisions in the Corps. Some 55,000 regular British soldiers will be assigned to ARRC, together with a substantial number of Territorial Army (see p. 139) and individual reservists.

Air Forces

The RAF makes a major contribution to NATO's Immediate and Rapid Reaction Forces. In all around 100 fixed wing aircraft and 40 helicopters are allocated to support these Reaction Forces. Tornado F3 and Rapier surface-to-air missiles form part of the Supreme Allied Commander Europe's Immediate Reaction Force, while Harrier, Tornado GR1 and GR1a provide offensive support and tactical reconnaissance to the Rapid Reaction Force. Chinook and Puma helicopters provide troop airlift facilities for the ARRC (see above) or other deployed land forces. Tornado F3 and Tornado GR1b aircraft provide air defence or anti-surface attack in support of NATO's maritime reaction forces.

Since 1991, the number of RAF squadrons in Germany has been reduced to four Tornado GR1 strike/attack squadrons, two Harrier offensive support squadrons and a Puma/Chinook support helicopter squadron at RAF Bruggen and RAF Laarbruch. It is intended that RAF Laarbruch will close in 1999, subject to consultation with the German authorities; the two Harrier squadrons and the support helicopters currently based there will be withdrawn to existing air bases in Britain. The four squadrons of Tornados, however, will remain at RAF Bruggen. These aircraft and personnel, alongside the continuing and significant Army presence in Germany, are a visible sign of Britain's continuing commitment to the defence of Europe.

Other Forces

Britain contributes to NATO's maritime augmentation forces. These will be held at the lowest state of readiness and in peacetime comprise ships mainly in routine refit or maintenance. It also contributes special forces to support reaction and main defence force deployments for surveillance, reconnaissance, offensive action and military assistance operations. The United Kingdom Amphibious Force, together with its Dutch counterpart, is assigned to the Supreme Allied Commander Atlantic for the reinforcement of Norway and could be deployed by the Supreme Allied Commander Europe, for example, with the ARRC. The Force is also a candidate for a range of WEU operations. Assisting these forces are RAF fighter aircraft and a strengthened air transport force.

Wider Security Interests

Military tasks within Defence Role Three are carried out to promote Britain's wider security interests. They may be undertaken unilaterally or multilaterally with support from NATO or directly for UN or CSCE operations.

United Nations Operations

Britain remains a major contributor to UN operations. Contingents are currently deployed in former Yugoslavia (see below), Cyprus, Iraq/Kuwait and Georgia; Britain has previously deployed contingents in Cambodia, the Western Sahara and Rwanda. The British manpower contribution to the UN force in Cyprus has been reduced by 50 per cent since 1992, although Britain remains the largest contributor.

Former Yugoslavia

Britain continues to make a substantial contribution to the UN Protection Force (UNPROFOR) in the former Yugoslavia, with over 3,300 ground troops deployed, including two infantry battalions, in central Bosnia as part of the humanitarian and peacekeeping mission. Another 3,000 Service personnel are deployed in the Adriatic; these include a Carrier Task group available to reinforce the two battalions if required and Royal Navy ships which contribute to joint NATO/WEU operations designed to enforce the UN arms embargo against the former Yugoslavia and trade sanctions against Serbia and Montenegro, supported by RAF maritime patrol aircraft. In addition, RAF Jaguars in Italy, together with Royal Navy Sea Harriers on the aircraft carrier, are available if needed to provide close support to UNPROFOR troops. RAF early warning aircraft, with Tornado F3s and their air-to-air refuelling support, continue operations to enforce the UN no-fly zone over Bosnia.

Other Operational Deployments

Royal Navy ships of the Armilla Patrol continue to provide reassurance and assistance to entitled merchant shipping in the Gulf area and regularly participate in maritime exercises with navies of Gulf states and coalition allies. The Patrol has conducted interception and boarding operations to ensure that ships do not breach UN sanctions on Iraq (see p. 122); these operations ceased in August 1994.

The number of operations against trafficking in illicit drugs has increased in recent years, especially in the Caribbean, where the West Indies Guardship and other

Royal Navy ships work closely with the authorities of the United States, the Dependent Territories and the Regional Security System to combat drug trafficking. Primary responsibility for this work rests with other government departments but the armed forces assist where this can be done without detriment to the performance of other military tasks.

British Garrisons

A British garrison is maintained in Brunei at the request of the Brunei Government. The withdrawal of the British garrison in Belize, originally maintained to deter and, if necessary, defend against, possible Guatemalan aggression, was completed at the end of September 1994. This was made possible by Guatemalan recognition of Belize as a sovereign and independent state in 1991 and the establishment of diplomatic relations between the two countries. However, a British military presence will be maintained in Belize in the form of the British Army Training Support Unit, Belize, which is geared to provide training (jungle, conventional and adventure) to deployments from Britain from October 1994.

Military Assistance

During 1993–94, some 4,000 students from 97 countries attended military training courses in Britain. On 1 January 1994, nearly 400 British Service personnel were on loan in 37 countries, their duties including the provision of assistance, advice and training for armed forces. British armed forces also participated in almost 200 exercises and training periods in 22 countries outside Europe in 1993.

NUCLEAR FORCES

The Royal Navy's independent nuclear deterrent remains the ultimate guarantee of Britain's security. The current submarine-launched Polaris strategic force is assigned to NATO but remains at all times under the control of the British Government; it enables Britain to provide a second independent centre of decision-making within NATO, thereby enhancing deterrence.

The Polaris force now comprises two nuclear submarines, each capable of carrying 16 Polaris missiles armed with improved British nuclear warheads. The Polaris force is being replaced by four British-built submarines, each of which will carry Trident missiles purchased from the United States. A four-boat force will ensure that one boat is always at sea, invulnerable to pre-emptive attack. Trident's nuclear warheads are British-designed and built. Two Trident submarines have been manufactured, with the first, HMS *Vanguard*, entering service at the beginning of the year.

The Government is committed to maintaining only the minimum deterrent level required for Britain's security. Each Trident submarine will deploy no more than 96 warheads and possibly significantly fewer. On current plans, the explosive power of each submarine will not be much changed from Polaris. When Trident is fully in service, the explosive power of Britain's operational nuclear inventory will be over 25 per cent lower than it was in 1990.

The armed forces also possess sub-strategic nuclear weapons, which provide a link between strategic and conventional forces. Following the end of the Cold War, Britain has made substantial reductions in these weapons, including the elimination of tactical maritime nuclear weapons and a reduction of over 50 per cent in the stockpile of WE177 free-fall nuclear bombs. The remaining WE177s are deployed on dual-capable Tornado aircraft, all of which are available to NATO. In addition, Britain plans to exploit the flexibility and capability of Trident to provide the vehicle for delivery of its sub-strategic deterrent, once the WE177 leaves service.

UNITED KINGDOM FORCE STRUCTURES

Defence Equipment Programme

Modern equipment is essential if one of the key aims of Britain's force restructuring programme is to be achieved, namely that of increasing the flexibility and mobility of the armed forces. The successful outcome of the Defence Costs Study (see p. 140) has enabled the British Government to preserve the front line (and its essential operational support) and to make a number of important improvements to its capability. Current and planned front line improvements for the Royal Navy equipment programme include:

- introduction of Trident submarines to replace Polaris;

- substantial updating of existing nuclear-powered submarines and an invitation to tender for the design and building of a second batch of Trafalgar Class submarines;

- a substantially modernised destroyer and frigate fleet;

- a follow-on batch of 7 Sandown Class single role minehunters;

- introduction of a new helicopter carrier to enhance Britain's amphibious forces;

- 18 new Sea Harrier F/A2 aircraft and the upgrading of in-service Sea Harriers to F/A2 standard; and

- invitations to tender for the design and building of a replacement for the assault ships *Fearless* and *Intrepid*.

The Army front line is being enhanced by:

- Challenger 2 tanks, which are expected to enter service in 1995;

- a new attack helicopter to replace the Lynx;

- the Multiple Launch Rocket System and the AS90 self-propelled howitzer, replacing Abbot and M–109 guns;

- improved Rapier short-range missiles;

- the new Starstreak high velocity close air defence missile;

- a new medium-range anti-tank missile; and

- a new generation of combat radios.

Improvements for the Royal Air Force include:

- The Eurofighter 2000 from the beginning of the next century;

- upgrading of the Tornado GR1 aircraft;

- programmes to enhance the RAF's inventory of air-launched missiles;
- planned purchase of additional support helicopters; and
- plans to upgrade or replace the Hercules C130 fleet.

THE ARMED FORCES

Commissioned Ranks

Commissions, either by promotion from the ranks or by direct entry based on educational and other qualifications, are granted for short, medium and long terms. All three Services have schemes for school, university and college sponsorships.

Commissioned ranks receive initial training at the Britannia Royal Naval College, Dartmouth; the Royal Military Academy, Sandhurst; or the Royal Air Force College, Cranwell. This is followed by specialist training, which may include degree courses at service establishments or universities.

Higher training for officers is currently provided by the Royal Naval College and Joint Services Defence College, Greenwich; the Army Staff College, Camberley; and the Royal Air Force Staff College, Bracknell. The Defence Costs Study (see p. 140) concluded that courses should be subsumed into a tri-Service course which will reinforce the joint approach to the tactical and operational levels of conflict. As such, the Joint Services Command and Staff College will be established in 1997 at either Camberley or Greenwich. The Higher Command and Staff Course, currently conducted at Camberley, will remain as a focus for the study of the operational level of command, but will be expanded to 30 students to increase the joint aspect.

Non-commissioned Ranks

Engagements for non-commissioned ranks in the Army and the RAF range from 6 months to 22 years; they can be for a maximum of 37 years in the Royal Navy and 32 years in the Royal Marines. There is a wide choice of engagement length and terms of service. Subject to a minimum period of service, entrants may leave at any time, at 18 months' notice (12 months for certain engagements). Discharge may also be granted on compassionate or medical grounds, by purchase or on grounds of conscience.

Throughout their Service careers, non-commissioned personnel receive basic training supplemented by specialist training. Study for educational qualifications is encouraged and Service trade and technical training lead to nationally recognised qualifications.

Reserve Forces

Reserve forces are a central component of Britain's armed forces. They include members who become reservists following a period of regular service (regular reserve); others are volunteers who train in their spare time. Volunteer reserve forces include the Royal Naval Reserve, the Royal Marines Reserve, the Territorial Army, the Royal Auxiliary Air Force and the Royal Air Force Volunteer Reserve. Reserves are available to support regular forces, either as units or as individuals, in time of tension or war. In particular, reserves can provide skills and units not available or required in peacetime. Reserves are also a valuable link between the Services and the civil community.

In April 1994, regular reserves totalled around 259,600 and volunteer reserves and auxiliary forces some 71,100.

ADMINISTRATION

The Defence Budget

The estimated defence budget for 1994–95 is £22,890 million, with expenditure plans for 1995–96 and 1996–97 of £22,130 million and £22,230 million respectively. The Government anticipates a reduction of around 16 per cent in real terms between 1990–91 and 1996–97, excluding costs of redundancies and the Gulf War. Britain spent 3.7 per cent of Gross Domestic Product on defence in 1993; this is expected to fall to 2.9 per cent by 1996–97.

Defence Management

Within the Ministry of Defence, a civilian–military Defence Staff is responsible for defence policy and strategy, operational requirements and commitments. Each Service Chief of Staff reports through the Chief of the Defence Staff to the Defence Secretary on matters related to the fighting effectiveness, management, efficiency and morale of his Service. The management of the three Services is exercised through the executive committees of their Service Boards, which are chaired by their respective Chiefs of Staff and act in accordance with centrally determined policy objectives and budgets. The Office of Management and Budget handles budgets and resources. Purchase of equipment and spares is dealt with by the Procurement Executive. As a result of the Defence Costs Study, changes are planned in defence management, under which a head office would be created, composed of a unified Central Staff and three small headquarters staffs supporting the individual Chiefs of Staff; under these proposals the titles of 'Office of Management and Budget' and 'Defence Staff' would be abolished.

Since 1991, military and civilian managers have been given greater responsibility to determine the most efficient use of their allocated resources. This approach aims to promote better value for money and to provide clear direction and accountability for local managers. Under Defence Costs Study proposals, further responsibilities will be delegated to Commands and budget holders outside London.

Defence Procurement

About 40 per cent of the defence budget is spent on military equipment, including the procurement of spares and associated costs. The aim is to meet the operational requirements of the armed forces by procuring equipment, works and services from the suppliers offering the best value for money, taking all relevant factors into account. When assessing options, particular consideration is given not just to the initial procurement cost of a project, but also to the costs that could be necessary to support it through its Service life. Competition is fundamental to obtaining value for money and takes place wherever possible. In general, competitions are open to prime and sub-contractors from overseas. Britain also seeks to promote the creation of an open market for defence equipment within Europe.

International Procurement Collaboration

International collaborative projects are becoming increasingly important as equipment development and production costs increase and defence budgets reduce. Britain favours such co-operation wherever it makes economic and military sense by reducing costs and improving standardisation. It, therefore, plays an active role in NATO's Conference of National Armaments Directors, which promotes equipment collaboration between NATO members. Britain is also a member of the WEU's Western European Armaments Group, which is the main European forum for consultations about armaments.

Current collaborative programmes include:

- the Eurofighter 2000 development (with Germany, Italy and Spain);
- anti-tank guided weapons (with Belgium, France, Germany and the Netherlands);
- a common new generation frigate (with France and Italy);
- the Multiple Launch Rocket System (with the United States, Germany, France and Italy); and
- the EH 101 helicopter (with Italy).

The Defence Costs Study

The 1993–1994 Defence Costs Study was a radical and comprehensive examination of all aspects of support to the front line. Its aims were to identify support area cost savings without reducing front line effectiveness. Twenty major studies and 13 minor ones were commissioned, covering all aspects of the Ministry of Defence's business, other than the front line itself. In addition to the key elements dealt with in earlier parts of this chapter, others include:

- a proposed reorganisation of the Ministry's Head Office, involving a reduction in Head office staff from a planned level of 5,200 in 1995 to 2,500–2,700 in London in 1998;
- establishment of the Employment Services Agency as the first point of contact for suitable candidates for the armed forces. Potential recruits would then be sent to regional Defence Careers Information Offices for more specific career counselling. This process would replace the existing network of regional Service Careers Information Offices;

- further development and streamlining of contracting methods;
- integration of the five existing defence telecommunications networks into a single coherent service and adoption of a more flexible approach to information technology and communications systems procurement; and
- rationalisation of spares stores and storage.

The Defence Costs Study succeeded in identifying ways of saving of some £750 million a year in 1996–97 and more thereafter, without reducing Britain's fighting capability. There will be no reduction in the front line and the forward equipment programme has been protected.

Further Reading

Britain, NATO and European Security. Aspects of Britain series, HMSO, 1994.

The Government's Expenditure Plans 1994–95 to 1996–97. Cm 2501. Departmental Report by the Ministry of Defence. HMSO 1994.

Defending Our Future: Statement on the Defence Estimates 1993. HMSO, 1993.

Statement on the Defence Estimates 1994. HMSO, 1994.

Front Line First—the Defence Costs Study. HMSO, 1994.

Economic Affairs

11 Economy

Having emerged from the recent recession, the British economy has been growing since 1992, with inflation having been brought down to its lowest level for 25 years. The current economic climate is also characterised by rising output, falling unemployment, an upward trend in retail sales, an all-time high level of manufacturing productivity and increased business confidence. A prime objective of government economic policy is to achieve sound public finances by exerting tight control over public expenditure.

National Economy

From 1981 to 1989 the British economy experienced eight years of sustained growth at an annual average rate of over 3 per cent. Subsequently, Britain in common with other major industrialised nations was severely affected by recession. In 1990 growth in Britain slowed to 0.6 per cent, and in 1991 gross domestic product (GDP) fell by 2.3 per cent. GDP rose slightly in the second half of 1992 as economic recovery began. Following growth of 1.9 per cent during 1993, GDP in the second quarter of 1994 reached a level 3.8 per cent higher than a year earlier.

The economy is benefiting from low interest rates: at 5.75 per cent in September 1994, base interest rates are among the lowest in the European Union (EU).

ECONOMIC BACKGROUND

The economy is primarily based on private enterprise, and government policy is aimed at

encouraging and expanding the private sector, which accounts for about 80 per cent of output and around 75 per cent of employment.

Values for some of the main economic indicators in selected years since 1983 are shown in Table 11.1. For further information see the Statistical Annex on pp. 516–17.

Inflation

During most of the 1950s and the 1960s the inflation rate in Britain rarely rose above 5 per cent. However, in 1971 inflation reached double figures, climbing to 27 per cent in 1975. Contributory factors included oil price rises in 1973 and increases in the money supply and public spending. Inflation fell in the early 1980s and stayed low for a number of years. However, it picked up towards the end of the decade and the annual rate rose to 10.9 per cent in September and October 1990.

Inflation has declined substantially since this peak. The Retail Prices Index (RPI—

Table 11.1: Economic Indicators

	1983	1988	1993
Gross domestic product[a]	440,888	537,215	548,559
Exports[a]	96,689	121,197	140,386
Imports[a]	93,954	137,443	153,402
Consumers' expenditure[a]	261,200	334,591	348,687
Gross domestic fixed capital formation[a]	71,845	105,164	96,611
Percentage increase in Retail Prices Index	n.a.	4.9	1.6
Workforce in employment (000s)	n.a.	26,128	25,244
Percentage of workforce unemployed	n.a.	8.0	10.4

Sources: *United Kingdom National Accounts 1994 Edition; Economic Trends; Employment Gazette.*
[a] £ million at 1990 market prices.
n.a. = not available.

often referred to as 'headline' inflation—which measures the change in the price of goods and services purchased by households in Britain) fell to 2.4 per cent in August 1994, one of the lowest rates for 25 years and some way below the EU average.

For the RPI excluding mortgage interest payments ('underlying' inflation), the annual rate was 2.3 per cent in August 1994, which is the lowest figure since November 1967 and within the bottom half of the Government's target range of 1 to 4 per cent (see p. 149).

Output

Output has been recovering since the second half of 1992, both for the economy as a whole and for manufacturing. GDP rose in the second quarter of 1994, for the ninth consecutive quarterly period; it increased by 3.8 per cent year-on-year, the strongest growth rate since the end of 1988, with production, construction and service sectors all showing solid growth. Manufacturing output in the three months to July 1994 increased by 3.9 per cent, compared with the same period a year earlier. The Government forecasts that GDP will rise by 2.75 per cent during 1994 and 1995.

After the oil price rises of 1973–74, manufacturing output dropped sharply. It later increased, but, in the wake of another oil price rise and stagnation in the world economy, it fell back again in the late 1970s and early 1980s. A period of steady growth occurred until 1990, but output fell significantly during the recent recession.

Table 11.2: Output and Employment (Indices: 1990 = 100)

	Output		Employment[a]	
	Index 1992	Index 1993	Index 1992	Index 1993
Agriculture, forestry and fishing	106.8	103.5	92.9	91.8
Production industries	95.9	97.9	88.3	84.6
of which: Electricity, gas and water	105.6	109.9	93.0	87.0
Mining and quarrying	106.5	115.0	83.5	64.6
Manufacturing	94.0	95.3	88.1	85.2
Construction	88.2	87.2	83.8	76.8
Services	99.0	101.3	98.6	98.1
GDP	97.4	99.4		
Employees in employment			95.3	93.7

Sources: *United Kingdom National Accounts 1994 Edition* and *Employment Gazette*
[a] Employment figures relate to Great Britain and cover employees in employment at June on a seasonally adjusted basis.

Table 11.3: Gross Domestic Product by Industry[a]

	1983		1993	
	£ million	per cent	£ million	per cent
Agriculture, hunting, forestry and fishing	5,429	2.1	10,373	1.9
Electricity, gas and water supply	8,682	3.3	13,994	2.6
Mining and quarrying, including oil and gas extraction	20,234	7.7	12,147	2.2
Manufacturing	64,738	24.8	118,294	21.7
Construction	15,929	6.1	29,221	5.4
Wholesale and retail trade, repairs, hotels and restaurants	33,491	12.8	78,348	14.3
Transport, storage and communications	19,727	7.6	46,263	8.5
Financial and business activities, real estate and renting	49,645	19.0	133,956	24.5
Public administration, defence and social security	18,599	7.1	38,199	7.0
Education, health and social work	22,997	8.8	54,457	10.5
Other services	13,752	5.3	31,292	5.7
Total	273,223	104.6	569,544	104.3
Adjustment for financial services	− 11,893	−4.6	− 23,741	−4.3
Statistical discrepancy	−105	–	317	–
GDP at factor cost	261,225	100.0	546,120	100.0

Source: *United Kingdom National Accounts 1994 Edition*
[a]Before provision for depreciation but after deducting stock appreciation.
Note: Differences between totals and the sums of their component parts are due to rounding.

Largely as a result of exploitation of North Sea oil and gas, energy output in 1986 was about twice the level of ten years earlier. Oil output passed its peak of the mid-1980s and fell back until 1992, when it increased by about 3 per cent; in 1993 recovery was even stronger, with a 6 per cent rise.

Recent decades have generally seen the fastest growth in the services sector. Services account for around 65 per cent of GDP, compared with about 50 per cent in 1950. Manufacturing contributes less than 25 per cent of GDP, compared with over a third in 1950. Table 11.2 compares output and employment in 1992 and 1993, and Table 11.3 compares GDP by industry in 1983 and 1993.

Productivity

Growth in manufacturing output per head in Britain in the 1980s was faster than in all other leading industrialised countries: between 1980 and 1990 it increased by an average of 4.6 per cent a year. In the three months to July 1994, it was at a record level, up 4.8 per cent on a year earlier following a 3.8 per cent increase in 1993. Output per head in the whole economy rose by 3.2 per cent in 1993.

Investment

From 1983 until 1989 fixed investment increased by about 8 per cent a year on average, with particularly rapid growth of over 10 per cent a year between 1986 and 1988. With the recession, investment declined between 1990 and 1992, but during 1993 it rose by 0.4 per cent and by 4.5 per cent in the second quarter of 1994, compared with a year earlier.

Over the decade 1980–90 the private sector's share of fixed investment grew from 73 to 84 per cent, due in part to privatisation (see pp. 195–6). In the same period, there was a rise in the share of investment undertaken by the services sector and a fall in that carried out by manufacturing.

An improvement in the quality of investment contributed to a rise in the late 1980s in the net real rate of return on capital employed in non-oil industrial and commercial companies to the highest levels for 20 years. Profitability declined in 1990 and 1991, but there was a recovery in 1992, when net profitability amounted to 7 per cent. Corporate earnings continued to recover in 1993, when net profitability reached 8 per cent. Table 11.4 shows investment by industrial sector.

Employment

The workforce in employment fell by around 2 million in the early 1990s following an increase of over 3 million between 1983 and June 1990. With the economic recovery, there are signs that employment levels have stabilised at an earlier stage than in previous cycles.

Unemployment had also increased during the early 1990s, and it reached nearly 3 million on a seasonally adjusted basis in late 1992. Since then unemployment has fallen by 376,000 and in August 1994 it was 2.6 million—9.2 per cent of the workforce— the lowest for over two years (see p. 176).

Overseas Trade

Britain has an open economy in which international trade plays a vital part. The Government welcomed the successful outcome of the Uruguay round of multilateral trade negotiations held under the auspices of the General Agreement on Tariffs and Trade (see p. 170). The share of GDP accounted for by exports of goods and services has increased from around 20 per cent in the early 1960s to 25 per cent. Similar rises have occurred in most other developed countries, reflecting the growing importance of international trade in an increasingly interdependent world economy.

Britain is a major exporter of aerospace products, electrical and electronic equipment, chemicals, oil and many types of machinery. It is also one of the world's largest importers of agricultural products, raw materials and semi-manufactures. For the last 11 years Britain has had a deficit on visible trade. In 1993 it stood at more than £13,000 million on a seasonally adjusted basis, reflecting in part weakness in Britain's key overseas markets. However, non-oil exports are now showing firm growth: in the three months to June 1994 they were up by 10 per cent compared with a year previously.

Substantial net earnings on invisible transactions kept the current account of the balance of payments in surplus in most years up to 1986, but it has been in deficit since

Table 11.4: Gross Domestic Fixed Capital Formation (Investment) by Sector 1993

	£ million at market prices	£ million at 1990 prices	Index at 1990 prices (1990 = 100)
Agriculture, hunting, forestry and fishing	1,174	1,142	83.5
Mining and quarrying, including oil and gas extraction	5,092	5,693	121.1
Electricity, gas and water	6,084	6,211	131.0
Manufacturing	12,165	10,989	77.2
Construction	812	745	77.2
Services	46,446	48,809	87.3
Dwellings	19,467	19,238	89.7
Transfer costs	3,475	3,784	88.9
Whole economy	**94,715**	**96,611**	**89.8**

Source: *United Kingdom National Accounts 1994 Edition.*

then. The contribution made by invisibles to the current account partly reflects Britain's position as a major financial centre. The surplus on invisibles was £2,800 million in 1993, although this is at a lower level than in the mid-1980s. In 1993 exports of services were valued at around 30 per cent of exports of goods.

Membership of the EU has had a major impact on Britain's pattern of trade. Between 1972 and 1993 the share of Britain's exports of goods going to other members of the Union rose from 33 to 53 per cent. Imports followed a similar trend, growing from 36 to 50 per cent. Trade with the People's Republic of China and Japan, as well as with the newly industrialised countries, including Singapore, Korea, Taiwan and Malaysia, has also risen significantly.

Inward Investment

Britain is recognised as an attractive location for inward direct investment and 13,000 overseas companies are currently operating in Britain, including more than 3,500 from the United States, over 1,000 from Germany and 200 from Japan. This reflects its membership of the EU and proximity to other European markets, its stable labour relations and comparatively low personal and corporate taxation. Overseas-owned firms are offered the same incentives as British-owned ones.

In recent years Britain has attracted the greatest share of inward investment into the European Union, including more than 40 per cent of Japanese investment and almost 40 per cent of US investment. Furthermore, it is second only to the United States as a destination for international direct investment.

Energy

With the exploitation of oil and natural gas from the Continental Shelf under the North Sea, Britain is self-sufficient in energy in net terms and expects to remain so for some years. In 1993 it was the world's tenth largest oil producer and the extraction of oil and gas accounted for some

4 per cent of GDP, while crude oil and petroleum products accounted for 7 per cent of visible exports.

The benefits to the balance of payments began to appear in the second half of the 1970s and in 1980 Britain had its first surplus on oil trade. Exports, mainly to other EU countries, are equivalent to over half of domestic oil production. They are partly offset in balance-of-payments terms by imports of other grades of crude oil from the Middle East and elsewhere.

ECONOMIC STRATEGY

The Government's policy is to ensure sustainable economic growth through low inflation and sound public finances. Following the suspension in 1992 of sterling's membership of the exchange rate mechanism (ERM) of the European Monetary System, the Government set out a new policy framework for its counter-inflation strategy. This includes a target of keeping underlying inflation within a range of 1 to 4 per cent, bringing it down to the lower part of this range by the end of the present Parliament.

The Government's economic policy is set in the context of a medium-term financial strategy, which is reviewed each year. Within this strategy, monetary and fiscal policies are designed to defeat inflation. Short-term interest rates remain the essential instrument of monetary policy. Fiscal policy is set over a medium-term horizon to support monetary policy.

Macroeconomic policy is directed towards keeping down the rate of inflation as the basis for sustainable growth, while microeconomic policies seek to improve the working of markets and encourage enterprise, efficiency and flexibility through measures such as privatisation, deregulation and tax reforms (see below).

Monetary Policy

Monetary policy is aimed at achieving the Government's objectives for inflation. Monetary policy takes time to influence inflation: hence, interest rate decisions are based on an assessment of the prospects for underlying inflation in 12 to 24 months' time. That assessment is based on a range of monetary indicators and other data. The main monetary indicators are the growth of 'narrow money', as measured by M0, and 'broad money', M4.[1] Medium-term target ranges have been set at 0 to 4 per cent for M0 and 3 to 9 per cent for M4. Movements in the exchange rate and asset prices, especially house prices, are also taken into account.

The Government's view is that re-entry into the ERM cannot be considered until there has been greater convergence between the monetary policy requirements of all EU economies and the Government is satisfied that the system will be operated to the benefit of all its members. It will not consider rejoining the ERM in the foreseeable future.

Fiscal Policy

The objectives of the Government's fiscal policy are to ensure sound public finances, return the budget towards balance by the end of the decade, and reduce the share of public expenditure in national income. The deficit is expected to fall as the economy continues to recover; the tax measures in the March and November 1993 Budgets, combined with tight control of public expenditure, will reinforce this trend.

Within the overall policy of moving towards a balanced budget over the medium term, the Government aims to reduce taxes when possible so as to leave people with more of their own money. The basic rate of income tax has been cut from 33 to 25 per cent, and a new lower rate of income tax of 20 per cent now applies on the first £3,000 of taxable income.

Supply-side Policies

While macroeconomic policy is directed towards ensuring sustainable growth through low inflation and sound public finances, the Government has sought to improve the supply response, and thus the efficiency, of the economy through microeconomic policies. Action has been taken to expose more of the economy to market forces. Direct controls—for example, on pay, prices, foreign exchange, dividend payments and commercial credit—have been abolished and competition in domestic markets strengthened.

Steps have been taken to reduce regulatory burdens on business and to reduce the number of administrative obstacles facing small firms and self-employed people (see p. 196). Where there is evidence of market failure, particular efforts have been made to improve the flow of investment funds to small firms, assist innovation in industry and attract industry to the inner cities. Measures have been implemented to encourage saving and share ownership.

Two new tax-free investments have helped to encourage wider share ownership and saving:

- Personal Equity Plans (PEPs), which allow investment in shares, unit trusts and investment trusts. Up to £9,000 a year can be invested by each person: £6,000 in a general PEP and £3,000 in a single company PEP. Nearly 2.9 million general PEPs have been opened since the scheme started in 1987, involving investment of £9,260 million. In 1992–93, 770,000 general PEPs and 140,000 single company PEPs were opened.

- TESSAs (Tax Exempt Special Savings Accounts), which provide tax relief to encourage small savers. They allow investment with a bank or building society of up to £9,000 over five years. Nearly 3.9 million TESSAs have been opened since the introduction of the scheme in 1991, with a value of over £13,000 million.

---

[1] M0 is notes and cash in circulation with the public and banks' holdings of cash and their operational balances at the Bank of England. M4 is notes and cash in circulation with the public together with all sterling deposits held with banks and building societies by the rest of the private sector.

A White Paper issued in May 1994, designed to improve business competitiveness, contains over 60 new measures, many relating to improving education and training and the performance of small businesses (see p. 197).

A substantial number of activities have been transferred from the public sector to the private sector by privatisation and contracting out. In addition, the Government is seeking greater efficiency and value for money in the public sector through market testing and competitive tendering, efficiency reviews and scrutinies, and better financial management.

Labour Market

The Government has sought to improve work incentives by reducing personal income tax rates, raising tax thresholds and reforming the benefits system. It has also, through the tax system, encouraged the extension of share ownership among employees. A scheme of income tax relief has been introduced to encourage the spread of profit-related pay. The Government has taken steps to achieve a more balanced legal framework for industrial relations. It has expanded training opportunities and put in place a new training framework, with a greater role for employers, so that training better reflects local needs. Obstacles to the mobility of labour have also been reduced.

Economic Management

HM Treasury has prime responsibility for the formulation and conduct of economic policy, which it carries out in conjunction with the Bank of England (the central bank) and the Departments of Trade and Industry, Employment, the Environment, Transport, and the Ministry of Agriculture, Fisheries and Food. The Bank of England is now responsible for deciding the precise timing of interest rate changes following the Governor of the Bank of England's monthly meeting with the Chancellor of the Exchequer, who continues to make policy decisions about whether to change rates.

Several other bodies deal with specific aspects of economic policy and the

regulation of certain sectors of the economy. These include bodies such as the Office of Fair Trading and the Monopolies and Mergers Commission.

On major matters of public policy, such as the broad economic strategy, and on the economic problems it faces, the Government makes known its policies and keeps in touch with developments throughout the economy by means of informal and continuous links with the chief industrial, financial and other interests. Final responsibility for the broad lines of economic policy rests with the Cabinet.

To assist in the process of economic forecasting, the Government set up a Panel of Independent Forecasters in 1992. The Panel publishes a full range of forecasts on the main economic indicators.

NATIONAL INCOME AND EXPENDITURE

The value of all goods and services produced in the economy is measured by GDP. This may be expressed either in terms of market prices (the prices people pay for the goods and services they buy) or at factor cost (the cost of the goods and services before adding taxes and subtracting subsidies). It can also be expressed in current prices or in constant prices (that is, removing the effects of inflation to measure the volume of growth in the economy). In 1993 GDP at current factor cost totalled £546,120 million. Between 1983 and 1993 the index of GDP at constant factor cost increased by 24 per cent.

Table 11.5 gives figures for GDP, at both current market prices and current factor cost. It also shows the components of two other main aggregates, gross national product and national income.

Table 11.6 shows the categories of total final expenditure in 1993. Consumers' expenditure accounted for one-half of total final expenditure, and exports of goods and services for nearly one-fifth.

Personal Incomes and Expenditure

Personal disposable income consists of personal incomes after deductions—mainly

Table 11.5: Gross Domestic Product, Gross National Product and National Income

	£ million 1983	£ million 1993
Total final expenditure	382,775	796,380
less imports of goods and services	−77,588	−166,266
GDP at market prices	304,456	630,023
plus net property income from abroad	2,830	3,062
Gross national product at market prices	307,286	633,085
less factor cost adjustment (taxes less subsidies)	−43,231	− 83,903
GDP at factor cost	261,225	546,120
Net property income from abroad	2,830	3,062
Gross national product at factor cost	264,055	549,182
less capital consumption	−36,150	− 65,023
National income (net national product at factor cost)	227,905	484,159

Source: *United Kingdom National Accounts 1994 Edition*
Note: Differences between totals and the sums of their component parts are due to rounding.

taxation and social security contributions. This rose fairly steadily from £205,511 million in 1983 to £462,178 million at current prices in 1993. Personal disposable income in 1993 was 5 per cent higher in real terms than in 1992. Consumers' expenditure amounted to 87.8 per cent of post-tax personal income in 1993, compared with 87.2 per cent in 1992.

Consumers' expenditure rose by 2.6 per cent in real terms between 1992 and 1993. Table 11.7 shows the changing pattern of consumers' expenditure between 1983 and 1993. Declining proportions are being spent on food, tobacco, clothing and footwear, and fuel and power. Over the longer term, as incomes rise, people tend to spend increasing proportions on services. Spending on leisure pursuits and tourism, health and financial services have all shown significant growth in recent years. Housing, food, alcoholic drink, clothing and footwear, and fuel and power together accounted for about 42 per cent of the total in 1993.

The ratio of savings to personal disposable income declined substantially during the 1980s, from a peak of 13.4 per cent in 1980 to 5.7 per cent in 1988. However, since then it has more than doubled to 12.8 per cent in 1992, before falling to 12.2 per cent in 1993.

Sources of Income

The proportion of total personal pre-tax income accounted for by income from employment was 61 per cent in 1993; average gross weekly earnings in April 1994 in Great Britain were £362 for full-time male workers and £262 for full-time female workers. The three other main sources of personal income were self-employment (11 per cent), rent, dividends and interest (12 per cent), and social security benefits and other current grants from government (15 per cent).

Public Finance

Public expenditure covers expenditure by both central and local government. Central government expenditure includes money spent on goods and services, and in payments to people, for example, social security and pensions.

General government expenditure (see p. 154) is expected to be over £290,000 million in 1994–95 (see Table 11.8). The Government's policy is to maintain tight control of public spending, so that general government expenditure as a share of GDP declines.

The diagram on p. 157 shows the main categories of expenditure, together with the main sources of revenue. The government departments with the largest spending programmes are:

Table 11.6: Total Final Expenditure in 1993 at Market Prices

	£ million	per cent
Consumers' expenditure	405,639	50.9
General government final consumption	138,224	17.4
Gross domestic fixed capital formation	94,715	11.9
Value of physical increase in stocks and work in progress	−197	–
Total domestic expenditure	638,381	80.2
Exports of goods and services	157,999	19.8
Total final expenditure	**796,380**	**100.0**

Source: *United Kingdom National Accounts 1994 Edition*

- the Department of Social Security (with expenditure of £67,600 million in 1993–94, excluding cyclical social security);
- the Department of the Environment (£39,430 million, of which £29,350 million was on local government);
- the Department of Health (£30,120 million); and
- the Ministry of Defence (£23,440 million).

The tough controls on public expenditure mean that savings are being sought in all areas. Savings have been made in a number of areas, such as defence, housing, transport and social security. Nevertheless, additional resources are being devoted to priority areas, including health and education.

Education accounts for about 40 per cent of local authority spending; law and order, housing and other environmental services, personal social services, social security, and roads and transport take up most of the remainder.

General government expenditure (excluding privatisation proceeds), as a proportion of gross domestic product (GDP), fell from over 47 per cent in 1982–83 to under 40 per cent in 1989–90. The recent recession led to a rise in the

Table 11.7: Consumers' Expenditure in 1983 and 1993 at Market Prices

	1983	1993	
	per cent	per cent	£ million
Food (household expenditure)	15.1	11.4	46,327
Alcoholic drink	7.1	6.0	24,395
Tobacco	3.3	2.7	10,829
Clothing and footwear	6.5	5.7	23,322
Housing	15.1	15.4	62,316
Fuel and power	5.0	3.6	14,618
Household goods and services	6.5	6.4	26,160
Transport and communications	17.5	17.2	69,624
Recreation, entertainment and education	9.2	10.0	40,537
Other goods and services	13.5	19.4	78,521
Other items[a]	1.0	2.2	8,991
Total	**100.0**	**100.0**	**405,639**

Source: *United Kingdom National Accounts 1994 Edition*
[a] Household expenditure overseas plus final expenditure by private non-profit-making bodies, minus expenditure by foreign tourists in Britain.
Note: Differences between totals and the sums of their component parts are due to rounding.

Table 11.8: Public Expenditure Plans

	1994–95	1995–96	1996–97
	£ thousand million		
Central government expenditure	172.9	179.9	184.4
Local authority expenditure	71.7	73.7	75.6
Financing requirements of nationalised industries	3.2	2.4	1.9
Reserve	3.5	7.0	10.5
Control total	251.3	263.0	272.3
Cyclical social security	14.6	15.2	16.0
Central government debt interest	22.4	24.5	25.5
Accounting adjustments[a]	8.9	9.8	11.0
General government expenditure, excluding privatisation proceeds	297.1	312.4	325.2
Privatisation proceeds	–5.5	–2.5	–1.0
General government expenditure	291.6	309.9	324.2

Source: HM Treasury.

[a] A number of adjustments are needed to relate the Government's forecast for public expenditure to the broader concepts of general government expenditure.

Note: Differences between totals and the sums of their component parts are due to rounding.

ratio, to 45 per cent in 1993–94, but it is forecast to decline to 42.5 per cent by 1996–97.

Between 1987–88 and 1990–91 the public sector was in surplus so that the Government repaid debt. The Public Sector Borrowing Requirement (PSBR) rose rapidly during the early 1990s, largely reflecting the impact of the recession, and in 1993–94 amounted to £46,000 million, 7.25 per cent of GDP. The PSBR is forecast to fall to £36,000 million in 1994–95 (see Table 11.9), 5.25 per cent of GDP. Tight control over public expenditure and fiscal measures announced in the March and November 1993 Budgets are intended to reinforce the tendency of the PSBR to fall further as the economy recovers, so that the PSBR should be close to zero by 1998–99.

Private Finance Initiative

The private finance initiative was launched in 1992. Its aim is to get the public and private sectors working together more effectively by mobilising the private sector to become involved in the provision of capital assets and the supply of services traditionally regarded as being exclusively handled by the public sector. The initiative follows on from privatisation, market testing and contracting out. It reflects the shift in the role of the public sector from a provider to a purchaser of services. This should lead, the Government believes, to projects being better designed and managed. The total estimated value of projects which the Government currently expects to proceed under the initiative is over £6,000 million. Examples include the Channel Tunnel Rail Link (see p. 293), the upgrading of the West Coast main line railway between London and Glasgow (see p. 291), two new prisons (see p. 97) and a wide variety of health projects.

The Government has set up the Private Finance Panel (containing high-level representatives from the public and private sectors) to encourage greater participation in the initiative and seek solutions to any problems which might arise.

PUBLIC EXPENDITURE TERMS

The three main public expenditure totals are general government expenditure, the 'control total' and Supply expenditure.

General Government Expenditure

General government expenditure, excluding privatisation proceeds, is the total spending of

Table 11.9: Projected Public Expenditure, Receipts and Borrowing Requirement

£ thousand million

	1993–94 (provisional outturn)	1994–95	1995–96
General government expenditure	278.9	291.6	309.9
of which: public expenditure control total	*242.7*	*251.3*	*263.0*
General government receipts	232.3	254.3	280.7
of which: taxes	*175.5*	*194.1*	*217.7*
social security contributions	*38.8*	*42.9*	*45.7*
Public sector borrowing requirement (PSBR)	46.0	36.1	27.9
PSBR as percentage of GDP	7.25	5.25	4

Source: *Summer Economic Forecast 1994*

central and local government, including central government support for nationalised industries and other public corporations. It is the key public spending aggregate and is used in the medium-term financial strategy (see p. 156), where public spending is set in the context of broader economic policy. As it is usually less affected by institutional differences, it is considered as the most appropriate measure for making international comparisons.

Control Total

The control total is used by the Government for the purposes of planning and control. The Government seeks to achieve its wider medium-term objective—expressed in terms of general government expenditure excluding privatisation proceeds—by controlling spending within this total. The control total includes:

- expenditure for which central government is itself responsible;
- the support it provides or approves for local authority expenditure;
- local authority self-financed expenditure;
- the external financing requirements of public corporations, including nationalised industries; and
- a reserve to cover unanticipated expenditure.

It excludes the items of expenditure most affected by the economic cycle—debt interest and cyclical social security. By excluding

these items, the Government is able to set firm limits on the growth of the control total.

Supply Expenditure

Supply expenditure is financed out of money voted by Parliament in the Supply Estimates (see p. 156). About 87 per cent of all Supply expenditure counts in the control total. The main element of the control total not funded through Supply Estimates is expenditure financed from the National Insurance Fund.

CONTROL OF PUBLIC EXPENDITURE

The Government's objective is that public expenditure (measured by general government expenditure, excluding privatisation proceeds) should grow by less than the economy as a whole over time, while value for money is constantly improved.

In 1992 it announced a new system of public expenditure control aimed at reducing the share of national income taken by public spending. Annual ceilings are set for the growth of the control total, in line with the Government's medium-term objectives. By restricting real growth in the control total to below 1.5 per cent, the Government should ensure that the ratio of general government expenditure to national income will fall over time.

This 'top-down' approach separates decisions on overall public expenditure levels from the allocation between programmes.

Departmental spending decisions are based on allocating available resources within agreed ceilings for aggregate spending; resources are devoted to priority areas, with an emphasis on obtaining maximum value for money. Together with the move to a unified budget (see below), the new framework represents an important reform of fiscal planning procedures.

Fundamental Expenditure Reviews

The Government announced in 1993 that it would conduct in-depth reviews of all public expenditure by each government department. This work goes beyond traditional Public Expenditure Survey arrangements. It examines long-term trends in spending on individual programmes to assess whether these are sustainable. It seeks out areas from which the Government might withdraw or where expenditure should be targeted more effectively. Early results of the first four reviews—into social security, health, education and the Home Office— helped to inform the decisions taken during the 1993 Public Expenditure Survey affecting the departments concerned. The next series of reviews will cover employment and transport programmes, the legal departments, Trade and Industry, Inland Revenue, Customs and Excise, HM Treasury and urban expenditure.

Planning Cycle and the Unified Budget

A new planning cycle has taken effect with the introduction of the unified Budget arrangements in November 1993, under which the Government presents taxation and spending proposals to Parliament at the same time to allow comparison. The Budget now covers both the Government's taxation plans for the coming financial year and its spending plans for the next three years. The proposals are announced to the House of Commons by the Chancellor of the Exchequer in the Budget statement and are published in the *Financial Statement and Budget Report*. This report also contains a review of recent developments in the economy, together with an economic forecast, and sets out the fiscal

and monetary framework within which economic policy operates. This is the medium-term financial strategy.

The Budget statement is followed by the moving of a set of Budget resolutions in which the proposals are embodied. These resolutions are the foundation of the Finance Bill, published in December. The Provisional Collection of Taxes Act 1968 allows the tax authorities to collect taxes provisionally, at the levels provided by the Budget proposals, pending enactment of the Finance Bill.

For two taxes—income tax and corporation tax—annual Ways and Means resolutions followed by Finance Bill clauses are required to maintain their existence, since they are annual rather than permanent taxes. Tax changes can be made at other times, either by specific legislation or by the use of the regulator, which permits limited changes between Budgets in the rates of VAT (value added tax—by up to 25 per cent) and of the main excise duties (by up to 10 per cent).

Estimates

The annual Public Expenditure Survey conducted by HM Treasury provides the basis for the Estimates which each government department submits to the Treasury, giving details of its cash requirements for the coming financial year. After Treasury approval, these Supply Estimates are presented to Parliament. Parliamentary authorisation is required for the major part of the new spending plans for the year ahead announced in the unified Budget. Parliament approves them as part of the annual Appropriation Act. Supplementary Estimates may also be presented to Parliament during the course of the year. Individual reports setting out expenditure plans for government departments are published around February.

If any Supply Estimate is overspent, the Committee of Public Accounts (see p. 158) may investigate before Parliament is asked to approve any Excess Vote to balance the account. In each parliamentary session, up to three 'Estimates days' are available for debates on the Supply Estimates, following scrutiny by select committees of the House of Commons.

Cash Limits

The Government sets cash limits on just over 60 per cent of Supply expenditure and is extending the coverage of limits whenever possible. The imposition of cash limits indicates that the Government intends to avoid extra provision for programmes even in the event of unexpected increases in costs. They cover the major part of grants to local authorities, which are financed out of Supply expenditure. Cash limits also apply to some expenditure not voted in the Estimates.

Running cost limits are imposed on the administrative costs of central government, which are identified separately in the Estimates. Any overspending of cash or running cost limits leads to an investigation into the causes and, where appropriate, a reduction in the limits in the following year.

Those Estimates not subject to cash limits mainly finance demand-led services like income support from the Department of Social Security. In such cases, once policy and rates of payment are determined, expenditure depends on factors beyond the

direct control of government, such as the number of eligible recipients.

Examination and Audit of Public Expenditure

Examination of public expenditure is carried out by select committees of the House of Commons. These study in detail the activities of particular government departments and require the attendance of ministers and officials for cross-examination. Audit of the Government's spending, which follows up the control inherent in parliamentary approval of the Estimates, is exercised through the functions of the Comptroller and Auditor General, the head of the National Audit Office.

Comptroller and Auditor General

The Comptroller and Auditor General, an officer of the House of Commons appointed by the Crown, has two distinct functions. As Comptroller General, he or she is responsible for ensuring that all revenue and

Government Receipts and Expenditure 1993–94

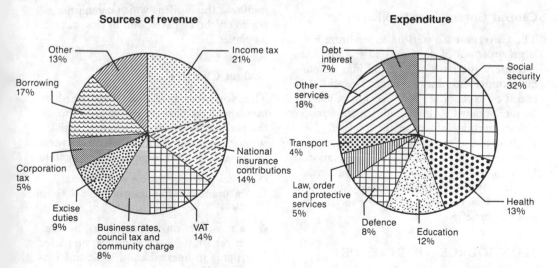

Note: As a result of rounding and omission of minor items, percentages do not add up to 100.

Source: HM Treasury.

other public money payable to the Consolidated Fund and the National Loans Fund (see below) is duly paid and that all payments from these funds are authorised by statute. As Auditor General, he or she must certify the accounts of all government departments and executive agencies and those of a wide range of other public sector bodies; scrutinise the economy, efficiency and effectiveness of their operations; examine revenue accounts and inventories; and report the results of these examinations to Parliament.

Committee of Public Accounts

The Committee of Public Accounts considers the accounts of government departments, executive agencies and other public sector bodies; the Comptroller and Auditor General's reports on them; and on departments' use of their resources. The Committee takes evidence from the heads of departments, agencies and other public sector bodies and submits reports to Parliament. The Government's formal replies to the reports are presented to Parliament in the form of Treasury minutes, and the reports and minutes are usually debated annually in the Commons.

Central Government Funds

The Government's sterling expenditure is largely met out of the Consolidated Fund, an account at the Bank of England into which tax receipts and other revenues are paid. Any excess of expenditure over receipts is met by the National Loans Fund, which is another official sterling account at the Bank of England and is the repository for funds borrowed by the Government. The National Insurance Fund, into which contributions are paid by employers and employed people, is used mainly to pay for social security benefits.

MAIN SOURCES OF REVENUE

The main sources of revenue are:

- taxes on income (including profits), which include personal income tax, corporation tax and petroleum revenue tax;

- taxes on expenditure, which include VAT and customs and excise duties; and

- National Insurance contributions, which give entitlement to a range of benefits.

Other sources are stamp duties; inheritance tax; capital gains tax; and the council tax and business rates.

Taxation Policy

The Government's programme of tax reform has sought to create a climate in which business can thrive and individual initiative is rewarded. Its aims include:

- keeping the overall tax burden as low as possible through firm control over public expenditure;

- reducing marginal tax rates of income and profits to sharpen incentives to work and create wealth;

- maintaining a broad tax base, which helps to keep tax rates low and avoids distorting commercial decisions; and

- shifting the balance of taxation from taxes on income to taxes on expenditure.

The Government also aims to simplify the administration of the tax system and minimise the burdens which compliance places on the taxpayer, and to close tax loopholes.

Budget Changes

The November 1993 Budget contained a number of tax changes designed to broaden the tax base and increase revenue, while supporting government policy objectives on health and the environment. They include:

- a 2.5 per cent tax on most general insurance premiums paid from 1 October 1994;

- a new duty on air passengers, to take effect from November 1994, of £5 for flights to internal and EU destinations and £10 elsewhere;

- increased road fuel duties, which are to be raised by at least 5 per cent in real terms in future Budgets;

- higher tobacco duties, which will grow by at least 3 per cent in real terms in future Budgets; and
- a series of measures, estimated to raise around £2,000 million over three years, to block tax avoidance schemes.

Collection of Taxes and Duties

The Inland Revenue assesses and collects the taxes on income, profits and capital, and stamp duty. HM Customs and Excise collects the most important taxes on expenditure (VAT and most duties). Vehicle excise duty is the responsibility of the Department of Transport. National Insurance contributions are the responsibility of the Department of Social Security, although they are generally collected by the Inland Revenue. The council tax and business rates are collected by local authorities.

Taxes on Income

Income Tax

Taxes on individual incomes are generally progressive in that larger incomes bear a proportionately greater amount of tax. Income tax is imposed for the year of assessment beginning on 6 April. From April 1994 the new lower rate of 20 per cent was widened to the first £3,000 of taxable income. The basic rate of 25 per cent applies to the next £20,700 of taxable income. A rate of 40 per cent is levied on taxable income above £23,700. These rates apply to total income, including earned and investment income.

A number of allowances and reliefs reduce the amount of a person's taxable income compared with gross income. All taxpayers, irrespective of sex or marital status, are entitled to a personal allowance against income from all sources. Married women pay their own tax on the basis of their own income. In addition, there is a married couple's allowance, which may be allocated to either partner or they may receive half each. Wives are entitled to claim half of the allowance as of right. For 1994–95 the values of the main allowances are £3,445 for the

personal allowance and £1,720 for the married couple's allowance. Since April 1994 tax relief for some allowances, including the married couple's allowance, has been restricted to 20 per cent, and this will be reduced to 15 per cent in 1995–96.

Among the most important of the reliefs is that for mortgage interest payments on borrowing for house purchase up to the statutory limit of £30,000. Since April 1994 relief has been restricted to the lower rate of 20 per cent, and this will be limited to 15 per cent in 1995–96. It is usually given 'at source', that is, repayments which the borrower makes to the lender are reduced to take account of tax at the basic rate and the tax refund is then passed directly by the tax authorities to the building society or bank making the loan rather than to the individual taxpayer.

Employees' contributions to their pension schemes also qualify for tax relief within limits laid down by Parliament.

Most wage and salary earners pay their income tax under a Pay-As-You-Earn (PAYE) system whereby tax is deducted and accounted for to the Inland Revenue by the employer, in a way which enables employees to keep as up to date as possible with their tax payments.

The assessment and collection of personal taxation will be simplified from 1996–97. The option of self-assessment will be extended to all who fill in tax returns (about 9 million people). The changes will allow taxpayers to calculate their own liability to tax, and will introduce a uniform set of dates for the payment of income tax and capital gains tax. They will also replace the 'preceding year' basis of income tax for the self-employed by a simpler 'current year' basis; people becoming self-employed from April 1994 will be taxed on the latter basis.

In general, income tax is charged on all income which originates in Britain—although some forms of income are exempt, such as certain social security benefits—and on all income arising abroad of people resident in

Britain. Interest on certain British government securities belonging to people not ordinarily resident in Britain is exempt. Britain has entered into agreements with many countries to provide relief from double taxation; where such agreements are not in force unilateral relief is often allowed. British residents working abroad for the whole year benefit from 100 per cent tax relief.

Corporation Tax

The rates of company tax in Britain are lower than in most other industrialised countries. Companies pay corporation tax on their income and capital gains after deduction of certain allowances and reliefs. A company which distributes profits to its shareholders is required to pay advance corporation tax (ACT) to the Inland Revenue. This ACT can be set against the company's liability to corporation tax, subject to a limit. If resident in Britain, a shareholder receiving dividends from companies resident in Britain is entitled to a tax credit. This satisfies some or all of the shareholder's liability to income tax on his or her dividend income, or is paid to shareholders not liable to tax.

The main rate of corporation tax is 33 per cent, with a reduced rate of 25 per cent for small companies (those with profits below £300,000 in a year). Marginal relief, so that a company's overall rate is between the main rate and the small companies' rate, is allowed for companies with profits between £300,000 and £1.5 million. Expenditure on plant and machinery, on scientific research and on industrial and agricultural buildings qualifies for annual allowances.

Petroleum Revenue Tax

Petroleum revenue tax (PRT), deductible in computing profits for corporation tax, is charged on profits from the production—as opposed, for example, to the refining—of oil and gas in Britain and on its Continental Shelf under licence from the Department of Trade and Industry. Each licensee of an oilfield is charged on the profits from that field after deduction of certain allowances and reliefs. New fields given consent for

development on or after 16 March 1993 are not liable to PRT. The PRT rate for existing fields was reduced from 75 to 50 per cent from 1 July 1993.

Inheritance Tax

Inheritance tax is charged on the value of estates at the time of death and is also immediately chargeable on certain lifetime transfers. The majority of business assets are now exempt from inheritance tax, so that most family businesses can be passed on without a tax charge. Tax is charged at a single rate of 40 per cent above the threshold for inheritance tax of £150,000.

There are several important exemptions. Generally, transfers between spouses are exempt, and gifts and bequests to British charities, major political parties and heritage bodies are also normally exempt.

Capital Gains Tax

Capital gains realised on the disposal of assets are liable to capital gains tax or, in the case of companies, to corporation tax. For 1994–95, individuals are exempt from tax in respect of total net gains of up to £5,800 in any one year and most trusts on gains of up to £2,900. Gains are treated as the taxpayer's top slice of income, and are therefore charged at the individual's highest income tax rate or the company's corporation tax rate.

Only gains arising since March 1982 are subject to tax and the effects of inflation are allowed for when measuring gains. Some assets, including the principal private residence, are normally exempt. Gains on government securities and certain corporate bonds are exempt from the tax, as are gains on shares owned under Personal Equity Plans (see p. 150). This last exemption is designed to encourage wider share ownership.

Taxes on Expenditure

Value Added Tax

VAT is a broadly based expenditure tax, chargeable at 17.5 per cent. It is collected at each stage in the production and distribution of goods and services by taxable persons. The final tax is borne by the consumer. When a taxable person purchases taxable goods or services, the supplier charges VAT—the taxable person's input tax. When the taxable person supplies goods or services, the customers are then in turn charged VAT, which is the taxable person's output tax. The difference between the output tax and the input tax is paid to, or repaid by, Customs and Excise.

The annual level of turnover above which traders must register for VAT was raised from £37,600 to £45,000 in December 1993. Certain goods and services are relieved from VAT, either by being charged at a zero rate or by being exempt:

- Under zero rating, a taxable person does not charge tax to a customer but reclaims any input tax paid to suppliers. Among the main categories where zero-rating applies are goods exported to other countries, and goods shipped as stores on ships and aircraft; most food; water and sewerage; domestic and international passenger transport; books, newspapers and periodicals; construction of new residential buildings; young children's clothing and footwear; drugs and medicines supplied on prescription; specified aids for handicapped people; and certain supplies by or to charities.

- For exempt goods or services, a taxable person does not charge any output tax but is not entitled to reclaim the input tax. The main categories where exemption applies are many supplies of land and buildings; insurance; postal services; betting; gaming (subject to certain important exceptions); lotteries; finance; much education and training; and health and welfare.

VAT was introduced on domestic fuel and power at 8 per cent from April 1994 and will be charged at the full standard rate from April 1995. As well as being a revenue-raising measure, this extension of VAT is expected to encourage energy conservation and help to contribute to Britain's commitments on global warming.

Customs Duties

Customs duties are chargeable on goods from outside the EU in accordance with its Common Customs Tariff. The introduction of the single European market on 1 January 1993 means that goods can move freely across internal frontiers between different member states, without making customs entries at importation or stopping for routine fiscal checks. For commercial consignments, excise duty and VAT are charged in the member state of destination, at the rate in force in that state.

Excise Duties

Hydrocarbon oils used as road fuel bear higher rates of duty than those used for other purposes, although the rate of duty on unleaded petrol is lower than that on leaded. Kerosene, most lubricating oils and other oils used for certain industrial processes are free of duty. There are duties on spirits, beer, wine, made-wine (wine with added constituents, such as fruit juice), cider and perry, based on alcoholic strength and volume. Spirits used for scientific, medical, research and industrial processes are generally free of duty. Cigarette duty is charged partly as a cash amount per cigarette and partly as a percentage of retail price. Duty on other tobacco products is based on weight.

Duties are charged on off-course betting, pool betting, gaming in casinos, bingo and gaming machines. Rates vary with the particular form of gambling. Duty is charged either as a percentage of gross or net stakes or, in the case of gaming machines, as a fixed amount per machine according to the cost of playing it and its prize level. A 12 per cent duty on gross stakes will be levied on the new National Lottery due to start in November 1994 (see p. 493); there will be no tax on winnings.

Vehicle excise duty (VED) on a privately-owned motor car, light van or taxi with fewer than nine seats is £130 a year; for motor cycles it is £15, £35 or £55 a year, according to engine capacity. The duty on goods vehicles is levied on the basis of gross weight and, if over 12 tonnes, according to the number of axles; the duty is designed to ensure that such vehicles at least cover their share of the full costs of road use through the tax paid (VED and fuel duty). Duty on taxis and buses varies according to seating capacity.

Stamp Duty

Certain kinds of transfer are subject to stamp duty. These include purchases of houses, at 1 per cent of the total price if this exceeds £60,000, and instruments such as declarations of trust. Transfers by gift and transfers to charities are exempt.

Taxpayer's Charter

The Taxpayer's Charter, relaunched in 1991, was one of the first separate charters issued following the publication of the Citizen's Charter (see p. 67). It sets out the standard of service that people can expect from the Inland Revenue and Customs and Excise. Both departments should be fair, helpful, courteous, efficient and accountable, and keep taxpayers' financial affairs private.

Other Revenue

National Insurance Contributions

There are five classes of National Insurance contribution:

- Class 1—paid by employees and their employers;
- Class 1A—paid by employers on the cash equivalent of the benefit of cars and fuel provided to their employees for private use;
- Class 2—paid by the self-employed;
- Class 3—paid voluntarily for pension purposes; and
- Class 4—paid by self-employed people on their taxable profits between £6,490 and £22,360 a year (in addition to their Class 2 contribution).

Details of the rates of contribution are given in Chapter 25, Social Security, on p. 399.

Local Authority Revenue

Local authorities in Great Britain have four sources of income: grants from central government (which finances about 85 per cent of spending); non-domestic rates; council tax; and fees and charges.

Non-domestic rates are a tax on the occupiers of non-domestic property. The rateable value of property is assessed by reference to annual rents and reviewed every five years. In England and Wales the non-domestic rate is set nationally by central government and collected by local authorities. It is paid into a national pool and redistributed to local authorities in proportion to their population. In Scotland non-domestic rates are levied by local authorities. In Northern Ireland rates are not payable on industrial premises or on commercial premises in enterprise zones. Certain other properties in Northern Ireland, such as freight transport and recreational premises, are partially derated.

Domestic property is generally subject to the council tax, which replaced the community charge in April 1993. Each dwelling is allocated to one of eight valuation bands, based on its capital value in April 1991. Capital values are based on the amount each dwelling might have sold for on the open market, subject to certain assumptions, if it had been sold on 1 April 1991. Discounts are available for dwellings with fewer than two resident adults. A council tax payer on a low income may receive a rebate of up to 100 per cent of his or her tax bill. A transitional relief scheme aims to limit increases arising from the switch from the community charge to the council tax to a fixed amount for each valuation band.

In Northern Ireland, rates—local domestic property taxes based on the value of the property—are collected by local authorities.

PUBLIC SECTOR FINANCIAL OPERATIONS

The Government funds its borrowing requirement by selling debt to the private sector. The major debt instrument is known as gilt-edged stock as there is no risk of default. Gilt-edged stock is marketable and is widely traded. Pension funds and life insurance companies have the largest holdings. The Government publishes an annual remit, setting out how the Bank of England will sell 'gilts' on its behalf. Issues are mostly by auction (broadly monthly) or *ad hoc* 'tap' sales. Gilts include 'conventionals', which pay fixed rates of interest and redemption sums; index-linked stocks, on which principal and interest are linked to the movement in the Retail Prices Index; and floating-rate gilts, with payments linked to short-term interest rates.

An important additional source of government finance is the range of National Savings products (see p. 217), which are non-marketable and designed to attract personal savings.

Sterling Treasury bills are sold at a weekly tender; the majority have a maturity of three months. These are used to manage the money markets, rather than to meet the Government's borrowing needs. The Government has also issued bills denominated and payable in European Currency Units (ECUs) since 1988 and longer-dated ECU notes since 1992. The proceeds have been added to the official foreign exchange reserves rather than being used to finance public expenditure.

The bulk of public corporations' borrowing is funded by central government, although their temporary borrowing needs are met largely from the market, usually under Treasury guarantee. That part of local authority borrowing met by central government is supplied by authorisation of Parliament through the Public Works Loan Board from the National Loans Fund. The Board remains an independent body even though it is merged for administrative purposes with the former National Debt Office, forming the National Investment and Loans Office. Local authorities may also borrow directly from the market, both short-term and long-term, through a range of instruments. Some public corporations and local authorities borrow on occasion, under special statutory power and with Treasury consent, in foreign currencies.

Public Sector Debt

Public sector borrowing, or debt repayment, each year represents an addition to, or subtraction from, the net debt of the public sector. This debt is the consolidated debt of the public sector less its holdings of liquid assets. Public sector debt held outside the public sector amounted to £249,600 million at the end of March 1993. This represented 40 per cent of GDP in 1992–93, compared with 50 per cent in 1979.

Further Reading

Financial Statement and Budget Report, annual report, HMSO.
United Kingdom National Accounts, annual report, HMSO.

12 Overseas Trade

Overseas trade has been of vital importance to the British economy for hundreds of years. Although small in area and accounting for only about 1 per cent of the world's population, Britain is the fifth largest trading nation in the world. As a member of the European Union (EU), it is part of the world's largest established trading group, which grew even bigger when five other Western European countries joined with the EU in January 1994 to create the European Economic Area (EEA).

Britain exports more per head than the United States (US) and Japan; its overseas sales of goods and services are equivalent to about a quarter of its gross domestic product (GDP). Invisible earnings of British companies place Britain in the top three countries in the international league table of overseas invisibles earners. Britain is the world's second biggest overseas investor and the leading destination for inward investment into the EU.

VISIBLE TRADE

In 1993 Britain's exports of goods were valued at about £121,400 million and its imports of goods at £134,600 million on a balance-of-payments basis (see Table 12.1). Between 1992 and 1993 the volume of exports rose by 3 per cent and their value by 13 per cent. Over the same period imports grew by 4 per cent by volume and 12 per cent in terms of value.

Commodity Composition

Britain has traditionally been an exporter of manufactured goods and an importer of food and basic materials. In 1970 manufactures accounted for 85 per cent of its exports; this fell to around 67 per cent by the mid-1980s as North Sea oil exports increased their share. The proportion of manufactures in exports has since risen, to 82 per cent in 1993. Britain has not, however, had a surplus on manufactures since 1982. Machinery and transport equipment account for about 40 per cent of exports and a similar proportion of imports. Aerospace, chemicals and electronics have become increasingly significant export sectors, while textiles have declined in relative importance.

Since the mid-1970s North Sea oil has made a substantial contribution to Britain's overseas trade both in terms of exports and import substitution. In 1993 exports of fuels in volume terms were about five times their

Table 12.1: Overseas Trade 1991–93

	1991	1992	1993
Value (£ million)[a]			
EXPORTS			
Goods	103,413	107,343	121,414
of which:			
Oil	6,757	6,652	7,981
Other goods	96,656	100,691	113,433
Services	30,821	33,134	36,585
Goods and services	**134,234**	**140,477**	**157,999**
IMPORTS			
Goods	113,697	120,447	134,623
of which:			
Oil	5,549	5,104	5,519
Other goods	108,148	115,343	129,104
Services	27,113	29,045	31,643
Goods and services	**140,810**	**149,492**	**166,266**
Volume indices (1990 = 100)			
EXPORTS			
Goods			
All goods	101.2	103.7	106.9
Non-oil goods	101.2	103.5	105.8
Services	93.1	98.1	100.5
Goods and services	**99.3**	**102.4**	**105.4**
IMPORTS			
Goods			
All goods	94.7	100.9	104.6
Non-oil goods	94.3	101.1	104.6
Services	94.8	99.1	98.2
Goods and services	**94.7**	**100.6**	**103.5**
Unit value indices (1990 = 100)			
EXPORTS			
All goods	101.4	103.5	114.8
Non-oil goods	102.3	105.0	116.9
IMPORTS			
All goods	101.2	102.1	110.5
Non-oil goods	101.7	102.9	111.8
TERMS OF TRADE[b]			
All goods	100.2	101.4	103.9
Non-oil goods	100.6	102.0	104.6

Source: *United Kingdom Balance of Payments 1994 Edition*
[a]Balance-of-payments basis.
[b]Export unit value index as a percentage of import unit value index.

Table 12.2: Sector Analysis of Visible Trade 1993[a]

£ million

	Exports	Imports	Visible balance
Food, beverages and tobacco	9,136	13,314	–4,178
Basic materials	2,267	5,046	–2,779
Oil	7,981	5,519	2,462
Other mineral fuels and lubricants	448	1,423	–975
Semi-manufactured goods	35,450	34,558	892
Finished manufactured goods	64,464	73,356	–8,892
Commodities and transactions not classified according to kind	1,668	1,407	261
Total	**121,414**	**134,623**	**–13,209**

Source: *United Kingdom Balance of Payments 1994 Edition*
[a]Balance-of-payments basis.

1975 level; imports were around three-quarters of the 1975 figure. The share of fuels in exports rose from 4 to 22 per cent in the mid-1980s, falling back to 7 per cent in 1993. The import share decreased from 18 per cent in 1975 to 13 per cent in the mid-1980s and to 5 per cent in 1993. North Sea oil and gas production has now passed its peak of the mid-1980s, when exports of fuels accounted for over 20 per cent of total exports. In 1993 the surplus on trade in oil amounted to a little under £2,500 million.

Imported manufactures have taken a greater share of the domestic market in

Geographical Distribution of Trade 1993

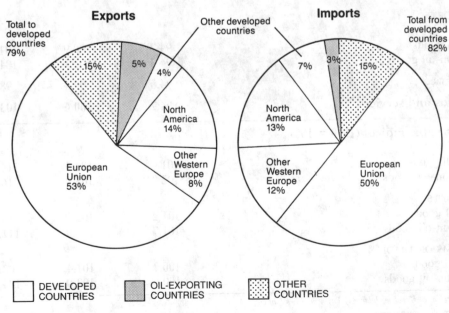

Differences between totals and the sums of their component parts are due to rounding.
Source: *United Kingdom Balance of Payments.*

166

Table 12.3: Commodity Composition of Visible Trade 1993[a]

£ million

	Exports	Imports
Food and live animals	5,661	11,574
Beverages and tobacco	3,270	2,117
Crude materials	2,098	4,953
of which: Wood, lumber and cork	22	1,108
Pulp and waste paper	24	541
Textile fibres	495	481
Metal ores	611	1,165
Fuels	8,228	7,303
Petroleum and petroleum products	7,789	5,749
Coal, gas and electricity	435	1,553
Animal and vegetable oils and fats	118	477
Chemicals	17,297	12,911
of which: Organic chemicals	4,370	3,104
Inorganic chemicals	1,216	985
Plastics	2,461	3,244
Manufactures classified chiefly by material	17,331	21,733
of which: Wood and cork manufactures	128	431
Paper and paperboard manufactures	1,830	3,721
Textile manufactures	2,585	4,000
Iron and steel	3,135	2,540
Non-ferrous metals	1,913	2,908
Metal manufactures	2,278	2,560
Machinery and transport equipment	48,340	53,291
Mechanical machinery	15,025	11,822
Electrical machinery	20,672	23,839
Road vehicles	8,303	14,387
Other transport equipment	4,344	3,235
Miscellaneous manufactures	14,812	20,124
of which: Clothing and footwear	2,698	5,961
Scientific and photographic	4,756	4,682
Other commodities and transactions	1,594	1,257
Total	**118,742**	**135,740**

Source: *Monthly Digest of Statistics*

[a]On an overseas-trade-statistics basis, seasonally adjusted. This differs from a balance-of-payments basis in that, for imports, it includes the cost of insurance and freight, and, for both exports and imports, includes returned goods.

recent decades. The share of finished manufactures in total imports rose from 25 per cent in 1970 to 54 per cent in 1993, while the share of basic materials fell from 15 to 4 per cent between 1970 and 1993. The percentage of food, beverages and tobacco in total imports has been dropping since the 1950s, reaching 10 per cent in 1993, as a result both of the increasing extent to which

food demand has been met from domestic agriculture and the decline in the proportion of total expenditure on food.

Geographical Distribution

Britain's overseas trade is mainly—and increasingly—with other developed countries. In 1970 these accounted for 73 per cent of

Table 12.4: Britain's Main Markets and Suppliers 1993[a]

	Value (£ million)	Share (per cent)
Main markets		
Germany	15,979	13.2
United States	15,351	12.7
France	12,076	10.0
Netherlands	8,061	6.7
Belgium/Luxembourg	7,100	5.9
Irish Republic	6,324	5.2
Italy	6,052	5.0
Spain	4,354	3.6
Sweden	2,883	2.4
Japan	2,656	2.2
Main suppliers		
Germany	20,163	14.6
United States	16,328	11.8
France	13,604	9.8
Netherlands	9,098	6.6
Japan	8,517	6.2
Belgium/Luxembourg	6,770	4.9
Italy	6,752	4.9
Irish Republic	5,525	4.0
Switzerland	4,738	3.4
Norway	4,159	3.0

Source: *Monthly Digest of Statistics.*
[a] On an overseas-trade-statistics basis, seasonally adjusted.

exports and a similar percentage of imports; by 1993 the shares were 80 and 82 per cent respectively. The proportion of Britain's trade with non-oil developing nations has been broadly constant over the last 20 years: in 1993 they accounted for 15 per cent of its trade.

In 1972, the year before Britain joined the European Community, around a third of Britain's trade was with the other 11 countries which made up the European Union in 1994. The proportion rose to around one-half in 1993 (see p. 166). Western Europe as a whole took three-fifths of British exports in 1993.

EU countries accounted for seven of Britain's top 10 export markets and six of the 10 leading suppliers of goods to Britain in 1993 (see Table 12.4). In 1990 Germany overtook the US to become Britain's biggest overseas market; Germany is also Britain's largest single supplier. In 1993 it took 13 per cent of Britain's exports and supplied 15 per cent of its imports.

There have been a number of other changes in the pattern of Britain's overseas trade in recent years. The growth in wealth of the oil-exporting countries during the 1970s led to a sharp increase in their imports from all sources, and by the early 1980s they were taking about 12 per cent of Britain's exports. However, by 1993 their share of British exports and imports had fallen to 5 and 3 per cent respectively.

Exports to Japan, which is presently Britain's tenth largest export market, rose by 19 per cent in 1993. Japan has steadily increased its share of Britain's imports and now accounts for around 6 per cent. In 1993 there was also a sizeable increase— around 30 per cent—in Britain's exports to other expanding markets in the Asia-Pacific Rim. Hong Kong, Malaysia, Singapore, Korea, Taiwan and Thailand, together with the People's Republic of China and the Philippines, all showed strong growth in exports from Britain in 1993.

INVISIBLE TRANSACTIONS

Transactions in invisible trade fall into three main groups:

- internationally tradeable services;
- investment income on external assets; and
- non-commercial transfers.

Britain accounts for 6 per cent of the world's exports of services and 14 per cent of its investment income. Its earnings from invisible trade in 1993 were £116,000 million, with earnings from services alone of £36,600 million.

Services range from banking, insurance and stockbroking, tourism, and shipping and aviation to specialist services such as engineering consultancy, computer programming and training. Financial services make a major contribution to overseas earnings; net overseas receipts were £15,600 million in 1993. Britain's trade in services has been in surplus for about 200 years, excluding war periods.

Earnings on external assets and liabilities have rarely been in deficit; transfers, however, have almost always been in deficit. For invisible trade as a whole, the deficit of general government is more than offset by the substantial surplus of the private sector (including public corporations), resulting in an overall surplus. General government transactions are relatively unimportant in either the services or the investment income accounts but they form the greater part of the transfers account. In 1993 the private sector had a surplus of £11,500 million on invisible trade while government had a deficit of £8,600 million.

Earnings from private sector services rose in value by 10 per cent in 1993 to £36,200 million; debits, at £29,300 million, were 11 per cent higher than a year previously. The surplus on private sector investment income was £4,900 million in 1993. The deficit on private sector transfers was £270 million, while that on government transfers was £4,800 million.

COMMERCIAL POLICY

Britain is an active member of the European Union. It remains committed to the open multilateral trading system and to the further liberalisation of world trade. To this end it has taken a leading part in the activities of such organisations as the General Agreement on Tariffs and Trade (GATT), the International Monetary Fund (IMF) and the Organisation for Economic Co-operation and Development (OECD).

General Agreement on Tariffs and Trade

GATT has provided a framework of rules for the conduct of international trade since 1947.

Table 12.5: Britain's Invisible Transactions 1993

		Credits	Debits	£ million Balance
Private sector and public corporations		110,828	99,328	**11,500**
Services		36,151	29,311	6,840
of which:	Sea transport	3,843	4,301	−458
	Civil aviation	5,075	5,526	−451
	Travel	8,951	12,257	3,306
	Financial and other services	18,282	7,227	11,055
Investment income		72,627	67,697	4,930
Transfers		2,050	2,320	−270
General government		5,172	13,774	**−8,602**
Services		434	2,332	−1,898
Investment income		1,413	3,281	−1,868
Transfers		3,325	8,161	−4,836
Total invisible transactions		**116,000**	**113,102**	**2,898**

Source: *United Kingdom Balance of Payments 1994 Edition.*

Around 120 countries already belong and more are expected to join. The European Commission acts on behalf of Britain and its EU partners in GATT negotiations.

> The eighth and most recent GATT round—the Uruguay round—was launched in 1986 and successfully concluded in December 1993. It was the largest-ever international trade negotiation and will reduce tariffs on goods and liberalise trade in services and agriculture. Creation of a World Trade Organisation will put the new system on a permanent institutional footing. An OECD/World Bank report has estimated that world annual output will be boosted by more than US$270,000 million after ten years as a result of the agreement.

The main features of the new agreement, which is likely to be brought into force in late 1995, are as follows:

- There will be overall tariff reductions across all countries of about 40 per cent (tariff reductions by the EU will average over 33 per cent) and member states have undertaken not to raise tariffs again on 95 per cent of world trade.
- With the formation of the General Agreement on Trade in Services, services are to be brought within the framework of GATT multilateral trade rules. Any remaining restrictions on trade in services will be made transparent and non-discriminatory.
- Agriculture will come under the rules of multilateral trade for the first time; there will be a 36 per cent reduction in tariffs as well as substantial cuts in subsidies.
- Agreed multilateral rules will govern trade-related intellectual property rights, providing protection for holders of patents, copyrights and designs.
- Trade in textiles, where restrictions on imports have been allowed under the Multi-Fibre Arrangement (MFA—see p. 171) to balance the interests of exporters and importers, will be reintegrated into GATT over ten years.

Single European Market

The single European market 'opened for business' on 1 January 1993, with the essential legislation in place for the free movement of goods, services, people and capital within the EU. Member states are now concentrating on ensuring that the market operates efficiently in practice and completing work in energy and telecommunications liberalisation. Among the changes from January 1993 were the following:

- the ending of routine customs clearance of commercial goods at national frontiers;
- the introduction of the right to trade financial services throughout the EU on the basis of a single home authorisation 'passport' (see p. 116); and
- deregulation of airlines, with national flag carriers losing preferential treatment.

> On 1 January 1994 the EU implemented an agreement with five members of the European Free Trade Association (EFTA)—Austria, Finland, Iceland, Norway and Sweden—on the creation of the European Economic Area. The EEA forms a free trade area with 370 million consumers, and the free movement of goods, services and capital.

Austria, Finland, Norway and Sweden have successfully applied to join the Union; accession is due on 1 January 1995.

Other Agreements

The EU has association and co-operation agreements with virtually all non-member countries with a Mediterranean coastline, plus Jordan; these give preferential access to EU markets. Non-preferential co-operation agreements have also been made with countries in South Asia and Latin America, as well as with the People's Republic of China, the Association of South East Asian Nations, the Andean Pact and the Central American states. Trade relations with the developing countries of Africa, the Caribbean and the Pacific are governed by the Lomé

Convention, which gives these countries tariff-free access, subject to certain safeguards, to the EU for industrial goods and most agricultural products.

Tariff preference is also given to developing countries under the Generalised System of Preferences. This applies to most industrial products and to agricultural produce and textiles. The scheme concentrates benefits on poorer producers and countries.

Association agreements are in place between the EU and Poland, Hungary, the Czech Republic, Slovakia, Bulgaria and Romania. They are designed to facilitate closer political and economic ties and the eventual creation of a free trade zone with a view to those countries becoming full members of the EU. Trade and economic co-operation agreements have also been signed with Albania, Slovenia and the Baltic states. Partnership and co-operation agreements have been concluded with Russia, Ukraine and Kazakhstan.

CONTROLS ON TRADE

With the completion of the single European market, all routine border controls and requirements for accompanying Customs documents were removed for trade between the members of the EU. This has substantially cut travel times and costs; for example, journey times from Britain to Italy have been reduced by up to 24 hours.

Import Controls

Individual national quantitative restrictions are inconsistent with the single European market and following the removal of internal frontiers they will be largely abolished. A system of Union-wide quotas is under discussion between the European Commission and member states. Quantitative restrictions on textiles stem from the MFA, under which there is a series of bilateral agreements. A small number of quantitative restrictions are also maintained against non-GATT countries.

Imports of certain other goods are restricted in order to protect human, animal or plant life or health. These include firearms and ammunition; nuclear materials; certain

drugs; explosives (including fireworks); endangered wildlife and certain agricultural, horticultural and food products.

Export Controls

The great majority of British exports are not subject to any government control or direction except for presentation and declaration to HM Customs and Excise to enable them to exercise necessary controls and collect overseas trade statistics. Controls govern the export of goods associated with biological, chemical and nuclear weapons and missiles. There are also controls on the export of firearms, military equipment and of dual-use industrial goods—those that can be used for both civil and military purposes.

Other controls include those for health certification purposes on certain animals, meat and fish exported to another EU member; on endangered animal and plant species; and on antiques and works of art, including photographic material, documents, manuscripts and archaeological items.

The Co-ordinating Committee for Multilateral Export Controls (COCOM), of which Britain is a member, has already agreed on extensive relaxation in East–West controls because of the political changes in Eastern Europe. The break-up of the former Soviet Union is expected to reduce these controls still further.

Britain is a member of the Australia Group and of the Missile Technology Control Regime, international bodies which aim to prevent the spread of weapons of mass destruction. Britain has issued a list of countries of concern, along with lists of controlled goods and technologies used in the production, handling or storage of nuclear, chemical and biological weapons and missile technology which may not be exported. Also listed are controlled dual-use items.

GOVERNMENT SERVICES

The Government assists exporters by creating conditions favourable to the export trade and by providing practical help, advice and financial support. This includes a wide range of services and assistance to meet the requirements of exporters, especially small and medium-sized enterprises.

Export Promotion Services

Overseas Trade Services (OTS) comprises the leading government departments engaged in export promotion, including the Department of Trade and Industry (DTI), the Foreign & Commonwealth Office (FCO), the Industry Department of the Welsh Office, Scottish Trade International and the Industrial Development Board of Northern Ireland. There are around 2,000 staff worldwide, based at the DTI in London, in 11 regional offices around Britain and at 201 diplomatic posts overseas. In England the development of local Business Links (see p. 197) will make OTS more accessible to potential users. In a White Paper on business competitiveness (see p. 194), issued in May 1994, the Government announced that it would increase the number of Business Links and of private-sector export consultants (see below).

OTS gathers and disseminates export intelligence, helps in researching potential markets and at trade fairs, and supports firms participating in trade missions. In 1993–94 around £186 million was spent on support for exporters.

A major reorganisation of the DTI's export services was announced in 1993. Its main elements included:

- devising export strategies for Britain's top 80 export markets;

- separating export promotion from trade policy work;

- setting up two export promotion divisions—one dealing with North and South America and Western and Eastern Europe, including the former Soviet Union, and another covering the Asia Pacific region, including Japan and Australasia, South Asia, the Middle East and Africa.

The new export promotion divisions work closely with 100 'export promoters' seconded from private industry, as well as with the British Overseas Trade Board (BOTB), the BOTB's Area Advisory Groups and with FCO posts abroad. The BOTB's aims are to:

- help guide the Government's export promotion efforts, including the provision of export services; and
- provide advice on policy issues affecting international trade and exports.

The BOTB's Area Advisory Groups, which are made up of business people with expert knowledge of trade with particular world markets, provide advice on the world's main trading areas. The Overseas Projects Board advises on major project business overseas and the Small Firms Committee on matters relating to small businesses. Nearly 200 businessmen and women are involved in the Board's work.

OTS pays special attention to the promotion of exports to its top priority areas in Western Europe, North America, and Japan and the Asia Pacific Rim. These three areas contain the world's largest and richest markets, and account for around four-fifths of Britain's exports. Emerging markets in other areas are also being targeted.

British Invisibles

British Invisibles is an organisation which promotes the international activities of financial institutions and business services. Its role is to suggest and, where possible, implement measures for boosting invisible earnings in Britain and abroad. It also seeks to increase awareness of London as an international financial centre and of the role of the service sector in the British economy.

ECGD

ECGD (Export Credits Guarantee Department) is a government department, responsible to the President of the Board of Trade. It helps exporters overcome many of the risks of selling and investing overseas. ECGD supports projects and capital goods and services exported on medium- and long-term credit by:

- insuring exporters and financing banks against the risk of non-payment by overseas buyers;
- giving interest rate support to banks, allowing exporters access to funds at fixed, often favourable, rates of interest; and

- providing reinsurance to private-sector credit insurance covering exports sold on short-term credit.

In order to encourage investment in less developed countries, especially in Eastern Europe, ECGD also insures against the main political risks, such as war, expropriation and restrictions on repatriation of profits.

Particular attention is being paid to increasing cover for rapidly-growing exports to countries like Hong Kong, China, Indonesia, South Africa and Malaysia.

ECGD's Insurance Services Group, dealing with exports sold on credit terms of less than two years, was sold to the private sector in 1991.

BALANCE OF PAYMENTS

The balance-of-payments statistics record transactions between residents of Britain and non-residents. The transactions are classified into two groups: current account, and transactions in Britain's external assets and liabilities, sometimes known as the capital account. The current account records trade in goods (visible trade) and services, including finance, tourism and transport, transactions in investment income, and transfers (invisible trade). Capital transactions include inward and outward investment, overseas transactions by banks in Britain, external borrowing and lending by residents in Britain and drawings on and accruals to the official reserves.

Britain has no exchange controls; residents are free to acquire foreign currency for any purpose, including direct and portfolio investment overseas. There are also no controls on the lending of sterling abroad and non-residents may freely acquire sterling for any purpose. Gold may be freely bought and sold. Exchange controls were abolished in 1979, and Britain meets in full its obligations on capital movements under an OECD code and under EC directives.

The current account has been in deficit since 1986. Since 1983 Britain has had a deficit on visible trade; however, it has traditionally run a surplus on trade in invisibles. At £13,200 million in 1993, the deficit on visible trade was virtually the same as in the previous year. The invisibles surplus fell from £3,300 million to £2,900 million. The surplus on services increased by £800 million; that on investment income fell by £1,200 million; and the deficit on transfers was, at £5,100 million, almost exactly the same as in 1992.

Inward and Outward Investment

The Government welcomes both outward and inward investment.[1] Outward investment helps to develop markets for

---

[1] A distinction needs to be made between capital flows and capital holdings. Flows comprise transactions resulting in a change of ownership of financial assets and liabilities between British residents and non-residents, while holdings are measured by the total values of British external assets and liabilities at the end of the year. Income earned on external assets and liabilities is dealt with in the section on invisibles.

Table 12.6: Britain's Balance of Payments 1989–93

£ million

	1989	1990	1991	1992	1993
Current account					
Visible trade balance	24,683	−18,809	−10,284	−13,104	−13,209
Invisible transactions balance	2,171	−226	2,108	3,273	2,898
Current balance	−22,512	−19,035	−8,176	−9,831	−10,311
Transactions in assets and liabilities					
British external assets	−90,583	−80,680	−20,717	−82,219	−158,450
British external liabilities	110,219	98,873	29,336	85,588	166,763
Balancing item	2,876	842	−443	6,462	1,998

Source: *United Kingdom Balance of Payments 1994 Edition.*
Note: Differences between totals and the sums of their component parts are due to rounding.

British exports while providing earnings in the form of investment income. Inward investment is promoted by DTI's Invest in Britain Bureau (IBB—see p. 202) as a means of introducing new technology, products, management styles and attitudes; creating or safeguarding employment; and increasing exports or substituting imports. In recent years Japanese investment in the automotive industries has helped transform these industries in Britain.

The IBB's annual report for 1993–94 shows 404 inward investment decisions in that year, projects that will create or safeguard 96,000 jobs. Inward investment is playing an increasingly important role in Britain's economy, with overseas firms providing 17 per cent of all manufacturing jobs, 23 per cent of net output and 33 per cent of net capital expenditure. At present Britain has around 40 per cent of US and Japanese investment in the EU.

Inward direct investment (investment in branches, subsidiaries and associated companies) in 1993 was £9,500 million, little changed from 1992. In 1993 direct investment overseas by British residents was £17,300 million, compared with £11,100 million in 1992. Outward portfolio investment was £85,600 million (£27,400 million in 1992). The inflow of portfolio investment into Britain amounted to £40,000 million.

External Assets and Liabilities

At the end of 1993 Britain's identified external assets exceeded identified external liabilities by £20,300 million, compared with £10,600 million a year earlier. Net assets of the private sector and public corporations amounted to £40,800 million and net liabilities of general government to £20,500 million.

Direct investment assets overseas of British residents totalled £172,500 million at the end of 1993 and portfolio investment £423,200 million. At the end of 1992, 81 per cent of direct investment was in developed countries, with 37 per cent in the United States and 26 per cent in the EU. Direct investment in Britain by overseas residents amounted to £130,900 million at the end of 1993 and portfolio investment to £256,600 million. At the end of 1992, investment from developed countries accounted for 97 per cent of overseas direct investment in Britain: 40 per cent originated in the United States and 31 per cent in the EU.

Further Reading

Overseas Trade. Aspects of Britain series, HMSO, 1994.
United Kingdom Balance of Payments 1994 Edition. Central Statistical Office, HMSO.

13 Employment

Britain has a higher proportion of the adult population in work—70 per cent—than any other large European country. The labour market has changed considerably in recent years, with a growing proportion working in services. Nearly three-quarters of employees now work in the service sector, compared with around one-fifth in manufacturing. Other major changes have been the growing proportion of women in the workforce and the rise in part-time employment. Industrial relations have been transformed, and the number of stoppages in 1993 was the lowest on record.

PATTERNS OF EMPLOYMENT

The total workforce in 1994 was around 28 million. The workforce in employment in June 1994 totalled 25.2 million (see Table 13.1), of whom 21.4 million (10.8 million men and 10.6 million women) were classed as employees in employment.

In the early 1990s employment fell as a result of the recession. With the economic recovery (see p. 145), this decline ceased in 1993 and, according to the Labour Force Survey, there was an increase of 80,000 in the number of people in employment in Great Britain on a seasonally adjusted basis between winter 1993–94 and spring 1994.

Women account for a growing proportion of the workforce in employment and in June 1994 they represented 49.6 per cent of employees in employment. The proportion of women in work in Britain is well above the

Table 13.1: Workforce in Employment in Britain

				Thousands, seasonally adjusted, June	
	1984	1989	1992	1993	1994
Employees in employment	21,229	22,670	21,851	21,493	21,397
Self-employed	2,669	3,486	3,196	3,166	3,266
HM Forces	326	308	290	271	250
Work-related government training programmes	175	462	325	311	319
Workforce in employment	24,399	26,926	25,661	25,241	25,232

Source: *Employment Gazette*

Table 13.2: Employees by Main Sector in Britain (at June)

	1989	1992	1993	1994
Thousands				
Service industries	15,610	15,735	15,656	15,699
Manufacturing industries	5,208	4,521	4,369	4,330
Energy and water supply	465	403	354	315
Other industries	1,388	1,191	1,113	1,053
Per cent of employees				
Service industries	68.9	72.0	72.8	73.4
Manufacturing industries	23.0	20.7	20.3	20.2
Energy and water supply	2.1	1.8	1.6	1.5
Other industries	6.1	5.5	5.2	4.9

Source: Department of Employment.

Note: From September 1991 certain local authority employees were reclassified from services to other industries. Accordingly, the figures for 1992, 1993 and 1994 are not strictly comparable with those for 1989.

EU average, being exceeded only by Denmark. Many employers have developed policies to help women to return to the labour market. The Government is encouraging voluntary action by employers to increase the employment opportunities for women. It has joined the 'Opportunity 2000' campaign and in 1994 launched a new regional initiative in England, 'Fair Play for Women' (see p. 36).

'Teleworking'—people working from home using information technology— is becoming more widespread. About 11 per cent of employers are employing workers based at home and more are planning to adopt teleworking. There are about 60 'telecottages' in Britain. These are rural centres providing a variety of information technology and telecommunications facilities for business and community users. A report by the Department of Employment on teleworking found that managers of telework schemes expressed a high level of satisfaction with teleworkers.

Recent trends show a continued fall in full-time employment and a growth in part-time employment. Since 1984 part-time employment in Great Britain has risen by 1.1 million to 6 million in spring 1994, about 24 per cent of those in employment. The proportion in part-time employment was 46 per cent of women, compared with 7 per cent of men. About 50 per cent of married women work part-time, compared with just over 30 per cent of non-married women.

Self-employment is increasing again, following a decline during the recession. About 3.2 million people are self-employed in Great Britain, 22 per cent more than in 1984. The sectors with the highest concentrations of self-employed people are agriculture and construction.

Government Policy

The Government has taken a number of steps to change the labour market, with the aim of creating an economic climate in which business can flourish and create more jobs. These include:

- increasing the flexibility of the labour market, for example, adopting flexible working patterns for more employees;

- removing burdens on employers and workers, including regulatory barriers which hinder recruitment; and

- encouraging better training, especially by setting up employer-led Training and Enterprise Councils and, in Scotland, Local Enterprise Companies (see pp. 178–9).

The Government supports a social dimension to the European Union (see p. 110) which gives priority to the creation and development of jobs and takes into account the different employment patterns and practices in member states.

Employment by Sector

As in other industrialised countries, there has been a marked shift in jobs from manufacturing to service industries (see Table 13.2). Between 1955 and 1994 the proportion of employees in employment engaged in service industries more than doubled, to 73 per cent. In June 1994, 15.3 million people were employed in services in Great Britain, over 2.1 million more than in 1983 (see Table 13.3). Financial services, education, medical services, retail distribution, and hotels and catering experienced significant increases. Employment in some services, however, particularly transport and communications, has fallen.

Manufacturing industry accounted for 42 per cent of employees in employment in 1955, but by 1994 the proportion had fallen to 20 per cent. Nearly all manufacturing industries have experienced a decline in employment as productivity has increased and as markets for manufactured goods have

changed. Traditional manufacturing industries, such as steel and shipbuilding, have experienced particularly large falls in employment. In June 1993 employment in the main manufacturing sectors in Great Britain included:

- 605,000 in mechanical engineering;
- 601,000 in office machinery, electrical engineering and instruments;
- 488,000 in food, drink and tobacco;
- 465,000 in timber, wooden furniture, rubber and plastics;
- 447,000 in paper products, printing and publishing; and
- 425,000 in textiles, leather, footwear and clothing.

Occupational Changes

There has been a gradual move away from manual occupations towards non-manual occupations, which now account for nearly three-fifths of jobs. The main growth areas have been in managers and administrators, in selling and in the personal and protective service occupations. Self-employment is highest in craft and related occupations

Table 13.3: Employees in Employment in Services in Great Britain

Thousands, seasonally adjusted, June

	1983	1988	1991	1992	1993
Wholesale distribution and repair	1,125	1,169	1,132	1,095	1,082
Retail distribution	1,982	2,159	2,315	2,309	2,255
Hotels and catering[a]	911	1,078	1,198	1,176	1,161
Transport	900	870	901	884	867
Postal services and telecommunications	424	430	428	409	372
Banking, finance, insurance, business services and leasing[a]	1,846	2,431	2,628	2,604	2,656
Public administration[a]	1,861	1,922	1,948	1,793	1,792
Education[a]	1,526	1,680	1,702	1,832	1,830
Medical and other health services, veterinary services	1,251	1,389	1,493	1,554	1,544
Other services[a]	1,302	1,698	1,654	1,694	1,711
All services	13,130	14,841	15,395	15,343	15,258

Source: *Employment Gazette*
[a]Industries affected by the reclassification of some local authority employees in September 1991. Accordingly, the figures for June 1992 and 1993 for these services are not strictly comparable with those for earlier years.

(30 per cent of those in this sector in Great Britain in spring 1994), followed by managers and administrators (20 per cent).

Unemployment

Since December 1992 there has been a recovery in the labour market, and unemployment in Britain had fallen by 376,000 by August 1994. The fall in unemployment started at an earlier stage in the economic cycle, reflecting a number of factors, including an improvement in the functioning of the labour market (following measures such as deregulation), more young people staying on in education, and greater efficiency in the placing of unemployed people into work by the Employment Service. In August 1994 unemployment totalled 2.6 million, 9.2 per cent of the workforce. It ranged from 7.1 per cent in East Anglia to 13.0 per cent in Northern Ireland.

The Government has introduced a wide range of measures to help combat unemployment. In 1994–95 about 1.5 million opportunities on employment and training schemes are being offered to help unemployed people. Recently introduced measures include:

- Community Action, providing 50,000 opportunities for people to do voluntary work of benefit to the community on a part-time basis while they actively look for work; and
- four pilot 'Workstart' measures, which are designed to test the effectiveness of paying recruitment subsidies to employers to encourage them to recruit the long-term unemployed.

In addition, a new Jobseeker's Allowance is planned (see p. 406), which is intended to improve the way in which unemployed people receive help.

TRAINING, EDUCATION AND ENTERPRISE

Employers in Britain spend over £20,000 million a year on employee training and development. The Government funds a number of training, enterprise and vocational education programmes. Its training strategy is designed to increase Britain's prosperity by stimulating enterprise and developing excellence in skills. Individuals are being encouraged to train by means of tax reliefs and loan schemes. Britain is acknowledged as an innovative world leader in open and flexible learning, for example, through the Open University and the Open College (see p. 428).

In May 1994 the Government announced a series of measures, costing about £300 million over the three years to 1997–98, designed to boost vocational education and training. They include:

- new accelerated modern apprenticeships (see p. 181);
- £63 million to update the managerial, supervisory and technical skills of 24,000 key employees in small firms so that they can pass on their skills to others (see p. 180);
- £23 million to provide a week of work experience for every young person before they leave education and to improve links between schools and business;
- better careers education and guidance for young people; and
- measures to update and strengthen vocational qualifications.

Training and Enterprise Councils

There are 82 Training and Enterprise Councils (TECs) in England and Wales. They are independent companies run by local business leaders. They are accountable to Government through their contracts and are subject to regular monitoring by Government Offices for the Regions.

The objective of TECs is to develop the skilled and enterprising workforce necessary for sustaining economic growth and prosperity. Their special focus is to strengthen the skill base and assist local enterprise to expand and compete effectively.

As well as running training and enterprise programmes previously run by the Government, TECs promote the importance of training as a business strategy.

For 1994–95, £1,700 million has been provided to TECs to deliver the range of Department of Employment programmes including Training for Work and Youth Training (see below). They also contract with the Department of Trade and Industry to deliver enterprise and business assistance programmes (see Chapter 14) and can compete for contracts under the Government's Single Regeneration Budget (see p. 355).

Local Enterprise Companies

A separate network of 22 Local Enterprise Companies (LECs) exists in Scotland. These have wider-ranging responsibilities than the TECs, covering economic development and environmental improvement. LECs operate the same major training programmes as TECs, but, unlike them, have no responsibility for work-related further education. They run under the supervision of the two enterprise bodies: Scottish Enterprise and Highlands and Islands Enterprise (see p. 200).

Industry Training Organisations

Industry Training Organisations (ITOs) act as the focal point for training matters in their particular sector of industry, commerce or public service. Their role is to ensure that the skills needs of their sectors are being met and that occupational standards are being established and maintained for key occupations. There are over 120 independent ITOs, covering sectors employing about 85 per cent of the civilian workforce. The National Council of Industry Training Organisations, a voluntary body set up to represent the interests of ITOs, aims to improve the effectiveness of these bodies, for example, by encouraging good practice.

National Targets for Education and Training

The National Targets for Education and Training were launched by the Confederation of British Industry in 1991 and were agreed by over 100 national and local organisations, including all TECs, LECs and ITOs, and other major education, training and employer bodies. The Government supports the targets and in 1993 established the independent National Advisory Council for Education and Training Targets (NACETT); a parallel body operates in Scotland. The remit of NACETT is to monitor progress towards the targets, advise the Government on performance and policies which influence progress towards them, and promote appropriate investment by employers.

The targets, currently under review, cover both young people and the workforce as a whole. Among the 'foundation targets' are:

- that by 1997 at least 80 per cent of all young people attain NVQ/SVQ Level 2 (see p. 425) or its academic equivalent in their foundation education and training; and

- that by 2000, 50 per cent of young people should attain NVQ/SVQ Level 3 or its academic equivalent, as a basis for further progression.

Training for Work

The Training for Work programme has the objective of helping long-term unemployed people to find jobs and to improve their work-related skills through the provision of relevant training and structured work activity based on a careful assessment of individual needs. Training is carried out by training providers under contract with the local TEC or LEC. Each new participant receives an individually adapted package of training and/or structured work activities. The programme focuses more closely on the long-term unemployed than its predecessors. About 114,000 places for Training for Work are available in Great Britain in 1994–95, when the programme is expected to help up to 272,000 people.

Investors in People

The Investors in People initiative aims to encourage employers to develop the potential of all employees in line with business goals. It is based on a rigorous national standard. TECs and LECs provide advice and information to help organisations to work towards the standard. By August 1994 about 1,000 employers had achieved the Investors in People standard, and over 9,700 had made a formal commitment to work towards it.

Improving the Training Market

The Improving the Training Market programme is aimed at bringing about change and improvements in the operation of the vocational education and training systems. Priority has been given to encouraging investment in skills, helping people to improve their employment prospects and supporting the implementation of new qualifications.

National Training Awards

The National Training Awards aim to complement TEC and LEC activities and the competition is designed to promote good training practice by example, rewarding companies which have carried out exceptionally effective training. Around 80 corporate awards and approximately 20 individual awards are presented to national winners, who are selected from 200 regional winners.

Skill Choice

The Skill Choice initiative was introduced in 1993 and is intended to persuade individuals of the benefits of training and to encourage them to take greater responsibility for their own career development. Individuals are offered credits which they can use to buy guidance and assessment services; part of the cost is being met by the Government. In the initial stage a number of TECs and LECs are involved, providing credits to 250,000 people in the two years 1993–94 and 1994–95.

Career Development Loans

People who live in, or intend to undertake vocational training in, Great Britain can apply to one of three major banks for a Career Development Loan. Deferred repayment loans of £200 to £8,000 can help to pay for vocational courses lasting up to two years, or two years of a longer course. More than 50,000 people have borrowed over £138 million through the programme to pay for training. A substantial expansion of the programme is in progress.

Small Firms Training Loans

The Small Firms Training Loans scheme was introduced in June 1994. Firms with 50 or fewer employees may apply to one of three major banks for a loan. Loans of between £500 and £125,000 are available to pay for a wide range of training and training-related expenses. Repayments are deferred for up to 13 months. In 1994–95 up to 3,000 loans are available.

Training for Young People

The Government guarantees the offer of a suitable training place to all 16- and 17-year-olds who want one and are not going into full-time education or a job. Currently the main work-based training provision is Youth Training (YT). Young people receive careers guidance in the form of training appropriate to their needs and draw up an individual training plan in conjunction with the Careers Service. The delivery of training is arranged through TECs and LECs. YT provides the opportunity to acquire a broad-based vocational education and to achieve a vocational qualification at NVQ Level 2 (see p. 425) or a credit towards one.

Youth Credits

Youth Credits, which operate within the broad framework of YT, are intended to offer young people more individual choice and a greater sense of personal responsibility when buying training. Each credit has a financial value and can be presented to an employer or training provider in exchange for training. Youth Credits have been extended since their introduction on a pilot basis. During 1995 they will become available from TECs throughout England and Wales, and the equivalent scheme, Skillseekers, will become available throughout Scotland from LECs. Credits are the mechanism by which 16- and 17-year-old school and college leavers have access to the new apprenticeships (see below).

Modern Apprenticeships

In November 1993 the Government announced its intention to bring in 'Modern Apprenticeships' from 1995; the first prototype schemes were launched in September 1994. They are designed to build on the best features of existing apprenticeships and to increase significantly the number of young people trained to technician, supervisory and equivalent levels. When Modern Apprenticeships are fully available, about 150,000 young people in England are expected to be in training. The aim is for over 40,000 young people in England to achieve qualifications at NVQ Level 3 or above each year through work-based training.

Accelerated Modern Apprenticeships

Accelerated Modern Apprenticeships, which were announced in May 1994 and will be developed alongside Modern Apprenticeships, will provide high-level training for those aged 18 and 19. By 2000 this is expected to produce an extra 30,000 skilled and qualified technicians, supervisors and craftspeople each year.

Education Initiatives

A major government objective is to raise the motivation and attainment of young people to achieve their full potential and develop the skills needed by the economy. This requires close working relationships between industry and education. A number of education initiatives are being implemented, including the Technical and Vocational Education Initiative, Education Business Partnerships, Compacts and the National Record of Achievement. Details are given in Chapter 26.

Vocational Qualifications

The proportion of the workforce with qualifications, gained either in school or further education, is growing. Between 1984 and 1993 it rose from 63 per cent to 79 per cent.

The National Council for Vocational Qualifications (NCVQ), established in 1986, has been charged with reforming and rationalising vocational qualifications. New National Vocational Qualifications (NVQs) have been established in England, Wales and Northern Ireland (see p. 425). In Scotland the Scottish Vocational Education Council (SCOTVEC) has established parallel Scottish Vocational Qualifications (SVQs).

NVQs and SVQs are designed mainly for people in the workplace, although they can also be studied full-time. They are job-specific, based on national standards of competence set by industry and are assessed in the workplace. There are five levels within the NVQ and SVQ framework (see p. 425). NVQs and SVQs at levels 1 to 5 to cover 90 per cent of the employed workforce are expected to be in place by the end of 1995. The 1994 White Paper on competitiveness (see p. 194) announced a review of the top 100 NVQs/SVQs by the end of 1995 and of all NVQs/SVQs by the end of 1997–98.

Northern Ireland

The Training and Employment Agency, an executive agency within the Department of Economic Development, has primary responsibility for training and employment services. Its overall aim is to assist economic growth by ensuring the provision and operation of training and employment services that contribute to Northern Ireland companies becoming more competitive and individuals obtaining the skills and competences needed to secure employment. The Agency works closely with employers and is encouraging each main sector of industry to form a sectoral representative body to represent the opinions of employers and others on training needs. It has also established sectoral working groups to develop training strategies.

Northern Ireland has its own range of training and employment programmes. These include:

- the Action for Community Employment programme, which provides temporary jobs with a training input for long-term unemployed people;
- the Job Training programme, a programme devised to help unemployed adults compete for available jobs; and
- the Youth Training programme, an integrated training programme for those aged 16 and 17 which aims to develop the occupational competence of young people entering the labour market.

RECRUITMENT AND JOB-FINDING

There are a variety of ways in which people can find jobs. In winter 1993–94, according to the Labour Force Survey, the main methods used by people who had found their current job in the previous three months were:

- hearing from someone else who worked there (31 per cent);
- replying to advertisements (25 per cent);
- direct approaches to employers (16 per cent); and
- visiting a Jobcentre (9 per cent).

Government Employment Services

The Government provides a range of services to jobseekers through the Employment Service, an executive agency within the Department of Employment. These include:

- a network of local offices, at which people can find details of job opportunities;
- advice and guidance so that people can find the best route back into employment, for example, by training; and
- a range of special programmes.

The Employment Service has over 1,200 Jobcentres and unemployment benefit offices, and employs about 47,000 staff. Jobcentres are now being integrated with the benefit offices to provide a comprehensive service to unemployed people. By mid-1994 over 900 integrated offices had been established. In 1993–94 the Employment Service placed 1.64 million unemployed people into jobs and conducted over 7 million advisory interviews to help people find appropriate work or places on employment and training programmes.

The Jobseeker's Charter contains a number of provisions governing the standard of service to users. These include provisions on the speed of service, and ensuring that vacancies on display boards at offices are up to date and are available, and that those entitled to benefit receive the correct payments promptly.

Advisory Services

Help for unemployed people is provided through the main jobcentre services, which provide access to vacancies, employment advice and training opportunities. Advisers provide unemployed people with information on employment and training opportunities available locally. New Client Advisers interview newly unemployed people to check their eligibility for benefit. Together with the unemployed person, they agree a 'Back to Work Plan', which shows them the best course of action. These plans are reviewed at every advisory interview.

Under the Restart programme, everyone who has been unemployed for six months or longer is asked to attend a Restart interview with a claimant adviser. The adviser and unemployed person discuss that person's circumstances, with the aim of helping him or her back into work as soon as possible.

The Service has a number of programmes, some of which are designed to help the long-term unemployed. These include:

- Jobclubs, where participants are given training and advice in job-hunting skills and have access to facilities to help an intensive job search;
- Restart courses, designed to rebuild self-confidence and motivation, and including help with job-hunting skills; and

- Jobplan workshops, which are designed to enable those unemployed for a year to assess their skills, qualities and training needs, and to act as an introduction to future job and training options.

Help for People with Disabilities

All of the Employment Service's programmes make provision for people with disabilities. Services for people with disabilities are now being delivered through local integrated specialist teams—Placing Assessment and Counselling Teams. They are supported by nine regional Ability Development Centres, which carry out training and development work, and provide special advice for employers who may be considering employing people with disabilities. A wide range of programmes, such as one offering sheltered employment opportunities, is available for people with disabilities who need specialist help.

Employment Agencies

There are many private employment agencies, including several large firms with many branches. The total value of the market has been estimated at about £8,000 million a year.

The main trade body for the employment agency industry is the Federation of Recruitment and Employment Services, which regulates the activities of its members by means of a Code of Good Recruitment Practice and by specialist section codes of practice.

The law governing employment agencies is less restrictive than that of most other EU countries. Agencies must be licensed by the Secretary of State, and abide by specified standards of good conduct. They are generally prohibited from charging fees to people for finding or seeking to find jobs, although there are conditional exceptions for entertainment and modelling agencies. There were over 14,800 licence holders at the end of March 1994.

The Deregulation and Contracting Out Bill (see p. 197) proposes the abolition of licensing requirements, but there would be

powers to prohibit people from operating agencies when necessary. Agencies would still have to comply with statutory standards of conduct, including the general prohibition on charging fees to jobseekers.

TERMS AND CONDITIONS OF EMPLOYMENT

Employment Rights

Employment protection legislation provides a number of safeguards for employees. For example, most employees have a right to a written statement setting out details of the main conditions, including pay, hours of work and holidays.

Employees with the necessary period of continuous employment with their employer (normally two years) are entitled to lump-sum redundancy payments if their jobs cease to exist (for example, because of technological improvements or a fall in demand) and their employers cannot offer suitable alternative work. Where employers are insolvent, redundancy payments are met directly from the National Insurance fund.

New maternity rights were established by the Trade Union Reform and Employment Rights Act 1993 and apply to pregnant employees whose babies arrive on or after 16 October 1994. They implement an EC directive and coincide with new legislation on maternity pay (see p. 402). All pregnant employees, regardless of length of service, have the right to 14 weeks' statutory maternity leave with all their non-wage contractual benefits maintained, and protection against dismissal because of pregnancy. Existing rights are preserved.

Minimum periods of notice when employment is to be terminated are laid down for both employers and employees. Most employees who believe they have been unfairly dismissed have the right to complain to an industrial tribunal, provided they have the necessary qualifying period of employment. If the complaint is upheld, the tribunal may make an order for re-employment or award compensation.

Legislation forbids any employment of children under 13 years of age, and employment in any industrial undertaking of children who have not reached the statutory minimum school-leaving age, with some exceptions for family undertakings.

Equal Opportunities

The Race Relations Act 1976 makes it generally unlawful to discriminate on grounds of colour, race, nationality (including citizenship) or ethnic or national origin, in employment, training and related matters. The Department of Employment operates a nationwide Race Relations Employment Advisory Service. Its objective is to promote the Government's policies aimed at combating racial discrimination in employment and promoting fair treatment and equality of opportunity in employment. Advisers provide employers with advice and practical help in developing and implementing effective equal opportunity strategies.

The Sex Discrimination Act 1975, as amended, makes it generally unlawful in Great Britain to discriminate on grounds of sex or marital status when recruiting, training, promoting, dismissing or retiring staff. The Equal Pay Act 1970 makes it generally unlawful to discriminate between men and women in pay and other terms and conditions of employment. The Act was significantly extended in 1984 to meet EU requirements by providing for equal pay for work of equal value.

Practical advice to employers and others on the best arrangements for implementing equal opportunities policies in Great Britain is given in codes of practice from the Commission for Racial Equality and from the Equal Opportunities Commission (see p. 36), while the Department of Employment has also published practical guidance to employers on how to make equal opportunities an integral part of management practice.

Northern Ireland

Similar legislation to that in Great Britain on equal pay and sex discrimination applies in Northern Ireland; there is at present no legislation on race relations, but this is under review. Discrimination, both direct and indirect, in employment on grounds of religious belief or political opinion is unlawful. The Fair Employment Commission has the task of promoting equality of opportunity and investigating employment practices, with powers to issue legally enforceable directions. The Fair Employment Tribunal adjudicates on individual complaints of religious or political discrimination and enforces the Commission's directions. All but the smallest employers are required to monitor the religious composition of their workforces and periodically to review their employment practices. Where fair participation is not being enjoyed by both Protestants and Roman Catholics, the introduction of 'affirmative action' measures must be considered.

Earnings

According to the Department of Employment's New Earnings Survey, the average weekly earnings, unaffected by absence and including overtime payments, in April 1994 of full-time employees on adult rates were £326. Earnings were higher for non-manual employees (£360) than for manual employees (£263). Managerial and professional groups are the highest paid. The industries with the highest average weekly earnings were energy and water supply (£427) and banking, finance, insurance, business services and leasing (£381).

Overtime and other additional payments are particularly important for manual employees, for whom such additional payments represented over one-fifth of earnings. About 49 per cent of manual employees and 19 per cent of non-manual employees received overtime payments.

The rate of increase in earnings has recently been running at a relatively low level. In the year to July 1994 the underlying average increase for the economy as a whole was about 3.75 per cent.

Fringe Benefits

A variety of fringe benefits are used by employers to provide additional rewards to their employees, including schemes to encourage employee financial participation in their companies, pension schemes, private medical insurance, subsidised meals, company cars and childcare schemes.

Many employees are covered by pension schemes provided by their employers. Such benefits are more usual among clerical and professional employees than among manual workers. Nearly 11 million people in Britain are members of occupational schemes.

Company cars are provided for employees in a wide variety of circumstances. It is estimated that around 1.8 million people have a company car and around half of these receive fuel for private motoring in their cars.

The Government has introduced tax reliefs to encourage employers to set up financial participation schemes, and give employees a direct financial stake in the business they work for.

Profit-related pay (PRP) schemes link part of pay to changes in a business's profits. PRP schemes have increased considerably and by the end of March 1994 over 7,000 schemes were registered with the Inland Revenue. They covered nearly 1.8 million people, 54 per cent more than in March 1993. Employee share schemes allow employees to receive low-cost or free shares from their employer without paying income tax. By the end of March 1993 about 3.1 million employees had benefited from all-employee profit sharing and Save-As-You-Earn (SAYE) share option schemes.

Hours of Work

Most full-time employees have a basic working week of between 34 and 40 hours, and work a five-day week. When overtime is taken into account, average weekly hours worked in Great Britain in April 1994 were 41.6 for men and 37.6 for women. Average hours worked by full-time and part-time employees and the self-employed were 39.7 for men and 26.5 for women in spring 1994. Hours worked tended to be longest in agriculture, transport and communications, and construction, and shortest in most service industries. More men than women work overtime, and those in manual occupations generally work more overtime than employees in non-manual jobs.

In general, there are no limits on hours worked by adults except in a few occupations (such as for drivers of goods and public service vehicles).

The Government is challenging in the European Court a draft EC directive which includes proposals for a maximum 48-hour working week.

Holidays with Pay

There are no general statutory entitlements to holidays, and holiday entitlements are frequently determined by negotiation. Recent decades have seen a considerable increase in holiday entitlements. In 1961, 97 per cent of full-time manual employees were entitled to two weeks a year. Nowadays, holiday entitlements (excluding public holidays) generally provide for at least four weeks' paid holiday a year. Over three-quarters of manual employees covered by nationally negotiated agreements have basic holiday entitlements of 21 to 24 days, with a significant number having five weeks or more. Non-manual workers tend to have longer holidays than manual workers. Holiday entitlements may also be dependent upon length of service.

INDUSTRIAL RELATIONS

The structure of industrial relations in Britain has been established mainly on a voluntary basis. The system is based chiefly on the organisation of employees and employers into trade unions and employers' associations, and on freely conducted negotiations at all levels.

Trends in Bargaining and Pay

There has been a considerable reduction in

the proportion of employees and workplaces where pay is determined by collective bargaining. The proportion of employees covered by major collective agreements declined from about 55 per cent in the mid-1970s to 31 per cent in 1993. Private sector employees are much less likely to be covered by collective bargaining than are public sector employees. National agreements covering over 1.2 million employees have ended since 1986 in sectors such as engineering, banking, the multiple food trade, electricity supply and water supply.

Where agreements in the private sector are industry-wide, they are often supplemented by local agreements in companies or factories (plant bargaining). These company or plant agreements frequently produce pay rates which are higher than the minima set by national agreements, as well as other detailed terms and conditions of employment. Where there is no collective bargaining, pay is usually determined by management at local level.

Another trend has been the growth in systems linking pay to performance. A substantial majority of medium and large employers make some use of performance-related pay systems such as merit pay, financial participation (see p. 185) and individual payment by results. Private sector organisations are more likely to use performance-related pay than public sector bodies.

The Government is committed to the further development of performance-related pay in the public sector as part of its wider objectives for improving the quality of the public services as set out in the Citizen's Charter (see p. 67). Performance-related pay is being extended in areas such as the Civil Service and education. Greater pay flexibility is also being encouraged in other ways, such as the delegation of pay determination to many departments and agencies in central government, to self-governing trusts in the National Health Service and to grant-maintained schools.

'New-style' agreements, often associated with overseas-owned companies, have become more widespread. Features normally include flexibility in working practices, recognition of a single union for all of a company's employees and 'single status', involving the elimination of the traditional distinction between managers, supervisors and other employees.

Employee Involvement

Employers practise a wide variety of methods of informing and consulting their employees, not only through committees but also through direct communication between management and employees. These methods include:

- employee bulletins and reports;
- briefing systems;
- quality circles;
- financial participation schemes; and
- attitude surveys.

The Government is, however, opposed to the EU's proposals for statutory requirements on some multinational employers to inform and consult their employees, and for worker participation in decision-making through works councils. It believes that companies should be free to develop employee involvement arrangements which are appropriate to their own circumstances and the needs of their employees.

Trade Unions

Trade unions have members in nearly all occupations. They are widely recognised by employers in the public sector and in large firms and establishments. As well as negotiating pay and other terms and conditions of employment with employers, they provide benefits and services such as educational facilities, financial services, legal advice and aid in work-related cases. In recent years many unions have extended considerably the range of services for members.

There has been a decline in trade union membership, and by the end of 1992 total union membership was 9 million, about 35 per cent of employees. The decline reflects the moves away from manufacturing and public services, both of which have a relatively high level of membership, and the growth in part-time employment. Union membership is higher among male employees (38 per cent) than among female employees (31 per cent) and in large workplaces. Mergers have resulted in a fall in the number of unions, and several unions are discussing possible mergers.

UNISON, with about 1.5 million members, is the biggest union in Britain. It was formed in 1993 from a merger of three unions: the Confederation of Health Service Employees, the National Union of Public Employees and the National and Local Government Officers' Association. Other unions with over 500,000 members are:

- the Transport and General Workers Union (with 1 million members);
- the Amalgamated Engineering and Electrical Union (884,000);
- GMB (799,000)—a general union with members in a range of public and private sector industries; and
- Manufacturing Science Finance (552,000).

At the end of 1993 there were 287 trade unions on the list maintained by the Certification Officer, who, among other duties, is responsible for certifying the independence of trade unions. To be eligible for entry on the list a trade union must show that it consists wholly or mainly of workers and that its principal purposes include the regulation of relations between workers and employers or between workers and employers' associations.

Trade union organisation varies widely, but there is usually a national executive council or committee. Many unions also have regional and district organisations, while local branches cover one or more workplaces. Elected workplace representatives are often called 'shop stewards'. Where two or more unions have members in the same workplace, shop stewards' committees may be formed to discuss matters of common concern.

Trades Union Congress

In Britain the national body of the trade union movement is the Trades Union Congress (TUC), founded in 1868. Its affiliated membership comprises 69 trade unions, which together represent some 7.3 million people, or about 80 per cent of all trade unionists in Britain.

The TUC's objectives are to promote the interests of its affiliated organisations and to improve the economic and social conditions of working people. It deals with all general questions which concern trade unions, both nationally and internationally, and provides a forum in which affiliated unions can collectively determine policy. There are six TUC regional councils for England and a Wales Trades Union Council. The annual Congress meets in September to discuss matters of concern to trade unionists. A General Council represents the TUC between annual meetings.

In March 1994 the TUC launched a programme of change designed to promote trade unionism and increase its influence on the nation's affairs. The TUC's immediate priorities include:

- campaigning for full employment and job security;
- developing links with government and other bodies;
- developing union services in areas such as education, health and safety, pensions and training; and
- strengthening work on Europe, for example, on workers' rights.

The TUC plays an active part in international trade union activity, through its affiliation to the International Confederation of Free Trade Unions and the European Trade Union Confederation. It also nominates the British workers' delegation to the annual International Labour Conference.

Scotland and Northern Ireland

Trade unions in Scotland also have their own national central body, the Scottish Trades Union Congress, which in many respects is similar in constitution and function to the TUC. Trade unions in Northern Ireland are represented by the Northern Ireland Committee of the Irish Congress of Trade Unions (ICTU). Most trade unionists in Northern Ireland are members of organisations affiliated to the ICTU, while the majority also belong to unions based in Great Britain which are affiliated to the TUC. The Northern Ireland Committee of the ICTU enjoys a high degree of autonomy.

Legal Framework

The Government's reforms of industrial relations and trade union law have helped to change the balance of power between trade unions and employers, and between trade unions and their own members. For example, since 1980 employers have been free to decide whether or not to bargain with a trade union or continue to do so. Legislation is consolidated in the Trade Union and Labour Relations (Consolidation) Act 1992, as amended by the most recent Act, the Trade Union Reform and Employment Rights Act 1993.

There were 649,000 working days lost in 211 stoppages of work as a result of industrial action in 1993 (see Table 13.4), the lowest number of stoppages since records began in 1891.

Union Membership and Non-membership Rights

All individuals have the right under the law not to be dismissed or refused employment (or the services of an employment agency) because of membership or otherwise of a trade union. Individuals who believe that they have been dismissed or refused employment on such grounds may complain to an industrial tribunal. All employees who are union members also have the right not to have union membership subscriptions deducted from their pay unless they have authorised this, and renew this at least every three years.

The Conduct of Union Affairs

The law requires a trade union to elect every member of its governing body, its general secretary and its president. Elections must be held at least every five years and be carried out by a secret postal ballot under independent scrutiny. Any union member who believes that the union has not complied with the statutory requirements may complain to the courts or to the Certification Officer.

A trade union may establish a political fund if it wishes to use its money for what the law defines as 'political objects'. If a union wishes to set up a political fund, its members must first agree in a secret ballot a resolution adopting those political objectives as an aim of the union. The union must also ballot its members every ten years to maintain the fund. Union members have a statutory right to opt out of contributing to a political fund.

The law also gives all union members a statutory remedy if unjustifiably disciplined by their union, for example, for refusing to come out on strike or for crossing a picket

Table 13.4: Industrial Disputes 1983–1993

	Working days lost (thousands)	Working days lost per 1,000 employees[a]	Workers involved (thousands)	Number of stoppages
1983	3,754	178	574	1,364
1988	3,702	166	790	781
1991	761	34	176	369
1992	528	24	148	253
1993	649	30	385	211

Source: Department of Employment
[a]Based on the mid-year (June) estimates of employees in employment.

line. Members also have the right to inspect their union's accounting records and obtain an annual statement from the union about its financial affairs.

Industrial Action

For most of the 20th century trade unions enjoyed wide immunity protecting them from legal proceedings for organising industrial action, so that the organisation of almost any industrial action was protected. Legislative reforms have restricted the scope of these immunities. To have the benefit of statutory immunity (that is, to be 'lawful'), the organisation of industrial action must now be wholly or mainly in contemplation or furtherance of a trade dispute between workers and their own employer, and must not:

- involve workers who have no dispute with their own employer (so-called 'secondary' action);
- involve unlawful forms of picketing;
- be to establish or maintain a union-only labour agreement (the 'closed shop'); or
- be in support of any employee dismissed while taking unofficial industrial action.

Before calling for industrial action, a trade union must first obtain the support of its members in a secret postal ballot and must notify employers of its intention to conduct such a ballot. The union must also provide employers, in writing, with at least seven days' notice of official industrial action following a ballot, and with details of the ballot result.

Any trade union member has the right to restrain the union from calling on him or her, and other members, to take action unless a properly conducted secret ballot has supported the action. Anyone deprived of goods or services because of unlawful organisation of industrial action has the right to obtain a court order to stop this happening.

Employers' Organisations

Many employers in Britain are members of employers' organisations, some of which are wholly concerned with labour matters, although others are also trade associations concerned with commercial matters in general. With the move away from national pay bargaining, many employers' associations have looked at their functions and have moved towards concentrating on areas such as supplying information for bargaining purposes and dealing with specialist questions.

Employers' organisations are usually established on an industry basis rather than a product basis, for example, the Engineering Employers' Federation. A few are purely local in character or deal with a section of an industry or, for example, with small businesses; most are national and are concerned with the whole of an industry. In some of the main industries there are local or regional organisations combined into national federations. At the end of 1993, 123 listed and 130 unlisted employers' associations were known to the Certification Officer.

Most national organisations belong to the Confederation of British Industry (see p. 193), which represents directly or indirectly some 250,000 businesses.

Advisory, Conciliation and Arbitration Service

The Advisory, Conciliation and Arbitration Service (ACAS) is an independent statutory body which has a general duty of promoting the improvement of industrial relations. ACAS seeks to discharge its responsibilities through the voluntary co-operation of employers, employees and, where appropriate, their representatives. Its main functions are collective conciliation, provision of arbitration and mediation facilities, advisory mediation services for preventing disputes and improving industrial relations through the joint involvement of employers and employees, and providing an information service. ACAS also conciliates in disputes on individual employment rights.

In 1993 ACAS:

- received 1,211 requests for collective conciliation, with a further 163 requests referred to arbitration or mediation;

- dealt with nearly 69,600 individual conciliation cases;

- made nearly 4,000 advisory visits;

- assisted with 529 joint working exercises; and

- dealt with almost 481,400 enquiries through its public enquiry points.

In Northern Ireland the Labour Relations Agency, an independent statutory body, provides services similar to those provided by ACAS in Great Britain.

HEALTH AND SAFETY AT WORK

Health and safety standards in Britain are among the best in the world. Recent statistics indicate a reduction in the rate of major and other reported injuries to employees. In 1992–93 the number of deaths from accidents at work fell to 430, the lowest figure recorded. The decline reflects improvements in safety, together with a change in industrial structure away from old heavy industries which tend to have higher risks. About 18 million working days a year are lost as a result of work-related injuries.

> The Health and Safety Commission has conducted a review of all health and safety legislation to assess its relevance. The review, published in May 1994, looked at the impact on business, and whether repeal or simplification would be possible without endangering health and safety standards. As a result, it is recommending a substantial simplification of legislation, including the removal of nearly 100 regulations identified as no longer necessary.

The principal legislation is the Health and Safety at Work etc. Act 1974. It imposes general duties on everyone concerned with work activities, including employers, the self-employed, employees, and manufacturers and suppliers of materials for use at work. Associated Acts and regulations deal with particular hazards and types of work. Employers with five or more staff must prepare a written statement of their health and safety policy and bring it to the attention of their staff.

The Control of Substances Hazardous to Health Regulations 1988 constitute one of the most important sets of regulations made under the 1974 Act. They replaced a range of outdated legislation by a comprehensive and systematic approach to the control of exposure to virtually all substances hazardous to health. These include chemicals, fumes, dust and micro-organisms.

Six new sets of health and safety regulations came into force at the beginning of 1993, giving effect in Britain to various EC directives. Most of the requirements in the regulations clarify existing health and safety law and make it more explicit. The regulations cover:

- the management of health and safety;

- the provision and use of work equipment;

- personal protective equipment;

- manual handling;

- display screen equipment; and

- general health, safety and welfare in the workplace.

Health and Safety Commission

The Health and Safety Commission (HSC) has responsibility for developing policy on health and safety at work, including proposals for new or revised regulations and approved codes of practice. The HSC has an obligation to consult those who would be affected by such proposals and makes recommendations to the appropriate Secretary of State.

The HSC has a number of advisory committees covering subjects such as toxic substances, genetic modification and the safety of nuclear installations. There are also several industry advisory committees, each of which deals with a specific sector of industry.

Health and Safety Executive

The Health and Safety Executive (HSE) is the primary instrument for carrying out the HSC's policies and has day-to-day responsibility for enforcing health and safety law, except where other bodies, such as local authorities, are responsible. Its field services and inspections over the country as a whole are carried out by the Field Operations Division. This incorporates the Factory, Agricultural and Quarries inspectorates, together with the regional staff of the Employment Medical Advisory Service (which provides advice on medical aspects of employment problems), and the Field Consulting Groups, which provide technical support to the inspectorates. The HSE also includes:

- the policy divisions covering health, safety and strategic considerations;

- the Technology and Health Services Division, which provides technical advice on industrial health and safety matters; and

- the Health and Safety Laboratory, which provides scientific and medical support and testing services, and carries out research.

In premises such as offices, shops, warehouses, restaurants and hotels, health and safety legislation is enforced by inspectors appointed by local authorities, working under guidance from the HSE. Some other official bodies work under agency agreement with the HSE.

Northern Ireland

The general requirements of the Northern Ireland health and safety legislation are broadly similar to those for Great Britain. They are enforced mainly by the Department of Economic Development and the Department of Agriculture through their health and safety inspectorates, although the district councils have an enforcement role similar to that of local authorities in Great Britain. There is a Health and Safety Agency, roughly corresponding to the HSC but without its policy-making powers, and an Employment Medical Advisory Service.

Further Reading

Employment. Aspects of Britain series, HMSO, 1994.

Employment Gazette. Department of Employment. Monthly. Harrington Kilbride plc.

Essentials of Health and Safety at Work. HSE Books, 1994.

Labour Force Survey Quarterly Bulletin. Department of Employment.

14 Industry and Government

Private enterprises are responsible for over three-quarters of total economic activity. Since 1979 the Government has privatised nearly 50 major businesses and reduced the state-owned sector of industry by about two-thirds. The Government is taking measures to cut unnecessary regulations imposed on business, and operates schemes which provide direct assistance or advice mainly to small and medium-sized businesses.

STRUCTURE AND ORGANISATION

In some sectors a small number of large companies and their subsidiaries are responsible for a substantial proportion of total production, notably in the vehicle, aerospace and transport equipment industries. Private enterprises account for by far the greater part of activity in the agricultural, manufacturing, construction, distributive, financial and miscellaneous service sectors. The private sector contributed 76 per cent of total domestic expenditure in 1993, general government 23 per cent and public corporations 1 per cent.

About 250 British industrial companies each have an annual turnover of over £500 million. The annual turnover of the biggest company, British Petroleum (BP), makes it the 11th largest industrial group in the world and the second largest in Europe. Five British firms are among the top 20 European Union (EU) companies in terms of capital employed.

Industrial Financing

Over half of companies' funds for investment and other purposes are generated internally. Banks are the chief external source of finance, but companies have increasingly turned to equity finance. The main forms of short-term finance in the private sector are bank overdrafts, trade credit and factoring (making cash available to a company in exchange for debts owing to it).

Types of medium- and long-term finance include bank loans, mortgaging of property and the issue of shares and other securities to the public through the London Stock Exchange. The leasing of equipment may also be regarded as a form of finance. Other sources of finance for industry include the Government, the EU and specialist financial institutions, like financing and leasing, factoring and venture capital companies.

Venture Capital

Venture capital, or private equity capital, is a

major source of funding for the start-up, expansion or the management buy-out or buy-in (see below) of a company. Venture capital is provided by major institutions and is managed by independent fund and investment managers and wholly owned subsidiaries or divisions of large financial institutions such as banks. The British Venture Capital Association (BVCA) has 115 full members.

> Over £10,000 million has been invested by venture capital companies in 11,700 businesses since 1983, with £1,400 million being invested in 1,200 businesses in 1993.

Buy-ins and Buy-outs

In the late 1980s there was a rise in the number of buy-outs, in which the staff or management of a company raise the finance to purchase it, and buy-ins, whereby the staff or management of one firm purchase another. Buy-outs and buy-ins accounted for 63 per cent of venture capital investments by BVCA members in Britain in 1993.

Taxation

Rates of corporate taxation have been progressively reduced in recent years. The main rate of corporation tax is 33 per cent, with a reduced rate of 25 per cent for small firms (see p. 197—those with annual profits of less than £300,000). For companies with profits of between £300,000 and £1.5 million, the overall corporation tax rate is between the main rate and the rate for small firms. Expenditure on business plant and machinery, industrial building, and scientific research qualifies for annual allowances against profit for tax purposes.

A new Enterprise Investment Scheme, which succeeds the Business Expansion Scheme, is designed to encourage equity investment in unquoted trading companies—usually small concerns. It provides relief on investments at a rate of 20 per cent as well as income or capital gains tax relief on losses. The Government has also proposed a new venture capital trust scheme. This would permit pool savings and capital gains from investment in unquoted trading companies; investors would receive dividends and capital gains free of tax.

INDUSTRIAL ASSOCIATIONS

Confederation of British Industry

The Confederation of British Industry (CBI) is the largest employers' organisation in Britain, representing about 250,000 companies from all sectors, which together employ over 60 per cent of Britain's workforce. Membership ranges from the smallest to the largest companies in manufacturing, agriculture, construction, distribution, mining, finance, retailing, insurance, and other sectors. Most national employers' organisations, trade associations, and some chambers of commerce are members.

The CBI aims primarily to ensure that the Government, national and international institutions and the public understand the needs, intentions and problems of business, so as to create a climate of opinion in which business can operate efficiently and profitably. It campaigns to lessen the burdens on business, tackle handicaps on competition, and help improve the performance of companies. It offers members a forum, a lobby and a range of advisory services. The CBI also conducts surveys of activity in manufacturing, distribution, financial services, the regions, innovation, and pay and productivity. It has 12 regional offices and an office in Brussels. The CBI is the British member of the Union of Industrial and Employers' Confederations of Europe.

British Chambers of Commerce

The British Chambers of Commerce (BCC) represents business views to the Government at national and local levels. It promotes local economic development—for example, through regeneration projects, tourism, inward investment promotion and business services, including overseas trade missions, exhibitions and training conferences. It also provides member firms with information about overseas buyers and product sourcing. The BCC represents over 214,000 businesses in over 230 chambers of commerce and trade throughout Britain.

Institute of Directors

The Institute of Directors (IOD) has more

than 48,600 members worldwide, including 31,200 members in Britain, many of whom are in the small business sector. The IOD provides business advisory services on a range of matters affecting company directors, such as corporate management, insolvency and career counselling, and represents the interests of members to authorities in Britain and the EU. It also offers a full training programme of courses and lectures.

Trade and Employers' Organisations

Trade associations consist of companies producing or selling a particular product or group of products. They exist to supply common services, regulate trading practices and represent their members to government departments.

Employers' organisations are usually concerned with the negotiation of wages and conditions of work in a particular industry, although an institution may combine this function with that of a trade association.

GOVERNMENT RELATIONS WITH INDUSTRY

The Government believes that economic decisions are best taken by those competing in the market place, and that government should encourage enterprise and create the right climate for markets to work better.

The Department of Trade and Industry (DTI) is the department mainly responsible for the Government's relations with industry and commerce. Specific responsibilities include technology and innovation, overseas trade and export promotion (outlined in Chapter 12), competition policy and consumer affairs, regional industrial development, small firms, company legislation and patents. Through the Invest in Britain Bureau (see p. 202), it gives advice and assistance to overseas companies on locating in Britain. The Scottish, Welsh and Northern Ireland Offices are responsible for industrial policies in their areas.

The Government has reorganised the DTI so that it relates more closely to individual sectors of business. In 1992 the DTI specified its objectives as:

- identifying business needs through close contact with individual sectors;
- ensuring these needs are taken into account by Government and the EU;
- identifying influences on competitiveness at home and abroad;
- working for global trade liberalisation worldwide and helping businesses take advantage of market opportunities at home and abroad;
- widening choice and stimulating enterprise by promoting competition and privatisation;
- maintaining confidence in markets and protecting consumers by fair regulation;
- reducing unnecessary regulatory and administrative burdens on business;
- promoting innovation and best practice in quality, design and management;
- fostering the creation and development of small and medium-sized businesses;
- responding to the needs of different regions and areas with special difficulties; and
- taking account of environmental issues when developing government policies and stimulating an effective business response to environmental developments.

Competitiveness White Paper

A White Paper, issued in May 1994, contains a programme of new measures to help British business compete effectively in world markets. They are devoted to improving education and training, helping small firms to be more innovative and to increase exports, boosting regional economies and attracting more inward investment. Some of the more important measures are covered in this chapter, and also in Chapter 13.

Education and Training

A well-educated and well-trained workforce is considered essential for economic growth, particularly at a time of intense international competition and rapid technological advance. The Government takes measures to see that education and training are broadly based and

The Dome of the Rock in Jerusalem, recently restored by Mivan, an international construction company based in Antrim, Northern Ireland. Special automated machinery was designed to tackle the complex work, and over $1 million worth of gold was applied to the 1,500 sq m surface of the dome.

Pharmacist James Lofthouse invented Fisherman's Friend lozenges in 1865 to relieve the bronchial ailments suffered by trawlermen in the fishing port of Fleetwood, Lancashire. Now 85 per cent of production is exported, and the company has won a Queen's Award for Export three times in the past ten years.

THE CHANNEL TUNNEL

1994 marked the start of services through the Channel Tunnel.

Some idea of the scale of the project can be gained from this view of the approach road to the Coquelles terminal near Calais, France. Signs direct drivers into the correct lanes.

Vehicles are carried between the two terminals on purpose-built shuttle trains. The layout of the terminal allows cars to be driven straight onto the train.

The Eurostar trains have been specially designed to provide services between London, Paris and Brussels. Much longer than other passenger trains in Britain, they are capable of running using different systems of overhead and third-rail electrification.

The official inauguration of the tunnel took place on 6 May 1994. The ceremony, which included a journey through the tunnel, was performed by Her Majesty The Queen and President Mitterand of France.

The Channel Tunnel has been commemorated in these special postage stamps symbolising the joining of the two countries, designed jointly by the Royal Mail and La Poste, the French post office.

WORLD WAR II REMEMBERED

VE Day, London 1945.

Veterans gather on the
beach at Arromanches
in Normandy, France,
for a service to
commemorate the D-Day
landings.

that people of all ages can acquire relevant knowledge and skills. Education–business co-operation is constantly being improved (see p. 422).

New initiatives on education and training outlined in the competitiveness White Paper include:

- improved careers guidance for secondary level students;
- a strengthening of academic and vocational qualifications;
- extra funding to support work experience for school students;
- new accelerated apprenticeships; and
- funding for small firms to train people as trainers.

Training and Enterprise Councils and Local Enterprise Companies

The Government has set up a network of 82 business-led Training and Enterprise Councils (TECs) in England and Wales and 22 Local Enterprise Companies (LECs) in Scotland. TECs and LECs are independent companies run by boards of directors, the majority of whom are drawn from private sector business. Grants are made available to TECs to enable them to provide a range of training, vocational education and enterprise programmes on behalf of the Government. LECs encourage investment in the development of skills throughout the workforce and invest directly in training, particularly for school-leavers and the long-term unemployed. In addition, they offer a range of advisory and training services to businesses, including schemes to enhance the expertise of managers.

Single European Market

The Government believes that the completion of the single European market, which was achieved by the end of 1992 (see p. 117), will benefit the economy of each member state, and that the removal of trade barriers should lead to a reduction in business costs as well as increasing competition and stimulating efficiency, benefiting consumers and encouraging the creation of jobs and wealth.

Ratification of the European Economic Area (EEA) has extended the single market to Austria, Finland, Iceland, Norway and Sweden; the EEA has around 370 million consumers.

Specific benefits of the single market include:

- increased consumer choice;
- removal of barriers to trade through mutual recognition of standards and harmonisation where appropriate;
- liberalisation of public procurement;
- the right to trade financial services throughout the EEA on the basis of a single authorisation 'passport' (see p. 170);
- mutual recognition of professional and vocational qualifications; and
- a reduction in export bureaucracy.

Privatisation

The Government believes that the best way to improve the performance of public sector companies and nationalised industries is to expose them to market forces, through privatisation and the promotion of competition. Privatisation has also provided an opportunity for the Government to widen and deepen share ownership by encouraging both employees and the general public to take a direct stake in industry. In major flotations, employees in privatised companies are normally given a preferential right to buy shares in the new privatised companies.

Since 1979 the Government has privatised almost 50 major businesses, with net proceeds to the end of 1993–94 of about £55,000 million. Recent privatisations include the electricity industry in Northern Ireland and the Government's residual shareholding in BT (British Telecom). British Coal is being privatised and legislation is being introduced to enable the private sector to operate rail services. In addition, the ten companies operating London's buses are being sold to the private sector. Privatisation is also being extended to non-core government activities and other public sector areas.

Table 14.1: Major Government Sales

	Year of sale	Net equity proceeds (£ million)
BAA	1987	1,182
BT	1984–93	13,900
British Aerospace	1981–85	390
British Airways	1987	853
British Gas	1986–90	5,293
British Petroleum	1979–87	6,084
British Steel	1988	2,425
Britoil	1982-85	962
Cable and Wireless	1981-85	1,021
Rolls-Royce	1987	1,031
Water companies (England and Wales)	1989	3,454
Regional electricity companies (England and Wales)	1990 }	7,123[a]
Electricity generating companies (England and Wales)	1991	
Scottish electricity companies	1991	2,828[a]
BT secondary share sale	1991	5,128
Northern Ireland Electricity	1992–93	704[a]
BT secondary share sale	1993	5,335[a]

Source: HM Treasury
[a] Gross proceeds

Benefits

The economy has benefited through higher returns on capital in the privatised industries, which can no longer pre-empt or command resources from elsewhere in the economy but must compete for funds in the open capital markets. Privatised companies have welcomed the freedom to raise finance in private sector capital markets.

The consumer has benefited from downward pressure on prices and from rising standards of service. The Government has established a system of independent regulation for the privatised utilities. For each of the privatised utility sectors, such as telecommunications or gas, there is a regulatory body which has a wide range of powers and duties to promote competition and the interests of consumers. These include considering all complaints and representations about the company's services. Each privatised utility has a pricing policy which usually limits annual price increases to no more than the rate of inflation.

Nationalised Industries

The remaining major nationalised industries are British Rail, the Post Office, London Transport and Nuclear Electric. Their managing boards are appointed by ministers who have power to give general directions but are not involved in day-to-day management. Managing boards and staffs of nationalised industries are not civil servants.

The Government considers that nationalised industries should act as commercial enterprises and has set policies with which they are expected to conform. These involve:

- clear government objectives;
- regular corporate plans and performance reviews;
- agreed principles relating to investment appraisal and pricing;
- financial targets and performance aims;
- external financing limits; and
- systematic monitoring.

Deregulation

The Government's aim is to reduce or simplify administrative and legislative burdens on business, particularly small businesses, where the burden of compliance is most demanding. A small firms 'litmus test' has been introduced to help ensure that compliance costs for new regulations are not unduly high. Deregulation helps businesses to contain costs, operate more efficiently and trade more competitively.

Under a Deregulation Initiative, the Government is reducing burdens on business by:

- achieving better regulation, and cutting unnecessary regulation and the cost of compliance with essential regulation;
- ensuring that the views of business, and potential costs of compliance, are taken into account in framing new regulations and in negotiating EU proposals;
- improving official awareness of the needs of business through training and better consultation and communication; and
- improving the quality of service to business generally, whether provided by central or local government.

Proposed regulations, including EC directives, must take account of the costs they would impose on business. The existing 3,500 regulations affecting companies are being reviewed by government departments with the help of business people. The Deregulation and Contracting Out Bill enables the Government to amend or repeal primary legislation imposing unnecessary burdens on business.

Small Firms

Small businesses make a major contribution to the economy. Firms with fewer than 100 employees account for 50 per cent of the private sector workforce and 27 per cent of turnover. More than 96 per cent of the 2.7 million firms in Britain employ fewer than 20 people, representing over 30 per cent of the workforce. Industries with the fastest growth rates between 1979 and 1992 were in the services sector, particularly finance, property, and professional and business services.

The Government runs schemes giving either direct assistance or guidance on business problems affecting small firms. In addition to DTI schemes such as those available under the Enterprise Initiative, TECs offer small and medium-sized enterprises a comprehensive package of business and training support, including business information and advice services, business counselling for new and existing companies, and business skills training programmes.

The White Paper on business competitiveness contains a package of measures to help small businesses. A network of private-sector export consultants will be expanded to 70. Innovation and technology counsellors are to be recruited by Business Links (see below), who will be able to offer Innovation Credits worth up to £1,000 a year to buy in services for improving innovation. In addition, a series of measures will be implemented to help tackle the problem of late payment.

Business Links

The Business Link concept was launched by the DTI in 1992. The Department is setting up a network of around 200 business advice centres—Business Links—to bring together in a single point of access organisations supporting enterprise, such as local companies, TECs, chambers of commerce, local authorities and enterprise agencies. They offer a full range of business advisory services to established medium-sized and small firms. Services include development of business skills, business 'health checks' and advice and information on exporting, technology transfer, innovation and design. They are envisaged not as a government scheme but as a network of local partnerships, in which larger firms can make contacts and expertise available to smaller firms. By the end of 1995 it is expected that every company in England will have easy access to a Business Link.

The Government is to contract out all consultancy services (see below) at present run by the DTI to Business Links.

In Scotland arrangements for providing integrated business advice are slightly different. LECs play a significant role, individually and in their partnerships with other agencies, and several local Business Information Centres have been opened.

Enterprise Initiative

The Enterprise Initiative brings together a

wide range of the services that the DTI provides for industry and commerce. The consultancy scheme encourages small and medium-sized businesses to use outside consultancy services as a regular part of their management strategy and offers short-term consultancy support in design, marketing, manufacturing and services systems, quality, business planning, and financial and management information systems. About 10,400 consultancy projects were completed in 1993–94, bringing the total number of completions to over 65,000.

In Scotland and Wales the consultancy scheme is delivered by Enterprise Services Scotland (a subsidiary of Scottish Enterprise —see p. 200) and the Welsh Development Agency (see p. 200).

Consultancy is available to most manufacturing and service businesses with fewer than 500 employees. In the Assisted Areas (see below) and Urban Programme Areas, half of the costs of a project are met; elsewhere the rate is one-third. The Enterprise Initiative scheme will be phased out by 1995–96 and a new flexible consultancy and diagnostic service is to be established nationwide. This will help businesses to analyse their strengths and weaknesses and the options open to them as well as identifying available support. Additionally, a trial consultancy brokerage service is being set up, using data and experience gathered under the Enterprise Initiative scheme.

Small Firms Schemes

The Support for Products Under Research scheme (SPUR) offers grants to businesses with up to 250 employees for new product and process development demonstrating a significant technological advance. In 1993–94 a total of £12 million was awarded to 139 projects. The Small Firms Merit Award for Research and Technology (SMART) is an annual competition providing grants to individuals and businesses with fewer than 50 employees in support of innovative technological projects with commercial potential. In 1993–94 grants were made to 180 new projects.

Other government help to small firms includes:

- the Small Firms Loan Guarantee Scheme, which helps businesses with viable proposals to obtain finance where conventional loans are unavailable as a result of a lack of financial security or previous performance; the scheme provides banks and other financial institutions with a government guarantee on a certain percentage (70 or 85 per cent) of the loan in return for a premium payment; (since 1981, 37,000 loans valued at £1,200 million have been guaranteed);

- an initiative to encourage informal investment for small firms from a wider range of sources. The Government is providing support to TECs and other organisations to bring together investors and small firms; and

- the Business Start-Up scheme, enabling unemployed people to claim an allowance while establishing a new business.

REGIONAL INDUSTRIAL DEVELOPMENT

Industrial policy is designed to encourage enterprise and economic growth in all areas of Britain. However, where additional help is needed, it is provided under the Enterprise Initiative. Help is focused on the Assisted Areas (Development Areas and Intermediate Areas), which cover around 34 per cent of Britain's working population. The promotion of inward investment is a key element in the Government's regional policy.

Following a review of the Assisted Areas, in 1993 the Government announced a number of changes. The review took into account a wide range of factors, including levels of unemployment and the nature of the problems faced in each area. Some regions, such as Wales, which have experienced a relative improvement in unemployment levels, now have less of their area covered by Assisted Areas. Areas which have become eligible for regional aid include parts of the South East, such as inner areas of London and some coastal towns affected by high unemployment; and areas in the East Midlands and Yorkshire affected by coal mine closures (see p. 256).

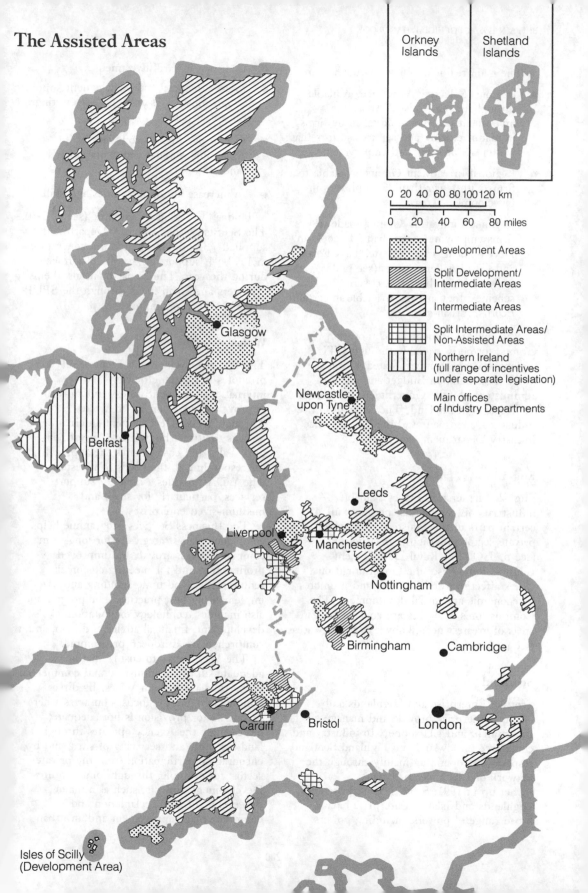

The Assisted Areas

Orkney Islands

Shetland Islands

0 20 40 60 80 100 120 km

0 20 40 60 80 miles

Development Areas

Split Development/
Intermediate Areas

Intermediate Areas

Split Intermediate Areas/
Non-Assisted Areas

Northern Ireland
(full range of incentives
under separate legislation)

Main offices
of Industry Departments

Glasgow

Newcastle
upon Tyne

Belfast

Leeds

Liverpool

Manchester

Nottingham

Birmingham

Cambridge

Cardiff

Bristol

London

Isles of Scilly
(Development Area)

The main regional policy instruments are:

- Regional Selective Assistance, available throughout the Assisted Areas, for investment projects undertaken by firms in manufacturing and services sectors that will create or safeguard employment;

- Regional Investment Grants, available to firms with fewer than 25 employees in Development Areas;

- Regional Innovation Grants, made to firms employing fewer than 50 people in Development, Intermediate, Task Force and City Challenge areas (see p. 335), as well as some other areas covered by EU schemes; they are also available in certain Scottish urban areas.

Regional Investment and Innovation Grants, formerly available through DTI regions, have been incorporated within the Single Regeneration Budget and are administered by the Government Offices for the Regions in England, The Scottish Office Industry Department and the Welsh Office Industry Department (see p. 335).

England

English Partnerships makes available industrial and commercial premises in certain parts of the Assisted Areas where private sector provision is insufficient (see p. 336). The Rural Development Commission advises the Government on issues affecting rural England and promotes its economic and social development. The Commission's resources are concentrated in areas of greatest need, known as priority areas (see p. 338).

Scotland

Scottish Enterprise and Highlands and Islands Enterprise provide and manage government and EU support to industry and commerce, in lowland and highland Scotland respectively, operating mainly through the network of LECs (see p. 195).

Set up in 1991, Scottish Enterprise and Highlands and Islands Enterprise have a broad range of powers, including powers:

- to attract inward investment;

- to give financial and management support to new businesses and to assist existing ones to expand;

- to improve the environment by reclaiming derelict and contaminated land; and

- to increase job opportunities and skills.

Under the Urban Programme (see p. 340), The Scottish Office Industry Department supplied £38 million for urban regeneration in 1993–94, supporting over 1,200 projects during the year. The Department also helps exporters and small firms through the SPUR and SMART programmes (see p. 198).

Wales

The Welsh Development Agency (WDA) promotes industrial efficiency and international competitiveness and aims to improve the environment in Wales. Through Welsh Development International, it seeks to attract high-quality investment into Wales and co-ordinates the approach for responding to the needs of investors. The WDA provides a range of support services, particularly for small and medium-sized enterprises.

The Business Services programme helps companies plan strategically for long-term competitiveness, growth and improved profitability, and for meeting customer requirements, and understanding and implementing best practice. The programme also includes technology exploitation, skills development, financial advice and help, and a comprehensive European programme.

The WDA aims to ensure that an adequate supply of industrial and commercial property is available in Wales. Its direct building programme focuses on areas where private sector provision is not adequate; increasingly the Agency operates through land assembly and servicing of sites, and by encouraging participation from the private sector, for example, through joint ventures. Development projects, such as a major programme of land reclamation and environmental improvement and an urban development programme, aim to regenerate selected areas by opening up development opportunities for private enterprise.

The Rural Prosperity Programme includes comprehensive action plans to develop specific rural areas. There are also initiatives and schemes to stimulate new rural enterprise and business growth. The Development Board for Rural Wales supplies factories, housing and advice for small businesses.

Northern Ireland

Development policy in Northern Ireland is the responsibility of the Department of Economic Development and is delivered through various agencies, including:

- the Industrial Development Board, which deals with overseas companies considering Northern Ireland as an investment location, as well as the development of local companies with more than 50 employees;

- the Local Enterprise Development Unit, which promotes enterprise and the development of small businesses;

- the Industrial Research and Technology Unit, providing advice and assistance on research and development, innovation and technology transfer; and

- the Training and Employment Agency, which helps with in-company training and management development.

A variety of schemes are available to help companies with marketing, exporting, product development and design, improved productivity and quality, training, and research and development. The full range of assistance is made available to those companies which are able to demonstrate development potential and a prospect of long-term competitive growth. Where appropriate, this assistance includes capital grants, loans and share capital investment. The Industrial Development Board also offers stocks of land and industrial premises for purchase or lease. There is exemption from local property taxes for manufacturing premises.

European Union Regional Policy and Aid

The EU seeks to reduce disparities between regions. The principal responsibility for helping poorer areas remains with national authorities, but the EU complements schemes by providing grants and loans from a number of sources, including the European Regional Development Fund.

The European Investment Bank (see p. 119) offers loans for public and private capital investment schemes. Assisted projects typically include improvements to and building of roads of regional and national importance; construction of trans-European transport links (like the Channel Tunnel); and factory construction.

> EU Structural Funds, especially the European Regional Development Fund (ERDF), play an important role in regional development. Three areas—Northern Ireland, the Highlands and Islands, and Merseyside—are eligible for assistance to regions whose development is lagging behind; they will receive around £2,000 million of EU funding over the period 1994–99. The ERDF also provides finance for areas of industrial decline and for rural development. Structural Funds are being made available to areas suffering from a decline in the coal, shipbuilding, steel, textile and defence industries.

INWARD INVESTMENT

The Government encourages overseas investment in Britain, recognising the many benefits it brings to the industrial base and the economy as a whole. Some of Britain's new manufacturing techniques and management attitudes were introduced by inward investors, which also create new employment and help boost Britain's balance of payments through increased exports and lower imports. Many overseas firms, such as Ford, Vauxhall and Black & Decker, are now household names in Britain. Overseas companies are responsible for 17 per cent of British manufacturing employment, 23 per cent of net output and 33 per cent of net capital expenditure.

Overall policy and the co-ordination of overseas promotion of inward investment are the responsibility of the Department of Trade and Industry's Invest in Britain Bureau (IBB), which represents Britain as a whole. It is supported in Britain by several territorial and regional bodies and overseas it operates through British Embassies, High Commissions and Consulates-general.

Inward investment has long been successful for foreign-owned companies operating in Britain and for Britain itself. The year 1993–94 saw a consolidation of Britain's position as the preferred location in Europe for internationally-mobile investment, with the IBB recording announcements of over 400 new projects and around 100,000 associated jobs during that period.

According to the latest official figures, Britain's share of US investment into Europe for the period 1951–93 stood at 43 per cent and its share of Japanese investment into Europe for the same period at 41 per cent. German government figures reveal German investment into Britain of 12 per cent, second only to investment into the United States.

A growing proportion of inward investment has been through expansion or reinvestment by existing investors. This trend is likely to continue as firms restructure or rationalise their European operations. The IBB and its regional partners give high priority to 'caring for' existing foreign investors, to ensure that they are aware of the advantages of remaining and expanding in Britain.

Similar advice and assistance to that provided in England is available through:

- Locate in Scotland, operated jointly by The Scottish Office Industry Department and Scottish Enterprise;

- Welsh Development International, the investment arm of the Welsh Development Agency; and

- the Industrial Development Board in Northern Ireland.

REGULATION OF MARKETS

While preferring to let markets operate as freely as possible, the Government recognises that intervention may sometimes be needed to ensure that markets are open and fair. The Government therefore seeks to control restrictive or anti-competitive practices.

Government policy provides for the regulation of monopolies, mergers, anti-competitive practices and restrictive trade practices. The Office of Fair Trading, headed by its Director General, administers the legislation on competition, consumer protection including consumer credit, fair trading and resale price maintenance. Among other things, it takes action against monopolies, cartels, anti-competitive practices and unfair trading; examines company mergers for adverse effects on competition; and scrutinises rules and practices of regulatory bodies in sectors such as financial services.

The Government has taken measures to increase competition in professional services by tackling restrictive practices. The opticians' monopoly on the dispensing of spectacles and the solicitors' monopoly on conveyancing have been ended. Certain professional groups (for example, accountants, solicitors, veterinary surgeons, stockbrokers, doctors, dentists and surveyors) have eased restrictions on advertising by their members, and rules on fee scales have been made more liberal in a number of areas. Legislation has also provided for greater competition in the provision of legal services. Building societies are now allowed to offer a greater range of services. Legislation exists to offer greater protection to investors. The Securities and Investments Board (see p. 212) is empowered to set out general principles governing the conduct of investment business.

European Community rules provide for free and fair competition in trade between member states. Enforcement of these rules is primarily the responsibility of the European Commission, which has powers to investigate and terminate alleged infringements and to impose fines. The competition authorities in Britain liaise closely with the Commission.

The Government announced in 1993 that it proposed to strengthen the law against anti-competitive practices, including increasing the investigative powers of the Director General of Fair Trading. The Government also remains committed to reforming the law on restrictive agreements.

Monopolies

The Director General of Fair Trading and the President of the Board of Trade can refer monopolies for investigation by the Monopolies and Mergers Commission, an independent body. Its members are drawn from a variety of backgrounds and include industrialists, lawyers, economists and trade unionists. The governing legislation defines a monopoly situation as one in which at least a quarter of the market for a particular product or service in Britain, or part of it, is supplied or consumed by a single person, company or a group of connected companies, or by two or more people acting in a way which prevents, restricts, or distorts competition.

If the Commission finds that a monopoly situation operates, or could be expected to operate, against the public interest, the President of the Board of Trade has powers to take action to remedy the adverse effects. Alternatively the Director General may be asked to negotiate undertakings. In 1993 the Commission reported on ten monopoly references; four further monopoly references were under investigation at the end of 1993.

Mergers

In most cases judgment of the advantages and disadvantages of mergers is left to the parties involved, with the market determining the outcome. The great majority of mergers are not considered to pose a threat to competition and are allowed to take place. However, under the Fair Trading Act 1973, the President of the Board of Trade can refer mergers for

investigation by the Monopolies and Mergers Commission if they could lead to a significant reduction in competition or otherwise raise matters of public concern.

A merger is defined as occurring when two or more enterprises come under common ownership or control. It qualifies for investigation by the Commission where:

- a market share of 25 per cent or more in Britain or a substantial part of it is created; or

- the total value of gross assets to be taken over exceeds £70 million.

After considering advice from the Director General of Fair Trading, the President of the Board of Trade may refer a merger or proposed merger to the Commission. The primary criterion of the Government's referral policy is the possible effects on competition in Britain, taking into account the international dimension of competition. If the Commission finds that a merger or proposed merger may be expected to operate against the public interest, the President of the Board of Trade can prohibit it or allow it subject to certain conditions being met. Alternatively, the Director General may be asked to obtain suitable undertakings from the companies involved to remedy the adverse effects identified. If the merger has already taken place, the President of the Board of Trade can take action to reverse it. There are special provisions for newspaper and water company mergers.

The Companies Act 1989 made changes to merger control procedures. These provided for:

- a voluntary procedure for pre-notification of proposed mergers which offers prompt clearance of straightforward cases; and

- acceptance of enforceable undertakings by the parties concerned to divest assets in order to obviate the need for a full investigation by the Commission.

Large mergers with an EU dimension, assessed by reference to turnover, come under the exclusive jurisdiction of the European Commission, with provision for referral back to national authorities in certain difficult circumstances. The Commission can ban them if it concludes that they create or strengthen a dominant position which would significantly impede effective competition within the EU or a substantial part of it.

Anti-competitive Practices

The Director General of Fair Trading can investigate any course of conduct by a business which appears to be anti-competitive. He or she must publish a report on the investigation and, if it concludes that a practice is anti-competitive, undertakings may be offered by the business responsible for the conduct. If a suitable undertaking is not given, the matter may be referred to the Monopolies and Mergers Commission to establish whether the course of conduct is an anti-competitive practice and if so whether it operates against the public interest. In the case of an adverse finding by the Commission, the President of the Board of Trade has powers to take remedial action. Firms with a turnover of less than £10 million, or which have a market share of less than 25 per cent, are exempted from investigation under the Competition Act.

Restrictive Trade Practices

Most commercial agreements containing restrictions on matters such as prices and other conditions of sale and parties or areas to be dealt with have to be notified to the Director General of Fair Trading for registration. Failure to register an agreement within the required period means that the restrictions are void and unenforceable and the parties may be liable to legal proceedings. Legal proceedings are normally initiated by the Director General against blatantly anti-competitive agreements which have not been notified as required by law.

Once an agreement has been registered, the Director General is under a general duty to refer it to the Restrictive Practices Court. If an agreement goes to the Court, it must declare the restrictions contrary to the public interest unless the parties can satisfy it that the agreement is in the public interest, using set criteria ('gateways'). Restrictions declared contrary to the public interest by the Court are void, and the Court has the power to order the parties not to implement them.

In practice, however, the great majority of agreements never reach the Court because the parties elect to give up the restrictions because they are not significant enough to warrant referral to the Court.

Resale Price Maintenance

With two exceptions—books and certain pharmaceuticals—it is unlawful for suppliers to notify dealers of a minimum resale price for their goods or to make it a condition of supply that their goods be sold at a specified price. Similarly, it is also unlawful for suppliers to seek to impose minimum resale prices by withholding supplies of goods or by discriminating against price-cutting dealers in other ways. The Director General of Fair Trading, or anyone affected, can take proceedings in the civil courts.

Consumer Protection

Consumer protection is an integral element in the fair operation of markets. The Government believes that consumers' interests are best served by open and competitive markets offering the widest choice of goods and services. There are, however, laws to ensure that consumers are adequately protected.

Legislation covers the sale of goods, the supply of goods and services, and the way that goods and services are described. The marking and accuracy of quantities are regulated by weights and measures legislation. The Food Safety Act 1990 and, for Northern Ireland, the Food Safety (NI) Order 1991 contain measures to improve food safety and to protect consumers. Another law provides for the control of medical products, and certain other substances and articles, through a system of licences and certificates. Under EC legislation, it is a criminal offence to supply unsafe consumer products. A range of public safety information for consumers has been made available by the DTI.

The Director General of Fair Trading promotes good trading practices and acts against malpractices. Under the Fair Trading Act 1973, the Director General makes recommendations for legislative or other changes to stop practices adversely affecting consumers' economic welfare, encourages trade associations to adopt codes of practice promoting consumers' interests, takes action against traders who persistently breach the law to the detriment of consumers, and disseminates consumer information and guidance.

Under the Consumer Credit Act 1974, those engaging in consumer credit or hire businesses, or ancillary businesses such as credit broking, debt collection, debt counselling and credit reference agencies, require licences. The Director General is responsible for administering the licensing system, including revoking the licences of those unfit to hold them. He or she also has powers to ban people from engaging in estate agency, and to take court action to prevent the publication of misleading advertisements.

The EU's consumer programme covers activities such as health and safety, protection of the consumer's economic interests, promotion of consumer education and strengthening the representation of consumers. The views of British consumer organisations on EU matters are represented by the Consumers in Europe Group (UK). British consumer bodies are also represented on the European consumer 'watchdog' body, the Bureau Européen des Unions de Consommateurs.

Consumer Advice and Information

Advice and information on consumer matters are given by Citizens Advice Bureaux, trading standards or consumer protection departments of local authorities (in Northern Ireland the Department of Economic Development), and, in some areas, by specialist consumer advice centres.

The independent, non-statutory National Consumer Council (and associated councils for Scotland and Wales), which receives government finance, presents the consumer's view to government, industry and others. The General Consumer Council for Northern Ireland has wide-ranging duties in consumer affairs in general.

Consumer bodies for the rail industry and for some privatised utilities investigate questions of concern to the consumer. Some trade associations in industry and commerce have established codes of practice. In addition, several private organisations work to further consumer interests. The largest is the Consumers' Association, funded by the subscriptions of its 800,000 members.

Company Law

All British companies are registered with the Registrar of Companies in Cardiff, Edinburgh or Belfast, depending on whether a company's registered office is in England or Wales, Scotland or Northern Ireland. Legislation deals with capital structure, rights and duties of directors and members, and the preparation and filing of accounts. Most corporate businesses are 'limited liability' companies. The liability of members of a limited company is restricted to contributing an amount related to their shareholding or to their guarantee where companies are limited by guarantee. In the case of unincorporated businesses, such as sole proprietorships or partnerships, individuals are personally liable for any business debts, except where a member of a partnership is a limited liability company or a limited member of a limited partnership.

Companies may be either public or private. A company must satisfy certain conditions before it can become a public limited company (plc). It must:

- be limited by shares or guarantee and have a share capital;

- state in its memorandum of association that it is to be a public limited company;

- meet specified minimum capital requirements; and

- have as the suffix to its name the words 'public limited company' or 'plc'.

All other British companies are private companies and are generally prohibited from offering their shares to the public. Companies with a place of business or branch in Britain, but which are incorporated overseas, are also required to register.

Laws relating to companies are designed to meet the need for proper regulation of business, secure open markets and create safeguards for those wishing to invest in companies or do business with them. They take account of EC directives on company law, and company and group accounts and their auditing. The Government's aim is to achieve these objectives while imposing as small a burden as possible on business. Hence, it has removed from certain types of small firms the statutory obligation to have their accounts audited and it intends to introduce a simple procedure for dissolving private companies that are no longer operational.

The 1992 Cadbury Committee Report on the management of companies contains a Code of Best Practice for company boards, underpinned by a Stock Exchange requirement for firms to state whether they are complying with the Code and giving reasons for areas of non-compliance. The Report is based on the need for effective management and for checks and balances to prevent abuses of power.

Insider dealing in shares is a criminal offence. Inspectors may be appointed to investigate possible insider dealing. Throughout Britain there is a licensing procedure to ensure the professional competence, integrity and independence of people acting as trustees of bankrupt individuals, or as liquidators, receivers or administrators of insolvent companies.

MANAGEMENT INITIATIVES

The DTI works with other government departments and with industry to improve management education and to spread awareness about best management practices through schemes such as the Enterprise Initiative (see p. 197).

Another programme, 'Managing in the 90s', offers advice to managers in small and medium-sized businesses on design, quality, production and purchasing, and materials management. It focuses on innovation and management practices in manufacturing.

Management Development and Industrial Training

Management education is on offer at many universities and colleges of higher and further education. Some regional management centres have been established in England and Wales by associations of these colleges, and there are several similar organisations in Scotland. Universities run full-time postgraduate programmes at business schools such as those of London, Manchester, Durham, Warwick and Strathclyde universities.

The British Institute of Management encourages excellence in management. Other bodies are concerned with standards and training in specialised branches of management. The employer-led Management Charter Initiative (MCI) is the operating arm of the National Forum for Management Education and Development and the leading industrial body for management standards. More than 1,800 employers, representing a quarter of the total workforce, are members of the MCI, which has 90 local networks working with local employers.

Placement Schemes

The Teaching Company Scheme (TCS) provides industrially relevant training for young graduates over a two-year period while they undertake key technology transfer projects in companies under the joint supervision of academic and company staff. There are over 500 TCS partnerships in progress at any one time. The Senior Academics in Industry Scheme supports the placement of senior academic staff into firms for six months, where they work directly on projects which will benefit from their research experience; smaller firms are given preference.

QUALITY AND STANDARDS

The Government is urging business to consider quality at all stages of design, production, marketing and delivery to customers.

Through its support for consultancy projects, the Government helps small and medium-sized firms to learn about and apply quality management techniques based on a national standard—BS EN ISO 9000—meeting international requirements. In order to increase customer confidence, companies are encouraged to obtain assessment and registration to this standard. The competence and performance of organisations undertaking such certification are officially accredited by the President of the Board of Trade through the National Accreditation Council for Certification Bodies. Companies certified by accredited bodies are permitted to use the national 'crown and tick' accreditation mark. The DTI's Register of Quality Assessed Companies lists accredited certification bodies and companies assessed by them.

British Standards Institution

The British Standards Institution (BSI), incorporated by Royal Charter, is the British member of the European and international standards organisations. It works with industry and government to produce standards of the required quality, relevant to the needs of the market, internationally respected, and suitable for public purchasing and regulatory purposes.

Government support for the BSI is directed particularly towards European and international standards work. Common standards contribute to the aim of removing technical barriers to trade in the EU. About 5,000 of the 13,000 British Standards are now identical with European or international standards. The Kitemark is the BSI's registered certification trade mark.

Measurement Standards

The DTI is responsible for policy relating to the National Measurement System. Through its contractors, it provides many of the physical measurement standards and associated calibration facilities necessary so that measurements in Britain are made on a common basis and to the required accuracy. Contractors include three DTI executive agencies: the National Physical Laboratory, the Laboratory of the Government Chemist, and the National Weights and Measures Laboratory. Links with laboratories in other countries ensure international compatibility in standards and measurement, essential for overseas trade and technological co-operation. The National Measurement Accreditation Service (NAMAS) is the national accreditation service for calibration and testing laboratories. For example, NAMAS-accredited calibration laboratories offer calibration of scientific instruments and supply official certificates in, primarily, the physical, chemical and engineering fields.

Design

Design is a key commercial tool for companies to become more profitable through the design of products and services which add value and improve performance. The British design consultancy industry has an annual estimated turnover of £1,000 million and employs around 18,000 people, mainly in small consultancies of up to six designers.

The DTI's design policy and promotion unit encourages firms to invest in design which can contribute to international competitiveness. The Design Consultancy Scheme, part of the Enterprise Initiative, helps smaller companies to use a design consultant. Between 1988 and 1993 about 5,300 design projects were commissioned, of which 4,900 have been completed.

The DTI also supports the benefits of good design through the Design Council, an independent body governed by Royal Charter. In 1993 the Government announced that the Council would be reorganised into a smaller body acting primarily as a provider of analysis and advice on design policy to government, business and others. Design services for industry in England will in future be supplied through Business Links (in Scotland, through Scottish Design), with financial support from the DTI.

Awards to Industry and Commerce

The Queen's Awards for Export and Technological Achievement recognise outstanding performance in their respective fields. Awarded annually, they are valid for five years and are granted by the Queen on the advice of the Prime Minister, who is assisted by an Advisory Committee consisting of senior representatives from industry, commerce, the trade unions and government departments. Any self-contained 'industrial unit' in Britain is eligible to apply, regardless of size, provided it meets the scheme's criteria. The Queen's Award for Environmental Achievement was launched in 1993.

Other awards include the Export Award for Smaller Businesses (for firms employing fewer than 200 people) and the MacRobert Award for engineering in Britain made by the Fellowship of Engineering for successful technological innovation.

INNOVATION

Innovation—the successful exploitation of new ideas—is vital in maintaining an economy based on competitive wealth creation. Through its Innovation Unit, which includes 20 seconded industrialists, the DTI seeks to influence the thinking of business, education, the media and Government, as well as the general public, by:

- strengthening the partnership between Government and industry;

- improving commercial exploitation of Britain's science and technology base;

- facilitating exchange of technology between business sectors;

- improving management of innovation in business by spreading best practice;

- improving communications between investors and business regarding innovation;

- increasing appreciation of the importance of innovation within education at all levels;

- encouraging a more positive attitude to innovation, as well as to science and technology;

- informing the public of the importance of innovation in wealth creation;

- developing better access to technical help, especially for small and medium-sized companies; and

- ensuring consistency and co-operation in the delivery of innovation schemes and services provided by the DTI and other government departments.

The Government's Technology Foresight Programme will help focus the attention of business and Government on commercially viable R & D (see p. 310). Networks of local (Nearnet) and national (Supernet) centres of innovation support are being set up through Business Links. The Government is also strengthening industry and university partnerships through increased funding for joint research. At present about 70 universities and 700 firms are engaged in collaborative research.

In Northern Ireland the Industrial Research and Technology Unit has a similar role to that of the DTI's Innovation Unit. It seeks to improve the competitiveness of industry by encouraging innovation, industrially relevant R & D and technology transfer. It does this through the provision of scientific services and the delivery of research and development support programmes, such as its Compete Development Programme and Science and Technology Programme.

Industrial and Intellectual Property

The Government supports innovation by protecting the rights of the originators of inventions, industrial designs, trade marks and copyright in literary, artistic and musical works. These matters are the responsibility of the Patent Office, which includes the Design Registry and the

Trade Marks Registry. The Patent Office is an executive agency of the DTI. Patent protection is also available under the European Patent Convention and the Patent Co-operation Treaty. Benefits may be claimed in other countries by virtue of separate conventions on industrial property, literary and artistic works, and music and broadcasting. Recent measures include:

- the adoption of EC directives on copyright which harmonise rental and lending rights, the rights of performers, record producers and broadcasters, and legal protection of computer programs. The directive on computer programs has been implemented into British law.

- a regulation on patents to create a supplementary protection certificate for medicinal products.

Further Reading

Competitiveness: Helping Business to Win. Cm 2563, HMSO 1994.

Government and Industry. Aspects of Britain series, HMSO, 1995.

Small Firms in Britain 1994. Department of Trade and Industry, HMSO, 1994.

15 Finance and Other Service Industries

The service industries, which include finance, retailing, tourism and business services, contribute about 65 per cent of gross domestic product and over 70 per cent of employment. Britain is responsible for about 10 per cent of the world's exports of services: overseas earnings from services in Britain amounted to around 30 per cent of the value of exports of manufactures in 1993. The number of employees in services rose from over 13 million in 1982 to 15.7 million by 1994, much of the rise being accounted for by growth in part-time (principally female) employment.

Average real disposable income per head increased by more than three-quarters between 1971 and 1993 and this was reflected in a rise in consumer spending on financial, personal and leisure services and on the maintenance and repair of consumer durables. Demand for British travel, hotel and catering services rose as real incomes in Britain and other countries increased. The spread of home ownership, particularly during the 1980s, increased demand for legal and estate agency services.

Britain is a major financial centre, housing some of the world's leading banking, insurance, securities, shipping, commodities, futures, and other financial services and markets. Financial services are an important source of employment and overseas earnings. Business services include advertising, market research, management consultancy, exhibition and conference facilities and computing.

By the year 2000, tourism is expected to be the world's biggest industry, and Britain is one of the world's leading tourist destinations. The industry is Britain's second largest, employing about 7 per cent of the workforce. Retailing is also a major employer and Britain has an advanced distribution network. An important trend in retailing has been the growth of out-of-town shopping centres.

Banking, finance, insurance, business services and leasing accounted for around one-fifth of Britain's total output in 1993, a share which has risen substantially over the last decade.

A notable trend in the services sector is the growth of franchising, an operation in which a company owning the rights to a particular form of trading licenses them to franchisees, usually by means of an initial payment with continuing royalties. The main areas include cleaning services, film processing, print shops, hairdressing and cosmetics, fitness centres, courier delivery, car rental, engine tuning and servicing, and fast food retailing.

Financial Services

Historically the financial services industry in Britain has been located in the famous 'Square Mile' in the City of London. This remains broadly the case, even though the markets for financial and related services have grown and diversified greatly. Manchester, Cardiff, Liverpool, Leeds, Edinburgh and Glasgow are also financial centres. 'The City', the collection of markets and institutions in and around the Square Mile, is noted for having:

- the greatest concentration of foreign banks in the world;

- a banking sector that accounts for about a fifth of total international bank lending;

- one of the world's largest international insurance markets;

- the largest centre in the world for trading overseas equities;

- the world's largest foreign exchange market;

- one of the world's largest financial derivatives markets;

- the greatest concentration of international bond dealers;

- important markets for transactions in commodities; and

- a full range of ancillary and support services—legal, accountancy and management consultancy—which contribute to London's strength as a financial centre.

Banking, finance and insurance accounted for 13 per cent of all employment in Great Britain in 1994. British financial institutions' net overseas earnings amounted to £15,600 million in 1993.

DEVELOPMENT OF FINANCIAL SERVICES

The growth in international movements of capital in the 1960s and 1970s mainly took the form of increased bank lending and foreign exchange trading. London became the international centre of this activity, particularly in the eurocurrency markets (see p. 222), and the number of overseas banks represented in London is larger than in any other financial centre. During the 1980s, with increasing international competition in financial services and developments in technology, London's securities markets grew rapidly. Edinburgh also developed as a centre for fund management.

Some traditional distinctions between financial institutions have been eroded, so that single firms supply a broader range of services, both in domestic and international markets. Major landmarks in the deregulation of Britain's financial services in recent years include:

- the abolition of exchange controls in 1979;

- the ending in 1980 of the supplementary special deposits scheme, which was designed to curb bank lending;

- the abolition in 1981 of the Reserve Asset Ratio requirement, under which banks had to hold 12.5 per cent of their deposits as liquid assets with the Bank of England;

- the abolition of hire purchase restrictions in 1982;

- the Building Societies Act 1986 (see p. 216); and

- 'Big Bang', also in 1986 (see p. 221).

There has since been further deregulation affecting, for instance, building societies (see p. 215) and friendly societies (see p. 216).

SUPERVISION

HM Treasury is the government department with responsibility for financial services. In particular, it is responsible for legislation covering the supervision of banks, building societies, friendly societies and investment businesses, which are subject to the regulatory system established under the Banking Act 1987 (see p. 213), the Building Societies Act 1986 (see p. 216) and the Financial Services Act 1986 (see below). The Treasury also oversees the Securities and Investments Board (SIB—see below).

The Department of Trade and Industry (DTI) is responsible for company law and insolvency matters, and for investigations and prosecutions under the Financial Services, Insolvency and Companies Acts. Investigations are carried out with the Serious Fraud Office (see p. 510). DTI's responsibilities also include prudential supervision of insurance undertakings, European Community (EC) insurance directives, insurance interests in the Organisation for Economic Co-operation and Development (OECD) and the General Agreement on Tariffs and Trade (GATT), and general questions affecting the insurance industry. It also has powers to investigate 'insider dealing'—securities trading carried out on the basis of privileged access to relevant information.

The Treasury negotiates and implements EC directives relating to financial services and is responsible for arrangements with overseas regulators for exchanging information. Various EC directives give or will give banking, insurance and investment services firms the freedom to operate throughout the European Union (EU) on the basis of their home state authorisation. The European Economic Area (EEA) agreement extends the principles of the single market to Austria, Finland, Iceland, Norway and Sweden.

The Treasury is also charged with encouraging international liberalisation in financial services both bilaterally and through GATT and the OECD. Following the successful conclusion of the Uruguay round of GATT talks in 1993, financial and other services will be subject to the principles of multilateral trade rules.

International supervisory forums include the Basle Committee on Banking Supervision and the International Organisation of Securities Commissions (IOSCO). IOSCO is the primary international meeting place for regulatory authorities. Its 1992 conference, held in London, approved a set of principles for the supervision of financial conglomerates and released guidelines for clearing and settlement systems in energy markets.

The main provisions of the Financial Services Act came into force in 1988; and most of the Act's powers are delegated to the SIB. Under the Act, investment businesses (those dealing in, arranging, managing or giving advice on investments or operating collective investment schemes) require authorisation and are subject to rules on the conduct of business and other rules made under the legislation. The SIB has recognised a number of self-regulating organisations (SROs) and recognised professional bodies (RPBs). It has a duty to assist SROs and RPBs to fulfil their regulatory functions. Most investment businesses are authorised under the Act by virtue of membership of one of these. The SROs are:

- the Investment Management Regulatory Organisation (IMRO), whose members include merchant banks and pension fund managers with mainly corporate clients;

- the Securities and Futures Authority (SFA), whose members include member firms of the London Stock Exchange, as well as futures brokers and dealers, and eurobond dealers; and

- the Personal Investment Authority (PIA), which came into operation in July 1994, is the main single regulator for retail investment services covering the marketing and provision of advice on products like life assurance, pension funds, unit trusts and investment trusts. All retail firms are encouraged to join the PIA, which is expected to deliver improved standards of investor protection; however, there remains the option of direct regulation by the SIB.

Other information relating to supervision and regulation is contained in the following section and in the sections dealing with the various types of financial institutions and markets.

BANK OF ENGLAND

The Bank of England was established in 1694 by Act of Parliament and Royal Charter as a corporate body. Its entire capital stock was acquired by the Government in 1946. The Bank acts as banker to the Government, holding its main accounts, managing Britain's reserves of gold and foreign exchange, arranging new government borrowing and managing the stock of its existing debt. The Bank's main objectives are to:

- ensure the soundness of the financial system through the direct supervision of banks and specialised City institutions;

- promote the efficiency and competitiveness of the financial system, especially in domestic and international payment and settlement systems; and

- provide advice on and implement the Government's monetary policy.

The Banking Act 1987 assigns the Bank of England the overriding objective of protecting depositors. To this end institutions intending to take deposits from the public must gain authorisation from the Bank and submit to its continued supervision. Under the Financial Services Act 1986, the Bank is also responsible for overseeing money-market institutions (see p. 221). The Bank's supervision is 'prudential'—it sets minimum standards for authorised institutions but offers no guarantee that those institutions will not fail or that investors or depositors will be compensated in full. The Banking Act established the Deposit Protection Fund, financed by contributions levied on the banking system; this entitles depositors to limited compensation if an authorised bank fails. In order to be and remain authorised, an institution has to satisfy the Bank that it has:

- adequate capital and liquidity;

- a realistic business plan;

- adequate systems and controls;

- adequate provision for bad and doubtful debts; and

- that its business is carried out with integrity and skill, and in a prudent manner.

The Bank is the Government's agent for selling marketable debt. It maintains the register of holdings of government securities on behalf of the Treasury, and manages the Exchange Equalisation Account holding the Government's official reserves of gold, foreign exchange, Special Drawing Rights (SDRs—claims on the International Monetary Fund) and European Currency Units (ECUs). The reserves are used to check undue fluctuations in the exchange value of sterling and to enable government departments to meet their foreign currency needs.

The Bank is able to influence money-market conditions through its dealings with the discount houses (see p. 217), which developed in the 19th century as bill brokers for industrialists. Discount houses hold mainly Treasury, local authority and commercial bills, and negotiable certificates of deposit financed by short-term loans from the banks. If on a particular day there is a shortage of cash in the banking system as a result, for example, of large tax payments, the Bank relieves the shortage either by buying bills from the discount houses or by lending directly to them. This permits banks to replenish their cash balances at the Bank by recalling some of their short-term loans to the discount houses. The Bank's dealings with the discount houses give it powerful influence over short-term interest rates.

The Bank of England has the sole right in England and Wales to issue banknotes. The note issue is no longer backed by gold but by government and other securities. Three Scottish and four Northern Ireland banks also issue notes. These issues, apart from a small amount specified by legislation for each bank, must be fully covered by holdings of Bank of England notes and coinage. Responsibility for the provision of coin lies with the Royal Mint, a government trading fund which became an executive agency in 1990.

The Bank of England seeks to ensure that Britain's financial markets are efficient and competitive. To this end it runs two securities settlement systems with in-built payment arrangements—the Central Gilts Office and the Central Moneymarket Office. A permanent body of market and legal practitioners—the Financial Law Panel—has been established by the Bank to help find practical solutions to problems of legal uncertainty in the wholesale financial markets.

BANKS AND BUILDING SOCIETIES

In addition to banks, the chief institutions offering banking services are the building societies and the National Savings Bank. The 'single passport' system created by the European Community Second Banking Directive allows 'credit institutions' (banks and building societies) to operate throughout the EEA on the basis of their home-state authorisation.

A useful distinction can be made between 'retail' and 'wholesale' banking. Retail banking is primarily for personal customers and small businesses. Its main services are cash deposit and withdrawal facilities, and money transmission systems. Competition between the banks and the building societies in providing money transmission services to individuals has increased during the last two decades and is expected to intensify further (see p. 216). Building societies can also offer money transmission services to companies.

Wholesale business involves taking large deposits at higher rates of interest, deploying funds in money-market instruments (see p. 221) and making large loans and investments. Nearly all banks in Britain engage in some wholesale activities and some, such as the merchant and overseas banks, centre their business on them. Many such wholesale dealings are conducted on the inter-bank market, that is, between banks themselves.

In 1994 there were 389 institutions authorised under the Banking Act 1987, including clearing banks, investment banks, branches of overseas banks from outside the EEA, discount houses and banking subsidiaries of both banking and non-banking institutions from Britain and overseas. Additionally, there were 97 branches of banks from EEA countries entitled to take deposits in Britain; such 'European authorised institutions' are authorised by the relevant authority in their home country. Of this total of 486 banks, around 320 were members of the British Bankers' Association, the main representative body for British banks.

Retail Banks

The major retail banks have a significant branch network, offering a full range of financial services to both individuals and companies. Among services generally available are interest-bearing current accounts; deposit accounts; and various kinds of loan arrangements. In addition, there is a full range of money transmission facilities that increasingly feature plastic card technology.

The major banks in England and Wales are Barclays, Lloyds, Midland, National Westminster, the TSB Group and Abbey National; and in Scotland the Bank of Scotland and the Royal Bank of Scotland. Other important retail banks are the Clydesdale Bank, the Co-operative Bank, the Yorkshire Bank and Alliance & Leicester Giro (formerly Girobank). Northern Ireland is served by branch networks of four major banking groups.

With the growth of financial services and a relaxation of restrictions on competition among financial institutions, the major banks have diversified their services. They are lending more money for house purchases, and most now own finance houses, leasing and factoring companies, merchant banks, securities dealers, insurance companies and unit trust companies.

The banks offer loan facilities to companies; since the 1970s they have provided more medium- and long-term loans than they did formerly. They have become important suppliers of finance for small firms. A loan guarantee scheme is supported by the banks, under which 70 per cent (85 per cent in certain cases) of the value of bank loans to small companies is guaranteed by the Government. Some banks have set up special subsidiaries to provide venture capital for companies (see p. 220). Most retail banks maintain overseas subsidiaries, which may account for a substantial proportion of their business, and are active in eurocurrency markets (see p. 221).

The total liabilities/assets of the retail banks amounted to over £540,000 million in 1994. Liabilities are made up of sterling deposits, foreign currency deposits, items in suspense or transmission, and capital and other funds. The banks' main liquid assets consist of money at call (mainly short-term loans to discount houses), their holdings of Treasury and other bills, short-dated British government securities and balances at the Bank of England. They also hold a proportion of their assets as portfolio investments (mainly longer-dated British government securities) or trade investments.

The main retail banks operate through over 12,100 branches and sub-branches in Britain. National Westminster has the largest number, with 2,545 branches, followed by Barclays (2,119), Lloyds (1,860), Midland (1,713), TSB (1,321), the Royal Bank of Scotland (752), Abbey National (686), Bank of Scotland (455), Clydesdale Bank (314), Yorkshire Bank (270) and the Co-operative Bank (109). Around three-quarters of adults in Britain have a current account and over one-third a deposit account.

Payment Systems

Apart from credit and debit card arrangements, the main payment systems are run by three separate companies operating under an umbrella organisation, the Association for Payment Clearing Services (APACS), of which 23 banks and building societies are members. One covers bulk paper clearings—cheques and credit transfers. A second deals with high-value clearings for same-day settlement, namely the nationwide electronic transfer service Clearing House Automated Payment System (CHAPS) and the cheque-based Town Clearing (which operates only in the City of London). A third covers bulk electronic clearing for standing orders and direct debits. Membership of each of these clearing companies is open to any bank, building society or other financial institution meeting the criteria for appropriate supervision and volume of transactions.

Plastic Card Technology

All the major retail banks and building societies have substantial networks of automated teller machines, which give customers access to cash and other services for up to 24 hours a day. Almost 18,500 machines were in operation at the end of 1993.

The banks and major building societies also offer their customers cheque guarantee cards—typically for amounts up to £100. The cards entitle holders to cheque-cashing facilities in participating institutions and guarantee retailers that transactions up to the specified guarantee limit will be honoured. Uniform eurocheques supported by a eurocheque card are available from all major banks. These standard-format cheques may be used to obtain cash or make payments in Britain, elsewhere in Europe and in a few other overseas countries. The cheques are made out in the currency of the country in which they are being used, with a guarantee limit of the equivalent of £100 per cheque.

Credit cards issued by major retail banks and building societies are a popular means of payment and are widely accepted throughout Britain and overseas. Most cards are affiliated to one of the two major international credit card organisations, Visa and MasterCard. Some of the major retail stores issue their own cards, which operate like credit cards. A charge card, like a credit card, enables the holder to make retail payments, but there is either no credit limit or a very high limit, and the balance must be settled in full on receipt of a monthly statement.

As well as the traditional paper-based systems for making retail payments by credit or charge cards, an increasing number of stores and garages now provide EFTPOS (see p. 226) facilities. Using debit cards, payments can be deducted directly from the purchaser's bank account. Most cards are affiliated either to Visa or to the Switch organisation, which is based in Britain.

Home Banking

A growing number of banks and building societies offer home banking services whereby customers use a telephone or personal computer to obtain account information, make transfers and pay bills. Midland's First Direct is one such service.

Building Societies

Building societies are mutual institutions, owned by their savers and borrowers. They raise short-term deposits from savers, who are generally able to withdraw their money on demand or at short notice. The societies make long-term loans, mostly at variable rates of interest, against the security of property—usually private dwellings purchased for owner-occupation. They are the major lenders for house purchase in Britain and are the main repository for the personal sector's liquid assets. Around 60 per cent of adults have building society savings accounts.

Competition between the building societies and other financial institutions has increased in the last decade. A variety of savings schemes have been established, and a growing number of societies provide current account facilities such as cheque books and automated teller machines.

There are 84 registered societies, of which 83 are members of the Building Societies' Association. Building societies' assets totalled £281,000 million at the end of 1993; about £33,000 million was advanced in new mortgages in the course of the year. The three largest—the Halifax, Nationwide and Woolwich—account for about one-half of the total assets of all societies.

The Building Societies Act 1986 enabled societies to diversify into banking and other services. Up to 25 per cent of a society's commercial assets may be used for purposes other than loans on first mortgage of owner-occupied houses, including as much as 15 per cent in other types of asset such as unsecured loans. Directly or through subsidiaries, societies may offer services within the general areas of banking, investment, insurance, trusteeship, executorship and estate agency. The Government has decided to allow societies to raise up to 50 per cent (up from 40 per cent) of their funds on the wholesale market; set up subsidiaries to make loans to businesses not secured on land; and wholly own a general insurance firm offering buildings and contents insurance as well as mortgage payments protection policies. However, their main business will continue to be financial and housing-related services.

The 1986 Act established the Building Societies Commission to carry out the prudential supervision of building societies. It also made provision for a society to seek the approval of its members to convert into a public limited company. In this event the society becomes an authorised institution under the Banking Act 1987 (see p. 214) and is then supervised by the Bank of England. Abbey National pursued this course and no longer contributes to building society statistics.

The Council of Mortgage Lenders is a trade body established in 1989 for all mortgage lending institutions, including building societies, insurance companies, finance houses and banks.

Friendly Societies

Friendly societies have traditionally been unincorporated societies of individuals, offering their members a limited range of financial services, particularly provision for retirement and against loss of income through sickness or unemployment. The Friendly Societies Act 1992 enabled friendly societies to incorporate, take on new powers and offer a broad range of financial services through subsidiaries.

Merchant Banks

Merchant banks have traditionally been concerned primarily with accepting, or guaranteeing, commercial bills and with sponsoring capital issues on behalf of their customers. Today they undertake a diversified range of activities. After the 'Big Bang' some merchant banks acquired securities trading operations. Merchant banks have important roles in equity and debt markets and the provision of advice and financial services to industrial companies, especially where mergers, takeovers and other forms of corporate reorganisation are involved. Management of investment holdings, including trusts, pensions and other funds, is also an important function of merchant banks. The sector is split between independent houses and those which are part of larger banking groups.

Overseas Banks

A total of 286 banks incorporated overseas are represented in Britain. Of these, 24 are from the United States and 28 from Japan. A total of 78 institutions incorporated in Britain are subsidiaries of overseas companies. They offer a comprehensive banking service in many parts of the world and engage in the financing of trade not only between Britain and other countries but also between third-party countries.

British-based Overseas Banks

A small number of banks have their head offices in Britain, but operate mainly abroad, often specialising in particular regions. Standard Chartered, which is represented in Asia, Africa and the Middle East, is the major example of this type of bank.

Discount Houses

There are seven discount houses authorised under the Banking Act 1987. These are specialised institutions unique in their function and central position in the British monetary system. They act as financial intermediaries between the Bank of England and the rest of the banking sector, promoting an orderly flow of short-term funds. They guarantee to tender for the whole of the weekly offer of the Government's Treasury bills, which are instruments to raise funds over a period of up to six months. In return for acting as intermediaries, the discount houses have secured borrowing facilities at the Bank of England, acting as 'lender of last resort'. Assets of the discount houses consist mainly of Treasury and commercial bills, negotiable certificates of deposit and short-term loans. Their liabilities are for the most part short-term deposits.

National Savings Bank

The National Savings Bank is run by the Department for National Savings, a government department. It contributes to government borrowing and aims to encourage saving by offering personal savers a range of investments, designed to meet various requirements. Important products include:

- Savings Certificates, which either pay a fixed rate of interest alone or a lower fixed rate of interest combined with index-linking;

- Premium Bonds, where interest is paid in the form of prizes chosen by lottery;

- Income and Capital Bonds;

- Children's Bonus Bonds, which are designed to accumulate capital sums for those under 21;

- Ordinary and Investment Accounts, where deposits and withdrawals can be made at post offices throughout Britain;

- FIRST Option Bonds, launched in 1992, which offer a guaranteed rate of interest that is fixed for one year; and

- Pensioners' Guaranteed Income Bonds, where interest is paid monthly and rates are fixed for five years at a time.

With the exception of FIRST Option Bonds, interest on National Savings products is paid without deduction of tax at source. Certain National Savings products offer tax exempt returns. In some cases the best returns are paid to those who leave their savings untouched for several years. In August 1994 the total amount of money invested in National Savings was over £50,000 million.

INSURANCE

London is the world's leading centre for insurance and for placing international reinsurance; it handles an estimated 20 per cent of the general insurance business placed on the international market. There are two broad categories of insurance: long-term life insurance, where contracts may be for periods of many years; and general insurance, including accident and short-term life insurance, where contracts are for a year or less. Authorised insurance companies are supervised by the Department of Trade and Industry under the Insurance Companies Act 1982.

In addition to the British companies and Lloyd's (see p. 218), a large number of overseas companies are represented, with which many British companies have formed close relationships. Some British companies confine their activities to domestic business but most large companies undertaking general business transact a substantial amount overseas through branches and agencies or affiliated local companies.

Over 820 companies are authorised to carry on one or more classes of insurance business in Britain. About 450 companies belong to the Association of British Insurers (ABI). Some companies are mutual institutions, owned by their policy holders. Insurance is also available from certain friendly societies (see p. 216).

EC directives introducing the 'single-licence' system in insurance came into force in July 1994. Life and non-life insurers may operate throughout the EEA on the basis of authorisation in their home state. Separate directives cover reinsurance, motor insurance and co-insurance.

Long-term Insurance

As well as providing life cover, life insurance is a vehicle for saving and investment because premiums are invested in securities and other assets. About 30 per cent of adults have life assurance policies. The net long-term insurance premium income of companies representing about 99 per cent of the British market in 1993 was over £56,000 million from their worldwide operations. Long-term insurance is handled by 194 companies.

General Insurance

General insurance business is undertaken by insurance companies and by underwriters at Lloyd's. It includes fire, accident, general liability, short-term life, motor, marine, aviation and transport risks. Total ABI member company premium income worldwide in 1993 was £34,000 million, of which £21,000 million was earned in Britain.

Lloyd's

Lloyd's, the origins of which go back to the 17th century, is an incorporated society of private insurers in London. Although its

activities were originally confined to marine insurance, a considerable worldwide market for the transaction of other classes of insurance business, such as aviation and motor insurance, has been built up.

Lloyd's is not a company but a market for insurance administered by the Council of Lloyd's and Lloyd's Regulatory and Market Boards. Business is carried out for individual elected underwriting members, or 'names', trading with unlimited liability in competition with each other and with insurance companies. From January 1994 corporate members with limited liability have been trading alongside individual members. Both are required to satisfy certain financial requirements and maintain set levels of deposits at Lloyd's.

For the 1994 year of account, there was total market capacity of £10,900 million provided by 18,022 members grouped into 179 syndicates. Each syndicate is managed by an underwriting agent responsible for appointing a professional underwriter to accept insurance risks and settle claims on the syndicate members' behalf. With the exception of motor insurance business, insurance may only be placed through accredited Lloyd's brokers, who negotiate with Lloyd's syndicates on behalf of the insured. Reinsurance constitutes a large part of Lloyd's business.

Lloyd's net premium income in 1991, the most recent year for which figures are available, was £6,000 million.

Lloyd's has suffered severe losses in recent years, partly as a result of a series of natural disasters, including the storms in Britain in October 1987, the *Exxon Valdez* oil tanker disaster off the coast of Alaska in 1989, and Hurricane Andrew, which struck Florida and Louisiana in 1992; the recent recession has also adversely affected trading.

Institute of London Underwriters

The Institute of London Underwriters was formed in 1884, originally as a trade association for marine underwriters. It now provides a market where member insurance companies transact marine, energy, commercial transport and aviation business. The Institute issues combined policies in its own name on risks which are underwritten by member companies. The gross premium income processed by the Institute's member companies in 1993 was £2,460 million. About half of the 80 member companies are branches or subsidiaries of overseas companies.

Insurance Brokers

Insurance brokers acting on behalf of the insured are a valuable part of the company market and play an essential role in the Lloyd's market. Smaller brokers mainly deal with the general public or specialise in a particular type of commercial insurance. Medium to large brokers almost exclusively handle commercial insurance, with the largest dealing with risks worldwide. Some brokers specialise in reinsurance business, serving as intermediaries in the exchange of contracts between companies, both British and overseas, and often acting as London representatives of the latter.

The Insurance Brokers (Registration) Act 1977 makes provision for the voluntary registration and regulation of insurance brokers by the Insurance Brokers Registration Council. Only those registered with the Council can use the title 'insurance broker'. In 1994 15,340 individuals were registered with the Council, through 2,100 partnerships or sole traderships and 2,600 limited companies.

Insurance may be broked without registration with the Council so long as the title 'insurance broker' is not used. There are about 7,000 non-registered intermediaries operating under the Association of British Insurers' code of practice.

INVESTMENT

Investment Funds

Britain has a great deal of expertise in fund management, which involves managing funds on the investor's behalf, or advising investors on how to invest their funds. The main types of investment fund include pension schemes, life assurance, investment trusts and unit trusts.

Pension Funds

All occupational pension schemes are established under trust law to protect the interests of members and most pay benefits related to final salary. Benefits are funded in advance by employer (and wholly employee) contributions, which are held and invested by trustees on behalf of beneficiaries. Pension funds are major investors in securities markets. Total British pension fund net assets were worth in the region of £460,000 million at the end of 1993; pension funds hold around 30 per cent of securities listed on the London Stock Exchange. Since 1986, members of occupational pension schemes have been able to opt out and set up a personal pension scheme. Over 13 million people belong to occupational pension schemes and more than 5 million to personal pension schemes.

Investment and Unit Trusts

Investment trust companies, which offer the opportunity to diversify risk even on a relatively small investment, are listed on the London Stock Exchange and their shares are traded in the usual way. They must invest mostly in securities, and the trusts themselves are exempt from capital gains tax. Assets are purchased mainly out of shareholders' funds, although investment trusts are also allowed to borrow money for investment. There were 292 members of the Association of Investment Trust Companies in August 1994, with £38,000 million worth of assets under management.

Authorised unit trusts are open-ended mutual or pooled investment vehicles which place funds in a wide range of securities markets all over the world. As with investment trusts, investors with relatively small amounts to invest are able to benefit from diversified and expertly managed portfolios. The industry has grown rapidly during the last decade, and in 1993 there were over 1,500 authorised unit trusts. By May 1994 total assets were £95,000 million. Unit trust management groups are represented by the Association of Unit Trusts and Investment Funds and regulated by IMRO. The trusts themselves are authorised by the SIB.

Personal Equity Plans

Personal equity plans (PEPs) were introduced to encourage shareholding by individuals. Dividends and capital gains on shares held in a PEP are exempted from income tax and capital gains tax, and withdrawals from plans are normally tax free (see p. 158).

SPECIAL FINANCING INSTITUTIONS

Several specialised institutions offer finance and support to personal and corporate sector borrowers. These borrowers are found in both the public and the private sectors. Among public sector agencies are Scottish Enterprise, Highlands and Islands Enterprise, the Welsh Development Agency, the Industrial Development Board for Northern Ireland and ECGD (Export Credits Guarantee Department—Britain's official export credit insurer). The part of ECGD that handled the export of capital goods sold on short-term credit was privatised in 1991 and is now dealt with by NCM Credit Insurance.

Some private sector institutions were set up with government support and with financing from banks and other financial institutions. They may offer loan finance or equity capital. The main private sector institutions are described below.

Finance and Leasing Companies

In 1992 the Finance Houses Association and the Equipment Leasing Association formed a single new representative body, the Finance and Leasing Association (FLA). This represents the interests of companies offering motor finance, consumer credit, and business finance and leasing. The FLA's 108 members undertook new business worth £13,455 million in 1993.

Factoring Companies

Factoring comprises a range of financial services which provide growing companies with a flexible source of finance in exchange for the outstanding invoices due to them. Factoring has developed as a major financial service since the early 1960s, covering international activities as well as domestic trade. Member companies of the Association of British Factors and Discounters handled business worth £19,700 million in 1993.

Venture Capital Companies

Venture capital companies offer medium- and long-term equity financing for new and developing businesses when such funds are not easily or directly available from traditional sources, such as the stock market or banks. The British Venture Capital Association has 115 full members and makes up virtually all the industry. Many venture capital companies are subsidiaries of other financial institutions, including banks, insurance companies and pension funds. The largest of Britain's venture capital companies is 3i.

FINANCIAL MARKETS

The City of London has a variety of financial markets. They include the London Stock Exchange, the foreign exchange market, the financial futures and options market, eurobond and eurocurrency markets, Lloyd's insurance market (see p. 218), and bullion and commodity markets. The securities markets are supervised jointly by the Treasury, the Bank of England, SIB and the London Stock Exchange, among others.

London Stock Exchange

The London Stock Exchange has its main administrative centre in London, as well as centres in Belfast, Birmingham, Leeds, Glasgow and Manchester. As a result of a set of reforms implemented in 1986 and known popularly as 'Big Bang', the Exchange has changed radically in recent years. The main reforms were as follows:

- the Exchange's rules on membership were altered to allow corporate ownership of member firms;
- the system under which dealers charged fixed minimum scales of commission to investors was abolished in favour of negotiated commissions;
- dealers were permitted to trade in securities both on their own behalf, as principals, and on behalf of clients, as agents, these two roles formerly having been kept distinct; and
- a screen-based price quotation system was introduced and led to the closing of the trading floor.

The London Stock Exchange is one of the largest in the world in terms of the number and variety of securities listed. It accounts for 10 per cent of equity trading worldwide. More than 8,000 securities are listed; in 1993 these had a market value of almost £3,300,000 million. About 2,400 company securities are listed, including those of a growing number of leading overseas companies, with a value of around £2,800,000 million. The remainder is made up of British and overseas government and corporate stocks as well as eurobonds (see p. 221).

Throughout the 1980s a trend towards the 'securitisation of debt' developed, with major borrowers increasingly raising funds by issuing securities rather than by seeking out bank loans. In recent years the largest market for new issues has been that for companies' securities, including issues of shares resulting from the Government's privatisation programme.

The gilt-edged market allows the Government to borrow money by issuing loan stock through the Bank of England. The Stock Exchange offers a secondary market where investors can buy and sell gilts.

European Community Directives

The London Stock Exchange altered its rules in 1990 to conform to EC directives on listing particulars, prospectuses and mutual recognition. The major effect of the EC directive on Mutual Recognition of Listing Particulars is that, subject to certain limitations, each member state is required to recognise listing particulars accepted in another member state. In order to put British companies on an equal footing with those in other EU countries, the Exchange reduced the minimum trading record requirement for full listing from five years to three.

Money Markets

The London money markets comprise the interbank deposit markets plus a range of other instruments, usually short-term in maturity. They are wholesale in the sense that the participants are professional operators dealing in substantial amounts of money.

Banks are the major participants in these markets, and are supervised by the Bank of England. The Bank also supervises other institutions which operate in the foreign exchange and other wholesale money markets. In close consultation with market participants, the Bank has issued the London Code of Conduct, which defines the instruments that comprise the wholesale money markets and the standards and dealing procedures which participants should follow.

Since 1986, large companies have been permitted to issue sterling commercial paper (SCP), which takes the form of negotiable bearer debt securities with a maturity of up to one year. The range of qualifying issuers of SCP has broadened since 1986 to include, for example, banks, building societies and overseas public authorities.

Euromarkets

These are markets in currencies lent or invested outside their domestic marketplace, particularly as a means of financing international trade and investment. Transactions can thus be carried out in eurodollars, eurodeutschemarks, euroyen and so on. London is at the heart of the euromarkets and houses most of the major international banks and securities firms.

The euromarkets developed in the late 1950s following the restoration of convertibility between the major currencies, partly to avoid incurring the costs of exchange control and other regulations. In recent years distinctions between markets have been breaking down and the euromarkets form a major part of the wider international money and capital markets. Participants in the markets include multinational trading corporations, financial companies, governments and international organisations like the World Bank and the European Investment Bank.

The euro-securities markets have grown considerably in recent years because the instruments traded on them, including eurobonds, euro-medium-term notes (EMTNs) and euro-commercial paper, are seen as flexible alternatives to bank loans. EMTN programmes were introduced in 1986, and EMTN issues rose sevenfold between 1990 and 1993. British building societies are prominent among EMTN issuers. There is a growing private sector market in ECU-denominated deposits, securities and eurobonds.

Foreign Exchange Market

London is the world's biggest centre for foreign exchange trading, with an average daily turnover of about US $300,000 million. In terms of currencies traded, it has the most diversified exchange market in the world.

The foreign exchange market consists of telephone and electronic links between the participants, which include banks, other financial institutions and several foreign exchange broking firms acting as intermediaries between the banks. It provides those engaged in international trade and investment with foreign currencies for their transactions. The banks are in close contact with financial centres abroad and are able to quote buying and selling rates for both immediate ('spot') and forward transactions in a range of currencies and maturities. The forward market enables traders and dealers who, at a given date in the future, wish to receive or make a specific foreign currency payment, to contract in advance to sell or buy the foreign currency involved for sterling at a fixed exchange rate.

Derivatives

Financial derivatives are contracts to buy or sell, at a future date, financial instruments such as equities, bonds or money-market instruments. They offer a means of hedging against changes in prices, exchange rates and interest rates. Derivatives include futures (agreements to buy or sell financial instruments or physical commodities at a future date), options (the right to buy or sell financial instruments or physical commodities for a stated period at a predetermined price) and 'over-the-counter' products, including swaps. A foreign exchange swap can convert a money-market instrument in one currency into a money-market instrument in another—a dollar deposit into a sterling deposit, for example.

The use of derivatives has grown rapidly and instruments have become more complex, especially as advances have been made in information technology and links between markets and institutions strengthened. Between 1992 and 1993 the turnover on London's futures and options exchanges grew by 38 per cent to reach 155 million contracts. LIFFE (see below) accounted for almost two-thirds of the contracts traded in 1993 and the London Metal Exchange (see p. 223) accounted for about a fifth.

Financial Futures and Options

Banks, other financial institutions, brokers and individual traders are members of the London International Financial Futures and Options Exchange (LIFFE), which trades at the Cannon Bridge development. Futures contracts cover the purchase or sale of a fixed amount of a commodity at a given date in the future at a price agreed at the time of trade. There is also dealing in options on the equity of prominent British companies and in stock index options. LIFFE has the most internationally diverse range of financial futures and options products of any exchange in the world.

London Bullion Market

Around 60 banks and other financial trading companies comprise the London gold and silver markets, which, like the foreign exchange market, trade by telephone or other electronic means. Five of the members of the London Bullion Market Association meet twice daily to establish a London fixing price for gold—a reference point for worldwide dealings. The silver fixing is held once a day. Although much interest centres upon the fixings, active dealing takes place throughout the day. London and Zurich are the main world centres for gold dealings.

Commodity, Shipping and Freight Markets

Britain is a major international centre for commodities trading and the home of many of the related international trade organisations. At the London Commodities Exchange, futures in grains and potatoes are traded, as are futures and options on 'soft' commodities (cocoa and coffee). White sugar, raw sugar and dry freight index futures contracts are also traded. The London Metal Exchange is the primary base metals market in the world, trading both spot and forward contracts in aluminium, aluminium alloy, copper, lead, nickel, tin and zinc. The International Petroleum Exchange is Europe's only energy futures exchange. The Baltic Exchange, which finds ships for cargoes and cargoes for ships throughout the world, is the world's leading international shipping market.

Other Services

DISTRIBUTION AND SALES

Distribution

Distributing goods to their point of sale by road, rail, air and sea is a major economic activity, accounting for about a sixth of national income. In 1993 there were 3.3 million employees in the distributive and allied trades in Great Britain. The large retailers and wholesalers of food, drink and clothing operate, either directly or through contractors, extensive distribution networks.

Wholesaling

There were 127,000 businesses, with a turnover valued at £224,000 million (see Table 15.1), engaged in wholesaling and dealing in Great Britain in 1992.

In the food and drink trade almost all large retailers have their own buying and central distribution operations. Elsewhere in the trade, voluntary 'symbol' groups (for example, Spa and VG) have been formed by wholesalers and small independent retailers. This has helped many smaller retail outlets, including traditional 'corner shops' and village stores, to stay in business as it has given them the advantages of bulk buying and co-ordinated distribution.

Table 15.1: Wholesale Trade in Great Britain 1992

	Number of businesses	Turnover[a] (£ million)
Food and drink	15,971	48,070
Petroleum products	968	19,805
Clothing, furs, textiles and footwear	10,440	10,148
Coal and oil merchants	2,976	3,225
Builders' merchants	4,197	8,160
Agricultural supplies and livestock dealing	2,889	7,471
Industrial materials	6,129	23,791
Scrap and waste products	3,470	2,233
Industrial and agricultural machinery	9,211	17,726
Operational leasing	2,468	1,831
Other goods	68,008	81,318
Total wholesaling and dealing	126,729	223,777

Source: *Business Monitor SDA26. Wholesaling, 1992*
[a] Excludes value added tax.

London's wholesale markets play a significant part in the distribution of foodstuffs. New Covent Garden is the main market for fruit and vegetables, Smithfield for meat and Billingsgate for fish.

The Co-operative Movement has its own distribution organisation, the Co-operative Wholesale Society (CWS). Retail co-operative societies buy from the CWS, which is their main supplier. The CWS is also a major retailer in Scotland, Northern Ireland, the Midlands and south-east, and northern England.

Retailing

The retail market in Britain is highly competitive. In 1991 there were 232,000 retail businesses, with 342,000 outlets, in Great Britain (see Table 15.2). During recent years the large multiple retailers have grown considerably in Britain, reducing numbers of stores but increasing outlet size and diversifying their product ranges. Some, like Marks and Spencer and the supermarket groups J. Sainsbury and Tesco (see below), have opened branches or made franchise arrangements abroad, especially on the European continent. Decline has been particularly evident among small independent businesses and retail co-operative societies (see above). Of the 25 largest retailers in Western Europe, more than one-third are British.

The biggest multiple retailers in the grocery market are J. Sainsbury, Tesco, Argyll (which includes Safeway) and Asda. These four groups had a market share of 38 per cent in 1992–93. Other important groups are Waitrose and Morrisons. Kwik Save is the leading discount food retailer. Since 1991 several overseas discount food retailers, such as Aldi and Netto, have entered the British market.

Retail co-operative societies are voluntary organisations controlled by their members, membership being open to anyone paying a small deposit on a minimum share. There are 4,600 retail co-operative outlets, over half of which sell food and groceries.

Alcoholic drinks are sold mainly in specialist 'off licences' and supermarkets, the former accounting for 51 per cent of sales and the latter 49 per cent. The selling of alcohol is closely controlled by law and only permitted between certain hours. The principal off licence chains are Cellar Five, Oddbins, Threshers and Victoria Wine.

Table 15.2: Retail Trade in Great Britain 1991

	Number of businesses	Number of outlets	Number of people engaged ('000s)	Turnover[a] (£ million)
Single-outlet retailers	205,641	205,641	759	35,560
Small multiple retailers	25,510	65,574	305	16,233
Large multiple retailers	894	71,107	1,303	87,797
Food retailers	62,009	82,572	813	51,485
Drink, confectionery and tobacco retailers	49,109	61,528	274	13,664
Clothing, footwear and leather goods retailers	27,321	56,571	289	13,134
Household goods retailers	49,248	67,987	322	21,718
Other non-food retailers	38,322	54,033	261	12,919
Mixed retail businesses	4,163	13,145	376	25,348
Hire and repair businesses	1,873	6,485	33	1,323
Total retail trade	232,045	342,321	2,367	139,590

Source: *Business Monitor SDA25. Retailing, 1991.*
[a] Includes value added tax.

The leading mixed retail businesses include Marks and Spencer, Boots, Kingfisher (which includes Woolworth), Storehouse, W. H. Smith, Argos, Littlewoods, Savacentre (J. Sainsbury), John Menzies, Sears, Burton Group and House of Fraser.

About 18 million people regularly buy all kinds of goods and services through mail order catalogues like Freemans, Great Universal Stores, Empire and Littlewoods. In 1993 sales by general mail order totalled £4,200 million, 3 per cent of all retail sales. The largest selling items are clothing, footwear, furniture, household textiles and domestic electrical appliances.

Shopping Facilities

Britain has a wide range of complementary shopping facilities inside and outside town and city centres. One of the most significant trends in retailing has been the spread of superstores (of which there are around 900). While the 100 largest retailers account for 62 per cent of retail sales, there continues to be a demand for the products and services provided by small, specialised shops.

The main multiple grocery companies have experienced strong competitive pressures and have turned their attention to town centres with smaller outlets aimed at the convenience market. Examples include Tesco's 'Metro' format and J. Sainsbury's 'Capital' stores. Also, retailers of non-food goods, such as DIY products, toys, furniture and electrical appliances, sportswear, and office and computer products, have built outlets away from town and city centres, particularly to attract shoppers with cars. There is also a strong trend towards grouping retail warehouses into retail parks, often with food and other facilities.

Regional out-of-town shopping centres have been established on sites offering good access and parking facilities. One of the first was the Metro Centre at Gateshead, which is the largest of its kind in Europe. Other centres include Meadowhall in Sheffield and the Lakeside Centre at Thurrock in Essex, both opened in 1990. About one-half of total food sales are accounted for by superstores away from

town centres, compared with a fifth at the beginning of the 1980s.

Warehouse clubs, an idea recently introduced from the United States, offer cut priced branded products by selling a limited range in bulk quantities, typically from spartan, hangar-like, outlets. So far, however, they have had a limited impact.

All new retail development requires planning permission from the local government planning authority. These authorities must consult the appropriate central government department before granting permission for developments of 20,000 sq m (215,000 sq ft) or more. The Government's policy is to encourage the provision of a broad range of shopping facilities to the public, while ensuring that the effects of major new retail development do not undermine the viability and vitality of existing town centres.

Rental Services

A broad range of rental services, many franchised, are on offer in towns and cities throughout Britain. These include hire of cars and other vehicles, televisions and video cassette recorders, household appliances such as washing machines and tumble dryers, tools and heavy decorating equipment (ladders, floor sanders and so on) and video films and computer games. Retailing of many types of service is dominated by chains, though there are still independent operators in most fields.

Auction Houses

Britain attracts buyers and sellers from around the world and has a long tradition of expertise and innovation in auctioneering. Its chief auction houses are active in the international auction markets for works of art, trading on their acknowledged expertise. The two largest houses, Sotheby's and Christie's, are established worldwide. In 1994 Sotheby's celebrated its 250th anniversary. Sotheby's handled sales valued at £885 million in 1993, while Christie's sales were valued at £728 million. Phillips and Bonhams are also prominent auctioneers.

Other Trends

Many of the large multiple groups sell a much greater number of goods and services than previously. However, in some cases extensive diversification has proved unprofitable and, for example, large food retailers are increasing their range of foods instead. More emphasis is also being placed on selling own-label goods (which now account for up to one-half of total sales) and environmentally friendly products, including organic produce. Most superstores and supermarkets offer fresh food, such as meat, fish, vegetables and, in many cases, bread baked on the premises, as well as packaged foods. The major supermarket chains also have their own petrol stations at some of their bigger outlets.

'Stores within stores' are becoming more common; for example, sportswear and sports goods retailers are to be found in many of the big mixed retail stores, while Laura Ashley, the furnishings and fabrics retailer, has opened facilities in Homebase.

Several large retailers have issued their own credit cards for regular customers in an attempt to encourage sales, particularly of high-value goods. Marks and Spencer also offers financial services.

Information Technology

Information technology has become increasingly central to distribution and retailing. Computers are used to monitor stock levels and record sales figures through developments such as electronic point-of-sale (EPOS) systems. EPOS systems read a bar-code, printed on the retail product, that holds price and product information and can be used to generate orders for stock replenishment as well as totalling up bills and providing a receipt for customers.

Techniques such as 'just-in-time' ordering, in which produce arrives at the store at the last possible moment before sale, have become widespread as a result. Most large retailers have set up electronic data interchange (EDI) systems; these enable their computers to communicate with those of their suppliers, and transmit orders and invoices electronically, so reducing errors and saving time.

EFTPOS (electronic funds transfer at point of sale) systems enable customers to pay for purchases using debit cards which automatically transfer funds from their bank account. Several major EFTPOS schemes are well established and the number of terminals, which currently stands at about 275,000, is growing rapidly.

Vehicle, Vehicle Parts and Petrol Retailing

In Great Britain in 1994 there were 275,300 people employed in retailing motor vehicles and parts, and in petrol stations. Many businesses selling new vehicles are franchised by the motor manufacturers. Drive-in fitting centres sell tyres, exhaust systems, batteries, clutches and other vehicle parts; the largest chains include Kwik-Fit and Associated Tyre Services.

Over one-third of the 19,000 petrol stations are owned by oil companies. The three companies with the largest number of outlets are Shell, Esso and BP. Unleaded petrol accounts for over half of petrol sold. The majority of petrol stations are self-service. The majority of outlets sell diesel fuel.

HOTELS, PUBLIC HOUSES AND CATERING

The hotel and catering trades, which include public houses (pubs) and licensed bars, employ 2.4 million people in Great Britain, including:

- 327,000 in pubs and bars;

- 295,000 in restaurants, cafés and snack bars;

- 289,000 in hotels and other residential establishments; and

- 138,000 in clubs.

Around 165,000 self-employed people also work in these sectors.

There are 52,000 hotels in Great Britain. The largest hotel business is Forte, with 344 hotels in Britain. As well as catering and leisure interests, Forte has substantial overseas interests. At the other end of the scale, numerous guest houses and hotels each have fewer than 20 rooms. Holiday centres, including holiday camps with full board, self-catering centres and caravan parks, are run by Butlins, Holiday Club, Center Parcs, Warner Holidays and Pontin's.

Britain has a very wide range of restaurants, offering cuisine from virtually every country in the world. Chinese, Indian, Italian and Greek restaurants are among the most popular. 'Fast food' restaurants are becoming more widespread; these specialise in hamburgers, chicken, pizza and a variety of other foods to be eaten on the premises or taken away. The most well-known chains, many of which are US-owned, include Wimpy (hamburgers), McDonald's (hamburgers), Burger King (hamburgers), KFC and Pizza Hut. Traditional fish and chip shops are the other main providers of cooked take-away food. Sandwich bars proliferate in towns and cities, typically in areas where there are high concentrations of office workers.

There are about 69,000 public houses, which mainly sell beer, wines, soft drinks and spirits to adults for consumption on the premises, although an increasing number also provide hot and cold food and many have special separate facilities where children are allowed. Some are owned by the large brewing companies, which either provide managers to run them or offer tenancy agreements; these pubs tend to sell just their own brands of beer, although some also offer 'guest' beers. Others, called 'free houses', are independently owned and managed and frequently serve a variety of beers. Wine bars are normally smaller than pubs and tend to specialise in wine and food; they more closely resemble bars in other parts of Europe.

Permitted opening hours for some 100,000 licensed premises in England and Wales were extended in 1986; the more popular pubs and bars now open from 11.00 am to 11.00 pm from Monday to Saturday (on Sunday pubs may only open between 12.00 and 3.00 pm and 7.00 and 10.30 pm). The introduction of liquor licences for 'café-style' premises has been proposed, which would allow children under 14 to accompany their parents to places where alcoholic drinks are available. In Scotland a similar type of licence called a 'refreshment licence' has been available since 1976, and licensed premises can apply for a 'children's certificate' permitting children to accompany an adult on the premises within certain hours.

TOURISM AND TRAVEL

In the region of 1.5 million people are employed in tourism, and the industry contributes £30,000 million annually to the economy—about 5 per cent of gross domestic product. Britain is one of the world's six leading tourist destinations and by the year 2000 tourism is expected to be the biggest industry in the world.

Between 1980 and 1990 the number of overseas visits to Britain grew by 50 per cent. In 1993 there were 19.1 million overseas visitors to Britain, who spent £9,200 million. An estimated 64 per cent of visitors came from Europe and 17 per cent from North America. Business travel accounts for about one-fifth of all overseas tourism revenue. Britain's tourist attractions include theatres, museums, art galleries, and historic houses, as well as shopping, sports and business facilities.

Domestic tourism was worth £12,400 million in 1992 (see p. 38). Of British residents opting to take their main holiday in Britain, around half choose a traditional seaside destination. Short breaks, valued at about £2,000 million in 1992, make up an increasingly significant part of the market, with shopping accounting for about a third of all expenditure on day trips. Scotland has several skiing resorts.

The British have traditionally travelled widely. Most British holiday-makers wishing to go overseas buy 'package holidays' from travel agencies, where the cost covers both transport and accommodation. The most popular package holiday destinations are Spain, France and Greece. Long-haul holidays to places like the United States, the Caribbean and Australia are becoming more popular as air fares come down. Winter skiing holidays to resorts in Austria, France, Italy and Switzerland and other countries inside and outside Europe continue to attract large numbers of Britons.

There are around 7,200 travel agencies in Britain, of which 98 per cent belong to the Association of British Travel Agents (ABTA). Although most travel agents are small businesses, there are a few large firms, such as Lunn Poly and Thomas Cook, which have hundreds of branches. Computerised information and booking systems are used extensively in travel agencies. There are also 629 tour operator members of ABTA; about half are both retail agents and tour operators. ABTA operates financial protection schemes to safeguard its members' customers and maintains codes of conduct drawn up with the Office of Fair Trading. It also offers a free consumer affairs service to help resolve complaints against members and an independent arbitration scheme for tour operators' customers.

Tourist Authorities

The Department of National Heritage is responsible for tourism in England, and the Scottish, Welsh, and Northern Ireland Offices have responsibility for tourism in their respective countries. The government-supported British Tourist Authority (BTA) promotes Britain overseas as a tourist destination and encourages the development of tourist facilities in Britain to meet the needs of overseas visitors. The tourist boards for England, Scotland, Wales and Northern Ireland encourage the development and promotion of domestic tourism and work with the BTA to promote Britain overseas.

The BTA and the national tourist boards inform and advise the Government on issues of concern to the industry. They also help businesses and public sector bodies to plan by researching and publicising trends affecting the industry. The national tourist boards work closely with regional tourist boards, on which local government and business interests are represented. The national tourist boards

offer financial assistance to the industry. There are 800 or so Tourist Information Centres in Britain, operating an information service for visitors.

Three accommodation classification and grading schemes are operated by the national tourist boards:

- the Crown scheme for hotels, guest houses, inns, bed and breakfast and farmhouse holiday accommodation. A new Lodge category has been introduced for purpose-built accommodation alongside motorways and major roads;
- the Key (Dragons used in Wales) scheme for self-catering holiday homes; and
- the Quality 'Q' scheme for holiday caravan, chalet and camping parks.

Common standards are applied throughout Britain. All participating establishments are inspected every year.

BUSINESS SERVICES

Exhibition and Conference Centres

Britain is one of the world's three leading countries for international conferences—the others being the United States and France. London and Paris are the two most popular conference cities. A total of 110 towns and cities in Britain now have facilities for conferences and exhibitions.

Among the most modern purpose-built conference and exhibition centres are the International Conference Centre in Birmingham and the Queen Elizabeth II and Olympia Conference Centres, both in London. Others are situated in Brighton (East Sussex), Harrogate (North Yorkshire), Bournemouth (Dorset), Cardiff, Birmingham, Manchester, Nottingham and Torquay (Devon). In Scotland both Glasgow and Aberdeen have exhibition and conference centres, and an International Conference Centre is being built in Edinburgh. Other large exhibition facilities are situated in London at the Barbican, Earls Court/Olympia, Alexandra Palace and Wembley Arena.

Many of the larger sites belong to a marketing group, the British Conference and

Exhibition Centres Export Council. Cardiff International Arena is a 5,000-seat multi-purpose facility which opened in 1993.

Advertising

Britain is a major centre for creative advertising, and multinational corporations often use advertising created in Britain for marketing their products throughout Europe. British agencies have strong foreign links through overseas ownership and associate networks. Spending on advertising in 1993 amounted to £9,155 million. The press accounted for 56 per cent of the total, television for 29 per cent, direct mail for 10 per cent, posters for 3 per cent, and commercial radio and cinema for the rest. The largest advertising expenditure is on food, retail and mail order services, motor vehicles and financial services. Advertising expenditure on the top 100 brands rose by almost 10 per cent in 1993 to a little over £1,000 million; the biggest spenders in 1993 included BT, Ford, Vauxhall, McDonald's and J. Sainsbury. British television advertising receives many international awards.

Campaigns are planned by 1,300 advertising agencies which, in some cases, in addition to their creative, production and media buying roles, also offer integrated marketing services, such as consumer research and public relations. Britain is home to two of the world's largest agencies—Saatchi and Saatchi and WPP Group. Other leading agencies include J Walter Thompson and Abbott Mead Vickers BBDO.

Government advertising campaigns— recruitment for the armed services, health promotion, road safety and so on—are organised in the main by the Central Office of Information, an executive agency (see p. 512), which is able to secure large discounts because of its centralised buying power.

Computing Services

The computing services industry comprises software houses; production of packaged software; consultancy; facilities management; processing services; and the provision of complete computer systems. It also includes companies providing information technology education and training, independent maintenance, contingency planning and recruitment, and contract staff.

The turnover of companies in the Computing Services Association, which represents about 75 per cent of the industry in Britain, totalled more than £6,000 million in 1993. Important areas for software development include data and word processing, telecommunications, computer-aided design and manufacturing, defence and consumer electronics.

Management Consultancy

Management consultants provide business solutions by giving advice and technical assistance to business and government clients. Typically, consultants identify and investigate problems and opportunities, recommend appropriate action and help to implement recommendations. Many British-based consultancies operate internationally; the most recent trend has been for the largest firms to set up offices in Eastern Europe and the Pacific Rim. The 35 member firms of the Management Consultancies Association are among the largest in the industry and account for more than half of management consultancy work; they range from Andersen Consulting and CMG Management, with a strong technical bias, to Coopers & Lybrand and PA Consulting group, which specialise in market/industry sectors. In 1993 the member firms earned £750 million in Britain and £125 million overseas.

Market Research

A wide range of domestic and overseas clients, including government bodies, use Britain's advanced market research facilities. Britain accounts for about 10 per cent of worldwide market research spending. The Association of Market Survey Organisations is the main trade organisation, with 30 member companies; in 1993 its members earned £330 million out of an estimated total research industry turnover in excess of £500 million.

16 Manufacturing and Construction Industries

Introduction	230	Construction	243
Sectors of Manufacturing	231		

Britain became the world's first industrialised country in the mid-19th century. Wealth was based on manufacturing iron and steel, heavy machinery and cotton textiles, and on coal mining, shipbuilding and trade. Manufacturing still plays an important role and Britain excels in high-technology industries like pharmaceuticals, electronics, aerospace and offshore equipment, where British companies are among the world's largest and most successful. The British construction industry has made its mark around the world and has continued to be involved in some of the most prestigious domestic and international building projects, such as the Channel Tunnel.

Introduction

Manufacturing accounted for 22 per cent of gross domestic product (GDP) in 1993 and for about the same percentage of employment. About 82 per cent of visible exports consisted of manufactured or semi-manufactured goods. Almost all manufacturing is carried out by private-sector businesses.

In 1993 manufacturing output was 12 per cent higher than in 1986, but 4 per cent lower than in 1990 (see Table 16.2). The

Table 16.1: Manufacturing—Size of Businesses by Turnover and Employment

Annual turnover (£'000)	Number of businesses[a] 1993	Employment size	Number of businesses[a] 1993	Employment 1991
1–34	26,838	1–9	90,672	280,805
35–49	12,894	10–19	13,934	194,481
50–99	25,598	20–49	14,314	437,656
100–249	33,176	50–99	5,628	390,344
250–499	19,633	100–199	3,234	448,027
500–999	13,974	200–499	2,138	656,131
1,000–1,999	9,208	500–999	686	469,360
2,000–4,999	7,230	1,000+	516	1,381,514
5,000–9,999	3,100			
10,000+	4,024			
Total	155,675	Total	131,122	4,258,318

Source: *Size Analysis of United Kingdom Businesses 1993. Business Monitor PA 1003*
[a]Defined as legal units, which includes companies, partnerships, sole proprietors, general government and non-profit-making bodies.

recent recession led to a decline in manufacturing output of 0.9 per cent in 1992, but in 1993 output rose by 1.7 per cent. Employment in manufacturing in Britain fell from 5.2 million in 1986 to 4.4 million in 1993. Total capital investment in manufacturing was £12,165 million in 1993, comprising £10,146 million in plant and machinery, £1,253 million in new building work and £766 million in vehicles.

The construction industry contributed 5 per cent of GDP and employed about 1.2 million people in 1993, 4 per cent of the total number of employees. Between 1992 and 1993 output fell by almost 2 per cent, following much larger declines in 1991 and 1992 as recession continued to affect the industry. Total domestic fixed capital investment was £812 million.

Sectors of Manufacturing

Relative sizes of the main sectors are shown in Tables 16.1 and 16.2. Table 16.3 indicates output and investment. A more detailed description of the some of the main sectors is given below.

Mineral and Metal Products

British producers delivered 15.1 million tonnes of finished steel in 1993, of which 52 per cent was exported. Over the past ten years annual steel industry exports have doubled, to 7.8 million tonnes, creating a favourable balance of trade in steel products.

The major areas of steel production are in south Wales and northern England, with substantial further processing in the Midlands. Major restructuring in the steel industry took place during the 1980s and early 1990s. Productivity and efficiency have improved and the industry is now one of the lowest-cost producers in Europe. The number of people employed in the steel industry in 1993 was 40,000, compared with 88,000 in 1981.

British Steel is the fourth largest steel company in the world, producing about three-quarters of Britain's crude steel. The company's output is based on flat steel products, plate, heavy sections and tubes. These are used principally in the construction, automotive, engineering, transport, metal goods, packaging and energy industries.

Table 16.2: Indices of Manufacturing Output (1990 = 100)

1992 Standard Industrial Classification Category	Share of output 1990 (weight per 1,000)	1989	1992	1993
Food and beverages	29	98.9	100.5	101.2
Tobacco products	2	96.3	107.4	100.3
Textiles and leather products	14	102.5	89.6	89.8
Wood and wood products	7	101.5	86.1	87.2
Pulp, paper products, printing and publishing	25	97.8	95.8	98.9
Solid and nuclear fuels, oil refining	6	103.0	110.7	112.8
Chemicals and synthetic fibres	24	100.3	104.8	107.4
Rubber and plastics products	10	97.2	96.7	100.8
Other non-metallic mineral products	11	105.2	86.6	89.7
Basic metal and metal products	21	102.8	86.4	86.1
Machinery and equipment	27	97.8	84.8	84.0
Electrical and optical equipment	30	99.8	95.6	101.5
Transport equipment	28	101.7	91.1	88.2
Other manufacturing	3	98.5	84.7	80.3
Total	**237**	**100.2**	**94.0**	**95.3**

Source: *United Kingdom National Accounts 1994 Edition*

Other important steel producers in Britain include United Engineering Steels, Allied Steel and Wire, Co-Steel Sheerness, the Glynwed Group and the specialist stainless steel producer Avesta Sheffield. Products manufactured by these companies include reinforcing bars for the construction industry, wire rod, hot rolled and cold finished bars, engineering steels and other special steels for the aerospace and offshore oil and gas industries.

Output of non-ferrous metals and their alloys in 1993 included primary and secondary (recycled) aluminium and copper, as well as aluminium and copper and copper alloy semi-manufactures. The production of metal relies mainly on imported ores and recycled material of both domestic and overseas origin.

Britain is a major producer of specialised alloys for high-technology requirements in the aerospace, electronic, petrochemical, and nuclear and other fuel industries. Titanium and titanium alloys, which are light, strong and flexible, are used in aircraft production, power generation and North Sea oil production. Nickel alloys are utilised in aero-engines for high-temperature environments.

In recent years considerable progress has been made in producing 'superplastic' alloys, which are more ductile and elastic than conventional alloys. Aluminium lithium, developed by British Alcan Aluminium, is also ideal for use in aircraft, being lighter, stronger and more rigid than normal aluminium.

There is also an important sector producing copper and copper alloy semi-manufactures for use in a wide variety of products like electric wire and cable, tube and fittings for plumbing, and valves and components for the engineering and transport industries.

Ceramics

The ceramics industry manufactures clay products, such as domestic pottery, sanitaryware and tiles, and clay pipes for the building trade. Domestic pottery production includes china, earthenware and stoneware. Tableware is produced in Stoke-on-Trent.

> **Britain is the world's leading manufacturer and exporter of fine bone china, like Wedgwood, Spode and Royal Doulton.**

Table 16.3: Output and Investment in Manufacturing

1992 Standard Industrial Classification category	Gross output (£ million) 1993	Gross domestic fixed capital formation (£ million) 1993
Solid and nuclear fuels, oil refining	2,709	559
Chemicals and synthetic fibres	13,626	
Other non-metallic mineral products	4,483	3,004
Basic metals and metal products	8,954	
Machinery and equipment	12,973	
Electrical and optical equipment	15,397	3,786
Transport equipment	11,794	
Food and beverages	15,912	
Tobacco products	1,255	
Textiles and leather products	6,619	
Wood and wood products	3,336	4,816
Pulp, paper products, printing and publishing	13,852	
Rubber and plastics products	5,958	
Other manufacturing	1,424	
Total	**118,292**	**12,165**

Source: *United Kingdom National Accounts 1994 Edition*

Research is being conducted into ceramics for use in housebuilding and diesel and jet engines. Important industrial ceramics invented in Britain include silicon carbides and sialons, which can withstand ultra-high temperatures.

Glass Products

Flat glass is manufactured through the float glass process, which was developed by Pilkington Brothers and licensed to glassmakers throughout the world. Pilkington has also produced an energy-saving window glass which reflects room heat without impairing visibility. United Glass is a leading manufacturer of bottles and other glass containers. Glass-reinforced cement composites for the construction industry were invented in Britain in the early 1970s and are made under licence in over 40 countries.

China Clay

Britain is the world's biggest exporter of china clay (kaolin), four-fifths of which is used in paper-making. In 1993, 2.2 million tonnes were sold overseas. The main company is ECC International, part of the English China Clays Group.

Chemicals and Related Products

Britain's chemical industry is at the forefront of modern technology, spending the equivalent of about 5 per cent of total sales on research and development (R & D). It is the third largest chemical industry in Europe. The nation's fourth biggest manufacturing industry, it provides direct employment for 303,000 people. Around a half of its output of principal products is exported, making it Britain's greatest single export earner. Exports in 1993 were worth £17,300 million, while imports (mainly consisting of plastics and organic chemicals) were valued at £12,900 million.

Many major chemical companies in Britain are multinationals; several are subsidiaries of overseas companies and others are specialist manufacturers of pharmaceuticals, such as Glaxo and Wellcome. Imperial Chemical Industries (ICI) is the sixth largest chemical company in the world, with a range of 8,000 products. In a major restructuring programme, ICI was demerged into two companies in 1993 to form 'new' ICI, built around industrial chemicals, paints, materials and explosives, and a separate company, Zeneca, comprising ICI's pharmaceuticals, agrochemicals and seeds, and specialities businesses.

Traditionally, Britain has been a major producer of basic industrial chemicals, such as inorganic and basic organic chemicals, plastics and fertilisers, which together comprise around two-fifths of output. The most rapid growth in recent years has been in speciality chemicals, particularly pharmaceuticals and cosmetics.

Sales of the principal products of organic chemicals amounted to £3,664 million in 1992 and those of other basic industrial chemicals to £6,716 million. The most important products sold in the organic chemicals range are ethylene, propylene and benzene.

Much inorganic chemical production consists of relatively simple bulk chemicals, such as sulphuric acid and metallic and non-metallic oxides, serving as basic materials for industry. Speciality chemicals include industrial gases, essential oils and flavourings, adhesives and sealants, and explosives, including those used for car safety airbags. Investment in environmentally safe products and processes, such as substitutes for chlorofluorocarbons (CFCs), is increasing.

A large proportion of world R & D in agrochemicals is conducted in Britain. Notable British discoveries include diquat and paraquat herbicides, pyrethroid insecticides, systemic fungicides and aphicides, genetically-engineered microbial pesticides and methods of encouraging natural parasites to eradicate common pests in horticulture.

Exports of soap and toilet preparations in 1993 were valued at £1,691 million, compared with imports of £1,011 million. Total sales amounted to £4,173 million in 1992. This sector includes soap and synthetic detergents, dominated by Lever Brothers (part of Unilever) and by the US-owned Proctor and Gamble. Boots and SmithKline Beecham (the latter is jointly owned by British and United States interests) are significant producers of perfumes, cosmetics and toilet preparations.

Plastics

Total annual turnover of the plastics industry is estimated at £13,200 million; exports reached £2,700 million in 1993. Around 180,000 people are employed in the industry, three-quarters in the processing or conversion sector. About 3,900 firms are engaged in plastics processing—the conversion of plastics materials into finished, semi-finished or sub-assemblies of final products. Production includes housewares and semi-finished products for the automotive, domestic appliance, mechanical goods, construction and business equipment industries.

Paints

Sales of paint, varnishes and painters' fillings were worth £1,718 million in 1992. ICI is the world's second largest paint manufacturer. Among its specialised products are new ranges of synthetic resins and pigments, powder coatings, non-drip and quick-drying paints and paints needing only one top coat. Its best-known consumer product is the 'Dulux' paint range. Two of the more recent innovations have been solid emulsion paint and a temporary water-based finish which can be removed easily by chemical treatment, for vehicle bodies and road markings.

Pharmaceuticals

Britain is the world's fourth biggest exporter of medicines, after Germany, Switzerland and the United States. It has some of the largest multinational manufacturers, as well as medium-sized and smaller specialist companies. Total sales in 1993 were around £7,000 million, of which £3,685 million was accounted for by overseas sales. The main overseas markets are Western Europe and North America, with Japan an expanding market.

Employing over 80,000 people directly, pharmaceuticals support employment for 250,000 people in such related activities as research, distribution and retailing. The industry invested more than £1,500 million in R & D in 1993. This sum amounts to 20 per cent of British manufacturing industry's R & D and represents 8 per cent of total world expenditure on medicines research. Progress in devising vaccines has helped to reduce dramatically the impact of infectious diseases, such as whooping cough, mumps and measles.

Britain is home to two of the world's top 15 pharmaceuticals groups, Glaxo and SmithKline Beecham. British firms make five of the world's 20 best-selling medicines, including Glaxo's ulcer treatment Zantac, the world's best-selling medicine, and ICI's (now Zeneca's) beta-blocker Tenormin, for treating high blood pressure. Among Zeneca's newer products are Zestril (for combating high blood pressure), Zoladex (a prostate cancer therapy) and Diprivan (an anaesthetic).

Other major developments pioneered in Britain are semi-synthetic penicillins and cephalosporins, both powerful antibiotics, and new treatments for asthma, arthritis, migraine and coronary heart disease. SmithKline Beecham, which manufactures four of the world's top-selling antibiotics, has developed Augmentin, used to treat a range of infections that have become resistant to antibiotics. Glaxo's Zofran, an anti-nausea drug used to counter the unpleasant side-effects of cancer treatments, is one of the company's most successful new medicines.

British companies lead in the development of molecular graphics, which contribute to the rational design of new and improved medicines through a computer-aided technique for analysing the structures of complicated organic molecules using a visual display unit.

A growing trend is the production of generic drugs. These are versions of branded drugs whose patents have expired. They are mostly unbranded and cheaper than the branded originals. About 40 per cent of doctors' prescriptions are for generic drugs.

Biotechnology

Biotechnology has improved the specificity of pharmaceuticals through greater understanding of disease at the molecular level. It has enabled companies to manufacture products using genetic modification. Britain has made major advances in the development of drugs such as human insulin and interferons, genetically-engineered vaccines, and in the production of antibiotics by fermentation; alternative bacteriocidal drugs based on Nisin, a food preservative made in Britain; agricultural products such as infection-resistant crops; and medical diagnostic devices, including the world's best-selling biosensor.

Major companies such as Zeneca, Wellcome, Glaxo and SmithKline Beecham undertake extensive research in biotechnology. A second generation of vaccines based on recombinant DNA technology includes SmithKline Beecham's Engerix-B vaccine against hepatitis. Therapies based on correcting the function of defective genes are under development. Diseases being targeted include those where a single defective gene needs correcting, such as cystic fibrosis, and those where there are genetic and environmental components, like cardio-vascular disease.

Specialist products of Britain's small and medium-sized biotechnology firms comprise, among other items, medical diagnostics and microbial pesticides. The British company Celltech was the first licensed by the United States Government for the large-scale production of monoclonal antibodies, proteins which can seek out a particular substance in the body. They are used to diagnose diseases, identify different blood types and can be employed in the treatment of a range of conditions, including cancer.

Fibres

The main types of synthetic fibre are still those first developed: regenerated cellulosic fibres such as viscose, and the major synthetic fibres like nylon polyamide, polyester and acrylics. Extensive research continues to produce a wide variety of innovative products with characteristics designed to meet market needs; antistatic and flame-retardant fibres are examples. More specialist products include the aramids (with very high thermal stability and strength), elastanes (giving very high stretch and recovery) and melded fabrics (produced without the need for knitting or weaving).

Britain's second biggest chemical company, Courtaulds, has developed a new, solvent-spun, biodegradable fibre, Tencel, which is twice as strong as cotton while being soft enough to be used by designers of luxury garments.

Mechanical Engineering and Metal Goods

Exports of mechanical machinery—at £15,000 million—represented 13 per cent of total visible exports in 1993. Output includes pressure vessels, heat exchangers and storage tanks for chemical and oil-refining plant, steam-raising boilers (including those for power stations), nuclear reactors, water and sewage treatment plant, and fabricated steelwork for bridges, buildings and industrial installations.

Britain is among the world's major producers of tractors, which make up around three-quarters of the country's total output of agricultural equipment. Sales of wheeled tractors in 1993 were valued at £1,100 million. Leading tractor manufacturers include Massey Ferguson and Ford.

Widely used technical innovations include computer-controlled tractors, a highly efficient pesticide sprayer and combined mower/conditioners that reduce the drying time for grass. Much new machinery is designed for use in a variety of conditions to meet the needs of overseas farmers.

Britain is the world's eighth largest producer of machine tools. Almost all are purchased by the engineering, aerospace, automotive, and metal goods industries. Total sales of metal-working machine tools reached almost £900 million in 1993. British manufacturers have made technological advances in probes, sensors, co-ordinate measuring devices, laser melting and the installation of flexible manufacturing systems. Computer numerical-controlled machines account for an increasing proportion of output. The 600 Group is the biggest British machine tool company.

Most sales of textile machinery are to export markets. British innovations include computerised colour matching and weave simulation, friction spinning, high-speed computer-controlled knitting machines and electronic jacquard attachments for weaving looms. Bonas Machine Company of Gateshead, producer of electronic jacquards, exports 90 per cent of its £35 million annual turnover, to more than 75 countries.

Britain's mining and tunnelling equipment industry leads in the production of coal-cutting and road-heading (shearing) equipment, hydraulic roof supports, conveying equipment, flameproof transformers, switchgear, and subsurface transport equipment and control systems. J.C. Bamford is the world's leading manufacturer of backhoe loaders and telescopic handlers. Sales of construction equipment, such as excavators and backhoe loaders, rose sharply in 1993, to over £1,500 million.

The mechanical handling and lifting equipment industry produces cranes and transporters, lifting devices, escalators, conveyors, powered industrial trucks and air bridges, as well as electronically-controlled and automatic handling systems. In 1993 sales in this sector were worth £2,500 million. Britain is also a major producer of industrial engines, pumps, valves and compressors, and of pneumatic and hydraulic equipment. Companies like Babcock manufacture steam generators and other heavy equipment for power plants. Despite an overall decline in the castings industry, some foundries have been investing in new melting, moulding and quality control equipment.

Electrical, Electronic and Instrument Engineering

Making extensive use of the most advanced technologies, the electrical engineering industry manufactures products for the electricity supply sector, including power plant, cable transformers and switchgear, and lighting, plugs and sockets. The domestic electrical appliance sector is dominated by a few large firms, such as Thorn EMI.

Britain has the fourth largest electronics industry in the world. Products include computers, communications equipment and a broad range of components.

The major electronic consumer goods produced are radio and television sets, and high-fidelity audio and video equipment. Several Japanese companies, including Sony, have established manufacturing bases in Wales, making television sets, video recorders and compact disc players. In the audio field British manufacturers like Quad have a reputation for high-quality goods, but are less strong in the mass market.

Computers

This sector produces an extensive range of systems, central processors and peripheral equipment, from large computers for large-scale data-processing and scientific work to mini- and microcomputers for control and automation systems and for home, educational and office use. In 1993 exports reached a record level, around £4,000 million.

The Trax, a novel design of supercomputer processor with a wide range of applications, including high-definition television and defence systems, was originally developed at Brunel University, near London.

Britain makes 40 per cent of Europe's desktop computers. Nearly half of computers and peripheral equipment intended for export are made in Scotland. Several leading overseas manufacturers of data-processing equipment—for example, IBM, Unisys and Compaq—have established manufacturing plants in Britain. Britain's biggest computer manufacturer is the largely Japanese-owned ICL. Other companies, such as Psion, have concentrated on developing new products for specialised markets. These include hand-held, pocket-sized computers, increasingly used by company sales forces, and notebook and pen computers.

British firms make communications software for portable and mainframe computers. The world's first modem (computer telephone link) for portable computers was designed in Britain. Psion is a pioneer of the 'palmtop' computer, which has the equivalent power of a desktop machine. A Scottish firm, Calluna, has designed an extremely small disc drive for use in notebook-sized computers.

British firms and research organisations, with government support, have been involved in the development and application of the family of 'three-five' semiconductor materials, such as gallium arsenide; these are used in a number of microwave devices and in the production of faster-working computers. Major advances are being made by British firms in the field of 'virtual reality', a three-dimensional computer simulation technique with a host of industrial and other applications. It is being used to design buildings and a range of products, including cars, pharmaceuticals and machine tools.

Communications Equipment

Britain's main communications products are switching and transmission equipment, telephones and terminals. As the telecommunications market has become fully liberalised (see p. 302), there has been a growing demand for equipment and services. GPT is Britain's foremost telecommunications manufacturer; its product range includes PBXs (private branch exchanges), transmissions systems and videoconferencing equipment.

Innovative work is being stimulated by the expansion of cable television and the growth in value added network services. There has been rapid expansion in the market for cellular telephones since the second half of the 1980s.

Transmission equipment and cables for telecommunications and information networks include submarine and high-specification data-carrying cables. Supported by a technically advanced cable industry, BT has led in the development of optical fibre communications systems and has paved the way for simpler and cheaper optical cables by laying the first non-repeatered cable over 100 km (62 miles) long, and by developing the first all-optical repeater.

More than half of the world's undersea communications cables have been made and laid by STC Submarine Systems, which, with its US and French partners, completed the laying of the first transatlantic optical fibre cable in 1988. Now part of Canada's Northern Telecom, STC is building the first fibre-optic cable linking Canada and Europe. The cable, which will be made in Britain and the United States, will carry up to 30,000 telephone calls simultaneously down each of two pairs of optical fibres.

Britain also has a world lead in the transmission of computerised data along telephone lines for reproduction on television screens.

Another sector of the industry manufactures radio communications equipment, radar, radio and sonar navigational aids for ships and aircraft, thermal imaging systems, alarms and signalling equipment, public broadcasting equipment and other capital goods. Radar was invented in Britain and British firms are still in the forefront of technical advances. Racal Avionics' X-band radar for aircraft ground movement control is in use at airports in several countries. Solid-state secondary surveillance radar, manufactured by Cossor Electronics, is being supplied to 50 overseas civil aviation operators. Cable and Wireless's submarine cable-laying robot 'CIRRUS', which can work at depths of up to 1 km (3,280 ft), is controlled entirely by a computer on its mother ship.

Medical and Other Electronic Equipment

A range of electronic measurement and test equipment is made in Britain, as well as analytical instruments, process control equipment, and numerical control and indication equipment for use in machine tools. Companies such as GEC and Oxford Instruments produce electronic medical equipment, like ultrasound scanners, electromyography systems and patient monitoring systems for intensive and coronary care and other uses. Britain pioneered magnetic resonance imaging.

The indigenous electronics components industry is supplemented by subsidiaries of leading overseas companies. An area of rapid change in which Britain is particularly strong is the manufacture of advanced components, such as integrated circuits.

The instrument engineering industry makes measuring, photographic, cinematographic and reprographic equipment; watches, clocks and other timing devices; and medical and surgical instruments.

Overseas sales of scientific and photographic equipment were worth £4,700 million in 1993.

Motor Vehicles

Just under 2 million new cars and commercial vehicles were sold in 1993. Production has recovered following the recession, with sales of new cars up by around 12 per cent on the previous year. Car output is dominated by seven groups, accounting for 99 per cent of the total: Rover (which became a subsidiary of BMW in March 1994), Ford (including Jaguar), Vauxhall, Peugeot-Talbot, Honda, Nissan and Toyota. The remainder is in the hands of smaller, specialist producers such as Rolls-Royce, whose cars are renowned for their quality and durability. Rover's production includes the highly successful Land Rover four-wheel drive vehicle and the 600 range of family cars, launched in 1993. A total of more than 530,000 passenger cars was exported by the industry in 1993. Nissan was the biggest car exporter that year.

A period of major change has accompanied the arrival of the three major Japanese manufacturers—Nissan, Toyota and Honda—which have invested heavily in 'state of the art' plants. Japanese inward investment has introduced new management techniques and production methods into the sector. The established motor vehicle manufacturers and components suppliers are restructuring as a result.

The motor components industry consists of over 2,000 companies, such as GKN, Lucas and Bosch, and is ranked as one of Britain's major industries.

Total sales of motor vehicle bodies and parts amounted to £5,900 million.

Shipbuilding and Marine Engineering

The largest shipbuilding and shiprepairing sector is warships and support vessels. In addition to meeting all the needs of the Royal Navy, warship yards build and convert ships for overseas governments.

The Shipbuilders and Shiprepairers' Association estimates that the order books of British merchant shipbuilders for new building were worth around £250 million at the end of 1993; merchant shiprepairers had a turnover of £120 million in 1993. The marine equipment industry is a major contributor to the shipbuilding industry, as equipment installed in a ship's hull accounts for about 50 per cent of its total cost. It offers a complete range of products, from diving equipment to sophisticated navigational systems, around 70 per cent of which is exported.

More than two decades of oil and gas exploitation in the North Sea have generated a major offshore industry (see p. 249). Shipbuilders and fabricators build floating production units and semi-submersible units for drilling, production and emergency/maintenance support, drill ships, jack-up rigs, modules and offshore loading systems. UIE Scotland, Highland Fabricators, John Brown and McDermott Scotland are among the larger manufacturers and designers.

Several thousand firms supply other products needed by the offshore industry—such as diving equipment and helicopters—as well as services, including consultancy, design, project management, and R & D to the offshore industry. Their experience of North Sea projects has enabled them to establish themselves in oil and gas markets throughout the world.

Aerospace

Britain's aerospace industry is the third largest in the Western world, after the United States and France. With around 200 member companies of the Society of British Aerospace Companies employing 134,500 people, it had a turnover in 1993 of about £10,300 million. Exports totalled nearly £6,400 million and contributed more than £2,300 million in net terms to the balance of payments. Aircraft and parts account for around three-fifths of overseas sales, with engines and parts, missiles and aerospace equipment (including satellite equipment) making up the rest. The impact of recession on the civil aerospace market and reductions in defence orders following the ending of the Cold War, accompanied by fierce international competition in the defence products market, have led to further rationalisation and consolidation of the aerospace industry. Collaborative development of civil and military aircraft, as well as aviation equipment and satellites, is increasing to save on the costs of long-term programmes.

The industry's activities cover designing and constructing airframes, aero-engines, guided weapons, simulators and space satellites, flight controls including 'fly-by-wire' and 'fly-by-light' equipment (see p. 309), avionics and complex components, with their associated services. In order to improve fuel economy, engine and airframe manufacturers use lighter materials such as titanium and carbon-fibre composites (see p. 232), combined with advanced avionics and improved aerodynamic techniques.

Britain pioneered the development of hovercraft and remains a world leader in their technology and production. Westland Aerospace hovercraft range from large commercial craft to smaller, 10-passenger models. Slingsby Aviation builds hovercraft for passenger transport, cargo, ambulance and rescue, and surveying.

Civil Aircraft

As one of the leading British exporters of manufactured goods, British Aerospace (BAe) produces both civil and military aircraft, as well as guided weapons and components. Civil aircraft include the Avro RJ family of regional quiet-jet airliners and the 64-seat Jetstream ATP (advanced turboprop) airliner, which is being developed as the 70-seat Jetstream 61, the 29-seat Jetstream 41 and 19-seat Jetstream Super 31.

BAe has a 20 per cent share of the European consortium Airbus Industrie, which had a turnover of £8,700 million in 1993. BAe designs and supplies the wings for the whole family of Airbus airliners, from the smallest short- to medium-haul A320 series

(the first civil airliner to use fly-by-wire controls—see p. 309) to the large long-range four-engined A340 introduced into service in 1993. Together with other international aerospace organisations, BAe is studying the feasibility of developing a successor to the Concorde supersonic airliner and an ultra high-capacity aircraft.

Short Brothers of Belfast (now Canadian-owned) is engaged in the design and production of civil aircraft, advanced nacelle (engine casings) systems and components for aerospace manufacturers as well as the provision of aviation support services. It designs and builds the wings for the Fokker 100 and 70 jetliners and is a partner in manufacturing the 50-seat Canadair Regional Jet airliner; the Learjet 45, a small business jet aircraft; and the Bombardier Global Express long-range business jet. Pilatus Britten-Norman manufactures the Islander light utility aircraft, which has had sales in over 100 countries.

Military Aircraft and Missiles

British Aerospace is one of the world's top defence companies. More than four-fifths of its military production was exported in 1993. It includes the Harrier, a unique vertical/short take-off and landing (V/STOL) military combat aircraft. BAe also produces the Hawk fast-jet trainer and, with McDonnell Douglas, the Goshawk T45 carrier jet trainer. It has a 33 per cent share in the development of the Eurofighter 2000, a co-operative venture between Britain, Germany, Italy and Spain, which had its maiden flight in March 1994.

The Tornado combat aircraft is built by a company set up jointly by BAe, Alenia of Italy and Deutsche Aerospace. A £5,000 million order for 48 Tornado bombers for Saudi Arabia was confirmed in 1993, making it one of Britain's biggest ever export deals. The United States Air Force has chosen Slingsby Aviation's T67 Firefly trainer aircraft as its new basic trainer. Slingsby also designs and makes aerospace components and parts for airships.

Together with its Airbus partners, BAe is examining the possibility of designing and manufacturing a new large military transport aircraft.

BAe and Shorts are major suppliers of tactical guided weapon systems for use on land, at sea and in the air.

Helicopters

In addition to producing aerospace equipment, Westland manufactures the Sea King and Lynx military helicopters. In collaboration with Agusta of Italy, it is developing the multi-role EH101 three-engine helicopter, which will be delivered to the Royal Navy and the Italian Navy by 1996–97. The company is also a leading manufacturer of composite helicopter blades.

Aero-engines

Rolls-Royce is one of the world's three major manufacturers of aero-engines, with a turnover in 1993 of £2,100 million for its aerospace division. The company's civil engine group produces engines for airliners and regional, executive and corporate jets. Rolls-Royce RB211-535 engines have been selected by over 80 per cent of airlines for their Boeing 757 airliners.

The company's latest large engine, the Trent, is aimed at the new generation of wide-body twin-engined airliners, such as Boeing's 777 and the Airbus A330. The Trent 800 variant is the most powerful engine Rolls-Royce has produced and has already run at over 100,000 lb thrust.

Rolls-Royce is a partner in the five-nation International Aero Engine consortium, which produces the low-emission V2500 aero-engine, now in service on the Airbus A320.

The military engine group of Rolls-Royce produces engines for both aircraft and helicopters, and is a partner in the EJ200 engine project for the Eurofighter 2000.

The company also produces gas turbines for power generation, for oil and gas pumping and marine propulsion. Turnover of Rolls-Royce's industrial power wing amounted to almost £1,400 million in 1993.

Aviation Equipment

Around one-third of the aerospace industry is devoted to designing and manufacturing aviation equipment. British firms have made significant technological advances. Manufacturers like Dowty, GEC-Marconi, Lucas, Smiths Industries, Racal and BAe provide equipment and systems for engines and aircraft—propellers, navigation and landing systems, engine and flight controls, electrical generation, mechanical and hydraulic power systems, cabin furnishings, flight-deck controls and information displays, including head-up displays (HUDs), of which GEC-Marconi is the world's largest manufacturer.

British firms have made important advances in developing ejection seats, firefighting equipment and flight simulators, as well as fly-by-wire and fly-by-light technology, where control surfaces are moved by means of automatic electronic signalling and fibre optics respectively, rather than by mechanical means. Fly-by-wire is being used on the Airbus A330 and A340 as well as the A320 and its derivatives. Britain's aerospace companies provide radar and air traffic control equipment and ground power supplies to airports and airlines worldwide.

Satellite Equipment

Over 400 companies in Britain are engaged in space activities. The industry is strong in the manufacture of satellites and ground infrastructure for satellite systems and in the analysis and exploitation of data from satellites. Matra-Marconi Space is one of the world's leading producers of communications satellites. It was the prime contractor for all such satellites built for the European Space Agency (ESA), and for the Marecs and Inmarsat-2 series of maritime communications satellites. It built payload pallets for the United States Space Shuttle and supplies SPELDA, a structure that enables the ESA's Ariane 4 launcher to carry two spacecraft on the same mission. Work is now in progress on ESA's latest Cluster and SOHO scientific spacecraft and the company is acting as prime contractor for the European Polar Platform. The first of ESA's new generation of environmental monitoring missions, ENVISAT IV, is due for launching in 1998 and uses the European Polar

Platform. Matra-Marconi Space is also the main contractor for two Skynet 4 Stage 2 military communications satellites due to come into operation in 1998.

Matra-Marconi Space has acted as main contractor on many telecommunications payloads, for example, for ESA. In addition, it was prime contractor for the principal radar instrument on the ESA's European Remote Sensing Satellites ERS-1 and ERS-2.

A new Earth Observation Data Centre processes data from ERS-1 and other satellites, and is helping to develop the market for earth observation data. GEC Ferranti Defence Systems produces the inertial guidance system for the European Ariane launcher and Pilkington Space Technology is the world's leading producer of solar cell coverglasses for satellites. Several companies, such as the National Remote Sensing Centre, Logica, Data Sciences, EOS and Cray Electronics, are involved in processing earth observation data, and a wide range of smaller companies specialise in its interpretation.

Food and Drink

Britain has a large food and drink manufacturing industry, which has accounted for a growing proportion of total domestic food supply in recent decades. In the last few years, it has increased productivity and undergone restructuring, partly in order to take advantage of the single European market. Approximately 500,000 people are employed in the industry.

Frozen and prepared chilled foods, annual sales of which stand at over £3,600 million and £1,800 million respectively, other convenience foods, yoghurts, dairy desserts and instant snacks have formed the fastest-growing sector of the food market in recent years. The market in health and slimming foods continues to expand. Companies have introduced new low-fat and fat-free spreads and ice creams to meet consumer demand. There has also been a rise in sales of organically-grown produce as well as products for vegetarians (soya-based foods, for instance).

British firms are at the forefront of innovation in the food industry. They support research and development programmes to ensure that products and production methods meet the highest safety standards and the expectations of consumers. New foods, including 'healthy' alternatives, and better packaging are constantly being developed.

Around 60 per cent of liquid milk in Britain is distributed through a doorstep delivery system employing about 80,000 people; the proportion is, however, declining. Household milk consumption per head— 2.23 litres (3.9 pints) a week—is among the highest in the world. Consumption of skimmed and semi-skimmed milk continues to rise as people seek to reduce the fat content in their diet.

Milk for manufacturing purposes goes principally into butter, cheese, condensed milk, dried whole and skimmed milk, cream and other products like yoghurt. The British dairy industry accounted for 56 per cent of butter supplies to the domestic market in 1993 and 68 per cent of cheese supplies. Butter exports in 1993 were worth £122 million. The other main exports are skimmed milk powder and whole milk powder, valued at £178 million in total.

About 80 per cent of bread is manufactured in large bakeries; the total bread market is valued at £3,000 million a year. A significant increase in the varieties available, a greater awareness of the nutritional value of bread and the growth of the sandwich market have helped stabilise consumption. Exports of biscuits were valued at £224 million in 1993 and those of chocolate confectionery at £253 million.

Of major significance among the alcoholic drinks produced in Britain is Scotch whisky, which is one of Britain's top export earners. There are 110 distilleries in Scotland, where the best known brands of blended Scotch whisky, such as J & B, Johnnie Walker, Famous Grouse and Teachers, are made from the products of single malt and single grain whisky distilleries. About four-fifths of Scotch whisky production is exported, to over 200 countries. The value of whisky exports was £2,100 million in 1993, Europe taking 40 per cent and the United States 14 per cent by volume.

In 1993 purchases of beer in Britain reached £13,600 million, about 3 per cent of consumers' expenditure. The brewing industry has six major national brewery groups, and about 160 regional and local brewers. British malt, which is made almost entirely from home-grown barley, is used by brewers throughout the world. Demand for traditional cask-conditioned ales ('real ale') continues to rise, while lager now accounts for just over half of all beer sales. In the last few years there has been a shift towards stronger bottled beers, a significant proportion of which are imported. Cider is made primarily in south-west England, Gloucester, Hereford and Worcester.

There are around 450 vineyards and 150 wineries in Britain (mainly in southern England), producing an average of 1.75 million litres of wine a year.

The soft drinks industry—comprising carbonated drinks, concentrates, fruit juices, and natural mineral and bottled waters—is the fastest growing sector of the grocery trade, with an annual turnover of about £6,000 million.

Tobacco

The British tobacco industry manufactures nearly all the cigarettes and tobacco goods sold in Britain. Almost all domestic output is provided by three major manufacturers (Imperial Tobacco, Gallaher and Carreras Rothmans). The industry specialises in the production of high-quality cigarettes made from flue-cured tobacco and achieves significant exports. Europe, the Middle East and Africa are important markets.

Textiles and Clothing

These products make a substantial contribution to the British economy in terms of employment, exports and turnover. Together with the footwear and leather industries, they employ around 415,000 people, equal to about 10 per cent of manufacturing employment. For textiles, there is a high degree of regional concentration, particularly in the North West, West Yorkshire (mainly wool), the East Midlands (knitwear), Scotland and Northern Ireland. The clothing industry is scattered throughout Britain, with significant concentrations in Manchester, Leicester and London. The main products are yarn, woven and knitted fabrics, apparel, industrial and household textiles, and carpets based mainly on wool, cotton and synthetic fibres. Exports of textiles, clothing and footwear totalled over £5,000 million in 1993.

The textile and clothing industry has around 12,000 firms, comprising a few large multi-process companies and two of the world's largest firms—Coats Viyella and Courtaulds Textiles—as well as a large number of small and medium-sized firms.

Increased investment in new machinery and greater attention to design, training and marketing have helped the industry to raise competitiveness. New technologies, largely designed to improve response times and give greater flexibility in production, are being used throughout the industry.

The Multi-Fibre Arrangement (MFA) of the General Agreement on Tariffs and Trade (GATT—see p. 170) allows a measure of restraint on imports into the European Union from low-cost countries; however, the MFA is being phased out over 10 years under the latest GATT settlement, reached in 1993 (see p. 170).

Britain's wool textile industry is one of the largest in the world, with two main branches making woollen and worsted (fine wool fabric often used for making suits). Synthetic fibre is sometimes blended with wool. West Yorkshire is the main producing area, but Scotland is also famous as a specialised producer of high-quality yarns, tweeds and cloth. Raw wool is scoured and cleaned in Britain in preparation for spinning. British mills also process rare fibres such as cashmere. Sales of the woollen and worsted industry amounted to £1,400 million in 1993.

Low-cost competition has cut progressively into British markets for cotton and allied products. Production includes yarn and fabrics of cotton, synthetic fibres and cotton-synthetic mixes, with large-scale dyeing and printing of cotton and synthetic fibre fabric. The linen industry is centred in Northern Ireland.

The high quality and variety of design make Britain one of the world's leading producers of woven carpets. Over half the value of carpet and rug output is made up of tufted carpets. Woven carpets, mainly Axminster, account for most of the remaining sales. There is a higher wool content in woven types, although in these, too, considerable use is being made of synthetic fibres.

Industrial textiles account for an increasing proportion of the industry's output, covering products such as conveyor belting and geotextiles used in civil engineering. Many of these are non-woven. Synthetic polypropylene yarn is used in the manufacture of carpet backing and ropes, and woven into fabrics for a wide range of applications in the packaging, upholstery, building and motor vehicle industries.

The clothing industry is labour intensive, involving about 7,700 companies. While a broad range of clothing is imported from Europe and Asia, British industry supplies over half of domestic demand. Exports have risen since the British fashion designer industry regained prominence during the 1980s and traditional British tailoring enables clothing companies such as Burberry's to compete overseas. The hosiery and knitwear industry comprises about 1,500 companies, mainly in the east Midlands and Scotland.

Other Manufacturing

There are 105 paper and board mills employing 26,000 people. Among the largest British groups are Arjo Wiggins Appleton, St Regis and BPB Paper and Packaging. Production has been concentrated in large-scale units to enable the industry to compete more effectively within the single European market. Between 1985 and 1993 output increased by 41 per cent. Over half the industry is made up of forestry product companies from Scandinavia, North America, Australia and elsewhere. There has been a significant trend towards waste-based packaging grades. Usage of recycled waste paper is increasing and research is helping to extend it. In 1993 the total amount of waste paper used in British newspapers accounted

for 73 per cent of newsprint produced. Waste paper provides over half of the industry's fibre needs.

Employment in the paper products, printing and publishing industries is about 450,000. Most of the printing and publishing industry's employment and output is concentrated in firms based in south-east England. Mergers have led to the formation of large groups in newspaper, magazine and book publishing. Reed Elsevier, one of the world's biggest publishing businesses, resulted from a merger between Reed International and the Dutch company Elsevier in 1993. More than £2,700 million worth of books were sold in Britain in 1993. The book-publishing industry is a major exporter, selling one-third of production in overseas markets. Security printers (of, for example, banknotes and postage stamps) are important exporters, the major company being De La Rue.

About half of all rubber tyres and inner tubes sold by British manufacturers in 1993 went overseas. Tyre manufacturers include subsidiaries of United States and other overseas companies.

Construction

Construction work is carried out by private contractors and public authorities employing their own labour. From 1990 the industry was in recession, with employment falling from 1.8 million to 1.3 million in 1992. In 1993–94 there were signs of recovery, with new orders on an upward trend, although employment continued to fall. The Department of the Environment assists British construction and building products and materials firms to secure overseas contracts (see p. 245) by, for instance, arranging inward and outward trade missions.

Most work is done by private firms, 98 per cent of which employ fewer than 25 people. While only 95 out of a total of 206,000 firms employ more than 600 people directly, these companies undertake about one-fifth of all construction in Britain. Some larger firms own quarries and factories for materials manufacture, and sophisticated plant. Some undertake responsibility for all stages of projects from initial design to finished building. Efficiency and productivity in construction have benefited from greater off-site fabrication of standardised components and from computerised techniques such as electronic load safety measures for cranes, distance measuring equipment, computerised stock ordering and job costing, and computer-aided design.

Building Materials and Products

A vast range of products is used in the construction process, from glass and bricks to tiles and bathroom fittings. These materials are estimated to make up around 40 per cent of the value of construction output. In 1993 sales of construction materials were worth around £20,000 million, with exports amounting to £2,500 million.

Most crushed rock, sand and gravel that is quarried by the aggregates industry is used in construction. The brick industry, one of Britain's oldest, is regarded as the world's most technically advanced: in the late 1980s over £300 million was invested in improving production. Portland cement, a 19th-century British innovation, is the most widely used chemical compound in the world.

Britain is a world leader in the manufacture of glass used in windows, doors and cladding. Pilkington developed the float process for manufacturing distortion-free flat glass (see p. 232), which is licensed throughout the world. Substantially more energy efficient, flat glass is used to allow more light into buildings and to provide insulation against heat loss in winter. The manufacture and supply of windows and doors is carried out by a large number of companies operating in one of three distinct product sectors—timber, metal (aluminium and steel) and UPVC.

Project Procurement, Management and Financing

The common basis of procurement is a lump-sum contract with provision for variation. The largest projects are often carried out under the direction of construction managers or management contractors. Clients generally employ architects, project managers or civil engineers to advise on the feasibility of projects, draw up plans, and inspect and supervise the construction work.

Private and public sector projects are managed in a variety of ways. Most clients invite construction firms to bid for work by competitive tender, having used the design services of a consultant. The successful contractor will then undertake on-site work with a number of specialist sub-contractors. Alternative methods of contracting are becoming more common: for example, contracts might include subsequent provision of building maintenance or a comprehensive 'design-and-build' service, where a single company accepts responsibility for every stage of a project.

The Government provides substantial work for the construction industry. Recently, a number of schemes have been built and paid for by private consortia, which then charge the public for their use for a fixed period of time before transferring ownership back to the public sector; these are known as 'BOOT' ('Build, Own, Operate and Transfer') schemes. An example is the toll bridge over the River Thames at Dartford, Kent (see p. 287).

Major Construction Projects in Britain

The most important recent construction project is the Channel Tunnel, the largest single civil engineering project ever undertaken in Europe (see p. 293). Completed in 1993, its estimated cost was about £10,000 million. Building work was carried out by a consortium of ten French and British contractors working together as Transmanche Link (TML). The tunnel is nearly 50 km (31 miles) long and is 70 m (230ft) below sea level at its deepest. Associated projects include a new international station at Waterloo in London and an international terminal at Folkestone.

Other major building projects in hand or recently completed are the M25 motorway widening scheme; the A55 Conwy Tunnel in Wales; the extensive development in London's Docklands; and the Sizewell B nuclear power station in Suffolk. Both Stansted and Manchester airports have been substantially redeveloped. There has also been large-scale redevelopment of sports stadiums, including Twickenham and Murrayfield (in Edinburgh) rugby grounds, and Manchester United and Arsenal football grounds.

> A £20 million stadium for a football ground at Millwall in south-east London, completed in 1993, was the first major new stadium to be built in Britain since the end of the Second World War.

Housing

During 1993 construction of 185,000 dwellings was started in Great Britain, up by nearly a fifth on the 1992 figure. Starts by private enterprise were 142,000, by housing associations 41,000 and in the public sector almost 2,000. Around 174,000 dwellings were completed: over 137,000 by the private sector, 34,000 by housing associations and 2,000 by the public sector. The total value of new housing orders was nearly £6,500 million.

Building Regulations

The Department of the Environment's building regulations prescribe minimum standards of construction in England and Wales. Administered and enforced by local government, the regulations apply to new building, the installation or replacement of fittings, and alterations and extensions to existing buildings. There are similar controls in Scotland and Northern Ireland. An alternative to local authority building control was introduced in 1984; under this there is a system of private certification of compliance with building regulations. The British Standards Institution is making Britain's contribution to the drafting of European standards, which are increasingly replacing national construction standards.

Research and Advisory Services

The Building Research Establishment, an

executive agency of the Government, provides advice and research services to the Government on the design, construction and performance of buildings together with the health and safety of people in and around buildings. Its areas of expertise include prevention and control of fires and protection of the environment. It has a key role in developing European codes and standards and has strong links with a variety of international organisations. Major construction and materials firms, universities, colleges and research associations, as well as the British Board of Agrément, carry out research and provide advisory services. The Building Centre provides exhibition and information services on materials, products, techniques and building services.

Overseas Contracting and Consultancy

British companies are engaged in many major projects throughout the world and have been in the forefront of innovative methods of management contracting and construction management. Contractors and consultants undertake the supervision and all or part of the construction of a project. Consultants are involved in the planning, design and supervision of construction projects. British contractors and consultants have a reputation for integrity and independence.

British contractors are currently undertaking, or have recently completed, work in 123 overseas countries and have a permanent presence in 95 of them. In 1992 they won new international business valued at £2,900 million, securing more new business in Asia—a major growth region—than any of their European competitors. Important international contracts won in 1993–94 included:

- a management contract for EXPO '98 in Lisbon ($1,000 million);
- a major share in an international contract to build a second bridge over the Tagus river in Portugal (£550 million);
- a tunnelling contract for the Cairo waste water project (£95 million);
- a contract to build a prestige apartment block in Egypt (£64 million);

- a management contract for the redevelopment of Kowloon station in Hong Kong (£60 million); and

- a contract to construct a 30-storey hotel and office tower in Mexico City (£50 million).

British engineering consultants were engaged in over 3,000 projects in more than 140 countries, having offices in 78 of those countries. In 1993 members of the Association of Consulting Engineers were involved in new work overseas valued at almost £30,000 million. The capital value of projects under way at the end of 1993 or completed during the year was £66,000 million. British consulting engineers had

estimated gross earnings in 1993 of £605 million from overseas commissions. The three largest categories of work covered roads, bridges and tunnels; thermal power stations; and water supply. The largest markets were the Far East, Africa, India and the Middle East. Major international projects include:

- Sabiya power station in Kuwait (£1,100 million);

- Yang Pu city development project in China (£1,000 million);

- Hong Kong Route 3 country park section (£1,000 million); and

- Oresund bridge crossing in Denmark (£800 million).

Further Reading

The Aerospace Industry. Aspects of Britain series, HMSO, 1993.
Overseas Trade. Aspects of Britain series, HMSO, 1994.

17 Energy and Natural Resources

Energy production is a vital part of Britain's economy. It directly employs about 270,000 people—6 per cent of industrial employees. Offshore oil and gas also provides employment for 250,000 in support industries—building oil rigs, designing platforms and pipelines, operating boats and helicopters, etc. The energy sector accounts for 5 per cent of gross domestic product (GDP), 11 per cent of total investment and 42 per cent of industrial investment. It contributes £1,500 million a year to the balance of payments. It also includes three of Britain's ten largest companies—Shell, BP and British Gas.

Energy Resources

Britain has the largest energy resources of any country in the European Union (EU) and is a major world producer of oil and natural gas—called primary sources. The other main primary sources are coal, nuclear power and some water power; secondary sources (derived from primary sources) are electricity, coke and smokeless fuels, and petroleum products. In 1993 Britain was a net exporter of fuels in volume terms— 4.2 million tonnes of oil equivalent— representing a surplus of £1,250 million. Coal still supplies a significant, but declining, proportion of the country's energy needs—25 per cent of total inland consumption in 1993. Nuclear power provided about 25 per cent of electricity supplied by the British electricity companies in 1993.

Ownership and Exploitation

With the major exceptions of gold, silver, oil and natural gas (owned by the Crown), and coal (and associated minerals), minerals in Great Britain are mainly privately owned. In Northern Ireland gold and silver are owned by the Crown, while rights to exploit petroleum and other minerals are vested in the Department of Economic Development.

On the United Kingdom Continental Shelf (UKCS; see map, p. 252) the right to work all minerals except coal is vested in the Crown. The exclusive right to extract coal, or license others to do so, both on land in Great Britain and under the sea, is currently vested in the British Coal Corporation. Normally, ownership of minerals belongs to the owner of the land surface, but in some areas, particularly those with a long history of mining, these rights have become separated.

Mining and quarrying are usually carried out by privately owned companies.

ENERGY POLICY

The President of the Board of Trade (who heads the Department of Trade and Industry—DTI) and the Secretary of State for the Environment are responsible for energy matters in Great Britain, except for electricity in Scotland, which is under the Secretary of State for Scotland. The Secretary of State for Northern Ireland is responsible for all energy matters there.

The aim of the Government's energy policy is to ensure secure, diverse and sustainable supplies of energy in the forms that people and businesses want, and at competitive prices. Health, safety and environmental policies, as well as EU and other international commitments, have also to be borne in mind.

Key elements are to:

- encourage competition among producers and choice for consumers, and establish a legal and regulatory framework to enable markets to work well;
- ensure service in a commercial environment, with consumers paying the full cost of energy resources they consume;
- privatise state-owned industries where possible, thus exposing them to the discipline of capital markets;
- promote energy efficiency; and
- promote wider share ownership.

The independent regulators' main role is to encourage the development of competition and to protect the interests of consumers by administering price controls and enforcing standards of service.

Privatisation

British Gas, Britoil, Enterprise Oil, and the non-nuclear electricity supply industry in Britain are in the private sector. The Coal Industry Bill, now before Parliament, contains the Government's proposals for restructuring and privatising British Coal. The Citizen's Charter commitment aims to give customers of privatised utilities fair treatment and strengthens the powers of regulators. Customers are to be compensated when standards are not met and greater competition introduced into the gas industry.

International Commitments

Britain is actively engaged in international collaboration on energy questions, notably through its membership of the EU and of the International Energy Agency (IEA; part of the Organisation for Economic Co-operation and Development, with 23 member countries). The European Energy Charter is a multilateral treaty which aims to set a legal framework for energy investment and trade with Russia and other economies in transition.

Britain supports the continuing development of the single market in energy, in particular through the removal of obstacles to trade in the EU's gas and electricity markets.

Energy Report

The Government published its first annual energy report, to provide information for business and investment, in 1994. It deals with trends in supply and demand, licensing activity, and regulatory developments in the energy sector as it moves towards a fully competitive market for all fuels.

An independent energy advisory panel advises on the preparation of the report. Energy suppliers and users serve on the panel.

ENERGY CONSUMPTION

During 1982–93, when Britain's GDP rose by about 28 per cent, final energy consumption on a 'heat supplied' basis increased by only 11 per cent. Energy consumption by final users in 1993 amounted to 152.3 million tonnes of oil equivalent[1] on a 'heat supplied' basis, of which transport consumed 33 per cent, industrial users 24 per cent, domestic users 30 per cent, and commerce, agriculture and public services 13 per cent.

---

[1] 1 tonne of oil equivalent = 41,868 gigajoules.

Table 17.1: Inland Energy Consumption (in terms of primary sources)[a]

million tonnes oil equivalent

	1983	1988	1991	1992	1993
Oil	68.1	74.7	78.1	77.8	79.7
Coal	68.6	70.1	67.1	63.4	55.1
Natural gas	47.1	51.5	54.0	54.8	62.4
Nuclear energy	13.5	16.6	17.4	18.5	21.5
Hydro-electric power	0.4	0.4	0.4	0.5	0.4
Net imports of electricity	–	1.1	1.4	1.4	1.4
Total	197.7	214.4	218.5	216.4	220.5

Source: Department of Trade and Industry

[a]Adjustments in the figures for recent years are the result of methodological review.

Note: Differences between totals and the sums of their component parts are due to rounding.

ENERGY EFFICIENCY

Britain's consumers spend about £50,000 million a year on energy. The Energy Efficiency Office (EEO), part of the Department of the Environment (DOE), estimates that 20 per cent—or £10,000 million—could be saved through measures involving little, if any, cost. Energy efficiency improvements offer a fast, cost-effective means of reducing carbon dioxide (CO_2) emissions. The EEO encourages investment in energy efficiency improvements through various programmes. It provides consumers with the necessary information to make energy efficiency improvements, and gives grants where the need is greatest. The EEO budget for 1994–95 has been increased to over £100 million.

The Best Practice programme researches and disseminates technical information. It aims to generate savings of £800 million a year by 2000. It also aims to increase the capacity of Combined Heat and Power (CHP) to 5,000 megawatts[2] (MW) by 2000. CHP is the simultaneous generation of electricity and heat in a single process. It is significantly more efficient than conventional generation, makes substantial energy cost savings and emits less CO_2.

The EEO operates two grant schemes. The Home Energy Efficiency Scheme gives advice and grants to householders on low incomes or over the age of 60 for draught-proofing and loft and water tank insulation. The Energy Management Assistance Scheme helps small and medium-sized companies to improve their energy efficiency.

Among the EEO's publicity initiatives, the 'Making a Corporate Commitment' campaign underlines the need for senior management to commit itself to responsible energy management. More than 1,600 organisations have so far joined. Publicity campaigns, which include television and press advertising, tell householders how they can help combat global warming by improving the energy efficiency of their homes.

Other work includes the promotion of home energy labelling and energy labelling of domestic appliances. In addition, the DOE's Green House Demonstration Programme has established a network of energy efficiency demonstration schemes across England to encourage local authorities to develop and apply energy efficiency to their housing. The Programme ended in March 1994, but local authorities are now required to include energy efficiency as an integral part of their housing strategies and investment programmes.

Revisions to the Building Regulations, including double glazing, improved insulation, heating controls, and home energy labelling, are also under consideration.

The independent Energy Saving Trust, set up by the Government, British Gas and the electricity companies, develops new programmes to promote the efficient use of energy.

[2] 1 MW = 1,000 kilowatts (Kw).

OIL AND GAS

Britain has substantial oil and gas reserves offshore on the UKCS. The trend in offshore oil and gas developments is towards the exploitation of smaller reservoirs, and advances in science and technology have made this a more economic proposition.

The Government must approve all plans for the development of oil and gas fields. It has granted exploration and production licences as a result of 14 offshore licensing rounds since 1964. By the end of 1993, 5,250 wells had been or were being drilled in the UKCS: 2,428 development wells, 1,756 exploration wells and 1,066 appraisal wells.

Oil and Gas Licensing

In the 14th round, announced in June 1993 and the biggest in terms of blocks available and applications received since 1971–72, 484 blocks were offered. Applications were received for 128 blocks and 110 were awarded. These include blocks in the English Channel, Cardigan Bay, Solway Firth and the North Channel. There is interest in the more mature areas of the UKCS. Blocks were also licensed in frontier acreage in the south-west approaches. For the first time, companies were asked to state their environmental policies in their licence applications. The 15th round, announced in April 1994, includes all available unlicensed acreage in the Southern Basin and in the central North Sea. Nominations for a 16th round were also invited.

Offshore Supplies

The Oil and Gas Projects and Supplies Office (OSO) of the DTI works to ensure fair commercial opportunities for Britain in all oil and gas markets. It also encourages reduction of the cost of oil and gas developments, to improve the competitiveness of the UKCS.

All oil companies, their suppliers and the DTI are partners in an initiative which aims to reduce capital costs by at least 30 per cent within two or three years.

Research

The Offshore Energy Technology Board advises the OSO on its offshore technology programme. A number of universities, research institutes and private-sector companies carry out oil-related research. Funding comes from private sector oil and supplies companies, OSO, the Marine Technology Directorate Ltd and the Petroleum Science and Technology Institute. The Offshore Technology Park in Aberdeen comprises several research facilities.

> Export levels are increasing, with some companies now exporting as much as 50 per cent of their turnover. About one-third of all orders placed (worth over £2,000 million a year) are for overseas.

Economic and Industrial Aspects

In 1993 UKCS oil and gas production accounted for about 1.4 per cent of Britain's gross national product at factor cost. Total revenue from the sale of oil and gas produced from the UKCS in 1993 is estimated to have been £8,700 million and £3,600 million respectively. Taxes and royalty receipts attributable to UKCS oil and gas are estimated to have been £1,350 million in 1993–94. The British supplies industry wins about 75 per cent of UKCS contracts—worth about £5,000 million a year.

Gross capital investment from British sources in the oil and gas extraction industry amounted to some £4,700 million in 1993. This was about 20 per cent of British industrial investment and 5 per cent of gross domestic fixed capital formation. Total investment between 1965 and 1993 came to about £57,000 million (£101,000 million at 1993 prices). Some 34,200 people were employed offshore in September 1993.

Offshore Safety

The Offshore Safety Act 1992 raises the maximum penalties for certain offences against health and safety regulations. The Act also completes the statutory transfer of offshore safety responsibilities to the Health and Safety Executive (HSE). Government funding for the HSE's Offshore Safety Division will reach £35 million in 1994–95.

OIL

Before the 1970s Britain was almost wholly dependent for its oil supplies on imports, the only indigenous supplies coming from a few land-based oilfields. However, the first notable offshore discovery of oil in the UKCS was made in 1969 and the first oil brought ashore in 1975. Output of crude oil and natural gas liquids (NGLs) in Britain in 1993 averaged 2.06 million barrels (about 274,205 tonnes) a day, making Britain the world's tenth largest producer.

North Sea Fields

There were 62 offshore fields producing crude oil at the end of February 1994, and 20 new offshore development projects (seven of them for oil) were approved during 1993.

The fields with the largest cumulative production totals are Forties and Brent. Ninian, Piper, Beryl, Fulmar, Magnus and Claymore are other high-producing fields. Production from most large fields is controlled from production platforms of either steel or concrete which have been built to withstand severe weather, including gusts of wind of up to 260 km/h (160 mph) and waves of 30 m (100 ft). The Petroleum Act 1987 lays down measures to be taken when offshore installations and pipelines are abandoned.

The Government's oil policy encourages exploration, development and investment—to maximise economic oil production for the foreseeable future. Remaining recoverable reserves of UKCS oil in the 'proven' plus 'probable' categories amount to 1,406 million tonnes, while the total remaining potential of the UKCS could be nearly 6,000 million tonnes on current estimates.

Structure of the Oil Industry

About 250 private sector companies, including many large oil firms, operate in Britain or engage in work in the UKCS. Exploration and development of the UKCS are carried out by the private sector. The Government receives royalties from UKCS oil.

The two leading British oil companies are British Petroleum (BP) and Shell Transport and Trading, which has a 40 per cent interest in the Royal Dutch/Shell Group of Companies. BP and Shell are the two largest industrial companies in Britain in terms of turnover.

Land-based Fields

Onshore production of crude oil and NGLs is much less significant than offshore production. In 1993 it was 3.9 million tonnes, 85 per cent of which came from Britain's largest onshore field at Wytch Farm (Dorset). In addition to minor production from various mining licensees, other onshore fields include Welton (Lincolnshire) and Wareham (Dorset). Small, independent companies play an increasingly prominent role in onshore exploration. At the end of 1993, 176 landward petroleum licences were in force, covering an area of 24,331 sq km (9,489 sq miles).

Refineries

Britain's refinery industry is one of the most modern and efficient in Europe. In 1993 the refinery sector processed 96.3 million tonnes of crude and process oils (4.3 per cent more than in 1992), a figure close to maximum capacity. About 80 per cent of output is in the form of lighter, higher-value products such as gasoline, DERV and jet kerosene. By comparison, the proportion of Western European output accounted for by these higher-value products is about 70 per cent.

Consumption

Deliveries of petroleum products for inland consumption (excluding refinery consumption) in 1993 included 23.8 million tonnes of motor spirit, 9.7 million tonnes of kerosene, 19.6 million tonnes of gas and diesel oil (including DERV fuel used in road vehicles), 10.8 million tonnes of fuel oil and 11.9 million tonnes of other products.

Oil

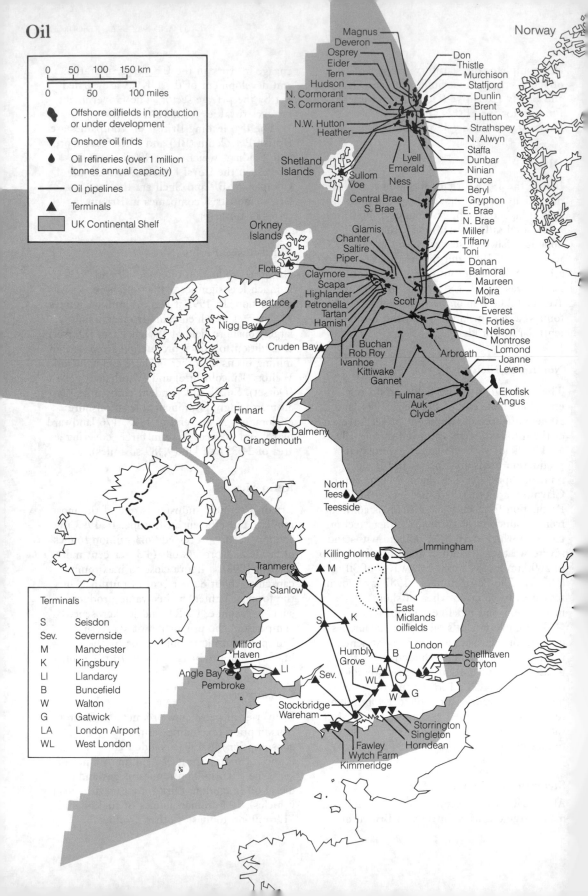

Norway

Scale:
- 0, 50, 100, 150 km
- 0, 50, 100 miles

Legend:
- Offshore oilfields in production or under development
- Onshore oil finds
- Oil refineries (over 1 million tonnes annual capacity)
- Oil pipelines
- Terminals
- UK Continental Shelf

Oilfield labels (north to south):
Magnus, Deveron, Osprey, Eider, Tern, Hudson, N. Cormorant, S. Cormorant, N.W. Hutton, Heather, Don, Thistle, Murchison, Statfjord, Dunlin, Brent, Hutton, Strathspey, N. Alwyn, Staffa, Dunbar, Ninian, Bruce, Beryl, Gryphon, E. Brae, N. Brae, Miller, Tiffany, Toni, Donan, Balmoral, Maureen, Moira, Alba, Everest, Forties, Nelson, Montrose, Lomond, Joanne, Leven, Ekofisk, Angus

Shetland Islands, Sullom Voe, Lyell, Emerald, Ness, Central Brae, S. Brae

Orkney Islands, Flotta, Glamis, Chanter, Saltire, Piper, Claymore, Scapa, Highlander, Petronella, Tartan, Hamish, Scott

Beatrice, Nigg Bay, Cruden Bay, Buchan, Rob Roy, Ivanhoe, Kittiwake, Gannet, Arbroath, Fulmar, Auk, Clyde

Finnart, Dalmeny, Grangemouth

North Tees, Teesside

Killingholme, Immingham, Tranmere, Stanlow, M, S, K, East Midlands oilfields, London, Shellhaven, Coryton, Milford Haven, Humbly Grove, B, LA, WL, Angle Bay, Pembroke, LI, Sev., W, G, Stockbridge, Wareham, Storrington, Singleton, Horndean, Fawley, Wytch Farm, Kimmeridge

Terminals

S	Seisdon
Sev.	Severnside
M	Manchester
K	Kingsbury
LI	Llandarcy
B	Buncefield
W	Walton
G	Gatwick
LA	London Airport
WL	West London

Table 17.2: Oil Statistics

million tonnes

	1983	1988	1991	1992	1993
Oil production:[a]					
land	0.3	0.8	3.7	4.0	3.9
offshore	114.6	113.7	83.1	85.2	90.2
Refinery output	70.9	79.8	85.5	85.8	89.6
Deliveries of petroleum products for inland consumption	64.5	72.3	74.5	75.5	75.8
Exports (including re-exports):					
crude petroleum, natural gas liquids (NGLs) and feedstocks	69.9	73.3	55.1	57.6	64.2
refined petroleum products	13.3	15.8	19.4	20.2	23.1
Imports:					
crude petroleum, NGLs and feedstocks	30.3	44.3	57.1	57.7	61.7
refined petroleum products	9.9	9.2	10.1	10.6	10.0

Source: Department of Trade and Industry
[a] Crude oil plus condensates.

Trade

Britain's refinery sector has set new records for exports in each of the last three years. In 1993, it exported over 25 million tonnes of refined petroleum products and NGLs (separated at North Sea terminals), nearly 30 per cent of its output (worth £3,000 million to the balance of payments). Virtually all exports went to Britain's partners in the EU and the IEA, the largest markets being France, Italy, the Irish Republic, the Netherlands and Germany, and, outside the EU, the United States.

Oil Pipelines

Oil pipelines brought ashore about 80 per cent of offshore oil in 1993. Some 1,930 km (1,199 miles) of major submarine pipeline brings oil ashore from the North Sea oilfields. Major crude oil onshore pipelines (from harbours, land terminals or offshore moorings to refineries) include those connecting Grangemouth to Finnart, Cruden Bay to Grangemouth, and Purbeck to Southampton. Onshore pipelines also carry refined products to major marketing areas; for example, a 423-km (263-mile) pipeline runs from Milford Haven to the Midlands and Manchester, while similar pipelines also run from Fawley to Wolverhampton and from Lindsey to north London. Chemical pipelines include one from Mossmorran to Grangemouth and another (405 km—252 miles) from Grangemouth to Stanlow.

GAS

Public supply of manufactured gas in Britain began in the early 19th century in central London. For many years gas was produced from coal, but during the 1960s growing imports of oil brought about production of town gas from oil-based feedstocks. Following the first commercial natural gas discovery in the UKCS in 1965 and the start of offshore gas production in 1967, supplies of offshore natural gas grew rapidly and by 1977 natural gas had replaced town gas in the public supply system in Great Britain. Up to the end of 1993 some £14,870 million had been spent on developing natural gas resources on the UKCS and 962,000 million cubic metres had been produced. Britain is the world's fifth largest gas producer.

Structure

The gas industry in Great Britain, in state ownership since 1949, was privatised in 1986. British Gas plc supplies gas to consumers in accordance with its authorisation as a public gas supplier under the Gas Act 1986. It is currently the only public gas supplier. Over 30 independent companies supply gas to industrial and commercial customers in competition with British Gas. The regulatory regime for the private gas sector places responsibility on the Office of Gas Supply (OFGAS) for ensuring that British Gas is operating within the terms of its authorisation. The Act also established the Gas Consumers' Council, independent of both British Gas and OFGAS, and responsible for investigating consumer complaints.

At the end of 1993, British Gas was instructed to separate its transport and supply businesses. It is also the Government's intention to phase competition into the domestic gas market from 1996.

Production

In 1993 indigenous production of natural gas amounted to 65,488 million cubic metres. This included 3,919 million cubic metres of gas used for drilling, production and pumping operations on North Sea production platforms and at terminals. Total availability of UKCS gas amounted to 60,682 million cubic metres—17.8 per cent higher than in 1992. In addition, about 4,600 million cubic metres of gas were imported from Norway. Some 640 million cubic metres were exported. British natural gas accounts for about a quarter of total primary fuel consumption in Britain. Natural gas from the three most prolific of the 48 offshore gasfields—Leman, Indefatigable (South) and the Hewett area—accounted for over half the cumulative total gas produced in the UKCS. In addition to supplies from gasfields, associated gas delivered to land via the Far North Liquids and Associated Gas System (FLAGS) and from Alwyn North made further significant contributions. Gas from the South Morecambe field in the Irish Sea and from the twin North Sean and South

Sean fields is used to augment supplies to meet peak demand in winter.

There are various methods of natural gas storage, including salt cavities and storage facilities for liquefied natural gas. The partially depleted Rough field is used as a major gas store. Gas is drawn from the national transmission system in summer and injected into the Rough reservoir—for rapid recovery during periods of peak winter demand.

Reserves

Remaining recoverable gas reserves in present discoveries are estimated at between 630,000 million and 1.92 million million cubic metres. If possible gas from existing discoveries and potential future discoveries are added, the remaining total reserves are estimated to be in the range of 1.06 million million to 3.5 million million cubic metres. Indigenous offshore natural gas reserves are likely to meet most of the British demand well into the next century.

Transmission

The British Gas national and regional high-pressure pipeline system of some 265,000 km (164,660 miles) transports natural gas around Great Britain. It is largely supplied from four North Sea shore terminals, and one in Barrow-in-Furness (Cumbria). The high-pressure transmission system is inspected regularly.

Newly built natural gas pipelines, run by independent operators, run from Horndean to Barking and from Theddlethorpe to Killingholme.

Consumption

Sales of natural gas in Britain totalled 668 terawatt[3] hours (TWh) in 1993. About 49 per cent of this is for industrial and commercial purposes, the remainder being for domestic use by 18 million consumers. Gas is used extensively in industries requiring the control of temperatures to a fine degree of

---

[3] 1 TW = 1,000 gigawatts. 1 GW = 1,000 MW.

Gas

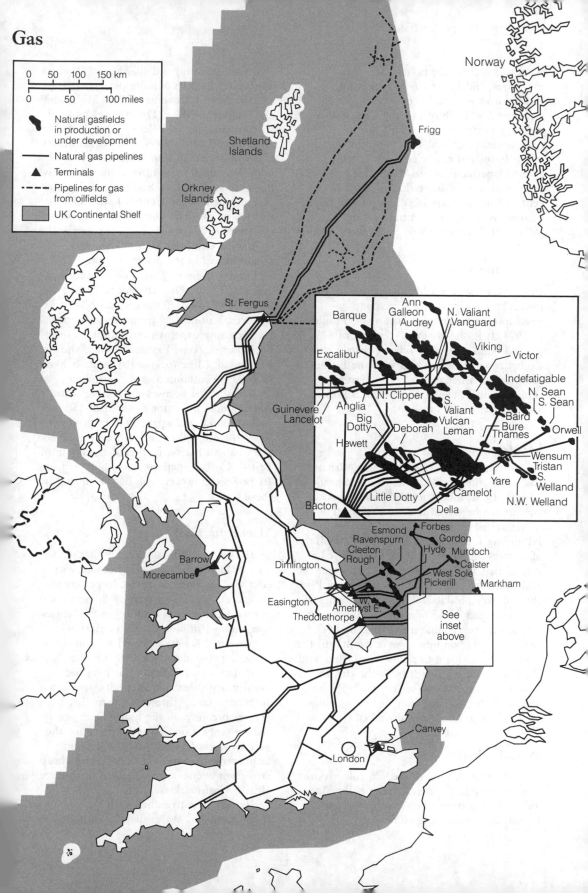

Legend:
- 0 50 100 150 km
- 0 50 100 miles
- Natural gasfields in production or under development
- Natural gas pipelines
- ▲ Terminals
- Pipelines for gas from oilfields
- UK Continental Shelf

Norway

Shetland Islands

Orkney Islands

Frigg

St. Fergus

Inset:

Barque
Ann
Galleon
Audrey
N. Valiant
Vanguard
Excalibur
Viking
Victor
Indefatigable
N. Sean
S. Sean
Guinevere
Lancelot
Anglia
N. Clipper
S. Valiant
Vulcan
Baird
Bure
Thames
Orwell
Big Dotty
Deborah
Leman
Hewett
Wensum
Tristan
S. Welland
Yare
Little Dotty
Camelot
N.W. Welland
Bacton
Della

See inset above

Esmond
Forbes
Ravenspurn
Gordon
Cleeton
Hyde
Murdoch
Rough
Caister
West Sole
Pickerill
Markham
Dimlington
Barrow
Morecambe
Easington
Amethyst E.
W.
Theddlethorpe

Canvey

London

accuracy, such as the pottery and glass industries, and in certain processes for making iron and steel products.

Some 226 TWh of this gas were sold to industry in Britain, and 103 TWh to commercial (including other non-domestic) users. Industrial gas prices have fallen by about 25 per cent in real terms since privatisation, and domestic prices by 22 per cent. An increasingly large part of domestic demand is for gas for central heating. In 1993, 340 TWh were sold to domestic users.

Development

British Gas has a worldwide reputation for gas technology, with a research and development programme costing £80 million in 1993. It is one of seven sponsors of a plan to build a pipeline linking Britain with Zeebrugge in Belgium and with the European gas market. Among its overseas activities, the company is exploring for gas in Poland and Bulgaria.

COAL

Despite the size of recent cutbacks, Britain has one of the world's most technologically advanced coal industries. Coal mining in Britain can be traced back to Roman times. Taxes raised on its sale helped pay for rebuilding London, and St Paul's Cathedral, after the Great Fire of 1666. Coal played a crucial part in the industrial revolution of the 18th and 19th centuries. In its peak year, 1913, the industry produced 292 million tonnes of coal, exported 74 million tonnes and employed over 1 million workers. In 1947 (when 200 million tonnes were produced) the coal mines passed into public ownership, and the National Coal Board (now the British Coal Corporation) was set up. In 1955 there were 850 British Coal collieries in operation; by 1992 the number had dwindled to 50.

Privatisation

In 1993, British Coal offered 28 collieries for lease/licence to the private sector. By May 1994, six had been taken over by private mining companies: Clipstone

(Nottinghamshire) and Rossington (South Yorkshire) by RJB Mining plc; Trentham (Staffordshire), Coventry (West Midlands) and Markham Main (Derbyshire) by Coal Investments plc; and Betws (Dyfed) by Betws Anthracite Ltd. In 1994, the Coal Industry Bill will enable 16 remaining deep and 32 opencast mines to be offered for sale in five businesses—based on Scotland, Wales, the North East and the Central Coalfield (in two parts). The Government is also offering for sale seven further collieries closed by British Coal, but kept on care and maintenance, to the private sector.

Grants of about £900 million were made available by the Government to British Coal in 1993–94 to offset the cost of colliery closures, redundancy payments and other restructuring expenses carried out to meet declining markets. Payments under the Redundant Mineworkers Payments Scheme in 1993–94 amounted to £33.1 million.

British Coal licenses the private sector to work mines employing fewer than 150 men underground, and opencast sites producing less than 250,000 tonnes. A new public body, the Coal Authority, is to take on certain of British Coal's functions, including licensing. Its powers, however, will not be subject to these limits.

Market for Coal

In 1993–94 inland consumption of coal was 84.7 million tonnes, of which about 75 per cent was by power stations, 10 per cent by coke ovens and 5 per cent by domestic users. British Coal sales of coal to power stations totalled 46.1 million tonnes in 1993–94. Exports in 1993–94 were 1.1 million tonnes, while imports amounted to 18.4 million tonnes.

Britain's coal industry has long been heavily dependent on electricity generation. Increasing competition in this market has put greater pressure on the coal industry to reduce costs. Long-term contracts for the supply of gas for electricity generation, improvement in nuclear output, and cheaper coal from overseas, have helped to squeeze British Coal markets.

By agreement reached with the generators in England and Wales in 1993, British Coal will supply 160 million tonnes of coal over five years. British Coal has also signed contracts with the Scottish electricity industry for the supply of more than 2 million tonnes of Scottish coal a year through to 1998. These contracts will be reallocated to successor companies on privatisation.

Production

In 1993–94 total output of 59.9 million tonnes comprised 42.5 million tonnes of British Coal deep-mined coal, 13.5 million tonnes from its opencast mines and 3.9 million tonnes from licensed mines (deep and opencast).

British Coal's investment programme amounted to £149 million in 1993–94. A new colliery, Asfordby (Leicestershire), is being designed for the combined longwall/continuous mine production strategy, employing approximately 450 people and producing about 1.75 million tonnes a year. Another colliery, Maltby (South Yorkshire), has been redeveloped and will absorb Silverwood colliery during 1994.

Employment in British Coal deep mines has been reduced from about 138,000 in 1985 to 10,700 at the end of March 1994, including a reduction of 27,000 mining jobs in the year 1993–94 alone. Since 1984, British Coal, through its job creation arm, British Coal Enterprise, has helped create job opportunities for 100,000 people in areas where mining was previously the main source of employment.

Research

Clean coal technologies, such as fluidised bed boilers, are now widely employed to reduce pollutant emissions in industry. Two advanced systems, integrated gasification/combined cycle and pressurised fluidised bed combustion, are also being developed. In 1993–94 the DTI more than doubled its annual contribution for coal research and development to £7 million. The work includes over 100 projects with British industry and universities, and also collaboration with overseas organisations. The coal liquefaction plant at Point of Ayr (Clwyd) converts 2.5 tonnes of coal a day into petrol, diesel and other transport fuels.

ELECTRICITY

England and Wales

The privatised electricity supply industry in England and Wales consists of two main generating companies, the National Grid Company (NGC) and 12 regional electricity companies (RECs). The two main non-nuclear generators, National Power and PowerGen, the publicly owned nuclear generator, Nuclear Electric plc, and other generators and importers sell electricity to suppliers through a market known as the pool. The NGC operates the transmission system—bulk transfer of electricity across the national grid—and owns the pumped storage stations at Dinorwig and Ffestiniog. It is owned by the RECs through a holding company.

Distribution and supply of electricity are the business of the RECs. Distribution involves transfer of electricity from the national grid and its delivery, across local systems, to consumers. Supply is the purchase of electricity from generators and its sale to customers. Each REC is authorised to supply any premises within its own area. The RECs and the main generators hold second-tier licences to supply customers throughout the country—but only those with a maximum consumption of 100 kW. Other companies have also entered this complex market by obtaining a second-tier licence.

The Government plans to sell its 40 per cent shareholding in each of National Power and PowerGen during 1994–95.

Scotland

Industry restructuring in Scotland created three companies. ScottishPower plc and Scottish Hydro-Electric plc generate, transmit, distribute and supply electricity. They are also contracted to buy all the output from Scottish Nuclear Ltd, a government-owned company which operates the nuclear power stations at Hunterston (Strathclyde) and Torness (Lothian), and have contracts to share the output from each other's generation capacity. Opportunities exist for electricity trading in the pool (see above).

Electricity

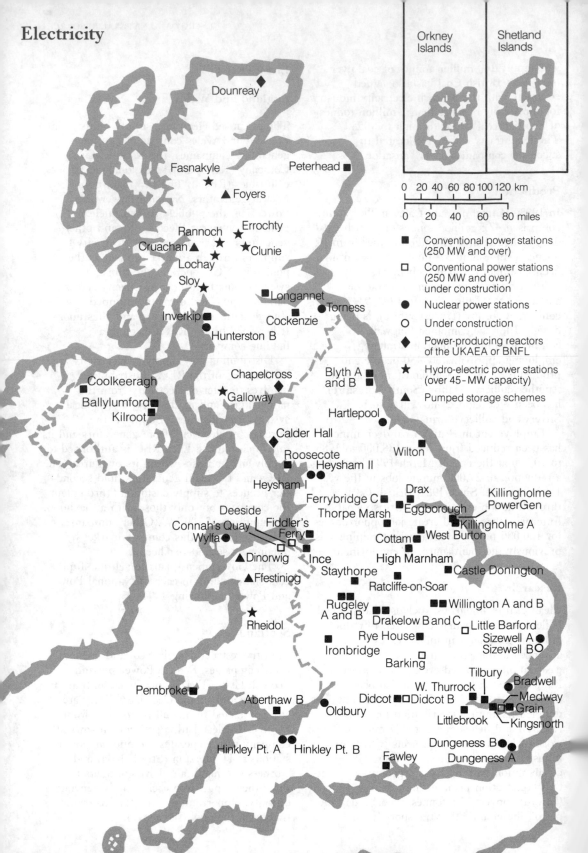

Orkney Islands

Shetland Islands

	km
0 20 40 60 80 100 120	km
0 20 40 60 80	miles

■ Conventional power stations (250 MW and over)

□ Conventional power stations (250 MW and over) under construction

● Nuclear power stations

○ Under construction

◆ Power-producing reactors of the UKAEA or BNFL

★ Hydro-electric power stations (over 45 – MW capacity)

▲ Pumped storage schemes

Dounreay

Fasnakyle

Foyers

Peterhead

Rannoch

Errochty

Cruachan

Clunie

Lochay

Sloy

Longannet

Torness

Inverkip

Cockenzie

Hunterston B

Coolkeeragh

Chapelcross

Blyth A and B

Ballylumford

Galloway

Kilroot

Hartlepool

Calder Hall

Wilton

Roosecote

Heysham II

Heysham I

Drax

Ferrybridge C

Killingholme PowerGen

Thorpe Marsh

Eggborough

Deeside

Connah's Quay

Fiddler's Ferry

Killingholme A

Wylfa

Cottam

West Burton

Dinorwig

Ince

High Marnham

Staythorpe

Castle Donington

Ffestiniog

Ratcliffe-on-Soar

Rugeley A and B

Willington A and B

Drakelow B and C

Little Barford

Rheidol

Rye House

Sizewell A

Ironbridge

Sizewell B

Barking

Tilbury

Bradwell

Pembroke

W. Thurrock

Medway

Aberthaw B

Didcot

Didcot B

Grain

Oldbury

Littlebrook

Kingsnorth

Hinkley Pt. A

Hinkley Pt. B

Dungeness B

Fawley

Dungeness A

Associated Functions

Certain service and co-ordinating functions for the industry are undertaken by the Electricity Association, jointly owned by the electricity companies of Great Britain. Regulation of the industry is the responsibility of the Office of Electricity Regulation, headed by the Director General of Electricity Supply, whose duties include the promotion of competition and the protection of consumer interests.

Northern Ireland

Northern Ireland's four power stations were transferred to the private sector in 1992. The flotation of Northern Ireland Electricity (NIE) plc in 1993 completed the privatisation of the industry. Regulation is shared between the Department of Economic Development and the Director General of Electricity Supply (NI).

Consumption

In 1993 sales of electricity through the distribution system in Britain amounted to 282,764 GWh. Domestic users took 36 per cent of the total, industry 34 per cent, and commercial and other users the remainder.

Generation

National Power owns 36 operational fossil-fuelled power stations, which generate about 40 per cent of the electricity supplied to the transmission and distribution networks in England and Wales. PowerGen's 19 operational fossil-fuelled power stations generate about 30 per cent. The nuclear stations in Great Britain generate almost 22 per cent.

In 1993–94, 49 per cent of electricity used in Scotland was produced by Scottish Nuclear's two stations. In addition to nuclear generation, Scotland's electricity needs are met from hydro, coal and gas generation, using gas from the Miller field at Peterhead power station—a total output capacity of 9,900 MW. Scottish Nuclear sells 74.9 per cent of its output to ScottishPower and the rest to Hydro-Electric.

Non-nuclear power stations owned by Britain's major power producers consumed 67.4 million tonnes of oil equivalent in 1993, of which coal accounted for 56 per cent and oil 6 per cent.

Independent generators are allowed to compete on equal terms with the major generators and have equal access to the grid transmission and local distribution systems. National Power and PowerGen

Table 17.3: Generation by and Capacity of Power Stations owned by the Major Generating Companies in Britain

	Electricity generated (GWh)			Per cent	Output
	1983	1988	1993[a]	1993	capacity (MW)
Nuclear plant	45,776	58,867	84,433	16.6	11,274
Other steam plant	208,514	222,887	210,597	73.5	46,836
Gas turbines and oil engines	356	464	359	3.7	2,018
Pumped storage plant	1,897	2,121	1,437	4.1	2,787
Natural flow hydro-electric plant	3,892	4,121	3,522	2.0	1,327
Renewables other than hydro	–	1	165	0.1	65
Total	260,436	288,511	300,514	100	64,306
Electricity supplied (net)[a]	241,305	266,711	281,175		

Source: Department of Trade and Industry

[a] Electricity generated less electricity used at power stations (both electricity used on works and that used for pumping at pumped-storage stations).

Note: Differences between totals and the sums of their component parts are due to rounding.

have agreed to sell about 6,000 MW of their fossil-fuelled plant by 1996—to increase both the number of independent generators and competition in generation.

To control acid emissions National Power and PowerGen are fitting flue gas desulphurisation (FGD) equipment to their existing coal-fired power stations at Drax (North Yorkshire) and Ratcliffe on Soar (Leicestershire). ScottishPower expects to fit FGD at its main coal station, Longannet. In addition, a ten-year programme to control nitrogen oxide (NO_x) emissions through the installation of low-NO_x burners at 12 major power stations in England and Wales is in progress. ScottishPower is fitting low-NO_x burners at Longannet.

For new stations the trend is towards the construction of combined cycle gas turbines (CCGTs). They are cheaper, and take less time, to build than other types of station. Their use of natural gas, low in sulphur, also helps to reduce acid and CO_2 emissions. In England and Wales, 18 such stations over 50 MW are commissioned or under construction. Some 8 per cent of electricity in Britain was derived from gas in 1993.

The NGC, together with Electricité de France, runs a 2,000-MW cross-Channel cable link, providing the capacity for the transmission of electricity between the two countries. The link has generally been used to supply baseload electricity—the minimum amount that needs to be generated—from France to England, but a contract concluded in 1993 provides for exports from England at times of peak demand in France.

Transmission lines linking the Scottish and English grid systems enable cross-border trading. This interconnector is run jointly by the NGC and ScottishPower. Capacity at the Scottish end of the interconnector has been increased from 850 MW to 1,600 MW. NIE plc and ScottishPower have plans to construct a 250-MW interconnector between Scotland and Northern Ireland, to come into use in 1997.

Nuclear Power

In 1956 the world's first industrial-scale nuclear power station, at Calder Hall (Cumbria), began to supply electricity to the national grid. It, together with the Magnox station at Chapelcross (Dumfries and Galloway), is still operated by British Nuclear Fuels plc (BNFL). There are also 12 commercial nuclear power stations operated by Nuclear Electric and Scottish Nuclear. The former has five Magnox stations (with capacities ranging from 245 to 950 MW) and five Advanced Gas-cooled Reactor stations (AGRs; ranging from 1,010 MW to 1,250 MW). Scottish Nuclear operates two 1,320 MW AGR stations. Nuclear Electric has also built Britain's first pressurised water reactor (PWR; 1,175 MW) at Sizewell (Suffolk). Three commercial Magnox stations (one each in England, Wales and Scotland) have been shut down and are being decommissioned.

Nuclear power generation increases diversity of energy supply and helps maintain its security, and nuclear stations produce no sulphur dioxide (SO_2), NO_x or CO_2. The Government wishes to maintain the nuclear option, provided nuclear power can demonstrate that it is competitive with other sources.

In England and Wales the 'fossil fuel levy' is set at 10 per cent of electricity sales. Most of the revenue raised is to pay a premium to nuclear generators, as the cost of producing energy from nuclear sources is greater than that of producing it from fossil fuel sources. The levy is expected to raise £9,100 million up to 1997–98 to help cover the unavoidable costs associated with the operation of existing stations. A small but growing proportion goes to pay a premium to renewable generators.

British Nuclear Fuels

BNFL provides services covering the whole nuclear fuel cycle. It is wholly owned by the Government.

BNFL's thermal oxide reprocessing plant (THORP) began operations in March 1994. Built at a cost of £2,800 million, including its share of associated facilities, THORP reprocesses spent fuel from British and overseas oxide reactors. Environmental protection plant costing £600 million was brought on stream at the same time. BNFL has begun supplying fuel for the PWR at

Sizewell and has contributed its waste management and decommissioning expertise to international joint ventures. A subsidiary company, BNFL Inc, was established in the United States in 1990 and has won environmental restoration contracts with the United States Department of Energy.

UK Atomic Energy Authority

Since 1994 the UK Atomic Energy Authority (UKAEA) has been reorganised into two: AEA Technology and UKAEA (Government Division). AEA Technology operates as a commercial business, providing science and engineering services to the nuclear industry worldwide and to other industrial sectors. UKAEA (Government Division) is responsible for the safe management and decommissioning of AEA's nuclear facilities, radioactive waste management, fuel reprocessing and the Government's nuclear research and development programme.

Nuclear Research

Most of DTI's nuclear expenditure is on the decommissioning of redundant nuclear research and development facilities. These include research and demonstration power reactors, such as the Winfrith (Dorset) Steam Generating Heavy Water Reactor, the Windscale (Cumbria) AGR, the Dounreay (Highland) Fast Reactor and the Prototype Fast Reactor. The radioactive wastes arising from this programme are safely and cleanly managed until their final disposal in purpose-built and authorised facilities.

The Government plans to spend £16 million in 1994–95 on fusion research. About half of this is the cost of the EU Joint European Torus (JET) nuclear project at Culham (Oxfordshire). The remaining half goes to fund a national programme of fusion research carried out by the AEA as part of the EU fusion programme.

DTI also funds assessments of advanced reactor safety, international safety standards and the transfer of technology to help improve nuclear safety in the former Soviet Union, and in central and eastern Europe. In 1993 it contributed £8.25 million to the European Bank for Reconstruction and Development to finance safety improvements at the higher-risk nuclear plants in those countries.

Nuclear Safety

Britain has a rigorous system of nuclear safety regulation, enforced by the HSE's Nuclear Installations Inspectorate, which ensures that high standards of safety are incorporated into the design, construction, operation, maintenance and decommissioning of all nuclear plant, and eventual disposal of resulting wastes. While the safety of such plant in Britain is the ultimate responsibility of the nuclear operator, the Inspectorate has the power to shut down a plant if it thinks it unsafe and may also require improvements to an installation if it believes the appropriate standards of safety are not being met.

Discharges of radioactive waste have to be kept within the limits and conditions set by authorisations granted under the Radioactive Substances Act 1993. Within maximum dose limits, operators of nuclear facilities are required to keep discharges as low as is reasonably achievable and failure to do so makes them liable to prosecution.

Emergency Plans

The precautions taken in the design and construction of nuclear installations in Britain, and the high safety standards in their operation and maintenance, reduce the chance of accidents which might affect the public to an extremely low level. However, all operators are required, as a condition of their site licences, to prepare emergency plans, including those for dealing with an accidental release of radioactivity. These are regularly tested in exercises under the supervision of the Nuclear Installations Inspectorate.

International conventions have been established on the early notification of a nuclear accident which may have possible transboundary effects, and on the mutual provision of assistance in the event of a nuclear accident or radiological emergency.

NEW AND RENEWABLE SOURCES OF ENERGY

Renewable energy sources provide about 6 per cent of EU primary energy production. The Government encourages development of new and renewable technologies which promise to become economically attractive and environmentally acceptable—to contribute to:

● diverse, secure and sustainable energy supplies;

● a reduction in the emission of pollutants; and

● internationally competitive renewables industries.

It is working towards a figure of 1,500 MW (3 per cent of Britain's current capacity) of new electricity generating capacity from renewable energy sources, for Britain as a whole, by 2000. Renewables might, though, be able to supply up to 20 per cent of Britain's 1991 electricity needs by 2025. By the end of 1991 two renewables orders for England and Wales under the non-fossil fuel obligation (NFFO, which currently supports renewables to the extent of about £60 million a year) had resulted in contracts for 197 projects, with a total capacity of over 600 MW. By March 1994, 138 of these projects were generating 306 MW. The first Northern Ireland NFFO order, for nearly 16 MW of renewables capacity (mainly wind), was made in March 1994. The third NFFO renewables order for England and Wales, and the first Scottish renewables order, were also set in train for a prospective total of 330 to 440 MW.

Research and development policy concentrates resources on key technologies—energy from coppice and waste, wind, solar and fuel cells—and aims to increase their appeal to investors. Emphasis on technology transfer continues. Expenditure on the Government's renewables programme for 1994–95 is just under £20 million. Planning policy requires the environmental benefits of wind and other renewables to be taken into account, but also stresses the need to protect the local environment.

International collaboration is undertaken through multilateral and bilateral arrangements within the IEA and the EU. These include:

● JOULE, which supports research into economically viable and environmentally sound energy technologies;

● THERMIE, which aims to promote innovative energy technologies in energy efficiency, renewable energy and clean coal and hydrocarbons; and

● ALTENER, which is designed to foster development of renewable sources in the EU, and increase trade in products, equipment and services.

Wastes and Biomass

These offer the largest potential resource of any renewable and are likely to be among the earliest exploited. By March 1993, 82 waste/biomass projects had begun to operate under the first two renewables NFFO orders, with a combined output of 235 MW. The main energy sources used to generate electricity are: municipal and industrial wastes (with potential for up to 10 per cent of electricity supply by 2025), landfill gas, agricultural and forestry wastes and energy crops.

Wind Energy

This has the potential to contribute perhaps 30 TWh a year to electricity supply by 2025. Under the first two NFFO renewables orders, contracts were placed for 58 wind energy projects, with a total declared net capacity (DNC—a measure of average output) of 96 MW. By March 1994, 29 projects (comprising some 370 wind turbines—53 MW DNC, largely in Wales and north-west England) had been commissioned and were generating to the grid. Another 6.5 MW DNC were under construction. In response to public concern about the visual impact of wind farms and possible noise from turbines, the Government expects to see no more than about 20 wind farms in the third NFFO renewables order later in 1994.

Solar

Britain's solar energy resource is potentially large, but also diffuse, and there is much unplanned use of solar gain. Estimates suggest that such use contributes up to 150 TWh a year to energy needs in buildings. The photovoltaic (PV) industry shows promise in the export market. The Government is assessing the potential of buildings-integrated PV systems, where PV units would be placed in the façades of domestic and commercial buildings, which are likely to be the most promising application.

Hydroelectricity

Large-scale hydro schemes account for about 2 per cent of generation in Britain, with most to be found in Scotland. The Government has provided funding of up to half the cost of an initial feasibility study for small-scale hydro schemes (below 5 MW). In March 1994, 27 small-scale hydro projects were generating under renewables NFFO arrangements, with a combined output of 19 MW.

Other Technologies

The Government has spent over £70 million on research, development and demonstration in geothermal, tidal and wave power. It has concluded that these technologies have limited potential to contribute commercially to energy supplies in the next few decades. They have therefore been allocated to a 'watching brief' category. No further commitments will be made once current programmes have been completed.

Non-fuel Minerals

Although much of Britain's requirements for industrial raw materials is met by imports, the non-fuel minerals it produces make an important contribution to the economy. Output of non-fuel minerals in 1992 totalled 320 million tonnes, valued at £1,748 million. Construction raw materials, in particular aggregates, form the bulk of the value of non-fuel minerals production. The total number of employees in the extractive industry was some 40,000 in 1992.

Table 17.4: Production of Some of the Main Non-fuel Minerals

million tonnes

	1983	1987	1992
Sand and gravel	107.0	117.8	98.9
Silica sand	4.0	4.0	3.6
Igneous rock	36.9	46.0	57.7
Limestone and dolomite	94.0	113.7	107.9
Chalk[a]	12.4	13.4	9.2
Sandstone	14.7	16.4	14.9
Gypsum	2.9	3.4	2.5
Salt, including salt in brine	6.3	7.1	6.1
Common clay and shale[a]	22.4	18.3	12.2
China clay	2.5	3.1	2.5[b]
Ball clay	0.6	0.7	0.7
Fireclay	0.7[a]	0.9	0.6
Iron ore	0.4	0.3	0.0
Potash	0.5	0.7	0.9
Fluorspar	0.1	0.1	0.1
Fuller's earth	0.2	0.2	0.2

Source: *British Geological Survey, United Kingdom Minerals Yearbook 1992*

[a] Great Britain only.

[b] Moisture-free basis.

Some Minerals Produced in Britain

Orkney Islands

Shetland Islands

talc

talc

0 20 40 60 80 100 120 km

0 20 40 60 80 miles

● Major metallic and industrial mineral workings

▲ Major mineral deposits (unworked)

marble

● silica sand

▲ barytes ▲ gold

barytes
▲
gold

● silica sand

● silica sand

gold ● salt
▲
diatomite

fluorspar, lead
NORTHERN PENNINE
OREFIELD

gypsum ●
barytes

salt ● potash

silica sand ●

SOUTHERN
PENNINE
OREFIELD

zinc, copper, lead, silver ▲   silica sand ●

fluorspar, barytes, lead

salt ●
salt ●

gypsum ●

gold ▲
CHESHIRE
SALTFIELD

gypsum ●

silica sand ●

silica sand
●

silica sand ●

fuller's earth ●
fuller's earth ●
silica sand ●

fuller's earth ●

▲
fuller's earth   silica sand ●

fuller's earth ●

gypsum ●

ball clay ●

china clay ●   ball clay ●   ball clay ●

china clay ●   china clay ●
▲
tungsten, tin

tin ●

Exploration

The Government is seeking to restrict the growth in England of quarries supplying rock, and sand and gravel for building. It also expects the construction industry to double the use of recycled material, and to reduce its dependence on aggregates extracted on land from 80 to 68 per cent by 2006. Coastal superquarries from outside England may make an increased contribution to aggregates requirements in the future. Scottish Office guidelines on minerals working in Scotland include a policy that there should be no more than four superquarries in Scotland over the period to 2009.

The British Geological Survey is carrying out a long-term programme for the DTI aimed at identifying areas with mineral potential. Gold exploration by the private sector has decreased, but continues, especially in Scotland, Northern Ireland and south-west England. In Wales small-scale production of gold takes place at the Gwynfynydd and Clogau mines. Reports by the Mineral Reconnaissance Programme, funded by the DTI, include a description of a gold-bearing fault zone in Glen Clova in the south-east Scottish highlands. It has been traced over 1.6 km and may extend over 10 km.

Production

In terms of value, production of limestone and dolomite was estimated at £486 million in 1992, sand and gravel £425 million, clays £277 million, igneous rock £245 million, potash £68 million, sandstone £65 million, salt £49 million, chalk £38 million, silica sands £36 million, gypsum and anhydrite £18 million, fuller's earth £14 million, fluorspar £9 million and tin £7 million. In 1992 the production of metals in non-ferrous ores totalled 3,000 tonnes, mainly tin from Cornwall. South Crofty, the one remaining Cornish mine and one of the very few sources of tin in the EU, produced 2,232 tonnes of tin-in-concentrate in 1992, equivalent to about 20 per cent of Britain's demand. Some lead and a little zinc are produced as by-products of fluorspar.

Water

Britain's water supplies are obtained partly (about 75 per cent) from surface sources such as mountain lakes, reservoirs and river intakes, and partly (about 25 per cent) from groundwater. About 99 per cent of the population in Great Britain and 97 per cent in Northern Ireland are served by the public water supply system. Water put into the public supply system (including industrial and other uses) in England and Wales amounted to about 16,757 megalitres (Ml) a day in 1993, of which average domestic daily consumption per head was 150 litres. An average of 2,206 Ml a day was supplied in Scotland in 1992–93.

Some 45,176 Ml a day were abstracted in England and Wales in 1992, of which public water supplies accounted for 17,958 Ml a day. The electricity generating companies and other industry took 20,287 Ml a day. Agriculture took 412 Ml a day.

England and Wales

The Secretaries of State for the Environment and for Wales, the Director General of Water Services and the National Rivers Authority (NRA) are the principal regulators. The Drinking Water Inspectorate regulates drinking water quality. The Minister of Agriculture, Fisheries and Food and the Secretary of State for Wales are responsible for policy relating to land drainage, flood protection, sea defence, and the protection and development of fisheries.

Water Companies

The ten water service companies have statutory responsibilities for water supply, its quality and sufficiency, and for sewerage and sewage treatment. The supply-only companies, of which there were 29 in the private sector in 1989, now number 21. They supply water to about a quarter of the population.

The Water Industry Act 1991 allows the water companies to determine their own methods of charging. An alternative to the charging system based on rateable values, however, must be found by the year 2000. In the Government's view, water metering is potentially the fairest way of paying for water, even though it would take time to introduce and would not be appropriate everywhere. In general, companies require new properties to have metered supplies.

A system of economic regulation and guaranteed standards of service is overseen by OFWAT, the office of the Director General of Water Services. It has a duty to ensure that water companies are able to finance the carrying-out of their statutory obligations; it also promotes economy and efficiency within the water industry and, where appropriate, competition; and it also has to protect the interests of customers and to ensure that there is no undue preference or discrimination in the fixing of charges. The Director General also sets limits to the rate at which water companies can increase their prices.

The Water Supply (Water Quality) Regulations 1989 define wholesomeness and incorporate the requirements of the EC's drinking water directive. They impose physical, chemical and microbiological standards for water intended for domestic and food production purposes. The task of the Drinking Water Inspectorate is to ensure that drinking water is wholesome and that companies comply with the Regulations. Of 3.75 million tests carried out in 1992, 98.7 per cent came within the legal limits.

National Rivers Authority

The NRA is a non-departmental public body with statutory duties and powers in relation to water resources, pollution control, flood defence, fisheries, recreation, conservation and navigation in England and Wales. The water environment for which it has responsibility includes all rivers, lakes, reservoirs, estuaries, coastal waters and water stored naturally underground. The NRA's consent is needed for abstraction of water and discharge of effluent.

Development Projects

The water industry in England and Wales has a ten-year investment programme costing £30,000 million at 1992–93 prices. Thames Water's 80-km (50-mile) distribution system to meet the growing demand for water in London is due for completion in 1996. North West Water has a 25-year investment programme to clean up the polluted rivers of the Mersey Basin.

Water is an increasingly scarce resource, yet consumption is forecast to rise by as much as 43 per cent in 30 years. South-east England, for example, where five years of winter rainfall well below the long-term average ended in 1992, receives 14 per cent of Britain's rainfall, yet contains about 30 per cent of its population.

The NRA encourages companies to promote efficient water use and to reduce leakage (estimated at about 25 per cent in 1994)—thus helping to remove the need for land-consuming and expensive reservoirs. More household meters would, the NRA says, curb demand.

Scotland

In Scotland responsibility for public water supply, sewerage and sewage disposal rests with the nine regional and three islands councils ('the water authorities'). In addition, the Central Scotland Water Development Board (CSWDB) is responsible for providing water in bulk to five regional councils in central Scotland. In 1993–94 the Board supplied authorities with an average 271 Ml a day. Parliament is considering a Bill which would create three public water authorities to take over provision of these services from the local authorities on 1 April 1996 and would also dissolve the CSWDB on that date. An independent representative body for consumers would also be established.

The Secretary of State for Scotland is responsible for promoting conservation of water resources and provision by water authorities and water development boards of adequate water supplies. He has a duty to promote the cleanliness of rivers and other inland waters, and the tidal waters of Scotland. River purification authorities have a statutory responsibility for water pollution control. Water is charged for according to type of consumer: domestic consumers pay council water charges or metered charges; non-domestic consumers pay non-domestic water rates, or metered charges. For sewerage services, domestic consumers pay through the council tax, and non-domestic consumers pay non-domestic sewerage rates and, where appropriate, trade effluent charges. Charges and rates are decided by each authority.

Scotland has a relative abundance of unpolluted water from upland sources.

Northern Ireland

The Department of the Environment for Northern Ireland is responsible for public water supply and sewerage throughout Northern Ireland. It is also responsible for the conservation and cleanliness of water resources and, with the Department of Agriculture, may prepare a water management programme with respect to water resources in any area. There is a domestic water charge which is contained in the regional rate, while agriculture, commerce and industry pay metered charges. There are abundant potential supplies of water for both domestic and industrial use. An average of 680 Ml of water a day was supplied in 1993–94.

Research

Several organisations and centres of expertise provide water research services to government, the NRA, water companies and the Scottish river purification boards.

The Water Research Centre, a private company, has a large programme of research into, for example, environmental issues and drinking water safety.

Research carried out by institutes of the Natural Environment Research Council embraces river modelling, water quality, climate change, effects on resources and the impact of pollution on freshwater.

Among its various roles the Institute of Hydrology studies the statistics of floods and droughts.

Further Reading

The Energy Report 2: Oil and Gas Resources of the United Kingdom 1994. Department of Trade and Industry. HMSO.

Digest of United Kingdom Energy Statistics 1994. Department of Trade and Industry. HMSO.

United Kingdom Minerals Yearbook 1993. British Geological Survey. HMSO.

Digest of Environmental Protection and Water Statistics. No. 16, 1994. Department of the Environment. HMSO.

Energy and Natural Resources. Aspects of Britain series. HMSO, 1992.

18 Agriculture, the Fishing Industry and Forestry

British agriculture is noted for its high level of efficiency and productivity. In 1993 Britain was self-sufficient in 58 per cent of all types of food and animal feed, and in 73 per cent of indigenous-type food and feed. In 1994 the proportion of agricultural land covered by the Environmentally Sensitive Areas (ESAs) scheme increased by 15 per cent with the designation of a further 12 areas. Other plans encourage organic farming and public access to set-aside land and ESAs. Completion of the GATT Uruguay round negotiations in December 1993 created the basis for freer trade in agricultural produce and a reduction in subsidies.

Agriculture

In 1993 British agriculture employed 2.2 per cent of the total workforce. Food, feed and beverages accounted for about 11 per cent of Britain's imports by value, compared with about a quarter in the 1960s. The agricultural contribution to gross domestic product was £7,600 million in 1993, 1.4 per cent of the total. Britain is a major exporter of agricultural produce and food products, agrochemicals and agricultural machinery.

The Government aims to foster an efficient and sustainable agriculture industry through the provision and sponsorship of research, development and advisory services; provide financial support where appropriate; implement measures to control disease, pests and pollution; and improve marketing arrangements for food and food products. It also promotes high standards of animal welfare, and the balancing of environmental

protection with the needs of economic development. The latter includes conservation of the countryside's natural beauty and promotion of its enjoyment.

In accordance with the Citizen's Charter, annual performance targets which emphasise quality of service are set for the executive agencies of the Ministry of Agriculture, Fisheries and Food (MAFF; see p. 275). Farmers and crofters in Scotland have similar targets.

Land Use

The area of agricultural land has been declining, although there has been a reduction in the net rate of loss in recent years. In 1993 there were 11.3 million hectares (28 million acres) under crops and grass. A further 5.8 million hectares (14.4 million acres) were used for rough grazing, most of it in hilly areas. Soils vary from the thin poor ones of highland Britain to the rich fertile soils of low-lying areas such as the fenlands of eastern England. The climate is generally temperate, though rainfall distribution over Britain is uneven. The South East receives only about 600 mm a year, compared with over 1,500 mm in parts of west Scotland, Cumbria and Wales. Unsettled and wet weather during 1993 on the whole produced plentiful grass for grazing and conservation, but hampered progress with the harvest and autumn fieldwork.

Land Use in Britain

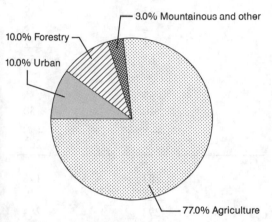

- 3.0% Mountainous and other
- 10.0% Forestry
- 10.0% Urban
- 77.0% Agriculture

Farming

In 1993 there were some 244,200 farm holdings in Britain (excluding minor holdings), with an average size of 70.2 hectares (173.4 acres)—again excluding minor holdings. About two-thirds of all agricultural land is owner-occupied. Some 44 per cent of holdings are 8 European size units (ESU)[1] or smaller.

Labour productivity has increased by over 30 per cent over the past ten years. Total income from farming (that of farmers, partners, directors and their spouses, and family workers—see Table 18.1) was estimated at £3,953 million in 1993, 41 per cent more than in 1992—largely because of a rise of 17.6 per cent (worth £948 million) in the industry's net product and a further fall, of £237 million, in interest paid.

[1] ESUs measure the financial potential of the holding in terms of the margins which might be expected from crops and stock. 8 ESU is judged the minimum for full-time holdings.

At the end of 1992 the industry's capital stock amounted to some £30,830 million, of which buildings and works made up over two-thirds. The overall stock of fixed capital is about 4 per cent down on 1982–84.

Agricultural Land Use 1993

TOTAL AREA ON AGRICULTURAL HOLDINGS

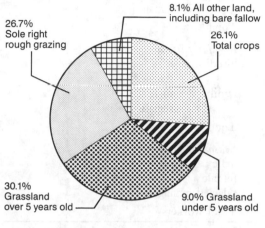

- 8.1% All other land, including bare fallow
- 26.7% Sole right rough grazing
- 26.1% Total crops
- 30.1% Grassland over 5 years old
- 9.0% Grassland under 5 years old

CROPS

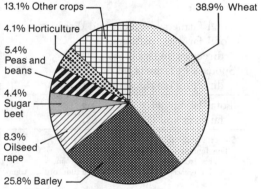

- 13.1% Other crops
- 38.9% Wheat
- 4.1% Horticulture
- 5.4% Peas and beans
- 4.4% Sugar beet
- 8.3% Oilseed rape
- 25.8% Barley

PRODUCTION

Home production of the principal foods is shown in Table 18.2 as a percentage by weight of total supplies (that is, production plus imports minus exports).

Livestock

Over half of full-time farms are devoted mainly to dairy farming or to beef cattle and sheep. The majority of sheep and cattle are

Table 18.1: Labour Force in Agriculture

	'000 persons 1982–84 Average	'000 persons 1993
Workers		
Regular whole time		
hired: male	121	74
female	11	11
family: male	30	22
female	5	3
Total	166	110
Regular part-time		
hired: male	19	19
female	23	19
family: male	12	13
female	7	7
Total	61	57
Seasonal or casual		
male	57	58
female	40	30
salaried managers[a]	8	8
Total workers	332	263
Farmers, partners and directors		
whole-time	203	176
part-time	88	108
Total farmers, partners and directors	292	284
Total farmers, partners, directors and workers	624	547
Spouses of farmers, partners and directors (engaged in farm work)	75	78
Total labour force (including farmers and their spouses)[b]	699	625

Source: *Agriculture in the United Kingdom 1993*
[a] This figure relates to Great Britain only.
[b] Figures exclude schoolchildren and most trainees.
Note: Differences between totals and the sums of their component parts are due to rounding.

reared in the hill and moorland areas of Scotland, Wales, Northern Ireland and northern and south-western England. Beef fattening occurs partly in better grassland areas, as does dairying, and partly on arable farms. British livestock breeders have developed many of the cattle, sheep and pig breeds with worldwide reputations, for example, the Hereford and Aberdeen Angus beef breeds, the Jersey, Guernsey and Ayrshire dairy breeds, Large White pigs and a number of sheep breeds. Developments in artificial insemination and embryo transfer have enabled Britain to export semen and embryos from high-quality donor animals. Livestock totals are given in Table 18.3.

Cattle and Sheep

Cattle and sheep constitute more than 40 per cent of the value of Britain's agricultural gross output. Dairy production is the largest

Table 18.2: British Production as a Percentage of Total New Supplies

Food Product	1982–84 average	1993 (provisional)
Beef and veal	98	102
Eggs	99	98
Milk for human consumption (as liquid)	100	99
Cheese	70	72
Butter	63	72
Sugar (as refined)	55	62
Wheat	106	120
Potatoes	91	91

Source: MAFF

part of the sector, followed by cattle and calves, and then fat sheep and lambs. Most dairy cattle in Britain are bred by artificial insemination. In 1993 the average size of dairy herds was 64 (excluding minor holdings), while the average yield of milk per dairy cow was 5,304 litres (1,211 gallons). Average household consumption of liquid (including low-fat) milk per head in 1993 was 2.18 litres (3.83 pints) a week.

About two-thirds of home-fed beef production originates from the national dairy herd, in which the Friesian breed is predominant. The remainder is derived from suckler herds producing high-quality beef calves in the hills and uplands, where the traditional British beef breeds, such as Hereford and Aberdeen Angus, are raised. Imported breeds include the Charolais,

Limousin, Simmental and Belgian Blue. In 1993 the size of the beef-breeding herd continued to expand. The increase to December 1993 more than offset the further decrease in the dairy herd.

Britain has a long tradition of sheep production, with more than 60 breeds and many cross-bred varieties. Research has provided vaccine and serum protection against nearly all the epidemic diseases. Sheepmeat production is the main source of income for sheep farmers, and wool provides a small additional return.

Grass (including silage) covers most British agricultural land and supplies 60–80 per cent of the feed for cattle and sheep. Grass production has been enhanced by the increased use of fertilisers, methods of grazing control, and improved herbage

Table 18.3: Livestock and Livestock Products

	1982–84 average	1991	1992	1993 (provisional)
Cattle and calves ('000 head)	13,249	11,866	11,804	11,729
Sheep and lambs ('000 head)	33,980	43,621	43,998	43,901
Pigs ('000 head)	7,962	7,596	7,609	7,754
Poultry ('000 head)[a]	80,220	94,664	91,965	98,469
Milk (million litres)	15,943	13,654	13,527	13,576
Eggs (million dozen)[b]	983	822	812	807
Beef and veal ('000 tonnes)	1,053	1,023	967	876
Mutton and lamb ('000 tonnes)	291	418	392	382
Pork ('000 tonnes)	745	797	806	826
Bacon and ham ('000 tonnes)	206	176	167	177
Poultry meat ('000 tonnes)	822	1,074	1,077	1,080

Source: MAFF
[a] Includes ducks, geese and turkeys. Figures for the latter are for England and Wales only.
[b] Hen and duck eggs.

conservation for winter feed. Rough grazings are used for extensively grazed sheep and cattle, producing young animals for fattening elsewhere.

A harmonised identification system being introduced throughout the European Union (EU) will enable animals to be traced to their farm of origin, for disease control purposes and for checking payments made under the Common Agricultural Policy (CAP).

Pigs

Pig production occurs in most areas but is particularly important in East Anglia and Yorkshire. There is an increasing concentration into specialist units and larger herds—19 per cent of farms account for 79 per cent of the pig herd.

Poultry

High husbandry standards and use of improved genetic stock have helped to increase efficiency in poultry meat production. In 1992 acquisitions—larger companies buying up smaller concerns—resulted in a more efficient industry, which remains able to supply the continuing increase in demand, also partly satisfied by imports. Poultry production in 1993 was 1.08 million tonnes, dominated by broilers. Broiler production, at 838,000 tonnes, was 8,000 tonnes below the level for 1992. Broilers from the 8 per cent of holdings with over 100,000 table birds account for well over a half of the total population. Production of hen eggs fell from 806 million dozen in 1992 to 800 million dozen in 1993. A decline in demand has led to lower production as well as fewer imports. Britain remains broadly self-sufficient in poultry meat and eggs (see p. 271).

Table 18.4: Main Crops

	1982–84 average	1991	1992	1993 (provisional)
Wheat				
Area ('000 hectares)	1,766	1,981	2,067	1,759
Production ('000 tonnes)	12,029	14,363	14,095	12,890
Yield (tonnes per hectare)	6.81	7.25	6.82	7.33
Barley				
Area ('000 hectares)	2,115	1,393	1,297	1,164
Production ('000 tonnes)	10,669	7,627	7,365	6,038
Yield (tonnes per hectare)	5.04	5.47	5.68	5.19
Oats				
Area ('000 hectares)	115	104	101	92
Production ('000 tonnes)	519	523	502	479
Yield (tonnes per hectare)	4.53	5.04	5.01	5.23
Potatoes				
Area ('000 hectares)	196	177	180	170
Production ('000 tonnes)	6,737	6,267	7,802	7,117
Yield (tonnes per hectare)	34.40	35.50	43.80	41.70
Oilseed rape				
Area ('000 hectares)	222	440	421	377
Production ('000 tonnes)	688	1,278	1,166	1,011
Yield (tonnes per hectare)	3.11	2.90	2.76	2.68
Sugar beet				
Area ('000 hectares)	201	196	197	197
Production ('000 tonnes)	8,840	7,673	9,300	8,550
Yield (tonnes per hectare)	44.67	39.14	47.21	43.40

Sources: *Agriculture in the United Kingdom 1993*, and *Agricultural Census, June 1993*

Animal Welfare

The welfare of farm animals is protected by legislation and it is an offence to cause unnecessary pain or distress to commercially reared livestock. Detailed regulations require owners of intensive units to arrange for the daily inspection of their stock and the equipment on which it depends. The law bans close confinement crates for keeping veal calves, and is phasing out close confinement systems for keeping pigs. There are further controls to safeguard the welfare of animals in markets, during transport and at slaughter. The Farm Animal Welfare Council, an independent body set up by the Government, advises on legislative or other changes. Britain continues to lead in pressing for higher standards of animal welfare, particularly during transport, throughout Europe.

Crops

The farms devoted primarily to arable crops are found mainly in eastern and central-southern England and eastern Scotland. The main crops are shown in Table 18.4. In Britain in 1993—the first full year to have been affected by the set-aside arrangements introduced as part of the 1992 CAP reforms—cereals were grown on just over 3 million hectares (7.5 million acres), an area 13 per cent down on 1992. Production, at 19.5 million tonnes, was 2.6 million tonnes down on 1992. Production of wheat, barley and oats fell in 1993, but higher yields were recorded for wheat and oats.

Between 40 and 50 per cent of available domestic wheat supplies (allowing for imports and exports) are normally used for flour milling, and a similar amount for animal feed. About a third of barley supplies are used for brewing, malting and distilling (there were plentiful supplies of good-quality malting barley in 1993), and virtually all the remainder for animal feed.

Large-scale potato and vegetable cultivation can be found on the fertile soils throughout Britain, often with irrigation. Principal areas are the peat and silt fens of Cambridgeshire, Lincolnshire and Norfolk;

the sandy loams of Norfolk, Suffolk, West Midlands, Nottinghamshire, South Yorkshire and Lincolnshire; the peat soils of South Lancashire; and the alluvial silts of parts of the Thames and Humber valleys. Early potatoes are produced in Shropshire, Pembrokeshire, Cornwall, Devon, Essex, Kent and Cheshire. Production of high-grade seed potatoes is confined to Scotland, Northern Ireland and the Welsh borders.

Sugar from home-grown sugar beet provides just over 60 per cent of home needs, most of the remainder being refined from raw cane sugar imported under the Lomé Convention (see p. 171).

Horticulture

In 1993 the land utilised for horticulture (excluding potatoes, peas for harvesting dry and mushrooms) was about 187,000 hectares (462,095 acres). Vegetables grown in the open accounted for 67 per cent of this, orchards for 17 per cent, and soft fruit and ornamentals (including hardy nursery stock, bulbs and flowers grown in the open) each for 7 per cent. More than one vegetable crop is, in some cases, taken from the same area of land in a year, so that the estimated area actually cropped in 1993 was 254,400 hectares (628,620 acres).

Mushrooms are the single most valuable horticultural crop, with a farm gate value of £165 million in 1993. Apples are also a significant crop. Output (of dessert and cooking apples) reached 319,000 tonnes.

Field vegetables account for 55 per cent of the value of horticultural output and are widely grown throughout the country. Most horticultural enterprises are increasing productivity with the help of improved planting material, new techniques and the widespread use of machinery. Some field vegetables, for example, are raised in blocks of compressed peat or loose-filled cells, a technique which reduces root damage and allows plants to establish themselves more reliably and evenly.

Glasshouses are used for growing tomatoes, cucumbers, sweet peppers, lettuces, flowers, pot plants and nursery stock. Widespread use is made of automatic control of heating and ventilation, and semi-automatic control of watering. Energy-efficient glasshouses use thermal screens, while low-cost plastic tunnels extend the season for certain crops previously grown in the open.

Organic Farming

The Government is encouraging the development of organic farming and growing, to respond to consumer demand and benefit the environment. It implements EU organic standards, supports a considerable research programme and aids conversion to organic production under a regulation which obliges EU members to adopt schemes beneficial to the environment (see below).

The organic production and processing standards are implemented by the United Kingdom Register of Organic Food Standards, which has a board of independent experts appointed by ministers.

FOOD SAFETY

EU food law harmonisation covers food safety, fair trading and informative labelling. The Government carries out research and surveillance to identify any risks. Food law enforcement falls mainly to local authorities.

In particular, MAFF has programmes to promote food safety and against diseases affecting food supply. Its expenditure on food safety research in 1994–95 is about £10 million. The link between diet, nutrition and health is one of the main subjects studied.

Among the groups assisting MAFF on food safety, the Steering Group on Chemical Aspects of Food Surveillance oversees a programme which encompasses pesticides and veterinary residues. The Steering Group on the Microbiological Safety of Food is surveying the entire food chain—from producer to consumer.

EXPORTS

Provisional data for 1993 suggest that the volume of exports related to agriculture (food, feed and drink) dropped by 7.2 per cent, when their value amounted to £8,361 million. The main markets are Western Europe, North America and the Middle East. Exports include speciality products such as fresh salmon, whisky (exports to the EU alone were worth over £765 million), biscuits, jams and conserves, as well as beef and lamb carcasses and cheese. Export promotion is headed by Food From Britain, an organisation funded by MAFF and industry.

One of the world's largest agricultural events, the annual Royal International Agricultural Exhibition, held at Stoneleigh in Warwickshire, enables visitors to see the latest techniques and improvements in British agriculture. Some 175,000 visitors attended in 1994, of whom 5,500 were from overseas. Other major agricultural displays include the Royal Smithfield Show, held in London, which exhibits agricultural machinery, livestock and carcasses; the Royal Highland Show; the Royal Welsh Show; and the Royal Ulster Agricultural Show. There are also important regional shows.

MARKETING

The Government's food marketing initiative encourages a partnership approach—between companies, or between individual growers, for example—throughout the agriculture and food industries. The Marketing Development Scheme, successor to the Group Marketing Grant, was introduced in 1994 under powers provided by the Agriculture Act 1993. The new scheme provides non-capital grants (for development of best practice and training, for example, and other proposals that do not involve capital expenditure) up to £150,000. Departments also operate EU grant schemes to help capital investment aimed at improving the processing of agricultural and fishery products.

Agricultural goods are marketed by private traders, producers' co-operatives and some marketing boards. The Agriculture Act 1993 ends the milk marketing schemes in Britain. In November 1994 a co-operative, Milk Marque, inherited certain assets of the Milk Marketing Board for England and Wales. The Act provides for the termination of the Potato Marketing Scheme, but no decision has been taken to invoke this provision.

Marketing arrangements for wool continue to be administered by the British Wool Marketing Board.

> In 1993–94 MAFF approved Group Marketing Grant projects for over 50 producer groups, with a total turnover between them of over £530 million.

Much agricultural and horticultural produce, such as grain, fruit and vegetables, is handled by marketing co-operatives and other farmers' businesses; these had a turnover of some £3,000 million in 1993.

In Scotland separate marketing measures are being developed to improve sales of agricultural and fish products, especially overseas. The Scottish Food Strategy Group has recommended a single Quality Mark for Scottish food and drink.

ROLE OF THE GOVERNMENT

Four government departments have joint responsibility for agriculture and fisheries matters—MAFF; the Scottish Office Agriculture and Fisheries Department; the Welsh Office; and the Department of Agriculture for Northern Ireland.

Common Agricultural Policy

The CAP aims to ensure stable markets and a fair standard of living for producers, and to assure regular supplies of food at reasonable prices. For many commodities support prices are set annually; there are also levies on imports to maintain internal market prices. Surpluses are bought by intervention boards (the Intervention Board executive agency in Britain) to be stored and sold when appropriate. Intervention stocks can be disposed of within the EU where this can be done without disrupting internal markets.

Exports, from the market and intervention stocks, are facilitated by the provision of export refunds to bridge any gap between EU prices and world prices. In some cases there are also direct payments to producers—for example, the arable area payments scheme (see below), the suckler cow premium, the beef special premium and the ewe annual premium. The support prices, as well as rates of levy, export refunds and other aids, are set in European Currency Units and are converted into the currencies of the member states at fixed rates of exchange—'green rates'. These green rates are kept broadly in line with market rates in accordance with an agreed formula.

Public Expenditure under the CAP by the Intervention Board and the Agricultural Departments

FORECAST 1993/94

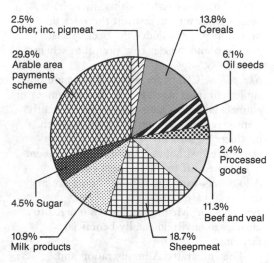

2.5% Other, inc. pigmeat

29.8% Arable area payments scheme

13.8% Cereals

6.1% Oil seeds

2.4% Processed goods

11.3% Beef and veal

18.7% Sheepmeat

10.9% Milk products

4.5% Sugar

Nearly all the EU's agricultural expenditure (£28,000 million in 1994) is channelled through the European Agricultural Guidance and Guarantee Fund. The Fund's guarantee section finances market support arrangements, while the guidance section provides funds for structural reform—for example, farm modernisation and investment—and payments to assist certain farmers to change to alternative enterprises.

In Britain's view, the cost of the CAP, which accounts for over 50 per cent of the EU's budget, remains excessive. To achieve a more market-oriented CAP and the ending of costly surpluses, the Government is seeking further reductions in price support. It also considers that quota systems as an alternative method of controlling production impede economic development.

Reforms

Those agreed in 1992 have been implemented for arable crops (see p. 272), beef and sheep. Commitment to environmental protection, which Britain secured as part of the CAP, has been followed in a number of areas.

Beef. The phased reductions in the categories of beef animals eligible for intervention, the intervention price and the annual ceilings for intervention purchases in Britain had the effect of reducing significantly the quantities of beef entering intervention in 1994. To compensate for this, there have been significant increases in the rates of premium payable under the beef special premium and suckler cow premium schemes since 1993.

Sheepmeat. Claims for ewe premium are now subject to individual quotas on the number of animals eligible. Quota may be permanently transferred or temporarily leased between producers. Normally, when quota is transferred without the holding, 15 per cent is siphoned off to the national reserve. Allocations from the national quota are made to special case categories.

Environment. Member states are obliged to encourage environmentally beneficial farming.

The Integrated Administration and Control System is designed to ensure uniform enforcement of the reformed CAP and to reduce the scope for fraud.

GATT Uruguay Round

The Final Act of the GATT Uruguay Round of multilateral trade negotiations was signed in April 1994 (see p. 170). The agreement (to come into effect in 1995) brings agriculture fully within GATT disciplines for the first time. It

- limits expenditure on agricultural subsidies: (a) overall domestic support will be 20 per cent below that in 1986–88; (b) outlays on export subsidies will be cut by 36 per cent by comparison with 1986–90; and subsidised export volumes must fall by 21 per cent from their level in 1986–90;

- aims to open up more markets by converting all barriers to agricultural imports into tariffs—to be reduced by an average of 36 per cent over six years; existing tariffs will, similarly, be cut by an average of 36 per cent by 2000; and

- requires signatories to the Agreement to introduce reduced tariff import quotas equal to 3 per cent of consumption in any agricultural product sector, rising to 5 per cent by 2000.

Price Guarantees, Grants and Subsidies

Expenditure in Britain in 1993–94 on CAP market regulation and on price guarantees, grants and subsidies was estimated at £287 million and £2,727 million respectively.

Farmers are eligible for grants aimed at environmental enhancement of their farms and pollution control. Hill and upland farmers can also benefit from payments per head on cattle and sheep, known as hill livestock compensatory allowances (HLCAs). The Marketing Development Scheme (see p. 273) helps farmers and growers to develop effective marketing skills.

In Less Favoured Areas (LFAs), where land quality is poor, farmers benefit from enhanced rates of grant and special payments on livestock. Their purpose is to support the continuation of livestock farming in hills and uplands, thus conserving the countryside and maintaining a viable population in the LFAs.

Farmers in LFAs are expected to receive some £550 million in subsidy from all sources in 1994. A rise in their incomes of some 70 per cent in 1992–94 has brought about a reduction in payments to them of HLCAs from £130 million in 1992–93 to £105 million in 1993–94.

Smallholdings and Crofts

In England and Wales county councils let smallholdings to experienced people who want to farm on their own account. Councils may lend working capital to them. At 31 March 1993 there were about 5,180 smallholdings in England and 890 in Wales. Land settlement in Scotland has been carried out by the Government, which, while now seeking to dispose of holdings to its sitting tenants, still owns and maintains 119,000 hectares (293,800 acres) of land settlement estates, comprising 1,446 crofts and holdings.

In the crofting areas of Scotland (the former counties of Argyll, Inverness, Ross and Cromarty, Sutherland, Caithness, Orkney and Shetland) much of the land is tenanted by crofters (smallholders). They enjoy the statutory protection provided by crofting legislation and can benefit from government schemes which exist to support and help crofting communities—such as agriculture and livestock improvement schemes. Most crofters are part-time or spare-time agriculturalists using croft income to supplement income from activities such as weaving, fishing, tourism and other occupations. The Crofters Commission has a statutory duty to promote the interests of crofters.

Agricultural Landlords and Tenants

Approximately 35 per cent of agricultural land in England and Wales is rented. Here the Government plans to simplify the legal framework on the leasing of land. In Scotland, the proportion is somewhat higher—50 per cent of farmland is rented—partly because of the relatively large areas of common grazings tenanted by crofters.

Most farms in Northern Ireland are owner-occupied, but, under a practice known as 'conacre', occupiers not wishing to farm all their land let it annually to others. About one-fifth of agricultural land is let under this practice and is used mainly for grazing.

Agriculture and Protection of the Countryside

During 1993 Britain secured EU agreement that member states should be able to attach appropriate environmental conditions to the payment of livestock subsidies. Further progress was made in improving the environmental potential of set-aside.

Environmentally Sensitive Areas

The ESA scheme (see Table 18.5) encourages farmers to maintain or adopt environmentally beneficial agricultural practices in parts of the country where the landscape, wildlife or historical features are of national importance. ESAs are regularly reviewed and information on their economic and environmental impact is published. The newest, designated in 1994, include Dartmoor and the Cotswold Hills in England, Preseli and the Clwydian Range in Wales, the Argyll Islands and Shetland Islands of Scotland, and the Sperrins and Slieve Gullion in Northern Ireland.

Participation in the ESA scheme is voluntary. Farmers enter into ten-year agreements with the relevant agriculture department. An agreement specifies the agricultural management practices to be carried out. Each ESA has varying tiers of entry, from basic care and maintenance to more extensive forms of management and environmental restoration. Details also vary, but participants may not convert grassland to arable and are subject to restrictions on fertiliser and chemical usage.

Most ESAs also restrict the numbers of stock on the land as well as operations such as the timing of cultivation. The annual

Table 18.5: ESAs – as at 31 March 1994

	Number of ESAs	Agreements	Land designated '000 hectares	Areas covered by agreements ('000 acres)	Payments to farmers in 1993–94 (£ '000)
England	22	4,761	1,148 (2,836)	272 (667)	16,548
Wales	7	80	520 (1,285)	64 (158)	1,541
Scotland	10	822	1,439 (3,556)	106 (262)	963
Northern Ireland	5	863	248 (613)	16 (39)	586

Sources: MAFF; Welsh Office; Scottish Office; Northern Ireland Office

payments are designed to compensate for reduced profitability, through the adoption of these less intensive production methods, and for the further work some management practices require. Additional payments are made for distinct items (such as hedgerows and stone wall renewal) set out in conservation plans, and for allowing public access to suitable farmland.

Other Schemes

The Farm Woodland Premium Scheme offers incentives to farmers to plant woodlands on agricultural land. Trees planted on arable or improved grassland qualify for annual payments of up to £250 a hectare for either ten or 15 years, depending on the type of woodland created. Between 1 April 1992 and 31 March 1994, applications to plant nearly 17,400 hectares (43,000 acres) of woodland in Britain were approved. Three-quarters of this area will be planted with broadleaved trees.

Under the arable area payment scheme, growers can claim area-based payments on cereals, oilseeds and protein crops. In order to qualify, growers must set aside part of the area on which they have claimed payment. In 1993 over 62,000 applications were received in Britain for some 4.1 million hectares (10.1 million acres).

The Farm and Conservation Grant Scheme, part-funded by the EU, provides grants to farmers for pollution control equipment and environmental improvements (such as hedges and stone walls). Since 1989 some £182 million has been paid to farmers in Britain, of which £138 million was for installing and improving waste handling facilities.

As well as expanding the scope of the existing ESA scheme the Government has introduced a Habitat Scheme, offering payments to farmers to promote nature conservation on their farms by taking carefully selected areas of land out of production for 20 years and managing them in environmentally beneficial ways. It has also launched a Nitrate Sensitive Areas Scheme, which will help protect selected groundwater sources used to supply drinking water, and an Organic Aid Scheme to help farmers wishing to convert to organic production.

Subject to EU approval, two further schemes will be introduced during 1994:

- a Countryside Access Scheme to increase opportunities for public access on set-aside land; and

- a Moorland Scheme aimed at protecting and improving the condition of heather and other shrubby moorland.

Proposals for Scotland, Wales and Northern Ireland are along broadly similar lines. By the time they come fully into effect, annual expenditure on these new measures in Britain will exceed £100 million.

Farm Diversification

Many farmers have diversified into non-agricultural enterprises to increase their incomes. A study by Exeter University in 1991 estimated that nearly 80,000 jobs on farms were reliant on non-agricultural activities. The most common are leisure amenities such as golf courses, tourist accommodation, or riding. Often these are small-scale, with low financial returns. In contrast, many farmers run large-scale farm shops which make a substantial contribution to their income. In 1994 board and lodging for holidaymakers on farms in England and Wales brought in some £70 million and benefited the rural economy by £115 million.

Agricultural Training

ATB-Landbase, an independent company, acts as the Industry Training Organisation (see p. 179) for the agriculture and horticulture industries. ATB-Landbase oversees the industry's training needs and arranges training through its network of providers and instructors. It operates under a contract with the Government, which provides the funding. At local level Local Enterprise Companies and Training and Enterprise Councils (see p. 178) help develop business skills. ATB-Landbase also arranges training in wider rural skills, business management and the management of shows and similar events. The agricultural colleges and independent instructors also help train in the agricultural and horticultural businesses.

Professional, Scientific and Technical Services

In England and Wales ADAS (Food, Farms, Land and Leisure), an executive agency, provides professional, scientific and technical services for agriculture and its ancillary industries. Most types of advice and servicing are on a fee-paying basis, although initial advice to farmers on conservation, use of land for woodlands and animal welfare is available free. The Government also funds the Farming and Wildlife Advisory Growers to provide free initial conservation advice. Similar services in Scotland come from the Scottish Office Agriculture and Fisheries Department through the Scottish Agricultural College. In Northern Ireland they are available from the Department of Agriculture's agriculture and science services.

CONTROL OF DISEASES AND PESTS

Farm Animals

Safeguarding Britain's high animal health status includes measures to prevent the import of disease in live animals, genetic material, meat and other animal products. From 1 January 1993 internal frontier controls within the EU were replaced by intensified checks at points of origin and spot checks at destinations, together with a system of checks on imports from third countries. Further measures have been taken against any increased risk:

- continuous surveillance at all English south and east coast ports;

- targeting consignments from countries where there is disease; and

- stepped-up routine checks, at destinations, on 50–60 per cent of all imported livestock.

There is evidence that measures to control bovine spongiform encephalopathy (BSE) are working. The incidence of BSE is down to very low levels in cattle under five years old.

Professional advice and action on the statutory control of animal disease and the welfare of farm livestock are the responsibility of the government State Veterinary Service, whose veterinary investigation centres also advise private practitioners treating animals on the farm.

Rabies

Special measures apply to prevent rabies entering Britain. Dogs, cats and certain other mammals are subject to import licence and six months' quarantine. From July 1994 commercially traded dogs and cats which satisfy strict conditions are allowed entry without quarantine from other EU states. There are severe penalties for breaking the law. No cases of rabies outside quarantine have occurred in Britain since 1970.

Fish

The fisheries departments operate statutory controls to prevent the introduction and spread of serious diseases of fish and shellfish. These controls include the licensing of live fish imports, the licensing of deposits of shellfish on the seabed, and movement restrictions on sites where outbreaks of notifiable diseases have been confirmed.

Plants

The agriculture departments are responsible for limiting the spread of plant pests and diseases and for preventing the introduction of new ones. They issue the health certificates required by other countries to accompany plant material exported from Britain, and authorise growers who wish to sell on the EU's single internal market. Certification schemes encourage the development of healthy and true-to-type planting stocks.

Pesticides

All pesticides must be approved for their safety and efficacy. There are strict controls on the supply, storage and use of pesticides, and their maximum residue levels in food. Controls on pesticides are the joint responsibility of six government departments on the basis of advice from the independent Advisory Committee on Pesticides. Arrangements for the approval of pesticides in Britain are being integrated into an EU-wide system under the terms of a directive on pesticides authorisations.

Veterinary Medicinal Products

The manufacture, sale and supply of veterinary medicinal products are controlled by legislation. Licences are issued by the Veterinary Medicines Directorate on behalf of the agriculture and health ministers for products that have been approved on the basis of safety, quality and efficacy. Independent expert advice on these criteria and on suspected adverse reactions is provided by the Veterinary Products Committee. Approval of veterinary medicines is being harmonised under an EU-wide system from 1995.

The Fishing Industry

The fishing industry provides 55 per cent by quantity of British fish supplies, and is an important source of employment and income in a number of ports. Cod, haddock, whiting, herring, plaice and sole are caught in the North Sea off the east coasts of Scotland and England; mackerel, together with cod and other demersal fish (caught on or near the bottom of the sea), are found off the west coast of Scotland; sole, plaice, cod, herring and whiting in the Irish Sea; and mackerel, sole and plaice off the south-west coast of England. Nephrops, crabs, lobsters and other shellfish are taken from the inshore waters all around the coast. A fleet also operates in distant waters—around Greenland and north Norway, for example.

Fish Caught

In 1993 demersal fish accounted for 53 per cent by weight of total British landings, pelagic fish (caught near the surface) for 36 per cent and shellfish for 11 per cent. Landings of all types of fish (excluding salmon and trout) by British fishing vessels totalled 727,000 tonnes. Cod and haddock represented 13 and 11 per cent respectively of the total value of demersal and pelagic fish landed, while anglerfish, plaice and mackerel (each with 8 per cent), hake (6 per cent) and whiting (5 per cent) were the other most important sources of earnings to the industry. The quayside value of landings of all sea fish, including shellfish, by British vessels in 1993 was £517 million.

The Fishing Fleet

At the end of 1993 the British fleet consisted of 11,108 registered vessels, including 451 deep-sea vessels longer than 24.4 m (80 ft).

Among the main ports from which the fishing fleet operates are Aberdeen, Peterhead, Fraserburgh (Grampian), Lerwick (Shetland), Kinlochbervie, Ullapool (Highland), North Shields (Tyne and Wear), Hull, Grimsby (Humberside), Lowestoft (Suffolk), Brixham (Devon), Newlyn (Cornwall), and Kilkeel, Ardglass and Portavogie (Northern Ireland).

The Government aims to conserve fish stocks, taking account of biological and environmental considerations and of marine ecology. Its primary purpose is to create the

Table 18.6: Imports and Exports of Fish

			tonnes
	1992	1992[a]	1993[a]
Imports			
Salt-water and shellfish[b]	420,377	331,114	313,149
Freshwater fish	52,973	49,838	41,654
Fish meals	237,350	177,965	208,856
Fish oils	na	95,332	108,984
Exports and re-exports			
Salt-water fish and fish products	398,860	155,694	116,150
Freshwater fish	22,665	2,615	2,981

Sources: MAFF; Scottish Office; Northern Ireland Office
[a] Figures do not contain trade within EU.
[b] Fresh, frozen, cured and canned.

best opportunities for Britain's fishermen. In accordance with measures to conserve fish stocks announced in 1992 all commercial fishing vessels now have to be licensed. However, implementation of restrictions on days at sea has been suspended pending a ruling from the European Court of Justice. Government financial support for decommissioning vessels is continuing.

Fish Farming

Fish farming is centred on Atlantic salmon and rainbow trout, which are particularly suited to Britain's climate and waters. Production of salmon and trout has grown from less than 1,000 tonnes in the early 1970s to 48,691 tonnes of salmon (all in Scotland) and 15,000 tonnes of trout in 1993. Scotland produces the largest amount of farmed salmon (with a first-sale value of £170 million) in the EU. Shellfish farming concentrates on molluscs such as oysters, mussels, clams and scallops, producing an estimated 5,700 tonnes a year.

The fish and shellfish farming industries make an important contribution to rural infrastructure, especially in remote areas such as the Highlands and Islands of Scotland. In 1993 the industries were estimated to have a combined wholesale turnover of some £205 million. Production is based on almost 1,195 businesses operating from some 1,890 sites and employing more than 5,000 people.

Administration

The fisheries departments are responsible for the administration of legislation concerning the fishing industry and for fisheries research. The safety and welfare of crews of fishing vessels and other shipping matters are provided for under legislation administered by the Department of Transport.

The Sea Fish Industry Authority is concerned with all aspects of the industry, including consumer interests. It undertakes research and development, provides training, and encourages quality awareness. It also administers a government grant scheme for fishing vessels, to promote a safe, efficient and modern fleet.

Fishery Limits

British fishery limits extend to 200 miles or the median line (broadly halfway between the British coast and the opposing coastline of another coastal state), measured from baselines on or near the coast of Britain. Only British vessels may fish within 6 miles of the coast. Certain other EU member states have fishing rights between 6 and 12 miles in certain areas and for named species, as British vessels have in other member states' coastal waters. Outside 12 miles EU vessels may fish against agreed EU quotas in named areas, while the only non-EU countries whose vessels may fish in EU waters are those with which the EU has reciprocal fisheries agreements (Norway, Sweden and the Faroes) which define areas and quantities of species of permitted catch.

Common Fisheries Policy

Britain plays an active role in the implementation and development of the EU's Common Fisheries Policy (CFP). The CFP's system for the conservation and management of the EU's fishing resources means that total allowable catches are set each year in order to conserve stocks. Decisions are based on independent scientific advice. These catch levels are then allocated between member states on a fixed percentage basis, taking account of traditional fishing patterns. Activity is also regulated by a number of technical conservation measures, including minimum mesh sizes for towed nets and net configuration restrictions, minimum landing sizes and closed areas designated mainly to protect young fish. Each member state is responsible for enforcement of the rules on its own fishermen and those of other member states in its own waters. National compliance with EU regulations is monitored by EU inspectors.

The CFP also covers the common organisation of the market in fishery and aquaculture products and policies on the size and structure of the EU fleet.

CFP provisions are supplemented by a number of fisheries agreements between the EU and third countries, the most important for Britain being the agreements with

Norway, Greenland and the Faroe Islands. EU catch quotas have also been established in the international waters of the north-west Atlantic and around Spitzbergen (Svalbard).

Fish and Shellfish Hygiene

Community legislation sets minimum hygiene standards for the production and marketing of fish and shellfish. Live bivalve molluscs (oysters, mussels and cockles) can be marketed only if they come from areas classified by the Government according to strict microbiological standards.

Salmon and Freshwater Fisheries

Salmon and sea-trout are fished commercially in inshore waters around the British coast. Eels and elvers are also taken commercially in both estuaries and freshwater. Angling for salmon and sea-trout (game fishing) and for other freshwater species (coarse fishing) is popular throughout Britain. There is no public right to fish in freshwater lakes and rivers in Great Britain. In England and Wales those wishing to fish such waters must first obtain permission from the owner of the fishing rights and a licence from the National Rivers Authority. In Scotland salmon fishing is administered by district salmon fishery boards. In Northern Ireland fishing is licensed by the Fisheries Conservancy Board for Northern Ireland and the Foyle Fisheries Commission in their respective areas, and 65 public angling waters, including salmon, trout and coarse fisheries, are accessible to Department of Agriculture permit holders.

Research

The total government-funded programme of research and development in agriculture, fisheries and food in 1994-95 amounts to about £320 million. This includes funding by MAFF, the Scottish Office Agriculture and Fisheries Department, the Department of Agriculture for Northern Ireland and the Office of Science and Technology. The Government funds research essential for the public good—for example, into food safety,

human health, animal welfare and flood protection. It also funds research which seeks to encourage an efficient and competitive industry consistent with high standards of consumer protection and care for the environment. It looks to industry to fund those areas of research where individual firms or ventures benefit directly. Research is carried out in a network of organisations, including research institutes, specialist laboratories and higher education institutions.

Agriculture and Food

The Biotechnology and Biological Sciences Research Council (BBSRC), formed in 1994 (see p. 313), absorbed the work of the former Agricultural and Food Research Council (AFRC). The BBSRC also took over responsibility for biological science from the former Science and Engineering Research Council. Research work has been guided by the recommendations of the independent Priorities Board for Research and Development in Agriculture and Food.

The BBSRC receives funds from the science budget through the Office of Science and Technology, and income from work commissioned by MAFF, by industry and by other bodies. It carries out research in its eight institutes and in higher education through its grants scheme.

ADAS carries out research and development under commission from MAFF and works under contract for other bodies. These undertakings are carried out at research farms across England and Wales, and through regional centres or on clients' premises.

MAFF also commissions research at its other agencies—the Central Veterinary Laboratory and the Central Science Laboratory (which incorporated the Food Science Laboratories in 1994). The five Scottish Agricultural and Biological Research Institutes, funded by the Scottish Office Agriculture and Fisheries Department, cover areas of research complementary to those of the BBSRC institutes, while including work relevant to the conditions of northern Britain. Development work in Scotland is carried out by the Scottish Agricultural College, which operates from three centres.

In Northern Ireland basic and applied research is done by the Department of Agriculture in its specialist research divisions and at its three agricultural colleges. It also has links with the Queen's University of Belfast and the Agricultural Research Institute of Northern Ireland.

Fisheries and Aquatic Environment

MAFF laboratories deal with marine and freshwater fisheries, shellfish, marine pollution, fish farming and disease. It also commissions research work from the Natural Environment Research Council, the Sea Fish Industry Authority and a number of universities. MAFF has two seagoing research vessels. In Scotland, the Scottish Office Agriculture and Fisheries Department undertakes a similar, and complementary, range of research and also has two seagoing vessels. The Department of Agriculture laboratories in Northern Ireland undertake research on marine and freshwater fisheries, and also have a seagoing research vessel.

Forestry

Woodland covers an estimated 2.4 million hectares (5.9 million acres) in Britain: about 7 per cent of England, 15 per cent of Scotland, 12 per cent of Wales and 5 per cent of Northern Ireland—about 10 per cent of the total land area and well below the 25 per cent average for the whole of Europe.

Britain's forestry programme aims to:

- protect forest resources;

- increase their value and promote the market for home-grown timber;

- conserve woodland as a home for wildlife and rare and endangered species;

- improve the environment;

- develop opportunities for recreation;

- enhance landscape and cultural heritage;

- promote appropriate management and training; and

- encourage public understanding and participation.

Doubling of the forest area since 1919 has meant substantial growth in Britain's wood processing industry. Since the early 1980s nearly 250,000 hectares (618,000 acres) of new woodland have been created. Forestry employs more than 40,000 people. Britain's woodlands produce about 7 million cubic metres (240 million cubic feet) of wood a year—about 15 per cent of total consumption. The Government plans to spend £283 million supporting the management of state and private forests and their expansion in the three years 1994–95 to 1996–97.

The area of productive forest in Great Britain is 2.18 million hectares (5.38 million acres), 39 per cent of which is managed by the Forestry Commission. The rate of new planting in 1993–94 was 1,385 hectares (3,422 acres) by the Commission and 15,875 hectares (39,228 acres) by other woodland owners, with the help of grants from the Commission, mainly in Scotland. In 1993–94, 10,780 hectares (26,638 acres) of broadleaved trees were planted, a practice encouraged on suitable sites. Much new planting is by private owners.

The volume of timber harvested on Commission lands in 1993–94 totalled 4.3 million cubic metres (152 million cubic feet).

The Commission's Woodland Grant Scheme pays grants to help create new woodlands and forests and regenerate existing ones. Management grants under the scheme contribute to the cost of managing woodlands to provide silvicultural, environmental and social benefits. Supplements are available for planting community woodlands and for planting on better land.

The Forestry Commission and Forestry Policy

The Forestry Commission, established in 1919, is the government department responsible for forestry in Great Britain. The Commissioners advise on forestry matters and are responsible to the Secretary of State for

Scotland, the Minister of Agriculture, Fisheries and Food, and the Secretary of State for Wales.

Within the Commission, the Forestry Authority controls tree felling, provides grants and advice to private woodland owners, and sets standards for the forestry industry as a whole. Forest Enterprise develops and manages the Commission's forests and forestry estate, as a multiple-use resource, supplying timber, opportunities for recreation, and enhancing nature conservation and the forest environment. After a major review of forestry in 1993–94, Forest Enterprise is to become an executive agency within the Forestry Commission, which is to remain in the public sector. A Policy and Resources Group sees to parliamentary business, policy development, and European and international liaison.

The Commission has sold 108,619 hectares (268,403 acres) of plantation and plantable land since 1981 and has, at the Government's request, to dispose of 100,000 hectares (247,000 acres) during the 1990s. The Commission is financed partly by the Government and partly by receipts from sales of timber and other produce, and from rents.

Forestry Initiatives

Plans for three Community Forests[2] in England—Thames Chase (east of London), Mercia (Staffordshire) and Great North (Tyne and Wear)—have been approved. A new national forest in the English Midlands (500 sq km; 200 sq miles) is being

---

[2] The Forestry and Countryside Commissions and local authorities plan to create Community Forests near certain towns—as recreational and productive woodlands in areas that at present do not have them.

established. Plans are also in hand to restore Sherwood Forest (Nottinghamshire). As part of its rural initiative (see p. 338), the Government is encouraging local communities to participate in the development of 350 sq km (135 sq miles) of existing forest in the valleys of south Wales—about 20 per cent of the land area—which is owned by the Forestry Commission. Community forests are also being promoted and developed in Scotland and Northern Ireland.

Forestry Research

The Forestry Authority maintains two principal research stations, at Alice Holt Lodge, near Farnham (Surrey), and at Bush Estate, near Edinburgh, for basic and applied research into all aspects of forestry. Aid is also given for research work in universities and other institutions. A database on forestry and tree-related research in Great Britain has been compiled by the Forestry Research Co-ordination Committee and is updated annually.

The Forestry Authority conducts an annual forest health survey which monitors the effects of stress factors on broadleaves and conifers.

Forestry in Northern Ireland

The Department of Agriculture may acquire land for afforestation and give financial and technical assistance for private planting. The state forest area has grown steadily since 1945. By 1993, 62,115 hectares (153,424 acres) of plantable land had been acquired, of which 60,823 hectares (150,233 acres) were planted. There were 16,000 hectares (39,520 acres) of privately owned forest. Some 430 professional and industrial staff work in state forests.

Further Reading

Agriculture, Fisheries and Forestry, Aspects of Britain series, HMSO, 1993.
Agriculture in the United Kingdom 1993. HMSO.
Forestry Commission. Annual report. HMSO.

19 Transport and Communications

Britain's transport and communications infrastructure is developing rapidly. The opening of the Channel Tunnel (see p. 293) has linked the rail transport system of Great Britain to that of the European mainland. Rail services are being privatised. Britain's road network is developing, with the emphasis on upgrading existing routes rather than building new motorways. Investment at seaports and airports and in air traffic control equipment continues to expand capacity and ease the international movement of people and goods. Britain's telecommunications infrastructure continues to develop, with 45 new licences granted to new operators for fixed links since 1991.

Transport

There has been a considerable increase in passenger travel in recent years. Travel in Great Britain rose by 31 per cent between 1983 and 1993. Travel by car and van rose by 40 per cent and air travel was up 75 per cent. However, travel by motor cycle, pedal cycle and by bus and coach has been declining. In all, car and van travel accounts for 86 per cent of passenger mileage within Great Britain, buses and coaches for about 6 per cent, rail for 5 per cent and air less than 1 per cent. The amount of freight hauled by road increased by 39 per cent between 1983 and 1993.

Car ownership has also risen substantially. In all, 68 per cent of households in Great Britain had the regular use of one or more cars in 1992; 23 per cent had the use of two or more cars. At the end of 1993 there were 24.8 million vehicles licensed for use on the roads of Great Britain, of which 20.8 million were cars (including 2.2 million company cars); 1.9 million light goods vehicles; 590,000 other goods vehicles; 740,000 motor cycles, scooters and mopeds; and 153,000 buses and coaches.

ROADS

Total motor traffic for 1993 is estimated at 410,200 million vehicle-km. The total road network in Britain in 1993 was 388,714 km (233,300 miles). Trunk motorways accounted for 3,200 km (1,900 miles) of this, less than 1 per cent, and other trunk roads for 14,500 km (8,700 miles), or about 3.7 per cent. However, motorways carry about 15 per cent of all traffic and trunk roads about 17 per cent. Combined, they carry over half of all goods vehicle traffic in Great Britain.

A Road User's Charter was published in April 1994, setting out the standards expected of the new Highways Agency (see below) on motorways and trunk roads. These cover matters such as safety and security on the road network, the maintenance and improvement of the network, and answering queries and complaints.

Management

Responsibility for trunk roads in Great Britain, including most motorways, rests in England with the Secretary of State for Transport, in Scotland with the Secretary of State for Scotland and in Wales with the Secretary of State for Wales. Central government meets the majority of the costs of construction and maintenance. In April 1994 a new executive agency of the Department of Transport, the Highways Agency, took over responsibility for building, improving and maintaining motorways and trunk roads in England. Its total budget is about £2,000 million in 1994–95.

The main highway authorities[1] for non-trunk roads are presently:

- in England, the county councils, the metropolitan district councils and the London borough councils;

- in Wales, the county councils; and

- in Scotland, the regional or islands councils.

---

[1] The structure of local government in Great Britain is currently under review (see p. 72), which could affect these arrangements.

In Northern Ireland the Department of the Environment for Northern Ireland is responsible for the construction, improvement and maintenance of all public roads.

Research on transport issues, such as congestion, safety and infrastructure, is carried out by the Transport Research Laboratory (TRL). This is an executive agency of the Department of Transport, but the Government announced in March 1994 that it intends to privatise the TRL in 1995–96. Universities and other higher education institutions, consultants and industry also undertake research, while some is done collaboratively within EU programmes.

Road Programme

In March 1994 the Government announced the findings of a review of its programme to improve the motorway and trunk road network. Schemes in the programme have been assessed for priority. The most important projects will be implemented more quickly. By contrast, 49 schemes that were no longer environmentally acceptable or not needed in the foreseeable future have been withdrawn, while preparation work is being suspended on 67 others. In particular, the number of proposals for building new publicly-funded trunk routes has been sharply reduced to only six.

In spring 1994, 55 motorway and trunk road schemes were under construction in England and 273 further schemes were in

Table 19.1: Road Length (as at April 1993)

kilometres

	Public roads	All-purpose trunk roads and trunk motorways	Trunk motorways[a]
England	278,841	10,471	2,689
Scotland	52,023	3,123	254
Wales	33,612	1,698	120
Northern Ireland	24,238	2,338	113
Britain	**388,714**	**17,630**	**3,176**

Source: Department of Transport

[a] In addition, there were 47 km (29 miles) of local authority motorway in England and 31 km (20 miles) in Scotland.

preparation. Expenditure of about £1,360 million on new trunk road construction is planned for 1994–95, with 22 new schemes due to start. The trunk road maintenance programme is £670 million. The Department of Transport is supporting 269 major local authority road schemes, including 35 new schemes. A total of £329 million of government grant is available to support local authority road schemes in England in 1994–95.

Road communications in Wales will benefit from the second Severn crossing, the recent completion of the M4 motorway and improvements to the A55 and A465 roads. The A55 is now dual carriageway across the mainland. The Welsh Office's trunk roads and transport programme for 1994–95 totals £194 million. A total of £64 million is also being made available to support major local authority road schemes in Wales.

The Government has committed £500 million over three years to new road construction in Scotland. The main priorities within the trunk road programme are the completion of the Glasgow to Carlisle motorway, which is now well advanced, and of the motorway network in central Scotland. These routes provide important links for commerce and industry to the south and to mainland Europe. The Government's future strategy also includes a series of 'route action plans' designed significantly to improve safety and journey times on specific major routes. The possibility of a privately funded second road bridge across the Firth of Forth is being considered as part of a package of measures in the area. A total of £175 million is also being made available to provide for local authority capital expenditure on roads and transport schemes in Scotland.

In Northern Ireland the emphasis is on improving arterial routes, constructing more bypasses, and improving roads in the Belfast area, including the construction of a new cross-harbour link planned for the mid-1990s.

Private Finance

The Government is encouraging greater private sector involvement in the design, construction, operation and funding of roads. Privately funded schemes recently completed or being undertaken include:

- a crossing of the River Thames at Dartford, which opened to traffic in late 1991 and links into the M25 London orbital motorway;

- a second crossing of the River Severn, which should be completed by 1996;

- a relief road north of Birmingham, which will be the first overland toll route in Britain; and

- a bridge under construction between the mainland of Scotland and Skye.

In 1993 the Government issued a consultation paper on the wider application of tolls on routes between cities and on ways of involving private finance. It has also announced plans to develop an electronic tolling system, which has attracted considerable interest from industry.

Licensing and Standards

The Driver and Vehicle Licensing Agency (DVLA) maintains official records of drivers and vehicles in Great Britain. At the end of 1993 it held records on 35.5 million drivers and 25 million licensed vehicles. New drivers of motor vehicles must pass a driving test before getting a full licence to drive.

The Driving Standards Agency is the national driver testing authority in Great Britain. It also supervises professional driving instructors and the compulsory basic training scheme for learner motor cyclists. Minimum ages are:

- 16 for riders of mopeds, drivers of small tractors, and disabled people receiving a mobility allowance;

- 17 for drivers of cars and other passenger vehicles with nine or fewer seats (including that of the driver), motor cycles and goods vehicles not over 3.5 tonnes permissible maximum weight;

- 18 for goods vehicles over 3.5, but not over 7.5, tonnes; and

- 21 for passenger vehicles with over nine seats and goods vehicles over 7.5 tonnes.

Before most new cars and goods vehicles are allowed on the roads, they must meet a number of safety and environmental requirements, based primarily on standards drawn up by the EU. This form of control, known as type approval, is operated by the Vehicle Certification Agency.

The Vehicle Inspectorate is the national testing and enforcement authority. It meets this responsibility mainly through:

- annual testing and certification of heavy and light goods vehicles, buses and coaches;

- administration of the 'MOT' testing scheme, under which cars, motor cycles and some light goods vehicles of 3,000–3,500 kg (59–68 cwt) design gross weight are tested at private garages authorised as test stations;

- roadside enforcement checks of roadworthiness, overloading and drivers' hours;

- carrying out, on behalf of the Traffic Commissioners, investigations and assessments of operators' vehicle maintenance arrangements; and

- the investigation of serious accidents and vehicle defects, and overseeing vehicle recall campaigns.

In Northern Ireland the Driver and Vehicle Testing Agency (DVTA) is responsible for testing drivers and vehicles under statutory schemes broadly similar to those in Great Britain. Private cars five or more years old are tested at DVTA centres.

Road Safety

Although Great Britain has one of the highest densities of road traffic in the world, it has a good record on road safety, with the lowest road accident death rate in the EU. Figures for 1993 show that 3,814 people were killed on the roads (down 10 per cent on 1992 and the first time since records were kept that the figure has been below 4,000), 45,000 seriously injured and 257,200 slightly injured. This compares with nearly 8,000 deaths a year in the mid-1960s. Several factors, such as developments in vehicle safety standards, improvements in roads, the introduction of legislation on seat-belt wearing and drinking and driving, and developments in road safety training, education and publicity, have contributed to the long-term decline in serious casualties.

> The introduction of automatic cameras to detect speeding and traffic light offences has had considerable safety benefits. In west London, for example, speed cameras have led to an 18 per cent drop in accidents and a 37 per cent drop in fatal or serious injuries in their first full year of operation.

The Government's aim is to reduce road casualties by one-third by the end of the century, compared with the 1981–85 average. Priority is given to reducing casualties among vulnerable road-users (children, pedestrians, cyclists, motor cyclists and the elderly), particularly in urban areas, where about 75 per cent of road accidents occur. For example, the child road safety campaign encourages drivers to slow down when children are likely to be about, particularly in urban areas. Other strategies for achieving lower casualties are improvements in highway design, better protection for vehicle occupants, encouraging the use of cycle helmets and measures to combat drinking and driving.

Traffic in Towns

Traffic management schemes are used in many urban areas to reduce congestion, create a better environment and improve road safety. Such schemes include, for example, one-way streets, bus lanes, facilities for pedestrians and cyclists, and traffic-calming measures such as road humps and chicanes to constrain traffic speeds in residential areas. It is now also possible for local authorities to introduce 20 mph (32 km/h) zones, subject to central government consent. Over 100 have been set up in the few years since they became possible.

Many towns have shopping precincts designed for the convenience of pedestrians, from which motor vehicles are excluded for all or part of the day. Controls over on-street parking are enforced through excess charges and fixed penalties, supported where appropriate by powers to remove vehicles. In parts of London wheel clamping is also used to immobilise illegally parked vehicles.

In 1992 the Government announced the designation of a network of priority 'red routes' in London about 480 km (300 miles) long, the first of which was scheduled to come into operation during 1994. Red routes, to be marked by red lining and special signs, will be subject to special stopping controls and other traffic management measures, strictly enforced with higher penalties. The Traffic Director for London has been appointed to co-ordinate the introduction and operation of the priority routes throughout London. A pilot scheme in north and east London, introduced in 1991, has caused significant falls in journey times and greater reliability for buses, with a consequent rise in passenger numbers.

The Government has also set up a wide-ranging study into urban traffic congestion, including the lessons to be learnt from improvements to traffic management in other countries, and the question of 'congestion charging' in London and other cities.

ROAD HAULAGE

Road haulage traffic by heavy goods vehicles amounted to 128,600 million tonne-km in 1993, 6 per cent more than in 1992. There has been a move towards larger and more efficient vehicles carrying heavier loads— about 80 per cent of the traffic, measured in tonne-km, is now carried by vehicles of over 25 tonnes laden weight. Much of the traffic is moved over short distances, with 73 per cent of the tonnage being carried on hauls of 100 km (62 miles) or less. Public haulage (private road hauliers carrying other firms' goods) accounts for 72 per cent of freight carried in Great Britain in terms of tonne-km. In 1993 the main commodities handled by heavy goods vehicles were:

- crude minerals (310 million tonnes);
- food, drink and tobacco (300 million tonnes); and

- building materials (153 million tonnes).

Road haulage is predominantly an industry of small, privately owned businesses. There were about 125,300 holders of an operator's licence in March 1994, operating 404,200 heavy goods vehicles. Nearly 90 per cent of operators have fleets of five or fewer vehicles. The biggest operators in Great Britain are NFC plc, P & O Industrial Services Division, LEP Group plc, Ocean Group plc and Transport Development Group plc.

Licensing and Other Controls

In general, those operating goods vehicles or trailer combinations over 3.5 tonnes gross weight require a goods vehicle operator's licence. Licences are divided into restricted licences for own-account operators carrying goods connected with their own business, and standard licences for hauliers operating for hire or reward. Proof of professional competence, financial standing and good repute is needed to obtain a standard licence. Responsibility for granting licences rests with seven independent Traffic Commissioners. The Deregulation and Contracting Out Bill, at present before Parliament, contains proposals to simplify the operator licensing system, while maintaining protection of the environment and road safety. In Northern Ireland own-account operators do not require a licence, although this matter is under consideration.

Regulations lay down limits on the hours worked by drivers of goods vehicles, and minimum rest periods. Tachographs, which automatically record speed, distance covered, driving time and stopping periods, must be fitted and used in most goods vehicles over 3.5 tonnes gross weight in Great Britain. Speed limiters must also be fitted to heavy lorries. Originally these had to be set to limit speed to 60 mph (97 km/h). However, from January 1994 a programme began to reduce this gradually to 56 mph (90 km/h).

International Road Haulage

International road haulage has grown rapidly and in 1993 about 1.4 million road goods vehicles were ferried to mainland Europe or the Irish Republic. Of these, 394,800 were powered vehicles registered in Britain. In 1993 British vehicles carried almost 11 million tonnes internationally, more than double the amount carried in 1984. About 95 per cent of this traffic was with the European Union.

International road haulage within the EU was fully liberalised in January 1993. 'Cabotage' (the operation of domestic road haulage services within a member state by a non-resident) will be fully liberalised in 1998. Until then, quotas of permits are available which allow cabotage anywhere within the EU. Haulage with countries outside the EU takes place under bilateral agreements, most of which allow unrestricted numbers of British lorries into the country concerned, although some require permits. The European Conference of Transport Ministers issues a limited but increasing number of permits which allow free access to, and transit across, a number of countries in Central and Eastern Europe. The British quota for 1995 is 174, an increase of 75 over 1994 levels.

PASSENGER SERVICES

Buses

Outside London, almost all bus services in Great Britain are now provided by companies in the private sector, ranging from major groups with over 1,000 vehicles to small operators with fewer than five. Outside London there are very few restrictions on operators providing services. Local authorities subsidise the provision of extra services which are socially necessary but uneconomic, after competitive tendering.

London Transport (LT) is a statutory corporation responsible for providing public transport in London. Its main operating subsidiaries are London Buses Ltd (LBL) and London Underground Ltd. LT, which provides 600 bus routes, already involves the private sector in the provision of bus services, and private sector companies operating under contract to LT now run a quarter of all London's bus routes. The Government is planning to privatise LBL. One of its subsidiaries was sold in January 1994, three

more in September 1994 and the Government is planning to sell the remainder in 1994–95. In the longer term deregulation is proposed. Provision would be made for the operation of socially necessary but uneconomic services and the continuation of a London-wide concessionary travel scheme.

The Department of Transport has allocated about £20 million over the period 1992–94 for local authority bus priority measures. These include bus lanes, traffic light priority signalling, and park and ride schemes. A further £6.2 million has been allocated in 1994–95 to local authorities in London. This funding, up from £3.3 million in 1993–94, will also enable detailed design work for a 720-km (450-mile) bus priority network in the capital, which will cover nearly 70 per cent of the areas where buses are most delayed.

To assist passengers new information systems are being provided. For example, in Southampton a bus passenger information system known as Stopwatch provides information to passengers at 30 stops.

In Northern Ireland subsidiaries of the publicly owned Northern Ireland Transport Holding Company provide almost all road passenger services. Citybus Ltd operates services in Belfast, and Ulsterbus Ltd operates most of the services in the rest of Northern Ireland. These companies have about 300 and 1,000 vehicles respectively.

Coaches

In Britain long-distance coach services are provided by companies in the private sector. There are no restrictions on routes served or the number of vehicles operated. A national network of routes is maintained by the National Express company, largely through franchised operations. Passenger comfort in coaches has been improved in recent years.

While all regular, and some shuttle, overseas coach services still require authorisation or permission from the authorities of the countries to or through which they travel, most tourist services within the EU have been liberalised. Operators no longer need prior permission to run either holiday shuttle services, where

ASTRONOMY

A photograph of Jupiter taken by scientists at the
Royal Greenwich Observatory at Roque de los Muchachos
in the Canary Islands (pictured here). The photograph, taken
using the William Herschel 4.2 metre telescope, shows the
effects of the recent collisions with Comet Shoemaker Levy 9.

Major conservation and recreation areas

Legend:
- National Parks
- Forest Parks
- Areas of Outstanding Natural Beauty (National Scenic Areas in Scotland)
- Heritage Coast (Coastal Conservation Zones in Scotland)
- National Trails – – – –
- World Heritage Sites ▫

SCOTLAND

Speyside Way

West Highland Way

Southern Upland Way

NORTHERN IRELAND

Northumberland

North York Moors

Cleveland Way

Wolds Way

Lake District

Yorkshire Dales

Pennine Way

Peak District

Snowdonia

Offa's Dyke Path

Peddars Way and Norfolk Coast Path

The Broads

(Special protected area)

WALES

ENGLAND

Pembrokeshire Coast

Brecon Beacons

Pembrokeshire Coast Path

Ridgeway

Thames Path

North Downs Way

South Downs Way

Exmoor

Dartmoor

South West Coast Path

South West Coast Path

0	20	40	60	80	100 km

0	20	40	60 miles

Islands

Islands

Agricultural land use

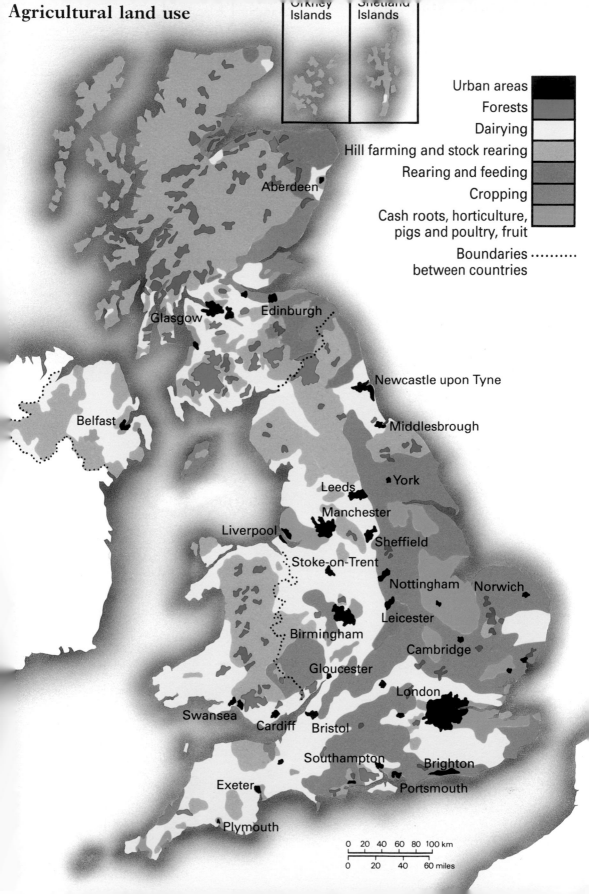

Orkney Islands

Shetland Islands

Legend:
- Urban areas
- Forests
- Dairying
- Hill farming and stock rearing
- Rearing and feeding
- Cropping
- Cash roots, horticulture, pigs and poultry, fruit
- Boundaries between countries ··········

Aberdeen

Glasgow

Edinburgh

Newcastle upon Tyne

Belfast

Middlesbrough

York

Leeds

Manchester

Liverpool

Sheffield

Stoke-on-Trent

Nottingham

Norwich

Leicester

Birmingham

Cambridge

Gloucester

London

Swansea

Cardiff

Bristol

Southampton

Brighton

Portsmouth

Exeter

Plymouth

0 20 40 60 80 100 km

0   20   40   60 miles

ARCHAEOLOGY

The discovery of a 500,000–year-old leg bone in a quarry in Boxgrove, Sussex, is one of the most important archaeological finds in Europe. Examination of the bone at the Palaentology Laboratory of the Natural History Museum, London, has revealed that the man, alive during the temperate stage of the Ice Age, was over 1.83 m (6 ft) tall and weighed over 75.5 kg (12 stone).

A scientist at Glasgow University meticulously cleans fossilised dinosaur eggs recently discovered in Inner Mongolia. Special scanning equipment is being developed to examine an egg still embedded in the stone, as it is believed that it may contain an embryo.

accommodation is included as part of the package, or occasional coach tours to, from or within another member state. Since January 1993 passenger cabotage has been allowed for tours where a single vehicle carries the same group of passengers throughout a journey. From January 1996, this freedom will be extended to all non-regular services.

Taxis

There are about 56,000 licensed taxis in Great Britain, mainly in urban areas; London has about 17,500. In London and several other major cities taxis must be purpose-built to conform to very strict requirements and new ones have to provide for people in wheelchairs. In many urban districts drivers must have passed a test of their knowledge of the area. At present, a local authority can only limit the number of licensed taxis if it is satisfied that there is no unfulfilled demand for taxis in its area.

Private hire vehicles with drivers ('minicabs') may be booked only through the operator and not hired on the street. In most areas outside London private hire vehicles are licensed. The Government launched a review of the taxi licensing regime in England and Wales in October 1993.

There are about 4,000 licensed taxis in Northern Ireland. Licences are issued by the Department of the Environment for Northern Ireland on a basis broadly similar to that in Great Britain.

RAILWAYS

Railways were pioneered in Britain: the Stockton and Darlington Railway, opened in 1825, was the first public passenger railway in the world to be worked by steam power. The main railway companies in Great Britain were nationalised in 1948, coming under the control of the British Railways Board (BR). Now arrangements for a privatised railway network are being introduced.

Privatisation

The Government's approach, enshrined in the Railways Act 1993, includes:

- the franchising of all BR's existing passenger services to the private sector;
- the transfer of BR's freight and parcels operations to the private sector;
- the creation of a new right of access to the rail network for private operators of both passenger and freight services;
- the separation of track from train operations, under which Railtrack—a government-owned company—is responsible for operating all track and infrastructure, and passenger services are operated by BR until they are franchised;
- the appointment of a Rail Regulator to oversee the fair application of arrangements for track access and charging, and a Franchising Director responsible for negotiating, awarding and monitoring franchises;
- opportunities for the private sector to lease stations; and
- improved grant arrangements for individual rail services or groups of services.

Railtrack is seeking the involvement of private sector finance to improve the network—for example, bids from private consortia are being sought for the modernisation of the West Coast Main Line.

BR has restructured its passenger services into 25 train operating units as a basis for the privatised railway network. The Government has set the Franchising Director a target of awarding the first six franchises by the end of 1995 and for over half of BR's current passenger services to be franchised by April 1996. Future responsibility for rolling stock provision will pass to the private sector in 1995, with the sale of BR's three rolling stock leasing companies. These lease stock to the operators, including to BR pending franchising.

Three new, competing rail freight companies, each with a geographic heartland, were set up in autumn 1993 and will be privatised in 1995. The Government invited bids for the Freightliner container traffic business in May 1994. The two rail parcels businesses are also being sold to the private sector.

New regulations require rail operators to prepare a 'safety case' to demonstrate that safe practices will be followed at all times; these cases are monitored by Railtrack. Railway employees who undertake work with safety implications are required to be fit and competent. The Railway Inspectorate, part of the Health and Safety Executive (see p. 190), is responsible for validating Railtrack's own safety case.

> The first six passenger services to be franchised will be: the East Coast Main Line; the Gatwick Express; the Great Western Main Line; the London, Tilbury and Southend line; ScotRail; and the South Western division of Network SouthEast.

Operations

In 1993–94 BR's turnover, including financial support and income from other activities but excluding internal transactions, was £3,646 million. It received grants of £930 million as compensation for the public service obligation to operate sections of the passenger network that would not otherwise cover their cost.

As part of the Citizen's Charter initiative, BR published its Passenger's Charter. Compensation is payable to passengers when service falls by more than a small margin below these standards. Under the privatisation proposals, franchisees will be required to produce their own charters, which will be expected at least to match the standards achieved by BR.

Investment

There has been substantial investment in Britain's railways in recent years. BR's programme totalled £1,206 million in 1993–94. Major areas of expenditure included rolling stock and facilities for Channel Tunnel traffic from the opening of the tunnel (see p. 293).

In October 1993 BR announced its first rolling stock leasing deal. Under this, 41 new Networker trains are being acquired for lines in Kent and Essex. The trains are being financed by ABB, their builder, which will receive an annual leasing payment for their use.

Passenger Services

The passenger network (see map facing inside back cover) comprises a fast inter-city

Table 19.2: Railway Operations

	1989–90	1990–91	1991–92	1992–93	1993–94
Passenger journeys (million)	758	763	740	745	713
Passenger-km (million)	33,648	33,191	32,057	31,693	30,362
Freight traffic (million tonnes)	143	138	136	122	103
Trainload and wagonload traffic (million net-tonne km)	16,742	15,986	15,347	15,509	13,764
Assets at end of period:					
Locomotives	2,095	2,030	1,896	1,794	1,688
High Speed Train power units	197	197	197	197	197
Other coaching units	13,833	13,631	12,925	12,309	11,802
Freight vehicles[a]	21,970	20,763	19,877	15,912	13,871
Stations (including freight and parcels)	2,598	2,615	2,556	2,543	2,553
Route open for traffic (km)	16,588	16,584	16,558	16,527	16,535

Source: British Railways Board.
[a]In addition, a number of privately owned wagons and locomotives are operated on the railway network for customers of British Rail.

network, linking the main centres of Great Britain; local stopping services; and commuter services in and around the large conurbations, especially London and south-east England. InterCity 125 trains, travelling at maximum sustained speeds of 125 mph (201 km/h), are the world's fastest diesel trains. With the introduction of electric InterCity 225 trains, Britain now has more services running at over 100 mph (160 km/h) than any other country in Europe.

About 30 per cent of route-mileage is electrified, including the East Coast Main Line linking London and Edinburgh. A new generation of diesel multiple-unit trains has been introduced on regional services, while the first of a new generation of electric Networker trains entered service in Kent in 1992, and 674 coaches were in service by mid-1994.

Freight

Over 90 per cent of rail freight traffic by volume is of bulk commodities, mainly coal, coke, iron and steel, building materials and petroleum. The opening of the Channel Tunnel has presented an important opportunity for non-bulk freight movement. The Government makes grants to encourage companies to move goods by rail rather than road; over 200 schemes have been helped since 1975 at a cost of over £80 million in cash terms. A total of £43 million has been set aside for freight facilities and track access grants in England alone over the period 1994–95 to 1996–97. Freight users have had rights of open access to the rail network since April 1994. This allows the introduction of services by new rail freight operators and companies operating on their own account.

Northern Ireland

In Northern Ireland the Northern Ireland Railways Company Ltd, a subsidiary of the Northern Ireland Transport Holding Company, operates the railway service on about 330 km (206 miles) of track. It published a revised passenger charter in 1992. This includes a compensation scheme that operates if targets for punctuality and reliability are not met.

Channel Tunnel

The Channel Tunnel, the largest civil engineering project in Europe to be financed by the private sector, was officially inaugurated by Her Majesty the Queen and President Mitterrand of France in May 1994. Freight services began later the same month and passenger services began in October 1994. The project, which is estimated to have cost about £10,000 million, was undertaken by Eurotunnel, a British–French group which has a 65-year operating concession from the British and French governments. Construction was carried out for Eurotunnel by Transmanche Link, a consortium of ten British and French construction companies.

Eurotunnel Services

Eurotunnel operates shuttle trains through one-way twin rail tunnels between the terminals near Folkestone and Calais, with the journey taking about 35 minutes from platform to platform. These trains provide a drive-on, drive-off service, with separate shuttle trains for passenger and freight vehicles. Car and coach passengers stay with their vehicles during the journey. Lorry drivers travel separately from their vehicles, in a club car at the front of the shuttle. When full services are established, Eurotunnel plans to run passenger shuttle services every 15 minutes and freight shuttle services every 20 minutes at peak periods. As traffic grows, it should be possible for the frequency of services to be increased.

Railway Services

About £1,400 million has been invested in new passenger and freight rolling stock and infrastructure improvements for Channel Tunnel services. Once a full service is operating, about 30 Eurostar high-speed trains will run each day between the London terminal at Waterloo and Paris or Brussels. Daytime passenger services from the Midlands, northern England and Scotland to Paris and Brussels should begin operating from the end of 1995. Overnight services from London, south Wales, Scotland, the Midlands, the North West and the South West to the continent should also start from 1995. A part-privately funded international station is also being built at Ashford in Kent, scheduled for completion by the end of 1995.

Freight services through the Channel Tunnel are operating from a network of regional terminals to major industrial centres on the Continent. Four terminals—in . London, Glasgow, Manchester and Birmingham—started operations when the Tunnel opened. Because of infrastructure improvements and advanced wagon designs, over 90 per cent of standard continental swap-bodies will be able to travel over the lines between the tunnel and the British terminal network, even though the British loading gauge is smaller than the continental gauge. The terminal facilities allow the easy transfer of freight between road and rail.

A new rail link between London and the Channel Tunnel is proposed to meet the forecast growth in demand for through rail services. Most of the route for the rail link was announced by the Government in January 1994, with the remaining sections being announced in April. The route passes through Kent, crossing the River Thames near Dartford. It then runs through the east of London to a second London terminal at St Pancras.

It is expected that a Bill will be introduced for the construction of the rail link. The £2,700 million project will be a public–private sector joint venture, with the Government hopeful of appointing a private sector partner early in 1995.

Railways in London

London Underground Ltd (LUL) operates services on 408 km (254 miles) of railway, of which about 170 km (106 miles) are underground. The system has 248 stations, with 467 trains operating in the peak period. About 735 million passenger journeys were made on London Underground trains in 1993–94. LUL has a charter that sets out standards of service to passengers and a compensation scheme that applies when delays of 15 minutes or more occur within LUL's control. The most recent version was published in June 1994, setting more demanding performance targets.

Major investment in the Underground is under way or planned. Work started in October 1993 on an extension of the Jubilee Line to Stratford (east London) via Docklands and the north Greenwich peninsula. The extension is scheduled to open in 1998. A proposed CrossRail scheme would link Paddington with Liverpool Street via a tunnel which would be used by full-sized overground, rather than smaller, Underground trains. A line from Chelsea to Hackney is also being considered. Total LUL investment in new lines will be £527 million in 1994–95, of which most will be spent on the Jubilee Line but with some planning work on CrossRail. LUL has also applied for an Order to build a northern extension to the East London Line to Dalston, where it would link with BR's North London Line. Much work is also under way updating the existing system, including a £750 million modernisation of the Central Line, scheduled for completion by early 1995, and the refurbishment of over 200 trains at a cost of £195 million.

The Docklands Light Railway (DLR), a 23-km (14-mile) route with 27 stations, connects the City of London with Docklands, Beckton and Stratford. An extension is planned to Greenwich and Lewisham, subject to private finance being available. Approval is also being sought for the Croydon Tramlink, which would connect Croydon with Wimbledon, Beckenham and New Addington.

Other Urban Railways

The Glasgow Underground traverses a 10-km (6–mile) loop in central Glasgow. Other light rail lines include:
● the Tyne and Wear Metro, which connects Newcastle upon Tyne city centre with Newcastle Airport, Gateshead, North and South Shields, Heworth and Jarrow, with an extension planned to Sunderland; and

- the 31-km (19-mile) Greater Manchester Metrolink, which connects Manchester city centre with Altrincham and Bury, with extensions planned to Salford Quays, Oldham, Rochdale, Manchester Airport and Ashton-under-Lyne.

Traditional tramcars also operate between Blackpool and Fleetwood.

The first phase of the South Yorkshire Supertram, which connects Sheffield city centre with Middlewood, Hillsborough, Halfway and Meadowhall, began commercial operations in March 1994. The majority of the £240 million construction cost was met by the Government. The system is the responsibility of South Yorkshire Supertram Ltd, a subsidiary of the South Yorkshire Passenger Transport Executive. Once the full system is operational, it will be privatised.

Further light rail schemes are proposed. Parliamentary approval has been given to the first lines of the Midland Metro, which will connect Birmingham with Wolverhampton, the National Exhibition Centre and Birmingham Airport, and for the Leeds Supertram. Approval is being sought for the Greater Nottingham Rapid Transit scheme.

Private Railways

There are over 100 small, privately owned passenger-carrying railways in Great Britain, mostly operated on a voluntary basis and providing limited services for tourists and railway enthusiasts. The main aim of most of these railways is the preservation and operation of steam locomotives. They are generally run on old BR branch lines, but there are also several narrow-gauge lines, mainly in north Wales.

INLAND WATERWAYS

Inland waterways are popular for recreation, make a valuable contribution to the quality of Britain's environment, play an important part in land drainage and water supply, and are used to a limited extent for freight-carrying. The most significant amounts of freight are carried on the rivers Thames, Forth, Humber and Mersey and the Manchester Ship Canal.

The publicly owned British Waterways is responsible for 3,200 km (2,000 miles) of waterways in Great Britain. The majority of waterways are primarily for leisure use, but about 620 km (385 miles) are maintained as commercial waterways. British Waterways is developing its historical heritage for recreational and commercial use, often in conjunction with the private sector. In 1993–94 British Waterways' turnover amounted to £82 million, including a government grant of £49.3 million to maintain its waterways to statutory standards.

SHIPPING AND PORTS

In March 1994 British companies owned 668 trading vessels of 13.6 million deadweight tonnes. Among the ships owned by British companies were 168 vessels totalling 8.6 million deadweight tonnes used as oil, chemical or gas carriers and 471 vessels totalling 4.9 million deadweight tonnes employed as dry-bulk carriers, container ships or other types of cargo ship. About 72 per cent of British-owned vessels are registered in Britain or British dependent territories such as Bermuda.

The tonnage of the British-registered trading fleet has been declining. In recognition of this, measures to encourage British shipowners to register their vessels in Britain have recently been introduced. These include the simplification of registration law, a proposed relaxation of officer nationality rules, and the extension of the existing financial assistance for officer cadets to include junior officers studying for higher certificates. Fiscal changes announced in 1993 enabled shipowners to carry forward tax charges resulting from ship sales to set against further investment within a three-year period.

Cargo Services

About 94 per cent by weight (76 per cent by value) of Britain's overseas trade is carried by sea. In 1992 British seaborne trade amounted to 311 million tonnes (valued at £178,000 million) or 1,240,000 million tonne-km (770,000 million tonne-miles). British-registered ships carried 19 per cent by weight and 36 per cent by value. Tanker cargo accounted for 44 per cent of this trade by weight, but only 7 per cent by value; dry cargoes including foodstuffs and manufactured goods accounted for 84 per cent by value.

Virtually all the scheduled cargo-liner services from Britain are containerised. The British tonnage serving these trades is dominated by a relatively small number of private sector companies and, in deep-sea trades, they usually operate in conjunction with other companies on the same routes in organisations known as 'conferences'. The object of these groupings is to ensure regular and efficient services with stable freight rates, to the benefit of both shipper and shipowner. In addition to the carriage of freight by liner and bulk services between Britain and the rest of Europe, there are many roll-on, roll-off services to carry cars, passengers and commercial vehicles.

Passenger Services

In 1993 there were 35 million international sea passenger movements between Britain and the rest of the world, compared with about 87 million international air movements. Almost all the passengers who arrived at or departed from British ports travelled to or from the continent of Europe or the Irish Republic. In 1993 about 96,000 people embarked on pleasure cruises from British ports. Traffic from the southern and south-eastern ports accounts for a substantial proportion of traffic to the continent of Europe. The main British operators are Sealink Stena Line, P & O and Hoverspeed, although not all their vessels are under the British flag. Services are provided by roll-on, roll-off ferries, hovercraft, hydrofoils and high-speed catamarans. There has been a trend towards larger vessels in recent years as the ferry companies prepare for competition from the Channel Tunnel.

Domestic passenger and freight ferry services also run to many of the offshore islands, such as the Isle of Wight, the Orkney and Shetland islands, and the islands off the west coast of Scotland. It is estimated that in 1992 there were about 36 million passengers on such internal services.

Merchant Shipping Legislation and Policy

The Government's policy is one of minimum intervention and the encouragement of free and fair competition. However, regulations administered by the Department of Transport provide for marine safety and welfare, the investigation of accidents and the prevention and cleaning up of pollution from ships.

Britain also plays a significant role in the formulation of shipping policy within the EU. All international services and most cabotage services within the EU have been liberalised. Full cabotage liberalisation will be achieved over the next ten years. Work is progressing well to introduce the measures in the programme to improve maritime safety and prevent pollution.

Ports

There are about 80 ports of commercial significance in Great Britain, and in addition there are several hundred small harbours that cater for local cargo, fishing vessels, island ferries or recreation. There are three broad types of ports—trust ports owned and run by a board constituted as a trust, those owned by local authorities and company-owned ports. Most operate with statutory powers under private Acts of Parliament. Major ports controlled by trusts include Aberdeen, Dover, Ipswich, Milford Haven and Tyne. Local authorities own many small ports and a few much larger ports, including Portsmouth and the oil ports in Orkney and Shetland. The Ports Act 1991 facilitates the transfer of trust ports fully to the private sector; Clyde, Forth, Medway, Tees and Hartlepool and the Port of London Authority dock undertaking at Tilbury have already moved to the private sector.

Associated British Ports Holdings PLC (a private sector company) operates 22 ports, including Cardiff, Grimsby and Immingham, Hull, Newport, Southampton and Swansea. Together its ports handled 106 million tonnes of cargo in 1993. Other major ports owned by companies include Felixstowe, Liverpool, Manchester and a group of ferry ports, including Harwich (Parkeston Quay) and Stranraer.

Port Traffic

In 1993 traffic through the ports of Britain amounted provisionally to 507 million tonnes, comprising 157 million tonnes of exports, 192 million tonnes of imports and 158 million tonnes of domestic traffic (which included offshore traffic and landings of sea-dredged aggregates). About 54 per cent of the traffic was in fuels, mainly petroleum and petroleum products.

Britain's main ports, in terms of total tonnage handled, are given in Table 19.3. Sullom Voe (Shetland), Milford Haven and Forth mostly handle oil, while the main ports for non-fuel traffic are Dover, Felixstowe, Grimsby and Immingham, Liverpool, London, and Tees and Hartlepool.

Container and roll-on, roll-off traffic in Britain has increased sixfold since 1970 to 99 million tonnes in 1993 and now accounts for over 77 per cent of non-bulk traffic. The leading ports for container traffic are

Felixstowe, London and Southampton. Those for roll-on, roll-off traffic are Dover (Britain's leading seaport in terms of the value of trade handled), Felixstowe, Portsmouth and Ramsgate.

Development

Most recent major port developments have been at east- and south-coast ports. For example, at Felixstowe a £50 million extension to the terminal was completed in 1990; a new £100 million terminal on the River Medway caters for deep-sea container traffic; and Dover has started on a £100 million programme to develop its western docks to meet the challenge of the opening of the Channel Tunnel. A new cool store has been opened at Tees and Hartlepool, and there are plans for a new grain terminal. A 16-hectare (40-acre) car terminal has been built at Tyne. Recent investment by Associated British Ports includes:

- an £18 million third berth at the Immingham oil terminal, opened in August 1994;

- a £13 million roll-on, roll-off terminal at Immingham due to be completed in April 1995;

- an £11 million roll-on, roll-off facility at Hull;

Table 19.3: Traffic Through the Principal Ports of Great Britain

million tonnes

	1978	1988	1989	1990	1991	1992	1993[a]
London	53.0	53.7	54.0	54.5	52.8	48.9	53.0
Tees and Hartlepool	34.1	37.4	39.3	40.2	42.9	43.4	43.0
Grimsby and Immingham	25.9	35.0	38.1	38.9	40.2	40.8	41.0
Sullom Voe	1.1	50.6	40.7	30.6	35.9	41.4	39.0
Milford Haven	41.2	33.3	33.0	32.2	35.7	35.6	36.0
Southampton	24.0	31.4	26.1	28.8	31.5	29.6	31.0
Liverpool	16.5	19.6	20.2	23.2	24.8	27.8	29.0
Forth	28.8	29.0	22.9	25.4	22.9	23.3	26.0
Felixstowe	4.8	15.6	16.5	16.4	16.1	17.0	20.0
Dover	5.5	10.4	13.5	13.0	12.0	13.1	14.0
Medway	20.5	12.7	13.6	15.9	16.1	14.3	14.0
Orkneys	15.6	8.0	4.5	8.6	9.2	8.5	12.0
Port Talbot	5.1	7.8	8.7	8.9	9.4	9.4	10.0

Source: Department of Transport
[a]Provisional.

- a £2.6 million terminal at Goole, inaugurated in March 1994; and
- two new cold-storage chambers at Cardiff, costing £1 million.

Purpose-built terminals for oil from the British sector of the North Sea have been built at Hound Point on the Forth, on the Tees, at Flotta and at Sullom Voe (one of the largest oil terminals in the world). Supply bases for offshore oil and gas installations have been built at several ports, notably Aberdeen, Great Yarmouth and Heysham.

Safety at Sea

The Department of Transport launched two new executive agencies concerned with marine safety in April 1994—the Coastguard Agency and the Marine Safety Agency. The former has taken over responsibility for HM Coastguard and the Marine Pollution Control Unit (see p. 360). The latter has taken over the former Surveyor General's Organisation and the Register of Shipping and Seamen. HM Coastguard is responsible for co-ordinating civil maritime search and rescue operations around the coastline of Britain. In a maritime emergency the coastguard calls on and co-ordinates facilities such as:

- coastguard helicopters and cliff rescue companies;
- lifeboats of the Royal National Lifeboat Institution (a voluntary body);
- Ministry of Defence aeroplanes, helicopters and ships; and
- merchant shipping and commercial aircraft.

Some locations around Britain are hazardous for shipping. A number of measures are taken to reduce the risk of collision, including the separation of ships in internationally agreed shipping lanes. The traffic separation scheme in the Dover Strait, one of the busiest seaways in the world, is one such scheme. It is monitored by radar from the Channel Navigation Information Service near Dover. Ships are encouraged to report their movements and these are tracked. Those found to be contravening the regulations are identified and action taken.

Following the loss of the tanker MV *Braer* off Sumburgh in the Shetland Islands in January 1993, the British Chamber of Shipping produced a voluntary code for the routeing and operation of tankers around Britain's coast. An inquiry reported in May 1994 with a number of recommendations, which the Government is considering. Many of these can only be achieved effectively by international action, and so the report has also been presented to the International Maritime Organization, the United Nations agency concerned with maritime matters.

> In 1993 HM Coastguard co-ordinated action in 9,611 incidents (including cliff rescues), in which 17,106 people were helped.

The lighthouse authorities, which between them control about 370 lighthouses and other lights and buoys, are:

- the Corporation of Trinity House, which covers England, Wales and the Channel Islands;
- the Northern Lighthouse Board, for Scotland and the Isle of Man; and
- the Commissioners of Irish Lights for Northern Ireland and the Irish Republic.

They are funded mainly by light dues levied on shipping in Britain and Ireland. The Ports Act 1991 provided for the transfer of certain lights and buoys to harbour authorities where these are used mainly for local rather than general navigation. Responsibility for pilotage within harbours rests with harbour authorities under the Pilotage Act 1987.

CIVIL AVIATION

Airlines are seeking opportunities for modernisation, and this is complemented by the work of the aviation authorities in negotiating new international rights and improving facilities such as air traffic control. British airlines are entirely in the private sector, as are a number of the major airports.

Air Traffic

Total capacity offered on all services by British airlines amounted to 25,100 million tonne-km in 1993: 18,600 million tonne-km on scheduled services and 6,500 million tonne-km on non-scheduled services. The airlines carried 40.1 million passengers on scheduled services and 25.6 million on charter flights; 87 million passengers travelled by air (international terminal passengers) to or from Britain, a 6 per cent increase on 1992.

The value of Britain's overseas trade carried by air in 1992 was about £44,120 million—20 per cent of exports by value and 18 per cent of imports. Air freight is important for the carriage of goods with a high value-to-weight ratio, especially where speed is essential.

British Airways

British Airways plc is one of the world's leading airlines. In terms of international scheduled services it is the largest in the world. During 1993–94 British Airways' turnover was £6,303 million (including £5,785 million from airline operations), and the British Airways group carried 30.5 million passengers on scheduled and charter flights both domestically and internationally.

The British Airways scheduled route network serves 155 destinations in 72 countries. Its main operating base is London's Heathrow airport, but services from Gatwick and regional centres such as Manchester and Birmingham have been expanding. Scheduled Concorde supersonic services operate from London Heathrow to New York, Washington and, in the summer, Toronto, crossing the Atlantic in about half the time taken by subsonic aircraft. In March 1994 British Airways had a fleet of 253 aircraft, the largest fleet in Western Europe, including seven Concordes and 59 Boeing 747s.

Other Airlines

Other major British airlines include:

- Air UK, which has 34 aircraft and is the only British airline to operate from all three main airports in the London area (Heathrow, Gatwick and Stansted);
- Britannia Airways, the world's largest charter airline, which carried 7.6 million passengers in 1993 and has 28 aircraft;
- British Midland, which operates a large network of scheduled services, and has 34 aircraft; and
- Virgin Atlantic, which operates scheduled services between Britain, seven North American destinations, Athens, Dublin, Hong Kong and Tokyo, with 12 aircraft.

Helicopters and Other Aerial Work

Helicopters are engaged on a variety of work, especially operations connected with Britain's offshore oil and gas industry. The main offshore operators in Britain are Bond Helicopters, British International Helicopters and Bristow Helicopters, with 43, 25 and 55 helicopters respectively. Light aircraft and helicopters are also involved in other important commercial activities, such as charters, search and rescue services, load-lifting, aerial surveying and photography, and police and air ambulance operations.

Aviation Policy

The Government's civil aviation policy aims to maintain high standards of safety and security and to achieve environmental improvements through reduced noise and other emissions from aircraft. It is concerned to promote the interests of travellers by encouraging a competitive British industry, and is committed to encouraging more international services to and from regional airports. The Government has taken the lead in the EU and with bilateral partners in negotiating freer arrangements within which airline competition can flourish; agreement was reached within the EU in 1992 on a further package of liberalisation measures, including increased freedom for airlines to set their own fares. New arrangements with an increasing number of countries are resulting in better provision of services at more competitive fares.

Civil Aviation Authority

The Civil Aviation Authority (CAA) is an independent statutory body, responsible for the economic and safety regulation of the industry and, jointly with the Ministry of Defence, for the provision of air navigation services. Its board members are appointed by the Secretary of State for Transport. The CAA's primary objectives are to ensure that British airlines provide air services to satisfy all substantial categories of public demand at the lowest charges consistent with a high standard of safety and to further the reasonable interests of air transport users.

Air Safety

British airlines have a good safety record. In all but three of the 11 years to 1992, there were no passenger fatalities in accidents involving fixed-wing commercially registered British aircraft in British airspace. In only one year in this period were there any fatalities associated with British-registered aircraft in foreign airspace.

Every company operating aircraft used for commercial air transport purposes must possess an Air Operator's Certificate, which the CAA grants when it is satisfied that the operator is competent to conduct the safe operation of its aircraft. The CAA's flight operations inspectors, who are experienced civilian pilots, together with airworthiness surveyors, check that satisfactory standards are maintained. All aircraft registered in Britain must be granted a Certificate of Airworthiness by the CAA before being flown. In this and many other aspects of its work, the CAA is increasingly working to standards developed with its European partners in the Joint Airworthiness Authorities.

Each member of the flight crew of a British-registered aircraft, every ground engineer who certifies an aircraft fit to fly, and every air traffic controller must hold the appropriate official licence issued by the CAA. To qualify for a first professional licence, a pilot must undertake a full-time course of instruction approved by the CAA—or have acceptable military or civilian flying experience—and pass ground examinations and flight tests.

Air Traffic Control and Navigation Services

Civil and military air traffic control over Britain and the surrounding seas, including a large part of the North Atlantic, is carried out by the National Air Traffic Services (NATS), jointly responsible to the CAA and the Ministry of Defence. NATS also provides air traffic control at most of the major British airports. In May 1994 the Government announced proposals for NATS to become a private sector contractor to the CAA, which would ensure continued high safety standards through regulation. Such a change would require legislation.

Britain plays a major role in European air traffic control developments through participation in a number of international forums. Britain has put forward several European initiatives, including the centralised management of traffic flows throughout Europe, which is being progressively implemented over the period 1991–95. Within Britain, NATS has an investment programme running at around £90 million a year, which includes the construction of a new air traffic control centre for England and Wales, due to be completed in 1996. The Government has also approved a new centre for Scotland.

Airports

Of the 148 licensed civil aerodromes in Britain, about one-fifth handle more than 100,000 passengers a year each. Of these, 13 handle over 1 million passengers a year each (see Table 19.4). In 1993 Britain's civil airports handled a total of 113.9 million passengers (112.3 million terminal passengers and 1.6 million in transit), and 1.4 million tonnes of freight. Heathrow airport is the world's busiest airport for international travel and is Britain's most important airport for passengers and air freight, handling 48 million passengers (including transit passengers) and 846,600 tonnes of freight in 1993. Proposals have been put forward for a fifth terminal, which will be the subject of a public inquiry and could eventually handle 30 million passengers a year. Gatwick is also one of the world's busiest international airports.

Ownership and Control

Seven airports—Heathrow, Gatwick, Stansted and Southampton in south-east England, and Glasgow, Edinburgh and Aberdeen in Scotland—are owned and operated by BAA plc. Together they handle about 71 per cent of air passengers and 82 per cent of air cargo traffic in Britain.

Many of the other airports are controlled by local authorities, including Manchester, which is the third largest airport in Britain. A total of 14 major local authority airports now operate as Companies Act companies. The Government is encouraging their privatisation. For example, East Midlands International Airport was sold by its local authority shareholders in August 1993. Belfast International Airport was scheduled to be sold in the second half of 1994.

The CAA has responsibility for the economic regulation of the larger airports, although the Government announced a review of the mechanics of the system in January 1994. The CAA has powers to take action to remedy practices considered to be unreasonable or unfair, in particular any abuse of an airport's monopoly position, and also to limit increases in charges to airlines at certain airports. All airports used for public transport and training flights must also be licensed by the CAA for reasons of safety. Stringent requirements, such as the provision

of adequate fire-fighting, medical and rescue services, must be satisfied before a licence is granted. Strict security measures are in force; these were tightened in April 1994 by new regulations requiring airlines to account for and authorise for carriage every item of hold baggage placed on board international flights originating in Britain. This will not only improve security but should also cut down on misrouted baggage.

Communications

The telecommunications industry is one of the most rapidly growing sectors of the British economy. Postal services also continue to be important, with the volume of mail in Britain growing rather than declining despite the growth in electronic means of communication in recent years, partly as a result of the growth in direct mail marketing.

TELECOMMUNICATIONS

Major changes have occurred since 1981, with the progressive introduction of competition into the markets for telecommunications equipment and services. In 1984 British Telecommunications (BT) was privatised, and it faces increasing competition in the provision of services over fixed links. A principal feature of the

Table 19.4: Passenger Traffic at Britain's Main Airports

million passengers

	1989	1990	1991	1992	1993
London Heathrow	39.6	42.6	40.2	45.2	47.9
London Gatwick	21.1	21.0	18.7	20.0	20.2
Manchester	10.1	10.1	10.1	12.0	13.1
Glasgow	3.9	4.3	4.2	4.8	5.2
Birmingham	3.3	3.5	3.2	3.8	4.2
Edinburgh	2.4	2.5	2.3	2.7	2.9
London Stansted	1.3	1.2	1.7	2.4	2.7
Aberdeen	1.7	1.9	2.0	2.2	2.3
Belfast International	2.2	2.3	2.2	2.3	2.2
Newcastle	1.5	1.6	1.5	2.0	2.1
Luton	2.8	2.7	2.0	2.0	1.9
East Midlands	1.5	1.3	1.1	1.3	1.4
Bristol	0.8	0.8	0.8	1.0	1.1

Source: Civil Aviation Authority.

regulatory regime is an independent industry regulator, the Director General of Telecommunications.

Duopoly Review

In 1991 a major review of government telecommunications policy resulted in the publication of a White Paper, *Competition and Choice: Telecommunications Policy for the 1990s*. This stated that the Government would end the 'duopoly policy', under which only two companies, BT and Mercury Communications, were permitted to run fixed-link telecommunications systems. Other important points of the review were:

- greater freedom for existing mobile telecommunications operators and the ability of cable television operators to provide telephone services in their own right;
- more effective and streamlined procedures for the interconnection of systems;
- guidelines for the introduction of 'equal access', by which customers can exercise choice over the trunk operator that carries their calls; and
- the establishment of a new regime for national numbering, and the modification of operators' licences to allow for the introduction of number portability.

Office of Telecommunications

The Office of Telecommunications (OFTEL), a non-ministerial government department, is the independent regulatory body for the telecommunications industry. It is headed by the Director General of Telecommunications, among whose functions are to:

- ensure that licensees comply with the conditions of their licences;
- initiate the modification of licence conditions by agreement or a reference to the Monopolies and Mergers Commission;
- promote effective competition in the telecommunications industry;

- provide advice to the President of the Board of Trade on telecommunications matters; and
- investigate complaints.

The Director General also has a duty to promote the interests of consumers in respect of prices, quality and variety in telecommunications services. Areas where customers have benefited include price cuts in BT's charges resulting from the price regulation formula, amounting to reductions of £500 million during the year ended July 1994. Written complaints and enquiries to OFTEL declined considerably in 1993. The number of written representations over disputed bills had decreased by more than half.

OFTEL has taken over responsibility for administering the national telephone numbering scheme. A major change will take place in April 1995 when an extra digit, 1, will be introduced after the initial 0 to all area dialling codes in Britain. Thus, for example, the 071 code for inner London will become 0171 and the 0232 code for Belfast will become 01232. OFTEL will also oversee the introduction of a limited 'number portability' scheme, enabling someone who wishes to change service provider at the same address to retain their existing number, rather than having to change it, as at present.

BT

BT runs one of the world's largest public telecommunications networks, including:

- 20.1 million residential lines;
- 6 million business lines;
- about 58,000 telex connections;
- more than 104,000 public payphones; and
- a wide range of specialised voice, data, text and visual services.

The inland telephone and telex networks are fully automatic. International direct dialling is available from Britain to 200 countries, representing 99 per cent of the world's telephones. Following the sale of its shares in three tranches between 1984 and 1993, the Government has only a residual stake in BT to enable it to meet outstanding commitments under the bonus scheme which accompanied the privatisation.

Network Modernisation

BT has invested more than £17,000 million in the modernisation and expansion of its network to meet the increasing demand for basic telephone services and for more specialised services. The company has more than 2 million km (1.2 million miles) of optical fibre laid in its network in Britain, a higher proportion than any other world operator. There are more than 3,650 digital and modern electronic exchanges serving about 80 per cent of telephone lines. The combination of digital exchange switching and digital transmission techniques, using optical fibre cable and microwave radio links, is substantially improving the quality of telephone services. It also makes possible a wider range of services through the company's main network.

General Services

BT's services include:

- a free facility for emergency calls to the police, fire, ambulance, coastguard, lifeboat and air-sea rescue services;
- directory enquiries;
- various chargeable operator-connected services, such as reversed-charge calls and alarm calls;
- an operator-handled Freefone service and automatic 'LinkLine' facilities that enable callers to contact organisations anywhere in Britain, either free or at local-call rates;
- Callstream, a premium-rate service which allows callers to obtain information from independent providers; and
- network services such as three-way calling, call waiting and call diversion, which are available to customers on digital exchanges.

Under a public payphone service modernisation programme, £165 million has been spent on modernisation and additional provision on sites convenient for travellers, such as railway stations and motorway service areas. A number of cashless call services are available, including the Phonecard service using prepaid cards and phones that accept credit cards. Phonecard payphones account for more than 19,000 of the total of 113,000 payphones. There are about 280,000 private rented payphones on premises to which the public has access and these are also being upgraded with push-button equipment.

Close co-operation between BT and the police has led to successes in the struggle against payphone attacks, usually by organised gangs. Between April and September 1993, attacks on payphones were down by 49 per cent on the same period in 1992, while the number of arrests was up by 58 per cent.

BT Electronic Information Services (an electronic mail and information service) forms part of the company's portfolio of global network services. Through links with other databases, a wide range of other services, such as company accounting and market research information, banking services, holiday booking and reservation facilities, insurance and financial markets information, and BT's telephone directories, are available.

International Services

BT is the second largest shareholder in the International Telecommunications Satellite Organisation (INTELSAT), of which 125 countries are members, and in the European Telecommunications Satellite Organisation (EUTELSAT). It is also a leading shareholder in the International Maritime Satellite Organisation (INMARSAT), with interests in a number of other consortia.

BT operates satellite earth stations in the London Docklands and at Goonhilly Downs (Cornwall), Madley (near Hereford) and Aberdeen. Its range of digital transmission services includes a number available overseas, including 'Satstream' private-circuit digital links covering North America and Western Europe using small-dish aerials, and an

'International Kilostream' private-circuit service available to the United States, Australia and most major business centres in Asia and the rest of Europe. Extensive direct-dial maritime satellite services are available for vessels worldwide. In-flight operator-controlled telephone call facilities are available via Portishead radio station near Bristol. Digital transmission techniques have been introduced for services to the United States, Japan, Hong Kong and Australia via the Madley and Goonhilly stations.

Recent advances in submarine cable design, with the use of optical fibre technology, have significantly increased capacity. A high-capacity transatlantic optical fibre cable (TAT 9), which cost about £250 million and can carry about 75,000 telephone calls simultaneously, came into operation in 1992 to supplement an earlier link.

Mercury Communications

Mercury Communications Ltd, which is part of the Cable and Wireless group and is 20 per cent owned by Bell Canada Enterprises, has constructed its own long-distance all-digital network comprising 6,600 km (4,100 miles) of optical fibre cables and 700 km (440 miles) of digital microwave links. The network runs from the north of Scotland to the south coast, linking over 100 cities and towns across Britain. Mercury now offers a service to over 90 per cent of the population, including both business and residential customers.

Major customers can have a direct digital link between their premises and the Mercury network. A number of routeing devices have also been developed to enable customers to use Mercury indirectly via their existing exchange lines. Businesses are also able to take advantage of savings plans and automatic discounts. There are Mercury-compatible phones which connect the caller to the network at the push of a button. In addition, many customers are now able to use the Mercury network by dialling an access code. Mercurycard phones can be found in city centres, airports and railway stations nationwide.

International services are provided by satellite communications centres in London's Docklands, in Oxfordshire and at Brechin in Scotland, as well as by submarine cable links to Europe and the United States.

Other Operators

Other operators include Kingston Communications, which is the long-established network operator for the Kingston upon Hull area of Britain. The duopoly review (see p. 302) allowed other would-be operators to apply for licences to provide telecommunications services over fixed links. By June 1994, the Government had received 87 applications, and 45 licences had been granted. The licensees include:

- COLT, which is focusing on business customers in the Greater London area;

- Energis, one of the first electricity companies to expand its interests into telecommunications, using its infrastructure as a platform for installing new optical fibre networks;

- Ionica, which is installing a new national network using radio to provide the final connection to customers;

- Sprint, the third-largest long-distance telephone company in the United States, which is seeking to expand its domestic and international services in Britain; and

- Vodafone, the well-established mobile operator, which was granted a licence for fixed services in December 1993.

It was announced in February 1994 that British satellite operators would be able to buy capacity on INTELSAT direct without having to go through BT.

Mobile Communications

The Government has encouraged the expansion of mobile telecommunications services. It has licensed Vodafone Ltd and Telecom Securicor Cellular Radio Ltd to run competing national cellular radio systems. Considerable investment has been made in establishing their networks to provide increased capacity for the growing numbers of cellular radio telephone users (over 2.2 million by May 1994). The two companies will also run the new pan-European mobile system, known as GSM, in Britain.

Britain was the first country to offer personal communications network (PCN) services, which are intended to allow the same telephone to be used at home, at work and as a portable wherever there is network capacity. PCNs operate in the frequency range around 1.8 gigahertz. The Mercury One-2-One service started in September 1993, and Hutchison Microtel's Orange service was launched in April 1994.

National Band Three Ltd is licensed to offer a nationwide trunked radio service, while 26 licences have now been awarded for London and regional services. Four licences to operate mobile data networks have also been granted, and another five to run nationwide paging networks.

Cable Television Franchises

The Government concluded in the duopoly review that cable operators should be able to offer voice telephony in their own right, which they could previously provide only in conjunction with BT or Mercury. All 65 local franchises in operation by the beginning of 1994 provided television programmes, but 43 also offered voice telephony services. By then, the cable operators had installed 314,000 telephone lines in Britain, compared with 2,200 lines in January 1991.

Cable & Wireless

Cable and Wireless plc provides a wide range of telecommunications in over 50 countries worldwide. Its main business is the provision and operation, through the companies of the Cable & Wireless federation, of public telecommunications services in over 30 countries and territories, including Hong Kong, the United States and Japan, under franchises and licences granted by the governments concerned. It also provides and manages telecommunications services and facilities for public and private sector

customers, and undertakes consultancy work worldwide. It operates a fleet of ten ships and three submersible vehicle systems for laying and maintaining submarine telecommunications cables. Its strategy is to build on its regional hubs in Asia, Western Europe and the Caribbean. It links these hubs through its worldwide network of cable and satellite communications.

POSTAL SERVICES

The Post Office, founded in 1635, pioneered postal services and was the first to issue adhesive postage stamps as proof of advance payment for mail.

The Royal Mail provides deliveries to 24.5 million addresses and handles over 64 million letters and parcels each working day, which comes to over 15,900 million items a year. About 750,000 parcels a day are handled. Mail is collected from over 100,000 posting boxes, as well as from post offices and large postal users.

Mail sorting is increasingly done through mechanised letter offices; about 80 are now in operation. The British postcode system is one of the most sophisticated in the world, allowing mechanised sorting down to part of a street on a postman's round and, in some cases, to an individual address.

Britain has good international postal services, with prices among the cheapest. Royal Mail International dispatches 691 million items a year, including 600 million by air. It has its own mail handling centre at Heathrow, which handles about four-fifths of outward airmail. It uses 1,400 flights a week to send mail direct to over 300 destinations worldwide.

Post Office Counters Ltd handles a wide range of transactions; it acts as an agent for the letters and parcels businesses, government departments, local authorities and Alliance & Leicester Giro—formerly Girobank, which was transferred to the private sector in 1990. There are just under 20,000 post offices, of which 800 are operated directly by the Post Office. The remainder are franchise offices or are operated on an agency basis by sub-postmasters.

Post Office Specialist Services

The Post Office offers a range of specialist services. Parcelforce 'Datapost', a door-to-door delivery service, provides overnight delivery throughout Britain and an international service to over 160 countries. 'Datapost Sameday' provides a rapid delivery within or between more than 100 cities and towns in Britain. The Philatelic Bureau in Edinburgh is an important outlet for the Post Office's philatelic business, including sales to overseas collectors or dealers. The British Postal Consultancy Service offers advice and assistance on all aspects of postal business to overseas postal administrations, and over 50 countries have used its services since 1965.

Competition in Postal Services

The Post Office has a monopoly on the conveyance of letters within Britain, but the President of the Board of Trade has the power to suspend the monopoly in certain areas or for certain categories of mail and to license others to provide competing services. He has suspended the monopoly on letters subject to a minimum fee of £1, and has issued general licences enabling mail to be transferred between document exchanges and allowing charitable organisations to carry Christmas cards.

The Government has been considering options for the future of the Post Office. In June 1994 the Government published a Green Paper, *The Future of Postal Services*, on the future of the Post Office. This set out options for the future of the Royal Mail, with the aim of increasing its ability to respond to new commercial challenges. One option was the sale of a majority stake to the public, employees and sub-postmasters; another was retention in the public sector with greater commercial freedom so far as was consistent with public sector status. In November 1994 it was announced that privatisation of the Royal Mail would not be pursued, although the Government is still seeking ways to improve its competitiveness.

Private Courier and Express Service Operators

Private-sector couriers and express operators are allowed to handle time-sensitive door-to-door deliveries, subject to a minimum fee of £1. The courier/express service industry has grown rapidly and the revenue created by the carriage of these items is estimated at over £3,000 million a year. Britain is one of the main providers of monitored express deliveries in Europe, with London an important centre for air courier/express traffic.

Further Reading

Competition and Choice: Telecommunications Policy for the 1990s. Cm 1461. HMSO, 1991.

The Future of Postal Services. Cm 2614. HMSO, 1994.

New Opportunities for the Railways. Cm 2012. HMSO, 1992.

Telecommunications. Aspects of Britain series, HMSO, 1994.

Transport and Communications. Aspects of Britain series, HMSO, 1992.

Transport Statistics Great Britain, annual report. HMSO.

20   Science and Technology

Britain has a long tradition of research and innovation in science, technology and engineering in universities, research institutes and industry. Its record of achievement is in many ways unsurpassed, from the contributions of Isaac Newton to physics and astronomy in the 17th century (theory of gravitation and three laws of motion) to advances in the 20th century such as the discovery of the structure of DNA and the development of the technique of *in vitro* fertilisation which led to the birth of the world's first 'test-tube baby' in 1978.

British achievements in science and technology in the 20th century include fundamental contributions to modern molecular genetics through the discovery of the three-dimensional molecular structure of DNA (deoxyribonucleic acid) by Francis Crick, Maurice Wilkins, James Watson and Rosalind Franklin in 1953 and of cholesterol, vitamin D, penicillin and insulin by Dorothy Hodgkin.

Notable contributions in other areas over the past 20 years have been made by Stephen Hawking in improving the understanding of the nature and origin of the universe; Brian Josephson in superconductivity (abnormally high electrical conductivity at low temperatures); Martin Ryle and Anthony Hewish in radio astrophysics; and Godfrey Hounsfield in computer assisted tomography (a form of radiography) for medical diagnosis.

Much pioneering work was done during the 1980s. For example, in 1985 British Antarctic Survey scientists discovered the hole in the ozone layer over the Antarctic. Also in 1985 Alec Jeffreys invented DNA fingerprinting, a forensic technique which can identify an individual from a small tissue sample. More recently there have been several British breakthroughs in genetics research, including the identification of the gene in the Y chromosome responsible for determining sex, and the identification of other genes linked to diseases, including cystic fibrosis and a type of inherited heart disease. Gene therapy has begun on the treatment of cystic fibrosis. The world's first pig with a genetically modified heart has been bred by scientists at Cambridge University, an important milestone in breeding animals as organ donors for people.

Nobel Prizes for Science have been won by over 70 British citizens, more than any other country except the United States. The two most recent (1993) prizewinners were Richard Roberts (medicine) and Michael Smith (chemistry).

Research and Development Expenditure

Total expenditure in Britain on scientific research and development (R & D) in 1992 was £12,619 million, 2.1 per cent of gross domestic product. About 50 per cent was provided by industry and 35 per cent by government. Significant contributions were also made by private endowments, trusts and charities. Industry also funds university research and finances contract research at government establishments. Some charities have their own laboratories and offer grants for outside research. Contract research organisations carry out similar R & D for companies and are playing an increasingly important role in the transfer of technology to British industry.

Total spending on R & D in industry amounted to £7,930 million in 1992. Of this total, British industry's own contribution was 71 per cent, with 14 per cent from government and the rest from overseas. The main areas of expenditure were electronics (29 per cent of the total); chemicals, including pharmaceuticals (26.5 per cent); and aerospace (12 per cent). Of the ten companies with the largest expenditure on R & D (see Table 20.1), four—Glaxo, SmithKline Beecham, Zeneca (formerly part of ICI) and Wellcome—are in pharmaceuticals.

Table 20.1: Company Expenditure on R & D

	R & D annual expenditure (£ million)	R & D as % of sales
Glaxo	739	15.0
SmithKline Beecham	575	9.3
Shell Transport and Trading	529	0.6
Unilever	518	1.9
Zeneca	490	11.0
GEC	398	7.1
Wellcome	326	16.0
Rolls-Royce	253	7.2
British Petroleum	237	0.7
BT	233	1.8

Source: DTI R & D Scoreboard

Note: R & D expenditure includes expenditure overseas.

Some examples of recent notable R & D projects in electronics, chemicals and aerospace are given below.

Electronics

British firms and research organisations, with government support, are leading in the development and application of the family of 'three-five' semiconductor materials (such as gallium arsenide). These materials have a wide variety of uses including lasers for optical fibre communications, microwave devices for satellite communications, and high-efficiency solar cells.

BT (British Telecom) is in the forefront of the development of optical fibre cable and recently developed the first all-optical repeater. Britain also has a world lead in the transmission of computerised data along telephone lines for reproduction on television screens. Up to 800 R & D projects are carried out by BT at any one time; a recent example is the development of a video handset with an optical telephone link. Around two-thirds of its research is in software engineering.

The transputer, a powerful 'computer on a chip', was designed and built in Britain. Several companies have developed powerful machines based on the transputer.

Chemicals

Research performed by the chemicals industry over the past few years has led to significant technological and commercial breakthroughs. ICI pioneered the microbial production of a biodegradable plastic, Biopol, and is at the forefront of global efforts to develop substitutes for chlorofluorocarbons (CFCs—see p. 362).

Pharmaceuticals is the most research intensive sector of the chemicals industry (see p. 232). Research conducted by Zeneca, Glaxo, SmithKline Beecham and Fisons has led to the development of the first successful beta blockers, drugs used in the treatment of cardiovascular conditions; semi-synthetic penicillins; vaccines; and treatments for cancer, asthma, migraine and arthritis. Glaxo is Britain's biggest pharmaceutical company, with a new £500 million research centre at Stevenage (Hertfordshire). It manufactures the world's best selling pharmaceutical, Zantac, which is used in the treatment of gastric ulcers.

Among a host of other research projects are the application of biotechnology to pharmaceuticals, disease-resistant crops, new forms of food, plant science, and the development of advanced materials such as engineering plastics. The biotechnology sector continues to grow, with an increasing number of companies engaged in the development and manufacture of products using genetic modification techniques.

Aerospace

Britain has led the world in many aspects of aerospace R & D over the past 80 years. Pioneering achievements include radar, jet engines, Concorde, automatic landing, vertical take-off and landing, flight simulators and ejector seats. British Aerospace, with Marconi and Dowty Boulton Paul, developed a system known as 'fly-by-wire', in which flying control surfaces are moved by electronic rather than mechanical means. GEC-Marconi developed the world's first optically signalled ('fly-by-light') system. The concept of head-up display (HUD) was pioneered and developed in Britain. This system electronically projects symbols into the pilot's view, avoiding the need to look down at instruments. GEC-Marconi has also developed a holographic HUD, which enables pilots to fly at high speeds at very low altitude in darkness.

GOVERNMENT ROLE

Science and technology issues are the responsibility of a Cabinet Minister, the Chancellor of the Duchy of Lancaster, acting on behalf of the Prime Minister. The Minister is supported by the Office of Science and Technology (OST)—part of the Office of Public Service and Science within the Cabinet Office; it is headed by the Government's Chief Scientific Adviser. The OST provides a central focus for the development of government policy on

science and technology, both nationally and internationally, including strengthening the science base and maximising its contribution to economic performance and the quality of life.

In addition to its role in overall science policy and co-ordination, the OST is responsible for the Science Budget and the six government-financed research councils (see pp. 311–15): the Engineering and Physical Sciences Research Council (EPSRC), the Particle Physics and Astronomy Research Council (PPARC), the Medical Research Council (MRC), the Natural Environment Research Council (NERC), the Biotechnology and Biological Sciences Research Council (BBSRC) and the Economic and Social Research Council (ESRC). OST funding provides assistance for research, through the research councils, in the following ways:

- awarding grants and contracts to universities and other higher education establishments and to research units;
- funding research council establishments;
- supporting postgraduate study; and
- subscribing to international scientific organisations.

The OST also provides support to universities (whose main source of funding is through the appropriate higher education funding council) through programmes administered through the Royal Society and the Royal Academy of Engineering (see p. 321).

Finance

Government finance for R & D goes to research establishments, higher education institutions and private industry, as well as to collaborative research programmes. Total net government R & D expenditure (both civil and defence) in 1992–93 was £5,199 million, of which £2,978 million was devoted to civil science. The Science Budget (see Table 20.2) totals £1,236.5 million for 1994–95. Government funding through the Science Budget has increased by over 20 per cent in real terms since 1984–85.

Table 20.2: Science Budget 1994–95

	£ million	%
EPSRC	364.0	29.4
MRC	269.2	21.8
PPARC	184.9	15.0
BBSRC	171.8	13.9
NERC	155.4	12.6
ESRC	58.9	4.8
Royal Society	20.1	1.6
Royal Academy of Engineering, OST initiatives and other payments	12.2	1.0

Source: Cabinet Office

Among government departments, the Ministry of Defence (MoD—see p. 317) has the largest research budget. The main civil departments involved are the Department of Trade and Industry (DTI—see p. 315), the Ministry of Agriculture, Fisheries and Food (MAFF—see p. 318) and the Department of the Environment (see p. 318).

Strategy

A White Paper, *Realising Our Potential: A Strategy for Science, Engineering and Technology*, published in 1993, contained the first major policy review on science for over 20 years. The Government's strategy, following the White Paper, is to improve Britain's competitiveness and quality of life by maintaining the excellence of science, engineering and technology in Britain and by:

- developing stronger partnerships with and between the science and engineering communities, industry and the research councils;

- supporting the science and engineering base in order to advance knowledge, increase understanding and produce highly educated and trained scientists and technologists;

- contributing to international research efforts, particularly European research;

- promoting the public understanding of science, technology and engineering; and

- ensuring government-funded research is conducted efficiently and effectively.

A number of changes to the organisation and direction of government-funded science, engineering and technology have been made following the White Paper:

- A new Council for Science and Technology has been set up, chaired by the Chancellor of the Duchy of Lancaster. Its members include senior people from industry and academic life. It provides independent advice to government on strategic issues of science and technology, including expenditure priorities.

- A new 'Forward Look', first published in April 1994, will be published by the Government each year. This gives industrialists and researchers a regular statement of the Government's strategy.

- A new Technology Foresight Programme, intended to strengthen links between industry, academia and government, is being established. It will influence private sector strategies; inform the work of the Council for Science and Technology, the Director-General of the Research Councils, the higher education funding councils and government departments; and help in the preparation of the annual Forward Look. The first results are expected in spring 1995.

- The research council system was restructured with effect from 1 April 1994 (see p. 311). Management structures have been modified, and councils now have part-time chairmen selected to bring in industrial and commercial experience. A Director-General of Research Councils within OST advises ministers on the performance and needs of the science and engineering base.

- The customer-contractor principle has been maintained and strengthened.

- The OST now plays the major role in co-ordinating science and technology issues involving more than one department.

- Special importance is now attached to co-ordination of European and other international negotiations.

A major policy initiative in the White Paper was the announcement of a campaign to promote the public awareness of science, engineering and technology. It has two aims:

- to make science and engineering more attractive to the general public and, in particular, young people; and

- in the longer term to boost the number of scientifically literate young people.

It also has the wider objective of improving the general public's understanding of scientific terms, concepts and issues. The first major event of the campaign was the national week of science, engineering and technology, held in March 1994. About 1,200 events were held in 230 towns and cities across Britain. These were organised, with financial support from the Government, by the British Association for the Advancement of Science. A second week is planned for March 1995. As part of the campaign, the Government also supports organisations and events such as the British Association's Annual Meeting and the Edinburgh International Science Festival (see p. 323).

The LINK initiative, for which the OST has lead responsibility, is designed to bridge the gap between industry and the research base for the benefit of the British economy. It encourages collaboration on high quality, commercially relevant research between industry and higher education institutions and other research base organisations. Under the initiative, government departments and research councils fund up to 50 per cent of the cost of research projects, with industry providing the remainder. The participating industrial partners in LINK projects are responsible for the commercial exploitation of research outcomes.

RESEARCH COUNCILS

Each research council is an autonomous body established under Royal Charter, with members of its governing council drawn from the universities, professions, industry and government. Councils conduct research through their own establishments and by supporting selected research programmes and projects, and training in universities and other higher education institutions. Two new councils—the EPSRC and the PPARC—were created, dividing between them most of the portfolio of the former Science and Engineering Research Council (SERC). A third new council, the Biotechnology and Biological Sciences Research Council, took over responsibility for the programme of the former Agricultural and Food Research Council and for the work of the SERC in biology and biotechnology.

In addition to funding from the OST, the research councils also receive income for research commissioned by government departments and from the private sector. Income from commissioned research is particularly important for the BBSRC and NERC: in these councils receipts in 1994–95 are expected to offset over 20 per cent of gross expenditure.

Engineering and Physical Sciences Research Council

The EPSRC, the largest research council, supports underpinning research in engineering and the physical sciences for a very wide range of industries, including electronics, chemicals, pharmaceuticals, transport, information technology, communications, construction, manufacturing, energy, aerospace, food, hotels and catering, banking, finance, leisure and retailing. About 80 per cent of the Council's research and training investment is spent in higher education institutions.

Priority areas on which the EPSRC is working are:

- innovative manufacturing and clean technology, underpinned by research in a range of generic technologies— information technology, materials, design, systems and production engineering and processing technology;

- high quality research and training in core engineering and physical science disciplines to maintain their health and to aid the EPSRC's initiatives and key technologies; and

- continuing access to high-quality national and international facilities for British researchers.

The EPSRC also has responsibility for the Daresbury Rutherford Appleton Laboratories (DRAL) at Chilton in Oxfordshire and Warrington in Cheshire. Since April 1994 these centres of specialised research have operated under common management. They provide experimental facilities too large and complex to be housed by individual academic institutions, and undertake contract research. For example, the DRAL at Chilton has one of the most powerful lasers devoted to civil research in Europe—Vulcan—which is capable of simulating conditions inside stars. The ISIS pulsed neutron source is used by scientific teams from over 20 countries, including those working on research on high-temperature superconductors. In recent years the Synchrotron Radiation Source at the DRAL at Daresbury has been responsible for establishing the structure of viruses that cause foot and mouth disease and sleeping sickness.

The world's first continuously variable wavelength, ultraviolet microscope has been installed at Daresbury. Funded by the EU, it will be used to provide 'optical slice' images through biological and other materials.

It is expected that the combined Rutherford Appleton and Daresbury laboratories will in due course form a self-standing institution independent of any single research council in terms of formal ownership, but with customers from five of the six research councils; a review is in progress.

The objectives of the EPSRC commit it to the industrial implementation of the technologies developed with the aid of the academic science base.

Particle Physics and Astronomy Research Council

The major task of the PPARC is to ensure continuity of the country's long tradition of excellence in research into fundamental physical processes through studies in particle physics, astronomy and astrophysics, and solar system science. The PPARC maintains four research establishments under common management: the Royal Greenwich Observatory at Cambridge, the Royal Observatory at Edinburgh and two overseas observatories on La Palma in the Canary Islands and on

Hawaii. The PPARC is a major source of funding for many of the leading university physics departments in Britain.

Specific research projects to be undertaken over the next decade include:

- physics of the 'Big Bang': the origin of mass and the nature of the fundamental particles and forces;
- symmetry of matter and anti-matter;
- structure and evolution of the universe since the 'Big Bang';
- the resolution of the 'missing mass' or 'dark matter' problem: the difference between the visible mass of the universe and that required to explain its physical properties;
- star formation and evolution;
- coupling of the Sun's emissions to the Earth's ionosphere and atmosphere; and
- the formation and evolution of the solar system.

Through the PPARC Britain is to take part in one of the most important ground-based astronomical projects of the 1990s: Gemini, an international collaboration to build two 8-metre telescopes that will give all-sky coverage from sites in Hawaii and Chile. Britain will be involved in the design, construction and instrumentation of the telescopes.

The Council's work is in fields where international co-operation is particularly important; substantial contributions are made to the European Space Agency (ESA) and the European Laboratory for Particle Physics (CERN—see p. 324), where the proposed Large Hadron Collider is a major research interest.

Biotechnology and Biological Sciences Research Council

BBSRC sustains a broad base of interdisciplinary research and training to underpin the biology-based industries—agriculture, pharmaceuticals, chemicals and food.

The Council operates underlying science-led research programmes organised in areas reflecting the different levels of biological structure and directed research programmes to develop further opportunities arising from such research. Science-led programmes include work on biomolecular science; genes; cell biology and biochemistry; plant, animal and microbial science; systems and engineering. Directed programmes include work on agricultural systems and on chemicals and pharmaceuticals (including the design, development and efficient manufacture of bioproducts) and research of relevance to the food industry. Research is carried out at eight institutes, at Horticulture Research International and in higher education institutions.

> Recombinant DNA technologies have helped to produce novel domestic animal vaccines against economically important diseases and these have been successfully commercialised. Advances in gene technologies have led to the development of fruit with improved storage capacity and hence longer shelf life in supermarkets. It is also possible to produce human pharmaceutical proteins such as blood clotting factors in animal milk, from which these proteins are easily extracted in a pure form. The use of biotransformations has led to the biosynthesis of industrially important pure chemicals which are key building blocks in some anti-viral agents.

BBSRC has an important role in the training of scientists and engineers: it has over 2,000 research studentships and 75 postdoctoral fellowships. Use is made of the two main mechanisms for supporting postgraduate training with an industrial orientation: CASE awards and awards under the Teaching Company Scheme (see p. 206).

Medical Research Council

The MRC is the main government agency supporting medical research. Its total budget in 1994–95 is £302 million. It promotes and supports research and training aimed at maintaining and improving human health, advancing knowledge and technology, and providing well-trained staff to meet the needs of user communities, including the providers of health care and the biotechnology, food, health care, medical instrumentation, pharmaceutical and other biomedical-related industries.

The MRC is unusual among the research councils in that about half its research expenditure is spent in its own institutes and units, which have close links with universities and medical schools, the rest being spent mainly in direct support of research in higher education institutions. The council has three large institutes—the National Institute for Medical Research at Mill Hill in London, the Laboratory of Molecular Biology at Cambridge and the Clinical Sciences Centre (opened in 1993) at Hammersmith Hospital, London—and 40 research units and a number of smaller teams.

Areas in which the MRC is conducting research include:

- Molecules and cells, and inheritance and development—work in these areas is contributing to the identification of novel cellular targets for new pharmaceutical agents and to the detection, prevention and treatment of diseases with a genetic component.

- Infections and immunity—these areas include work on developing new vaccines and identifying novel targets for antiviral chemotherapy. The Council has a major research programme on HIV infection and AIDS.

- Environment—the Council's strategy is to determine the health impact of particular environmental hazards; the MRC has established a research centre in Mechanisms of Human Toxicity in Leicester and, with the Departments of the Environment and Health, is establishing an Institute for Environmental Health.

- Cancer—the Council's activity is aimed at increasing basic understanding of tumour biology, developing methods of detecting cancer, identifying preventive strategies, and developing and evaluating better methods of early detection and treatment. The MRC's work complements that of the medical research charities and involves important international collaboration.

- Neurosciences and mental health—this is an area to which the Council commits very considerable expenditure in order to extend understanding of the central nervous system, explore diseases of the nervous system, and develop new methods of diagnosis, prevention and treatment. Support is given to research on psychoses (including schizophrenia), neuroses, dementia, addictions, child psychiatry and neurological disorders, all a severe burden on sufferers, their families and the National Health Service (NHS).

- Systems-oriented research—this concerns main body systems; particular areas are cardiovascular studies, haematology, respiratory disease, reproduction, calcium metabolism and bone disorders, rheumatology, dental research, nutrition and metabolism.

Scientists working at the MRC Human Genetics Unit in Edinburgh have succeeded in creating a strain of laboratory mice carrying the defective gene that causes cystic fibrosis. The Edinburgh mouse, unlike other models, closely mimics the early stages of lung disease in patients. The cystic fibrosis mouse has already proved valuable in developing and testing the safety and effectiveness of new drug and gene therapies before conducting clinical tests on people. These trials are being undertaken at the Royal Brompton Hospital, London.

- Health services and public health research—the Council's work is focused on implementing medical knowledge to improve health and address needs for which effective medical interventions exist or could soon be developed. The MRC's work complements that of the Health Departments, the NHS and the ESRC.

Natural Environment Research Council

NERC has an R & D provision of £155 million for 1994–95 and its wide-ranging activities fall into the following categories:

- Earth observation—advanced research methodology for measuring the properties of the Earth's atmosphere, land, sea and surface. Since April 1994 NERC's responsibilities cover support for the whole area of Earth observation, including instrument development;

- Earth sciences—structure, composition, processes and mineral resources of the Earth (geology, geophysics, geochemistry, palaeontology and aspects of physical geography);

- marine sciences—physical, chemical and biological characteristics and processes of the seas and sea floor;

- atmospheric sciences—physical and chemical processes determining weather and climate, atmospheric pollution and air-surface interactions;

- terrestrial and freshwater sciences— physical, chemical and biological characteristics and processes of land and freshwater;

- polar sciences—physical, chemical and biological aspects of the Antarctic and Arctic environments (atmospheric, cryospheric, marine, earth and life sciences).

The Council supports research in 15 NERC institutes, units and research centres as well as research and training in universities. It also provides a range of facilities for use by the environmental science community, including a research fleet. NERC institutes include the British Geological Survey, the Institute of Terrestrial Ecology, the Institute of Oceanographic Sciences Deacon Laboratory and the British Antarctic Survey.

A new national centre for oceanographic science and technology, the Southampton Oceanography Centre, will be opened in 1995. It is intended to be a world-class centre of excellence in this area and to be a national focus for research, training and support in oceanography, geology and aspects of marine technology and engineering.

NERC has a substantial income from commissioned research and other services making use of its expertise. Programmes such as those of the British Geological Survey are important for environmental conservation; the Land-Ocean Interaction Study is also important, as are programmes in marine, atmospheric and terrestrial and freshwater sciences and in Antarctic research.

> A comprehensive geological survey of Britain's inner continental shelf, undertaken by the British Geological Survey, has yielded a detailed picture of the area and associated natural resources. Britain is the first country to have completely mapped its offshore area in this way.

Economic and Social Research Council

ESRC, with an R & D provision of £60 million for 1994–95, supports research to increase understanding of social and economic change in order to enhance industrial competitiveness and the quality of life, and to contribute to the effectiveness of public services and policy. All research funded by ESRC is conducted in higher education institutions or independent research institutes.

The Council devotes a substantial part of its expenditure (£17.5 million is available for 1994–95) to high quality training in research to aid the development and maintenance of a first-class research capacity in the social sciences. Over 1,000 postgraduate students are supported by the Council through research training awards, advanced course awards and fellowships. Through its participation in the DTI's Teaching Company Scheme (see p. 206), ESRC promotes partnerships between social scientists and business by placing graduates in companies for short-term projects.

The main areas for the Council's research are economic performance, environmental change, social cohesion, government and public services, health and welfare, and human development and learning. The priority for the allocation of funds in the next three years will be work on the study and enhancement of innovation in the British economy. ESRC is a joint sponsor of an initiative, being managed by EPSRC, on innovation in manufacturing.

GOVERNMENT DEPARTMENTS

Department of Trade and Industry

Direct government support for research in industry is led by the Department of Trade and Industry (DTI). Although most industrial research and development is financed by industry itself, the DTI provides assistance where there is a sound case for doing so.

In 1993–94 it spent an estimated £310 million on R & D, covering general industrial innovation, aeronautics, space (see p. 319), nuclear and non-nuclear energy and support for statutory, regulatory and policy responsibilities. A further £113 million was allocated to technology transfer and related activities.

The largest part of the DTI's R & D expenditure on energy is on nuclear energy (an estimated £54 million in 1993–94), most of which is carried out by AEA Technology (see p. 261). The DTI also funds research in support of offshore oil and gas technology, coal technology and renewable energy.

DTI Industrial Innovation Programmes

The DTI's policy on science and technology builds on the commitment contained in the 1993 White Paper to improve the partnership between government, industry and the science base. Additional measures were set out in the 1994 White Paper on competitiveness (see p. 194). The balance of the DTI's industrial innovation programmes has shifted away from supporting technology generation towards concentrating on the exploitation and transfer of technology and the promotion of innovation. In particular, the DTI is:

- improving companies' access to local innovation services through Business Links (see p. 197);

- encouraging industry to collaborate with the science base in R & D projects under the LINK initiative (see p. 311);

- putting more effort into helping firms of all sizes work together to undertake R & D projects, including those under the EUREKA initiative (see p. 323);

- facilitating companies' access to technology from overseas and helping small and medium-sized concerns to identify technological opportunities and potential partners, both in Britain and overseas;

- continuing direct single-company support to smaller firms under the SMART competition and the SPUR scheme (see p. 198) for the development of new products and processes; and

- concentrating support from the DTI's innovation budget for industry R & D collaboration on those projects which will result in exceptional economic benefits.

To carry out these measures, the DTI's budget allocation for industrial innovation is £116.5 million in 1994–95.

Aeronautics

The DTI's Civil Aircraft Research and Demonstration Programme (CARAD) supports research and technology demonstration in the aircraft and aeroengine industry, helping it to compete effectively in world markets. The programme is part of a national aeronautics research effort, with over half of the research work supported being conducted in industry and the universities, and the remainder at the Defence Research Agency (see p. 317). Priority areas are aircraft exhaust emissions, advanced materials, and safety problems such as explosion hazards. In 1994–95 the provision for aeronautics is £18.7 million.

Launch Aid is a means of providing government assistance for specific development projects in the aerospace industry. The civil version of the EH101 British/Italian multi-role helicopter is receiving Launch Aid assistance, and a significant offer of Launch Aid has been made to Short Brothers for the Learjet 45 project for 1995–96 and 1996–97, while other Launch Aid projects are under consideration.

Industrial Research Establishments

The DTI has three research establishments. Their primary role is to provide the Government with an effective source of scientific and technological expertise. They supply technological services to industry, undertake research commissioned by industry, and are involved in a variety of international activities.

- The Laboratory of the Government Chemist (LGC) is the focus for chemical measurement within government. It provides both public and private sectors with a comprehensive service based on analytical chemistry and promotes sound chemical measurement in Britain in support of the National Measurement System.

- The National Engineering Laboratory (NEL) carries out a range of technical services, including R & D, testing and consultancies in engineering and related disciplines. It also maintains British Standards of flow measurement, which are of special importance in the oil and gas industries. The NEL manages technology transfer programmes for the DTI in open systems, as well as operating the National Wind Turbine Centre.

- The National Physical Laboratory (NPL) is Britain's national standards laboratory, with responsibility for maintaining national measurements for physical quantities. It supplies essential calibration and technology transfer services for industry, and undertakes research on standards for engineering materials and information technology. The NPL is also the base for the National Measurement Accreditation Service, which provides accreditation of calibration and testing laboratories in both the public and private sectors.

The three laboratories are now executive agencies (see p. 69). The Government has reviewed their operations and has decided that their future lies in the private sector:

- the LGC is to be established as an independent non-profit-making private sector company by the end of 1995–96;

- the NEL is to be sold during summer 1995; and

- proposals are to be invited for a management contractor to take over the NPL—the Government is considering possible alternative arrangements for the National Measurement Accreditation Service.

Technology Transfer

The DTI concentrates support on helping firms gain access to, and assimilate, technology; building up partnerships among firms; working with higher education; learning from overseas; and ensuring firms have the facilities to enable them to innovate and to do business better. It is significantly improving companies' access to science and technology by making innovation services available locally, for example, through Business Links (see p. 197). Many local innovation networks already exist which bring together expertise in higher education institutions, technical colleges, industrial research organisations and other bodies. The DTI intends to build on these networks and improve access to them for small and medium-sized establishments.

The DTI Innovation Unit works predominantly through the use of secondees from industry in six key areas, covering both government and the private sector, to stimulate wealth creation by encouraging a climate for innovation:

- encouraging the spread of best practice of innovation;

- commercial exploitation of the science base;

- improving industry–investor relations;

- encouraging innovation in education;

- improving the public understanding of innovation; and

- encouraging innovation in government.

DTI initiatives to enhance companies' awareness of management best practice will continue through the 'Managing in the 90s' programme (see p. 206). In addition, the Environmental Technology Best Practice Programme (see p. 356) aims to improve industrial competitiveness and reduce pollution. The DTI is developing a more comprehensive information service about technology overseas.

Ministry of Defence

Ministry of Defence provision for R & D in 1994–95 is £2,315 million. About £631 million of this is for medium and long-term applied research relevant to military needs, much of it carried out in the MoD's Defence Research Agency (DRA) and other smaller establishments. With the ending of the Cold War, the Government is committed to achieving a gradual reduction in real terms in spending on defence R & D.

Several research establishments merged to form the DRA in 1991. It is the largest single scientific employer in Britain. Its role is to provide scientific and technical services primarily to the Ministry but also to other government departments.

The DRA subcontracts about £200 million of research to industry and universities, ensuring that their know-how is harnessed to meeting military requirements. It also works closely with industry in order to ensure that scientific and technological advances are taken forward at an early stage into development and production. This technology transfer is not just confined to the defence industry but has also led to important 'spin offs' from defence into civil markets, in fields ranging from new materials and electronic devices to advanced aerodynamics. The latter in particular has been instrumental in giving Britain a leading role in civil aircraft design.

Recent innovations by the DRA include the development of an advanced composite rotor blade for the Lynx helicopter; and the invention of a special form of highly porous silicon, which can be made to emit light when irradiated with ultra-violet light and opens up the technology of silicon opto-microelectronics.

Other Government Departments

Ministry of Agriculture, Fisheries and Food

MAFF co-ordinates its research programme with The Scottish Office Agriculture and Fisheries Department, the Department of Agriculture for Northern Ireland and the research councils, particularly the BBSRC (see p. 313). It also covers the research interests of the Welsh Office Agriculture Department.

Its research programme reflects the Ministry's wide-ranging responsibilities for protecting and enhancing the rural and marine environment; protecting the public, especially in food safety and quality, flooding and coastal defence, and animal health and welfare; and improving the economic performance of the agriculture, fishing and food industries.

The budget for research expenditure in 1994–95 is £137 million. Research is contracted with research councils, the Ministry's agencies, non-departmental public bodies, higher education institutions and other organisations.

Department of the Environment

The Department of the Environment funds research in several policy areas: environmental protection, including radioactive substances; water; the countryside; planning and inner cities; local government; housing; building and construction; and energy efficiency. The three largest sub-programmes are those on pollution-related climate change, regional and urban air quality, and the safe disposal of radioactive waste. Total research expenditure in 1994–95 is estimated at £93.4 million.

Department of Health

The Department of Health has developed an R & D programme for the National Health Service (NHS) which will provide a scientific basis for the promotion of health and the provision of health care. A key aim is to increase the effectiveness of the NHS by creating a sound base from which strategies in health care, operational policy and management can be defined and practice improved. The Department also manages a Health and Personal Social Service research programme concerned with the needs of ministers and policy-makers, with emphasis on improving efficiency.

Overseas Development Administration

The Overseas Development Administration (ODA) commissions and sponsors research on topics relevant to those geographical regions designated as the primary targets of the aid programme and of benefit to the poorest people in those countries. Provision for R & D in 1994–95 is £85 million.

The ODA's support for R & D is organised into five main programmes, covering renewable natural resources; engineering-related sectors (water and sanitation, energy efficiency and geoscience, urbanisation and transport); health and population; economic and social development; and education.

R & D is also carried out as part of Britain's bilateral aid to particular countries. It draws upon a range of professional expertise in agencies such as the Transport Research Laboratory, the British Geological Survey and the Institute of Hydrology. The ODA contributes towards international centres and programmes undertaking R & D aimed at solving problems faced by developing countries. It also contributes to science and technology through the European Union. The EU's Science and Technology for Development programme seeks to stimulate simultaneous study in various parts of the world on specific scientific issues in health, nutrition and agriculture, which can contribute to progress in all developing countries.

The Scottish Office

The Scottish Office both contracts and itself undertakes a wide range of R & D commissions. Total R & D planned expenditure in 1994–95 is £73.3 million in support of its policy responsibilities, especially on agriculture, fisheries, health, the environment, education and home affairs. In some areas of work—medicine, agriculture and biological sciences, fisheries and marine science—research in Scotland is at the forefront internationally.

Space Activities

Britain's support for civil space research is co-ordinated by the British National Space Centre (BNSC), a partnership between various government departments and research councils. BNSC encourages industry to exploit opportunities in space, based on appraisal of project costs and potential technological and commercial benefits. Through BNSC, Britain spent around £171 million on space activities in 1993–94, mainly through DTI and research council financing. Around 63 per cent—£108 million—was devoted to programmes shared with the European Space Agency (ESA). The remainder supported a programme of R & D in industry, higher education institutions, government establishments and industry.

The major part of Britain's space programme is concerned with satellite-based Earth observation (remote sensing) for commercial and environmental applications. Britain has committed around £70 million to the ESA's ERS-1 satellite, which was launched in 1991. ERS-2, to which Britain has contributed £45 million, is due to be launched in December 1994. Britain provided two of the instruments on both satellites: a synthetic aperture radar (SAR) and an along track scanning radiometer (ATSR). The SAR is capable of providing high resolution images of the Earth with 24-hour coverage, irrespective of cloud cover conditions. The ATSR measures global sea surface temperature to a very high degree of accuracy. British remote sensing instruments are also being flown on other satellites, including the Upper Atmosphere Research Satellite, operated by the United States National Aeronautics and Space Administration (NASA).

The Earth Observation Data Centre at Farnborough (Hampshire), operated by the National Remote Sensing Centre Ltd, processes the data output from ERS-1 and other remote sensing spacecraft, and will do so for successor missions. It is also one of the ESA's four processing and archiving facilities which store and distribute remotely sensed data for both scientific and commercial purposes.

Britain is also contributing £284 million to the Polar Platform and ENVISAT-1 programmes. The ENVISAT payload, carrying a new generation of ESA environmental instruments, will fly on the British-led Polar Platform. For ENVISAT Britain is leading the development of an advanced action microwave instrument, and an advanced version of the precision instrument that measures infra-red emissions over land and sea.

In space science, Britain participates in all of the ESA's missions. These range from the Hubble Space Telescope, for which British Aerospace built the solar panels, to the Ulysses solar polar probe, which is the first spacecraft to overfly the poles of the sun. Britain is contributing substantially to the Cluster and SOHO missions to study the sun, the Earth's magnetosphere and the solar wind, and to the Infrared Space Observatory, all due for launch in 1995. It is also participating in the ESA's X-ray spectroscopy mission, due for launch in 1999.

There are bilateral agreements for space research between Britain and other countries, such as the United States through NASA, and Japan. British groups have been involved in developing, for example, the widefield camera for Germany's X-ray satellite ROSAT, a spectrometer for the Japanese-built Yohkoh satellite and an X-ray telescope for the Russian Spectrum-X mission.

In Europe, Britain is both a leading producer and user of satellite communications technology, exploiting commercially the expertise developed within the ESA's satellite communications programmes.

RESEARCH IN HIGHER EDUCATION INSTITUTIONS

The higher education funding councils in England, Scotland and Wales (see p. 426) are the largest single source of finance for higher education institutions in Great Britain. About

40 per cent of research carried out in higher education institutions is financed from resources allocated by these bodies. These funds pay for the salaries of permanent academic staff, who usually teach as well as carry out research, and contribute to the cost of support services. In Northern Ireland the institutions are funded by the Department of Education for Northern Ireland. The quality of research performance of departments is a key element in the allocation of funding.

The research councils also support research in higher education institutions in two main ways. First, they provide postgraduate awards to over 25 per cent of postgraduate students in science and technology. Secondly, they give grants and contracts to institutions for projects, particularly in new or developing areas of research, and for support units and facilities for research. The research councils have become responsible for meeting all the costs of the research projects they support in higher education institutions, except for costs associated with the salaries of permanent academic staff and the costs of premises and infrastructure.

The other main channels of support for scientific research in higher education institutions are government departments, charities and industry. The European Union also provides substantial funding. Institutions are expected to recover the full cost of short-term commissioned research from the Government and industry.

The high quality of research in higher education institutions, and their marketing skills, have enabled them to attract more funding from a larger range of external sources, especially in contract income from industry. Co-operation continues between the higher education institutions, industry and the Government in joint projects.

Institutions undertaking research with the support of research council grants have the rights over the commercial exploitation of their research, subject to the prior agreement of the sponsoring research council. They may make use of the expertise of the British Technology Group (see below) to patent and license their inventions.

Science Parks

Science parks are partnerships between higher education institutions and industry to promote commercially focused research and advanced technology. At the end of 1993 there were 45 such parks in operation, generally at or near universities, accommodating nearly 1,200 companies. Most are engaged in work on computing, electronics, instrumentation, robotics, electrical engineering, chemicals and biotechnology. Research, development and training activities are the most common activities, rather than large-scale manufacturing. The biggest science park is at Cambridge, with about 85 companies on site. Recently opened parks are situated at Oxford, Cranfield, Westlakes (Cumbria) and York.

A growing number of universities offer industry interdisciplinary research centres with exploitable resources. These include access to analytical equipment, library facilities and worldwide databases as well as academic expertise.

OTHER ORGANISATIONS

Charitable Foundations

Medical research charities provide a major source of funds for biomedical research in Britain. Their combined contribution in 1992–93 was about £320 million. The three largest contributors were the Wellcome Trust—the world's largest medical charity—with a contribution of £77 million, the Imperial Cancer Research Fund (£50 million) and the Cancer Research Campaign (£44 million).

British Technology Group

British Technology Group (BTG) is among the world's leading technology transfer companies. It promotes the profitable commercialisation of technology by:

● developing and protecting technology arising from research carried out by individuals, higher education institutions and other research organisations which it considers will be commercially viable;

- licensing the resulting intellectual property rights to companies throughout the world; and

- assessing the commercial potential of companies' proprietary technology and licensing this technology to other companies worldwide.

BTG administers about 10,000 patents covering around 1,400 technologies. In 1993–94 the Group's turnover was £29 million. The company is owned by a consortium consisting of BTG management, employees and financial institutions.

Professional Institutions and Learned Societies

There are numerous technical institutions and professional associations in Britain, many of which promote their own disciplines or the education and professional well-being of their members.

The Council of Science and Technology Institutes has seven member institutes representing biology, chemical engineering, chemistry, food science and technology, geology, hospital physics and physics. The Engineering Council promotes the study of all types of engineering in schools and other organisations, in co-operation with its 210 industry affiliates, which include large private sector companies and government departments. Together with 41 professional engineering institutions, the Council accredits courses in higher education institutions. It also advises the Government on a range of academic, industrial and professional issues.

More than 300 learned societies play an important part in promoting science and technology through meetings, publications and sponsorship.

Royal Society

The most prestigious learned society is the Royal Society, founded in 1660. It has over 1,100 Fellows and more than 100 Foreign Members. Many of its Fellows serve on governmental advisory councils and committees concerned with research. The Society's estimated net expenditure on science and

technology in 1994–95 is about £22 million. Almost 80 per cent of funding is derived from the Government, the remainder coming from private sources.

The Society encourages scientific research and its application through a programme of meetings and lectures, publications, and by awarding grants, fellowships and other funding. It recognises scientific and technological achievements through election to the Fellowship and the award of medals and endowed lectureships. As the national academy of sciences, it represents Britain in international non-governmental organisations and participates in a variety of international scientific programmes. It also facilitates collaborative projects and the exchange of scientists through bilateral agreements with academies and research councils throughout the world. It gives independent advice on scientific matters, notably to government, and represents and supports the scientific community as a whole.

The Society is increasingly active in promoting science understanding and awareness among the general public, as well as science education. It also supports research into the history of scientific endeavour.

Royal Academy of Engineering

The national academy of engineering in Britain is the Royal Academy of Engineering, founded in 1976. The Academy, which has about 970 Fellows, 57 Foreign Members and 12 Honorary Fellows, promotes the advancement of engineering for the benefit of the public. It receives a grant from the OST amounting to £2.2 million in 1994–95 and plans to raise over £5 million from other sources. Among the objectives of its programmes are the attraction of first-class students into engineering, raising awareness of the importance of engineering design among undergraduates, developing links between industry and higher education institutions, and increasing industrial investment in engineering research in higher education institutions.

Other Societies

In Scotland the Royal Society of Edinburgh,

321

established in 1783, promotes science by awarding scholarships, organising meetings and symposia, publishing journals and awarding prizes. It also administers fellowship schemes for post-doctoral research workers.

Three other major institutions publicise scientific developments through lectures and publications for specialists and schoolchildren. Of these, the British Association for the Advancement of Science (BAAS), founded in 1831, is mainly concerned with science, while the Royal Society of Arts, dating from 1754, deals with the arts and commerce as well as science. The Royal Institution, founded in 1799, also performs these functions and runs its own research laboratories.

The Committee on the Public Understanding of Science (COPUS), set up in 1986 by the Royal Society, the BAAS and the Royal Institution, acts as a focus for a wide-ranging programme in Britain to improve public awareness of science and technology. It recommends initiatives to its sponsoring bodies and promotes the activities of other organisations and institutions.

Zoological Gardens

The Zoological Society of London, an independent scientific body founded in 1826, runs London Zoo, which occupies about 15 hectares (36 acres) of Regent's Park, London. The Society is responsible for the Institute of Zoology, which carries out research in support of conservation. The Institute's work covers a wide range of topics, including ecology, behaviour, reproductive biology and conservation genetics.

> Many zoos play a vital role in programmes for reintroducing species of international importance, and some have a wider role in management plans for areas and species of conservation interest. For example, London Zoo is involved in 52 co-ordinated captive breeding programmes for exotic species and manages 29 such programmes.

Whipsnade Wild Animal Park near Dunstable (Bedfordshire) is also managed by the Society. Other well-known zoos include those at Edinburgh, Bristol, Chester, Dudley and Marwell (near Winchester).

Botanic Gardens

The Royal Botanic Gardens, founded in 1759, cover 121 hectares (300 acres) at Kew in west London and a 187-hectare (462-acre) estate at Wakehurst Place, Ardingly, in West Sussex. They contain the largest collections of living and dried plants in the world. Research is conducted into all aspects of plant life, including physiology, biochemistry, genetics, economic botany and the conservation of habitats and species. Kew has the world's largest seed bank for wild origin species and is active in programmes to return endangered plant species to the wild. It participates in joint research programmes in 52 countries.

The Royal Botanic Garden in Edinburgh, founded in 1670, is a centre for research into taxonomy (classification of species), for the conservation and study of living plants and for horticultural education.

Scientific Museums

The Natural History Museum, which includes the Geological Museum, has 60 million specimens ranging in size from a blue whale skeleton to minute insects. It is one of the world's principal centres for research into natural history, offering an advisory service to institutions all over the world. The museum is keen to promote public appreciation of nature conservation and in 1991 opened a major exhibition on ecology, illustrating the diversity of living species.

The Science Museum promotes understanding of the history of science, technology, industry and medicine. Its extensive collection of scientific instruments and machinery is complemented by interactive computer games and audio-visual equipment for visitors to use. In this way the museum explains scientific principles to the general public and documents the history of science, from early discoveries to space age technology. These two museums are in South Kensington,

HOUSING

The Community Self Build Agency helps people in housing need to build their own homes and at the same time to acquire new skills. Pictured here is the St John's Self Build Group, Newham, London, which hopes to have family accommodation ready for occupation by May 1995.

Clarion House, a development of 24 flats and houses in central London, built by Soho Housing Association in partnership with a commercial developer. Housing associations provide low cost housing for rent and for sale to those on low incomes and in the greatest housing need.

EDUCATION IN SCHOOLS

The United World College of the Atlantic, founded in 1962 on the South Wales coast, was the first international sixth form college in the world, and aims to promote international understanding through education.

Science is one of the core subjects of the National Curriculum. Here five year olds at Bewbush County First School in Crawley learn about weighing.

A gym lesson at Bushy Hill County Middle School, Guildford. Physical education is part of the curriculum of all state schools in Britain.

Secondary schools must offer at least one language of the European Union, usually French, German or Spanish.

MEDICINE

Leading British molecular geneticist Professor Bob Williamson of St Mary's Hospital Medical School, Imperial College, London, who has been jointly awarded the King Faisal International Prize for Medicine. Professor Williamson has pioneered new treatments for sufferers of inherited diseases, including muscular dystrophy and cystic fibrosis.

ECHO International Health Services, a non profit-making organisation, provides a complete range of medical supplies, including infant incubators, respirators, anaesthetic machines and wheelchairs, to areas in need around the world.

London. Other important collections include those of the Museum of Science and Industry in Birmingham, the Museum of Science and Industry in Manchester, the Museum of the History of Science in Oxford, and the Royal Scottish Museum, Edinburgh.

Science Festivals

Science festivals are a growing feature of local co-operative efforts to provide improved public understanding of the contribution made by science to everyday life. Schools, museums, laboratories, higher education institutions and industry contribute to a wide range of special events. The oldest and most widely publicised science festival is the British Association Annual Festival of Science, held at the end of summer at a British university.

> The largest science festival in a single city in the world is the Edinburgh International Science Festival. In 1994 the Festival included 16 exhibitions, 36 workshops and over 200 lectures; more than 200,000 people attended.

INTERNATIONAL COLLABORATION

Britain plays a key role in a wide range of major international scientific facilities and research programmes.

European Union

Since 1984 the EU has run a series of R & D framework programmes in several strategic sectors, with the aim of strengthening the scientific and technological basis of European industry and improving its international competitiveness. The Third Framework Programme lasted from 1990 to 1994, with a budget of 6,600 million ECUs (£5,079 million).

The Fourth Framework Programme, which is to run from 1994 to 1998, has an agreed expenditure ceiling of about £9,500 million, and Britain played a significant part in shaping its structure and priorities.

Britain helped to secure agreement that the EU should develop 'generic' technologies with a wide range of industrial applications, rather than just funding research projects to meet the needs of specific industrial sectors. The EU has also agreed that more resources should be devoted to disseminating technology from research projects to small and medium-sized enterprises.

Examples of the many EU research activities involving British organisations include the following programmes:

- Britain contributes to the EU Nuclear Fusion Programme, both by supporting a programme of research into fusion carried out by AEA at Culham, Oxfordshire, and by hosting the Joint European Torus (JET) project, also based at Culham. Countries participating in JET include the 12 members of the EU, Sweden and Switzerland.

- The EU's Information Technology Programme, formerly known as ESPRIT (European Strategic Programme for Research in Information Technology), is part of the Fourth Framework Programme. It is a shared-cost collaborative programme, designed to help build the services and technologies that underpin the information society, with a high emphasis on the needs and users of the market. The programme is open to companies, academic institutions and research bodies. Britain is currently involved in 369 projects.

Other International Activities

Over 500 British organisations participate in EUREKA, an industry-led scheme to encourage European co-operation in developing and producing advanced technology products with worldwide sales potential. Britain is currently involved in 257 projects. Major projects include research into a European standard for high-definition television and into semi-conductors. There are 23 members of EUREKA, including the 12 EU countries and the European Commission.

The COST (European Co-operation in the Field of Scientific and Technical Research) programme encourages the co-operation of national research activities across Europe, with participants coming from industry, academia and research laboratories. Transport, telecommunications and materials have traditionally been the largest areas supported. New areas include physics, neuroscience and forests and forestry products. There are currently 25 member states, including the 12 EU countries. Britain takes part in 84 of 102 current COST actions.

Britain is a member of CERN, the European Laboratory for Particle Physics, based in Geneva. Scientific programmes at CERN aim to test, verify and develop the 'standard model' of the origins and structure of the universe. There are 19 member states. The subscription to CERN is paid by the PPARC.

Similar arrangements apply to other international collaborations. Contributions to the high-flux neutron source at the Institut Laue-Langevin and the European Synchrotron Radiation Facility, both in Grenoble, are paid by the EPSRC. The PPARC is a partner in the European Incoherent Scatter Radar Facility within the Arctic Circle, which conducts research on the middle and upper atmosphere.

Through the MRC, Britain participates in the European Molecular Biology Laboratory (EMBL), based in Heidelberg, Germany. Britain has been chosen as the location for the European Bioinformatics Institute, an outstation of the EMBL. The Institute, to be based in Cambridge, will provide up-to-date information on molecular biology and genome sequencing for researchers throughout Europe. It will be funded jointly by the Wellcome Trust and the MRC, and will be fully operational by 1995.

The MRC pays Britain's contribution to the Human Frontier Science programme on behalf of all the research councils. The programme supports international collaborative research into brain function and biological function through molecular level approaches.

NERC's James Rennell Centre in Southampton is a focal point for Britain's contributions to the World Ocean Circulation Experiment, one of the major components of the World Climate Research Programme. NERC also supports Britain's subscription to the Ocean Drilling Program (ODP). In 1993 Britain was chosen as the location for the scientific planning office of the ODP's Joint Oceanographic Institute for Deep Earth Sampling. The office will be based at the University of Wales, Cardiff, for two years from October 1994.

Britain is a member of the science and technology committees of international organisations such as the OECD and NATO, for example, taking part in the OECD's Megascience Forum set up to look at global planning of large facilities and programmes, and of various specialised agencies of the United Nations.

Among non-governmental organisations, the research councils, the Royal Society and the British Academy were founder members of the European Science Foundation in 1974 and play a full part in its activities. The research councils also maintain, with the British Council, a joint office in Brussels to promote European co-operation in research. Staff in British Embassies and High Commissions promote contacts in science and technology between Britain and overseas countries and help to inform a wide range of organisations in Britain about science and technology developments overseas. There are science and technology sections in Paris, Bonn, Washington, Tokyo and Moscow.

The British Council (see p. 130) promotes better understanding and knowledge of Britain and its scientific and technological achievements. It encourages exchange of specialists, supplies specialised information, and fosters co-operation in research, training and education. The Council also identifies and manages technological, scientific and educational projects in developing countries.

Further Reading

Competitiveness: Helping Business to Win. Cm 2563. HMSO, 1994.

Forward Look of Government-funded Science, Engineering and Technology 1994. HMSO, 1994.

Realising Our Potential: A Strategy for Science, Engineering and Technology. Cm 2250. HMSO, 1993.

The Environment

21 Housing and Regeneration

The promotion of home ownership is central to government housing policy; owner-occupation in Great Britain rose from 49 per cent in 1971 to 67 per cent in 1994. There are many strategies in Britain to enhance the urban and rural environments and ensure the availability and diversity of suitable tenure. These include job creation, training, right-to-buy schemes, and improvements to security and lighting on estates. A new Single Regeneration Budget brings together many existing regeneration programmes in England. A total of £1,447 million will be spent from this in 1994–95, in addition to schemes outside this budget and regeneration programmes in Wales, Scotland and Northern Ireland.

Housing

The pattern of housing tenure has changed considerably in recent years, with a substantial increase in owner-occupation and some moderate growth in the private rented sector. Both public and private sectors build housing, but most dwellings are now built by the private sector for sale to owner-occupiers. Local authorities are being encouraged to see their housing role as more of an enabling one, working with housing associations and the private sector to increase the supply of low-cost housing for sale or rent without necessarily providing it themselves. Housing associations are now the main providers of new 'social housing'. This allows local authorities to concentrate their resources on improving the management of their own

stock. To stimulate the private rented sector, which has been declining for most of this century, rents on new private sector lettings in Great Britain were deregulated in 1988. This has helped to stop the decline, and the sector has grown to nearly 10 per cent of households.

Administration

The Secretary of State for the Environment in England and the Secretaries of State for Wales, Scotland and Northern Ireland are responsible for formulating housing policy and supervising the housing programme.

The construction or structural alteration of housing is subject to building regulations laid down by the Government. In addition, warranty arrangements provided by the

National House-Building Council cover many new houses. It sets standards and enforces them by inspection, and provides cover against major structural defects for at least ten years.

Home Ownership

Over the last 40 years the proportion of people owning their own homes has risen from 29 per cent to 67 per cent. The number of owner-occupied dwellings in Great Britain amounted to over 15.4 million at the end of 1992, compared with 4.1 million in 1950. Most council tenants have the right to buy the homes they occupy. With a few exceptions, secure public tenants with at least two years standing are entitled to buy their house or flat at a discount dependent upon the length of the tenancy. Similar provisions are made for Scotland and Northern Ireland. A total of 1.5 million council, housing association and New Town houses were sold in Great Britain between April 1979 and the end of 1993.

Local authorities have been asked to

encourage low-cost home ownership in a variety of ways. Scottish Homes has a scheme to encourage private developers to build for owner-occupation or market rents in areas they would not normally consider. In 1994–95 the planned investment in the scheme is about £33.5 million. The Northern Ireland Co-ownership Housing Association has developed shared ownership there. In Wales, detailed guidance for local authorities and housing associations on the range of low-cost home ownership initiatives available was issued at the end of 1993.

> The Government has made £110 million available for cash incentive schemes in England in 1994–95. In such schemes, local authority and housing association tenants are given grants to help them purchase housing in the private sector. The homes released by these tenants moving out are then available to be re-let to those families in greatest housing need.

Type of Accommodation Occupied

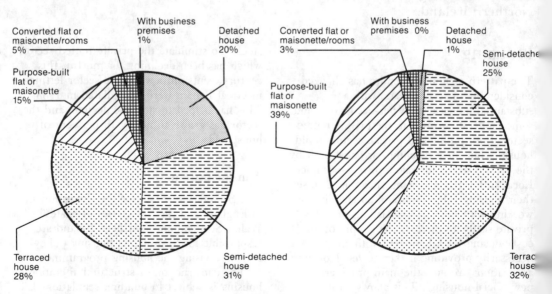

All households

- Converted flat or maisonette/rooms 5%
- With business premises 1%
- Detached house 20%
- Purpose-built flat or maisonette 15%
- Terraced house 28%
- Semi-detached house 31%

Local authority tenants

- Converted flat or maisonette/rooms 3%
- With business premises 0%
- Detached house 1%
- Semi-detached house 25%
- Purpose-built flat or maisonette 39%
- Terraced house 32%

Source: *General Household Survey 1992.*

Mortgage Loans

Most people buy their homes with a mortgage loan, with the property as security. Building societies are the largest source of such loans, although banks and other financial institutions also take a significant share of the mortgage market, while some companies make loans for house purchase available to their own employees. The amount that lenders are prepared to advance to a would-be house purchaser is generally calculated as a multiple of his or her annual income, typically up to two-and-a-half times earnings, and the term of the loan is commonly 25 years. Owner-occupiers get tax relief on interest payments on mortgages of up to £30,000 on their main home; since April 1994 this has been assessed at 20 per cent rather than the basic rate of 25 per cent, and from April 1995 will be assessed at 15 per cent.

High interest rates and problems of 'negative equity' caused by falling house prices in some regions created difficulties for many homebuyers in the late 1980s and early 1990s. A package of measures to protect homeowners from unnecessary repossession owing to arrears was announced by the Government in 1991. These include provision for benefits covering mortgage interest to be paid directly to lenders, and agreement with the mortgage lenders on the introduction of schemes to help borrowers in difficulty

Table 21.1: Average House Prices in Britain (£)

	New dwellings	All dwellings
1981	28,119	24,188
1982	28,205	23,644
1983	30,817	26,471
1984	33,080	29,106
1985	36,103	31,103
1986	43,562	36,276
1987	49,692	40,391
1988	61,873	49,355
1989	73,544	54,846
1990	75,037	59,785
1991	73,507	62,455
1992	73,190	60,821

Source: *Housing and Construction Statistics*

remain in their homes. Government figures show that mortgage possession orders in the first half of 1994 were 52 per cent down on the peak in the second half of 1991; figures from the Council of Mortgage Lenders show that the number of properties actually repossessed in the first half of 1994—at 25,000 less than 0.3 per cent of the number of mortgages—was 36 per cent lower than in the second half of 1991.

Social Housing

Public Sector Housing

Most of the public housing in Great Britain is provided by 460 local housing authorities. These are:

- the district councils in England and Wales, outside London;
- the London borough councils; and
- the district and islands councils in Scotland.

Public housing is also provided by the new town authorities, Scottish Homes (which has a stock of about 53,000 houses) and the Development Board for Rural Wales, although the latter is to transfer all its 1,200 houses to other social landlords by March 1996. The Northern Ireland Housing Executive is responsible for the provision and management of public housing in Northern Ireland. Public housing authorities in Great Britain own about 5 million houses and flats; the Northern Ireland Housing Executive owns 155,000 homes. Several local authorities have transferred all their housing stock to housing associations—involving 133,000 properties—and others are considering doing so.

Local authorities meet the capital costs of modernising their stock by:

- raising loans on the open market;
- borrowing from the Public Works Loan Board (an independent statutory body set up to make loans to local authorities);
- using part of the proceeds from the sale of local authority houses and other assets; or
- drawing on their revenue accounts.

Councils must maintain housing revenue accounts on a 'ring-fenced' basis to keep them separate from other council funds. Compulsory competitive tendering for local authority housing management is being phased in from April 1996 in England.[1] The Government provides local authorities in England and Wales with Housing Revenue Account Subsidy, worth nearly £4,400 million in England alone in 1994–95, mainly to cover the cost of rent rebates. Local authority housing investment programmes total over £1,500 million in England for 1994–95, and £295 million in Wales. In Scotland, Housing Support Grant of nearly £26 million is available for 1994–95; local authorities have been given £426 million in capital allocations to build new homes or improve existing ones. In Northern Ireland, the Housing Executive's capital programme is financed mainly by borrowing from government and receipts from house sales. In 1994–95 borrowing will total £86 million. Revenue expenditure is financed by rental income and by a government grant, which in 1994–95 is about £120 million.

Housing Associations

Housing associations, which are non-profit-making, are now the main providers of additional low-cost housing for rent and for sale to those on low incomes and in the greatest housing need. Many associations specialise in providing accommodation to meet the special needs of the elderly, disabled people and the mentally ill. The housing association sector is expanding rapidly; associations own, manage and maintain over 750,000 homes and about 65,000 hostel bed-spaces in England alone, providing homes for well over 1 million people; about 56,000 new homes for rent or shared ownership were provided in 1993–94.

People in housing need with insufficient income to obtain a mortgage for outright purchase may be able to buy a share in a house which a housing association has developed, or which they themselves have

chosen on the open market. They pay rent on the share retained by the association and may purchase it later if they wish. In Wales, the Government is also preparing to make available an assisted ownership scheme, under which the remaining share is provided by an interest-free loan from the housing association.

In Great Britain new housing schemes carried out by associations qualify for Housing Association Grant if the association concerned is one of about 2,800 registered with the Housing Corporation (in England), Scottish Homes or Housing for Wales. These three organisations are statutory bodies which supervise and pay grant to housing associations in their respective parts of Great Britain. Broadly similar assistance is available to associations in Northern Ireland.

The Government has increased the resources distributed to housing associations through the Housing Corporation's capital programme from £1,062 million in 1990–91 to about £1,500 million in 1994–95. The Government also aims to increase the amount of private finance being used by housing associations. This will allow more homes to be built with the available public resources than would otherwise be the case. It is anticipated that over 150,000 homes will be provided over the three years 1994–95 to 1996–97.

In 1994–95 Scottish Homes' approved development programme expenditure is £325 million, while it is expected that about £160 million of private finance will also be generated. Housing for Wales is managing a programme of £121 million in 1994–95, with a target of providing at least 3,900 new homes. On current plans, government provision to the housing association movement in Wales will be almost £500 million between 1991–92 and 1994–95. Private sector finance generated over the same period is forecast to reach almost £250 million. Northern Ireland's registered housing associations started 1,200 units of accommodation in 1993–94, and now have a stock of about 14,000 units for rent. They have a 1994–95 budget of £45 million, which, with an additional £9 million of private finance, is planned to provide

---

[1] This will come later in Scotland and Wales, following local government reorganisation.

1,000 new units of rented accommodation. Government plans provided for total funding of about £195 million over the period 1992–93 to 1995–96.

In England and Wales the rights of housing association tenants are protected under Tenants' Guarantees, which are issued by the Housing Corporation and Housing for Wales. They cover matters such as tenancy terms, principles for setting rent levels and the allocation of tenancies. Under these guarantees, tenants receive contractual rights in addition to their basic statutory rights, and associations are required to set and maintain rents at levels affordable by those in low-paid employment. In Scotland, similar non-statutory guidance, in the form of a model tenancy agreement, has been implemented as proposed jointly by Scottish Homes and the Scottish Federation of Housing Associations.

Following a Citizen's Charter commitment, the Government launched a Housing Association Tenants' Ombudsman Service in December 1993. The scheme, which covers England, allows independent investigation of tenants' complaints against their housing association, giving them a right similar to that for council tenants through the local government ombudsman. A similar scheme has been launched in Scotland, and one is being considered for Northern Ireland.

Other Voluntary Sector Bodies

As well as housing associations, other voluntary sector bodies have a role to play in housing matters. Such groups undertake a number of roles, for example advising people about their rights under housing law or encouraging energy efficiency in the home. To assist the work of such bodies the Government makes grants available. In England in 1994–95 a total of £306,000 is being made available to nine housing groups; in Scotland aid of nearly £852,000 in 1994–95 is being given to 17 voluntary bodies for work on homelessness and other housing matters.

Tenants' Rights

Legislation gives council tenants in England and Wales statutory rights, including security of tenure. Under the Tenants' Choice provisions, council tenants have the right to change their landlord. The effect of this is to increase choice for tenants, expose local authority housing to competition, and so raise service standards. Better management is also being provided through the new right to manage. This allows properly constituted tenants' associations the right to take over the management of their estates; 84 tenants' management organisations have been set up. The Leasehold Reform, Housing and Urban Development Act 1993 introduced a new right to improve, under which tenants can get compensation for improvements they carry out.

Government support is focused on tenants, through the housing benefit system, rather than on property. Depending on their personal circumstances, occupiers may qualify for housing benefit to help them pay their rent, whether their tenancy is public or private sector (see p. 332).

Housing for the Elderly

Sheltered housing, which comprises accommodation with an alarm system and the services of a resident warden, may be provided for elderly people who need support. Increasing emphasis is being placed on schemes to help elderly people to continue to live in their own homes, such as adaptations to existing housing to meet their needs. Home improvement agencies can help the elderly, people with disabilities and those on low incomes to carry out repairs and improvements to their properties. In England alone, over £4 million of government help in 1994–95 will go to support 125 home improvement agencies and a national co-ordinating body.

Rural Housing

Where there is an identified need for low-cost housing in rural areas, local authorities can exceptionally allow housing in areas where development would not normally be allowed, provided that the new housing can be reserved to meet those needs. The Housing Corporation has also funded a special rural programme to build houses in small villages: between 1989–90 and 1993–94 it approved the building of about 8,500 such homes. Housing for Wales has a major role in rural housing provision, targeting at least 25 per cent of its programme in rural areas. The Welsh Office also supports local authority schemes for rural housing undertaken in partnership with housing associations and others, for example, it announced £2.5 million of help for 15 schemes in April 1994. In Scotland, considerable progress is being made through the range of initiatives launched in 1990 as part of the Scottish Homes Rural Strategy. The Northern Ireland Housing Executive operates a rural strategy which directs special action both in public housing and also on the house renovation grant scheme for private housing, which it administers.

Privately Rented Housing

The number of households renting from private landlords declined to a low point of 8.6 per cent in the 1980s, but has now increased to 9.9 per cent. The Government's policy is to increase the availability of privately rented accommodation by removing disincentives to letting. To accomplish this, from January 1989 new private sector lettings were deregulated, and two new forms of tenancy were introduced:

- the assured tenancy, which gives the tenant long-term security in return for a freely negotiated market rent; and

- the assured shorthold tenancy (short assured tenancy in Scotland), which is for a fixed term of at least six months, again at a free market rent.

Tenants and most other residential occupiers may not be evicted without a court order. A 'Rent a Room' scheme encourages homeowners to let rooms to lodgers without having to pay tax on the rent they receive; rents of up to about £62 a week are now tax-free.

In Northern Ireland only certain pre-1956 properties subject to rent restriction come under statutory control. Rent levels are linked to those of the Northern Ireland Housing Executive. Both landlords and tenants may apply to a rent assessment committee for rent determination in cases where the current rent is considered to be inappropriate. Rent increases are allowed only for properties which meet a prescribed standard. The only assured tenancies in Northern Ireland are those on properties made available under the former Business Expansion Scheme; shorthold tenancies are available.

Improving Existing Housing

In urban areas of Britain slum clearance and redevelopment used to be major features of housing policy, but there has been a trend in recent years towards the retention of existing communities, accompanied by the modernisation and conversion of sub-standard homes. Housing conditions have improved considerably, but problems remain in some areas where there are concentrations of dwellings lacking basic amenities or requiring substantial repairs, and there are still some pockets of unfit housing for which demolition is the best solution. The emphasis now is on area renewal, with an integrated approach to renewal and renovation.

Estate Action Programme

The Estate Action programme, now part of the new Single Regeneration Budget (SRB—see p. 335), provides local authorities in England with additional resources to regenerate their run-down housing estates. These funds enable authorities to carry out an agreed package of measures on an estate, including physical refurbishment and improved management. By March 1993, Estate Action had made available £1,245 million to about 170 local authorities for over 1,000 schemes, improving about 400,000 homes. As part of this, the private sector has taken over and improved 24,000 homes and worked in partnership with local authorities in 300 schemes. The Estate Action budget in 1993–94 was £358 million,

and £373 million has been earmarked
within the SRB for Estate Action schemes
in 1994–95.

In Wales, Estate Partnership funding is
available to tackle the problems of selected
estates; £8.4 million of central government
money has been allocated for this in 1994–95
to supplement local authority and private
sector contributions.

Housing Action Trusts

Housing Action Trusts (HATs) focus
resources on some of the most run-down
areas of predominantly local authority
housing. The Government can designate a
HAT for a particular area or estate in
England or Wales, subject to a tenants' vote.
The HAT takes over responsibility for the
housing in its designated area in order to
renovate it, improve the housing
management, the environment and living
and social conditions, and stimulate local
enterprise. The tenants participate fully in
the work of a HAT. On completion of its
work, the Trust is wound up and its
property transferred to other owners and
managers, such as housing associations or
tenants' co-operatives, or back to the local
authority. Tenants are consulted on their
future landlords. Tenants as well as local
authorities may apply for the establishment
of a HAT. By August 1994 six HATs
had been established. Like Estate Action,
the HAT programme now forms part of
the SRB.

House Renovation Grants

About 1.6 million home renovation grants,
worth about £5,303 million, were paid in
respect of privately owned dwellings in
England and Wales between 1983 and 1993.
In England and Wales, local authorities give
mandatory renovation grants to enable unfit
dwellings to be brought up to the fitness
standard, with discretionary grants available
for a wider range of works. Grants of up to
100 per cent may be available, subject to a
test of the applicant's resources. Grants are
also available in certain circumstances for the
provision of facilities for disabled people and

for the repair of houses in multiple
occupation and of the common parts of
blocks of flats. Minor works assistance is also
available to help people in receipt of income-
related benefits, particularly the elderly, with
small-scale works.

In Scotland, local authorities give grants
for improvement and repair. Scottish Homes
also has the power to provide grants to
complement the role of local authorities in
private house renewal. In Northern Ireland,
grants are provided on a similar basis to that
in England and Wales through the House
Renovation Grants scheme, administered by
the Northern Ireland Housing Executive. In
isolated rural areas, a grant to replace
dwellings which cannot be restored is also
available through this scheme.

Renewal Areas

Renewal areas in England and Wales are
intended to provide a sharper focus to area
action, covering both renovation and selective
redevelopment and taking account of a range
of issues wider than just housing. Local
authorities can declare renewal areas where
certain conditions are met, such as the
physical condition of privately-owned houses
and the financial circumstances of their
owners. Authorities have additional powers to
buy land in renewal areas and to carry out
improvement works for which extra
government support is available.

In Scotland housing action area powers are
available for the improvement of areas in
which at least half the houses fail to meet a
statutory tolerable standard. Since 1975,
1,875 housing action areas have been
declared. Outside such areas in Scotland local
authorities have powers to apply
improvement orders to houses below the
statutory tolerable standard or lacking certain
basic amenities. Local authorities may also
give grants towards improving the
environment of mainly residential areas.

Considerable progress has been made in
improving housing conditions in Northern
Ireland. In total, 97 per cent of its dwellings
have all amenities, 91 per cent are classified
as fit and 89 per cent are in a good state of
repair. Urban renewal has been promoted

through redevelopment and housing action area activity. Since 1977, 53 housing action areas have been declared.

Homelessness

By law, local authorities have a duty to secure permanent accommodation for households which they accept as unintentionally homeless and in priority need. The latter category includes pregnant women, people with dependent children, and those who are vulnerable because of old age, mental or physical handicap or other special reasons. The number of homeless households in England has been falling since 1991 (see Table 21.2). In July 1994 the Government announced plans to reform the legislation on access to local authority and housing association tenancies, which would limit the duty of authorities to the provision of accommodation for a period of one year.

Over the period 1991–94, extra capital allocations have been given to housing authorities in Scotland for homelessness projects. In January 1994 the Government announced £4 million of additional funding to tackle homelessness in Wales. Local authorities were invited to present bids.

Table 21.2: Households in England Accepted as Homeless

1989[a]	122,180
1990[a]	140,350
1991[a]	144,780
1992	142,890
1993	134,190

Source: Department of the Environment
[a]1989, 1990 and first quarter 1991 figures are based on estimates in line with a new definition introduced in the second quarter of 1991.

Most homeless people have some form of accommodation, even though this may be temporary, overcrowded or otherwise unsatisfactory, and those entitled to rehousing are found accommodation by local authorities. Only a small proportion of the homeless are 'roofless'—that is, literally without accommodation and therefore forced to sleep rough. However, because there remains a number of people sleeping rough, especially in central London, the Government established the Rough Sleepers Initiative to tackle the problem in central London, with resources of £96 million. This has provided about 950 new places in short-term hostels and about 2,200 permanent and 700 leased places in accommodation for hostel dwellers to move on into. About £86 million has been made available to continue the Initiative until 1996, which will provide at least 1,500 more permanent homes, together with the professional help necessary to assist people to settle into a new life. Since 1990 more than £20 million has been spent by the Department of Health on the Homeless Mentally Ill Initiative, a programme to provide accommodation and psychiatric care for mentally-ill people who have been sleeping rough in central London. The Department has a three-year commitment to help with the running costs of the accommodation provided.

A voluntary sector count, held in May 1994, found that fewer than 270 people were sleeping rough in central London, compared with estimates of over 1,000 before the Rough Sleepers Initiative began.

Grants totalling £6.8 million are being made available to voluntary organisations which provide direct assistance to single people in need of accommodation. This includes £1.9 million to the National Homelessness Advice Service.

Regeneration

Economic trends in recent decades have altered the traditional locations and patterns of employment and brought profound changes to local economies. Many inner city areas have suffered from long-established industries moving out or closing, leaving problems of dereliction and unemployment. A report commissioned by the Government, *Assessing the Impact of Urban Policy*, was published in June 1994. It concluded that the gap between 57 urban priority areas and other places in England had narrowed in the period 1979–80 to 1990–91. Despite this progress, however, areas of deprivation still exist. Likewise, rural areas have had to adapt to declining employment in agriculture and the need in recent years to diversify away from farm production.

The Government is tackling urban problems in England with the new Single Regeneration Budget (SRB), announced in November 1993, which brings together 20 programmes from five government departments. Urban problems in Scotland, Wales and Northern Ireland are being tackled by Partnerships, the Programme for the Valleys and Belfast Action Teams respectively, as well as by many other government programmes. Other programmes and policies are addressing the needs of rural areas.

Single Regeneration Budget

The Secretary of State for the Environment has overall responsibility for the SRB. It is intended to promote more flexible and locally responsive forms of regeneration, building on the approach pioneered with the City Challenge initiative (see below). It came into operation in April 1994, with a budget of about £1,400 million in the first year. Existing commitments from the constituent programmes are being met, but as these commitments expire the money released will be allocated through a bidding procedure. There is about £100 million available for these bids in 1995–96.

As part of the same reforms, integrated Government Offices for the Regions (GORs) have been set up, combining the former regional offices of the Departments of the Environment, Employment, Trade and Industry, and Transport. There are also senior headquarters representatives in each office. The main programmes funded by the SRB are administered by the GORs. The work of the eight City Action Teams was subsumed within the GORs in April 1994. These teams were established to bring together officials of three government departments—Employment, Environment, and Trade and Industry—to ensure that their main programmes worked together effectively.

City Challenge

Under the City Challenge initiative, launched in 1991, local authorities were invited, in partnership with the private and voluntary sectors, local communities and government agencies, to submit imaginative and comprehensive plans for regenerating key neighbourhoods by tackling the problems of physical decay, lack of opportunity and poor quality of life. The best of these proposals are receiving government funding of £37.5 million over five years, subject to satisfactory progress being made towards achieving agreed targets and objectives.

There have been two rounds of the City Challenge competition. In the first pilot round, 11 of the 15 local authorities in England invited to submit bids were selected to draw up detailed plans for action, which commenced in April 1992. The 20 authorities successful in the second round competition began work on their five-year programmes in April 1993.

Over the five-year period to 1997–98, £1,162 million of City Challenge money is expected to attract over £3,000 million of private sector investment. A national evaluation of City Challenge is under way to measure the effectiveness of the initiative.

Task Forces

Task Forces were first set up in 1986 and are small teams which operate in the most deprived urban areas. They consist primarily of civil servants, but include secondees from local authorities and the private and voluntary sectors. Task Forces concentrate on the economic regeneration of designated inner city areas, by improving local people's employment prospects, by supporting training and education initiatives, and by identifying and removing barriers to their employment. They also aim to stimulate enterprise development and strengthen the capacity of communities to meet local needs. Once a Task Force area has improved prospects for continued regeneration and local organisations have been strengthened, the Task Force is closed. By March 1994 they had committed £148 million in support of 5,759 projects.

Urban Development Corporations

Twelve urban development corporations (UDCs) have been set up in England by the Government to reverse large-scale urban decline. The first two of these, London Docklands and Merseyside, were established in 1981. Ten others have since been set up: Birmingham Heartlands, Black Country (West Midlands), Bristol, Leeds, Central Manchester, Plymouth, Sheffield, Trafford Park (Greater Manchester), Teesside, and Tyne and Wear. These UDCs cover about 16,000 hectares (about 40,000 acres), and public expenditure on the programme will be £252 million in 1994–95.

By March 1994, the 12 English UDCs had led to the reclamation of 2,457 hectares (6,071 acres) of land, the construction of 27,500 homes, the construction of 5.4 million sq m (58.1 million sq ft) of industrial or commercial floorspace, and the creation of 152,300 permanent jobs. Private sector investment of £10,200 million had been attracted.

English Partnerships

English Partnerships, a new government regeneration agency, was launched in November 1993 and came fully into operation in April 1994. It was set up to promote the development of vacant, derelict and contaminated land throughout England. Its key objectives are to:

- stimulate local enterprise;
- create job opportunities; and
- improve the environment.

It will work in partnership with the public, private and voluntary sectors, and will be heavily involved in the Private Finance Initiative (see p. 153). It is funded within the SRB.

English Partnerships has taken over the work of English Estates and the Derelict Land Grant and City Grant programmes. For 1994–95, it has a budget of about £250 million, made up of grants from the Department of the Environment and receipts from its own activities. It is also eligible for assistance from the European Regional Development Fund (see p. 118). It has a land reclamation programme costing £102 million in 1994–95, including all the Derelict Land Grant commitments and more than 100 new schemes. The new schemes alone will reclaim 1,100 hectares (2,700 acres) of land by the end of the century.

English Partnerships will have a series of key output measures to ensure it meets its objectives. These will include the number of jobs created, the amount of private finance attracted and the area of land reclaimed.

Safer Cities

Higher than average crime rates, and the fear of crime, are particular problems in inner city areas. Safer Cities projects bring together all sections of the local community to tackle crime and the fear of crime. Since the programme's launch in 1988 over 3,600 crime prevention and community safety measures have been initiated, with funding of more than £22 million. The Government's objective is to double the number of Safer Cities projects established within the lifetime of the present Parliament. Nine new projects in England were announced in December 1993, and a further 20 projects are expected to be set up before the end of 1994. Examples of help include providing activities for young people otherwise likely to commit crime and fitting good quality locks to houses on estates with a high burglary rate. Successes include a 40 per cent reduction in burglaries on a Wolverhampton estate and a 60 per cent reduction in car crime in a Bradford car park.

Compacts

A number of schools/industry 'Compacts' have been introduced since August 1988 in many urban areas in England. Employers work with schools to guarantee a job with training for all school-leavers aged 16 to 18 who meet agreed targets for motivation and achievement. There are 50 Compacts in operation in inner city areas in England, with over 100,000 young people, 10,000 employers and 700 schools involved.

Regional Enterprise Grants

The Regional Enterprise Grant programme (see p. 200) has also been brought within the SRB. This supports investment and innovation projects in small firms in designated areas.

Other Measures

The first of a network of City Technology Colleges was opened near Birmingham in 1988; 15 are currently in operation. Intended to raise educational standards, the colleges are established jointly by government and industry. Although teaching the full National Curriculum (see p. 418), they emphasise science, technology and business understanding.

Training programmes such as Youth Training (see p. 180) and Training for Work (see p. 179) are helping many people in the inner cities. About one-third of the young people participating in Youth Training are from inner cities. There are about 110 Employment Service 'outreach' staff based in or visiting inner city areas, helping unemployed people look for jobs and encouraging them to participate in employment and training programmes. In 1992–93 there were about 500 inner city Jobclubs, many catering for people with literacy and numeracy or language difficulties. In addition, Employment Service regional directors have funds for innovative projects to help unemployed people in inner cities and other deprived areas back into work or training. Many of the independent Training and Enterprise Councils (see p. 195) are working in Task Force areas, City Challenge areas or other pockets of deprivation, and often play an important part in partnership approaches to regeneration.

The Government encourages tourism as a force for the improvement of inner city areas. Several major projects which create a cultural and artistic focus for inner city regeneration have been undertaken. Examples include the development of the Museum of Science and Technology in the Castlefields area of Manchester and the International Convention Centre in Birmingham. The English Tourist Board and regional tourist boards encourage promotional activities in inner city areas through local initiatives which bring together the tourist boards, local authorities, the private sector and other agencies.

In March 1994 the Government launched the Urban Forum, a new national body that brings together voluntary organisations involved in urban policy and regeneration. Its aim is to act as a communication channel between the voluntary sector and the Government, develop new ideas, and encourage local communities and voluntary groups to engage in regeneration partnerships.

City Pride

The Government announced its City Pride initiative in November 1993, at the same time as the establishment of the SRB. Civic and business leaders in three pilot cities— Birmingham, London and Manchester—have been invited to come forward with proposals for building on the strength of their areas. The GORs will work closely with the representatives of these cities.

European Union Programmes

Run-down areas in Britain benefit from the EU Structural Funds (see p. 118). These mainly come from the European Regional Development Fund (ERDF), which finances infrastructure projects and support for industry, among other things. Objectives for the Funds include regenerating areas affected by industrial decline and combating long-term unemployment, both problems common in inner city areas. The Department of the Environment is responsible for the co-ordination of ERDF programmes in the English regions. About £1,195 million has been allocated to declining industrial regions in England over the period 1994 to 1996.

Following a review of the Structural Funds, which took effect in January 1994, Merseyside qualifies for 'Objective 1' support—to promote economic development in underdeveloped regions. This justifies the highest level of Structural Funds support, and Merseyside stands to receive about £690 million from the Funds over the period 1994 to 1999.

Coalfield Areas Fund

The Coalfield Areas Fund was set up with the aim of alleviating the economic effects of colliery closures on local communities. A total of £5 million is being made available through the Fund in 1993–94 and 1994–95. This is supporting 36 projects put forward by 18 local authorities. It is estimated that about 1,700 jobs were created in 1993–94 and that about 46,000 sq m (494,000 sq ft) of new or improved business and commercial floorspace were provided.

Groundwork Trusts

Groundwork trusts, which work in partnership with public bodies, the private sector, voluntary organisations and individuals, aim to tackle environmental problems arising from dereliction and vandalism and to increase public awareness of the opportunities to change and improve local environments. Traditionally, such trusts have tended to concentrate on fringe urban or suburban areas, but increasingly they are also becoming involved in inner city areas. For example, a trust has recently been set up in the Hackney area of inner London. The Groundwork Foundation is a national body providing the trusts with advice and support.

Government funding for Groundwork in 1994–95 is £6 million in England; £401,000 is available in Wales. A target has been set of establishing 50 trusts in England and Wales by 1995, compared with 22 trusts in 1990–91.

Rural Development

The economy of the countryside has come under great pressure in recent years. Changes have included a greater tendency for commuters to live in rural areas, thus creating 'dormitory' villages, and the need for agricultural diversification following reform of the Common Agricultural Policy (see p. 275).

The Rural Development Commission (RDC) is the government agency set up to assist the economic and social development of the English countryside. It ensures that the needs and special circumstances of rural communities and businesses are taken into account when government policy is made. It has a local advisory role (particularly on planning matters), provides support for voluntary activity and assists selected activities in rural areas, such as housing, transport and village shops. The RDC spent £35.4 million in 1992–93 and its budget has been increased to £43 million for 1994–95.

A wide range of programmes is available, including:

- grants for the conversion of redundant buildings to workspace;
- business loans to top up funding for viable projects which cannot be completely financed by the private sector;
- measures to support the provision of affordable housing in the countryside;
- measures to support the provision of out-of-school childcare; and
- grants and loans for village halls.

The RDC's main economic programmes are concentrated in priority rural development areas (RDAs), which cover about 35 per cent of the area of England and take in over 2.7 million people. The Rural Challenge initiative, launched in February 1994, offers six awards, worth an extra £1 million a year, to these RDAs. Some rural areas are also eligible for help from the ERDF; a total of £381 million has been allocated to England over the period 1994 to 1999. The Government has put forward plans for the six English regions designated for this support.

Enterprise and Simplified Planning Zones

Since 1981 the Government has set up 33 enterprise zones. Each zone runs for a period of ten years from designation; most of the zones have therefore already reached the end of their lives. Benefits in the zones include:

338

- exemption from the national non-domestic rate (the local property tax payable by non-domestic property owners);
- 100 per cent allowances for corporation and income tax purposes for capital expenditure on industrial and commercial buildings; and
- a much simplified planning system.

In January 1995 there will be five zones operating, including two extensions. Three further zones are expected to be designated shortly afterwards in the East Midlands, East Durham and the Dearne Valley, South Yorkshire, in response to job losses in the mining industry. At present there is no intention to extend the enterprise zone scheme generally, although new zones may be created in exceptional circumstances.

Simplified planning zones (SPZs) can help local authorities to secure development in parts of their areas. An SPZ scheme, which also lasts for ten years, provides full planning permission for specified types of development. Like enterprise zones, from which the concept was derived, SPZs are useful as part of an overall package to generate private sector interest in an area. The procedures for establishing an SPZ were recently streamlined to encourage their use. By March 1993, there were six zones in operation.

Public Sector Land

The Department of the Environment is currently increasing its efforts to promote the sale and development of vacant and under-used public sector land. Information is being assembled on key sites with development potential, and where there are no firm plans to market or develop land, action will be taken to encourage and promote the sale of sites. Since 1989, registers of unused or under-used public sector land have been maintained by the owners. Under the 'Public Request to Order Disposal' scheme, members of the public are encouraged to request the Secretary of State to order public bodies to dispose of such land on the open market.

In January 1994 the rules governing the way local authorities can spend the proceeds of asset sales were altered to encourage the sale of surplus land. This has the effect of increasing the proportion of the proceeds that councils can spend on new capital projects in those cases where they have had to spend money preparing the land for sale.

Wales, Scotland and Northern Ireland

Wales

A new Strategic Development Scheme was launched in Wales in April 1994, into which the previous Urban Programme was subsumed. Funding is £55.5 million in 1994–95, and economic and environmental projects will receive priority. In addition, Urban Investment Grant encourages private-sector developments on derelict and run-down sites in urban areas; the 1994–95 budget is almost £8.7 million.

> The Government announced Urban Investment Grant for 11 development projects in the first six months of 1994. Public support of nearly £8 million will secure more than £45 million of private investment and create about 950 permanent jobs.

The Government aims to remove much of the remaining major industrial dereliction in Wales by the end of the 1990s. The Welsh Development Agency (see p. 200) may acquire and reclaim derelict land or make grants to local authorities for that purpose. Land use is also encouraged by the Land Authority for Wales, a statutory body with powers to make land available for development in circumstances where the private sector would find this difficult or impossible.

The first Programme for the Valleys, which ran from 1988 to 1993, was an extensive scheme of economic and urban regeneration, covering an area of about 2,200 sq km (860 sq miles) in the south Wales valleys. In April 1993 the Secretary of State for Wales launched a new five-year Programme. It builds on the success of the first Programme by continuing many of its measures, and also introducing new initiatives for the social, economic and environmental regeneration of the Valleys. The five aims of the new Programme are to:

- create more, better-quality jobs;
- improve training, education and transport, so that local people can benefit;
- improve the quality of the environment;
- improve the quality and choice of housing; and
- improve the health of local people.

The Cardiff Bay Development Corporation was set up in 1987 to bring forward redevelopment in an area of south Cardiff, once its commercial centre. By August 1994 the Corporation had received £220 million in government grant. Government support for the Corporation in 1994–95 will be £48 million. The Corporation's regeneration strategy includes the construction of a £147 million barrage across Cardiff harbour mouth, which will create a large freshwater lake and 12 km (7 miles) of waterside frontage. Work commenced on the barrage in May 1994 and is scheduled to be completed in 1998. It is expected that with the barrage more than 23,000 new jobs will be created in the Cardiff Bay area, 4,400 new homes built and over £1,200 million of private investment attracted.

Scotland

In 1988 the Government set out in the White Paper *New Life for Urban Scotland* its strategy for improving the quality of life for people living on peripheral estates in Scotland. Building on the experience gained from inner city regeneration schemes such as the Glasgow Eastern Area Renewal, the main aim of the strategy was to encourage residents to take more responsibility for the improvement of their own communities. A review of urban regeneration policy in Scotland was launched in October 1993, and decisions on the outcome are scheduled to be announced in late 1994.

The focus of regeneration effort is four Partnerships in areas of Dundee, Edinburgh, Glasgow and Paisley. These are led by The Scottish Office and involve other bodies and groups, including Scottish Enterprise (see p. 200), Scottish Homes (see p. 330), the local authorities, the private sector and the local communities. Their objectives include plans to:

- improve the quality and tenure mix of housing available to local people;
- improve employment prospects by providing increased avenues for training and further education; and
- tackle social and environmental problems on the estates.

> Almost 30 per cent of the housing stock in the Partnership areas has now been renovated, with over 6,500 homes refurbished and 1,300 new homes built. Local authority ownership has declined from 97 per cent to 73 per cent, with owner-occupation increasing from 2.5 per cent to 10 per cent and community ownership from less than 1 per cent to 12 per cent.

Other peripheral estates and inner city areas continue to receive substantial support through such sources as the Urban Programme, Scottish Homes and Scottish Enterprise. Scottish Homes is leading 11 Smaller Urban Renewal Initiatives, in which it is investing £24 million in 1994–95. The Government is committed to seeking ways to improve the Partnerships and to strengthening the Urban Programme in Scotland by emphasising those projects which form part of a concerted effort to assist a deprived area.

The Urban Programme has grown from £44 million in 1988–89 to £85 million in 1994–95. About 1,200 projects will be supported in 1994–95. Five Safer Cities programmes have been launched in Scotland, including schemes in Aberdeen, Edinburgh, Glasgow and Dundee. Four are still in existence, and £855,000 will be invested in them by central government in 1994–95.

The Local Enterprise Companies (LECs— see p. 195), working under contract to Scottish Enterprise, have substantial budgets and a flexible range of powers and functions to improve the environment and encourage business and employment in their areas. In particular, Scottish Enterprise operates a Local Enterprise Grants for Urban Projects scheme, which aims to encourage private sector investment for projects in deprived areas. The areas of need in which the scheme operates include the four Partnership areas, and other areas showing similar characteristics of deprivation. LECs can also support projects in their areas. Responsibility for derelict land reclamation rests with Scottish Enterprise, the LECs and Highlands and Islands Enterprise. They may acquire and reclaim land either by agreement or compulsorily; increasingly they seek to work with the private sector to bring land back into use.

The Compact scheme (see p. 337) has been introduced in Scotland, with 12 Compacts in operation. In all, 7,400 young people are involved with the Compacts, as are many of the 10,500 employers and business organisations in Education Business Partnerships in Scotland. The Training and Employment Grants scheme is designed to increase access to employment opportunities for young and long-term unemployed people.

Northern Ireland

Urban Development Grant is the principal urban regeneration measure in Northern Ireland, with projected expenditure of £3.6 million in 1994–95. It is targeted at the most run-down parts of Belfast and Londonderry. Grants may also be paid to landowners who restore or improve derelict sites in Northern Ireland.

A comprehensive development programme aims to revitalise the commercial areas of Belfast. In 1993–94 regeneration programmes have a combined allocation of over £34 million. Nine Action Teams have been established to tackle the problems of particularly deprived areas of the city. The 'Making Belfast Work' initiative, launched in 1988, is designed to reinforce the efforts to alleviate the economic, educational, social and environmental problems in the most disadvantaged areas of Belfast. In addition to extensive funding already allocated to mainstream departmental programmes, Making Belfast Work has provided a further £144 million approximately for the period 1988–89 to 1994–95. The Laganside Corporation was established in 1989 to regenerate Belfast's riverside area. Its government grant in 1993–94 is £5.3 million.

The Community Regeneration and Improvement Special Programme aims to regenerate disadvantaged smaller towns. It is jointly funded by the Department of the Environment for Northern Ireland and the International Fund for Ireland. A total of 33 small towns have been assisted since the programme was started in 1990.

Further Reading

Assessing the Impact of Urban Policy. HMSO, 1994.
Housing. Aspects of Britain series. HMSO, 1993.
New Life for Urban Scotland. HMSO, 1988.

Annual Reports
Building Societies Commission. HMSO.
Housing and Construction Statistics. HMSO.
The Housing Corporation. Housing Corporation.
The Rural Development Commission. RDC.

22 Planning and Conservation

Britain seeks to balance the demands for land from business, housing, transport, farming and leisure, and to protect the environment by means of a statutory system of land-use planning and development control. Government agencies and voluntary bodies work to conserve Britain's natural heritage and historic monuments; over 500,000 important buildings and 6,700 sites of special scientific interest receive statutory protection.

PLANNING

Direct responsibility for land-use planning in Great Britain lies with local authorities. The Secretaries of State for the Environment, Wales and Scotland have overall responsibility for the operation of the system. The Department of the Environment brings together the major responsibilities in England for land-use planning, housing and construction, countryside policy and environmental protection. The Welsh Office and The Scottish Office have broadly equivalent responsibilities. In Northern Ireland the Department of the Environment for Northern Ireland is responsible for planning matters through six divisional planning offices, which work closely with the district councils.

In England and Wales the departments provide national and regional guidance on planning matters, while strategic planning at the county level is the responsibility of the county councils. District councils are responsible for local plans and development control, except with regard to minerals and waste, which are 'county matters'.[1] In London and the former metropolitan counties, there is a unitary planning system. The boroughs and metropolitan districts prepare unitary development plans and are responsible for development control.

In Scotland, The Scottish Office provides national planning guidance. Planning functions are undertaken by regional and district councils, whose responsibilities are divided on a basis broadly similar to that in England and Wales. In the more rural regions and the islands, the regional and islands councils respectively have responsibility for all planning functions.

Development Plans

The Government is committed to a 'plan-led' system of development control. This has been

---

[1] Local government reorganisation (see p. 74) is likely to affect the division of responsibility for planning matters in many parts of the country.

reflected in recent legislation. The preparation of district-wide development plans is mandatory, and planning applications have to be determined in accordance with the statutory development plan, unless other material considerations indicate otherwise. This has, in effect, introduced a presumption in favour of proposals that accord with the development plan.

The present development plan system in England and Wales involves structure, local and unitary development plans:

- structure plans, setting out broad policies for the development and use of land, are adopted by county councils, which also draw up local plans for minerals and, in England, waste;

- local plans, prepared in general conformity with the adopted structure plan, and providing detailed guidance for development expected to start within about ten years, are adopted by district councils and National Park authorities; and

- unitary development plans, setting out both strategic and detailed land use and development policies, are adopted by metropolitan districts or London boroughs.

Members of the public are encouraged to become involved in the formulation of plan policies and proposals. They can formally object and make their case in public to an independent inspector.

In Scotland structure plans are prepared by regional or islands authorities, and local plans by those districts with planning responsibilities, and in some rural areas by regional planning and islands authorities. Under Northern Ireland's single-tier system, plans are prepared by the Department of the Environment for Northern Ireland.

When formulating their plans, planning authorities must take account of any strategic or regional guidance issued by the Secretary of State and any statements of government planning policy.

The Government's aim is for full use—having regard to the quality of the urban environment—to be made of urban land in existing towns and cities, so avoiding the need to develop 'green field' sites and reducing transport demands. In 1987, the most recent year for which reliable figures are available, virtually half of all new urban land uses involved land that was already urban.

> The Department of the Environment's Planning Policy Guidance note on transport, published in March 1994, aims to reduce the need to travel and to maximise the development potential of existing centres. The careful selection by local planning authorities of locations for new development, close to existing facilities and readily served by public transport, will reduce journey lengths and maximise the choice of means of transport other than the car.

Green Belts

'Green Belts' are areas intended to be left open and free from inappropriate development. Their purposes are to:

- restrict the sprawl of large built-up areas;

- safeguard the surrounding countryside;

- prevent neighbouring towns merging;

- preserve the special character of historic towns; and

- assist in urban regeneration.

They also have a recreational role. Green Belts have been established around major cities, including London, Aberdeen, Dundee, Edinburgh, Glasgow, Merseyside, Greater Manchester and the West Midlands, as well as several smaller towns. Some 1.5 million hectares (3.8 million acres) are designated as Green Belt in England and 150,000 hectares (370,000 acres) in Scotland. The Government attaches great importance to the protection of Green Belts and expects local planning authorities to do likewise when considering planning applications.

Development Control

Most development requires specific planning permission, apart from certain minor proposals. Applications are dealt with in the light of development plans and other material planning considerations, including national and regional guidance. In 1993 about 470,000 applications for planning permission were received in England alone; in total, about 370,000 applications were granted in this period. The Government has set local authorities a target of determining 80 per cent of applications within eight weeks. In recent years there has been steady progress towards this target (see Table 22.1).

Local planning authorities in England and Wales are required to publicise planning applications locally. Methods commonly used include site notices, newspaper advertising and notifying neighbours. In Scotland the applicant is required to notify the owners, occupiers and, in some cases, lessees of land and buildings adjoining the site of a proposed development when the application is submitted to the planning authority. Newspaper advertisement is required for certain types of development.

The applicant has a right of appeal to the Secretary of State if the local authority refuses planning permission, grants it with conditions attached, or fails to decide an application within eight weeks (or whatever longer period is agreed with the applicant). The great majority of appeals are decided on the basis of written submissions. However, either party has the right to be heard by an inspector (or 'reporter' in Scotland) at a public local inquiry or, where a less formal arrangement is appropriate, at a hearing. A local inquiry is usually held for more complicated or controversial applications. Similar provision is made in Northern Ireland for the hearing of representations at public inquiries; for planning applications which do not give rise to public inquiries, the applicant has a right of appeal to the independent Planning Appeals Commission.

The Secretaries of State can direct that a planning application be referred to them for decision. This power to 'call in' is generally exercised only for proposals which raise planning issues of national or regional importance. The applicant and the local planning authority have the right to be heard by a person appointed by the Secretary of State, and a public inquiry will normally be held. In Northern Ireland, major planning applications are dealt with under the Planning (NI) Order 1991, which allows for a public inquiry in certain circumstances.

Environmental Impact Assessment

Planning applications for certain types of development must be accompanied by an environmental impact assessment. This should describe the likely environmental effects and measures to minimise them. These statements are made available to the public and to statutory bodies such as the Countryside Commission and English Nature (see p. 348). The planning authority must take into consideration the environmental statement, and any representations received on it, before granting planning permission.

Table 22.1: Planning Applications and Decisions, England

	Total applications determined (thousands)	Percentage within eight weeks
1988–89	620	52
1989–90	595	46
1990–91	518	53
1991–92	483	60
1992–93	441	63
1993–94	448	65

Source: Department of the Environment

Recent legislation requires that local authorities take account of environmental considerations when drawing up their development plans. To assist them in this, in November 1993 the Government published a good practice guide on the environmental appraisal of development plans.

Architectural Standards

High standards in new building are encouraged by the Government, although it advises local planning authorities not to impose their architectural tastes on developers. The Department of the Environment, in collaboration with the independent Royal Institute of British Architects (RIBA) and the National House-Building Council, sponsors the biennial Housing Design Awards Scheme for England and Northern Ireland, with categories for renovation and new building. Scotland and Wales have similar award schemes. Royal Fine Art Commissions for England and Wales and for Scotland advise government departments, planning authorities and other public bodies on questions of public amenity or artistic importance.

The RIBA, the principal professional body for architects, together with the Architects Registration Council of the United Kingdom, exercises control over standards in architectural education and encourages high architectural standards in the profession. The Royal Incorporation of Architects in Scotland is allied to it, as is the Royal Society of Ulster Architects.

CONSERVATION

Britain has a long tradition of conservation, and for many years has had policies and laws designed to protect both its natural environment and built heritage. For example, the first Act of Parliament to protect old buildings, the Ancient Monuments Protection Act, was passed in 1882 and the Protection of Wild Birds Act in 1880. A wide variety of designations are used to protect areas, sites and monuments that are of special interest to conservationists, and various organisations work towards the conservation of differing aspects of Britain's national heritage.

Britain participated fully in the United Nations Conference on Environment and Development (UNCED), popularly known as the 'Earth Summit', held in Rio de Janeiro in June 1992, and is committed to carrying the process forward. Among the agreements reached was a framework convention on climate change (see p. 361), a convention on biodiversity (see p. 353), 'Agenda 21' (an action framework for the 21st century), a declaration setting out clear principles for sustainable development, and a declaration for the management of forests.

In January 1994, Britain published its national strategies for sustainable development, climate change (see p. 361), biodiversity (see p. 353) and forestry. The sustainable development strategy describes the likely state of the British environment over the next 20 years, the pressures on it and the ways in which various sectors of the economy might develop more sustainably. Britain's impact on the world environment is also described. The plan builds on the White Paper *This Common Inheritance* (see p. 346), but does not replace it, looking much more fundamentally at the rationale of different sectoral policies and opportunities that may be worth pursuing. The strategy includes the establishment of three bodies to assist policy on sustainable development:

- an independent advisory panel, which will be consulted on issues of major strategic importance to sustainable development;

- a 'round table', which will bring together interests such as business, local government and academics to discuss these matters with ministers; and

- a Citizens' Environment Initiative, an independent committee which will seek to persuade individuals and groups to commit themselves to sustainable development.

Administrative Arrangements

The Department of the Environment is responsible for countryside policy and environmental protection in England; the Department of National Heritage has responsibility for the listing of buildings and for scheduled ancient monuments. The Welsh Office, The Scottish Office and the Department of the Environment for Northern Ireland have broadly equivalent responsibilities. Agencies such as English Nature, English Heritage, the Countryside Commission and their equivalents carry out many functions on behalf of the Government. In addition, the local authorities and a wide range of voluntary organisations are actively involved in environmental conservation and protection.

This Common Inheritance

The environment White Paper *This Common Inheritance*, published in September 1990, was the first comprehensive statement by the Government of its policy on issues affecting the environment. It summarised more than 350 proposals for tackling such diverse issues as global warming, pollution control, the regulation of land use and planning, the rural economy, the countryside and wildlife. Three progress reports have been published. The most recent, published in May 1994, set out over 100 new commitments and listed progress on over 500 commitments from previous years.

Buildings and Monuments

Lists of buildings of special architectural or historical interest are compiled by the Government, in England with the advice of English Heritage. It is against the law to demolish, extend or alter the character of any 'listed' building without prior consent from the local planning authority or the appropriate Secretary of State. The local planning authority can issue temporary 'building preservation notices' to protect unlisted buildings that are at risk, allowing consideration to be given to listing. The Department of the Environment for Northern Ireland is directly responsible for the listing of buildings there.

Ancient monuments are similarly protected through a system of scheduling. English Heritage, the government agency responsible for the conservation of historic remains in England, has embarked upon a programme to evaluate all known archaeological remains in England. This is expected to result in a significant increase in the number of scheduled monuments. A similar effort is being made to increase the number of listed buildings and scheduled monuments in Wales.

Many of the royal palaces and parks are open to the public; their maintenance is the responsibility of the Secretaries of State for National Heritage and for Scotland. English Heritage manages about 400 properties on behalf of the Secretary of State for National Heritage, advises him on applications for consent to alter or demolish scheduled monuments and listed buildings, and gives grants for the repair of ancient monuments, historic buildings and buildings in conservation areas in England. Most of its monuments are open to the public. Government funding for English Heritage is £104 million in 1994–95.

In Scotland and Wales similar functions are performed by Historic Scotland, which

Table 22.2: Scheduled Monuments and Listed Buildings

	Listed buildings	Scheduled monuments
England	443,000	14,500
Wales	16,000	2,700
Scotland	41,000	6,000
Northern Ireland	8,000	1,100
Britain	**508,000**	**24,300**

Source: Department of National Heritage

cares for 330 monuments, and by Cadw: Welsh Historic Monuments, which manages 129, with advice from an Ancient Monuments Board and Historic Buildings Council for each country. Historic Scotland and Cadw are executive agencies within The Scottish Office and the Welsh Office respectively. The Department of the Environment for Northern Ireland has 173 historic monuments in its care, and is advised by a Historic Buildings Council and a Historic Monuments Council.

Local planning authorities have designated more than 8,000 'conservation areas' of special architectural or historic interest in England; there are over 400 in Wales, 674 in Scotland and 40 in Northern Ireland. These areas receive special protection through the planning system. Grants and loans are available from the appropriate historic buildings and monuments body for works which make a significant contribution towards the preservation or enhancement of a conservation area.

The National Heritage Memorial Fund helps towards the cost of acquiring, maintaining or preserving land, buildings, works of art and other items of outstanding interest which are also of importance to the national heritage. Government funding totals £8.7 million in 1994–95. It will also act as the distributing body for the heritage share of the proceeds from the National Lottery (see p. 493). In 1993–94 the Fund assisted in the preservation of 61 heritage items.

Industrial, Transport and Maritime Heritage

Britain was the first country in the world to industrialise on a large scale, and many advances in manufacturing and transport were pioneered in Britain. This has resulted in a large industrial heritage, the importance of which is being increasingly recognised. Key sites are scheduled or listed; one of the most important, the Ironbridge Gorge, where Abraham Darby (1677–1717) first smelted iron using coke instead of charcoal, has been designated a World Heritage Site (see p. 354). Other museums have also been set up, devoted to the preservation of industrial buildings and equipment.

Britain, which pioneered railways, has a fine heritage of railway buildings and structures, and there is an active movement to preserve it. Volunteers are very active in this. A large number of disused railway lines have been bought by railway preservation societies and returned to operation, often using preserved steam locomotives, and several railway museums have been established.

Reminders of Britain's maritime past are also preserved. The historic naval dockyard at Chatham has been opened to the public; at Portsmouth HMS *Victory*, Nelson's flagship, HMS *Warrior*, the world's first iron battleship, and the remains of *Mary Rose*, an early 16th-century warship, raised from the seabed in 1982, are open to the public. The Imperial War Museum has preserved the cruiser HMS *Belfast*, which is open to the public in the Pool of London. Isambard Kingdom Brunel's SS *Great Britain*, the world's first large screw-driven ship, is preserved in Bristol. A voluntary body, the Maritime Trust, has been established to preserve vessels and other maritime items of historic or technical interest. The Trust's vessels include the clipper *Cutty Sark* at Greenwich.

Voluntary Sector

Among the organisations which campaign for the preservation and appreciation of buildings are:

- the Society for the Protection of Ancient Buildings;
- the Ancient Monuments Society;
- the Georgian Group;
- the Victorian Society;
- the Twentieth Century Society;
- the Architectural Heritage Society of Scotland;
- the Ulster Architectural Heritage Society;
- the Architectural Heritage Fund; and
- the Council for British Archaeology.

While funded largely by private donations, the amenity societies have paid professional staff and statutory responsibilities, in recognition of which they receive government support.

The National Trust (for Places of Historic Interest or Natural Beauty), a charity with over 2 million members, owns and protects 230 historic houses open to the public, in addition to over 235,000 hectares (580,000 acres) of land in England, Wales and Northern Ireland. Scotland has its own National Trust. The Civic Trust makes awards for development and restoration work which enhances its surroundings. It undertakes urban regeneration projects and acts as an 'umbrella' organisation for nearly 1,000 local amenity societies. There are associate trusts in Scotland, Wales and north-east England.

The Countryside and Nature Conservation

Four government agencies are currently responsible for countryside policy and nature conservation in Great Britain:

- the Countryside Commission and English Nature, which both act in England;
- the Countryside Council for Wales (CCW); and
- Scottish Natural Heritage (SNH).

The Joint Nature Conservation Committee (JNCC) is the mechanism through which the three nature conservation agencies in England, Wales and Scotland fulfil their responsibilities for international nature conservation matters and those affecting Great Britain as a whole. The JNCC also undertakes research and sets standards for data, monitoring and other matters. It includes representatives from Northern Ireland and independent members, and has a supporting specialist staff.

Countryside Agencies

The Countryside Commission, the CCW and SNH are responsible for enhancing the natural beauty and amenity of the countryside and encouraging the provision of facilities for open-air recreation. They are expected to respect the needs of those who live and work in the countryside. Activities

aided by these bodies include the provision by local authorities (sometimes in association with other bodies) and private individuals of country parks and picnic sites, often within easy reach of towns; the provision or improvement of recreational paths; and the encouragement of amenity tree-planting schemes. The countryside agencies undertake research projects and experimental schemes, often working in consultation with local authorities and voluntary organisations. They give financial assistance to public, private and voluntary organisations, and individuals carrying out countryside conservation, recreation and amenity projects.

The Countryside Commission runs the Countryside Stewardship scheme, which offers incentives to farmers and other land managers to enhance valuable landscapes and habitats and improve access to the countryside. It now incorporates the Hedgerow Incentive Scheme. A total of 3,900 agreements have been made, covering 80,000 hectares (198,000 acres) and programmes involving 1,640 km (1,025 miles) of hedge restoration. The scheme is to transfer to the Ministry of Agriculture, Fisheries and Food in April 1996. In Wales an equivalent scheme is being run on a pilot basis by the CCW. Called Tir Cymen, it adopts a slightly different approach in that it applies to entire farms.

> Total funding for the countryside agencies in 1994–95 is £46 million for the Countryside Commission, £20.6 million for the CCW and £39.9 million for SNH. SNH's budget represents an increase of more than 10 per cent in cash terms.

The Countryside Commission recognises over 210 country parks and over 230 picnic sites in England. A further 35 country parks and about 30 picnic sites in Wales are recognised by the CCW. In Scotland there are 36 country parks, and many local authority and private sector schemes for a variety of countryside facilities have been approved for grant aid by SNH.

Nature Conservation Agencies

English Nature, the CCW and SNH are responsible for nature conservation in their areas. This includes:

- establishing and managing nature reserves;
- advising the Government;
- identifying and notifying Sites of Special Scientific Interest (SSSIs);
- providing general nature conservation information and advice;
- giving grants; and
- supporting and conducting research.

English Nature's funding for 1994–95 is £42 million.

There are over 300 national nature reserves covering some 190,000 hectares (468,000 acres) in Great Britain, and two statutory marine nature reserves, surrounding the islands of Lundy, off the Devon coast, and Skomer, off the coast of Dyfed. About 6,700 SSSIs have been notified in Great Britain for their plant, animal, geological or physiographical features. Local authorities have declared about 340 local nature reserves in England and 21 in Wales. The Environmentally Sensitive Areas scheme (see p. 277) also helps to protect wildlife.

In England, to assist those who have an interest or involvement in environmental planning and conservation action, English Nature has mapped and is describing 'Natural Areas'. These have a distinctive character that derives from the underlying geology, land forms, flora and fauna, and the land uses and settlement patterns of the area. The Natural Areas framework, which has been subject to public consultation, will underpin all of English Nature's work in future.

County wildlife trusts, urban wildlife trusts and the Royal Society for the Protection of Birds (RSPB) play an important part in protecting wildlife, having established between them over 2,000 reserves. The county and urban trusts are affiliated to a parent organisation, the Royal Society for Nature Conservation. The RSPB is the largest voluntary wildlife conservation body in Europe.

English Nature enters into land management agreements with owners and occupiers of SSSI land, increasingly to support management that is beneficial for its wildlife and natural features. Overall, English Nature's grant schemes provide more than £2 million to assist local action to sustain biodiversity and geodiversity.

In Northern Ireland both nature and countryside conservation are the responsibility of the Environment Service. In 1994–95 funding for its conservation measures is some £6.5 million. The Council for Nature Conservation and the Countryside advises the Department on nature conservation matters, including the establishment and management of land and marine nature reserves and the declaration of Areas of Special Scientific Interest. About 44 national nature reserves have been established and 40 Areas of Special Scientific Interest declared.

Wildlife Protection

Wildlife in Great Britain is protected principally by the Wildlife and Countryside Act 1981. This has:

- extended the list of protected species;
- restricted the introduction into the countryside of animals not normally found in the wild in Britain; and
- afforded greater protection for SSSIs and introduced provision for marine nature reserves.

There is also provision for reviews of the list of protected species to be conducted by the three official nature conservation agencies, acting jointly through the JNCC, every five years and for the revised list to be submitted to the Secretary of State for the Environment. In Northern Ireland separate legislation on species and habitat protection is in line with the rest of Britain.

Species Recovery and Reintroduction

Extensive research and management are carried out to encourage the recovery of populations of species threatened with extinction. The three nature conservation

349

agencies have also set up recovery programmes for a number of threatened species of plants and animals. English Nature's programme covers 25 species, including the dormouse, the Plymouth pear and the fen raft spider. The aim is to ensure the survival of self-sustaining populations of these species in the wild.

Schemes have been devised to reintroduce species into areas in which they used to be found. For example, the red kite had died out in England and Scotland, although it was still found in Wales and mainland Europe. An international project was co-ordinated by the JNCC and the RSPB to bring adult birds from Sweden and Spain and release them into the wild in areas which the species no longer inhabited. Other species reintroduced in recent years include the white-tailed sea eagle and the Large Blue butterfly. The Royal Botanic Gardens at Kew holds seeds from about 3,000 plant species which are extinct or under severe threat in the wild, and has had some success with reintroduction projects.

Tree Preservation and Planting

Tree preservation orders enable local authorities to protect trees and woodlands in the interests of amenity. Once a tree is protected, it is in general an offence to cut down, reshape or generally wilfully destroy it without permission. The courts can impose substantial fines for breaches of such orders. Where protected trees are felled in contravention of an order or are removed because they are dying, dead or dangerous, a replacement tree must be planted. Local authorities have powers to enforce this.

Tree planting is encouraged through various grant schemes. The planting of broadleaved trees has increased tenfold since 1985. Major new initiatives include a project to create a new national forest in the Midlands and 12 community forests near large towns and cities.

The Coast

Local planning authorities are responsible for planning land use at the coast; they also attempt to safeguard and enhance the coast's natural attractions and preserve areas of scientific interest. The protection of the coastline against erosion and flooding is administered centrally by the Ministry of Agriculture, Fisheries and Food, the Welsh Office and The Scottish Office. Operational responsibility lies with local authorities and the National Rivers Authority (see p. 266). Certain stretches of undeveloped coast of particular scenic beauty in England and Wales are designated as heritage coast; jointly with local authorities, the countryside agencies have designated 45 heritage coasts, protecting 1,525 km (948 miles). English Nature, through its Campaign for a Living Coast, provides funds for groups setting up voluntary marine nature reserves or producing management plans for England's estuaries. So far, seven voluntary marine nature reserves have been grant-aided and 21 estuary management plans produced, covering 70 per cent of England's total estuarine area. There are 29 marine consultation areas in Scotland. Statutory bodies taking decisions that affect these areas will be asked to consult SNH.

The National Trust, through its Enterprise Neptune campaign, raises funds to acquire stretches of coastline of great natural beauty and recreational value. About £18 million has been raised so far and the Trust now protects 850 km (528 miles) of coastline in England, Wales and Northern Ireland. The National Trust for Scotland also owns large parts of the Scottish coastline and protects others through conservation agreements.

National Parks, Areas of Outstanding Natural Beauty and National Scenic Areas

The Countryside Commission and the CCW can designate National Parks and areas of outstanding natural beauty (AONBs), subject to confirmation by the Secretaries of State for the Environment and for Wales respectively.

Ten National Parks have been established in England and Wales. Their aim is first to provide protection for the outstanding countryside they contain and secondly to provide opportunities for access and outdoor recreation. They are 'national' in the sense that they are of value to the nation as a whole. However, most of the land remains in private hands. Special National Park authorities have been set up, one for each park. Among other things, they:

- act as the development control authority for their areas;

- negotiate land management agreements and encourage farmers to manage their land in the traditional way;

- look after footpaths and negotiate agreements for public access; and

- set up information centres and employ rangers.

At present, most of these authorities are committees of county councils for the relevant areas. However, the Government has announced its intention to establish new independent authorities to run all the parks. This is designed to allow better protection

and management of the park areas. The Norfolk and Suffolk Broads have their own independent authority and enjoy protection equivalent to that of a National Park. It is intended that the New Forest in Hampshire should enjoy similar protection.

A total of 40 AONBs have been designated, covering around 19,600 sq km (7,600 sq miles) in England and 830 sq km (320 sq miles) in Wales. They comprise parts of the countryside which lack extensive areas of open country suitable for recreation and hence National Park status, but which nevertheless have an important landscape quality. Local authorities are encouraged to give special attention to AONBs in their planning and countryside conservation work.

In Scotland there are four regional parks and 40 National Scenic Areas, covering more than 10,000 sq km (4,000 sq miles), where certain kinds of development are subject to consultation with SNH and, in the event of a disagreement, with the Secretary of State for Scotland. Working parties have made

Broadleaved Tree-planting 1970-71 to 1991-92

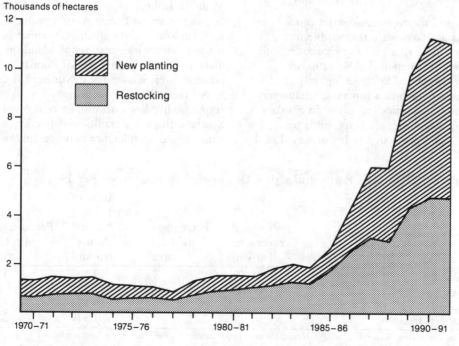

Source: Forestry Commission

recommendations for the management of the Cairngorms and for Loch Lomond and the Trossachs, two areas of outstanding natural importance in Scotland. The Government intends to announce decisions on these during 1994–95, and the increased funding for SNH (see p. 348) will enable the agreed recommendations to be implemented. In the wider countryside SNH provides grants for a range of countryside projects.

In Northern Ireland the Council for Nature Conservation and the Countryside advises the Department of the Environment for Northern Ireland on the preservation of amenities and the designation of areas of outstanding natural beauty. Nine such areas have been designated, covering 2,850 sq km (1,100 sq miles); seven areas are being managed as country parks and one as a regional park.

There are 11 forest parks in Great Britain, covering some 2,400 sq km (950 sq miles) and administered by the Forestry Commission. There are nine in Northern Ireland, where they are administered by the Forest Service of the Department of Agriculture.

Public Rights of Way and Open Country

County and metropolitan district councils in England and Wales are responsible for keeping public rights of way signposted and free from obstruction. Public paths are usually maintained by these highway authorities, which also supervise landowners' duties to repair stiles and gates. In Scotland, planning authorities are responsible for asserting and protecting rights of way. Local authorities in Great Britain can create paths, close paths no longer needed for public use and divert paths to meet the needs of either the public or landowners. Farmers in England and Wales are required by law rapidly to restore public paths damaged by agricultural operations. In England and Wales there are some 225,000 km (140,000 miles) of rights of way. There are 11 approved national trails in England and Wales, covering over 3,100 km (1,900 miles), and three approved long-distance routes in Scotland, covering about 580 km (360 miles). The Countryside Commission intends to help authorities bring all rights of way in England into good order by the end of the century, and a Parish Path Partnership scheme has been introduced, which is designed to stimulate local involvement and improvement. By early 1994, 27 local authorities had joined the scheme, which is receiving £3.8 million of government funding. The CCW is also establishing a network of public rights of way, and a Public Paths Campaign has been introduced.

There is no automatic right of public access to open country, although many landowners allow it more or less freely. Local planning authorities in England and Wales can secure access by means of agreements with landowners. If agreements cannot be reached, authorities may acquire land or make orders for public access. Similar powers cover Scotland and Northern Ireland; in Northern Ireland the primary responsibility lies with district councils. In Scotland there is a tradition of freedom to roam, based on tolerance between landowners

Table 22.3: National Parks and Other Designated Areas, December 1993

	National Parks area (sq km)	Percentage of total area	Areas of Outstanding Natural Beauty[a] (sq km)	Percentage of total area
England	9,631	7	19,595	15
Wales	4,098	20	833	4
Scotland	–	–	10,173	13
Northern Ireland	–	–	2,849	20

Sources: Countryside Commission, Scottish Natural Heritage, Department of the Environment for Northern Ireland
[a] National Scenic Areas in Scotland.

and those seeking reasonable recreational access to the hills.

Common land totals an estimated 600,000 hectares (1.5 million acres) in England and Wales, but a legal right of public access exists to only one-fifth of this area. Common land is usually privately owned, but people other than the owner may have various rights over it, for example, as pasture land. Commons are protected by law and cannot be built on or enclosed without the consent of the Secretaries of State for the Environment or Wales. There is no common land in Scotland or Northern Ireland.

Voluntary Sector

Many voluntary organisations are concerned to preserve the amenities of the countryside, including the Council for the Protection of Rural England, the Campaign for the Protection of Rural Wales, the Association for the Protection of Rural Scotland and the Ulster Society for the Preservation of the Countryside.

International Action

Britain plays a full part in international action to conserve wildlife. Its international obligations include the Berne Convention on the conservation of European wildlife and natural habitats, and EC directives on the conservation of wild birds (the Birds Directive) and of natural habitats and wild fauna and flora. The implementation of the latter directive, which came into force in 1994, entails the designation of Special Areas of Conservation (SACs). Together with Special Protection Areas (SPAs) designated under the Birds Directive, the SACs will contribute to a Community-wide network of protected sites to be known as 'Natura 2000'. Some 91 SPAs have already been designated.

Britain is also party to the Ramsar Convention on wetlands of international importance. A total of 86 sites in Britain have been designated under this convention, together with a further site in one of Britain's dependent territories. Other conservation measures promoted by the Government have included a ban (in conjunction with other EU countries) on the import of whale products and harp and hooded seal pup skins, and stricter controls for the protection of wild birds. Britain is a party to the Convention on International Trade in Endangered Species of Wild Fauna and Flora, which prohibits commercial trade in highly endangered species and regulates trade in less threatened species by means of a permit system.

The Convention on Biological Diversity was signed by over 150 countries, including Britain, at the June 1992 'Earth Summit'. It requires countries to develop national strategies for the conservation and sustainable use of biological diversity. Britain's action plan for implementing this was published in January 1994. Drawn up after extensive consultation, it provides a strategy for the protection of biodiversity in Britain in the next 10–20 years. The key objectives of this are to conserve and, where practicable, enhance:

- the overall population and natural ranges of native species and the quality and range of wildlife habitats and ecosystems;
- internationally important and threatened species, habitats and ecosystems;
- species, habitats and natural and managed ecosystems that are characteristic of local areas; and
- the biodiversity of natural and semi-natural habitats where this has been diminished over recent decades.

The plan commits the Government to increasing public awareness of the conservation of biodiversity and to contributing to biodiversity conservation on a European and global scale. A steering group which is taking forward these commitments will be responsible for developing a range of targets for key species and habitats for 2000 and 2010; these will be published in 1995.

The Darwin Initiative forms part of the measures announced by Britain at the UNCED meeting. It is intended to make British experience available to developing countries with important biological resources. Some £9 million will be made available over the first four years of the Initiative. By December 1993, 31 projects, totalling £3.7 million, had been approved.

Environmental Improvement

The Government assists local voluntary organisations to promote projects such as creating parks, footpaths and other areas of greenery in cities; conserving the industrial heritage and the natural environment; and recycling waste. The Department of the Environment makes grants through the Environmental Action Fund, managed by the Civic Trust, worth about £850,000 in 1994–95, to support projects with either direct or indirect environmental gains. The Civic Trust also manages a Local Projects Fund, from which some £300,000 will be available in 1994–95.

The Welsh Office has made £556,000 available in 1994–95 to voluntary organisations under its Environment Wales initiative. The Scottish Office Environment Department is making £400,000 available in 1994–95 to environmental organisations under its Special Grants (Environmental) Programme, and a further £435,000 to UK2000 Scotland, a partnership between central and local government, voluntary bodies and the private sector, which carries out practical environmental improvements. Scottish Enterprise and Highlands and Islands Enterprise (see p. 200) are responsible for environmental improvement and land reclamation in Scotland. The Government's programme of Environmentally Sensitive Areas (see p. 277) supports environmentally sensitive practices that protect and enhance the countryside.

World Heritage Sites

Britain is well represented in the World Heritage List, which was established under the World Heritage Convention to identify and secure lasting protection for those parts of the world heritage of outstanding universal value. So far 13 sites in Britain have been listed. These are:

- Canterbury Cathedral, with St Augustine's Abbey and St Martin's Church, in Kent;
- Durham Cathedral and Castle;
- Studley Royal Gardens and Fountains Abbey, in North Yorkshire;
- Ironbridge Gorge, with the world's first iron bridge and other early industrial sites, in Shropshire;
- the prehistoric stone circles at Stonehenge and Avebury, in Wiltshire;
- Blenheim Palace, in Oxfordshire;
- the city of Bath, in Avon;
- Hadrian's Wall;
- the Tower of London;
- the Palace of Westminster, Westminster Abbey and St Margaret's, Westminster, also in London;
- the islands of St Kilda, in Scotland;
- the castles and town walls of King Edward I, in north Wales; and
- the Giant's Causeway and Causeway Coast, in Northern Ireland.

Support for these sites under various programmes can be considerable. For example, projects assisted by the Welsh Office are under way to regenerate the town centres of both Caernarfon and Conwy in north Wales. Likewise, Durham Cathedral will receive £95,000 in government repair grant in 1994–95.

Further Reading

Conservation. Aspects of Britain series, HMSO, 1993.

Environmental Appraisal of Development Plans: a Good Practice Guide. HMSO, 1993.

Environmental Protection and Water Statistics. Annual report. HMSO.

Planning. Aspects of Britain series, HMSO, 1992.

This Common Inheritance: the Third Year Report. HMSO, 1994.

23 Control of Pollution

For more than a century Britain has been developing policies to protect the environment against pollution from industry and other sources. Laws were introduced at an early stage to control air and water pollution—for example, the Alkali Act 1863 and, more recently, the Clean Air Acts 1956 and 1968. Legislation, revised regularly to meet changing circumstances, sets out a wide range of powers and duties for central and local government, covering all types of pollution, from greenhouse gases to litter. Successes include a 69 per cent reduction in mercury inputs to coastal waters between 1985 and 1992, and a fall of over 40 per cent in sulphur dioxide emissions since 1970.

Introduction

Britain supports international co-operation on matters of environmental protection. Increasingly, much of Britain's legislation on pollution control is being developed in collaboration with other member states of the European Union and organisations such as the Organisation for Economic Co-operation and Development and the United Nations and its agencies. Britain is taking a leading position in the development of a European ecolabelling scheme. Recently, with increasing scientific understanding of global pollution problems, the Government has been considering how its own policies and actions can be further guided by the principle of 'sustainable development', the theme of a major United Nations conference in June 1992 (see p. 361). Assistance is also given to developing countries for environmental projects, while an Environmental Know How Fund was set up in 1992 to help Central and Eastern Europe and the former Soviet Union.

Britain has pledged £89 million to replenish the Global Environment Facility, a United Nations fund set up to help developing countries tackle global environmental problems. This includes a voluntary contribution to ensure that the Facility's target of $2,000 million is reached.

Administration

Executive responsibility for pollution control is divided between local authorities and central government agencies. Central government makes policy, exercises general budgetary control, promotes legislation and advises pollution control authorities on policy implementation. The Secretary of State for the Environment has general responsibility for co-ordinating the work of the Government on environmental protection. In Scotland and Wales the respective Secretaries of State are responsible for pollution control co-ordination within their countries. In Northern Ireland, this responsibility rests with the Department of the Environment for Northern Ireland. Local authorities also have important duties and powers. They are responsible for matters such as:

- collection and disposal of domestic wastes;

- keeping the streets clean from litter;

- control of air pollution from domestic and from many industrial premises; and

- noise and general nuisance abatement.

The National Rivers Authority (NRA) is responsible for monitoring water quality and the control of water pollution in England and Wales, on which it is expected to spend £88 million in 1994–95. In Scotland, the river purification authorities have statutory responsibility for water pollution control; the seven mainland authorities forecast expenditure of over £13 million in 1994–95. In Northern Ireland, water quality is monitored by the Environment Service of the Department of the Environment for Northern Ireland. In England and Wales Her Majesty's Inspectorate of Pollution (HMIP) has an important role in the control of emissions to land, air and water from certain industrial processes through the mechanism of 'integrated pollution control' (see p. 357). Her Majesty's Industrial Pollution Inspectorate (HMIPI) is the Scottish equivalent of HMIP.

The Government intends to introduce legislation to bring together the functions of HMIP and the NRA, together with those presently exercised by waste regulation authorities, into a single Environment Agency. Likewise, subject to legislation, a Scottish Environment Protection Agency would be set up to combine the functions of HMIPI, the river purification authorities and the waste regulation and some of the air pollution functions of the district and islands councils.

An independent standing Royal Commission on Environmental Pollution advises the Government on national and international matters concerning the pollution of the environment, on the adequacy of research and on the future possibilities of danger to the environment. So far it has produced 18 reports.

Business and Consumer Involvement

The Government has launched a number of initiatives to help business improve its environmental performance, ensure business concerns are taken into account when policy is made, and help consumers assess firms' environmental credentials. For example, the Government launched a new Environmental Technology Best Practice Programme in June 1994. It will concentrate on providing information to business about the cost-effective reduction of pollution and waste. Priority areas for the programme will be chosen in consultation with industry.

Advisory Committee on Business and the Environment

The Advisory Committee on Business and the Environment comprises 26 business leaders, appointed by the Government and serving in a personal capacity. Its roles are:

- advising the Government on environmental issues of concern to business;

- providing a link with international business initiatives on the environment; and

- helping to mobilise the business community through demonstrating good environmental practice.

Much of the Committee's work is carried on through working groups which concentrate on a particular area, for example transport or waste management.

British Standard on Environmental Management

In January 1994 the British Standards Institution (see p. 207) published BS7750, the world's first standard for environmental management systems. Having been tested in a wide range of businesses and other bodies, the standard can be used by any organisation. BS7750 shares many features of the widely-used BS EN ISO 9000—formerly BS5750—quality management standard.

Eco-management and Audit

In 1993 the European Union adopted a regulation setting up a voluntary EU-wide scheme of eco-management and audit, which will become fully operational throughout the EU in April 1995. Although it is intended primarily for the manufacturing, power and waste disposal sectors, Britain is extending its use to other sectors. An adaptation has been published for use by local government. Registration will be of individual sites[1] rather than companies' entire operations. A company or council must have an environmental policy before any of its sites or units can be registered. An essential component is an environmental management scheme, such as BS7750, which has been designed to be fully compatible with the scheme. Those seeking registration must have prepared and published an environmental statement which, together with the management system, needs to have been verified by an accredited independent body. A full cycle of review, verification and published statement must be conducted at least once every three years.

Each EU member state is required to have a competent body to maintain a register of sites. In Britain, the Department of the Environment is responsible.

[1] Or of operational units in the case of local authorities.

Ecolabelling

Increasingly consumers wish to take environmental considerations into account when buying goods. Britain has played a leading role in developing the EU ecolabelling scheme. This voluntary scheme aims to help consumers identify those products which are less harmful to the environment over their whole lifecycle. Member states are developing criteria for awarding ecolabels on a wide spectrum of consumer goods—apart from food, drink and pharmaceuticals, which have been excluded from the scheme. In 1993 Britain's ecolabelling board awarded the first European ecolabels to Hoover Ltd for washing machines in its 'New Wave' range.

Integrated Pollution Control

Under the Environmental Protection Act 1990, a system of 'integrated pollution control' (IPC) is being phased in to control certain categories of industrial pollution. The potentially most harmful processes are specified for IPC, and require authorisation from HMIP. The NRA is responsible for monitoring waters receiving discharges authorised under IPC. Emissions to air from more minor processes are controlled under a parallel system of local authority air pollution control In granting authorisation for releases under IPC, HMIP requires the use of the best available techniques not entailing excessive cost to prevent or minimise polluting emissions and to ensure that any releases are made harmless. The staff of the Inspectorate has been increased considerably to allow the full implementation of IPC.

In Scotland, IPC is administered by HMIPI jointly with the river purification authorities. In Northern Ireland broadly similar controls are exercised by the Environment Service, and proposals are being formulated for the introduction of a system of air pollution control similar to IPC.

The Government is pressing for the introduction of IPC on the British model within the EU.

Land

Certain local authorities are designated as waste collection, waste disposal or waste regulation authorities, responsible for different parts of the process of dealing with controlled wastes. Legislation has also established a licensing system for waste disposal sites, treatment plants and storage facilities receiving controlled wastes. It provides for a more intensive control system for special wastes, namely those which contain or consist of substances dangerous to life. HMIP, the NRA and the Hazardous Waste Inspectorate for Scotland may advise local authorities on how to improve their control of waste management and on how to work towards environmentally acceptable standards for dealing with hazardous wastes. In Northern Ireland, similar advice is offered to district councils by the Environment Service.

Part II of the Environmental Protection Act, which came into force in May 1994, strengthened existing controls on waste disposal. Responsibility for proper handling of waste falls on everyone who has control of it from production to final disposal or reclamation. Authorities are able to refuse licences if the applicant is not a fit and proper person. Operators now remain responsible for their sites until the waste regulation authority is satisfied that no future hazard is likely to arise. In England and Wales local authorities' waste disposal operations are being transferred to 'arm's length' companies or private contractors so as to separate them from the authorities' other jobs of setting policies and standards, and enforcement. The proposed Environment Agency would take over local authority waste regulation functions.

In Scotland, responsibility for the collection and disposal of refuse and the regulation of waste management activities remains with the district and islands councils, whose waste management function is examined by the Hazardous Waste Inspectorate. The proposed Scottish Environment Protection Agency would take over waste regulation. In Northern Ireland, responsibility for the collection, disposal and regulation of waste rests with the district councils.

In November 1993 the Government published a consultation paper on its proposals for dealing with polychlorinated biphenyls (PCBs), environmentally harmful chemicals whose main remaining use is in electrical transformers and capacitors. It is proposed that PCB stocks would have to be registered by the end of 1995 and destroyed by the end of 1999.

Litter

It is a criminal offence to leave litter in any public place in the open air or to dump rubbish except in designated places. The maximum penalty was raised in 1992 to £2,500. The Act also introduced new duties on local authorities to keep their public land as free of litter and refuse (including dog faeces) as practicable and new powers for the public to take action against those who fail to comply with their responsibilities.

To help counteract the problem of litter, financial support—totalling £2.9 million in 1994–95—is given to the Tidy Britain Group, which is recognised as the national agency for litter abatement. It provides a comprehensive litter abatement programme in collaboration with local authorities and the private sector. The Group secures sponsorship from industry to undertake litter abatement promotions and programmes such as its Neighbourhood Care Scheme.

London came out best in a recent litter survey carried out in nine European cities. The survey, which looked at four key types of central area, awarded London 77 points out of a possible total of 100, just ahead of Berne with 76 points.

Recycling and Materials Reclamation

The Government encourages the reclamation and recycling of waste materials whenever this is practicable; its target is for half of all recyclable household waste to be recycled by 2000. Under the Environmental Protection Act 1990, local authorities have to make plans for the recycling of waste. The Act also requires waste disposal authorities in England to pay 'recycling credits' to waste collection authorities to pass on the equivalent in disposal costs where waste is recycled. From April 1994 the credits were increased so that the full amount saved must be passed on. In Wales and Scotland, the same authorities handle waste collection and disposal. The Government has supported pilot recycling initiatives in Sheffield, Cardiff, Dundee and the county of Devon, which have tested a variety of collection and sorting methods.

Members of the public can deposit used glass containers for recycling in bottle banks. There are nearly 15,000 such sites in Britain, and over 1,000 can banks. There are also nearly 3,000 paper banks and, in some places, plastics or textiles banks. In addition, voluntary organisations arrange collections of waste material, and can be paid a recycling credit by the local authority for doing so.

Water

In general, it is against the law to allow any polluting matter to enter water in Britain except in accordance with a legal authorisation. In England and Wales the NRA's principal method of controlling water pollution is through the regulation of all effluent discharges into groundwaters, inland and coastal waters (except those releases subject to IPC, which are controlled by HMIP). Discharge consents issued by the NRA specify what may be discharged and set limits on the volume and content of effluent, in order to achieve appropriate water quality standards. The NRA maintains public registers containing information about discharge consents, authorisations from HMIP and water quality. HMIP maintains registers of authorisations and associated monitoring. Similar arrangements apply in Scotland, where control is exercised by the river purification authorities. In Northern Ireland the Environment Service is responsible for controlling water pollution.

Government regulations for a new system of classifying water quality in England and Wales came into force in May 1994. This system will provide the basis for setting water quality objectives. The objectives, which will be phased in gradually, will specify for each individual stretch of water the standards that should be reached and the target date for achieving them. The system of statutory water quality objectives will provide the framework for the NRA to set discharge consents. Once objectives are set, the NRA will be under a duty to use its powers to ensure that they are met.

Over the past 30 years, notable progress has been made in cleaning up the previously heavily polluted major estuaries of the east coast of England and Scotland—the Thames, Humber, Tees, Tyne and Forth—which now support varied populations of fish and other wildlife. A 25-year scheme, supported by the Government and the EU, aims to reduce river pollution and improve water quality throughout the Mersey river basin and estuary. Other major schemes in progress include programmes to improve water quality in the Clyde in Scotland and the Lagan in Northern Ireland.

More than 95 per cent of the population in Britain live in properties connected to a sewer, and sewage treatment works serve over 80 per cent of the population. In England and Wales the water industry is planning to spend about £14,000 million (at 1989 prices) up to the year 2000 on improving sewerage, sewage treatment and disposal, and a further £10,000 million within the period 2000–2005. Progressively higher treatment standards for industrial waste effluents and new measures to combat pollution from agriculture are expected to bring further improvements in water quality. In Scotland, sewage treatment and disposal come within the water and sewerage programme, which will total more than £728 million in the three years to 1995–96.

The Government is committed to meeting the requirements of a number of EC directives for the protection and improvement of water quality, for example on drinking water, bathing water (see p. 360), urban waste water, freshwater fisheries, and dangerous substances and groundwater.

Bathing Waters and Coastal Sewage Discharges

The Government has announced investment of around £2,200 million by the water industry to provide treatment of coastal sewage discharges and improve the quality of Britain's bathing waters. All but a handful of schemes in the bathing water improvement programme should be largely complete by the end of 1995. In the 1993 tests of bathing water quality, it was found that 80 per cent of identified bathing waters (365 out of 457) in Britain met the mandatory coliform bacteria standards of the EC bathing water directive, compared with 66 per cent of beaches in 1988. The Government expects virtually all bathing waters to meet the directive's standards by the end of 1995. Sea dumping of sewage sludge will be terminated by the end of 1998.

Marine Environment

In 1992 a new Convention for the Protection of the Marine Environment of the North East Atlantic was agreed in Paris. It covers both land and sea, sets targets for the introduction of additional safeguards for the area, and requires contracting parties to take all possible steps to prevent or eliminate pollution through an action plan subject to annual review. Britain is also a leading participant in the series of North Sea Conferences, an international forum of countries bordering the North Sea. Good progress is being made in meeting North Sea Conference targets for reducing the input of dangerous substances into the sea. For example, direct and riverine inputs of cadmium and mercury to coastal waters were more than halved between 1985 and 1992.

International action on the prevention of pollution from ships is taken through the International Maritime Organization (IMO). Britain applies international requirements to all ships in British waters and to British ships wherever they are. Enforcement is undertaken by the Department of Transport. Work is continuing within the IMO on further measures.

The Marine Pollution Control Unit (MPCU), part of the Coastguard Agency, is responsible for dealing with spillages of oil or other hazardous substances from ships at sea. The arrangements for dealing with pollution are set out in the Government's national contingency plan, developed and maintained by the MPCU. The Unit has at its disposal various counter-pollution facilities, including:

● remote sensing surveillance aircraft;
● aerial and seaborne spraying equipment;
● stocks of oil dispersants;
● mechanical recovery and cargo transfer equipment; and
● specialised beach cleaning equipment.

In order to minimise the environmental effect of offshore oil and gas operations, special conditions designed to protect the environment are included in licences for oil and gas exploration. These conditions are set in consultation with a number of bodies with environmental interests, including the relevant government departments and the Joint Nature Conservation Committee (see p. 348). Applicants for licences in sensitive areas are required to demonstrate that they have addressed the environmental concerns when developing their work programme. Before commencing offshore operations, the operators are required to have oil spill contingency plans. In addition, all discharges that contain oil are controlled under the Prevention of Oil Pollution Act 1971, and limits are set for the permissible level of oil discharged. In response to requests from the North Sea Conference, progressively tighter limits on oil discharged with drill cuttings have been set. This has resulted in the quantity of oil discharges from this source from installations in British waters falling from 18,500 tonnes in 1988 to 3,900 tonnes in 1993.

Britain ended the dumping of industrial waste at sea in 1992. Waste has not been licensed for incineration at sea since 1990. Under the North East Atlantic Convention, and the earlier convention it replaces, the dumping at sea of most types of waste will be phased out over the next few years. In February 1994 Britain announced that it was accepting an internationally-agreed ban on the sea dumping of low and intermediate level radioactive waste.

Air

Air quality in Britain has improved considerably in the last 30 years. Total emissions of smoke in the air have fallen by over 85 per cent since 1960. London and other major cities no longer have the dense smoke-laden 'smogs' of the 1950s and in central London winter sunshine has increased by about 70 per cent since 1958. However, new concerns have arisen, especially over the emissions from the growing number of motor vehicles and the possible impact on health. Measures have consequently been adopted to reduce substantially emissions from new vehicles (see p. 363).

Responsibility for clean air rests primarily with local authorities. Under the Clean Air Act 1993[2] and the Clean Air (Northern Ireland) Order 1981 they may declare 'smoke control areas' within which the emission of smoke from chimneys is an offence. About two-thirds of the dwellings in conurbations are covered by smoke control orders—around 6,340 are in force. Those industrial processes with the greatest potential for harmful emissions are controlled under the Environmental Protection Act 1990, in England and Wales by HMIP, and are becoming subject to IPC. Processes with a significant but lesser potential for air pollution require approval from local authorities. Also, under the Clean Air Act, local authorities control emissions of dark smoke from trade and industrial premises. The 1990 Act also provides local authorities in England and Wales with streamlined powers to deal with statutory nuisances, including smoke, dust and smells.

Britain's automatic air quality monitoring network is being extended and upgraded at a cost of £10 million. The target is for all major cities to be covered by the end of 1997. Since 1990, daily air pollution data from the monitoring network has been made available to the public by the Department of the Environment's Air Quality Bulletins. These give the concentrations of three main pollutants—ozone, nitrogen dioxide and sulphur dioxide—and grade air quality on a scale between 'very poor' and 'very good'. The information features in television and radio weather reports, and appears in many

national and local newspapers. The data are also available on a special free telephone number and on videotext systems.

A comprehensive government review of urban air quality is being undertaken. Three independent committees of experts are advising on different aspects of the problem, and are setting guidelines and targets for air quality. For example, in spring 1994 the introduction of air quality standards for benzene and ozone were recommended.

Climate Change

The greenhouse effect is a natural phenomenon keeping the earth at a temperature which can sustain life. But increasing man-made emissions of 'greenhouse gases', such as carbon dioxide (CO_2), methane and nitrous oxide (N_2O), are leading to greater concentrations of these gases in the atmosphere. In 1988 the United Nations Environment Programme and the World Meteorological Organisation established the Intergovernmental Panel on Climate Change (IPCC) to consider climate change and possible responses to it. Britain chairs the working group which assesses the scientific evidence on climate change. In its first report, the IPCC concluded that man-made emissions would lead to additional warming of the earth, and that, without any change in emissions, global average temperature would increase by about 0.3°C a decade, which would be faster than at any time over the past 10,000 years. Such changes could have major effects on the world. The IPCC is currently preparing an update of this assessment.

Britain played a leading role in the negotiations towards the United Nations framework convention on climate change, which was opened for signature at the Earth Summit in Rio de Janeiro in June 1992. This commits parties to the convention to devising and reporting on proposed measures to combat climate change. Chief among its obligations for developed countries is a commitment to prepare programmes aimed at returning emissions of greenhouse gases to 1990 levels by 2000. There is also a commitment to help

[2] This Act consolidated earlier legislation on air pollution, including the Clean Air Acts 1956 and 1968.

developing countries take measures to deal with the problem. The convention came into force in March 1994.

In January 1994 Britain published its national programme for combating the threat of global climate change. It is estimated that the measures in the programme will reduce emissions of CO_2 by 6 per cent, of methane by 10 per cent and of N_2O by 75 per cent by 2000. The programme includes:

- the introduction of VAT on domestic fuel and higher duties on road vehicle fuel;

- the creation of an Energy Saving Trust, which aims to promote the efficient use of energy, particularly in the home;

- tighter building regulations to promote the energy efficiency of new houses and business premises;

- government publicity on energy conservation in homes and businesses; and

- targets for energy saving in central and local government offices.

> Government funding for the Home Energy Efficiency Scheme is to be nearly doubled. The extra £35 million will enable the scheme to be extended to all pensioners and disabled people.

Britain is also conducting extensive research into global warming. The Department of the Environment's expenditure on research related to climate change will be £16 million in 1994–95. The research programme includes the work of the Hadley Centre for Climate Prediction and Research, which was opened in 1990 to build on the Meteorological Office climate modelling programme, and the construction of an advanced climate change detection instrument for launch on a satellite towards the end of the 1990s.

Ozone Layer

The Government is committed to the earliest possible phasing out of all ozone-depleting substances. Britain was one of the first 25 signatories to the Montreal Protocol, which deals with the protection of the ozone layer, and hosted the second meeting of the parties in 1990, which substantially strengthened the protocol. The protocol was further strengthened in 1992, and now requires chlorofluorocarbons (CFCs), 1,1,1 trichloroethane and carbon tetrachloride to be phased out by the end of 1995. The supply of halons was phased out by the end of 1993. There is provision for exemptions for any essential uses. Controls were also introduced on methyl bromide and on hydrochlorofluorocarbons (HCFCs—transitional substances with less ozone-depleting capacity than CFCs), which are needed in a number of areas if industry is to move away from CFCs quickly but which will themselves be phased out by 2030. European Community regulations require CFCs and carbon tetrachloride to be phased out by the end of 1994, again with exemptions for any essential uses, and are likely to impose controls on HCFCs and methyl bromide tighter than those in the protocol.

Emissions of Sulphur Dioxide and Oxides of Nitrogen

Sulphur dioxide (SO_2) and oxides of nitrogen (NO_x) are the main gases that lead to acid rain. The principal sources are combustion plants that burn fossil fuels, such as coal-fired power stations, and, for NO_x, road transport. National SO_2 emissions have fallen by over 40 per cent since 1970 and the Government has initiated a substantial programme to ensure that this fall continues. For example, under the EC directive on the control of emissions from large combustion plants, the Government has published a national plan setting out phased reductions in emissions from existing plants of NO_x to 1998 and of SO_2 to 2003. Negotiations on a new United Nations agreement on acid rain were expected to have reached a conclusion by mid-1994; Britain indicated its willingness to reduce sulphur emissions by 2005 by 70 per cent compared with 1980.

The damaging effect of acid depositions

from combustion processes on freshwaters and soils has been demonstrated by scientific research. The Government is spending about £10 million a year on an extensive research programme into the causes and effects of acid rain, and the likely results of possible abatement technologies. Lower emissions of SO_2 over the past 20 years (see graph) have led to the first signs of a decrease in acidification in some lochs in south-west Scotland.

Vehicle Emissions

There are about 25 million vehicles on Britain's roads, contributing substantially to Britain's total emissions of carbon monoxide (CO), hydrocarbons, NO_x and CO_2. A wide range of measures has been introduced by the Government to tackle vehicle emissions; these are expected to lead to a marked and progressive decline in pollutants from motor vehicles.

Britain has continued to be at the forefront of discussions within the EU on tightening up regulations on pollution from motor vehicles. Strict new emissions requirements came into force at the end of 1992, requiring new cars to be fitted with catalytic converters. As a result, there are now about 2.5 million cars on Britain's roads fitted with catalytic converters;

this figure will progressively increase as new cars are bought. Tests show that catalytic converters can reduce emissions of CO, hydrocarbons and NO_x by 70 per cent in good conditions. By the end of the 1990s, it is expected that NO_x emissions from cars will be back below their 1980 level. Equally stringent controls on emissions from vans and off-road vehicles will apply to vehicles first used from October 1994 onwards. Diesel-engined cars are subject to the same controls as petrol-engined cars and must also comply with a strict limit on particulates (smoke).

Britain has also pressed the EU to introduce stricter emission standards for heavy goods vehicles and buses. New emission limits came into force in October 1993 for new diesel-engined trucks and buses over 3.5 tonnes, reducing limits for CO, hydrocarbons and NO_x by 60, 50 and 45 per cent respectively and setting a limit on particulates. A further stage, to be implemented in 1996, will halve the particulate level.

A recently agreed EC directive, to be applied to cars from January 1997, will secure further reductions in CO, hydrocarbons, NO_x and particulates. These new standards represent a very substantial reduction from

Emissions of Sulphur Dioxide and Nitrogen Oxides

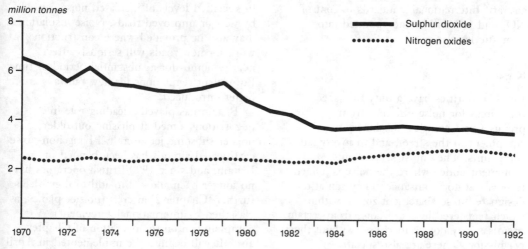

Source: Department of the Environment.

the 1991 levels. The directive also lays out a framework within which the European Commission will make further proposals for reducing car emissions from the year 2000.

The amount of lead in the air in Britain has fallen by 70 per cent since the permitted lead content in petrol was reduced in 1986 from 0.4 to 0.15 grammes a litre and unleaded petrol was introduced. Practically all petrol stations in Britain now sell unleaded petrol, and since 1990 new cars must be capable of running on it. The Government has encouraged the use of cleaner fuel by introducing a substantial tax differential in favour of unleaded petrol. Demand has risen rapidly, and unleaded petrol now accounts for over half of all petrol sold in Britain. By the year 2003 leaded petrol sales will be negligible.

To tackle CO_2 emissions, the Chancellor of the Exchequer in the November 1993 budget increased road fuel duties by 8 to 10 per cent and announced a long-term strategy of future annual increases averaging at least 5 per cent in real terms. This should save about 2.5 million tonnes of carbon in the year 2000, representing a quarter of the CO_2 emissions from all sources that Britain is required to save under the climate change convention.

Internationally developed standards have also been implemented in Britain to control the emission of smoke, vented fuel and unburned hydrocarbons from civil aircraft. International standards to control NO_x and CO will be incorporated into domestic legislation.

Noise

Local authorities have a duty to inspect their areas for noise nuisance from premises and vehicles, machinery or equipment in the street, and to investigate complaints. They must serve a noise abatement notice where the noise is judged to be a statutory nuisance. They can also designate 'noise abatement zones' within which registered levels of noise from certain premises may not be increased without their permission. There are also specific provisions in law to:

- control noise from construction and demolition sites;
- control the use of loudspeakers in the streets; and
- enable individuals to take independent action through the courts against noise amounting to a nuisance.

The majority of complaints relate to neighbour noise.

Tougher measures against noise were proposed in the environment White Paper (see p. 346). Many of its commitments were endorsed by an independent working party. It reported in 1990 with 33 recommendations, many of which have now been implemented. The Noise and Statutory Nuisance Act 1993 gave local authorities in Great Britain extra powers and duties to deal with noise nuisance in the street. The Government encourages the use of informal means of solving neighbour disputes, such as mediation. The Government also has an environmental noise research programme, spending on which is expected to be about £600,000 in 1994–95.

Regulations set out the permissible noise levels for various classes of new vehicle. Compensation may be payable for loss in property values caused by physical factors, including noise from new or improved public works such as roads, railways and airports. Regulations also require highway authorities to make grants available for insulation of homes that would be subject to specified levels of increased noise caused by new or improved roads. Noise insulation may also be provided where construction work for new roads will seriously affect nearby homes for a substantial period of time. Equivalent regulations for new railways are being introduced.

Britain has played a leading role in negotiations aimed at phasing out older, noisier subsonic jet aircraft. Flying non-noise certificated aircraft has been banned in Britain, and since 1990 British operators have no longer been allowed to add to their fleets further 'Chapter 2' aircraft (noisier planes, as classified by international agreement). A complete ban on the operation of Chapter 2 aircraft will begin to be implemented in April 1995, and it is intended to phase out all these types by April 2002. Various operational restrictions have been introduced to reduce noise disturbance further at Heathrow, Gatwick and Stansted, where the Secretary of State for Transport has assumed responsibility for noise abatement. These measures include:

- restrictions on the type and number of aircraft operating at night;
- the routeing of departing aircraft on noise-preferential routes; and
- quieter take-off and landing procedures.

For night flights in summer 1994, the Government introduced a control system combining a noise quota with a ceiling on the total number of movements. The population disturbed by aircraft noise[3] at Heathrow fell from 591,000 in 1988 to 429,000 in 1991, even though the number of air transport movements increased. This was largely because of the phasing out of older, noisier aircraft.

Under government proposals announced in 1993, airfield authorities will be given powers to enforce noise amelioration schemes. The Secretary of State would have powers to compel airfield authorities to prepare such a scheme. Local authorities would have powers to act against the owner of an airfield who did not take reasonable steps to ensure that an agreed scheme was operated effectively.

Radioactivity

Man-made radiation represents only a small fraction of that to which the population is exposed; most is naturally occurring. A large proportion of the man-made radioactivity to which the public is exposed comes from medical treatments, such as X-rays. Nevertheless, the man-made fraction is subject to stringent control. Users of radioactive materials must be registered by HMIP in England and Wales, and equivalents in Scotland and Northern Ireland, and authorisation is also required for the accumulation and disposal of radioactive

waste. The Health and Safety Executive (see p. 190), through its Nuclear Installations Inspectorate, is the authority responsible for the granting of nuclear site licences for major nuclear installations. No installation may be constructed or operated without a licence granted by the Executive.

The National Radiological Protection Board (NRPB) provides an authoritative point of reference on radiological protection. Following the accident at the Chernobyl nuclear power station in the then Soviet Union in 1986, the Government set up a national radiation monitoring network and overseas nuclear accident response system (RIMNET). An interim version began operating in 1988. A larger and more fully automated system, with 92 monitoring stations across Britain, became operational at the end of 1993.

In 1987 the Government announced measures to deal with the problem of radon, a naturally occurring radioactive gas which can accumulate in houses. These included a free survey by the NRPB for householders living in radon-affected areas. In 1990 the Government halved the level at which it recommends that householders take action to reduce radon in their homes. The NRPB has designated several 'radon-affected areas', for example, Cornwall, Devon, Northamptonshire and parts of Derbyshire and Somerset. Householders in these areas are eligible for free radon tests.

Radioactive Waste Disposal

Radioactive wastes vary widely in nature and level of activity, and the methods of disposal reflect this. Some wastes can be disposed of safely in the same way as other industrial and household wastes. UK Nirex Ltd is responsible for developing a deep disposal facility for solid low-level and intermediate-level radioactive waste. It is currently concentrating its detailed geological investigations on an area near the British Nuclear Fuels site at Sellafield, in Cumbria. As part of these studies, Nirex intends to construct an experimental rock laboratory, known as a 'rock characterisation facility'.

The Department of the Environment is

---

[3] That is, living within the 57 Leq noise contour, which is regarded as the onset of disturbance. Using the older, broadly comparable, 35 NNI measure, about 1.6 million people were affected in 1979.

sponsoring research, in collaboration with other countries, into disposal of high-level or heat-generating waste. This waste will first be stored in vitrified form for at least 50 years to allow the heat and radioactivity to decay.

Genetically Modified Organisms

Genetically modified organisms (GMOs) have many potential beneficial uses, for example, improving crops or clearing up contaminated land. However, their release to the environment could have harmful effects unless precautions are taken. The Environmental Protection Act 1990 and regulations which came into force in 1993 contain powers to ensure that any risks to the environment, including mankind, from the release of GMOs are prevented or minimised. The new legislation sets up a consent system for experimental releases of GMOs and for the EU-wide approval of GMO products. The Government recently announced, in the light of experience and developing knowledge, 'fast track' procedures for the approval of low-risk GMOs so that their benefits may be enjoyed as soon as possible with the least burden on industry consistent with safety.

Environmental Research

Research into environmental protection is essential to the Government's environmental policies. Its planned total spending on environmental research and development in 1993–94 was £300–£400 million, including work in areas such as renewable energy. The Department of the Environment expected to devote about £57 million in 1993–94 to research into subjects including:

- climate change;
- atmospheric pollution and its monitoring;
- toxic chemicals and GMOs;
- waste disposal; and
- water quality and health.

Other departments have substantial programmes, notably the Ministry of Agriculture, Fisheries and Food, The Scottish Office Agriculture and Fisheries Department and other official bodies such as the NRA and the Meteorological Office.

Research Councils

Basic and strategic research is carried out by the government-funded research councils (see pp. 311–15). All have a role in environmental protection research, but particularly important is the Natural Environment Research Council (NERC), which has a Science Budget allocation of £155 million in 1994–95. The NERC undertakes and supports research in the environmental sciences and funds postgraduate training. Its programmes encompass the marine, earth, terrestrial, freshwater, polar and atmospheric sciences. The NERC stresses international collaborative work on global environmental issues. For example, it is helping to develop global atmospheric climate models and strengthening atmospheric research in the Arctic. A major research programme, the Terrestrial Initiative in Global Environmental Research, aims to assess the likely impact of climate change on Britain and elsewhere. The NERC also co-ordinates the development and operation of the Environmental Change Network.

Further Reading

Pollution Control. Aspects of Britain series, HMSO, 1993.

Environment Protection and Water Statistics. Annual report. HMSO.

The UK Environment. HMSO, 1992.

This Common Inheritance—The Third Year Report. HMSO, 1994.

Social and
Cultural Affairs

24 Health and Social Services

Total spending on health and social services in 1994–95 is expected to be £38,223 million: £37,830 million on health and £394 million on social services. Total National Health Service spending in Britain was equivalent to 5.9 per cent of the gross domestic product in 1993–94, compared with 4.7 per cent in 1978–79. Recent developments include an expansion of the role of nurses in primary care, projects designed to improve health care in inner city areas and among ethnic minorities, and new procedures for assessing the care needs for individuals within the community.

The National Health Service (NHS) provides a full range of medical services which are available to all residents, regardless of their income. Local authority personal social services and voluntary organisations provide help and advice to the most vulnerable members of the community. These include elderly, physically disabled and mentally ill people, those with learning disabilities (mental handicap) and children in need of care.

Central government is directly responsible for the NHS, which is administered by a range of local health authorities and health boards throughout Britain, and for the social security system. Personal social services are administered by local authorities but central government is responsible for establishing national policies, issuing guidance and overseeing standards.

Joint finance and planning between health and local authorities aim to prevent overlapping of services and to encourage the development of community services.

Spending on the health service has increased substantially in real terms since 1980, and is planned to grow further over the next two years. More patients are being treated than ever before. Spending on the personal social services is determined by local authorities. Central government has restricted the total expenditure of individual local authorities, but spending has risen substantially in real terms since the late 1970s, reflecting the priority given to this sector.

The NHS health programme consists of:
- Hospital and Community Health Services (HCHS), providing all hospital care and a range of community health services;

- Family Health Services (FHS), providing general medical, dental, pharmaceutical and some ophthalmic services, and covering the cost of medicines prescribed by general practitioners (GPs);

- Central Health and Miscellaneous Services (CHMS), providing services most effectively administered centrally, such as welfare food (which includes free milk and vitamins to families with children under five, and expectant mothers, on income support) and support to the voluntary sector; and

- the administrative costs of the health departments.

Major Policy Developments

Reforms in Management

The NHS and Community Care Act 1990 introduced wide-ranging reform in management and patient care in the health and social care services. The NHS reforms, which came into effect in 1991, aim to give patients, wherever they live in Britain, better health care and greater choice of service, as follows:

1. Health authorities and health boards have been given a new role as purchasers of health care on behalf of their local residents, responsible for assessing local health care needs and ensuring the availability of a full range of services to meet identified health needs. They ensure that those needs are met within existing resources.

2. Each health authority is funded to buy health care for its local residents through arranging contracts with hospitals and other health service units in either the public or private sector. For the first time hospitals are directly funded for the number of patients they treat, making it easier for GPs to refer patients outside their area if treatment elsewhere is faster and better. However, powers exist for allocating resources where the urgent need for treatment does not allow NHS contracts to be arranged in advance.

3. The contracts agreed between health authorities and hospitals set out the quality, quantity and cost of the services to be delivered during the year. The contracts secured by each health authority are based on wide consultation with all local GPs.

4. Hospitals may apply to become self-governing NHS trusts (see p. 379), independent of local health authority control but remaining within the NHS. They are accountable to the relevant health department, treating NHS patients, and are funded largely through general taxation, under contracts with health authorities.

5. GPs from larger medical practices may apply to join the general practitioner fundholding scheme (see p. 377), under which they receive an annual budget directly from the health authority, enabling them to buy certain hospital services for their patients.

The reforms in community care provision, which came into force between 1991 and 1993, establish a new financial and managerial framework which aims to secure the delivery of good quality services in line with national objectives. They are intended to enable vulnerable groups in the community to live as independently as possible in their own homes for as long as they are able and wish to do so, and to give them a greater say in how they live and how the services they need should be provided. (For fuller details see p. 392.)

Broadly similar changes have been introduced under separate legislation in Northern Ireland, where health and personal social services are provided on an integrated basis by health and social services boards.

Patient's Charters

Patient's Charters are part of the health departments' response to the Citizen's Charter (see p. 67). Patient's Charters support the objectives of the NHS reforms: to improve standards of health care and sensitivity to patients in the NHS. They set out for the first time the rights of patients and the standards of care they can expect to receive from the NHS. Patients should know what they can expect from the NHS

Health Service Expenditure in England

NHS Gross Expenditure 1992–93 (estimate)

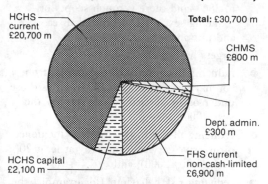

HCHS current £20,700 m

Total: £30,700 m

CHMS £800 m

Dept. admin. £300 m

FHS current non-cash-limited £6,900 m

HCHS capital £2,100 m

Hospital and Community Health Services Gross Current Expenditure by Sector 1990–91 (estimate)

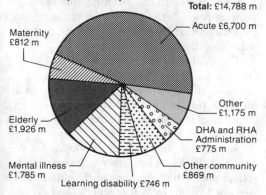

Total: £14,788 m

Acute £6,700 m

Maternity £812 m

Elderly £1,926 m

Mental illness £1,785 m

Learning disability £746 m

Other £1,175 m

DHA and RHA Administration £775 m

Other community £869 m

1. Other community services include health visiting, immunisation, screening, health promotion and community dental services.

2. Other services include ambulances, the blood transfusion service, mass radiography and the Service Increment for Teaching and Research (SIFTR).

Non-cash-limited Family Health Services Gross Expenditure 1991–92

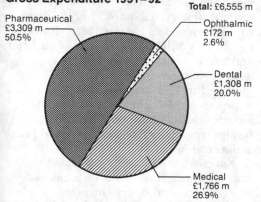

Total: £6,555 m

Pharmaceutical £3,309 m 50.5%

Ophthalmic £172 m 2.6%

Dental £1,308 m 20.0%

Medical £1,766 m 26.9%

Source: *Department of Health. The Government's Expenditure Plans 1994–95 to 1996–97.*

and the staff who provide services should understand what is expected of them. The responsibility for implementing the Patient's Charters rests with all parts of the NHS, English regions, purchasers and providers, and is carried out mainly through contract arrangements.

As well as restating the existing rights that patients have under the NHS, the Patient's Charter in England introduced three new rights. These are that patients must:

- be given detailed information on local health services, including quality standards and maximum waiting times;

- be guaranteed admission for treatment no later than two years from the date of being placed on a waiting list; and

- have any complaint about NHS services investigated, and receive a full reply as soon as possible.

In England the Patient's Charter also sets national charter standards. These are not legal rights but specific standards of service which the NHS aims to provide. These include respect for the individual patient; waiting times for ambulances, clinical assessment in accident and emergency departments and appointments in out-patient clinics; and cancellation of operations. Also included are local charter standards of service which health authorities aim to provide (see below).

Separate Patient's Charters have been developed for Scotland, Wales and Northern Ireland.

A new maternity services charter, describing key standards and rights, was published in April 1994. This is the first of a series of special documents based on the Patient's Charter. Others in preparation deal with long-term NHS care services and health services for children.

There are now initiatives on every aspect of the Patient's Charter—from setting up translation services in 140 languages to encourage access to services, to asking patients for their views on improving services.

All family health services authorities in

England have produced local charters. These include nationally set standards and targets for information to the public; transfer of patients' medical records; help to people wanting to change doctor; and effective handling of patients' complaints, suggestions and comments. GP practice staff are being encouraged to produce their own practice charters, setting out the standards of service they offer their patients.

In response to the Charter Right to Information, English regions have set up health information services. These can provide details of the times people have to wait for treatment for all specialties in local hospitals, as well as information from hospitals further afield (see p. 379).

The national health information service freephone receives nearly 400 calls every day.

Developing Health Strategies

The Government emphasises the importance of promoting health as well as treating illness. Preventive health services such as health education, and the responsibility that individuals have for their own health, play a major part in this. While great progress has been made in eliminating infectious diseases such as poliomyelitis and tuberculosis, there is still scope for greater success in controlling the major causes of early death and disability.

The White Paper *The Health of the Nation*, published in 1992, sets out a strategy for improving health in England. This is the first time a strategy has been developed for health in England and its long-term aim is to enable people to live longer, healthier lives. It sets targets for improvements in the following areas:

- coronary heart disease and stroke (the major cause of premature death in England);
- cancers (the second biggest cause of premature death);
- accidents (the commonest cause of death in those under 30);
- mental illness (a leading cause of ill-health and, through suicides, of death); and

- HIV/AIDS and sexual health (HIV/AIDS is perhaps the greatest new public health threat this century—see p. 386—and there is much scope for reducing sexually transmitted diseases and unwanted pregnancies).

Targets have been set for:

- reducing death rates (for example, from coronary heart disease and stroke in those under 65 by at least 40 per cent by the year 2000);
- reducing ill-health (such as the incidence of invasive cervical cancer by at least 20 per cent by 2000); and
- reducing risk behaviour (for example, the percentage of smokers to no more than 20 per cent of the population by 2000).

While the NHS has a central role in working towards the targets, the strategy also emphasises that there is a role for everyone in improving the nation's health.

The White Paper also sets out the Government's objective of ensuring the provision of effective family planning services for those people who want them. The conception rate for those under 16 years is a matter of particular concern.

Strategies have also been developed for Scotland, Wales and Northern Ireland which reflect the health variations in the different parts of Britain. In Wales, where the first of Britain's four national health strategies was published in 1990, areas for improvement include, among others: cancers; cardiovascular disease; maternal and early child health; physical disability; mental handicap and mental health; and injuries. Scotland's national strategy, published in 1991, places special emphasis on coronary heart disease, cancer, HIV/AIDS, accidents and dental and oral health, smoking, alcohol and drug misuse. Northern Ireland's strategy, published in 1991, sets targets for improvements in eight key areas which include circulatory diseases, cancers, respiratory diseases, child and maternal health and mental health.

National activity in England includes interdepartmental taskforces on accident prevention, nutrition, smoking, the workplace and physical activity, work with professional and voluntary bodies and the provision of guidance setting out a range of possible actions for each tier of the NHS. At local level, the NHS is being encouraged to form 'healthy alliances' for joint working with agencies ranging from the voluntary sector through to industry and the media. Progress towards the targets is monitored regularly and formally reviewed, and periodic progress reports are published.

A review of the first year's initiative in England,[1] published in November 1993, reports:

- a 9 per cent fall in the death rate from accidents among children aged under 15 towards a target of 33 per cent by 2005;
- a 4.8 per cent reduction in the death rate from coronary heart disease in people under 65 towards a target of at least 40 per cent by 2000; and
- a 3 per cent reduction in the death rate from lung cancer in men under 75 towards a target of at least 30 per cent by 2010.

Instances of negative trends include:

- the figures on the death rate from suicide, which show an increase of 0.9 per cent compared to a target of at least a 15 per cent reduction by 2000; and
- the figures on teenage smoking, which remain static.

The Government is working closely with the World Health Organisation (WHO) in presenting *The Health of the Nation* as one possible approach for other countries wishing to develop a strategic approach to improving health.

Improving London's Health Services

The Government's strategy to improve health services in the London area was launched in February 1993. It proposed to:

- develop better, local and accessible primary and community health services;
- provide a better-balanced hospital service, on fewer sites;

- streamline specialist services; and
- consolidate medical education and research, chiefly through mergers of free-standing undergraduate medical colleges with multifaculty colleges of London University.

As a result:

- a London Initiative Zone has been established as a focus for new investment and new approaches in primary health care and community-based services;
- regional health authorities are continuing to implement proposals for restructuring the acute hospital service in London;
- in late 1994 further plans to merge medical schools and postgraduate institutes with multifaculty colleges will be available. It has been agreed that fewer, larger specialist tertiary centres will offer the best means of providing excellence in treatment, care and research.

The National Health Service

The NHS is based upon the principle that there should be a full range of publicly provided services designed to help the individual stay healthy. The services are intended to provide effective and appropriate treatment and care where necessary while making the best use of available resources. All taxpayers, employers and employees contribute to its cost so that those members of the community who do not require health care help to pay for those who do. Some forms of treatment, such as hospital care, are provided free; others (see p. 375) may be charged for.

Growth in real spending on the health service is being used to meet the needs of increasing numbers of elderly people and to take full advantage of advances in medical technology. It is also used to provide more appropriate types of care, often in the community rather than in hospital, for priority groups such as elderly and mentally ill people and those with learning

[1] *The Health of the Nation—One Year On*. Department of Health. 1993.

disabilities. Increased spending has, in addition, been allocated to combat the growing problems arising from alcohol and drug misuse; and to remedy disparities in provision between the regions of Britain.

The Voluntary Sector

Government grant aid to voluntary organisations working in health and personal social services in England will exceed £19.5 million in 1994–95—an increase of more than 9 per cent on 1992–93. The grants go primarily to national organisations dealing with children, elderly people, carers and people from ethnic minorities, as well as those looking after people with mental illness, physical or learning disabilities, or suffering from the effects of HIV/AIDS or the misuse of alcohol or drugs. In Scotland grants to voluntary organisations in social welfare increased by 18 per cent in 1994–95, with grants to a wide range of bodies. Health authorities and local authorities have similar powers to make grants to local organisations.

Market Testing

The Government stresses the need for collaboration between the public and private health sectors and for improving efficiency in order to secure the best value for money and the maximum patient care.

Since 1983 the market testing of catering, domestic services, and laundry has produced cumulative savings of £1,000 million, which has been reinvested into direct personal care. NHS managers have already market-tested most non-clinical services, including administrative and financial services as well as various aspects of information technology and communications. They are now beginning to test clinical support services such as pathology and pharmacy.

Economies are also made in prescribing by restricting the use of expensive branded products in favour of cheaper but equally effective equivalent medicines.

ADMINISTRATION

The Secretary of State for Health in England and the Secretaries of State for Scotland, Wales and Northern Ireland are responsible for all aspects of the health services in their respective countries. The Department of Health is responsible for national strategic planning in England. It carries out its responsibility for providing services locally through the NHS Executive. The Scottish Office Home and Health Department, the Welsh Office and the Department of Health and Social Services in Northern Ireland have similar responsibilities.

District health authorities in England and Wales and health boards in Scotland are responsible for securing hospital and community health services in their areas. At present England also has regional authorities responsible for planning, resource allocation, major capital building work and certain specialised hospital services best administered on a regional basis. The health authorities and boards co-operate closely with local authorities responsible for social work, environmental health, education and other services. Family health services authorities (health boards in Scotland) arrange for the provision of services by doctors, dentists, pharmacists and opticians, as well as administering their contracts. Community health councils (local health councils in Scotland) represent local opinion on the health services provided.

In Northern Ireland health and social services boards are responsible for all health and personal social services in their areas. The representation of public opinion on these services is provided for by area health and social services councils.

In its continued drive to decentralise the NHS, the Government has announced proposals to streamline NHS management. These involve:

- creating a clear identity for the NHS Executive, within the Department of Health, as the headquarters of the NHS;
- abolishing the English regional health authorities (RHAs) and reorganising the NHS Executive to include eight regional offices, each headed by the regional director;
- appointing non-executive members of the NHS policy board to cover each of the eight regions; and

- enabling and encouraging mergers between district health authorities and family health services authorities.

As a first step towards the new structure, the number of RHAs was reduced from 14 to eight in April 1994, creating common boundaries with the planned new NHS Executive regional offices.

The changes would be expected to produce substantial savings in administrative costs and maximise the proportion of NHS spending devoted to direct patient care. Subject to parliamentary approval, the plans are expected to be fully in force by April 1996.

Finance

Over 82 per cent of the cost of the health service in Great Britain is paid for through general taxation. The rest is met from:

- the NHS element of National Insurance contributions, paid by employed people, their employers, and self-employed people (13.2 per cent);

- charges towards the cost of certain items such as drugs prescribed by family doctors, and general dental treatment (3.5 per cent); and

- other receipts, including land sales and the proceeds of income generation schemes (0.8 per cent).

Health authorities may raise funds from voluntary sources. Certain hospitals increase revenue by taking private patients, who pay the full cost of their accommodation and treatment.

Almost 80 per cent of medical prescription items are supplied free. Prescription charges do not apply to the following:

- children under 16 years (or young people under 19 and still in full-time education);

- expectant mothers and women who have had a baby in the past year;

- women aged 60 and over and men aged 65 and over;

- patients suffering from certain specified medical conditions;

- war and armed forces disablement pensioners (for prescriptions which relate to the disability for which they receive a war pension); and

- people in families who are receiving income support or family credit (see p. 406); and people or families with low incomes.

There are proportional charges for most types of NHS dental treatment, including examinations. However, women who were pregnant when the dentist accepted them for treatment or who have had a baby in the past year, anyone under the age of 18 (or 19 if in full-time education), people in families receiving income support or family credit, and people in families assessed as having a low income, do not have to pay.

Sight tests are free to children, people in families receiving income support or family credit, people in families assessed as having a low income and those with specified medical needs. Children, people on low incomes and those requiring certain complex lenses receive a voucher towards the cost of their spectacles.

Hospital medical staff are salaried and may be employed full time or part time. Family practitioners (doctors, dentists, optometrists and pharmacists) are self-employed and have contracts with the NHS. GPs are paid by a system of fees and allowances designed to reflect responsibilities, workload and practice expenses. Dentists providing treatment in their own surgeries are paid by a combination of capitation fees for treating children, continuing care payments for adults registered with the practice, and a prescribed scale of fees for individual treatments. Pharmacists dispensing from their own premises are refunded the cost of the items supplied, together with professional fees. Ophthalmic medical practitioners and ophthalmic opticians taking part in the general ophthalmic service receive approved fees for each sight test carried out.

Staffing

The NHS is one of the largest employers in the world, with a workforce of nearly 1 million people. Staff costs account for two-thirds of total NHS expenditure and 70 per cent of current expenditure on hospitals and community health services. The sharp fall in the numbers of directly employed ancillary staff and of maintenance and works staff reflects the continuing effect of competitive tendering (see p. 70). Between 1982 and 1992:

- the number of NHS medical and dental staff in England rose by 12.5 per cent to 58,816, while in Scotland the increase was 4.3 per cent to 7,904. In England on average the number of hospital medical consultants grew by 2.5 per cent a year and the number of junior doctors by 1.7 per cent. In Scotland on average the number of hospital medical consultants grew by 1.5 per cent a year and the number of junior doctors by 0.8 per cent.
- the number of scientific, professional and technical staff in England rose by 34 per cent;
- the number of nursing and midwifery staff, who make up 48 per cent of the NHS workforce, has decreased by 4 per cent since 1982. The drop in their numbers in 1992 reflects the the growth in bursaried students under the Project 2000 nurse training scheme (see p. 391). Project 2000 trainees have full student status and are not NHS employees.
- the number of general and senior managers has risen in recent years, which reflects the progressive introduction of management posts in a series of phased stages since 1986.

The Government's aim throughout the service is progressively to introduce greater pay flexibility to allow managers to relate pay to local markets and reward individual performance. A number of measures are being taken to provide a more effective workforce through better management development, education and training (see p. 379).

Health Service Commissioners

Health Service Commissioners (one each for England, Scotland and Wales) are responsible for dealing with complaints from members of the public about health service bodies. The three posts are at present held by one person, who is also Parliamentary Commissioner for Administration (Ombudsman—see p. 60). As Health Service Commissioner, he reports annually to Parliament.

The Health Service Commissioner can investigate complaints that a person has suffered injustice or hardship as a result of:

- a failure in a service provided by a health service body;
- a failure to provide a service which was the function of the health service body to provide; or
- a maladministration connected with action taken by or on behalf of a health service body.

The Health Service Commissioner's jurisdiction does not extend to complaints about clinical judgment, family practitioners, personnel matters and the use of a health authority's discretionary powers; separate procedures exist for these. In Northern Ireland the Commissioner for Complaints has a similar role.

An independent review of all aspects of NHS complaints procedures was published in May 1994. It recommends a single, speedy system to handle all types of complaint to replace current procedures, which are seen as too complex and fragmented.

FAMILY HEALTH SERVICES

The family health services are those given to patients by doctors, dentists, opticians and pharmacists of their own choice. They remain the first point of contact most people have with the NHS. Every year there are about 200 million consultations with family doctors and about 6 million people visit a pharmacy every day. Many of those who visit their family doctor or dentist need no clinical treatment but instead healthy lifestyle counselling and preventive health care advice. The Government's longstanding policy has been to build up and extend these services in order to improve health and relieve pressure on the far more costly secondary care sector (that is, hospital and specialist services).

GPs provide the first diagnosis in the case of illness and either prescribe a suitable course of treatment or refer a patient to the more specialised services and hospital consultants. About four-fifths of GPs in Britain work in partnerships or group practices, often as members of primary health-care teams. The teams also include health visitors and district nurses, and sometimes midwives, social workers and other professional staff employed by the health authorities. About a quarter of GPs in Great Britain and about half in Northern Ireland work in health centres, where medical and nursing services are provided. Health centres may also have facilities for health education, family planning, speech therapy, chiropody, assessment of hearing, physiotherapy and remedial exercises. Dental, pharmaceutical and ophthalmic services, hospital out-patient and supporting social work services, may also be provided.

There have been substantial increases in primary health care staff in recent years. For example, between 1978–9 and 1992–93 the number of GPs in England increased by 23.4 per cent (to almost 26,000); average patient list size fell by 16.9 per cent (to just under 2,000); and the number of family dentists increased by 26.4 per cent (to 15,000). The number of GP practice nurses increased ninefold—to 9,000—and the number of opticians increased by 24.5 per cent (to 6,600).

Special funds have been earmarked by the Government for improving the quality of primary health care in inner city areas. Efforts have also been made to improve health services for ethnic minority groups. These include new health projects in Britain's Chinese communities, a project in Cardiff for the Somali refugee community, and increased central funding for health information material to be produced in many minority languages.

An NHS ethnic health unit was set up in November 1993. Its aim is to ensure that people from different ethnic backgrounds derive full benefit from the *Health of the Nation* strategy (see p. 372), from local health purchasing policies, the Patient's Charter (see p. 371), the Care in the Community initiatives and the developing role of primary care.

The Government has welcomed a recent report which recommends ways in which the role of community pharmacists could be developed to increase their contribution to health care.

Recent Developments

GP Fundholders

GP practices with 7,000 patients or more (6,000 in Scotland and Northern Ireland) may apply for fundholding status. This is a voluntary scheme which gives larger medical practices the opportunity to manage sums of NHS money for the benefit of their patients. It aims to improve services for patients and enable GPs to explore more innovative methods of providing health care. GP fundholders are responsible for part of their own NHS budgets, enabling them to buy certain non-urgent hospital services. Prescription charges and part of the cost of running the practice are also covered. Fundholders may negotiate for services directly with hospitals from both public and private sectors in any district or regional health authority or health board in Britain. GP fundholders may buy NHS community nursing services for their patients, including district nursing and health visiting services and community psychiatric and community mental handicap nursing. In 1992–93 GP fundholders in England spent just over 1.5 per cent of their budget with non-NHS organisations.

By April 1994 some 8,800 GPs in over 2,000 practices in Great Britain had become fundholders, and 36 per cent of the population are now registered with a fundholding GP.

Contracts

The performance-related contract for GPs, introduced in 1990, is designed to raise standards of care, extend the range of services available to patients and improve patient choice. The changes are intended to make it easier for patients to see their GP at times convenient to them; easier for patients to change doctors; and to encourage doctors to practise more preventive medicine.

The new contract for dentists, introduced in 1990, aims at improving care and providing more information to patients about general dental services. As a result NHS dental care now includes preventive care as well as restorative treatment. All adult patients are now offered 'continuing care', and dentists are encouraged to practise more preventive dentistry for children. There are also incentives for dentists to undertake further training.

Clinical Audit

Clinical audit is a programme that requires all healthcare professionals to look systematically at the procedures used for diagnosis, care and treatment, examining how associated resources are used and investigating the effect care has on the outcome and quality of life for the patient.

The Government has so far allocated £221 million for clinical audit; more than 7,000 audit projects have been established.

Midwives, Health Visitors and District Nurses

Midwives provide care and support to women throughout pregnancy, birth and the post-natal period (up to 28 days after the baby is born). Midwives work in both hospital and community settings.

From October 1994 district nurses and health visitors in eight pilot schemes in England will be able to prescribe from a limited list of drugs and medical appliances. These schemes will be based in GP fundholding practices and are intended to reduce significantly the time patients have to wait for relief of their symptoms.

Health visitors are responsible for the preventive care and health promotion of families, particularly those with young children. They have a public health role, identifying local health needs and working closely with GPs, district nurses and other professions. District nurses give skilled nursing care to people at home or elsewhere outside hospital; they also play an important role in health promotion and education.

HOSPITAL AND SPECIALIST SERVICES

A full range of hospital services is provided by district general hospitals. These include treatment and diagnostic facilities for in-patients, day-patients and out-patients; maternity departments; infectious diseases units; psychiatric and geriatric facilities; rehabilitation facilities; and other forms of specialised treatment. There are also specialist hospitals or units for children, people suffering from mental illness, those with learning disabilities, and elderly people, and for the treatment of specific diseases. Examples of these include the world-famous Hospital for Sick Children (Great Ormond Street) and the Moorfields Eye Hospital, in London. Hospitals designated as teaching hospitals combine treatment facilities with training medical and other students, and research work.

Many of the hospitals in the NHS were built in the 19th century; some trace their origins to much earlier charitable foundations.

Much has been done to improve and extend existing hospital buildings and many new hospitals have been or are being opened. Since 1979 in Great Britain over 700 major building schemes, each costing £1 million or more, have been completed. A further 340 schemes are at various stages of development. This is the largest sustained building programme in the history of the NHS.

Recent policy in England and Wales has been to provide a balanced hospital service centred around a district general hospital, complemented as necessary by smaller, locally based hospitals and facilities.

The hospital service is now treating more patients a year than ever before. Between 1978–79 and 1992–93 lengths of stay for in-patients declined and the number of people treated as day patients more than trebled, to 1.8 million. In 1992–93 day cases accounted for 23 per cent of all hospital admissions in the general and acute specialities.

Waiting Times

Over the last few years there have been substantial reductions in the number of patients waiting more than 12 months for in-patient or day case treatment.

- In England in March 1994 fewer than 65,000 patients were waiting over a year for hospital treatment, compared with more than 200,000 in 1987. Since March 1988 the average waiting time has fallen from over nine months to less than five.

- In Scotland in 1993–94 the number of patients waiting over a year for hospital treatment fell by over 50 per cent to 4,193, while the number waiting for over two years fell by over 45 per cent to 1,830.

Regions are meeting the Patient's Charter guarantees of a maximum two-year wait for in-patient or day case treatment, and 18 months for hip or knee replacements or cataract operations. From April 1995 two new targets will be introduced to cover waiting times for coronary revascularisations and for first out-patient's appointment.

NHS Trusts

Under the NHS and Community Care Act 1990 hospitals and other health service units (for example, ambulance services and community health services) may apply to become independent of direct local health authority control and establish themselves as self-governing NHS Trusts. Parallel legislation was introduced in Northern Ireland to create Health and Social Services Trusts, which are broadly similar to NHS Trusts. The Trusts remain within the NHS, accountable to the appropriate Secretary of State and finally to Parliament. NHS Trusts are required to publish their business plans and annual reports and accounts, and to hold at least one public meeting a year.

Each NHS Trust is run by a board of directors. Trusts are free to employ their own staff and set their own rates of pay, although staff transferring to Trust employment retain their existing terms and conditions of service. Trusts are also free to carry out research and provide facilities for medical education and other forms of training. They derive their income mainly from NHS contracts to provide services to health authorities and GP fundholders. They may treat private patients and generate income provided this does not interfere with NHS obligations. By April 1994, 419 NHS Trusts were running in England, delivering around 96 per cent of NHS hospital and community health services. At the same date in Northern Ireland, 13 trusts were delivering over 70 per cent of the health and personal social services for the population.

Organ Transplants

Over the past 25 years there have been significant developments in transplant surgery in Britain. The United Kingdom Transplant Support Service Authority provides a centralised organ matching and allocation service. During 1993, 1,683 kidney transplants were performed. A similar service exists for corneas and, in 1993, 2,564 were transplanted.

Heart transplant operations have been conducted at Papworth Hospital in Cambridgeshire and Harefield Hospital in London since 1979. There are six other designated heart transplant centres in England, while Scotland's first unit opened in Glasgow in 1991.

A programme of combined heart and lung transplants is in progress and in 1993, 312 heart, 95 lung, and 39 heart/lung transplants were performed. The world's first combined heart, lungs and liver transplant operation was carried out at Papworth in 1987.

Commercial dealing in organs for transplant is illegal.

There are six designated liver transplant units in England and Scotland's first liver transplant centre opened in Edinburgh in 1992. In 1993 550 liver transplants were performed. A voluntary organ donor card system enables people to indicate their willingness to become organ donors in the event of their death. In March 1994 the Government launched a £1 million television campaign to encourage people to carry donor cards.

Blood Transfusion Services

Blood transfusion services are run by the National Blood Authority in England, the

Scottish National Blood Transfusion Service and the Common Health Services Agency in Wales.

Around 2.5 million donations are given each year by voluntary unpaid donors and separated into many different life-saving products for patients. Red cells, platelets and other products with a limited 'shelf life' are prepared at regional transfusion centres and the more complex processing of plasma products is undertaken at the Bio Products Laboratory in Elstree (Hertfordshire) and the Protein Fractionation Centre in Edinburgh.

Each of the three national bodies co-ordinates programmes for donor recruitment, retention and education, and donor sessions are organised regionally, in towns, villages and workplaces. Donors are normally aged between 18 (17 in Scotland) and 70. Regional transfusion centres are responsible for blood collection, screening, processing and regional blood banks. They also provide wide-ranging laboratory, clinical, research, teaching and advisory services and facilities. These are subject to nationally co-ordinated quality audit programmes.

Britain is completely self-sufficient in 'fresh' blood products and the National Blood Authority aims to meet fully the demand for plasma products in England. Scotland is already self-sufficient in all blood products.

Ambulance and Patient Transport Services

NHS emergency ambulances are available free of charge for cases of sudden illness or collapse, and for doctors' urgent calls. Rapid response services, in which paramedics use cars and motor cycles to reach emergency cases, have been introduced in a number of areas, particularly London and other major cities with areas of high traffic density. Helicopter ambulances serve many parts of England and an integrated air ambulance service is available throughout Scotland.

Non-emergency patient transport services are available to NHS patients considered by their doctor (or dentist or midwife) to be medically unfit to travel by other means. The principle applied is that each patient should be able to reach hospital in a reasonable time and in reasonable comfort, without detriment to his or her medical condition. In many areas the ambulance service organises volunteer drivers to provide a hospital car service for non-urgent patients.

Patients on income support, family credit or with low incomes may have their travelling expenses reimbursed. (In Scotland this also applies to patients in the Highland and Islands Development Area who travel 30 miles or more by land or five or more miles by sea to hospital.)

Rehabilitation

Rehabilitation services are available for elderly, young, and mentally ill people, and those with physical or learning disabilities who need such help to resume life in the community. These services are offered in hospitals, centres in the community and in people's own homes through co-ordinated work by a range of professionals.

Medical services may provide free artificial limbs and eyes, hearing aids, surgical supports, wheelchairs, and other appliances. Following assessment, very severely physically disabled patients may be provided with environmental control equipment which enables them to operate devices such as alarm bells, radios and televisions, telephones, and heating appliances. Nursing equipment may be provided on loan for use in the home.

Local authorities may provide a range of facilities to help patients in the transition from hospital to their own homes. These include the provision of equipment, help with cleaning, shopping and cooking care from domestic help workers, and professional help from occupational therapists and social workers. Voluntary organisations also provide services, complementing the work of the statutory agencies and widening the range of services.

Hospices

A number of hospices provide care for terminally ill people (including children), either directly in in-patient or day-care units or through nursing and other assistance in the patient's own home. Control of symptoms and psychological support for patients and their families form central features of the modern hospice movement, which started in Britain and is now worldwide. Some hospices are administered entirely by the NHS; the rest are run by independent charities, some receiving support from public funds. The number of voluntary hospices has more than doubled in the past ten years. There are over 150 hospices in England and Wales, providing over 2,500 beds; in Scotland 15 independent voluntary hospices providing almost 265 beds; and in Northern Ireland there are four independent hospices providing 76 beds.

The Government's aim has been to provide a level of public funding for the hospice movement which matches voluntary donations. In 1994–95, almost £48 million has been allocated to health authorities in England and Wales to enable them to offer increased support to hospices and similar organisations, including £6.3 million to enable them to arrange for drugs to be supplied to hospices without charge and £5.7 million to help them maintain levels of funding for in-patient voluntary hospices following the community care changes (see p. 392). In Scotland health boards have been allocated £2.7 million for 1994–95 to cover 50 per cent of the running costs of hospices in their areas and £436,000 has been provided for hospice pharmaceutical services. The National Council for Hospice and Specialist Palliative Care Services covers England, Wales and Northern Ireland; its Scottish counterpart is the Scottish Partnership Agency for Palliative and Cancer Care.

Private Medical Treatment

The Government's policy is to welcome cost-effective co-operation between the NHS and the independent sector in meeting the nation's health needs. It believes that this will benefit the NHS by adding to the resources devoted to health care and offering flexibility to health authorities in the delivery of services. Some health authorities share expensive facilities and equipment with private hospitals, and NHS patients are sometimes treated (at public expense) in the private sector to reduce waiting lists. The scale of private practice in relation to the NHS is, however, very small.

It is estimated that about three-quarters of those receiving acute treatment in private hospitals or NHS hospital pay-beds are covered by health insurance schemes, which make provision for private health care in return for annual subscriptions. Over 3 million people subscribe to such schemes, half of them within group schemes, some arranged by firms on behalf of employees. Subscriptions often cover more than one person (for example, members of a family); about 12 per cent of the population in Britain are covered by private medical insurance. The Government has introduced tax relief on private health insurance premiums paid by people aged 60 and over to encourage the increased use of private health facilities.

Many overseas patients come to Britain for treatment in private hospitals and clinics, and Harley Street in London is an internationally recognised centre for medical consultancy.

Parents and Children

Special preventive services are provided under the health service to safeguard the health of expectant mothers and of mothers with young children. Services include free dental treatment, dried milk and vitamins; health education; and vaccination and immunisation of children against certain infectious diseases (see p. 387). Pregnant women receive antenatal care from their GPs and hospital clinics, and women in paid employment have the right to visit the clinics during working hours. Some 99 per cent of women have their babies in hospital, returning home shortly afterwards to be attended by a midwife or health visitor and, where necessary, their GP.

The Government attaches great importance to improving the quality of maternity services, and to making them more responsive to women's wishes on how care is provided. Two government reports, one for England and Wales and one for Scotland, were published in 1993. They recommend giving women greater choice over the care they receive during pregnancy and childbirth. (See p. 518 for the new maternity services charter.)

A comprehensive programme of health surveillance is provided for pre-school children in clinics run by the community health authorities, and increasingly by GPs. This enables doctors, dentists and health visitors to oversee the physical and mental health and development of pre-school children. Information on preventive services is given and welfare foods are distributed. The school health service offers health care and advice for schoolchildren, including medical and dental inspection and treatment where necessary.

Child guidance and child psychiatric services provide help and advice to families and children with psychological or emotional problems.

In recent years special efforts have been made to improve co-operation between the community-based child health services and local authority social services for children. This is particularly important in the prevention of child abuse and for the health and welfare of children in care.

Human Fertilisation and Embryology

The world's first 'test-tube baby' was born in Britain in 1978, as a result of the technique of in vitro fertilisation. This opened up new horizons for helping with problems of infertility and for the science of embryology. The social, ethical and legal implications were examined by a committee of inquiry under Baroness Warnock (1984) and led eventually to the passage of the Human Fertilisation and Embryology Act 1990, one of the most comprehensive pieces of legislation on assisted reproduction and embryo research in the world.

This Act set up the Human Fertilisation and Embryology Authority (HFEA) to license and control centres providing certain infertility treatments, undertaking human embryo research or storing gametes or embryos. The HFEA maintains a code of practice giving guidance about licensed centres and reports annually to Parliament.

Commercial surrogacy agencies and advertising of, or for, surrogacy services are prohibited; legislation to ban the use of fetal ovarian tissue in fertility treatment is before Parliament.

Family Planning

Free family planning advice and treatment are available to women from family doctors and from health authority family planning clinics, which also make services available to men. The *Health of the Nation* White Paper recognises the need for providing effective family planning services for people who want them.

Abortion

The Abortion Act 1967, as amended in 1990, allows the ending of a pregnancy of up to 24 weeks by a doctor if two doctors consider that continuing the pregnancy would involve greater risk of injury to the physical or mental health of the woman (or to any existing children of the family of the pregnant woman) than having an abortion. There are three categories in which no time limit applies: where there is a risk of grave permanent injury to the physical or mental health of the woman; where there is a substantial risk of fetal handicap; or where continuing the pregnancy would involve a risk to the life of the pregnant woman greater than that of the pregnancy being terminated. The Act does not apply in Northern Ireland.

In 1992:

- 172,063 legal abortions were performed in England and Wales, compared with 179,522 in 1991 (representing a 4.2 per cent decrease). The figures for Scotland were 10,764 and 11,068 respectively;

- abortions performed in the NHS in England and Wales increased by 5.8 per cent to 79,634, while those performed in the non-NHS sector fell by 11.4 per cent to 92,429. In Scotland 98 per cent of abortions were preformed in the NHS; and

- some 6.7 per cent of all abortions in England and Wales were to non-residents. In Scotland the figure was only about 0.2 per cent.

Drug Misuse

The misuse of dangerous drugs, such as heroin, cocaine and amphetamines, is a

serious social and health problem, and the
Government has made the fight against such
misuse a major priority. Its strategy
comprises action to reduce the supply of
illicit drugs from abroad; to promote more
effective law enforcement by the police and
Customs services; and to maintain tight
controls on medicinal drugs that can be
misused. It also includes action to maintain
effective deterrents against misuse; to
develop effective programmes to treat and
rehabilitate misusers; and, through
educational programmes and publicity
campaigns, to prevent people who are not
misusers from starting.

Research on various aspects of drug misuse
is funded by several government departments.
The Government is advised on a wide range
of matters relating to drug misuse and
connected social problems by the Advisory
Council on the Misuse of Drugs.

In December 1993 the Central Drugs
Co-ordination Unit was set up to look at
existing government strategy in England and
to propose changes where appropriate.
Similarly, in Scotland a ministerial Drugs
Task Force was set up in April 1993 to
review existing arrangements for prevention,
provision of services and co-ordination. A
wide-ranging review of the effectiveness of
treatment services for drug misusers in
England was announced in April 1994.

Drug Statistics

Recent drug statistics show that between 1992
and 1993:

- the number of notified drug addicts in
  Britain increased by 13 per cent
  (to 28,000)—in line with the prevailing
  upward trend;.

- the proportion of those notified who are
  addicted to heroin, the most frequently
  reported drug, fell to below 70 per cent,
  but this is balanced by an increase in
  notifications of addiction to methadone,
  which now accounts for over 40 per cent
  of notifications;.

- fewer than 10 per cent were reported to
  be addicted to cocaine, although the
  proportion is increasing;

- in general the highest numbers of all
  categories of notified addicts are to be
  found in London and the north west of
  England; and

- the proportion of addicts injecting drugs
  rose slightly from 54 per cent to 56 per
  cent.

Prevention

The Government has run national mass
media campaigns since 1985 to persuade
young people not to take drugs, and to advise
parents, teachers and other professionals on
how to recognise and combat the problem.
They have included warning of the dangers
of heroin misuse and of the risks of
transmitting HIV, the virus which causes
AIDS (see p. 386), through the sharing of
injecting equipment. Since 1991–92 the focus
has changed to give greater emphasis to
locally-based campaigns.

At present the Drugs Prevention Initiative
provides funding for local drug prevention
teams in 20 areas in England, Wales and
Scotland. (A major restructuring takes place
from March 1995, when the Drugs
Prevention Initiative will be responsible for
12 teams in England.) Their task is to
strengthen community resistance to drug
misuse. Over 1,000 projects have been
supported since the Initiative began in 1989.
The 1994–95 budget for the initiative is
approximately £6 million.

The local teams have identified five main
prevention approaches which are being
pursued within the initiative:

- education and training;
- information and awareness raising;
- diversionary activities;
- supporting community development; and
- work with criminal justice agencies.

Working groups have been formed for
each of these themes to pool experience,
develop future work and identify areas
suitable for further research.

Separate measures have been introduced in
Scotland to discourage drug misuse through
publicity campaigns and action in the
education service and the community. The

recently established Drugline Scotland, a free government-funded telephone line, gives confidential advice.

The Government continues to make funds available for local education authorities in England and Wales to appoint staff to promote and co-ordinate preventive work in their areas, especially for anti-drug misuse work in schools. As part of the National Curriculum (see p. 418), children in primary and secondary schools receive education on the dangers of drug misuse.

Treatment and Rehabilitation

Funds have been made available to health authorities since 1986–87 for developing and expanding services for drug misusers. Further funding has also been allocated to help prevent the spread of HIV among and from injecting drug misusers. This includes schemes providing counselling and the exchange of clean for used injecting equipment—in England £2.7 million is being allocated in 1994–95 to expand the provision of needle exchange schemes within pharmacies. The total amount available to health authorities in 1994–95 is over £25 million. Similar projects are in progress in Scotland, where £7 million is made available each year for the support of drug misuse services.

Treatment for drug dependence is provided mainly on an out-patient basis. Many hospitals provide specialist treatment for drug misusers, mainly in psychiatric units, or have special drug treatment units. An increasing number of GPs also treat drug misusers, but only certain specialist doctors are licensed to prescribe heroin, cocaine and dipipanone (Diconal). All doctors must notify the authorities of any patient they consider to be addicted to certain controlled drugs, and guidelines on good medical practice in the treatment of drug misuse are issued to doctors.

Other Services

A number of non-statutory agencies work with and complement the health service provision. Advice and rehabilitation services, including residential facilities, for example,

are provided mainly by voluntary organisations. Support in the community is provided by the probation service and local social services departments (and in Scotland by social work departments).

Solvent Misuse

Government policy is directed towards preventing solvent misuse through the education of young people, parents and professionals and, where practicable, restricting the sales of solvent-based liquefied gas and aerosol products to young people. In England and Wales it is an offence to supply such substances to children under 18 if the supplier knows or has reason to believe they are to be used to cause intoxication. In Scotland proceedings can be taken under the common law.

Alcohol Misuse

Alcohol is consumed by over 90 per cent of the adult population. About 28 per cent of men and 11 per cent of women drink to an extent that may put their health at risk. An estimated 8 million working days each year are lost through alcohol-related absenteeism. The cost to British industry of alcohol misuse is estimated at £1,700 million a year, and the total cost to society at £2,500 million.

The Government's view is that the consumption of alcohol in sensible quantities and in appropriate circumstances provides many people with enjoyment. Drinking fewer than 21 units of alcohol a week by men and 14 units a week by women is unlikely to damage health. (A unit is 8 grammes of pure alcohol, roughly equivalent to half a pint of ordinary strength beer or lager; or a glass of wine; or a pub measure of spirits.) The British medical profession advises that sustained drinking above these levels progressively increases the health risk, and that drinking over 50 units a week by men and over 35 units by women is definitely dangerous.

The health strategies include targets for reducing the proportion of people drinking over sensible levels and set out a programme of action by government departments, health and local authorities, the independent sector, employers and the alcohol industry.

Part of the funds of the Health Education Authority (see p. 388) are for promoting the sensible drinking message in England, and equivalent bodies are similarly funded in other parts of Britain. At local level this requires co-ordinated action by a wide range of organisations with an interest in the use or misuse of alcohol.

Treatment and rehabilitation within the NHS include in-patient and out-patient services in general and psychiatric hospitals and specialised alcoholism treatment units. Primary care teams (GPs, nurses and social workers) and voluntary organisations providing treatment and rehabilitation in hostels, day centres and advisory services also play an important role.

The development of services to help problem drinkers and their families is being taken forward within the framework of community care. Local authorities are required to identify the need for alcohol misuse services in their area, and to list the services provided in their community care plans (see p. 392). They are then responsible for arranging for the needs of individuals with alcohol problems to be assessed, and for buying an appropriate course of care.

There is close co-operation between statutory and voluntary organisations. In England the voluntary agency Alcohol Concern, which is receiving a government grant of £1.58 million for 1994–95, plays a prominent role in training for professional and voluntary workers. It is improving the network of voluntary agencies and their collaboration with statutory bodies in the prevention of misuse.

Between 1991–92 and 1995–96 a total government contribution of £6 million is being allocated to Alcohol Concern for improving and extending the network of care, advisory and counselling services. In addition, a grant of £2.4 million is being paid to local authorities during 1994–95 to help voluntary agencies improve and extend provision for alcohol and drug misusers. The Scottish Council on Alcohol undertakes similar work in Scotland, with the help of a government grant (£185,000 in 1994–95).

Research and surveys on various aspects of alcohol misuse are funded by several government departments.

Smoking

Cigarette smoking is the greatest preventable cause of illness and death in Britain. It is associated with around 110,000 premature deaths and an estimated 50 million lost working days each year, and costs the NHS an estimated £10 million a year for the treatment of related diseases (for example, heart disease, lung cancer and bronchitis). In addition, smoking by pregnant women can cause low birth weight in infants. The Government is following an active health education policy supported by voluntary agreements with the tobacco industry (see below) aimed at reducing the level of smoking.

The Government aims to reduce adult smoking in England from the present 30 per cent to 20 per cent by the year 2000. A further aim has been to reduce smoking by young people by one-third between 1988 and the end of 1994. Smoking is also being tackled as a priority in Wales, Scotland and Northern Ireland and similar targets have been set for the year 2000.

A three-year national campaign, costing £4 million a year, started in 1994. Aimed at adult smokers, particularly parents, the campaign will emphasise the dangers of passive smoking. It will be backed up by local activities to help people to stop smoking. Education on the harmful effects of smoking is included in the National Curriculum for all pupils in publicly maintained schools in England and Wales.

The Government also supports the work of the voluntary organisation Action on Smoking and Health (ASH), whose services include a workplace services consultancy, offering advice and help to employers in formulating anti-smoking policies. The Government is committed to creating a smoke-free environment, with facilities where appropriate for those who wish to smoke, and has published a code of practice on smoking in public places. Health authorities have been asked to promote non-smoking as the normal practice in health service buildings and to give help and advice to people who want to give up smoking. The Independent Scientific Committee on Smoking and Health estimated that passive smoking, especially in the workplace and the home, may cause several hundred deaths through lung cancer every year.

Voluntary Agreements

Voluntary agreements between the Government and the tobacco industry regulate the advertising and promotion of tobacco products, and sports sponsorship by the industry. The agreement on tobacco advertising provides for the use on posters of six different health warnings about the dangers of smoking and contains measures to protect groups at particular risk, such as children, young people and women in their early child-bearing years.

Under a revised agreement, which runs for five years from 1994:

- health warnings on cigar and pipe tobacco advertisements are to be introduced for the first time;

- all permanent shopfront advertising is to be removed by the end of 1996;

- all poster advertising is to be banned from within a 200m radius of school entrances;

- all advertisements for cigarettes and hand-rolling tobacco are to be banned on buses and taxis; and

- permitted expenditure on cigarette poster advertising is to be reduced by 40 per cent.

The voluntary agreement on sports sponsorship covers levels of spending, restrictions on sponsorship of events chiefly for spectators under 18 years and controls over the siting of advertising at televised events.

Legislative Measures

It is illegal to sell any type of tobacco product to children; the maximum fine is £2,500. All tobacco advertising is banned on television and cigarette advertisements are banned on radio. Oral snuff products have been banned since 1993.

AIDS

Up to the end of June 1994 a total of 9,436 cases of AIDS had been reported in Britain, of whom 6,388 (68 per cent) had died; the total number of recognised HIV infections was 21,101. While this is recognised as a considerable underestimate of the true numbers of infections, attempts to contain the spread of HIV infection have nevertheless been successful and Britain now has one of the lowest estimated rates of HIV prevalence in Western Europe.

Government Strategy

The latest medium-term predictions (published in June 1993) show that new cases of AIDS among homosexual men are levelling out and declining among injecting drug misusers, but there is a steady increase in cases of HIV infection through heterosexual contact.

Key elements of the Government's strategy for dealing with the disease include:

- encouraging appropriate behaviour change by increased targeting of sections of the population at particular risk, including homosexual and bisexual men and drug misusers;

- sustaining and improving general public awareness;

- continuing to make HIV testing facilities more widely known, and encouraging health authorities to commission additional accessible HIV testing sites; and

- continued funding for the voluntary sector.

The Government's commitment to policies in this area is demonstrated by its inclusion of HIV/AIDS with sexual health as one of the five key areas in the *Health of the Nation* White Paper. HIV/AIDS has also been identified as a health priority in Scotland. A concerted approach is being maintained, spanning government, the NHS, local authorities and the voluntary sector (including women's groups, Britain's faith communities and organisations working with ethnic minorities).

RELIGION

Legislation allowing the ordination of women to the priesthood of the Church of England was passed in 1994. Here, Angela Berners-Wilson, the first woman to be ordained, celebrates the Eucharist at St Paul's Church, Bristol.

Muslim boys attend a class during Ramadan at the Jamia Mosque in High Wycombe, Buckinghamshire. There are nearly 500 mosques and prayer centres in Britain.

FOOD AND DRINK

The growing awareness in Britain of the importance of a healthy diet is encouraged by nationwide public information campaigns. Government guidelines recommend that more fruit, vegetables and starchy foods should be eaten instead of foods high in sugar and fat.

Denbies Wine Estate in Dorking, Surrey, has over 300,000 vines and 19 grape varieties. It produces over 1 million bottles of high-quality wine each year.

Shopping for food can now take place at times more convenient to the customer: new legislation, which came into force in summer 1994, has put an end to the anomalies surrounding Sunday retailing. Large stores like supermarkets may open for six hours a day, while smaller shops can open at any time.

Bottled water is increasingly popular in Britain. The export market is also expanding: Tŷ Nant, a company based in Dyfed, Wales, now sells 85 per cent of its spring water overseas.

Karen Dixon, who won the individual bronze medal in the World Three-Day Event Championship in The Netherlands. Britain's all-woman team won the gold medal.

England's 4 x 400 metres relay team, *(left to right)* Linda Keough, Sally Gunnell, Phylis Smith and Tracy Goddard, celebrate their gold medal win in the Commonwealth Games in Victoria, Canada.

In England NHS funding for HIV/AIDS increased from £214 million in 1993–94 to £225 million in 1994–95, and local authority funding increased from £12.4 million to £12.9 million. In Scotland over £19.5 million has been made available to health boards in 1994–95, in addition to their general allocations for HIV/AIDS related purposes.

Details of Britain's contribution to international co-operation on AIDS are given in Chapter 9.

Voluntary Organisations

Voluntary agencies concerned with HIV/AIDS include the Terrence Higgins Trust, London Lighthouse, Body Positive, National AIDS Trust, and Scottish AIDS Monitor, which promote knowledge about the disease and help people with AIDS and HIV. Both London Lighthouse and the Mildmay Mission Hospital, in London, provide hospice care and community support. The Government will continue distributing grants on a yearly basis, taking into account developing health priorities and the ability of voluntary bodies to raise funds from other sources for HIV/AIDS work.

Infectious Diseases

District health authorities (health boards in Scotland and Northern Ireland) carry out programmes of immunisation against diphtheria, measles, mumps, rubella, poliomyelitis, tetanus, tuberculosis and whooping cough. A new immunisation, 'Hib', was introduced in 1992, offering protection against invasive haemophilus disease, a major cause of meningitis in children under five years. As a result, Hib infections fell by over 70 per cent in the first quarter of 1993, compared with the same period in previous years.

Immunisation is voluntary, but parents are encouraged to protect their children. The proportion of children being vaccinated has been increasing since the end of 1978. GPs who achieve targets of 70 and 90 per cent uptake of child immunisation receive special payments (see p. 378).

The Public Health Laboratory Service provides a network of bacteriological and virological laboratories throughout England and Wales which conduct research and assist in the diagnosis, prevention and control of communicable diseases. Similar facilities are provided in Scotland by the Scottish Centre for Infection and Environmental Health and, as in Northern Ireland, by some hospital laboratories.

Cancer Care

Controlling cancer forms an enormous part of the NHS's work, consuming nearly 10 per cent of its total budget. In May 1994 the Government outlined proposals for reorganising the provision of cancer services. It proposes care at three levels:

- primary care, with detailed discussions between GPs and the hospital service to clarify patterns of referral and follow-up;
- designated cancer units, which should be created in many local hospitals and should be large enough to support multi-disciplinary clinical teams, with sufficient expertise and facilities to manage the more common cancers; and
- designated cancer centres to provide an extra range of specialised services in support of cancer units, and to treat less common cancers, or to provide treatments that are too technically demanding, too specialised, or too capital-intensive for the cancer units.

Cancer Screening

Breast cancer is recognised as a major health problem in Britain. Some 13,000 women die from it each year and 1 in 14 women in England will develop it. To help combat this, the Government has set up a national screening programme under which women aged between 50 and 64 are invited for mammography (breast X-ray) every three years by computerised call and recall systems.

Nearly 1,900 women die each year in Great Britain from cancer of the cervix, and the Government has, similarly, set up a nationwide cervical screening programme. All district health authorities in England and

Wales have computerised call and recall systems which enable all women aged between 20 and 64 to be invited to have a smear test at least every five years. Similar arrangements apply in Scotland (where the age range is 20 to 60) and in Northern Ireland. Deaths from cervical cancer in England and Wales have fallen since the programme began, dropping from 1,903 in 1987 to 1,647 in 1992. Special payments are made to GPs who achieve uptake targets for smear tests of 50 and 80 per cent. The response has been encouraging in many areas and the Government estimates that over 90 per cent of GPs now earn bonus payments for meeting cervical screening and childhood immunisation targets.

The reduction of deaths and illness from cancer is a key area in the Government's *Health of the Nation* White Paper. The targets set are:

- to reduce breast cancer deaths among women invited for screening by at least 25 per cent by the year 2000;
- to reduce the incidence of invasive cervical cancer by at least 20 per cent by the year 2000;
- to halt the year-on-year increase in the incidence of skin cancer by 2005; and
- to reduce the death rate for lung cancer under the age of 75 by at least 30 per cent in men and by at least 15 per cent in women by 2010.

Health Education

In England health education is promoted by the Health Education Authority, a part of the NHS. Its functions are to:

- advise the Government on health education;
- plan and carry out health education programmes in co-operation with health authorities and other bodies; and
- sponsor research and evaluation.

In addition, the Authority has the major executive responsibility for public education in Britain about AIDS. It also assists in the provision of training for HIV/AIDS workers, and provides a national centre of information

and advice on health education. Major campaigns carried out by the Authority include those focusing on coronary heart disease, smoking and alcohol misuse.

The Health Education Board for Scotland, with a budget of £6.6 million in 1994–95, the Welsh Health Promotion Authority (£3.2 million in 1994–95) and the Northern Ireland Health Promotion Agency are responsible for health education in their areas.

Almost all health authorities have their own health education service, which works closely with health professionals, health visitors, community groups, local employers and others to determine the most suitable local programmes. Increased resources in the health service are being directed towards health education and preventive measures. GPs receive special annual payments for health promotion programmes.

Healthier Eating

There has been growing public awareness in recent years of the importance of a healthy diet. The *Health of the Nation* White Paper followed the recommendations of the Committee on Medical Aspects of Food Policy (COMA) that people should reduce their average intakes of total fat and saturated fatty acids in order to reduce cardiovascular disease. It contained a number of dietary targets, and the Nutrition Task Force was established to devise a programme to achieve them. Launched in March 1994, the programme is being implemented through a number of project teams in information and education, catering, the NHS and the food chain. A report on obesity is due to be published in late 1994.

Nutritional labelling indicating the energy, fat, protein and carbohydrate content of food is being encouraged on a voluntary basis. The major supermarket chains and most food manufacturers have already introduced voluntary labelling schemes. The Government has issued guidelines on the labelling of food to show nutrient content in a standard format.

Current work by COMA includes a review of the relationship between diet and cardiovascular disease and between diet and cancer; matters relating to the nutrition of infants and children; and assessment of the nutritional implications of certain novel foods. Its recent reports have included comprehensive information on dietary reference values for food energy and nutrients (1991); and on the nutritional needs of elderly people (1992).

ENVIRONMENTAL HEALTH

Environmental health officers employed by local authorities are responsible for a range of functions, including the control of air pollution and noise, and food hygiene and safety. Their duties also cover the occupational health and safety aspects of a variety of premises, including offices and shops; the investigation of unfit housing; and in some instances refuse collection and home safety.

Doctors who specialise in community medicine and are employed by the health authorities advise local authorities on the medical aspects of environmental health, infectious diseases and food poisoning. They may also co-operate with the authorities responsible for water supply and sewerage. Environmental health officers at ports and airports carry out duties concerned with shipping, inspection of imported foods, and disease control. In Northern Ireland district councils are responsible for noise control; collection and disposal of refuse; clean air; and food composition, labelling and hygiene.

A new public body, the Institute for Environment and Health, was established by the Medical Research Council (see below) in 1993. It is concerned mainly with the chemical hazards to which people may be exposed through the environment.

Safety of Food

It is illegal to supply food unfit for human consumption or to apply any treatment or process to food which makes it harmful to health. Places where food or drink is prepared, handled, stored or sold must comply with certain hygiene provisions. Environmental health officers may take away for examination samples of any food intended for sale or human consumption. Specific

regulations control the safety of milk, meat, ice-cream and shellfish. The Food Safety Directorate within the Ministry of Agriculture, Fisheries and Food and the Health Aspects of the Environment and Food Division within the Department of Health ensure the safety and quality of Britain's food. The two Departments work closely with the food industry, environmental health departments and consumer bodies to ensure the provision of safe food in order to protect public health. (For further details on food safety, see Chapter 18.)

SAFETY OF MEDICINES

Only medicines which have been granted a product licence may be sold or supplied to the public. Licences are issued following scientific assessment by the Medicines Control Agency of the Department of Health. (The Veterinary Medicines Directorate of the Ministry of Agriculture, Fisheries and Food is similarly responsible for animal medicines).

A number of committees provide independent advice to Ministers. The Medicines Commission advises on matters connected with the safety of human and veterinary medicines; its duties also include hearing appeals from companies against advice that a product licence should not be granted. The Committee on Safety of Medicines and the Committee on Dental and Surgical Materials advise on the safety, quality and efficacy of medicinal products for human use.

In 1994, for example, a new homoeopathic registration scheme was set up, covering homoeopathic products for oral and/or external use. Registered products have to satisfy high standards of quality and safety although no evidence of efficacy is required.

RESEARCH

In 1993–94 the Department of Health in England spent an estimated £30 million on health and personal social services research, in addition to expenditure by the Medical Research Council (the main government agency for the support of biomedical and clinical research—see Chapter 20). Priority areas include research into health promotion and the prevention of ill health; environmental health; adult health; and child care.

Wales also participates in the Department of Health's programme of centrally commissioned research. A research and development strategy for the NHS in Scotland was published in 1993.

The NHS research and development programme aims to ensure that health service care is based on high-quality research relevant to improving the nation's health. The programme is managed by the regional health authorities, which are developing their own research plans. It is intended that up to 1.5 per cent of NHS expenditure will be used for research and development by 1997.

A new centre for primary health care research and development is being set up at Manchester University; the Department of Health will contribute £1.5 million a year.

The Department of Health is involved in international research and development, and takes part in the European Union's medical and public health research programme.

THE HEALTH PROFESSIONS

Doctors and Dentists

Only people on the medical or dentists' registers may practise as doctors or dentists in the NHS. University medical and dental schools are responsible for teaching; the NHS provides hospital facilities for training. Full registration as a doctor requires five or six years' training in a medical school and hospital, with a further year's experience in a hospital. For a dentist, five years' training at a dental school is required.

An extensive review of postgraduate medical education was carried out in 1992–93 and is expected to lead to considerable improvements in junior doctors' education and training, including a significant reduction in the time which individual doctors spend in the training grades.

The regulating body for the medical profession is the General Medical Council and, for dentists, the General Dental Council. The main professional associations are the British Medical Association and the British Dental Association.

Nurses

The minimum period of training required to qualify for registration as a first level nurse in general, mental health, mental handicap, or children's nursing is normally three years. Midwifery training for registered general nurses takes 18 months, and for others, three years. Health visitors are registered general nurses who have completed a one-year course in health visiting. District nurses are registered general nurses who practise within the community. They must complete a six-month course followed by a period of supervised practice in district nursing. In Northern Ireland health visitors, district nurses and schools', community psychiatric, community mental handicap and occupational health nurses undertake a one-year diploma course.

Project 2000 is the new system of nurse education and training, stemming from proposals put forward by the nursing profession in response to people's changing health care needs. The course is designed to give nurses a broader based education, emphasising health promotion as well as the care of the sick, and enabling them to work in either hospital or community without extensive further training. Implementation began in 1989 and all colleges now offer Project 2000.

The United Kingdom Central Council for Nursing, Midwifery and Health Visiting is responsible for regulating and registering these professions.

Pharmacists

Only people on the register of pharmaceutical chemists may practise as pharmacists. Registration requires three or four years' training in a school of pharmacy, followed by one year's practical experience in a community or hospital pharmacy approved for training by the Royal Pharmaceutical Society of Great Britain or the Pharmaceutical Society of Northern Ireland (regulatory bodies for the profession).

Opticians

The General Optical Council regulates the

professions of ophthalmic optician and dispensing optician. Only registered ophthalmic opticians (or registered ophthalmic medical practitioners) may test sight. Training of ophthalmic opticians takes four years, including a year of practical experience under supervision. Dispensing opticians take a two-year full-time course with a year's practical experience or follow a part-time day-release course while employed with an optician.

Other Health Professions

Chiropodists, dietitians, medical laboratory scientific officers, occupational therapists, physiotherapists and radiographers may, on qualification, apply for state registration. Each profession has its own board under the general supervision of the Council for Professions Supplementary to Medicine. Applications for a further two boards have been made from art, drama and music therapists and orthotists and prosthetists. State registration is mandatory for employment in the NHS and local authorities and is highly recommended in other public services and the private sector.

Dental therapists and dental hygienists are almost exclusively recruited from certified dental surgery assistants who have taken at least one year's training. Dental therapists then take a two-year training course and dental hygienists a one-year course; both carry out some simple dental work under the supervision of a registered dentist.

National and Scottish Vocational Qualifications (NVQs and SVQs—see p. 425) have been developed for health care support workers, ambulance personnel, operating department practitioners, physiological measurement technicians and administrative and clerical staff.

HEALTH ARRANGEMENTS WITH OTHER COUNTRIES

The member states of the European Economic Area have special health arrangements under which EEA nationals resident in a member state are entitled to receive emergency treatment, either free or at a reduced cost, during visits to other EEA countries. There are also arrangements for referral for specific treatment in certain circumstances and to cover people who go to work or live in other EEA countries. In addition, there are reciprocal arrangements with some other countries under which medical treatment is available to visitors to Britain if required immediately. Visitors are generally expected to pay if the purpose of their visit is to seek medical treatment. Visitors who are not covered by reciprocal arrangements must pay for any medical treatment they receive.

Personal Social Services

Personal social services assist elderly people, disabled people and their carers, children and young people, people with mental illness or learning disabilities, and families. Major services include skilled residential and day care, help for people confined to their homes, and the various forms of social work. The statutory services are provided by local government social services authorities in England and Wales, social work departments in Scotland, and health and social services boards in Northern Ireland. Alongside these providers are the many and varied contributions made by independent private and voluntary services. Much of the care given to elderly and disabled people is provided by families and self-help groups.

Demand for these services is rising because of the increasing number of elderly people, who, along with disabled and mentally ill people, or those with learning disabilities, can lead more normal lives in the community, given suitable support and facilities.

The shift away from long-term hospital care to care in the community is reflected in recent hospital statistics. Average length of stay in the geriatric hospital sector has declined by around 9 per cent a year since 1978. Personal social services staff increased by 23 per cent between 1978–79 and 1991–92, the most significant increases being in social work staff, day care and home helps. In the residential care group, numbers of staff in adult services in 1991–92 fell significantly for the first time.

Management Reforms

New policies on community care in England, Wales and Scotland have been implemented in stages under the NHS and Community Care Act 1990. In Northern Ireland similar arrangements were introduced in April 1993 under equivalent legislation. Many of the procedures which local authorities are implementing correspond to similar procedures being introduced in the NHS (see p. 373). Local authorities increasingly act as enablers and commissioners of services after assessing their populations' needs for social care.

- Since April 1991 inspection units have been responsible for inspecting local authority as well as private and voluntary sector residential care homes, and local authorities have had to have procedures for dealing with complaints about their social services.

- Since April 1992 local authorities have been obliged to produce community care plans after wide consultation with the NHS and other interests.

- Since April 1993 new procedures for assessing individuals' care needs and commissioning services to meet them have been introduced.

Local authorities are now responsible for funding and arranging social care in the community for people who require public support. This includes the provision of home helps or home care assistants to support people in their own homes, and making arrangements for residential and nursing home care for those no longer able to remain in their own homes. Previously, residents of these homes who obtained public funding received help principally through special higher levels of income support (see p. 405). In 1994–95 central government grant of over £1,000 million is being made available to local authorities for community care in England. This includes an extra £20 million for developing respite and domiciliary care.

Elderly People

Between 1981 and 1991 the number of people over 60 in Great Britain increased by about 500,000; little change is expected over the period 1991 to 1996. The number of people aged 75 and over in Britain is projected to rise from 3.9 million in mid-1993 to 4.5 million in mid-2003—an increase of 14 per cent.

Spending on health care for elderly people increased by 40.8 per cent in real terms between 1978–79 and 1990–91 and has remained broadly constant since 1991–92. Between 1978–79 and 1992–93 net spending on social services increased by 68.3 per cent in real terms. About 5 per cent of those aged 65 or over live in residential homes.

Services for elderly people are designed to help them live at home whenever possible. These services may include advice and help given by social workers, domestic help, the provision of meals in the home, sitters-in, night attendants and laundry services as well as day centres, lunch clubs and recreational facilities. Adaptations to the home can overcome a person's difficulties in moving about, and a wide range of equipment is available for people with difficulties affecting their hearing or eyesight. Alarm systems have been developed to help elderly people obtain assistance in an emergency. In some areas 'good neighbour' and visiting services are arranged by the local authority or a voluntary organisation.

Many local authorities provide free or subsidised travel for elderly people within their areas. Local authorities also provide residential care for elderly people and those in poor health.

As part of their responsibility for public housing, local authorities provide homes designed for elderly people; some of these developments have resident wardens. Housing associations and private builders also build such accommodation.

Disabled People

Britain has an estimated 6 million adults with one or more disabilities, of whom around 400,000 (7 per cent) live in communal establishments. Over the past ten years there has been increasing emphasis on rehabilitation and on the provision of day, domiciliary and respite support services to enable disabled people to live independently in the community wherever possible.

Local social services authorities help with social rehabilitation and adjustment to disability. They are required to identify the number of disabled people in their area and to publicise services. These may include advice on personal and social problems arising from disability, as well as occupational, educational, social and recreational facilities, either at day centres or elsewhere. Other services provided may include adaptations to homes (such as ramps for wheelchairs, and ground-floor toilets); the delivery of cooked meals; and help in the home. In cases of special need, help may be given with installing a telephone or a television. Local authorities and voluntary organisations may provide severely disabled people with residential accommodation or temporary facilities to allow their carers relief from their duties. Specially designed housing may be available for those able to look after themselves.

The Independent Living (1993) Fund is an independent and discretionary trust which provides financial help to very severely disabled people of working age to live independently in the community. The Fund works in partnership with local authorities, which are expected to make a contribution in the form of services equivalent to what they would have spent on residential or nursing care.

Some authorities provide free or subsidised travel for disabled people on public transport, and they are encouraged to provide special means of access to public buildings. Special government regulations cover the provision of access for disabled people in the construction of new buildings.

In 1991 the Government committed £3 million for a pilot scheme in England— the National Disability Information Project— designed to improve information services for disabled people, their carers and service providers. Twelve projects are being funded to explore ways in which the voluntary and statutory agencies can work together to provide information services aimed at satisfying the needs of users. Similar projects are being supported in Wales. A separate survey of the information needs of disabled people has been carried out in Scotland.

People with Learning Disabilities (Mental Handicap)

The Government's policy is to encourage the development of local services for people with learning disabilities and their families through co-operation between health and local authorities, and voluntary and other organisations.

Local authority social services departments are the leading statutory agency for planning and arranging services for people with learning disabilities. They provide short-term care, support for families in their own homes, residential accommodation and support for various types of activities outside the home. The main aims are to ensure that as far as possible people with learning disabilities can lead full lives in their communities and that no one is admitted to hospital unless it is necessary on health grounds.

The NHS provides specialist services where the general health needs of people with learning disabilities cannot be met by ordinary NHS services, and residential care for those with severe disabilities or whose needs can only effectively be met by the NHS.

Mentally Ill People

Government policy aims to ensure that people with mental illnesses should have access to all the services they need as locally as possible. These services should be based on a comprehensive network of health and social services facilities in each district. They should be community based and easily accessible.

While the total number of places for mentally ill people in the large hospitals has continued to fall, this has been matched by increasing provision of alternative places in smaller NHS hospitals, local authority accommodation and private and voluntary sector homes.

In England between 1982 and 1993:

- the number of homes and hospitals specialising in the care of mentally ill people grew from about 1,000 to almost 2,500;
- of 130 hospitals with over 100 beds open in 1961, 89 remained open; all but 22 of these had plans for closure by the end of the century; and
- the number of places available for mentally ill people remained in the region of 80,000.

Arrangements made by social services authorities for providing preventive care and after care for mentally ill people in the community include day centres, social centres and residential care. Social workers help patients and their families with problems caused by mental illness. In some cases they can apply for a mentally disordered person to be compulsorily admitted to and detained in hospital. The Mental Health Act Commission aims to provide improved safeguards for such patients. Similar arrangements apply in Wales, Scotland and Northern Ireland.

District health authorities (health boards in Scotland) are required to plan individual health and social care programmes for all patients leaving hospital and for all new patients accepted by the specialist psychiatric services. A specific grant of £36 million for 1994–95 to local authorities in England is designed to encourage them to increase the level of social care available to mentally ill patients, including those with dementia who need specialist psychiatric care in the community. In Scotland a similar scheme is supporting community projects to the value of £14 million in 1994–95.

The Government plans to introduce legislation to provide a new power of supervised discharge for mentally ill patients who need special support after they leave hospital. Under this patients who do not comply with their care programme may be recalled compulsorily to hospital. In addition supervision registers for discharged patients most at risk were introduced in April 1994. These are to be maintained by the providers of services for mentally ill people and will allow hospital staff to keep track of discharged patients.

The first government-backed national survey of mental illness began in April 1993 and will be completed in 1995. The survey, which covers adults aged 16 to 64 living in communal establishments as well as those living in private households, will estimate the prevalence of different types of mental illness and will identify the resulting social disabilities. It will also examine the varying use of health, social and voluntary care services, and the risk factors associated with mental illness. A review of mental health nursing reported in March 1994. The Government is considering its recommendations.

A three-year public information campaign began in spring 1993 to increase people's awareness and understanding about mental illness and suicide.

There are many voluntary organisations concerned with mental illness and learning disabilities, and they play an important role in providing services for both groups of people.

Help to Families

Social services authorities, through their own social workers and others in the voluntary sector, give help to families facing special problems. This includes services for families with children in need or at risk of harm or neglect including some who may need care away from their own families, and support for family carers who look after elderly and other family members in order to give them relief from their duties. They also help single parents. There are now many refuges run by local authorities or voluntary organisations for women, often with young children, whose home conditions have become intolerable. The refuges provide short-term accommodation and support while attempts are made to relieve the women's problems. Many authorities also contribute to the cost of support and counselling with families (such as marriage guidance) carried out by voluntary organisations.

Day Care for Children

Day care facilities for children under five are provided by local authorities, voluntary agencies and privately. In allocating places in their day nurseries and other facilities, local authorities give priority to children with special social, learning or health needs. Local authorities also register and inspect childminders, private day nurseries and playgroups in their areas and provide support and advice services. Day care figures for 1993 show the number of places for children in day nurseries and with childminders has continued to grow.

In 1993 the Government launched a £45 million scheme to help create childcare facilities in Great Britain for children over five after school hours and during the holidays. The scheme is operated through Training and Enterprise Councils and Local Enterprise Companies (see p. 195). These organisations are developing local partnerships with employers, schools, parents, local authorities and voluntary organisations.

Child Abuse

Cases of child abuse are the joint concern of a number of different agencies and professions. Area child protection committees provide forums for discussion and co-ordination and draw up policies and procedures for handling these cases. The Government's central training initiative on child abuse, established in England and Wales in 1986, consists of a variety of projects, including training for health visitors, school nurses, and local authority social services staff. Guidelines and training packs have been developed for those implementing the Children Act 1989 (see below). In Scotland the Government provides support for child abuse training at the University of Dundee and through a specific grant scheme.

The training initiative is now combined with a treatment initiative which began in 1990 to provide grant funding for a range of child abuse treatment projects.

In England, Wales and Northern Ireland children under the age of 14 called as witnesses in criminal cases involving certain violent and sexual offences are able to give evidence to courts through video recorded interview and television links, thus avoiding, wherever possible, the need for them to give evidence in open court in the presence of the alleged abuser. Similar arrangments are available in Scotland.

Children in Care

Local government authorities must provide accommodation for children who have no parent or guardian, have been abandoned, or whose parents are unable to provide for them.

The Children Act 1989, which came into effect in England and Wales in 1991, recasts the legislative framework for children's services, care and protection into a single coherent structure. It lays new duties on local authorities to safeguard and promote the welfare of children. Under the Act parents of children in care retain their parental responsibilities but act as far as possible as partners with the authority. There is a new requirement to prepare a child for leaving the local authority's responsibility and to continue to advise him or her up to the age of 21. Local authorities are required to have a complaints procedure with an independent element to cover children in their care.

The latest report on the working of the Children Act[2], published in May 1994, confirms that the number of children looked after by local authorities, and on a child protection register, continues to decline as local authorities respond to the Act's requirement that wherever possible children should remain at home with their families.

In England and Wales a child may be brought before a family proceedings court if he or she is neglected or ill-treated, exposed to moral danger, beyond the control of parents, or not attending school. The court can commit the child to the care of a local authority under a care order. Under the Children Act 1989 certain preconditions have to be satisfied to justify an order. These are that the child is suffering or is likely to suffer significant harm because of a lack of reasonable parental care or is beyond parental control. However, an order is made only if the court is also satisfied that this will positively contribute to the child's well-being and be in his or her best interests. In court

---

[2] *Children Act 1989. A Report by the Secretaries of State for Health and for Wales.* HMSO, £14.40.

proceedings the child is entitled to separate legal representation and the right to have a guardian to protect his or her interests.

All courts have to treat the welfare of the child as the paramount consideration when reaching any decision about his or her upbringing. The family proceedings court consists of specially trained magistrates with power to hear care cases as well as all other family and children's cases.

Recent concerns over standards of care in certain local authority children's homes have prompted a number of official inquiries whose recommendations are now being implemented. They include:

- Norman Warner's inquiry into the selection of staff in children's homes and the support and guidance available to them after appointment (1992);
- the Howe inquiry into staff conditions, management and training for all residential care staff in adult and children's homes (1992);
- the Skinner review of residential child care in Scotland (1992); and
- a report by the Social Services Inspectorate on children's homes in England (1993). This was the first national report to come from a team of SSI Inspectors and young people who had themselves been in care.

In Scotland children in trouble or in need may be brought before a children's hearing, which can impose a supervision requirement on a child if it thinks that compulsory measures are appropriate. Under these requirements most children are allowed to remain at home under the supervision of a social worker but some may live with foster parents or in a residential establishment while under supervision. Supervision requirements are reviewed at least once a year until ended by a children's hearing. A government White Paper, *Scotland's Children: Proposals for Child Care Policy and Law*, proposing reforms in Scottish child care policy and law, was published in 1993. In addition to proposed legislative changes, a number of improvements in child care services, policy and practice have already been made

through administrative means, increased funding and additional training of social work staff.

In Northern Ireland the juvenile court may place children who are in need of care, protection or control into the care of a fit person (including a health and social services board), or may make them subject to a supervision order. Children in trouble may be required to attend an attendance centre, be committed to a training school, or may be detained in a remand home. New child care legislation is being prepared in Northern Ireland which will reflect the changes introduced in England and Wales under the Children Act 1989 and will make a distinction between the treatment of children in need of care and young offenders.

Fostering and Children's Homes

When appropriate, children in care are placed with foster parents, who receive payments to cover living costs. Alternatively, the child may be placed in a local authority, voluntary or private children's home or other suitable residential accommodation, including boarding school. In Scotland local authorities are responsible for placing children in their care in foster homes, in local authority or voluntary homes, or in residential schools. Similar provisions apply in Northern Ireland. Regulations concerning residential care and the foster placement of children in care are made by central government.

Adoption

Local authorities are required by law to provide an adoption service, either directly or by arrangement with a voluntary organisation. Agencies may offer adoptive parents an allowance in certain circumstances if this would help to find a family for a child. Adoption is strictly regulated by law, and voluntary adoption societies must be approved by the appropriate Secretary of State. The Registrars-General keep confidential registers of adopted children. Adopted people may be given details of their original birth record on reaching the age of

18, and counselling is provided to help them understand the circumstances of their adoption. An Adoption Contact Register enables adopted adults and their birth parents to be given a safe and confidential way of making contact if that is the wish of both parties. A person's details are entered only if they wish to be contacted.

A government White Paper on adoption in England and Wales was published in 1993. It includes proposals to allow children aged 12 or over to agree to the making of their adoption order and to have the right to take part in their own adoption proceedings; simpler alternatives to adoption for step-parents, relatives or long-term foster parents; and streamlined arrangements for adopting from overseas.

In Scotland a consultation document on the review of adoption law was also published in 1993.

Social Workers

The effective working of the social services depends largely on professionally qualified social workers. Training programmes in social work are provided by universities and colleges of higher and further education. The Central Council for Education and Training in Social Work is the statutory body responsible for promoting and regulating social work training. A programme to introduce two-year courses leading to a new professional qualification, the Diploma in Social Work (DipSW), has been implemented. National Vocational Qualifications are being developed for other staff, including those in residential day and domiciliary care services.

Professional social workers (including those working in the NHS) are employed mainly by the social services departments of local authorities. Others work in the probation service, the education welfare service, or in voluntary and private organisations. In Scotland local authority social work departments provide most services, including those to the NHS and in probation and criminal justice. There is also a growing voluntary sector.

The Government is committed to improving social work training. In England alone it is providing £33.3 million in 1994–95 (£4.2 million in Scotland) through its training support programme to assist local authorities to train staff. Total spending by local authorities in England on social services training amounts to £46.9 million.

Further Reading

One Year On . . . : A Report on the Progress of the Health of the Nation. Department of Health, 1993.

On the State of the Public Health 1993. The Annual Report of the Chief Medical Officer of the Department of Health, HMSO, 1993.

Health in Scotland 1993. HMSO, 1993.

Social Welfare. Aspects of Britain series, HMSO, 1993.

25 Social Security

Administration	398	Arrangements with Other		
Contributions	399	Countries		408
Benefits	400			

Spending on social security is rising because of increasing numbers of beneficiaries, especially retirement pensioners, and long-term sick and disabled people. The value of retirement and most other long-term benefits has also increased in real terms since 1980. Planned spending in 1994–95 is £83,000 million—the Government's largest expenditure programme.

As part of its long-term review of public spending (see p. 155), the Government is examining the social security programme and reforming the structure of the present system to ensure it involves:

- better targeting of those in need;
- encouraging more self-provision; and
- providing more incentives to work.

The social security system is designed to secure a basic standard of living for people in financial need by providing income during periods of inability to earn (including periods of unemployment), help for families and assistance with costs arising from disablement. Nearly a third of government expenditure is devoted to the social security programme, which provides financial help for people who are elderly, sick, disabled, unemployed, widowed, bringing up children or on very low incomes.

Some benefits depend on the payment of contributions by employers, employees and self-employed people to the National Insurance Fund, from which benefits are paid. The Government also contributes to the Fund. The other social security benefits are non-contributory and are financed from general taxation; some of these are income-related (see p. 407). Appeals about claims for benefits are decided by independent tribunals.

ADMINISTRATION

Administration in Great Britain is handled by separate executive agencies of the Department of Social Security:

- the Benefits Agency, responsible for paying the majority of social security benefits;
- the Child Support Agency, responsible for collecting and enforcing maintenance payments for children (see p. 403);
- the Contributions Agency, responsible for handling National Insurance contributions;
- the Information Technology Services Agency, responsible for computerising the administration of social security;
- the Resettlement Agency, responsible for hostels for single homeless people; and
- the War Pensions Agency, set up in April 1994, responsible for delivering services to war pensioners.

The Employment Services Agency of the Employment Department pays unemployment benefits and income support to unemployed people on behalf of the Benefits Agency. The housing and council tax benefit schemes are administered by local authorities, which recover most of the cost from the Government.

In Northern Ireland contributions as well as social security benefits are administered by the Social Security Agency. The housing benefit scheme is administered by the Northern Ireland Housing Executive and the Rate Collection Agency; council tax does not apply in Northern Ireland.

A major programme to improve quality and customer service is in progress. The Benefits Agency, for example, is moving towards one-stop service delivery (a single contact point to handle each customer's business with the Agency where appropriate).

Anti-fraud Measures

Further measures are being introduced to improve the prevention and detection of social security fraud. These include:

- greater incentives to local authorities to prevent and detect fraud in the benefits they administer;

- better use of information technology; and

- better targeting of resources, and additional resources where necessary.

In 1994–95 the Benefits Agency is aiming to save £654 million through anti-fraud work.

Advice about Benefits

The demand for advice about benefits is partly met by the Freeline Social Security Service, which handles over 1 million calls each year. A complementary service, the Social Security Advice Line for Employers, handles some 3,500 calls a week. The Ethnic Freeline Service provides information on social security in Urdu, Punjabi and Chinese. There is also a freeline service in Welsh.

The Department of Social Security produces a wide range of leaflets and posters providing general information on entitlement and liability. These are available in English and a number of other languages.

CONTRIBUTIONS

Entitlement to National Insurance benefits such as retirement pension, sickness and invalidity benefit, unemployment benefit, maternity allowance and widow's benefit, is dependent upon the payment of contributions. There are five classes of contributions; **the rates given are effective from April 1994 to April 1995**:

- *Class 1—paid by employees and their employers.* Employees with earnings below £57 a week do not pay Class 1 contributions. Contributions on earnings of £57 a week and over are at the rate of 2 per cent of the first £57 of total earnings and 10 per cent of the balance, up to the upper earnings limit of £430 a week. Employers' contributions are subject to the same threshold. On earnings above the threshold, contributions rise in stages from 3.6 per cent of total earnings up to a maximum of 10.2 per cent when earnings are £200 or more a week; there is no upper earnings limit. The contribution is lower if the employer operates a 'contracted-out' occupational pension scheme (see p. 401).

- *Class 1A—paid by employers who provide their employees with car fuel and/or a car for private use.* A Class 1A contribution is payable on the cash equivalent of the benefit provided.

- *Class 2—paid by self-employed people.* Class 2 contributions are at a flat rate of £5.65 a week. The self-employed may claim exemption from payment of Class 2 contributions if their profits are expected to be below £3,200 for the tax year. Self-employed people are not eligible for unemployment and industrial injuries benefits.

- *Class 3—paid voluntarily to safeguard rights to some benefits.* Class 3 contributions are at a flat rate of £5.55 a week.

● *Class 4—paid by the self-employed on their taxable profits over a set lower limit (£6,490 a year), and up to a set upper limit (£22,360 a year) in addition to their Class 2 contribution. Class 4 contributions are payable at the rate of 7.3 per cent.*

Employees who work after pensionable age (60 for women and 65 for men) do not pay contributions but the employer continues to be liable. Self-employed people over pensionable age do not pay contributions.

BENEFITS

For most contributory benefits there are two conditions. First, before benefit can be paid at all, a certain number of contributions have to be paid. Second, the full rate of benefit cannot be paid unless contributions have been paid or credited to a specific level over a set period. A reduced rate of benefit is payable dependent on the level of contributions paid

or credited. For example, a great many of those receiving retirement pensions and widows' benefits receive a percentage-based rate of benefit. Benefits are increased annually in line with percentage increases in retail prices. The main benefits (payable weekly) are summarised below. **The rates given are those effective from April 1994 until April 1995.**

Retirement Pension

A state retirement pension is payable, subject to the satisfaction of contribution conditions, to women at the age of 60 and men at the age of 65. The Sex Discrimination Act 1986 protects employees of different sexes in a particular occupation from being required to retire at different ages. This, however, has not affected the payment of the state retirement pension at different ages for men and women.

The Government plans to equalise the

Social Security Expenditure: Great Britain 1993–94

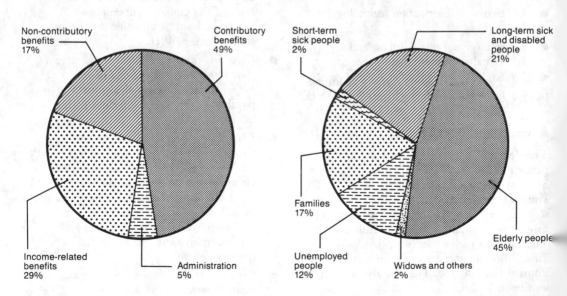

Analysis of planned expenditure 1993–94

Non-contributory benefits 17%
Contributory benefits 49%
Income-related benefits 29%
Administration 5%

Percentage of expenditure by broad groups of beneficiaries 1993–94

Short-term sick people 2%
Long-term sick and disabled people 21%
Families 17%
Unemployed people 12%
Widows and others 2%
Elderly people 45%

Source: *Social Security Departmental Report: The Government's Expenditure Plans 1994–95 to 1996–97.*

state pension age for men and women at 65. A White Paper published in December 1993 states that the change would start from 2010 and would be phased in over ten years. Women born before 6 April 1950 would not be affected; their pension age would remain at 60. The new pension age of 65 would apply to women born on or after 6 March 1955. Pension age for women born between these dates will move up gradually from 60 to 65.

The state pension scheme consists of a basic weekly pension of £57.60 for a single person and £92.10 for a married couple, together with an additional earnings-related pension. Pensioners may have unlimited earnings without affecting their pensions. Those who have put off their retirement during the five years after state pension age may earn extra pension. A non-contributory retirement pension of £34.50 a week is payable to people over the age of 80 who meet certain residence conditions, and who have not qualified for a contributory pension. People whose pensions do not give them enough to live on may be entitled to income support. Over 10 million people in Great Britain received a basic state pension in 1992.

Rights to basic pensions are safeguarded for people whose opportunities to work are limited while they are looking after a child or a sick or disabled person. Men and women may receive the same basic pension, provided they have paid full-rate National Insurance contributions when working. From April 1999 the earnings-related pension scheme will be based on a lifetime's revalued earnings instead of on the best 20 years. It will be calculated as 20 per cent rather than 25 per

Table 25.1: Estimated Number of Recipients of Benefits in Great Britain 1993–94[a]

Benefit	Contributory (C) or non-contributory (NC)	Thousands
Retirement pension	C	10,055
Widows' benefits	C	337
Unemployment benefit	C	584
Sickness benefit	C	155[b]
Invalidity benefit	C	1,509[b]
Maternity allowance	C	19[b]
Non-contributory retirement pension	NC	29
War pension	NC	267
Attendance allowance	NC	890
Disability living allowance	NC	1,167
Disability working allowance	NC	3
Invalid care allowance	NC	199
Severe disablement allowance	NC	322
Industrial injuries disablement benefit	NC	000[c]
Industrial death benefit	NC	24
Income support	NC	5,675
Child benefit	NC	
—numbers of children		12,522
—numbers of families		6,897
One-parent benefit	NC	873
Family credit	NC	447
Housing benefit	NC	
—rent rebate		3,037
—rent allowance		1,290
Council tax benefit	NC	6,550

[a] Average number of people receiving benefit at any one time.
[b] Estimate only; figures not available at time of going to print.
[c] Figures not available at time of going to print.

cent of earnings, to be phased in over ten years from 1999. The pensions of people retiring this century will be unaffected.

Occupational and Personal Pensions

Employers may 'contract out' their employees from the state scheme for the additional earnings-related pension and provide their own occupational pension instead. Their pension must be at least as good as the state additional pension. Joining an employer's contracted-out scheme is voluntary: employers are not free to contract out employees from the earnings-related pension scheme without the employees' consent. The State remains responsible for the basic pension.

Occupational pension schemes cover about half the working population and have nearly 11 million members. The occupational pension rights of those who change jobs before pensionable age, who are unable or who do not want to transfer their pension rights, are now offered some protection against inflation. Workers leaving a scheme have the right to a fair transfer value. The trustees or managers of pension schemes have to provide full information about their schemes.

Increasing numbers of pensioners receive income from occupational pensions and investment income. In 1990–91:

- 61 per cent had income from occupational pensions, compared with 43 per cent in 1979; and

- 76 per cent had income from savings, compared with 62 per cent in 1979.

Eighty-five per cent of pensioners now have income in addition to state benefits.

As an alternative to their employers' scheme or the state additional earnings-related pension scheme, people are entitled to choose a personal pension available from a bank, building society, insurance company or other financial institution. Some 7.8 million people have contracted out of the state earnings-related pension scheme and taken out personal pensions. In June 1994 the Government published a White Paper with its proposals for the future of occupational pensions. These are intended to enable occupational schemes to provide equal treatment between men and women and to make personal pensions more flexible and attractive to a broader age range.

A Pensions Ombudsman deals with complaints about maladministration of pension schemes and adjudicates on disputes of fact or law. A pensions registry helps people trace lost benefits.

Parents and Children

Most pregnant working women receive their statutory maternity pay directly from their employer for a maximum of 18 weeks. There are two rates:

- where a woman has been working for the same employer for at least two years, she is entitled to 90 per cent of her average weekly earnings for the first six weeks and to the lower rate of £48.80 a week for the remaining 12 weeks; and

- where a woman has been employed for between 26 weeks and two years, she is entitled to payments for up to 18 weeks at the lower rate.

Women who are not eligible for statutory maternity pay because, for example, they are self-employed, have recently changed jobs or given up their job, may qualify for a weekly maternity allowance of £44.55, which is payable for up to 18 weeks.

In 1992 the European Council of Ministers adopted a directive aimed at improving health and safety at work for pregnant women and nursing mothers. Legislation in Britain will be brought into line with the directive by October 1994. As a result:

- any woman who has worked for the same employer for 26 weeks will be entitled to statutory maternity pay, with the first six weeks paid at 90 per cent of average weekly earnings;

- the lower rate of statutory maternity pay will increase from £48.80 to £52.50; and

- all pregnant employees will have the right to take 14 weeks' maternity leave.

A payment of £100 from the social fund (see p. 406) may be available if the mother or her partner are receiving income support, family credit or disability working allowance (see p. 405). It is also available if a woman adopts a baby.

Non-contributory child benefit of £10.20 a week for the eldest qualifying child and £8.25 for each other child is the main social security benefit for children. Tax-free and normally paid to the mother, it is payable for children up to the age of 16 and for those up to 19 if they continue in full-time non-advanced education. In addition, one-parent benefit of £6.15 a week is generally payable to certain people bringing up one child or more on their own, whether as their parents or not. A non-contributory guardian's allowance of £11 a week for an orphaned child is payable to a person who is entitled to child benefit for that child. This is reduced to £9.80 if the higher rate of child benefit is payable for the child. In exceptional circumstances a guardian's allowance may be paid on the death of only one parent.

At the end of 1992 child benefit was paid for 12,425,000 children, an increase on the previous year of 134,000.

Child Support Agency

An estimated 1.3 million lone parents bring up over 2 million children in Britain. The Child Support Agency, which started work in April 1993, will—over a four-year phased timetable—replace the court system for obtaining maintenance for children. The Agency is responsible for assessing, collecting and enforcing child maintenance payments and for tracing absent parents. Assessments are made using a formula which takes into account each parent's income and essential outgoings.

Between April 1993 and March 1994 the Child Support Agency:

- took on 858,000 cases;
- traced over 28,000 absent parents in cases where the parent with care did not know their whereabouts and where other attempts to locate them had failed; and
- produced benefit savings of over £418 million.

Changes to the child support arrangements were introduced in February 1994 to take account of concerns raised by members of the public and MPs. These are designed to reduce the amount of child maintenance that many absent parents are required to pay and to give some families more time to adjust to increased bills.

Widows

Widows under the age of 60, or those over 60 whose husbands were not entitled to a state retirement pension when they died, receive a tax-free single payment of £1,000 following the death of their husbands, provided that their husbands had paid a minimum number of National Insurance contributions. Women whose husbands have died of an industrial injury or prescribed disease may also qualify, regardless of whether their husbands had paid National Insurance contributions.

A widowed mother with a young family receives a widowed mother's allowance of £57.60 a week with a further £9.80 for a child for whom the higher rate of child benefit is payable and £11 for each subsequent child. A widow's basic pension of £57.60 a week is payable to a widow who is 55 years or over when her husband dies or when her entitlement to widowed mother's allowance ends. A percentage of the full rate is payable to widows who are aged between 45 and 54 when their husbands die or when their entitlement to widowed mother's allowance ends. Special rules apply for widows whose husbands died before 11 April 1988. Entitlement continues until the widow remarries or begins drawing retirement pension. Payment ends if she lives with a man as his wife. Widows also benefit under the industrial injuries scheme.

A man whose wife dies when both are over pension age inherits his wife's pension rights just as a widow inherits her husband's rights.

Sick and Disabled People

Statutory Sick Pay and Sickness Benefit

A large variety of benefits is available for

people unable to work because of sickness or disablement. Employers are responsible for paying statutory sick pay to employees for up to a maximum of 28 weeks. There are two weekly rates—£47.80 or £52.50—depending on average weekly earnings. Employees who are not entitled to statutory sick pay can claim weekly state sickness benefit of £43.45 instead, as can self-employed people. Sickness benefit is payable for up to 28 weeks.

Invalidity Pension and Allowance

A weekly invalidity pension of £57.60—with additions of £34.50 for an adult dependant, £9.80 for the eldest child and £11 for each other child—is payable when statutory sick pay or sickness benefit ends. For the period to count towards receiving invalidity pension the contribution condition for sickness benefit must be satisfied. An invalidity allowance of up to £12.15 a week, depending on the age when incapacity began, may be paid, but this is offset by any entitlement to an additional invalidity pension.

The New Incapacity Benefit

The Social Security (Incapacity for Work) Act 1994 introduced a new **Incapacity Benefit** to replace sickness benefit and invalidity benefit. The Act comes into force on 13 April 1995.

The new benefit will have three rates:

- a lower rate of £43.45 a week for the first 28 weeks;

- a higher rate of £52.50 a week between the 29th and 52nd week; and

- a long-term rate of £57.60 a week from the 53rd week of incapacity.

It also comprises certain age additions and increases for adult and child dependants.

A new, more objective medical test of incapacity for work will also be introduced for incapacity benefit as well as for other social security benefits paid on the basis of incapacity for work. The new test will apply after 28 weeks' incapacity for work and will assess ability to perform a range of work-related activities rather than the ability to perform a specific job. Non-medical factors, such as education, skills and experience, will not be taken into account.

Severe Disablement Allowance

A severe disablement allowance of £34.80 plus an age-related addition of up to £12.15 a week may be payable to people under pensionable age. Those over 20 who are unable to work and are 80 per cent disabled but do not qualify for the National Insurance invalidity pension because they have not paid sufficient contributions may be entitled to severe disablement allowance. Additions for adult dependants and for children may also be paid.

Industrial Injuries Disablement Benefits

Various benefits are payable for disablement caused by an accident at work or a prescribed disease. The main benefit is industrial injuries disablement benefit; disablement benefit of up to £93.20 a week is usually paid after a qualifying period of 15 weeks if a person is 14 per cent or more physically or mentally disabled as a result of an industrial accident or a prescribed disease. If the person is incapable of work during the qualifying period, statutory sick pay or sickness benefit may be payable.

Basic disablement benefit can be paid in addition to other National Insurance benefits, such as sickness benefit or invalidity benefit. It can be paid whether or not the person returns to work and does not depend on earnings. The degree of disablement is assessed by an independent adjudicating medical authority and the amount paid depends on the extent of the disablement and how long it is expected to last. Except for certain progressive respiratory diseases, disablement of less than 14 per cent does not attract disablement benefit. In certain circumstances additional allowances, such as constant attendance allowance and exceptionally severe disablement allowance, may be payable. In some cases reduced earnings allowance may be payable.

Other Benefits

Disability living allowance (which replaced attendance allowance for people disabled before the age of 65 and mobility allowance) was introduced in 1992. It is a tax-free benefit with two components for people disabled before the age of 65 who need help with personal care or with mobility. The care component has three weekly rates—£45.70, £30.55 and £12.15. The mobility component has two rates—£31.95 and £12.15.

Motability, an independent charitable organisation, helps disabled drivers wanting to use the higher mobility component to obtain a vehicle or powered wheelchair on favourable terms. Applications for vehicles increased by 10 per cent in 1993–94 compared with the previous year. Almost 4 per cent of all cars registered in Britain in 1993 were bought under the Motability scheme, which currently has more than 180,000 customers.

A non-contributory, tax-free *attendance allowance* of £30.55 or £45.70 a week may be payable to people severely disabled at or after age 65, who have personal care needs, depending upon the amount of attention they require. The higher rate of attendance allowance and/or disability living allowance is paid to people who are terminally ill.

A non-contributory *invalid care allowance* of £34.50 weekly may be payable to people between 16 and pensionable age who cannot take up a paid job because they are caring for a person receiving either the higher or middle rate of disability living allowance care component or attendance allowance; an additional carer's premium may be paid if the recipient is also receiving income support, housing benefit or council tax benefit. It is estimated that some 1.5 million adults in Great Britain care for a disabled person for at least 20 hours a week.

Disability working allowance is an income-related tax-free benefit introduced in 1992. It provides help for some disabled people aged 16 or over who are working at least 16 hours a week or more on average and have an illness or disability which puts them at a disadvantage in getting a job.

Awards are for fixed periods of six months. To qualify a person must either:

- be getting disability living allowance, or an analogous benefit, such as constant attendance allowance under the war pensions or industrial injuries disablement scheme; or
- have an invalid three-wheeler or other vehicle under the NHS Act 1977; or
- have been entitled to one of the following in at least one of the 56 days before the date of claim: invalidity benefit; severe disablement allowance; or the disability premium with income support, housing benefit or council tax benefit.

Disability working allowance is available to single people, lone parents and couples. The rate depends on the person's income and size of family, and the ages of any children. The allowance is not payable if capital or savings exceed £16,000.

Unemployment Benefit

Unemployment benefit of £45.45 a week for a single person or £73.50 for a couple is payable for up to a year in any one period of unemployment. Periods covered by unemployment or sickness benefit, maternity allowance or some training allowances which are eight weeks or less apart, are linked to form a single period of interruption of work. Everyone claiming unemployment benefit has to be available for work, but unemployed people wishing to do voluntary work in the community may do so in some cases without losing entitlement to benefit. People seeking unemployment benefit must not have become unemployed voluntarily or have lost their job through misconduct. They are expected to look for work actively and must have good reasons for rejecting any job that is offered.

Income Support

Income support is payable to people who are not in work, or who work fewer than 16 hours a week, and whose financial resources are below certain set levels. It consists of a personal allowance ranging from £27.50 weekly for a single person or lone parent aged under 18 to

£71.70 for a couple, at least one of whom is aged over 18. Additional sums, known as premiums, are available to families, lone parents, pensioners, long-term sick and disabled people, and those caring for them who qualify for the invalid care allowance.

The income support scheme sets a limit to the amount of capital a person may have and still remain entitled. People with savings or capital worth more than £8,000 are ineligible; savings between £3,000 and £8,000 will reduce the amount received.

Although about half of fresh claims from unemployed people result in payment of unemployment benefit (see p. 405), a large proportion of those on the unemployment register at any one time rely partly or wholly on income support. This is either because they are disqualified from unemployment benefit or have not paid sufficient contributions to qualify for it, or because their entitlement to it has run out, or because they are entitled to income support as well as unemployment benefit.

Proposed Changes

The Government has announced proposals to introduce a new benefit—**Jobseeker's Allowance**—to replace unemployment benefit and income support for unemployed people from April 1996. This would be more clearly focused on helping unemployed people into work. All unemployed people would be required to enter into a jobseeker's agreement, committing them to a plan of action to seek work. Most recipients would be required to satisfy a means-test, and the benefit would be paid at rates determined by family circumstances on a similar basis to income support (see p. 405).

Housing Benefit

The housing benefit scheme assists people who need help to pay their rent (rent and/or domestic rates in Northern Ireland), using general assessment rules and benefit levels similar to those for the income support scheme. People whose net income is below certain specified levels qualify for housing benefit of up to 100 per cent of their rent.

Unlike income support (see p. 405), the housing benefit scheme sets a limit of £16,000 on the amount of capital a person may have and still remain entitled.

Council Tax Benefit

Council tax benefit helps people to meet their council tax payments. The scheme offers help to those claiming income support and others with low incomes. Subject to rules broadly similar to those governing the provision of income support and housing benefit (see above), people may receive rebates of up to 100 per cent of their council tax. At present over 5 million households receive such help. A person who is liable for the council tax may also claim benefit (called 'second adult rebate') for a second adult who is not liable to pay the council tax and who is living in the home on a non-commercial basis.

Recent Changes

In August 1994 a new residence test came into force, requiring claimants to establish that they are habitually resident in Britain before a claim for income support, housing benefit or council tax benefit can be paid. The test brings Britain into line with most other European countries, which already limit access to their benefit systems to those who have lived in the country for some time.

Family Credit

Family credit is payable to low-paid employed and self-employed working families with children. It is payable to couples or lone parents. At least one parent must work for a minimum of 16 hours a week. The amount payable depends on a family's net income (excluding child benefit) and the number and ages of the children in the family. A maximum award, consisting of an adult rate of £44.30 weekly, plus a rate for each child varying with age, is payable if the family's net income does not exceed £71.70 a week. The award is reduced by 70 pence for each pound by which net income exceeds this amount. In certain cases where children under 11 have formal childcare arrangements, up to £40 a week can be deducted from net income before family credit is assessed. Family credit is not payable if a family's capital or savings exceed £8,000.

Social Fund

Discretionary payments, in the form of loans or grants, may be available to people on low incomes for expenses which are difficult to meet from their regular income. There are three types:

- budgeting loans to help meet important occasional expenses;

- crisis loans for help in an emergency or a disaster; and

- community care grants to help people re-establish themselves or remain in the community and to ease exceptional pressure on families.

The total discretionary budget of £353 million for 1994–95 is £7 million higher than in the previous year.

The social fund also provides payments to help with the costs of maternity or funerals or with heating during very cold weather. These payments are regulated and are not

subject to the same budgetary considerations as other social fund payments.

War Pensions and Related Services

Pensions are payable for disablement or death as a result of service in the armed forces or for certain injuries received in the merchant navy or civil defence during wartime, or to civilians injured by enemy action. The amount paid depends on the degree of disablement: the pension for 100 per cent disablement is £98.90 a week.

There are a number of extra allowances. The main ones are for unemployability, restricted mobility, the need for constant attendance, the provision of extra comforts, and as maintenance for a lowered standard of occupation. An age allowance of between £6.60 and £20.40 is payable weekly to war pensioners aged 65 or over whose disablement is assessed at 40 per cent or more. Pensions are also paid to war widows and other dependants. (The standard rate of pension for a private's widow is £74.70 a week.)

The War Pensions Agency maintains a welfare service for war pensioners, war widows and other dependants. It works

Table 25.2: Tax Liability of Social Security Benefits

Not Taxable	Taxable
Attendance allowance	Income support paid to
Child benefit	unemployed people
Child's special allowance	Industrial death benefit
Disability living allowance	pensions
Disability working allowance	Invalid care allowance
Family credit	Retirement pension
Guardian's allowance	Statutory maternity pay
Housing benefit	Statutory sick pay
Income support[a]	Unemployment benefit
Industrial disablement benefit	Widowed mother's allowance
Invalidity benefit	Widow's pension
Maternity allowance	
One-parent benefit	
Severe disablement allowance	
Sickness benefit	
Social fund payments	
War disablement pension	
War widow's pension	

[a]That part of income support payable in place of unemployment benefit is taxable when paid to unemployed people who have to sign on, or to strikers or those directly interested in a trade dispute.

closely with ex-Service organisations and other voluntary bodies which give financial aid and personal support to those disabled or bereaved as a result of war.

Concessions

Other benefits for which unemployed people and those on low incomes may be eligible include exemption from health service charges (see p. 375), grants towards the cost of spectacles, free school meals and free legal aid.

Since April 1994 people on low incomes, as well as all pensioners, widows and long-term sick people on invalidity benefit, have received extra help to meet the cost of VAT on their fuel bills (see p. 407). In 1994–95 some 15 million people will benefit, at a cost of £381 million.

Reduced charges are often made to unemployed people, for example, for adult education and exhibitions, and pensioners are usually entitled to reduced transport fares.

Taxation

The general rule is that benefits which replace lost earnings are subject to tax, while those intended to meet a specific need are not (see Table 25.2). Various income tax reliefs and exemptions are allowed on account of age or a need to support dependants.

ARRANGEMENTS WITH OTHER COUNTRIES

As part of the European Union's efforts to promote the free movement of labour, regulations provide for equality of treatment and the protection of benefit rights for employed and self-employed people who move between member states. The regulations also cover retirement pensioners and other beneficiaries who have been employed, or self-employed, as well as dependants. Benefits covered include child benefit and those for sickness and maternity, unemployment, retirement, invalidity, accidents at work and occupational diseases.

Britain also has reciprocal social security agreements with a number of other countries which also provide cover for some National Insurance benefits and family benefits.

At the end of 1992 625,000 British national insurance pensions were paid overseas, at a cost of some £800 million.

Further Reading

Equality in State Pension Age. Cm 2420. HMSO, 1993.

Security, Equality, Choice: The Future for Pensions. Cm 2594-1. HMSO, 1994.

Social Welfare. Aspects of Britain series, HMSO, 1993.

Which Benefit? Leaflet FB2, issued by the Benefits Agency. Available free from social security offices, post offices or Employment Service Jobcentres.

26 Education

Over 9 million pupils attend about 29,900 state,[1] 1,800 special and 2,500 fee paying independent schools. They are taught by just over half a million teachers. The average pupil–teacher ratio is about 17:1, compared with 22:1 in 1970–71. There are over 25,000 nursery and primary schools and nearly 5,000 secondary schools. The proportion of young people entering higher education in universities and colleges has risen from one in eight in 1980 to more than one in four (one in three in Northern Ireland) and is expected to reach one in three by the year 2000 (more than two in five in Scotland and Northern Ireland). Continuing education for adults is provided by further education institutions, adult colleges and centres, and by universities, which have seen an increase in older students in recent years. Expenditure on education was £32,000 million in 1992–93.

INTRODUCTION

History

England and Wales

Although government grants for education were first made in 1833, it was the 1870 Education Act in England and Wales which originally enshrined the idea of compulsory elementary education with government aid. There were two types of elementary school —church voluntary schools and state schools provided by school boards. Attendance at school became compulsory in 1880 for children aged between five and ten, and the school leaving age was progressively raised to 14 by 1918.

A co-ordinated national system of education was introduced for the first time by the 1902 Education Act, under which local government became responsible for state education and for helping to finance the voluntary schools. The system was supervised by the Board of Education.

In 1944 a new Education Act raised the school leaving age to 15, and schools were divided into primary and secondary. All children were given a secondary education, and the newly created Ministry of Education was empowered to develop a national education policy. Local government remained responsible for administering the system. Children were allocated to different secondary schools on the basis of selection tests taken at the age of 11. In the 1960s and 1970s this system was gradually replaced by comprehensive schools, which

---

[1] For ease of reference the term 'state school' is used to cover schools maintained from public funds.

take pupils of all abilities. The school leaving age was raised to 16 in 1972–73.

Scotland

In Scotland an Act passed in 1872 transferred responsibility for education from the churches to elected school boards, which provided education for children between the ages of 5 and 13. In 1901 the school leaving age was raised to 14. An Act passed in 1918 replaced the boards by local government authorities and made the provision of secondary education mandatory for all children wanting it. Church schools were transferred to education authorities, while preserving their denominational character. The school leaving age was raised to 15 in 1947 and to 16 in 1972–73.

Northern Ireland

Education in Northern Ireland was brought into a single system by legislation passed in 1923, under which local government took over responsibility for its administration, supervised by the Ministry of Education. Secondary education remained largely in the hands of voluntary bodies, with assistance provided from public funds. Education was made compulsory for pupils between the ages of 5 and 14. The school leaving age was raised to 15 in 1947 and to 16 in 1972–73.

Reform

During the 1970s concern arose about the quality of education provided by Britain's schools and the lack of a formal national school curriculum. As a result, the three education systems are undergoing the most far-reaching reforms since 1945.

Administration

The Secretary of State for Education has overall responsibility for school and post-school education in England. The Secretaries of State for Scotland, Wales and Northern Ireland exercise similar responsibilities in those countries.

The government education departments are the Department for Education in England, the Welsh Office Education Department, the Scottish Office Education Department and the Department of Education for Northern Ireland. They formulate education policies and are also responsible for the supply and training of teachers.

Most state school education is the responsibility of education authorities, which are part of the local government system; the rest is provided by self-governing grant-maintained (GM) schools (see p. 411). In Northern Ireland the education service is administered locally by five education and library boards.

Education authorities pay teachers and other staff, provide and maintain buildings, and supply equipment and materials. Governing bodies in GM schools are responsible for these functions.

SCHOOLS

Finance

LEA-maintained Schools

Local education authorities (LEAs) in England and Wales are responsible for most of the public expenditure on schools; a large amount of this, however, is indirectly funded by the Government through the Revenue Support Grant, which is made to local government councils. Councils are free to decide how much of this grant should be distributed to education and the other services for which they have responsibility. There are also central Government grants supporting expenditure made by LEAs on items such as the National Curriculum (see p. 418), local management of schools, teacher recruitment, support for information technology and health education in schools. Finance also goes to inner city schools facing particularly severe problems.

Additional government grants are made for capital expenditure at voluntary-aided schools (see p. 411).

The rest of LEA expenditure on education is met by local taxes and by the non-domestic rates paid by business and commerce.

Grant-maintained Schools

State grant-maintained (GM) self-governing schools are not financed by LEAs, as they have chosen to opt out of LEA control (see below). Instead, the Funding Agency for Schools for England calculates and pays grants to GM schools from public funds and is responsible for financial monitoring. The Agency is responsible to the Secretary of State for Education, who appoints its members. Grant-maintained schools in Wales are financed by the Welsh Office.

Scotland and Northern Ireland

In Scotland most state schools are provided by the regional and islands councils, which are the education authorities; state self-governing schools are funded directly by the Government. The education authorities are financed in a similar way to those in England and Wales.

The costs of the education and library boards in Northern Ireland are met by the Department of Education.

School Management

England and Wales

There are three kinds of state school that are wholly or mainly supported from public funds:

- county schools, which are owned and funded by LEAs;
- voluntary schools, mostly established by religious denominations; the governors of some types of voluntary school contribute to capital costs; and
- self-governing GM schools (see below).

LEA-Financed Schools

Each LEA-maintained county and voluntary school has a governing body which includes governors appointed by the LEA, elected teacher and parent governors, and people co-opted from the local community. Voluntary schools also have governors from the church associated with the school.

All LEA county and voluntary schools manage their own budgets. LEAs allocate funds to the schools, largely on the basis of pupil numbers. The school governing body is responsible for overseeing spending and for most aspects of staffing, including appointments and dismissals. LEAs also fund special schools for pupils with special educational needs (see p. 415); all these schools will have full control over their budgets by April 1996.

Each LEA is responsible for deciding whether funds should be provided for nursery education.

Grant-maintained Status

Some 15 per cent of secondary schools in England are grant-maintained (GM) self-governing schools. GM status is achieved if the school's parents support the idea in a ballot and if the Secretary of State approves the school's proposals for GM status. Under the 1993 Education Act the governing bodies of non-GM state schools must consider each year whether or not to hold a ballot on GM status. If they decide not to hold a ballot, they must give reasons to parents for this decision.

The governing body for GM schools consists of parents, teachers and people from the community served by the school. The parent governors are elected by the parents of pupils at the school and the one or two teacher governors by the school's teachers. Governors take all decisions about school management, employ and pay staff, are responsible for school premises, and may acquire or dispose of land.

Some GM or voluntary aided secondary schools are technology colleges, which teach the National Curriculum and emphasise technology, science and mathematics. Governing body and financial arrangements are broadly similar to those of other GM or voluntary-aided schools. In addition, each college is sponsored by one or more companies or charitable trusts; the sponsors are represented on the governing body through sponsor governors. In April 1994, 25 schools were designated as technology colleges.

411

City Technology Colleges

There are 15 city technology colleges in England. These are non-fee-paying independent schools created by a partnership of government and private sector sponsors. The promoters own or lease the schools, employ teachers and other staff, and make substantial contributions towards the costs of building and equipment. There is no LEA involvement. The colleges teach the National Curriculum (see p. 418), but with an emphasis on mathematics, technology and science. There are over 11,000 pupils in city technology colleges.

Scotland

In Scotland school governing bodies are known as school boards and consist of elected parent and staff members as well as co-opted members. They are required to promote contact between parents, the school and the community, and are involved in the appointment of senior staff and the community use of school premises. They may also take on additional functions delegated from the education authority.

Plans are being made to ensure that devolved management is in place in primary and secondary schools by April 1996, and in special schools by April 1997. Devolved management does not have to be in place until 1 April 1998 for primary schools with full-time teaching headteachers.

Parents of children at state schools can opt for self-governing status following approval by a ballot; the school then receives funding directly from central government instead of the education authority. The first self-governing school came into existence in April 1994.

Northern Ireland

The main categories of school supported by public funds are:

- controlled schools, which are owned and financed 100 per cent by the education and library boards;

- voluntary maintained schools, most of which are owned by the Roman Catholic Church and largely financed from public funds;

- voluntary grammar schools, which may be owned by denominational or non-denominational bodies and are largely financed from public funds; and

- grant-maintained or controlled integrated schools, taking both Protestant and Roman Catholic pupils.

All publicly financed schools are managed by Boards of Governors, which include elected parents and teachers among their members.

Although all schools must be open to pupils of all religions, most Roman Catholic pupils attend Catholic maintained schools or Catholic voluntary grammar schools, and most Protestant children are enrolled at controlled schools or non-denominational voluntary grammar schools.

All recurrent expenditure (running expenses such as teachers' salaries) of voluntary maintained schools is met by the education and library boards. The Department of Education provides 85 per cent or 100 per cent of capital expenditure, the rate of grant paid being dependent on the constitution of the Board of Governors. Recurrent expenditure on voluntary grammar schools is met by the Department of Education, which also provides capital grants.

The Government has a statutory duty to encourage integrated education as a way of breaking down sectarian barriers. There are 21 integrated schools, with a total enrolment of 4,000 pupils—over 1 per cent of the school population. Integrated schools are financed by the Government. Existing controlled, maintained and voluntary grammar schools can apply to become integrated following a majority vote by parents.

The Council for Catholic Maintained Schools is responsible for employing teachers in Catholic maintained schools and for promoting effective control and management of these schools by the Boards of Governors.

All secondary schools and some 42 nursery schools and 605 primary schools are responsible for managing all costs, including staffing costs. The remaining 346 primary schools and 47 nursery schools have partially delegated budgets and are responsible for only non-staffing costs.

School Places

Education authorities are responsible for providing school places, with the exception of GM schools in England and Wales, where governing bodies are responsible.

Under the 1993 Education Act the Funding Agency for Schools in England may take on some responsibility for securing enough school places in individual LEA areas. In areas where between 10 and 75 per cent of pupils are being educated in GM primary or secondary schools, the LEA and the Agency may be jointly responsible. Once 75 per cent of primary or secondary pupils are in GM schools, the Agency may be solely responsible for the provision of school places. The Agency can only be involved in the provision of school places if the Secretary of State makes an order to that effect.

Table 26.1: School Pupils by Type of School in Britain

	1991–92
State schools	
Nursery	61,000
Primary	4,850,000
Secondary	3,535,000
Special schools	
(Full-time equivalent)	113,000
Independent schools	604,000
Total school places	**9,162,000**

Pupils

Parents are required by law to see that their children receive efficient full-time education, at school or elsewhere, between the ages of 5 and 16 in Great Britain and 4 and 16 in Northern Ireland. About 93 per cent of pupils receive free education financed from public funds, while the others attend independent schools paid for by fees from parents.

Boys and girls are taught together in most primary schools. More than 80 per cent of pupils in state secondary schools in England and Wales and about 66 per cent in Northern Ireland attend mixed schools. In Scotland nearly all secondary schools are mixed. Most independent schools (see p. 416) for younger children are mixed; the majority providing secondary education are single-sex, although the number of mixed secondary schools is growing.

Nursery and Primary Schools

Although there is no statutory requirement to educate under-fives, nearly 53 per cent of three- and four-year-olds in Britain attend nursery schools or classes. In addition, many children attend pre-school playgroups, most of which are organised by parents and incorporated in the Pre-School Playgroups Association.

Compulsory education begins at five in Great Britain and four in Northern Ireland, when children go to infant schools or departments; at seven many go on to junior schools or departments. The usual age for transfer from primary to secondary schools is 11 in England, Wales and Northern Ireland, but some local authorities in England have established first schools for pupils aged 5 to 8, 9 or 10, and middle schools for age-ranges between 8 and 14. In Scotland primary schools take children from 5 to 12, when they transfer to secondary schools. For information on independent schools, (see p. 416).

Secondary Schools

Around nine-tenths of the state secondary school population in Great Britain attend comprehensive schools. These take pupils without reference to ability or aptitude and provide a wide-ranging secondary education for all or most of the children in a district. English and Welsh schools can be organised in a number of ways. They include:

- those that take the full secondary school age-range, from 11 to 18;

- middle schools (see above); and

- schools with an age-range of 11 or 12 to 16, combined with a sixth-form or a tertiary college for pupils over 16.

Sixth-form colleges are schools which may provide non-academic courses in addition to academic ones. Tertiary colleges offer a range of full-time and part-time vocational courses for students over 16, as well as academic courses.

Most other children attend grammar or secondary modern schools, to which they are allocated after selection procedures at the age of 11.

Scottish secondary education is almost completely non-selective; the majority of schools are comprehensives covering the age-range 12 to 18.

In Northern Ireland secondary education is organised largely along selective lines, the 70 grammar schools admitting some 57,000 pupils on the basis of tests in English, maths and science. Some 88,000 pupils attend non-grammar secondary schools. Some secondary schools are run on a non-selective basis.

Rights of Parents

Parents must be given general information about a school through a prospectus and the school's annual report or, in Scotland, the school's handbook. They also have a statutory right to express a preference for a particular school for their child, and there is an appeal system if their choice is not met.

In England and Wales parents choosing among local secondary schools have the right to see:

- comparative tables showing the latest public examination results, vocational qualification results, rates of absence and amount of lesson time, school by school; and

- information in each school's prospectus on public examination results, vocational qualification results, attendance rates and the destinations of school leavers.

National comparative tables are published on state and independent secondary school performance throughout Britain.

Summaries of school inspection reports (see p. 422) are given to parents.

All state schools in England and Wales have to give parents a written annual report on their child's achievements, containing details about:

- the child's progress in all subjects and activities;

- the child's general progress and attendance record;

- the results of National Curriculum assessments and of public examinations taken by the child;

- comparative results of pupils of the same age in the school and nationally; and

- information about the arrangements for discussing pupils' school reports with teachers.

All parents are invited to an annual meeting in order to discuss the governors' annual report. They may raise any matters about the school with the governors and the headteacher.

When a pupil transfers to another school, a record of his or her academic achievements, other skills, abilities and progress in school is sent to the new school on request. Information about the pupil's latest assessments and examination results is sent automatically.

In Scotland national guidelines to schools on reporting to parents advise that they should provide information about their child's attainment in the various subjects, teachers' comments on his or her progress and details about steps to build on success or overcome difficulties. One main school report each year is advised, together with one brief update report. Parents have the opportunity to respond to the report and discuss the next steps at parent/teacher meetings.

The Northern Ireland reporting system to parents is broadly similar to that in England and Wales.

Failing Schools

If school inspectors in England and Wales identify a school failing to give its pupils an acceptable standard of education, the LEA can appoint new governors and withdraw delegated management from the school. Should these measures fail to work, central government can put the school under new management until its performance reaches a satisfactory level. The new management is financed from central government. After further advice from the schools inspectorate (see p. 422), the Secretary of State decides whether to end the new management's period of care for the school; if this is done, the school becomes grant maintained and self governing.

Ethnic Minority Children

Most school-aged children from ethnic minorities were born in Britain and tend to share the interests and aspirations of children in the population at large. Nevertheless, a substantial number still have particular needs arising from cultural differences, including those of language, religion and custom.

The education authorities have done much to meet these needs. English language teaching continues to receive priority, with a growing awareness of the value of bilingual support in the early primary years. Schools may teach the main ethnic minority community languages at secondary level in England and Wales as part of the National Curriculum. Schools have to take account of the ethnic and cultural backgrounds of pupils, and curricula should reflect ethnic and cultural diversity. Measures have been taken to improve the achievement of ethnic minority pupils, and to prepare all children, not just those of ethnic minority origin, for living in a multi-ethnic society.

Special Educational Needs

Special educational needs comprise learning difficulties of all kinds, including mental and physical disabilities which hinder or prevent learning. In the case of children whose learning difficulties are severe or complex, LEAs are required to:

- identify, assess and secure provision for their needs; and

- give parents the right to be involved in decisions about their child's special education.

If the LEA believes that it should determine the education for the child, it must draw up a formal statement of the child's special educational needs and the action it intends to take to meet them.

Parents have a right of appeal to the Special Educational Needs Tribunal if they disagree with the LEA decisions about their child's special educational needs. The Tribunal's verdict is final and binding on all parties.

Under the 1993 Education Act there are statutory time limits within which the LEA in England and Wales must carry out procedures for making assessments and statements. Similar timetables for Scotland are operated through guidance from the Scottish Office Education Department. A state school named in a statement of special educational needs is normally required to admit the child. The LEA has to consult the governors before naming the school.

Wherever possible, children with special educational needs are educated in ordinary schools. Placement in an ordinary school must be compatible with the needs of the child and with the provision of efficient education for the other children in the school. The LEA is required to comply with parents' choice of school unless this is inappropriate for the child or involves an inefficient use of resources.

A Code of Practice has been issued by the Government offering practical guidance to all state schools in England and Wales on how to identify, assess and monitor all pupils with special educational needs. All schools, LEAs and health and social services must take it into account when making provision for these pupils.

Each school must formulate a policy on pupils with special educational needs and must publish information about that policy. This will include information on:

- the name of the person responsible for co-ordinating day-to-day education for these pupils;

- admission arrangements;

- facilities for pupils;

- arrangements for providing a broadly based curriculum; and

- in-service training for teachers.

Annual reports to parents must report on the success of these policies.

In Scotland the choice of school is a matter for agreement between education authorities and parents. Legislation passed in 1986 and 1993 provided for earlier recording of special educational needs and gave parents improved rights on school choice for their children. New draft advice on the assessment and recording of children with special educational needs has recently been issued. This will be followed by a comprehensive package of advice and guidance for everyone involved in special education.

In Northern Ireland steps are being taken to introduce changes similar to those in England and Wales.

There are nearly 1,800 publicly maintained special schools (both day and boarding) in Britain for pupils with special educational needs. Some of these are run by voluntary organisations and some are established in hospitals. They cater for some 113,000 pupils. The pupil teacher ratio in special schools is 5.7 to 1 compared with 10.5 to 1 in 1970–71.

Health and Welfare of Schoolchildren

Physical education, including organised games, is part of the curriculum of all maintained schools, and in England and Wales playing fields must be available for pupils over the age of eight. Most secondary schools have a gymnasium.

Government health departments are responsible for the medical inspection of schoolchildren and for advice on, and treatment of, medical and dental problems. The education service seeks to help prevent and deal with juvenile drug misuse and to help prevent the spread of AIDS. In England and Wales government funds have supported the appointment of drugs and health education co-ordinators for schools, colleges and the youth service. In Scotland this is an education authority responsibility.

LEAs and GM schools are responsible for providing school meals for pupils. They are free to decide the nature of the meals service, taking account of local circumstances. They must provide free meals to pupils whose parents receive a social security benefit called income support (see p. 405) but must charge all other pupils for meals. Although LEAs do not have to provide milk to any pupil, they can offer subsidised milk to all pupils and many provide free milk to pupils of parents in receipt of income support. In Northern Ireland school meals must be provided for primary, special and grant-aided nursery school pupils.

LEAs must provide or arrange free of charge the transport they consider necessary to enable pupils living in their area to attend school. The most common grounds for this are distance, safety or pupils' special needs. LEAs may assist other pupils financially or carry them in spare places on school buses. LEAs must publish details each year about their transport policies.

Corporal punishment is prohibited by law in state schools in Britain, and for pupils in independent schools whose fees are met wholly or partly from public funds.

Independent Schools

Fee-paying independent schools must register with the appropriate education department and are open to inspection. They can be required to remedy serious shortcomings in their accommodation or teaching and to exclude anyone regarded as unsuitable to teach in or own a school. About 7 per cent of schoolchildren attend independent schools.

There are nearly 2,500 independent schools educating 600,000 pupils of all ages. They charge fees varying from around £300 a term for day pupils at nursery age to over £4,000 a term for senior boarding pupils. Many offer bursaries to help pupils from less well-off families. Such pupils may also be helped by LEAs—particularly if the authorities' own schools cannot meet the needs of individual children—or by the Government's Assisted Places Scheme, under which financial assistance is given according to parental income. Over 35,000 places are offered in England, Wales and Scotland under the scheme. The Government also gives income-related help with fees to about 550 pupils at five music schools and the

Royal Ballet School; there are also a limited number of similar scholarships at cathedral choir schools.

Independent schools range from small kindergartens to large day and boarding schools, and from new and, in some cases, experimental schools to ancient foundations. The 600 boys', girls' and mixed preparatory schools prepare children for entry to senior schools. The normal age-range for these preparatory schools is from seven-plus to 11, 12 or 13, but many have pre-preparatory departments for younger children. A number of independent schools have been established by religious orders and ethnic minorities.

Independent schools for older pupils—from 11, 12 or 13 to 18 or 19—include about 550 which are often referred to as 'public schools'. These belong to the Headmasters' Conference, the Governing Bodies Association, the Society of Headmasters and Headmistresses of Independent Schools, the Girls' Schools Association and the Governing Bodies of the Girls' Schools Association.

In Northern Ireland there are 21 independent schools educating nearly 1,000 pupils. These schools are subject to inspection by the Department of Education but do not receive any public funds.

Teachers

England and Wales

Teachers in state schools in England and Wales are appointed by LEAs or school governing bodies. They must hold qualifications approved by the Department for Education.

Formal teacher appraisal is being introduced in English and Welsh schools. By 1995 all teachers will have completed the first year of their two-year appraisal cycle, which is intended to assist professional development, strengthen the management of schools and improve the quality of education provided to pupils.

Consideration is being given to ways of ensuring that teachers' pay is more closely related to performance.

Almost all entrants to teaching in state schools in England and Wales complete an approved course of teacher training. These courses are offered by university departments of education as well as other higher education establishments (see p. 426). One of the two main qualifications is the four-year Bachelor of Education (BEd) honours degree. The other is the successful completion of a three-year degree course, topped up by a one-year Postgraduate Certificate in Education (PGCE) course.

Reform of Initial Teacher Training

Under new government reforms in England and Wales, schools will play a much larger part in initial teacher training by taking on more responsibility for planning and managing courses and for the selection, training and assessment of students, usually in partnership with institutions. They will train students to teach their specialist subjects, assess pupils and manage classes; they will also supervise students and assess their competence.

Consortia of schools will be able to run courses for postgraduate students if they wish to do so. Other courses, including all undergraduate courses, will be run by universities and colleges in partnership with schools.

From 1995–96, the Teacher Training Agency, established by 1994 legislation, will finance initial teacher training courses, ensure that national standards are met and promote teaching as a career. The Agency's objectives include:

- helping to raise teaching standards;
- improving the quality and efficiency of all routes into the teaching profession; and
- securing the involvement of schools in training courses.

In Wales, responsibility for the funding of initial teacher training will remain with the Higher Education Funding Council for Wales, which will also be able to fund such training in schools. This Funding Council will also assume responsibility for accrediting institutions and schools providing courses.

Other Training

Under the Licensed Teacher Scheme, a trainee teacher is appointed to the school, which provides training and pays a salary; on successful completion of a two-year period of in-service training, qualified teacher status is granted.

A recent report from the Office of Standards in Education (OFSTED—see p. 422) indicates that licensed teachers are generally achieving satisfactory levels of teaching competence.

Qualified teachers from other European Community countries are usually granted qualified teacher status.

Scotland

All teachers in education authority schools must be registered with the General Teaching Council (GTC) for Scotland. The GTC is responsible for disciplinary procedures under which teachers guilty of professional misconduct may be removed permanently or temporarily from the register. Advice is given by the GTC to the Secretary of State on teacher supply and the professional suitability of teacher-training courses.

All entrants to the teaching profession are graduates. New primary teachers qualify either through a four-year BEd course or a one-year postgraduate course at a higher education teacher-training institution. In addition, the University of Stirling offers courses which combine academic and professional training for intending primary and secondary teachers. Teachers of academic subjects at secondary schools must hold a degree containing two passes in the subjects which they wish to teach. Secondary teachers must undertake a one-year postgraduate training course. For music and technology, four-year BEd courses are also available, and for physical education all teachers take BEd courses.

Under new guidelines on initial teacher-training courses, students on the one-year postgraduate course for secondary teachers spend 22 weeks in school during their courses. In addition, the overall school placement for the undergraduate BEd degree for primary school teachers is 30 weeks over the four-year period of the course. The one-year postgraduate course for primary teachers remains unchanged; students will continue to spend 18 weeks in school and 18 weeks in college-based study.

All new pre-service and major in-service courses provided by teacher-training institutions must be approved by The Scottish Office Education Department and a validating body.

Education authorities have developed schemes to implement national guidelines for staff development and appraisal. Schemes must ensure that all teachers have been appraised at least once by the end of the 1995–96 school session.

Northern Ireland

Teacher training is provided by Queen's University, in Belfast, the University of Ulster and two colleges of education. The principal courses are BEd Honours (four years) and the one-year Postgraduate Certificate of Education. Education and library boards have a statutory duty to ensure that teachers are equipped with the necessary skills to implement education reforms and the Northern Ireland school curriculum.

School Curriculum

England and Wales

The National Curriculum consists of the core subjects of English, mathematics and science, as well as history, geography, technology, music, art, physical education and, for secondary school pupils, a modern foreign language. The scope of these subject areas is defined and amended through Parliamentary Orders.

In Wales the Welsh language constitutes a core subject in Welsh-speaking schools and a foundation subject elsewhere under the National Curriculum. The National Curriculum requirements for Welsh were introduced in 1990. The statutory requirement to teach Welsh to pupils aged 14 to 16 in non-Welsh-speaking schools has been temporarily suspended; nevertheless, schools have a statutory duty to prepare for a full implementation of this requirement from July 1999.

An Order has been laid before Parliament removing history and geography as compulsory subjects for 14–16 year olds, although schools will be encouraged to continue teaching these subjects. In Wales a modern foreign language and technology will also be optional subjects for 14–16 year olds. The introduction of modern languages as a compulsory subject for this group is being postponed until 1996, as is a revised curriculum on technology. These changes will increase the scope for developing new vocational courses intended for this age group.

Steps are being taken to lessen the administrative burden on teachers by simplifying the National Curriculum, while retaining the same range of core and other subjects. Under proposals published by the School Curriculum and Assessment Authority and the Curriculum and Assessment Authority for Wales (see p. 421) in May 1994, the content of the Curriculum would be reduced by releasing one day a week for schools to use at their discretion. The Curriculum would also be made far more manageable for teachers and give them significant professional discretion. Final advice will be given to the Government by the two Authorities in the autumn of 1994. The intention is that the new slimmed-down Curriculum will be introduced in September 1995 and September 1996. No further changes to the Curriculum will take place for five years.

National testing and assessment of pupils' performance at the ages of 7, 11 and 14 is being confined to the basics of English, mathematics and science. This also applies to Welsh in Wales. Pupils aged 16 are assessed by the General Certificate of Secondary Education (GCSE) examination. The Independent Appeals Authority for School Examinations hears written appeals against grades awarded in GCSE exams when the processes of the examining body concerned are exhausted.

Scotland

The content and management of the curriculum are not prescribed by statute and responsibility rests with education authorities and headteachers, though guidance is provided by the Secretary of State and the Scottish Consultative Council on the Curriculum. The Council has recommended that secondary level pupils should follow a broad and balanced curriculum consisting of English, mathematics, science, a modern European language, social studies, technological activities, art, music or drama, religious and moral education, and physical education.

A major programme of curricular review and development has been carried out for the 5 to 14 age-range. The Government has issued new guidance on English language, mathematics, expressive arts, Latin, modern languages, environmental studies and religious and moral education. Under new arrangements, standardised tests in English and mathematics are given to pupils in the 5–14 age group whenever they complete one of five levels. A major programme to extend modern language teaching to primary schools is in progress.

Provision is made for teaching in Gaelic in Gaelic-speaking areas and in some other areas where education authorities have identified this as a priority.

Pupils take the Scottish Certificate of Education (SCE) at Standard grade at the end of their fourth year of secondary education at the age of 16. The Higher grade is taken in the fifth and sixth year. Some pupils also sit examinations for the Certificate of Sixth Year Studies or take vocational National Certificate units (see p. 424).

Northern Ireland

The common curriculum in all publicly financed schools is based on six broad areas of study: English, mathematics, science and technology, the environment and society, creative and expressive studies, and, for secondary schools, language studies.

The school curriculum also includes six compulsory cross-curricular themes: cultural heritage, education for mutual understanding, health education, information technology, and, in secondary schools, economic awareness and careers education. The first theme is designed to help overcome distrust between the people of the Province by enabling pupils to understand the common and distinctive elements of their cultural heritage. The second is intended to teach pupils to understand other people's points of view and appreciate the benefits of resolving conflicts by non-violent means.

Statutory assessment arrangements are not yet in place. In 1992–93 pilot assessments were organised for pupils at the ages of 11 and 14 who had followed programmes of study in English, maths and science for three years. A second pilot programme was organised in 1993–94 covering pupils aged about 8, 11 and 14 and was substantially revised and simplified in the light of the first pilot.

As in England and Wales, the GCSE examination is used to assess 16-year-old pupils.

Religious Education and Collective Worship in Schools

In England and Wales state schools must provide religious education and a daily act of collective worship for all registered pupils. Every LEA has to produce an agreed religious education syllabus which must be reviewed every five years. Syllabuses must reflect Christianity while taking account of the other main religions practised in Britain.

In August 1993 the Government asked the School Curriculum and Assessment Authority to draw up national model syllabuses for religious education. These are intended to help LEAs to prepare syllabuses; they may adopt one of the models in full or draw on them when preparing the local syllabus. The Authority's work involved teachers as well as working groups comprising representatives of Christianity, Buddhism, Hinduism, Islam, Judaism and Sikhism.

Voluntary schools provide the opportunity for denominational religious education.

Parents have the right to withdraw their children from religious education classes and from collective worship.

Scottish education authorities are required to see that schools practise religious observance and give pupils religious instruction; parents may withdraw their children if they wish. Certain schools provide for Roman Catholic children but in all schools there are safeguards for individual conscience.

In Northern Ireland, too, schools must provide religious education and collective worship, although parents have the right to withdraw their children from both. In controlled schools clergy have a right of access which may be used for denominational instruction. In voluntary schools collective worship and religious education are controlled by the management authorities. The main churches have approved a core syllabus which is being taught to 12-, 13- and 14-year-old children and will be extended to 15- and 16-year-olds in 1995.

Sex Education

Under the 1993 Education Act state secondary schools in England and Wales are required to provide sex education for all pupils registered at the school. This includes education about HIV and AIDS and other sexually transmitted diseases. In state primary schools the governors are responsible for considering whether sex education should be offered to their pupils.

Sex education in state schools must encourage young people to have regard to moral considerations and the value of family life. Parents are entitled to withdraw their children from sex education classes other than those required by the National Curriculum Science Order. All state schools must publish in their prospectus a summary of the content and organisation of any sex education provided. The school governing body must keep and make available to parents on request a written statement of its policy on sex education.

In Scotland, Government guidance on sex education is provided to education authorities and headteachers, who are responsible for its content.

Curriculum Development and Assessment

The School Curriculum and Assessment Authority in England and the Curriculum and Assessment Authority for Wales are responsible for:

- keeping all aspects of the school curriculum and of school examinations under review;

- advising the Government on the curriculum, and assessment and examination arrangements; and

- publishing information about the curriculum.

All GCSE and other qualifications offered to pupils of compulsory school age in state schools in England and Wales must be approved by the Government. Associated syllabuses and assessment procedures must comply with national guidelines and be approved by the relevant curriculum and assessment authority.

In Scotland curriculum development is undertaken by the Scottish Consultative Council on the Curriculum in close consultation with the Scottish Office Education Department. The Scottish Examination Board liaises with the Council on links between the curriculum and assessment.

The Council for the Curriculum, Examinations and Assessment is responsible for the curriculum and its assessment in Northern Ireland.

Information Technology

The National Curriculum places a strong emphasis on the use of information technology (IT) to ensure that all children are well versed in the new technologies. In England the average number of pupils per microcomputer in primary schools in 1992 was 25 and for secondary schools was 13. The findings of a survey commissioned by the British Educational Suppliers Association suggest that in 1994 these figures have improved to 18 and 9 respectively. In Wales the average number of pupils per microcomputer in primary schools went down from 68 to 34 between 1988 and 1991; in secondary schools over the same period the average number decreased from 30 to 14.

In 1994–95 the Department for Education is providing grants for microcomputers, software and teacher training in secondary schools in the areas of mathematics, science, design and technology, and geography. Support is also being given to the development of primary pupils' ability to handle information technology; in addition, these funds will help children with special educational needs.

Other DFE projects have included funding for:

- development and use of CD-ROM technology in schools;

- evaluating portable computers and graphical calculators;

- investigating the potential of interactive multimedia technology as a teaching aid and assessing its full use for curriculum development in schools; and

- piloting integrated learning systems software to assess the potential for children's learning.

In Wales the Welsh Office also has a grant programme to support microcomputers in schools and has financed the installation of satellite television receiving equipment in all secondary schools. It is used to teach modern foreign languages and other subjects such as geography and science.

The Government also helps finance the National Council for Educational Technology, which promotes the effective use of new technologies throughout the educational system. The corresponding body in Scotland is the Scottish Council for Educational Technology.

In Scotland computing studies are included in the 5–14 national guidelines on environmental studies. In most secondary schools, first and second year pupils will take a short course in computing; third and fourth year pupils will choose between a Standard Grade course or a National Certificate module. Similarly, fifth and sixth year pupils will be able to choose between Higher Grade and a number of National Certificate modules.

In Northern Ireland, IT is one of the six compulsory educational themes forming part of the curriculum for all pupils of statutory school age in publicly financed schools.

Other Educational Aids

Teachers and pupils use a range of other aids in the classroom. Most schools have audio-visual equipment such as slide and overhead projectors. The BBC (British Broadcasting Corporation) and the independent broadcasting companies transmit radio and television programmes designed for schools. Teachers' notes, pupils' pamphlets and computer software accompany many broadcast series.

School Inspections

Various inspectorates report to the Government on the quality of education provided by schools.

England

In England the independent Office for Standards in Education (OFSTED) advises the Secretary of State on quality, standards and efficiency and regulates a new system of school inspections. The inspection cycle began in September 1993 for secondary schools and started in September 1994 for primary and other schools.

Every school has to be inspected every four years by a team of independent inspectors—headed by a registered inspector—containing educationists and lay people. Inspections take place according to agreed national standards monitored by OFSTED. Parents are sent a summary of the inspection report, which is published. School governing bodies have to prepare action plans to follow it up and then report back to parents on their progress.

OFSTED is headed by Her Majesty's Chief Inspector of Schools.

Wales

In Wales Her Majesty's Chief Inspector of Schools for Wales has similar functions to those of OFSTED. All schools are inspected every five years in the first instance.

Scotland

In Scotland HM Schools Inspectorate is responsible for independent and objective evaluation of education standards and for advising the Secretary of State. During inspections, the views and concerns of parents are taken into account by the inspectors. Full reports on inspections are published and a short summary given to parents. From 1994–95, each inspection team will contain lay people. The Inspectorate's Audit Unit collects, analyses and publishes evidence about the performance of schools and education authorities. Evidence is published on a comparative basis and recommendations are made for action and improvement.

Northern Ireland

School inspections in Northern Ireland are carried out by the Education and Training Inspectorate. Each school is subject to a major inspection once every five years. Before each general inspection, the Inspectorate meets with Boards of Governors and parents in order to take note of their concerns and comments. Parents are sent a summary of the inspection report which is published. Boards of Governors respond by indicating any action planned and submitting details of this to the Department of Education.

Schools, Careers and Business

One of the Government's key objectives is to help young people develop the skills the economy needs.

The Technical and Vocational Education Initiative (TVEI), applicable in England, Scotland and Wales, is designed to ensure that the school curriculum for 14- to 18-year-olds is made more relevant to adult and working life in a modern technological society. It is financed and administered by central government, working in close co-operation with LEAs. Over 1 million students are benefiting from TVEI in England.

Education Business Partnerships, consisting of representatives from industry, education and the wider community, aim to bring about closer links between education and industry in England and Wales, and ensure that young people develop the skills and attitudes to help them succeed in the labour market. They are supported by Training and Enterprise Councils, Local Enterprise Companies (see p. 178) and LEAs.

One of the main schemes managed by the Partnerships is the Teacher Placement Service (TPS), funded by the Department of Employment. The TPS organises placements in business for teachers to extend their professional and personal development, improve learning opportunities for young people, and provide better careers education services. Since 1989 some 100,000 teachers have been on placements.

Compacts bring together employers, young people, schools, colleges and other bodies involved in training in order to help young people achieve more at school, and to continue education and training after the age of 16. Under Compact schemes young people work towards agreed goals; in return for achieving them, employers provide a number of incentives.

Careers

Most schools have a written policy statement on careers education and guidance, a Careers co-ordinator and an agreement with the Government's Careers Service which contracts a range of organisations to provide a service responsive to the needs of local communities. The majority of contracts are with LEAs.

Careers services in schools and colleges are supported by materials produced by the Careers and Occupational Information Centre.

In Northern Ireland careers education is one of the six compulsory education themes forming part of the post-primary school curriculum. The Careers Service is part of the Training and Employment Agency.

All state secondary schools in England and Wales have to provide leavers with a National Record of Achievement setting out their school attainments, including public examination and National Curriculum assessment results. The Record is designed to give people a simple record of achievement in education and training throughout working life. In Scotland the Record is not compulsory, but it is available to all education authorities for issue to school leavers.

In Northern Ireland all pupils are issued with a record of achievement on leaving primary and secondary education.

EDUCATION AFTER 16

About 65 per cent of pupils choose to continue in education after 16. This takes place in school sixth forms, sixth form colleges, further education colleges, universities and other higher education institutions.

Broadly speaking, education after 16 is divided into further and higher education. Further and adult education is largely vocational and covers courses up to and including General Certificate of Education (GCE) A level and AS qualifications, GNVQ Advanced level or their equivalents (see p. 425). Higher education covers advanced courses at levels higher than GCE A level or equivalent.

Over 4 million people were enrolled on further education courses in 1992–93. By 1995–96, every 16- and 17-year-old leaving full-time education in Great Britain will be encouraged to undertake vocational education or training by the offer of a Youth Credit (see p. 180), enabling them to buy training from the establishment of their choice.

In 1992–93 there were 1.4 million home and overseas students in higher education, of whom 47 per cent were women (see p. 426).

In 1993 the Government published charters for the users of further and higher education in England, Wales and Scotland, chiefly students, parents and employers. These set out the standards of service which users should expect, including information about courses, financial support for students and complaints procedures if things go wrong. Further education colleges also have their own individual charters. A similar charter has been published in Northern Ireland.

Credit accumulation and transfer schemes

are in use in many English and Welsh post-school establishments. In Scotland a credit accumulation scheme covers courses in all further and higher education. Similar schemes in higher education in Northern Ireland are compatible with those of institutions in the rest of Britain.

The computer-based Educational Counselling and Credit Transfer Information Service (ECCTIS) provides prospective students and employers with access without charge to information about courses at over 700 universities and colleges throughout Britain. ECCTIS can be found at many careers centres, libraries, British Council offices and institutions of higher and further education.

Schools and Sixth-form Colleges

Having taken the GCSE examination (see p. 419), students in England, Wales and Northern Ireland can stay on at school or be educated in a further education college. Students in England and Wales can also study at sixth form colleges. They study for examinations which are the main standard for entry to higher education or professional training. These include the academic General Certificate of Education (GCE) Advanced (A) level, the Advanced Supplementary (AS) examination, Advanced General National Vocational Qualifications (GNVQs) and National Vocational Qualifications (NVQs). The GCE A level is taken at the age of 18 or 19 after two years' study; part of the qualification is based on course work and the rest on written test papers. Advanced Supplementary (AS) levels enable sixth-form pupils to study a wider range of subjects. Students specialising in the arts and humanities, for example, can continue to study mathematics and technological subjects at this level. Requiring the same standard of work as A levels, an AS level occupies half the teaching and study time of an A level.

Equality of status for academic and vocational qualifications is being promoted in England, Wales and Northern Ireland. The new GNVQs for young people in full-time education between the ages of 16 and 18 provide a broad-based preparation for a range of occupations and higher education and are designed to have parity of esteem with GCE A levels. There are three GNVQ levels—Advanced, Intermediate and Foundation. An Advanced GNVQ—called the vocational A level—requires a level of achievement equal to two GCE A levels. GNVQs may also be taken in combination with other qualifications such as GCE A levels or GCSEs (see p. 421).

Scotland

Pupils staying on at school after the end of compulsory education study for the Higher Grade Scottish Certificate of Education exam at the age of 16-18; passes at this grade are the basis for entry to higher education or professional training. However, entry is becoming more flexible as wider access to under-represented groups with non-standard qualifications is encouraged. The Certificate of Sixth Year Studies (CSYS) is for pupils who have completed their Higher grade main studies and who wish to continue studies in particular subjects.

A flexible system of vocational courses for 16- to 18-year-olds has been introduced in schools and colleges in disciplines such as business and administration, engineering and industrial production. These courses are also intended to meet the needs of many adults entering training or returning to education. The courses lead to the award of the non-advanced National Certificate, intended for students over 16 who have successfully completed a programme of vocational courses based on short study units. Similar unit-based courses are also available at advanced levels.

General Scottish Vocational Qualifications (General SVQs) are designed to meet the needs of 16- to 19-year-olds at school or in further education colleges. Broadly compatible with the GNVQs in the rest of Britain, General SVQs are a stepping-stone to higher education or further training.

In March 1994 the Government announced plans for a new system of courses and awards for fifth and sixth year pupils. Under these, Highers will remain but courses will be based on units called modules. Existing courses validated by the Scottish Examinations Board and the Scottish

Vocational Educational Council (SCOTVEC) will be drawn into a unified system of curriculum and assessment. Advanced Higher courses will be developed, incorporating and replacing the Certificate of Sixth Form Studies and building on Highers to provide coherent and challenging two-year, 320-hour courses.

Further Education Colleges

People over the age of 16 can also take courses in further education colleges. Much further education is work-related and vocational. The system is flexible and enables the student to acquire qualifications according to his or her abilities. Further education institutions supply much of the education element in government-sponsored training programmes such as Youth Training and Training for Work (see Chapter 11).

Table 26.2: Students enrolled on further and adult education courses in 1992–93 (Great Britain)

England	3,372,000
Scotland	310,449
Wales	202,868
Total	**3,885,317**

Note: In Northern Ireland 84,808 people were enrolled on vocational further education courses and 44,917 on non-vocational courses.

Many students on further education courses attend part time, either by day release or block release from employment or during the evenings. The system has strong ties with commerce and industry, and co-operation with business is encouraged by the Government and its agencies. Employers are normally involved in designing courses.

Courses are run by nearly 550 institutions of further education, many of which also offer higher education courses (see p. 426). In England and Wales each is controlled by an autonomous further education corporation and governing body with substantial representation from business. Scottish colleges are controlled by an autonomous board of management.

Funds are allocated to institutions by further education funding councils in England and Wales; part of the funding is not cash limited and is directly related to student numbers. The Scottish Office Education Department distributes funds to colleges in Scotland, partly on the basis of student numbers. In Northern Ireland further education colleges are financed via the education and library boards by the Department of Education. Other sources of income for colleges include services provided for employers and other clients.

Institutions in England and Wales are obliged to publish information about the use of their financial and other resources. Expenditure plans provide for a record 25 per cent rise in full-time equivalent student numbers in England and a 28 per cent rise in Wales over the three-year period from 1993. The number of full-time equivalent students in Scotland is projected to rise by more than 25 per cent between 1991 and 1996.

Funding Councils in England and Wales send out independent inspectors to assess the quality of the education provided by colleges. Inspectors publish reports containing quality assessments, and colleges are obliged to explain how they will put things right if there are major criticisms. Each college has to publish information about its examination results annually. Colleges in Scotland are inspected by the Schools Inspectorate and in Northern Ireland by the Education and Training Inspectorate.

Vocational Qualifications

The National Council for Vocational Qualifications (NCVQ) is establishing a new framework of National Vocational Qualifications (NVQs) in England, Wales and Northern Ireland. These are based on national standards that define the competence, knowledge and understanding that employers need. Awarding bodies have been reforming their qualifications for accreditation by the National Council.

The following five levels of NVQs have been established:

Level 1—Foundation
Level 2—Basic craft
Level 3—Technician, advanced craft, supervisor

Level 4—Higher technician, junior
management
Level 5—Professional, middle
management.

NVQs consist of units setting out the standards which the individual must reach in a range of job-related tasks. Performance of candidates is assessed by observation in the workplace. This assessment consists of practical work, oral questioning, course work and tests. NVQs are designed mainly for people in work, although they can also be studied in colleges and some schools.

NVQs at levels 1 to 4 are available in most occupations. The Government wants 50 per cent of young people to have reached NVQ level 3 by the year 2000.

In Scotland there is a similar system of Scottish Vocational Qualifications (SVQs).

NVQs and SVQs have equal recognition throughout Britain. The General NVQ and General SVQ system for full-time students in education is described on p. 424.

Examining Bodies

About 90 per cent of vocational qualifications in England, Wales and Northern Ireland are assessed by three examining bodies and accredited by the NCVQ.

The Business and Technology Education Council (BTEC) plans and administers a unified national system of courses at all levels; the most popular subjects are business, engineering and construction.

The City and Guilds of London Institute provides mostly part-time qualifications in areas such as engineering, construction, catering, hairdressing and community care.

The RSA Examinations Board is the largest provider of information technology qualifications throughout Britain and offers qualifications in areas ranging from management/customer service to retailing and wholesaling.

These three main vocational awarding bodies offer GNVQs and a wide range of NVQs, which will eventually replace most of their existing awards.

Other vocational qualifications are awarded by a large number of professional bodies.

The Scottish Vocational Education Council (SCOTVEC) is the main accreditation and awarding body in Scotland.

Higher Education

Higher education consists of degree and equivalent courses.

In order to maintain British expertise in technology, recent government schemes have sought to expand higher education and research in electronics, engineering and computer science by making available extra student places, and additional staff and research fellowships.

Higher education institutions are responsible for providing high quality education. The Higher Education Quality Council, financed by subscriptions from institutions, ensures that satisfactory quality control arrangements are in place. The Higher Education Funding Councils for England, Scotland and Wales (see below) carry out assessments of the education provided by institutions, publish regular reports on their findings and aim to ensure that any serious problems are put right by the university or college concerned. Acting on behalf of the Department of Education, the Higher Education Funding Council for England publishes reports on the quality of education in the two Northern Ireland universities.

Table 26.3: Full- and Part-time Students in Higher Education in Great Britain		
	1982–83	1992–93
Full time	553,000	934,200
Part time	296,600	474,700
Total	849,600	1,408,900

Finance

Higher education is largely financed by public funds, tuition fees for students paid through the awards system and income charged by institutions for research and other purposes.

Government finance for higher education institutions in England, Scotland and Wales is distributed by higher education funding councils responsible to their respective Secretary of State. In Northern Ireland grant is paid direct to the two universities by the Department of Education, following advice from the Northern Ireland Higher Education Council. The private University of Buckingham does not receive any public grants.

Finance from the funding councils helps meet the costs of teaching, research and related activities in all publicly funded universities and higher education colleges. In addition to teaching students, institutions undertake paid training, research or consultancy for commercial firms (see p. 428). Many establishments have endowments or receive grants from foundations and benefactors.

Student Grants and Loans

Over 90 per cent of full-time students resident in England and Wales on first degree and other comparable higher education courses are eligible for mandatory awards covering tuition fees and maintenance. There are also contributions from parents, assessed according to their income. Awards are made by LEAs in England and Wales. Similar schemes are administered by the Student Awards Agency for Scotland and the Northern Ireland education and library boards. The Government reimburses in full the amount spent by education authorities on mandatory student grants and fees. LEA grants for other courses are discretionary.

Most students on courses of full-time, non-postgraduate higher education can top up their grant with a loan to help pay their maintenance costs. Loans are not means tested and repayments are indexed to inflation. The scheme is designed to share the cost of student maintenance more equitably between students, parents and the taxpayer. In 1992–93 loans worth £227 million were made to 345,300 students in Britain, representing 41 per cent of those eligible. Loans are administered by the Student Loans Company in Glasgow.

Limited access funds administered by universities and colleges are available to people in cases where access to higher and further education might be inhibited by financial considerations or where students face real financial difficulties. In 1994–95, for example, there is provision of £26.7 million in England for this purpose.

Grants for postgraduate study are offered by the government education departments and by the research councils (see Chapter 19). Increasing numbers of scholarships are available from research charities, endowments and particular industries or companies.

Access Courses

Access and foundation courses provide a preparation and an appropriate test before enrolment on a course of higher education for prospective students who do not possess the standard entry qualifications (GCE A levels and equivalent qualifications). Many are from the ethnic minority communities. The growth of access courses has been very rapid in recent years; about 600 are now available nationwide.

The Scottish Wider Access Programme (SWAP) is designed to promote greater participation in higher education by mature students and those without the normal entry requirements. Successful completion of a SWAP course guarantees a higher education place.

Universities

There are some 90 universities, including the Open University. They are governed by royal charters or by Act of Parliament and enjoy academic freedom. They appoint their own staff, decide which students to admit, provide their own courses and award their own degrees. The universities of Oxford and Cambridge date from the 12th and 13th centuries, and the Scottish universities of St Andrews, Glasgow, Aberdeen and Edinburgh from the 14th and 15th centuries. All the other universities in Britain were founded in the 19th and 20th centuries. The 1960s saw considerable expansion in the number of new universities. The number of universities also jumped considerably in 1992, when polytechnics and some other higher education establishments were given the freedom to become universities and chose to exercise it.

Applications for first degree courses are usually made through the Universities and Colleges Admission Service (UCAS), in Cheltenham.

First degree courses are mainly full time and usually last three years in England, Wales and Northern Ireland. However, there are some four-year courses, and medical and veterinary courses normally require five years. All traditional first degree courses in Scotland require a minimum of three years' study. The ratio of staff to full-time students is about 1 to 12.5.

Universities offer courses in a wide range of subjects, including traditional arts subjects and science and technology. Some courses lead to the examinations of the chief professional bodies, and to qualifications such as those of the BTEC.

Many universities have close links with commerce and industry, with some students having a job and attending on a part-time basis.

Degree titles vary according to the practice of each university. In England, Wales and Northern Ireland the most common titles for a first degree are Bachelor of Arts (BA) or Bachelor of Science (BSc) and for a second degree Master of Arts (MA), Master of Science (MSc), and Doctor of Philosophy (PhD). In the older Scottish universities Master is used for a first degree in arts subjects. Uniformity of standards between universities is promoted by employing external examiners for all university examinations.

The Open University and other universities are responsible for validating degrees at higher education institutions without degree-awarding powers.

Most staff combine research with teaching duties and over half of postgraduate students are engaged on research projects. The Government is encouraging universities to co-operate closely with industry on research (see Chapter 20). Over 40 science parks have been set up by higher education institutions in conjunction with industrial scientists and technologists to promote the development and commercial application of advanced technology.

The Open University

The Open University is a non-residential university offering degree and other courses for adult students of all ages in Britain and the other member countries of the European Union. It uses a combination of specially produced printed texts, correspondence tuition, television and radio broadcasts and audio/video cassettes. For some courses, there are residential schools. There is a network of study centres for contact with part-time tutors and counsellors, and with fellow students. Formal academic qualifications are not required to register for most courses, but the standards of the University's degrees are the same as those of other universities. Its first degrees are the BA (Open) or the BSc (Open), which are general degrees awarded on a system of credits for each course completed. In 1994 there were some 91,000 registered undergraduates, and in all some 155,000 first degrees have been awarded since the University started its courses in 1970.

The University has a programme of higher degrees. The Bachelor of Philosophy (BPhil), Master of Philosophy (MPhil) and PhD are research degrees and the MA, MSc and Master of Business Administration (MBA) are awarded after successful completion of taught courses. About 9,000 students were registered on higher degree courses in 1994.

There are also programmes for professionals in education and the health and social welfare services, and for updating managers, scientists and technologists. Some of these are multi-media courses taught in a similar way to those in the undergraduate programme, and others are in the form of self-contained study packs. In 1994 about 8,000 students were following courses in these areas. The University's first Postgraduate Certificate in Education courses attracted 1,100 students.

The University has advised many other countries on setting up similar institutions. It has made a substantial contribution to the Commonwealth of Learning project, which brings together distance-teaching establishments and students throughout the Commonwealth, and to the European Distance Education Network. It is financed by the Higher Education Funding Council for England.

Further Education for Adults

Further education for adults is provided by further education institutions, adult centres and colleges run by LEAs, and voluntary bodies such as the Workers' Educational Association. The duty to secure it is shared by the further education funding councils and by LEAs.

The Councils fund formal academic and vocational courses, courses providing access to higher education and courses in basic literacy and numeracy, including English for speakers of other languages. LEAs are responsible for the less formal leisure and recreational courses. Both the Councils and the LEAs must take account of adult students with special educational needs.

University departments of continuing education also provide courses for adults.

ALBSU

The Adult Literacy and Basic Skills Unit (ALBSU) is concerned with adult literacy, numeracy and related basic skills in England and Wales. It provides consultancy and advisory services; funds local development projects, including research; publishes materials for teachers and students; and organises and sponsors staff training. Government funding of ALBSU was worth over £3 million in 1994–95.

The Government also supports two programmes managed by ALBSU, one of which is aimed at parents with literacy difficulties and their children. The other is the Basic Skills at Work programme, which helps unemployed people and those in work who cannot progress without improved basic skills.

National Organisation of Adult Learning

The National Organisation of Adult Learning —formerly the National Institute of Adult Continuing Education and still known as NIACE—is the national body representing adult learners in England and Wales. It convenes conferences, seminars and meetings, collects and disseminates information, conducts enquiries and research, undertakes special projects and works with other organisations.

Open and Distance Learning

The term 'open and distance learning' broadly means learning undertaken without the direct supervision of a tutor through use of various media such as television. More and more further education colleges are incorporating many distance learning materials and methods in their mainstream courses, thereby allowing increasing numbers of students to learn in ways which suit them best.

Open learning opportunities in further education were extended in 1987 by the formation of the Open College, an independent company set up with Government support, which brings together broadcasters, educationists and sponsors. It provides vocational education and training courses below degree level. The Open College of the Arts, also launched in 1987, offers foundation courses in the arts to those wishing to study at home.

Scottish Community Education Council

The Scottish Community Education Council advises the Government and promotes all community education matters, including adult literacy and basic education, and youth work.

EDUCATIONAL RESEARCH

Educational research is supported financially by government departments, the Economic and Social Research Council (see Chapter 20), philanthropic organisations, higher education institutions, teachers' associations and other agencies.

The major research institutions outside the universities are the autonomous National Foundation for Educational Research in England and Wales and the Scottish Council for Research in Education.

LINKS WITH OTHER COUNTRIES

Large numbers of people come to Britain from other countries to study, and British people work and train overseas. The British aid programme encourages links between educational institutions in Britain and developing countries.

There has been an expansion of interest in European studies and languages, with exchanges of teachers, schoolchildren and students taking place. Exchange of students is promoted by a European Union scheme (ERASMUS), under which grants are provided to enable Union students and those from countries belonging to the European Free Trade Association to study in other states. Over 25,000 students from Britain have benefited from the scheme.

The Union's LINGUA programme seeks to improve and widen competence in the use of foreign languages. It gives grants towards in-service training for teachers, study abroad for language students, joint educational projects and exchanges for young people undergoing professional, vocational and technical education; it also covers measures to develop language training materials for business.

The Action Programme for Education and Training for Technology (COMETT) aims to foster co-operation between higher education establishments and industry in the Union by training personnel, especially in small and medium-sized enterprises, in the application of advanced technology.

The EU's PETRA vocational training programme for young people organises training and work experience placements in other member states.

Union member states have created nine European schools, including one at Culham, Oxfordshire, to provide a multinational education for the children of staff employed in Union institutions.

Overseas Students in Britain

British universities and other further and higher education establishments have built up their strong reputation overseas by offering tuition of the highest standards, maintaining low student-to-staff ratios, and offering the most relevant courses and qualifications.

In 1992–93 there were 99,700 overseas students at publicly funded higher and further education institutions in Great Britain. Their numbers have increased by 76 per cent since 1982–83 and by 8 per cent since 1991–92. In Northern Ireland there

were more than 5,000 students from overseas in 1992–93.

In general, overseas students following courses of higher or further education in Britain pay fees covering the full cost of their courses.

Nationals of other member countries of the European Union generally pay the lower level of fees applicable to British students; if their courses are designated for mandatory awards, they may be eligible for fees-only awards from LEAs. Students attending Scottish institutions apply either to the Student Awards Agency for Scotland or the regional or island councils.

Government Scholarship Schemes

The Government makes considerable provision for foreign students and trainees under its overseas aid programme and through other award and scholarship schemes. In 1992–93 some 21,000 overseas students were supported at a cost of £147 million.

The Foreign & Commonwealth Office (FCO) finances the British Chevening Scholarships, a worldwide programme offering outstanding graduate students and young professionals the opportunity to spend a formative part of their careers studying at British universities and other academic institutions. In 1994–95 the FCO is spending some £30 million on about 5,000 scholarships for students from 146 countries.

There are also jointly funded scholarship schemes for overseas students co-sponsored by the FCO, business and industry, grant-giving foundations, churches and universities; some 800 scholarships were provided under these arrangements in 1993–94.

Outside the aid programme, the Overseas Research Students Awards Scheme, funded by the Department for Education, provides assistance for overseas full-time postgraduate students with outstanding research potential; these awards meet the difference between the home/European Union and overseas student fee levels.

Other Schemes

Many public and private scholarships and fellowships are available to students from overseas and to British students who want to study overseas. Among the best known are the British Council Fellowships, the Commonwealth Scholarship and Fellowship Plan, the Fulbright Scholarship Scheme, the Marshall Scholarships, the Rhodes Scholarships, the Churchill Scholarships and the Confederation of British Industry Scholarships. Most British universities and colleges also offer scholarships for which graduates of any nationality are eligible.

THE YOUTH SERVICE

The youth service—a partnership between local government and voluntary organisations—is concerned with the informal social education of young people.

Many of the voluntary organisations were established at the end of the 19th century and in the first decade of the 20th. In 1939 the Government first recognised the need for a youth service forming part of education and supported through LEAs. In 1944 the Education Act provided for the development of a service in England and Wales by LEAs in partnership with the voluntary organisations.

Local authorities maintain their own youth centres and clubs and provide most of the public support for local and regional voluntary organisations. The service is said to reach around 5 million young people, the voluntary organisations contributing a significant proportion of overall provision.

The Department for Education's Youth Service Unit gives grants to the national voluntary youth organisations to meet 50 per cent of the cost of programmes designed to promote access to the youth service, support training for voluntary youth workers and help improve the efficiency and effectiveness of the organisations.

Funded primarily by central government, England's National Youth Agency provides:

- support for those working with young people;

- information and publishing services; and
- support for curriculum development.

It is also responsible for the accreditation of training and staff development for youth workers.

The Welsh Office provides grant aid to national youth service bodies with headquarters in Wales and has established a Wales Youth Agency similar to the one in England.

In Scotland the youth service forms part of community education, which is promoted by the Scottish Community Education Council. The Scottish Office gives grants to voluntary youth organisations to assist them with their headquarters expenditure and staff training and development.

In Northern Ireland the education and library boards provide and fund youth clubs and outdoor activity centres, help pay the running costs of registered voluntary youth units, advise and support youth groups and assist young people visiting the rest of Britain, Ireland and overseas in connection with annual camps and award schemes. The Youth Council for Northern Ireland advises the education system on the development of the youth service, promotes provision of facilities and encourages cross-community activity among young people. It also helps co-ordinate youth service resources and provides funds to help voluntary youth organisations' headquarters meet their running costs.

Voluntary Youth Organisations

National voluntary youth organisations undertake a significant share of youth activities through local groups, which raise most of their day-to-day expenses by their own efforts. Many receive financial and other help from LEAs, which also make available facilities in many areas. The voluntary organisations vary greatly in character and include the uniformed organisations such as the Scouts and Girl Guides. Some organisations are church-based. Some also represent Jews and Muslims. Sport and the arts are catered for by various bodies. In Wales Urdd Gobaith Cymru (the Welsh League of Youth) provides cultural, sporting and language-based activities for young Welsh speakers and learners.

Thousands of youth clubs encourage their members to participate in sport, cultural and other creative activities. Some youth clubs provide information, counselling and advice.

Many local authorities and voluntary youth organisations have responded to new needs in society by making provision, for example, for the young unemployed, young people from the ethnic minorities, young people in inner cities or rural areas and those in trouble or especially vulnerable. Other areas of concern are homelessness and provision for handicapped young people.

Many authorities have youth committees on which official and voluntary bodies are represented. They employ youth officers to co-ordinate youth work and to arrange in-service training. There are also youth councils, which are representative bodies of young people from local youth organisations.

Youth Workers

In England and Wales a two-year training course at certain universities and higher education colleges produces qualified youth and community workers; several undergraduate part-time and postgraduate courses are also available. In Scotland one-, two- and three-year courses are provided at colleges of education. Students from Northern Ireland attend courses run in universities and colleges in Britain and the Irish Republic.

Other Organisations Concerned with Young People

Finance is provided by many grant-giving foundations and trusts for activities involving young people. The Prince's Trust and the Royal Jubilee Trust provide grants and practical help to individuals and organisations; areas of concern include urban deprivation, unemployment, homelessness, and young offenders. Efforts are also made to assist ethnic minorities.

The Duke of Edinburgh's Award Scheme challenges young people from Britain and other Commonwealth countries to meet certain standards in activities such as community service, expeditions, the development of personal interests, social and practical skills and physical recreation.

Voluntary Service by Young People

Thousands of young people voluntarily undertake community service designed to help those in need, including elderly and disabled people. Organisations responsible for community service, such as Community Service Volunteers, International Voluntary Service and the British Trust for Conservation Volunteers, receive grants from the Government. Many schools also organise community service work as part of the curriculum, and voluntary work in the community is sponsored by a number of churches.

Further Reading

Education After 16. Aspects of Britain series, HMSO, 1994.
Education Reforms in Schools. Aspects of Britain series, HMSO, 1994.

27 Religion

Everyone in Britain has the right to religious freedom without interference from the community or the State. Religious organisations and groups may own property, run schools, and promote their beliefs in speech and writing. There is no religious bar to the holding of public office.

INTRODUCTION

Most of the world's religions are represented in Britain, including large Hindu, Jewish, Muslim and Sikh communities, but Britain is predominantly Christian. Non-religious alternatives for humanists and atheists are offered by organisations such as the British Humanist Association and the National Secular Society.

Religious Freedom

Britain has a long tradition of religious tolerance. Freedom of conscience in religious matters was achieved gradually from the 17th century onwards. The laws discriminating against minority religious groups were gradually administered less harshly and then finally repealed. Heresy ceased to be a legal offence with the passage of the Ecclesiastical Jurisdiction Act 1677, and the Toleration Act 1688 granted freedom of worship to Protestant minority groups.

In 1828 the repeal of the Test and Corporation Acts gave nonconformists full political rights, making it possible for them to be appointed to public office. Roman Catholics gained political rights under the Roman Catholic Relief Act 1829, and the Jewish Relief Act 1858 enabled Jews to become Members of Parliament. The religious tests imposed on prospective students and academic staff of the universities of Oxford, Cambridge and Durham were successively abolished by Acts of 1854, 1856 and 1871. Similar restrictions on the staff of Scottish universities were formally removed in 1932.

The past 30 years have seen the acceptance of a wide variety of religious beliefs and of the traditions of large numbers of immigrants of different nationalities. Arrangements are made at places of work to allow the members of non-Christian religions to follow their religious observances.

Relations with the State

There are two established churches in Britain, that is, churches legally recognised as official churches of the State: in England the Church of England, and in Scotland the (Presbyterian) Church of Scotland. Ministers of the established churches, as well as clergy belonging to other religious groups, work in services run by the State, such as the armed forces, national hospitals and prisons, and are paid a salary for such services by the State. Voluntary schools provided by religious denominations may be wholly or partly maintained from public funds. Religious education in publicly maintained schools is required by law throughout Britain, as is a daily act of collective worship (see p. 420). Religious broadcasting is subject to some legislative controls (see p. 470).

The Government contributes towards the upkeep of nearly 300 redundant Church of England churches for which no alternative use can be found but which are of architectural or historic importance. The contribution for the period 1994 to 1997 will be about £7.2 million. In 1993 the Government launched the Historic Chapels Trust, which aims to preserve the redundant chapels and places of worship of other denominations and faiths.

The State does not contribute to general church expenses although some limited state aid does help repair historic churches; in 1993–94, for instance, English Heritage grants to churches totalled £10 million. Assistance is also given to meet some of the costs of repairing cathedrals and comparable buildings; some £4 million is being made available in each of the years 1994–95 and 1995–96. This funding is not restricted to Church of England buildings.

Involvement in Social Issues

Religious involvement in broader social issues was highlighted in the Church of England report *Faith in the City: A Call for Action by Church and Nation*, published in 1985. This led to the establishment in 1988 of the Church of England's Church Urban Fund, which aims to raise money for the Church's work in inner city and other priority areas. By June 1993 it had raised over £24.5 million and given grants to 550 inner city projects. Organisations belonging to other churches and religious groups are also closely involved with a wide range of social issues.

The Inner Cities Religious Council aims to provide faith communities with a new and effective way of working together in the inner cities and deprived urban areas in order to bring about real and lasting change. It is chaired by a government minister at the Department of the Environment and its members are drawn from the Christian, Hindu, Jewish, Muslim and Sikh faiths.

Statistics on Religious Affiliation

There is no standard information about the number of members of religious groups since questions are not normally asked about religious beliefs in censuses or for other official purposes, except in Northern Ireland. Each group adopts its own way of counting its members, and the membership figures in this chapter—supplied by the religious groups themselves—are therefore approximate.

There has been a fall in recent years in the number of full-time ministers and the number of adults recorded as members of most of the larger Christian churches. At the same time there has been significant growth in a range of independent churches, and in new religious movements. Surveys have also revealed that many people who do not belong to religious groups claim to be religious and say they believe in God.

ESTABLISHED CHURCHES

Church of England

The Church of England, founded by St Augustine in AD 597, became the established church during the Reformation in the 16th century. Its form of worship was set out in successive versions of the Book of Common Prayer from 1549 onwards. The Church of England's relationship with the State is one of mutual obligation, since the Church's privileges are balanced by certain duties it must fulfil.

The Monarch is the 'Supreme Governor' of the Church of England and must always be a member of the Church, and promise to uphold it. Church of England archbishops, bishops and deans of cathedrals are appointed by the Monarch on the advice of the Prime Minister, although the Crown Appointments Commission, which includes lay and clergy representatives, plays a decisive part in the selection of archbishops and diocesan bishops.

All clergy swear allegiance to the Crown. The Church can regulate its own worship. The two archbishops (of Canterbury and York), the bishops of London, Durham and Winchester, and 21 other senior bishops sit in the House of Lords. Clergy of the Church, together with those of the Church of Scotland, the Church of Ireland and the Roman Catholic Church, may not sit in the House of Commons.

The Church has two provinces: Canterbury, comprising 30 dioceses, including the Diocese in Europe; and York, with 14 dioceses. The dioceses are divided into archdeaconries and deaneries, which are in turn divided into about 13,000 parishes. There are, altogether, about 10,800 full-time stipendiary Church of England clergy—men and women—working within the diocesan structure, excluding mainland Europe. In 1991 an estimated 225,000 people were baptised into the Church in the two provinces, excluding the Diocese in Europe; of these, 180,000 were under one year old, representing 27 per cent of live births. In the same year there were 55,246 confirmations. Attendances at services on a normal Sunday are around 1.1 million. In 1991, 102,840 marriages were solemnised in the Church of England and the Church in Wales. These accounted for 66 per cent of all marriages with religious ceremonies, and 34 per cent of all marriages in England and Wales. Many people who rarely, if ever, attend services still regard themselves as belonging to the Church of England.

The central governing body is the General Synod, which comprises separate houses of bishops, clergy and lay members. Lay people are also concerned with church government in the parishes. The Synod is the centre of an administrative system dealing with such matters as missionary work, inter-church relations, social questions, and recruitment and training for the ministry. It also covers other church work in Britain and overseas, the care of church buildings and their contents, church schools (which are maintained largely from public funds), colleges and institutes of higher education, and voluntary and parish education.

The Church's investment income from historic sources is managed mainly by the Church Commissioners. Most of the remainder of the Church's income is provided by local voluntary donations.

The average annual stipend of a Church of England priest is about £12,800; the average value of additional benefits, including free housing and a non-contributory pension, is estimated to be about £9,000.

In November 1992 the General Synod voted in favour of legislation allowing the ordination of women to the priesthood. The measure was subsequently approved by both Houses of Parliament and received the Royal Assent. The first women priests were ordained in March 1994. The measure also provided for those unable to accept the ordination of women, including the payment of compensation to clergy who feel they have to leave the ministry of the Church. Two bishops have been appointed to provide additional pastoral care to those members and parishes of the Church who remain opposed to the ordination of women to the priesthood.

Church of Scotland

The Church of Scotland has a presbyterian form of government, that is, government by ministers and elders, all of whom are ordained to office. It became the national church following the Scottish Reformation and legislation of the Scottish Parliament, consolidated in the Treaty of Union 1707 and the Church of Scotland Act 1921, the latter confirming its complete freedom in all spiritual matters. It appoints its own office bearers, and its affairs are not subject to any civil authority.

The adult communicant membership of the Church of Scotland is 732,963; there are about 1,215 ministers serving in parishes. Both men and women may join the ministry. About 1,312 churches are governed locally by Kirk Sessions, consisting of ministers and elders. Above the Kirk Session is the Presbytery. The General Assembly, consisting of elected ministers and elders, meets annually under the presidency of an elected moderator, who serves for one year. The Monarch is normally represented at the General Assembly by the Lord High Commissioner.

There are also a number of independent Scottish Presbyterian churches, largely descended from groups which broke away from the Church of Scotland.

WALES

The Church in Wales became part of the Anglican Church at the Reformation. The Bible was translated into Welsh by Bishop Morgan in 1588. During the 18th and 19th centuries a powerful nonconformist (or Free Church—see below) movement developed throughout Wales: a census of religion in 1851 found that over 80 per cent of those at worship attended a nonconformist chapel. This strength was reflected in the disestablishment of the Church in Wales in 1920. The Church in Wales has some 101,000 members. The Church is responsible for the care of the country's medieval churches and cathedrals; at present only men may join its priesthood.

THE ANGLICAN COMMUNION

The Anglican Communion comprises 35 autonomous Churches in Britain and abroad, and three regional councils overseas with a total membership of about 70 million. In the British Isles there are four Anglican Churches: the Church of England, the Church in Wales, the Scottish Episcopal Church, and the Church of Ireland.

Every ten years the Lambeth Conference meets for consultation between all Anglican bishops. The last Conference was held in Canterbury in 1988. Presided over by the Archbishop of Canterbury, the Conference has no executive authority, but enjoys considerable influence. The Anglican Consultative Council, an assembly of lay people and clergy as well as of bishops, meets every two or three years and is intended to allow consultation within the Anglican Communion. The Primates Meeting brings together the senior bishops from each Church at similar intervals.

FREE CHURCHES

The term 'Free Churches' is often used to describe some of the Protestant churches in Britain which, unlike the Church of England and the Church of Scotland, are not established churches. Free Churches have existed in various forms since the Reformation, developing their own traditions over the years. Their members have also been known as dissenters or nonconformists. All the major Free Churches allow both men and women to become ministers.

The Methodist Church, the largest of the Free Churches, with nearly 410,000 adult full members and a community of more than 1.3 million, originated in the 18th century following the evangelical revival under John Wesley (1703–91). The present church is based on the 1932 union of most of the separate Methodist Churches. It has 3,601 ministers and 6,950 places of worship.

The Salvation Army was founded in the East End of London in 1865 by William Booth (1829–1912). Within Britain it is second only to the Government as a provider of social services. It is the largest provider of hostel accommodation, offering 4,000 beds every night. Other services include work with alcoholics, prison chaplaincy and a family tracing service which takes on 5,000 cases each year. The Army in Britain is served by 1,800 officers (ordained ministers) and runs more than 1,000 worship centres.

The Baptists first achieved an organised form in Britain in the 17th century. Today they are mainly organised in groups of churches, most of which belong to the Baptist Union of Great Britain (re-formed in 1812), with about 150,000 members, 2,300 ministers and 2,000 places of worship. There are also separate Baptist Unions for Scotland, Wales and Ireland, and other independent Baptist Churches.

The United Reformed Church, with some 111,000 members, 1,807 ministers and 1,803 places of worship, was formed in 1972 following the merger of the Congregational Church in England and Wales (the oldest Protestant minority in Britain, whose origins can be traced back to the Puritans of the 16th century) with the

Presbyterian Church of England, many of whose members are descended from Scottish Presbyterians. This was the first union of two different churches in Britain since the Reformation in the 16th century. In 1981 there was a further merger with the Reformed Association of the Churches of Christ.

Among the other Free Churches are the Presbyterian Church in Ireland, the Presbyterian (or Calvinistic Methodist) Church of Wales and the Union of Welsh Independents. There are also groupings of 'Black Majority' Churches.

ROMAN CATHOLIC CHURCH

The formal structure of the Roman Catholic Church in England and Wales, which ceased to exist after the Reformation, was restored in 1850. The Scottish Church's formal structure went out of existence in the early 17th century and was restored in 1878. However, throughout this period Catholicism never disappeared entirely. There are now seven Roman Catholic provinces in Great Britain, each under an archbishop, and 30 dioceses, each under a bishop (22 in England and Wales and eight in Scotland, independently responsible to the Pope). There are almost 3,300 parishes and about 7,300 priests (only men may become priests). Northern Ireland has six dioceses, some with territory partly in the Irish Republic. About one British citizen in ten claims to be a Roman Catholic. The Pope is represented diplomatically in Britain by an Apostolic Pro-Nuncio.

The Roman Catholic Church attaches great importance to the education of its children and requires its members to try to bring up their children in the Catholic faith. Almost 5 per cent of the teachers in Britain's 2,500 Catholic schools are members of religious orders. These orders also undertake other social work; about 250 Roman Catholic religious orders, congregations and societies are represented in Britain, as are congregations representing about 25 different nationalities who live in Britain. Most Catholic schools are maintained out of public funds.

OTHER CHRISTIAN CHURCHES

Other Protestant Churches include the Unitarians and Free Christians, whose origins are traceable to the Reformation, and the Pentecostalists, whose movement began in the early 20th century. The two main Pentecostalist organisations operating in Britain are the Assemblies of God (approximately 50,000 members) and the Elim Pentecostal Church (approximately 42,000 members). Recently both Pentecostal Churches have applied to join the Free Church Federal Council (see p. 439).

The Religious Society of Friends (Quakers), with about 18,000 adult members in Britain and 450 places of worship, was founded in the middle of the 17th century under the leadership of George Fox (1624–91). Silent worship is central to its life as a religious organisation. Emphasis is also placed on social concern and peace-making.

The Christian Brethren is a Protestant body organised in its present form by J. N. Darby (1800–82). There are two branches: the Open Brethren (with an estimated 43,500 members) and the Closed or Exclusive Brethren (with an estimated 7,600 members).

The Christian 'house church' movement (or 'new churches') began in the early 1970s and now has an estimated membership of almost 110,000. Services were originally held in private houses but now groups use a variety of hired buildings. These non-denominational congregations may come together as 'streams', of which some of the better known are New Frontiers, Pioneer and Ichthus.

Many Christian communities of foreign origin, including the Orthodox, Lutheran and Reformed Churches of various European countries, and the Coptic Orthodox Church and the Armenian Church, have established their own centres of worship, particularly in London. All these churches operate in a variety of languages. The largest is probably the Greek Orthodox Church, many of whose members are of Cypriot origin. It is represented in many cities throughout Britain.

There are also several other religious organisations in Britain which were founded in the United States in the last century. These include the Jehovah's Witnesses, the Church of Jesus Christ of the Latter-Day Saints (the Mormon Church), the Seventh-Day Adventists, the Christian Scientists and the Spiritualists.

OTHER RELIGIONS

The Jewish Community

Jews first settled in England at the time of the Norman Conquest and remained until banished by royal decree in 1290. The present community in Britain dates from 1656, having been founded by those of Spanish and Portuguese origin, known as Sephardim. Later more settlers came from Germany and Eastern Europe; they are known as Ashkenazim.

The present Jewish community in Britain, numbering about 300,000, is the second largest in Europe. It is divided into two main groups. Some 77 per cent of the majority Ashkenazi Jews are Orthodox and most acknowledge the authority of the Chief Rabbi. The Sephardi Orthodox element follow their own spiritual head. The recently established Masorti movement, the Reform movement, founded in 1840, and the Liberal and Progressive movement, established in 1901, account for most of the remaining 23 per cent.

Jewish congregations in Britain number about 350. About one in three Jewish children attend Jewish schools, some of which are supported by public funds. Several agencies care for elderly and handicapped people. The officially recognised representative body is the Board of Deputies of British Jews, which was established in 1760.

The Muslim Community

The most recent estimates suggest that Britain's Muslim population is between 1.5–2 million. The largest number originate from Pakistan and Bangladesh, while sizeable groups have come from India, Cyprus, the Arab world, Malaysia and parts of Africa. A growing community of British-born Muslims, mainly the children of immigrant parents, includes an increasing number of converts to Islam.

> There are nearly 500 mosques and numerous Muslim prayer centres throughout Britain. Mosques are not only places of worship; they also offer instruction in the Muslim way of life and facilities for educational and welfare activities.

The first mosque in Britain was established at Woking, Surrey, in 1890. Mosques now range from converted houses in many towns to the Central Mosque in Regent's Park, London, and its associated Islamic Cultural Centre, one of the most important Muslim institutions in the Western world. The Central Mosque has the largest congregation in Britain, and during festivals it may number over 30,000. There are also important mosques and cultural centres in Liverpool, Manchester, Leicester, Birmingham, Bradford, Cardiff, Edinburgh and Glasgow.

Many of the mosques belong to various Muslim organisations, and both the Sunni and the Shia traditions within Islam are represented among the Muslim community in Britain. Members of some of the major Sufi traditions have also developed branches in British cities.

The Sikh Community

A large British Sikh community, comprising over 300,000, originates mainly from India. The largest groups of Sikhs are in Greater London, Manchester, Birmingham, Nottingham and Wolverhampton. Sikh temples or gurdwaras cater for the religious, educational, social welfare and cultural needs of their community. The oldest gurdwara in London was established in 1908 and the largest is in Southall, Middlesex. There are over 140 gurdwaras in Britain.

The Hindu Community

The Hindu community in Britain comprises around 320,000 members and also originates largely from India. The largest groups of Hindus are to be found in Leicester, different areas of London, Birmingham and Bradford. The first Hindu temple or mandir was opened in London in 1962 and there are now over 150 mandirs in Britain.

Buddhism

The Buddhist community in Britain consists largely of adherents of British or Western origin. There are about 150 Buddhist groups in Britain and some 100 centres, with at least 15 monasteries and a number of temples. All the main schools of Buddhism are represented. The Buddhist Society promotes the principles of Buddhism; it does not belong to any particular school of Buddhism.

Other Religious Communities

Other religious communities include about 30,000 Jains, whose religion is of ancient Indian origin. A deresar, or Jain temple, opened in Leicester in 1988. The Zoroastrian religion, or Mazdaism, originated in ancient Iran. It is mainly represented in Britain by the Parsi community, who are by origin from the South Asian sub-continent. The Baha'i movement, originating in 19th-century Iran, regards all the major religions as divine in origin; there are an estimated 5,000 Baha'is in Britain.

New Religious Movements

A large number of new religious movements or cults, mainly established since the Second World War and often with overseas origins, are active in Britain. Examples include the Church of Scientology, the Transcendental Meditation movement and the Unification Church (popularly known as the 'Moonies'). In response to public concern about the activities of some of these cults the Government provided start-up funding from 1987 to 1993 for the Information Network Focus on Religious Movements, which is a group supported by the main churches. It seeks to provide objective information about new religious movements.

Further Reading

Religion. Aspects of Britain series, HMSO, 1992.

CO-OPERATION BETWEEN FAITHS

A number of organisations exist which seek to develop relations between different religions in Britain. They include the Inter-Faith Network for the United Kingdom, which links a wide range of organisations with an interest in inter-faith relations, including representative bodies from the Baha'i, Buddhist, Christian, Hindu, Jain, Jewish, Muslim, Sikh and Zoroastrian faith communities. Other organisations include the Council of Christians and Jews, which works for better understanding among members of the two religions and deals with issues in the educational and social fields.

Co-operation among the Churches

The Council of Churches for Britain and Ireland was established in 1990, replacing the former British Council of Churches and taking over its role as the main overall body for the Christian churches in Britain. The Council co-ordinates the work of its 30 member churches, which are also grouped in separate ecumenical bodies for England, Scotland, Wales and Ireland.

The Free Church Federal Council, with 20 member churches, includes most of the Free Churches of England and Wales. It promotes co-operation among the Free Churches (especially in hospital chaplaincy and in education matters) and is a channel for communication with government.

Inter-church discussions about the search for unity now take place through international as well as national bodies. The Roman Catholic, Orthodox and Lutheran Churches are represented on some of these, as are the Anglican and some of the Free Churches.

The Anglican Churches, the Church of Scotland and the main Free Churches are also members of the World Council of Churches. This organisation links some 310 churches in over 100 countries around the world.

28 The Arts

Artistic and cultural activity in Britain ranges from the highest professional standards to a wide variety of amateur performances and events. Thirty-six per cent of adults attend events in one or more of the major art forms; around 4 million people went to more than 650 professional arts festivals in Britain in 1993.

INTRODUCTION

Britain's artistic and cultural heritage is one of the richest in the world. The origins of English literature, one of the world's most influential bodies of writing, can be traced back to medieval times, while over the centuries Britain has amassed some of the finest collections of works of art. The performing arts also have a long and distinguished history.

London is one of the leading world centres for the arts. Other large cities, including Birmingham, Sheffield, Manchester, Edinburgh, Glasgow and Cardiff, have also sustained and developed their reputations as centres of artistic excellence in recent years. Arts festivals attract wide interest. Many British playwrights, composers, film-makers, painters, writers, actors, singers, musicians and dancers enjoy international reputations. They include, for example, Harold Pinter, Sir Colin Davies, Sir Andrew Lloyd Webber, David Hockney, Sir V.S. Naipaul, Vanessa Redgrave and Sir Ian McKellen. Television and radio bring a wide range of arts events to a large audience. At an amateur level, numerous groups and societies for the arts make use of local talent and resources.

Department of National Heritage

The Secretary of State for National Heritage, who is a member of the Cabinet, is responsible for arts policy. The office was created in 1992 and its holder heads the Department of National Heritage (see p. 441), which replaced the Office of Arts and Libraries as well as taking on a range of responsibilities from other departments. The Department determines government policy and administers government expenditure on national museums and art galleries in England, the Arts Council of England (see p. 442), the British Library and other national arts and heritage bodies. Other responsibilities include the regulation of the film industry, broadcasting, press regulation, the National Lottery and the export licensing of antiques.

The Secretaries of State for Wales, Scotland and Northern Ireland are responsible for the national museums, galleries and libraries in their countries, and for other cultural matters, including the running of their respective arts councils.

The Government's arts policies aim to:
- develop a high standard of artistic and cultural activity throughout Britain;
- encourage innovation; and

- promote public access to, and appreciation of, the arts, crafts and the cultural heritage.

The Department of National Heritage provides funds and advice, and encourages partnership with the private sector, including business sponsorship. National museums and galleries are given an incentive to increase their resources, for example, through trading and other activities. An important concept in funding policy is the 'arm's length' principle, by which government funds are distributed to arts organisations indirectly, through bodies such as the Arts Councils and the British Film Institute. This principle helps to avoid political influence over funding decisions by ensuring that funds are allocated by those best qualified to do so.

Local Authorities

Local authorities maintain around 1,000 local museums and art galleries and a network of over 4,000 public libraries. They also support many arts buildings, arts organisations and artistic events in their areas, providing grant aid for professional and voluntary organisations, including orchestras and theatre, opera and dance companies. They undertake direct promotions and contribute to the cost of new or converted buildings for the arts. In England revenue support from local authorities is estimated to be about £180 million a year. Arts education in schools, colleges, evening institutes and community centres is the responsibility of central government education departments, in partnership with local education authorities and voluntary bodies.

Finance

Planned central government expenditure through the Department of National Heritage, excluding sport, amounts to £920 million in 1994–95, of which £186 million is channelled through the Arts Council of England to support the performing and visual arts; over £80 million goes to the British Library. Grants are also made to the British Film Institute, the Crafts Council, certain other museums and arts bodies, and to the National Heritage Memorial Fund. The Fund helps organisations wishing to acquire, for the public benefit, land, buildings, works of art and other objects associated with the national heritage.

Planned 1994–95 expenditure by the Arts Councils for Scotland and Wales (see p. 442) is £23.8 million and £13.5 million respectively. The Scottish Office also aims to provide £44 million for Scotland's National Galleries and Museums and National Library, while the Welsh Office provides £23 million for Wales's National Museum and National Library. Planned spending by the Arts Council of Northern Ireland on the three major museums there amounts £16 million in 1994–95.

Business Sponsorship

Industrial and commercial companies offer vital sponsorship to a wide range of arts. The Business Sponsorship Incentive Scheme was introduced in Great Britain in 1984 in co-operation with the Association for Business Sponsorship of the Arts (ABSA) with the aim of raising the overall level of business sponsorship. (A similar scheme was set up in Northern Ireland in 1987.) Since its inception the scheme has brought nearly £79 million into the arts (including a government contribution of £25.7 million) and has attracted 3,600 first-time sponsors. An estimated 80 per cent of the awards have been made to arts organisations outside London. Between 1994–95 and 1996–97 the Government is making available £14.4 million to match new sponsorships.

Some recent business sponsorships include:

- a record £3.3 million agreement with the Royal Shakespeare Company, allowing for more international touring and the production of educational programmes in Britain (Allied Domecq);
- a Goya exhibition at the Royal Academy (*The Times* and Classic FM radio) and a Picasso exhibition at the Tate (Ernst & Young);
- BT's commitment of £500,000 to British orchestras; and

- WH Smith sponsorship of an Arts Council Childrens' Literature summer school in Oxford.

Further support is encouraged by tax concessions which allow companies and individuals to obtain tax relief on donations to arts charities. For example, under the Gift Aid scheme, single gifts of £250 and over in any one year qualify for tax relief.

Foundation for Sport and the Arts

The Foundation for Sport and the Arts was set up in 1991 by the Pool Promoters Association, with grants expected to total £60 million a year. About two-thirds of the revenue is used to benefit sport and the remainder to benefit the arts.

National Lottery

The new National Lottery (see p. 493) is expected to generate substantial funds for the arts, heritage, sports, charities and for a millennium fund to celebrate the year 2000. One-fifth of net proceeds of the lottery will go on the arts, including film and crafts.

Arts Councils

The main channels for government aid to the performing arts are the various independent Arts Councils. The Arts Council of Great Britain ceased to operate on 1 April 1994 and was succeeded by the Arts Councils of England, Scotland and Wales. The Scottish Arts Council and the Arts Council of Wales are now responsible to the Scottish and Welsh Offices respectively. Northern Ireland has its own independent Arts Council.

The aims and functions of these Arts Councils are to:

- develop and improve the knowledge, understanding and practice of the arts;
- increase their accessibility to the public; and
- advise and co-operate with government departments, local authorities and other organisations.

The Councils give financial help and advice to organisations ranging from the major opera, dance and drama companies; orchestras and festivals; to small touring theatres and experimental groups. They also provide funds for the training of arts administrators and help arts organisations to develop other sources of income, including box-office, trading profits, sponsorship and local authority support. They encourage contemporary and traditional dance, mime, jazz, literature, photography and art films, and help professional creative writers, choreographers, composers, artists and photographers. The Councils also promote art exhibitions and tours and make funds available for some specialist training courses in the arts. Emphasis is being placed on obtaining funds through partnership arrangements with local authorities and other agencies, and from commercial sources. As an extension of their responsibilities for funding the arts and arts organisations, the Councils promote the arts through broadcasting, film and video (see p. 452).

Developments in Arts Funding

In 1991 ten Regional Arts Boards were created to replace the 12 Regional Arts Associations in England. The Boards offer financial assistance to artists and arts organisations and advise on, and sometimes help to promote, arts activities. They are financed mainly by the Arts Council of England, with smaller sums from the British Film Institute and Crafts Council, as well as from local authorities. Through a system of forward planning and budgeting, the Boards are subject to a clearly focused system of financial accountability to their national funders. One-third of the members of each Board are nominated by local authorities. Boards also include representatives of the regional business community as well as others with expertise and interest in the arts.

The Boards have also been given responsibility for funding over 60 client organisations hitherto financed by the Arts Council of Great Britain. However, the Arts Council of England retains funding responsibility for the four national companies —the Royal Opera House, the English National Opera, the Royal Shakespeare

Company and the Royal National Theatre—as well as for the South Bank Centre. It also remains responsible for publishing works, for touring companies without a regional base and for other arts organisations which cannot be assessed on a regional level.

The Arts and Minority Communities

The arts activities undertaken by Britain's diverse communities embrace both traditional and new forms of artistic expression. In seeking to reflect and encourage this the former Arts Council of Great Britain devoted particular attention to black and Asian dance and drama. In 1990 ADiTi, a development organisation for South Asian dance, was launched in Bradford. The Council expanded its training to include arts administration and technical skills.

The Minorities Arts Advisory Service is an independent organisation which provides information on, and training in, the arts of these communities.

Arts and Disabled People

In a 1993 report the Arts Council of Great Britain expressed concern that the buildings where arts activities take place often fail to meet the needs of disabled people, despite sensitive planning of new buildings and a considerable amount of work undertaken by local authorities and arts venues.

The ADAPT Trust, a voluntary organisation set up in 1989, contributes towards the cost of making new facilities accessible to disabled people. Its funds are raised from government and private sector sponsorship, the largest contributions coming from the Carnegie (UK) Trust.

The Arts Council of England's Disability Unit produces the *Arts & Disability Directory*, which provides information on all aspects of arts and disability. The Unit also funds the *Disability Arts Magazine* and the National Disability Arts Forum.

The Arts Council of England's apprenticeship scheme gives disabled people the opportunity to acquire skills while working in major arts organisations. Apprenticeships now exist in the Royal Shakespeare Company, the Belgrade Theatre in Coventry, and the Bournemouth Orchestra.

Arts Centres

Over 200 arts centres in Britain give people the chance of enjoying and taking part in a range of activities, with educational projects becoming increasingly important. Nearly all arts centres are professionally managed and most are supported by volunteer groups. Most arts centres are converted buildings, including former churches, warehouses, schools, town halls and private houses. They are assisted mainly by Regional Arts Boards and local authorities, while the Arts Council of England funds two large centres in London—the South Bank Centre and the Institute of Contemporary Arts. Many theatres and art galleries also provide a focal point for the community by making available facilities for other arts.

British Council

The British Council (see p. 130) promotes a knowledge of British culture overseas and maintains libraries (including film libraries) in many of the 108 countries in which it is represented. The Visiting Arts Office, an autonomous body administered by the British Council, promotes foreign arts in Britain. It provides a clearing house for British and overseas arts organisations, advises on touring matters and makes awards for projects.

Broadcasting

BBC radio and television and the independent companies (see Chapter 29) broadcast a wide variety of drama, opera, ballet, and music; and general arts magazine programmes and documentaries. These have won many international awards at festivals such as the Prix Italia and Montreux International Television Festivals. Independent television companies also make grants for arts promotion in their regions.

Broadcasting is thus a major medium for making the arts available to the general public and is a crucial source of work for actors, musicians, writers, composers, technicians and others in the arts world. It has created its own forms—nothing like arts documentaries or drama series, for instance, exists in any other medium. Broadcasters commission and produce a vast quantity of new work. Television and radio provide critical debate, information and education about the arts.

The BBC also has six orchestras, which employ many of Britain's full-time professional musicians. Each week it broadcasts about 100 hours of classical and other music (both live and recorded) on its Radio 3 (FM) channel. BBC Radio 1 (FM) broadcasts rock and pop music 24 hours a day and a large part of the output of BBC Radio 2 (FM) is popular and light music. There are at present two national commercial radio stations:

- Classic FM, which broadcasts mainly classical music; and

- Virgin 1215, which plays broad-based rock music.

Much of the output of Britain's local radio stations consists of popular and light music.

The BBC regularly commissions new music, particularly by British composers, and sponsors concerts, competitions and festivals. Each summer it presents and broadcasts the BBC Promenade Concerts (the 'Proms'), the world's largest music festival, at the Royal Albert Hall. Classic FM sponsors the Royal Philharmonic Orchestra; it also organised a Summer Music Festival in 1994.

The Press

Many national and local newspapers devote considerable space to coverage of the arts, and developments in the arts are also covered in the ethnic minority press and in periodicals such as the *Spectator* and *New Statesman and Society* (see Chapter 29). Weekly 'listings' magazines, including *Time Out*, provide details of cultural and other events in London and other large cities.

There are also a large number of specialist publications which cover specific aspects of the arts, including the *Times Literary Supplement*, *Film Monthly*, *The Antique Collector* and *Opera*. A number of publications publish original literature, including the *London Magazine*, and *Granta*, which publishes fiction as well as cultural journalism. *New Musical Express (NME)* and *Melody Maker* cover rock and pop music. The newspaper *Stage and Television Today* is directed at professional actors and others in the industry.

Festivals

Some 650 professional arts festivals take place in Britain each year. The Edinburgh International Festival, featuring a wide range of arts, is the largest of its kind in the world. Other annual festivals held in Edinburgh include International Folk and Jazz Festivals and the Film and Television Festival. The Mayfest, the second largest festival in Britain, takes place in Glasgow. Some well-known festivals concentrating on music are the Three Choirs Festival, which has taken place annually for more than 260 years in Gloucester, Worcester or Hereford; the Cheltenham Festival, largely devoted to contemporary British music; and the Aldeburgh festival. Among others catering for a number of art forms are the Royal National Eisteddfod of Wales, the National Gaelic Mod in Scotland, the Belfast Festival at Queen's, and the festivals in Brighton, Buxton, Chichester, Harrogate, Llangollen, Malvern, Pitlochry, Salisbury, and York. Many much smaller towns also hold arts festivals. A major event in London is the Notting Hill Carnival, in which the Afro-Caribbean community plays a prominent part; over one million people visited the Carnival in 1993.

Arts 2000

Arts 2000 is an Arts Council initiative which celebrates the approach of the millennium. During each year between 1992 and 2000, a city, town or region in Britain is being nominated to celebrate a particular art form, concluding with the Year of the Artist in 2000.

- The East Midlands was the Region of Dance in 1993;

- Manchester is the City of Drama 1994,
- Swansea the City of Literature 1995;
- the Northern Region the Region of Visual Arts 1996;
- the Eastern Region the Region of Opera and Musical Theatre 1997; and
- West Yorkshire the Region of Photography and the Electronic Image 1988.

The nomination for the year of architecture and design 1999 will be announced in December 1994.

Arts 2000 is a competitive process judged by expert Arts Council selection committees. Winners are offered between £250,000 and £500,000 from Arts Councils' funds, and are expected to match this to create a wide-ranging and imaginative programme with a strong European context.

DRAMA

Britain is one of the world's major centres for theatre, and has a long and rich dramatic tradition. There are many companies based not only in London but in many other cities and towns; in addition numerous touring companies visit theatres, festivals and other venues, including arts and sports centres and social clubs. There were 67 companies in receipt of Arts Council subsidies in 1992–93 and well over 200 from regional arts boards.

> **Contemporary British playwrights who have received international recognition, with examples of their works, include:**
>
> - Harold Pinter—*The Caretaker, The Homecoming*;
> - Tom Stoppard— *Jumpers, Arcadia*;
> - Caryl Churchill—*Top Girls, The Skriker*; and
> - David Hare—*Plenty*, and the trilogy *Racing Demon, Murmuring Judges* and *The Absence of War*.

The musicals of Sir Andrew Lloyd Webber have been highly successful both in Britain and overseas; his more recent works are *The Phantom of the Opera* and *Sunset Boulevard*.

Among the best-known directors are Sir Peter Hall, Richard Eyre, Trevor Nunn, Adrian Noble, Jonathan Miller, Terry Hands and Deborah Warner, while the many British performers who enjoy international reputations include Sir John Gielgud, Sir Alec Guinness, Kenneth Branagh, Vanessa Redgrave, Sir Ian McKellen, Sir Derek Jacobi, Jonathan Pryce, Albert Finney, Dame Judi Dench, Juliet Stephenson, Helen Mirren, Simon Callow, Dame Diana Rigg and Dame Maggie Smith. British stage designers such as John Bury, Ralph Koltai and Carl Toms are internationally recognised.

Britain has about 300 theatres intended for professional use which can seat between 200 and 2,300 people. Some are privately owned, but most are owned either municipally or by non-profit-distributing organisations. Over 40 of these have resident theatre companies receiving subsidies from the Arts Councils and Regional Arts Boards. In summer there are also open air theatres, including one in London's Regent's Park and the Minack Theatre, which is on an open cliffside near Land's End in Cornwall.

Most theatres are commercially run and self-financing, relying on popular shows and musicals to be profitable. By contrast, companies funded by the Arts Councils tend to offer a variety of traditional and experimental or innovative productions. Experimental or innovative work is often staged in 'fringe' theatres in London and other cities; these are smaller theatres which use a variety of buildings, such as rooms in pubs.

The Theatres Restoration Fund provided £4 million in 1992–94 for renovating and repairing theatres. It focused on backstage projects for which no other funds were available. Theatres which were renovated included the Hackney Empire (London), the Queen's (Barnstaple) and the Miners' Institute (Wrexham). The Fund was financed jointly by the Government and the Wolfson Foundation and Family Charitable Trust.

London

London has about 100 theatres, 15 of them permanently occupied by subsidised companies. These include:

- the Royal National Theatre, which stages a wide range of modern and classical plays in its three auditoriums on the South Bank;

- the Royal Shakespeare Company, which presents plays mainly by Shakespeare and his contemporaries, as well as some modern work, both in Stratford-upon-Avon and in its two auditoriums in the City's Barbican Centre; and

- the English Stage Company at the Royal Court Theatre in Sloane Square, which stages the work of many new playwrights.

The largest concentration of London's commercial theatres is around Shaftesbury Avenue. West End theatre attendance was over 11.5 million in 1993; almost half of these went to modern musicals.

Table 28.1: Attendances at West End Theatres, 1987 and 1992

Type of Performance	Percentage 1987	1992
Modern musicals	28	51
Modern drama	13	10
Traditional musicals	17	8
Classical plays	7	8
Comedy	15	7
Opera/operetta	7	6
Ballet/dance	4	4
Thrillers/others	3	3
Revue/variety	2	2
Children's shows/ pantomimes	3	1

Source: City University Research for the Society of West End Theatres

In 1989 the partial remains of the Globe Theatre, where Shakespeare acted, and the Rose Theatre, where his plays were performed during his lifetime, were excavated on the south bank of the Thames; both have since been listed as ancient monuments. A modern reconstruction of the Globe Theatre, near its original site, is in progress.

Regional Theatres

Outside London most cities and many large towns have at least one theatre. Older theatres which have been restored include the Theatre Royal, Newcastle upon Tyne, which dates from the 18th century; and the Alhambra, Bradford; the Lyceum, Sheffield; the Theatre Royal, Bristol; and the Grand Opera House, Belfast, all dating from the 19th century. Others, such as the West Yorkshire Playhouse, Leeds, and the Theatre Royal, Plymouth, have been built to modern designs. Edinburgh's old Empire Theatre has undergone a major rebuilding and restoration scheme and has reopened as the Edinburgh Festival Theatre, providing an international venue for large-scale productions. Several universities have theatres which house professional companies playing to the general public.

Most regional repertory companies mount about eight to ten productions a year; several have studio theatres in addition to the main auditorium, where they present new or experimental drama and plays of specialist interest. Repertory theatres also often function as social centres by offering concerts, poetry readings and exhibitions, and by providing restaurants, bars and shops.

Regional theatre companies with major reputations include the Citizens' Theatre, Glasgow; the Royal Exchange, Manchester; Bristol Old Vic; West Yorkshire Playhouse; the Festival Theatre, Chichester; and Nottingham Playhouse, one of the first modern regional theatres. Successful productions from regional theatre companies often transfer to London's West End, while the largest regional theatres receive visits from the Royal National Theatre or the Royal Shakespeare Company. Cambridge Theatre Company, Oxford Stage Company and English Touring Theatre Company tour the English regions and worldwide.

Theatre for Young People

Unicorn Theatre for Children and Polka Children's Theatre, both in London, present plays specially written for children; and the Whirligig Theatre tours throughout Britain. The Young Vic Company in London and Contact Theatre Company in Manchester stage plays for young people. Numerous Theatre-in-Education companies perform in schools. Some of these companies operate independently—Theatre Centre, for example, plays in London and tours further afield. Others are attached to regional repertory theatres such as the Wolsey Theatre, Ipswich, and Greenwich Theatre. Most regional repertory theatres also mount productions for younger audiences, and concessionary ticket prices are generally available for those at school, college or university. There are also a number of puppet companies.

There has been a marked growth in youth theatres, which number more than 500 in England alone; both the National Youth Theatre in London and the Scottish Youth Theatre in Glasgow offer early acting opportunities to young people.

Dramatic Training

Training for actors, directors, lighting and sound technicians and stage managers is provided mainly in drama schools, among them the Royal Academy of Dramatic Art (RADA), the Central School of Speech and Drama, the London Academy of Music and Dramatic Art, and the Drama Centre (all in London); the Bristol Old Vic School, the Royal Scottish Academy of Music and Drama (Glasgow) and the Welsh College of Music and Drama (Cardiff). Theatre design courses, often based in art schools, are available for people wanting to train as stage designers. A number of universities and colleges offer degree courses in drama.

Amateur Theatre

There are several thousand amateur dramatic societies throughout Britain. They use a variety of buildings, including schools and public halls. Their work is encouraged by a number of organisations, such as the Central Council for Amateur Theatre, the National Drama Conference, the Scottish Community Drama Association and the Association of Ulster Drama Festivals. A nationwide umbrella body, the Voluntary Arts Network, was established in 1991. Amateur companies sometimes receive financial support from local government, Regional Arts Boards and other bodies.

MUSIC

People in Britain are interested in a wide range of music, from classical to different forms of rock and pop music. Jazz, folk, world and light music, and brass bands also have substantial followings.

The first National Music Day was held in 1992. During the second, in June 1993, over 1,100 separate events were organised, ranging from musical fêtes and marathons to activities involving local churches, schools and charities.

Orchestral and Choral Music

Seasons of orchestral and choral concerts are promoted every year in many large towns and cities. The principal concert halls in central London are the Royal Festival Hall in the South Bank Centre, next to which are the Queen Elizabeth Hall and the Purcell Room, which accommodate smaller scale performances; the Barbican Hall (part of the Barbican Centre for Arts and Conferences in the City of London); the Royal Albert Hall in Kensington; the Wigmore Hall, a recital centre; and St John's, Smith Square. A major new concert hall, the Symphony Hall, opened in Birmingham in 1991, and a new 2,400-seat international concert hall is to be built for Manchester's Hallé Orchestra; the Government is to contribute £22 million, about half the expected cost.

The leading symphony orchestras are the London Philharmonic, the London Symphony, the Philharmonia, the Royal Philharmonic, the BBC Symphony, the Royal Liverpool Philharmonic, the Hallé, the City of Birmingham Symphony, the Bournemouth Symphony, the Ulster and the Royal Scottish Orchestras and the BBC Welsh Symphony Orchestra. The BBC's six orchestras give broadcast concerts which are often open to the public. There are also chamber orchestras such as the English Chamber Orchestra, the Academy of St Martin-in-the-Fields, the Bournemouth Sinfonietta, and the Scottish Chamber Orchestra. Specialised ensembles include the Orchestra of the Age of Enlightenment, the English Baroque Soloists and the English Concert. The

London Sinfonietta and the Birmingham Contemporary Music Group specialise in contemporary music.

British conductors such as Sir Colin Davis, Vernon Handley, Sir Charles Mackerras, John Eliot Gardiner, Sir Simon Rattle, Christopher Hogwood, Jane Glover, and Sian Edwards reach a wide audience through their recordings as well as by their performances. The works of living composers such as Sir Michael Tippett, Sir Peter Maxwell Davies and Sir Harrison Birtwistle enjoy international acclaim. Other well-established composers include George Benjamin, John Tavener, Oliver Knussen, Jonathan Lloyd, Colin Matthews, Nigel Osborne, Robert Saxton, Mark-Anthony Turnage and Judith Weir. The Master of the Queen's Music, Malcolm Williamson, holds an office within the Royal Household with responsibility for organising and writing music for state occasions. Percussionist Evelyn Glennie and clarinettist Emma Johnson are among solo performers currently enjoying great acclaim.

The principal choral societies include the Bach Choir, the Royal Choral Society, the Huddersfield Choral Society, the Cardiff Polyphonic Choir, the Edinburgh International Festival Chorus and the Belfast Philharmonic Society. Almost all the leading orchestras maintain their own choral societies. The English tradition of church singing is represented by choirs such as those of King's College Chapel, Cambridge, and Christ Church Cathedral, Oxford, while other choirs such as the Roman Catholic Westminster Cathedral choir are also well known. There are many male-voice choirs in Wales and in certain parts of England.

Pop and Rock Music

Hundreds of hours of pop and rock music are broadcast through BBC and independent radio stations every week, while magazine programmes and occasional live or recorded concerts on television further promote pop and rock, which is by far the most popular form of musical expression in Britain.

In the 1960s and 1970s groups such as the Beatles, the Rolling Stones, Led Zeppelin and Pink Floyd achieved international success.

British groups continue to be popular throughout the world and are often at the forefront of new developments in music.

Some of the more recent groups, with examples of their recordings, include Take That (*Pray*), Stereo MCs (*Creation*), Jamiroquai (*Emergency on Planet Earth*), M People (*Renaissance*), and The Brand New Heavies (*Stay This Way*).

Well-known performers, with examples of recent recordings, include Phil Collins (*Serious Hits Live!*), Elton John (*The Last Song*), Annie Lennox (*Cold*), Mike Oldfield (*Sentinel*), and Dina Carroll (*Perfect Year*).

In recent years young black artists, including Seal, Roland Gift, Tasmin Archer, Field, and Ronny Jordan have furthered the development of popular music.

The pop and rock music industry continues to contribute significantly to Britain's overseas earnings through the sale of recordings, concert tours, and promotional material, including clothing and books. The recording industry in Britain has an estimated annual turnover of £1,000 million.

Jazz

Jazz has a large following in Britain and is played in numerous clubs and pubs. The London Jazz Festival attracts international stars such as the bandleader Django Bates, saxophonists Pharoah Saunders and Joshua Redman, and the singer Jean Carn. British musicians such as Barbara Thompson, Stan Tracey, Jason Rebello, Andy Sheppard and Courtney Pine have established strong reputations throughout Europe. Festivals of jazz music are held throughout Britain, including London, Cardiff Bay, Brecon, Edinburgh, Glasgow, and Birmingham. Jazz Services provides a national touring network.

Training

Professional training in music is given mainly at colleges of music. The leading London colleges are the Royal Academy of Music, the Royal College of Music, the Guildhall School of Music and Drama, and Trinity College of Music. The City University's music industry course provides training in business practice aimed specifically at musicians and music administrators. Outside London the main centres are the Royal Scottish Academy of Music and Drama in Glasgow, the Royal Northern College of Music in Manchester, the Welsh College of Music and Drama, Cardiff, and the Birmingham Conservatoire.

Other Educational Schemes

Many children learn to play musical instruments at school, and some take the examinations of the Associated Board of the Royal Schools of Music. Music is one of the foundation subjects in the National Curriculum (see p. 418). The National Youth Orchestras of Great Britain, of Scotland and of Wales and other youth orchestras have established high standards. Nearly a third of the players in the European Community Youth Orchestra come from Britain. There is also a National Youth Jazz Orchestra.

Youth and Music, an organisation affiliated to the international Jeunesses Musicales, encourages attendance by young people at opera, dance and concert performances.

OPERA

Interest in opera has been growing markedly in Britain since 1986, with an estimated 2.8 million of the adult population attending opera performances in 1993: an increase of 19 per cent. International singers such as Luciano Pavarotti, José Carreras and Placido Domingo have appeared in recent years at open air concerts in front of huge audiences.

Regular seasons of opera are held at the Royal Opera House, Covent Garden, London. The English National Opera stages opera in English at the London Coliseum. Scottish Opera has regular seasons at the Theatre Royal in Glasgow, and tours mainly in Scotland and northern England. Welsh National Opera presents seasons in Cardiff and other cities. Leeds-based Opera North tours primarily in the north of England, but also has recently staged Benjamin Britten's *Gloriana*, produced by Phyllida Lloyd, at Covent Garden. Opera Factory, the resident company at London's

South Bank, presents experimental work in opera and music theatre. English Touring Opera takes opera to towns throughout England. Opera Northern Ireland presents seasons at the Grand Opera House, Belfast, and tours the province.

An opera season for which international casts are specially assembled is held every summer at Glyndebourne in East Sussex. This is followed by an autumn tour by Glyndebourne Touring Opera, often using casts drawn from the chorus of the festival season. Work on a new enlarged 1,200-seat opera house, built on the same site at Glyndebourne at a cost of £33 million, was completed in record time for the 1994 season. All the funding came from private sources.

The National Opera Studio in London provides advanced training.

DANCE

An estimated 6 million people take part in dance, making it one of Britain's leading participatory activities, and audiences are attracted to a widening range of professional dance.

The Royal Ballet and the Birmingham Royal Ballet, English National Ballet and Northern Ballet Theatre, which rank among the world's leading companies, are supported by professional orchestras.

Subsidised Dance Companies

Subsidised dance companies include the Birmingham (formerly Sadler's Wells) Royal Ballet, which tours widely in Britain and overseas; English National Ballet, which divides its performances between London and the regions; Northern Ballet Theatre, which is based in Halifax and also tours; and Scottish Ballet, based in Glasgow.

The Arts Council of England also subsidises a wide range of other companies and dance organisations. Companies include Rambert Dance Company (Britain's oldest ballet company, which re-formed in 1966 as a leading contemporary dance company); Diversions (based in Cardiff); Adzido Pan African Dance Ensemble; Shobana Jeyasingh Dance Company, and Green Candle Dance

Company. Also subsidised is Dance Umbrella, which promotes an annual festival of contemporary dance in London. The three Arts Councils and the Regional Arts Boards support many smaller companies.

Lloyd Newson, Christopher Bruce, Richard Alston, Michael Clark, Jonathan Burrows, Shobana Jeyasingh and Siobhan Davies are among the foremost British choreographers. Leading dancers included Darcey Bussell, Marion Tait, Adam Cooper and Deborah Bull.

Training

Professional training for dancers and choreographers is provided mainly by specialist schools, which include the Royal Ballet School, the Central School of Ballet, the Laban Centre (University of London) and the London Contemporary Dance School; these, with many private schools, have helped in raising British dance to its present standard. Dance is a subject for degree studies at a number of institutions, including the Laban Centre, the University of Surrey, Dartington College of the Arts in Devon and Middlesex University.

Courses for students intending to work with community groups are available at several institutions. In 1991 the Royal Ballet began a scheme aimed to widen access to ballet training for children from a broader range of backgrounds, including ethnic minorities.

National Dance Agencies

A network of agencies for professional and amateur dancers has been established in Birmingham, Leeds, Nottingham, London, Newcastle upon Tyne, Swindon and Suffolk. The agencies, which receive Arts Council support, offer classes, provide information and advice, help to co-ordinate activities, and commission dance artists to create work. All ten Regional Arts Board areas now have a national dance agency or are preparing to set one up.

Other Educational Schemes

The Arts Council of England runs Taped, a scheme to finance dance videos for use in education, while the Video Place provides a library of videotape documentation of dance performances for viewing by promoters, choreographers, dancers, teachers and students.

All Government-funded dance companies provide dance workshops and education activities. Many have won awards for major projects, such as Phoenix Dance Company's 'Urban Exchange' and English National Ballet's 'Striking a Balance'. Ludus Dance Company, based in Lancaster, works mainly with young people; and Scottish Ballet Steps Out works in schools throughout Scotland. The Performing Arts and Technology School in Croydon, Surrey, offers studies in drama, music and dance to pupils aged from 14 to 18, with the emphasis on the application of technology to the performing arts.

The National Youth Music Theatre, which is based in London, gives young people between 11 and 18 the opportunity to perform music theatre under the guidance of professional directors and choreographers. All the work takes place in the school holidays.

The National Youth Dance Company and Yuva, the National South Asian Dance Youth Company, provide opportunities for young dancers to work with professionals and to create and perform dance. Similar opportunities exist for young people to join local youth dance companies throughout the country.

FILMS

British films, actors, and producers as well as the creative and technical services supporting them are widely acclaimed. In 1993 Emma Thompson won an Oscar as the best film actress for her role in *Howard's End*. Other British performers who enjoy international reputations include Sir Dirk Bogarde, Michael Caine, Sir Anthony Hopkins, Kenneth Branagh, Jeremy Irons, Dudley Moore, Michael York, Gary Oldman, Bob Hoskins, Liam Neeson, Alan Rickman, and Greta Scacchi.

There are approximately 1,800 cinema screens in Britain and estimated attendances are currently running at about 1.9 million a

ROYAL HERITAGE

The Grand Staircase at Buckingham Palace. The walls are set with full-length portraits, which include George III, Queen Charlotte, and William IV. The Palace was opened to the public for the first time in 1993; it attracted 377,000 visitors during the eight-week opening period.

The Crown Jewels have long been one of the main attractions at the Tower of London. A major development programme has recently been completed to offer better visitor facilities in the Jewel House, including the provision of moving walkways past some of the exhibits.

FILM AND ANIMATION

The main stage at Ealing Studios, London, is the setting for the top special effects being produced for a new and dramatic futuristic pan-European television game show called *Scavengers*, which is due to be screened in late 1994.

Sir John Gielgud, one of Britain's most respected actors. Now in his nineties, he still works tirelessly, making films and television dramas which reach a worldwide audience.

British animators have led the way in 3D and computer animation. Nick Park at Aardman Animations (pictured here) won an Oscar for the BBC-commissioned film *The Wrong Trousers*, featuring the characters Wallace and Gromit (below).

VISUAL ARTS

The Tate Gallery, St Ives, Cornwall, houses a collection of modern British works, and specialises in artists who have been associated with the area, such as Barbara Hepworth.

The new Glass Gallery at the Victoria and Albert Museum, London, houses Britain's national collection of glass. Over 6,000 items are on display, illustrating the history and development of glass over the last 4,000 years.

week. Seating capacity in cinemas increased during the late 1980s, due almost entirely to the rise in the number of multi-screen cinema complexes.

Cinema admissions in 1993 were estimated at 110 million—compared with 58.4 million in 1984. In London and other large cities a number of art or repertory cinemas show films which have not been more widely distributed. These include low budget films from Britain and abroad; other foreign films, often with English subtitles; and older films which are being shown again, sometimes in a newly edited form. Arts centres often include cinemas, and film societies use a range of buildings including, for example, public libraries.

Animation

The recent resurgence of interest in the cartoon film in Britain is due in part to the pioneering work of British animators, who have created 3D animation and computer animation. Television has proved an important source of production finance. Channel 4 Wales, for example, funded the animation of the opera *Carmen*, by the Italian-Welsh animator, Mario Cavalli. Nick Park's *The Wrong Trousers*, a BBC-commissioned film, won an Oscar in 1994; his *Creature Comforts* received an Oscar in 1991.

Government Support

An annual government grant (an estimated £17.1 million for 1994–95) is made to the British Film Institute and one of £1.2 million to the Scottish Film Council and the Scottish Film Production Fund. Since 1993 Britain has been a member of Eurimages, the Council of Europe's film co-production support scheme, contributing approximately £5.5 million over the first three years of membership. Eurimages aims to develop the European cinema and audio-visual industry by providing financial support for feature-length fiction films, creative documentaries and distribution. Within six months of Britain's membership eleven productions with British participation received loans worth £2.6 million.

British Film Commission

The British Film Commission was launched in 1991, with government funding of £3.5 million over four years. The Commission aims to attract film productions from overseas by offering a service to assist film-makers.

British Screen Finance

British Screen Finance, a private sector company, provides finance for new film-makers with commercially viable productions who have difficulty in attracting funding. The company, investing its own money together with contributions from the Government, part-finances the production of low- and medium-budget films involving largely British talent. It encourages the early stages of film project development and the production of short films. The Government is funding the company with £6 million between 1994 and 1996. Successful films supported by British Screen Finance include *The Crying Game* and *Orlando*.

British Film Institute

The development of film, video and television as art forms is promoted by the British Film Institute (BFI), founded in 1933, and in Scotland by the Scottish Film Council. The BFI offers some direct financial and technical help through its Production Board.

The BFI runs the National Film Theatre in London and the National Film Archive, and has the world's largest library of information on film and television. The BFI holds extensive international collections of books, periodicals, scripts, stills and posters. Its Education Department aims to enable as many people as possible to discover new ways of appreciating film, video and television.

The National Film Archive contains over 200,000 films and television programmes, including newsreels, dating from 1895. BFI South Bank comprises the Museum of the Moving Image, which traces the history of film and television, and the National Film Theatre. The latter has three cinemas showing films of historical, artistic or technical interest, and is unique in offering regular programmes unrestricted by commercial considerations. In November each year it hosts the London Film Festival, at which some 250 new films from all over the world are screened.

The BFI promotes, and helps to fund, a network of 34 regional film theatres, and is involved in establishing film and television centres with a range of activities and facilities. It also co-operates with the Regional Arts Boards and grant-aids their film work.

The Wales Film Council acts as the BFI's agent in Wales, and also receives funding from the Arts Council of Wales. The BFI's charter was recently extended to Northern Ireland, where the BFI works with the Northern Ireland Film Council (NIFC). The NIFC receives funds from the Arts Council of Northern Ireland.

Scottish Film Council

In Scotland the Scottish Film Council supports regional film theatres, administers the Scottish Film Archive, and promotes and provides material for media education. Together with the Scottish Arts Council, it has set up the Scottish Film Production Fund.

Children's Film

The Children's Film and Television Foundation produces and distributes entertainment films for children, shown largely through video and television.

The Children's Film Unit was founded in 1981. The Unit makes feature films for children (mainly for Channel 4) and runs weekly workshops for children on all aspects of film-making. The unit caters for about 50 children at any time and has produced 14 feature films.

The Northern Ireland Film Council funds an international film festival for young people.

Training in Film Production

The National Film and Television School is financed jointly by the Government and by

the film, video and television industries. It offers postgraduate and short course training for directors, editors, camera operators, animators and other specialists. The School enrols about 30 full-time students a year and about 500 on short course programmes. In 1994–95 it is receiving a government grant of £1.8 million.

The London International Film School, the Royal College of Art, and some universities and other institutions of higher education also offer training in film production.

Cinema Licensing and Film Classification

Cinemas showing films to the public must be licensed by local authorities, which have a legal duty to prohibit the admission of children under 16 to unsuitable films, and may prevent the showing of any film. In assessing films the authorities normally rely on the judgment of an independent non-statutory body, the British Board of Film Classification (BBFC), to which films must be submitted. The Board was set up on the initiative of the cinema industry to ensure a proper standard in films shown to the public. It does not use any written code of censorship, but can require cuts to be made before granting a certificate; on rare occasions, it refuses a certificate.

Films passed by the Board are put into one of the following categories:

- U (universal)—suitable for all;
- PG (parental guidance), in which some scenes may be unsuitable for young children;
- 12, 15 and 18, for people of not less than those ages; and
- Restricted 18, for restricted showing only at segregated premises to which no one under 18 is admitted—for example, licensed cinema clubs.

Videos

The BBFC is also legally responsible for classifying videos under a system similar to that for films. It is an offence to supply commercially a video which has not been classified or to supply it in contravention of its classification—for example, to sell or hire a video classified 18 to a person under the age of 18.

VISUAL ARTS

State support for the visual arts consists largely of funding for the national museums and galleries, purchase grants for municipal museums and galleries, and funding through local authorities, the Museums and Galleries Commission and the area museum councils. It also includes funding for the production, exhibition and distribution of work by contemporary artists and the development of audiences, channelled through the Arts Councils, the Crafts Council and the Regional Arts Boards, and grants towards the cost of art education. The Government encourages high standards of industrial design and craftsmanship through grants to the Design Council (see p. 207). All national museums and galleries are financed chiefly from government funds. They may charge for entry to their permanent collections and special exhibitions. All the national collections are managed by independent trustees.

Museums and art galleries maintained by local authorities, universities, independent museums and private funds may receive help in building up their collections through grants administered by the Museums and Galleries Commission (for England), the National Museums of Scotland and the Museum Councils in Wales and Northern Ireland. Financial and practical assistance to national and regional public and independent museums and galleries is also given by the Arts Councils and by trusts and voluntary bodies, including the Calouste Gulbenkian Foundation and the National Art Collections Fund.

Pre-eminent works of art are accepted by the Government in place of inheritance tax and are allocated to public galleries; recent acquisitions include paintings by Constable and Picasso, and manuscripts of two marches by Haydn. Financial help may be available from the National Heritage Memorial Fund (see p. 441), which is being allocated

£8.7 million by the Department of National Heritage in 1994–95. In recent years the Fund helped towards the acquisition of masterpieces by Hans Holbein and Jacques-Louis David (bought by the National Gallery), by El Greco (the National Gallery of Scotland), and by Gainsborough (the Tate Gallery and Gainsborough's House). The British Museum bought the Bowleaze Jewel and the Armada service (an Elizabethan silver-gilt dinner service), while the National Maritime Museum was able to buy an important collection of Lord Nelson's letters.

In collaboration with the Regional Arts Boards, the Arts Council of England provides strategic funding for museums and galleries, educational institutions from art schools and universities to schools, commercial galleries and publishers. It also supports touring exhibitions and the presentation of works of art commissioned for public spaces. The Arts Council of England's unique collection of 20th century British art, with the National Touring Exhibition Service, is managed on its behalf by the South Bank Board, which also runs the Hayward Gallery. The Council also supports the Institute of Contemporary Art in London and five other independent galleries: the Whitechapel and the Serpentine in London, Museum of Modern Art in Oxford, Ikon in Birmingham and Arnolfini in Bristol, as well as the newly formed Institute of International Visual Arts, based in London. The ten Regional Arts Boards provide direct support for artists and the Arts Council of England funds national organisations such as the National Artists Association and Axis, a national artists' database, and provides publishing opportunities for photographers and visual arts magazines.

Support for galleries is given by the Arts Councils in Scotland, Wales and Northern Ireland.

British artists, photographers and architects with international reputations include David Hockney, Lucian Freud, Sir Anthony Caro and Sir Eduardo Paolozzi. Younger artists with a similar standing include Richard Deacon, Tony Cragg and Anish Kapoor.

Museums and Art Galleries

About 80 million people a year, across all social groups, attend more than 2,000 museums and galleries open to the public, which include the major national collections and around 1,100 independent museums, some receiving support from local authorities.

Government provision for the national museums and galleries is £219.2 million in 1994–95. The Museums and Galleries Improvement Fund, which is jointly financed by the Government and the Wolfson Charities and the Family Charitable Trusts, is providing an annual budget of £4 million over five years from 1991–92 for refurbishment. The Fund is already supporting over 100 projects at national and other museums and galleries, including work in Glasgow, Merthyr Tydfil, Reading and Halifax.

The Government takes advice on policy from the Museums and Galleries Commission. The Commission also promotes co-operation between national and regional institutions. Ten area museum councils supply technical services and advice on conservation and the environment, display, documentation, and publicity.

In May 1994 the Government announced a wide-ranging review of its policy on museums and galleries in England. It is expected to announce its conclusions later in the year. The Government encourages the loan of objects from national and regional collections so that works of art can be seen by as wide a public as possible.

The Museum Training Institute is responsible for developing training standards and programmes within museums; the Arts Council of England supports an MA course at the Royal College of Art for curating and commissioning contemporary art and promotes professional practice among artists and curators.

Museums Association

The independent Museums Association, to which many museums and art galleries and their staffs belong, and which has many overseas members, facilitates exchange of information and discussion of matters relating to museums and galleries. It provides training, seminars and research; its publications include the monthly *Museums Journal*.

National Collections

The national museums and art galleries, many of them located in London, contain some of the world's most comprehensive collections of objects of artistic, archeological, scientific, historical and general interest. They are:

- the British Museum (including the ethnographic collections of the Museum of Mankind);
- the Natural History Museum;
- the Victoria and Albert Museum (the V&A, which displays fine and decorative arts);
- the Science Museum and its two regional institutes—the National Railway Museum (York) and National Museum of Photography, Film and Television (Bradford);
- the National Gallery (which houses western painting from around 1260 to 1920);
- the Tate Gallery, London (British painting and modern art);
- the Tate Gallery, Liverpool

Table 28.2: Visitors to National Museums and Galleries 1993–94 in England

	(million)
British Museum	6.25
Imperial War Museum	1.15
Museum of London	0.31
National Gallery	3.70
National Maritime Museum	0.51
National Museums and Galleries on Merseyside	1.20
National Portrait Gallery	0.60
Natural History Museum	1.75
Science Museum	2.64
Tate Gallery	2.55
Victoria and Albert Museum	1.44
Wallace Collection	0.17

Source: *Department of National Heritage Annual Report 1994*

- the Tate Gallery, St Ives (St Ives School and contemporary art)
- the National Portrait Gallery;
- the Imperial War Museum;
- the National Army Museum;
- the Royal Air Force Museum;
- the National Maritime Museum;
- the Wallace Collection (which includes paintings, furniture, arms and armour; and objets d'art); and
- the National Museums and Galleries on Merseyside.

The new Sainsbury Wing of the National Gallery provides a venue for major international touring exhibitions and other events. London is to be the location of the Tate's new museum of modern art. The V&A plans to open a branch in Bradford.

In Scotland the national collections are held by the National Museums of Scotland and the National Galleries of Scotland. The former include the Royal Museum of Scotland, the National Museum of Antiquities of Scotland, the Scottish United Services Museum and the Scottish Agricultural Museum, in Edinburgh; the Museum of Flight, near North Berwick; and the Museum of Costume at Shambellie House near Dumfries. A new Museum of Scotland is being built next to the Royal Museum to house the National Museums' Scottish collection. The National Galleries of Scotland comprise the National Gallery of Scotland, the Scottish National Portrait Gallery and the Scottish National Gallery of Modern Art.

The National Museum of Wales, which has opened new galleries at its main building in Cardiff, has a number of branches, including the Welsh Folk Museum at St Fagans and the Industrial and Maritime Museum in Cardiff's dockland.

Northern Ireland has two national museums: the Ulster Museum in Belfast and the Ulster Folk and Transport Museum in County Down.

Other Collections

Other important collections in London include the Museum of London; Sir John Soane's Museum; the Courtauld collection; and the London Transport Museum. The Queen's Gallery in Buckingham Palace has exhibitions of pictures from the extensive royal collection. The Royal Armouries, Britain's oldest museum, has been housed in the Tower of London for 900 years. A new headquarters for the collection is being built in Leeds. Due to open in 1996, the project is a pioneering joint public and private sector venture.

Most cities and towns have museums devoted to art, archaeology and natural history, usually administered by the local authorities but sometimes by local learned societies or by individuals or trustees. Both Oxford and Cambridge are rich in museums. Many are associated with their universities, such as the Ashmolean Museum in Oxford and the Fitzwilliam Museum in Cambridge.

Many private collections of art and antiques in historic family mansions, including those owned by the National Trusts and English Heritage (see p. 346), are open to the public.

An increasing number of open air museums depict the regional life of an area or preserve early industrial remains. These include the Weald and Downland Museum in West Sussex, and the Ironbridge Gorge Museum in Shropshire. Skills of the past are revived in a number of 'living' museums, such as the Gladstone Pottery Museum near Stoke-on-Trent and the Quarry Bank Mill at Styal in Cheshire.

Among the more recently opened museums are:

- the Museum of Science and Industry in Manchester;
- the Jorvik Viking Centre, a reconstruction of the Viking settlement in York;
- the Mary Rose Museum in Portsmouth, housing the restored wreck of the flagship of Henry VIII, which sank in 1545;
- the St Mungo Museum of Religious Life and Art in Glasgow, containing artefacts representing the world's major religions; and

- Eureka!, the first museum designed specifically for children, in Halifax, West Yorkshire.

The Burrell Collection in Glasgow houses world-famous tapestries, paintings and objets d'art. The Design Museum in London's Docklands contains a study collection of 20th century mass-produced consumer objects.

There are also a number of national art exhibiting societies, the most famous being the Royal Academy of Arts at Burlington House. The Academy holds an annual Summer Exhibition, where the works of hundreds of professional and amateur artists can be seen, and important exhibitions during the rest of the year. The Royal Scottish Academy holds annual exhibitions in Edinburgh. There are also children's exhibitions, including the National Exhibition of Children's Art.

Crafts

The crafts in Britain have an annual turnover estimated at £400 million. Government aid for the crafts, amounting to an estimated £3.2 million in 1994–95, is administered in England and Wales by the Crafts Council. The Council supports craftsmen and women by promoting public interest in their work, and encouraging the creation of works of contemporary craftsmanship. Grants are available to help with setting up workshops and acquiring equipment. The Crafts Council runs the national centre for crafts in London, which houses a gallery, reference and picture libraries, and a gallery shop. It organises the annual Chelsea Crafts Fair, and co-ordinates British groups at international trade fairs. Crafts Council exhibitions tour nationally and internationally, and grants are made to encourage exhibitions, projects and organisations. It also runs a craft shop at the Victoria and Albert Museum.

Funding is given to the Regional Arts Boards and the Welsh Arts Council for the support of crafts, and to Contemporary Applied Art, a membership organisation that holds exhibitions and sells work through its London gallery.

Craftworks, an independent company, is the crafts development agency for Northern Ireland, providing training, marketing and business counselling for the crafts sector. The Arts Council of Northern Ireland also provides funding for crafts promotion.

Training in Art and Design

Most practical education in art and design is provided in the art colleges and fine and applied art departments of universities: these include the Slade School of Art and Goldsmith's College of Art, London; and in further education colleges and private art schools. Many of these institutions award degrees at postgraduate level. Art is also taught at an advanced level at the four Scottish Central (Art) Institutions.

Courses at universities concentrate largely on academic disciplines such as the history of art. The leading institutions include the Courtauld and Warburg Institutes of the University of London and the Department of Classical Art and Archaeology at University College, London. The Open University also offers courses in art history, and theory of art. Art is one of the foundation subjects in the National Curriculum. The Society for Education through Art encourages, among other activities, the purchase by schools of original works of art by organising an annual Pictures for Schools exhibition.

The Open College of the Arts offers correspondence courses in art and design, painting, sculpture, textiles, photography and creative writing to people wishing to study at home.

Export Control of Works of Art

London is a major centre for the international art market, and sales of works of art take place in the main auction houses (two of the longest established being Sotheby's and Christie's), and through private dealers. Certain items are covered by export control. These are:
- works of art and collectors' items over 50 years old and worth £20,000 or more (£5,000 or more in the case of British historical portraits);
- photographic material over 50 years old and valued at £500 or more an item; and

- documents, manuscripts and archives over 50 years old, irrespective of value.

A licence from the Department of National Heritage is required before such items can be exported. If the Department's advisers recommend withholding a licence, the matter is referred to the Reviewing Committee on the Export of Works of Art. If the Committee considers a work to be of national importance it can advise the Government to withhold the export licence for a specified time to give a public museum, art gallery, or private collector an opportunity to buy at a fair price.

With the completion of the single European market in January 1993, there is concern that the removal of customs barriers for intra-community trade may facilitate the illicit export of national treasures. Discussions on methods of preventing this are in progress.

LITERATURE AND LIBRARIES

A number of literary activities receive public subsidy through the Arts Councils. In 1994, for example, this included continued support for a programme of tours by writers from other countries, innovative television films promoting reading, and support for literary magazines and independent publishers.

There are free public libraries throughout Britain (see p. 460), private libraries and several private literary societies. Book reviews are featured in the press and on television and radio, and numerous periodicals concerned with literature are published (see p. 479). Recognition of outstanding literary merit is provided by a number of awards, some of the most valuable being the Booker and Whitbread prizes. In 1993 Sir V.S. Naipaul was awarded the first David Cohen British Literature Prize for a lifetime's achievement by a living British writer. A part of the £40,000 prize, to be awarded every two years, will enable winners to commission new works from younger writers. Other awards to encourage young authors include those of the Somerset Maugham Trust Fund and the E. C. Gregory Trust Fund.

Many writers from overseas, often from Commonwealth countries, also live and work in Britain, writing books in English which have a wide circulation in Britain and overseas.

Distinguished British poets include Ted Hughes, the Poet Laureate (the Poet Laureate is a member of the Royal Household who receives an annual stipend from the Civil List—see p. 48; he may write commemorative verse if he wishes); Geoffrey Hill; Tony Harrison; James Berry; Seamus Heaney; Gavin Ewart; Wendy Cope; and Elizabeth Jennings.

Many British writers are internationally recognised. Well-known living novelists, with examples of their works, include.
- Sir Kingsley Amis–*Lucky Jim, Stanley and the Women*;
- Ian McEwan—*The Child in Time, Black Dogs*;
- Dame Muriel Spark—*The Prime of Miss Jean Brodie, and Memento Mori*;
- A. S. Byatt—*Possession: A Romance*.

English literature is taught extensively at schools, colleges and universities throughout Britain. Creative writing is also taught at a wide variety of institutions; one of the best known is the University of East Anglia, in Norwich, which also houses the British Centre for Literary Translation.

Authors' Copyright and Performers' Protection

Original literary, dramatic, musical or artistic works, films, sound recordings and broadcasts are automatically protected by copyright in Britain. This protection is also given to works from countries party to international copyright conventions. The copyright owner has rights against unauthorised reproduction, public performance, broadcasting and issue to the public of his or her work; and against dealing in unauthorised copies. In most cases the author is the first owner of the copyright, and the term of copyright is the life of the author and a period of 50 years after death (50 years from the year of release for films and sound recordings and 50 years from the year of broadcast for broadcasts).

The Copyright, Designs and Patents Act 1988 reformed copyright law and introduced the concept of moral rights, whereby authors have the right to be identified on their works and to object to derogatory treatment of them. The Act also updated the rights which protect performers against making and trading in unauthorised recordings of live performances, the term of protection for these rights being 50 years from the year in which the performance is given.

The term of protection will be extended from 50 to 70 years by July 1995.

Literary and Philological Societies

Societies to promote literature include the English Association and the Royal Society of Literature. The leading society for studies in the humanities is the British Academy for the Promotion of Historical, Philosophical and Philological Studies (the British Academy).

Other specialist societies are the Early English Text Society, the Bibliographical Society and several societies devoted to particular authors, the largest of which is the Dickens Fellowship. Various societies, such as the Poetry Society, sponsor poetry readings and recitals.

Libraries

The British Library

The British Library, the national library of Britain, is one of the world's greatest libraries. Its collections comprise over 18 million items—monographs, manuscripts, maps, newspapers, patents, stamps and recorded sound. Publishers must deposit there a copy of most items published or available in Britain.

The National Bibliographic Service processes material legally deposited at the Library for inclusion in catalogues and maintains a machine-readable database of bibliographical records from which is derived the British National Bibliography (a list of new and forthcoming British Books) and a range of automated bibliographical services.

The Research and Development Department is a major source of funding for research and development in library and information services.

The Library's Document Supply Centre at Boston Spa (West Yorkshire) is the national centre for inter-library lending within Britain and between Britain and countries overseas. It supplies 3.5 million requests a year, mostly from its own stock of 7 million documents.

The Library also has the self-supporting Centre for the Book, to promote awareness of books and their role in British life.

The British Library's new London headquarters at St Pancras is being built at a cost of £450 million, and will open in 1996. It will provide reading rooms for most of the Library's London-based collections— humanities, science, technology and industry; it will also house 330 km (208 miles) of shelves for 12 million books and specialist reading areas. The new Library aims to offer greatly improved services, including exhibition galleries, a bookshop, a lecture theatre and a conference centre.

Other Libraries

The National Libraries of Scotland and Wales, the Bodleian Library of Oxford University and the Cambridge University Library can also claim copies of all new British publications under legal deposit. The first phase of a new building for the National Library of Scotland was opened in 1989, accommodating a map library, lending services and the Scottish Science Library. The second stage is due to be open in May 1995.

Some of the national museums and government departments have important libraries.

- The Public Record Office in London and in Kew, Surrey, houses the records of the superior courts of law of England and Wales and of most government departments, as well as famous historical documents. The Office has many millions of documents, dating from the time of the Norman Conquest to the present day. Public records, with few exceptions, are available for inspection by members of the public 30 years after the end of the year in which they were created.

- The Scottish Record Office in Edinburgh and the Public Record Office of Northern Ireland, Belfast, serve the same purpose.

Besides a number of great private collections, such as that of the London Library, there are the libraries of the learned societies and institutions, such as the Royal Institute of International Affairs, the Royal Geographical Society and the Royal Academy of Music. The Poetry Library in the South Bank Centre, owned by the Arts Council of England, is a collection of 20th-century poetry written in or translated into English.

University Libraries

The university libraries of Oxford and Cambridge are unmatched by those of the more recent foundations. However, the combined library resources of the colleges and institutions of the University of London total 9 million volumes, the John Rylands University Library of Manchester contains 3.5 million volumes, Edinburgh 2.5 million, Leeds 2.3 million, and Birmingham, Glasgow, Liverpool and Aberdeen each have over 1 million volumes. Many universities have important research collections in special subjects—the Barnes Medical Library at Birmingham and the British Library of Political and Economic Science at the London School of Economics, for example. University libraries also have on-line access to library information worldwide.

Special Libraries

Numerous associations and commercial and industrial organisations run library and information services. Although most are intended primarily for use within the organisation, many can be used, by arrangement, by people interested in the area covered, and the specialist publications held are often available for inter-library lending.

Public Libraries

Local authorities in Great Britain and education and library boards in Northern Ireland have a duty to provide a free lending and reference library service, and Britain's network of more than 4,100 public libraries has a total stock of over 130 million books. Public libraries issue an average of ten books a year for every person in Britain. Of these, 56 per cent are works of fiction for adults. Over half of the total population are members of public libraries. Some areas are served by mobile libraries, and domiciliary services cater for people unable to visit a library

Many libraries have collections of compact discs, records, audio- and video-cassettes, and musical scores for loan to the public, while a number also lend from collections of works of art, which may be originals or reproductions. Most libraries hold documents on local history, and nearly all provide children's departments, while reference and information sections and art, music, commercial and technical departments meet the growing demands in these fields. The information role is one of increasing importance for many libraries, and greater use is being made of information technology, including microcomputers and reference databases.

The Government remains committed to providing a free basic library service—the borrowing and consultation of printed materials—but believes there is scope for greater private sector involvement. It makes available £250,000 a year to encourage new developments and increase efficiency. Priority is given to projects involving collaboration with other libraries and the private sector.

Public libraries charge for some services, such as research services and the lending of non-printed materials.

The Government is advised on library and information matters by four library and information services councils or committees, one for each constituent part of Britain. A new Commission was set up in 1994 to co-ordinate this advice.

The Government is reviewing the scope and value of services provided by public libraries in England and the feasibility of contracting out the delivery of some parts of their service.

The Library Association

The Library Association is the principal professional organisation for those engaged in library and information services. Founded in 1877, the Association has 25,000 members. It maintains a Register of Chartered Librarians and publishes books, pamphlets and an official journal.

The Library Association is the designated authority for the recognition of qualifications gained in other EU member states.

Public Lending Right Scheme

The Public Lending Right Scheme, introduced in 1979, gives registered authors the right to receive payment from a central fund (totalling £4.9 million in 1994–95) for the loans made of their books from public libraries in Britain. Payment is made in proportion to the number of times the authors' books are lent out. In 1992–93, 97 authors received the maximum payment of £6,000.

Books

In 1993 British publishers issued some 83,800 separate titles. The British publishing industry devotes much effort to developing overseas markets, and in 1993 the value of exports of British books amounted to £616.9 million

Among the leading organisations representing publishing and distribution interests are the Publishers Association, which has 200 members; and the Booksellers' Association, with 3,300 members. The Publishers Association, through its International Division, promotes the export of British books.

Historical Manuscripts

The Royal Commission on Historical Manuscripts, first established 1869, is the central investigatory and advisory body on manuscripts, records and archives other than the public records. It maintains the National Register of Archives and the Manorial Documents Register and advises owners, custodians and government; assists researchers; and co-ordinates the activities of bodies working in the field. It also publishes a series of *Guides to Sources for British History*.

The National Manuscripts Conservation Trust, established by the Commission and the British Library, provides grants to record offices, libraries and other owners of manuscripts and archives accessible to the public.

Further Reading

The Arts. Aspects of Britain series, HMSO, 1993.

Annual Report 1994. Department of National Heritage. Cm. 2511.

29 The Media

Television viewing is by far Britain's most popular leisure pastime: 94 per cent of households have a colour television set and 73 per cent a video recorder. People spend an average of over three and a half hours a day watching television, including video playbacks. The number of video tapes hired has declined for the past three years to about 6 million a week.

More daily newspapers, national and regional, are sold for every person in Britain than in most other developed countries. On an average day 60 per cent of people over the age of 15 read a national morning newspaper; about 70 per cent read a Sunday newspaper.

Television and Radio

Broadcasting in Britain has traditionally been based on the principle that it is a public service accountable to the people through Parliament. While retaining the essential public service element, it now embraces the principles of competition and choice.

Three public bodies have the main responsibility for television and radio services to which nearly everyone has access:

- the BBC (British Broadcasting Corporation) broadcasts television and radio programmes;

- the ITC (Independent Television Commission) licenses and regulates non-BBC television services, including cable and satellite services; and

- the Radio Authority licenses and regulates all non-BBC radio services, including cable and satellite.

These authorities work to broad requirements and objectives defined by Parliament, but are otherwise independent in their day-to-day conduct of business.

The government department responsible for overseeing the broadcasting system is the Department of National Heritage. The Secretary of State for National Heritage is answerable to Parliament on broad policy questions.

Television

There are four terrestrial television channels, offering a mixture of drama, light entertainment, films, sport, educational, children's and religious programmes, news and current affairs, and documentaries.

The BBC provides two complementary national networks—BBC 1 and BBC 2—which are financed predominantly by a licence fee. The ITC regulates two television services—ITV (Channel 3) and Channel 4—which complement each other and are largely funded by advertising. In Wales, S4C (Sianel Pedwar Cymru) broadcasts programmes on the fourth channel. All four channels broadcast on 625 lines UHF (ultra-high frequency) and over 99 per cent of the population live within range of transmission.

British television productions continue to win many international awards, and in 1993 film and television companies received £170 million in export earnings.

Radio

Practically every home has a radio, and the widespread ownership of portable sets (including personal stereos) and car radios means that people can listen to radio throughout the day. About 70 per cent of the population listen to the radio on a normal day and more than 85 per cent do so over the week.

The BBC has five national networks, which together transmit all types of music, news, current affairs, drama, education, sport and a range of features programmes. The Radio Authority regulates two national commercial radio stations; the award of the franchise for a third station took place in June 1994 (see p. 468).

There are 38 BBC local radio stations serving England and the Channel Islands, and regional and community radio services in Scotland, Wales and Northern Ireland. About 150 independent local radio (ILR) services are also in operation. More local stations are planned. Stations supply a comprehensive service of local news and information, sport, music and other entertainment, education and consumer advice. 'Phone-in' programmes allowing listeners to express their views on air are popular.

GOVERNMENT ROLE

During the last few years broadcasting in

Britain has seen radical changes. The availability of more radio frequencies, together with satellite, cable and microwave transmissions, has made a greater number of local, national and international services possible. Moreover, the technical quality of sound and pictures is improving.

In response to rapidly developing technology and rising public demand for a wide choice of programmes and services, the Government introduced the Broadcasting Act 1990 with the aim of making the regulatory framework for broadcasting more flexible and efficient, and giving viewers and listeners access to a wider range of services. At the same time the Act aimed to promote competition and to maintain high standards of taste and decency.

Changes Introduced by the Broadcasting Act

The Broadcasting Act 1990 overhauled the regulation of independent television and radio and opened the way for many more services.

In 1991 the IBA (Independent Broadcasting Authority) was replaced by the ITC (Independent Television Commission), the Radio Authority and a new transmission and engineering company, National Transcommunications Limited (see p. 463). At the same time the Cable Authority was made part of the ITC and the Radio Authority.

The ITC and the Radio Authority issue licences to commercial broadcasters and enforce rules to ensure diversity of ownership:

● The ITC awards major broadcasting licences by competitive tender to the highest bidders satisfying stipulated quality tests.

● The Radio Authority awards national radio licences by competitive tender. Local radio licences are not allocated by competitive tender; the success of licence applications is in part determined by audience demand, and the extent to which prospective stations would increase variety.

The ITC does not have the former IBA's detailed involvement in scheduling but has wider powers than the IBA to enforce licence conditions and ownership rules. Both organisations were initially able to take out government loans, but are obliged to repay these and to support themselves from licensing fees at the earliest possible date.

The 1990 Act made provision for setting up a new national independent television station, Channel 5, and three national commercial radio stations (see p. 467). Opportunities now also exist for launching hundreds of independent local radio and television channels.

The Broadcasting Act also provided for the former IBA's television and radio transmission networks to be privatised. In 1991 the IBA networks and other facilities were transferred to a new public company—National Transcommunications Limited (NTL). NTL was then sold for £70 million to a company formed for the purpose by Mercury Asset Management. NTL transmits television services for the independent television companies, Channel 4, S4C, and radio services for about 100 independent local radio stations.

Programming Obligations

Licence-holders of the independent television Channel 3 (and the proposed Channel 5) need to pass demanding quality tests (see p. 466). ITC regulations place a limit on the proportion of non-European material broadcast. Since January 1993 both the BBC and commercial television licensees have been required to ensure that at least 25 per cent of their original programming comes from independent producers.

Ownership Rules

The Broadcasting Act 1990 established clearer and more extensive ownership rules. These are designed to enable the ITC and the Radio Authority to keep ownership of the broadcasting media widely spread and to prevent unhealthy concentrations and cross-media ownership. Controlling ownership from outside the European Union is largely prohibited, and national newspapers are allowed relatively small stakes in direct broadcasting by satellite (DBS) channels,

Channels 3 and 5, and national and local radio (although these rules are being reviewed—see p. 475). Public telecommunications operators are not allowed to have controlling interests in any Channel 3, Channel 5, national radio or domestic satellite licence; and political bodies and local authorities are barred from holding licences.

> From 1 January 1994, a limited relaxation of the ITV (independent television) ownership rules allows a company to hold any two regional licences (except in London), a 20 per cent stake in a third company, and 5 per cent in any further licences.

Programme Standards

Recognising that broadcasting is an extremely powerful medium with the potential to offend, exploit and cause harm, the Act contains guarantees on programme standards which are extended to all British-based broadcasters. These guarantees cover taste, decency, accuracy and balance. Under the 1990 Act the Government can proscribe unacceptable foreign satellite services receivable in Britain. Anyone in Britain supporting such a service can now be prosecuted.

THE BBC

The constitution, finances and obligations of the BBC are governed by a Royal Charter and by a Licence and Agreement. The Corporation's board of 12 governors, including the chairman, vice-chairman and a national governor each for Scotland, Wales and Northern Ireland, is appointed by the Queen on the advice of the Government. The board of governors is ultimately responsible for all aspects of broadcasting by the BBC. The governors appoint the Director-General, the Corporation's chief executive officer, who heads the board of management—the body in charge of the daily running of the Corporation.

The BBC has a regional structure throughout Britain. The three English regions—BBC North, BBC Midlands & East and BBC South—and BBC Scotland, Wales and Northern Ireland make programmes for their local audiences as well as contributing to the national network.

The National Broadcasting Councils for Scotland, Wales and Northern Ireland advise on the policy and content of television and radio programmes intended mainly for reception in their areas. Ten Regional Councils in England advise the Board of Governors on the needs and concerns of audiences.

Finance

The domestic services of the BBC are financed predominantly from the sale of television licences. Households with a television must buy an annual licence costing £84.50 for colour and £28 for black and white. Over 20 million licences were current in May 1994; of these, around 19.5 million were for colour.

Licence income is supplemented by profits from trading activities, such as television programme exports, sale of recordings, publications and other merchandise connected with BBC programmes, hire and sale of educational films, film library sales, and exhibitions based on programmes. The BBC World Service (see p. 472) is financed by a grant-in-aid from the Foreign & Commonwealth Office (£175 million in 1994–95), while BBC World Service Television (see p. 472) is self-financing.

TV Licensing, a subsidiary company of the Post Office, undertakes the licence administration on behalf of the BBC. Since 1988 annual rises in the licence fee have been linked to the rate of inflation, and will continue to be until the end of 1996; this is intended further to improve the BBC's efficiency and encourage it to continue to develop alternative sources of revenue.

Future of the BBC

A government White Paper, entitled *The Future of the BBC: Serving the Nation, Competing Worldwide* was published in July 1994. It considered the BBC's future after the expiry of its current Royal Charter at the end of 1996 and proposed that:

- the BBC should remain a public service broadcaster, maintaining its current radio and television services, and this should be its main role. A new Royal Charter and Agreement should provide the framework for the BBC's activities for ten years from 1997;

- the BBC should be more accountable and responsive to its audiences, publishing objectives for its programmes and services;

- a reasonable proportion of the BBC's network programmes should be made in Scotland, Wales, Northern Ireland and the English regions;

- the licence fee should be the main source of income for the BBC's public services in Britain until at least 2001;

- World Service Radio should continue, funded by grant-in-aid;

- the BBC should develop its commercial activities in Britain and abroad, in partnership with the private sector, and should evolve into an international multimedia organisation. These commercial activities should be distinct from its public services, and should not be subsidised from the licence fee; and

- the Government and the BBC would explore options for injecting private finance into the Corporation's transmission services. Privatisation, either in whole or in part, would be among the options under consideration.

BBC Television

The two channels, BBC 1 and BBC 2, are scheduled in a complementary way to cater simultaneously for different interests. Although both services cover the whole range of television output:

- BBC 1 presents a wide range of programmes, including news and current affairs, major documentaries, sport, popular drama and light entertainment, and children's programmes;

BBC 2 presents music and the arts, new talent, innovative documentaries, sport, international films and serious drama, and is a forum for debate.

Apart from a break during the Second World War, the BBC has been providing regular television broadcasts since 1936. Together, BBC 1 and BBC 2 transmit over 12,800 hours of programmes a year for national and regional audiences.

Programmes for both networks are produced mainly in London. In 1993–94, 25 per cent of the expenditure on programmes shown nationally was represented by commissions placed with the regions. The BBC enters into agreements with overseas television corporations in order to share the cost of some new programmes.

BBC Select

BBC Select is the Corporation's specialist night-time television service. It is part of the BBC's Education Directorate and utilises the night hours on BBC 1 and BBC 2 to broadcast education, training, and professional information and updating programmes to specialist audiences.

BBC Select does not make any of the programmes that it broadcasts, but works with a variety of public bodies and charities to enable them to communicate with specific groups of people. Most programmes are 'open access' and free. They are designed for recording on video and viewing at a later date.

BBC Network Radio

BBC Network Radio serves an audience of 30 million a week in Britain, broadcasting around 38,000 hours of programmes each year on its five networks:

- BBC Radio 1 (FM) broadcasts rock and pop music 24 hours a day;

- BBC Radio 2 (FM) transmits popular music and light entertainment, also for 24 hours a day;

- BBC Radio 3 (FM) broadcasts mainly classical music, but presents jazz, drama, poetry, short stories and talks as well;

- BBC Radio 4 (broadcast with some differences on FM and LW) provides news and current affairs coverage, together with drama, comedy, documentaries and panel games; it also carries parliamentary coverage; and

- BBC Radio 5 Live (AM), which superseded Radio 5 in March 1994, is a 24-hour news and sport network.

INDEPENDENT BROADCASTING

Independent Television Commission

Like the Radio Authority and S4C, the ITC's constitution and finances are governed by the Broadcasting Act 1990. The ITC is responsible for licensing and regulating non-BBC television services operating in or from Britain. These include:

- ITV (Channel 3);

- Channel 4;

- the proposed Channel 5;

- cable and other local delivery services;

- independent teletext services; and

- satellite services transmitted from Britain.

Since January 1993, when the new Channel 3 licences came into effect, the ITC has ceased to broadcast programmes. These responsibilities have now passed to the new licensees. The ITC monitors the licences and licence conditions but is not involved in detailed scheduling of programmes.

The ITC is advised by committees on educational broadcasting, religious broadcasting, charitable appeals and advertising. Ten viewer consultative councils also comment on the commercial services' programmes.

ITV Programmes

The first regular ITV programmes began in London in 1955. ITV programmes are broadcast 24 hours a day throughout the country. About one-third of the output comprises informative programmes—news, documentaries, and coverage of current affairs, education and religion. The remainder cover sport, comedy, drama, game shows, films, and a range of other programmes with popular appeal. Over half the programmes are produced by the programme companies and ITN (Independent Television News—see below).

ITV (Channel 3) Programme Companies

ITV is made up of 15 regionally based television companies which are licensed to supply programmes in the 14 independent television geographical regions. Two companies share the contract for London, one providing programmes during weekdays and the other at the weekend. An additional ITC licensee provides a national breakfast-time service, transmitted on the ITV network.

The licensees operate on a commercial basis, deriving most of their revenue from selling advertising time. The financial resources, advertising revenue and programme production of the companies vary considerably, depending largely on the population of the areas in which they operate. Although newspapers may acquire an interest in programme companies, safeguards exist to ensure against concentration of media ownership, thereby protecting the public interest.

Each programme company plans the content of the programmes to be broadcast in its area. These are produced by the company itself, or by other programme companies or bought from elsewhere.

A common news service is provided by ITN. ITN has been appointed to supply a service of national and international news to the ITV network for a ten-year period from January 1993.

ITV Network Centre

The ITV Network Centre, which is wholly owned by the ITV companies, independently commissions and schedules those television programmes which are shown across the ITV network. Programmes are commissioned from the ITV companies as well as independent producers. The Centre also promotes the ITV network and co-ordinates developments in technology and training.

Licences

The ITV licences for Channel 3, which came up for renewal at the end of 1992, were awarded by the ITC in October 1991. Twelve existing franchise holders and four new companies were awarded licences.

Channel 3 licences are awarded for a ten-year period by competitive tender to the highest bidder who has passed a quality threshold. In exceptional cases a lower bid can be selected, for instance, where an applicant is able to offer a significantly better quality of service than that offered by the highest bidder.

There are safeguards for quality programming. Licensees are required to offer a diverse programme service, a proportion of good-quality programmes, as well as high-quality regional and national news and current affairs programmes, and children's and religious programmes. There is a statutory duty to present programmes made in and about the region. There is also a requirement for district and regional programming to be aimed at different areas within regions. Channel 3 licensees are obliged to operate a national programme network. Networking arrangements are subject to government approval so that anti-competitive practices are avoided.

Channel 4 and S4C

Channel 4, which began broadcasting in 1982, provides a national television service throughout Britain, except in Wales, which has a corresponding service—S4C (Sianel Pedwar Cymru). In January 1993 Channel 4 became a public corporation, licensed and regulated by the ITC, selling its own advertising time and retaining the proceeds. It was previously a public limited company owned by the ITC.

Channel 4's remit is to provide programmes with a distinctive character and to appeal to tastes and interests not generally catered for by Channel 3. It must present a suitable proportion of educational programmes and encourage innovation and experiment. Channel 4 commissions programmes from the ITV companies and independent producers and buys programmes from overseas. It broadcasts for around 139 hours a week, about half of which are devoted to informative programmes.

In Wales programmes on the fourth channel are run and controlled by S4C. Its members are appointed by the Government. S4C is required to see that a significant proportion of programming, in practice about 23 hours a week, is in the Welsh language and that programmes broadcast between 18.30 and 22.00 hours are mainly in Welsh. At other times S4C transmits national Channel 4 programmes.

Like Channel 4, S4C has sold its own advertising since January 1993. S4C is expected to cover only 10 per cent of its costs from advertising, with the remainder financed by the Government.

Gaelic TV Fund

The Gaelic Television Committee, appointed by the ITC, was set up under the Broadcasting Act 1990 to administer government finance for making television programmes in Gaelic. A fund of £8.7 million has been created and programmes thus financed came on screen from January 1993. The Fund has increased the output of Gaelic television programmes from 100 to about 300 hours each year.

Channel 5

A new national terrestrial television channel—Channel 5—was originally intended to come into operation in late 1994, financed through advertising, subscription or sponsorship. The ten-year licence was to be awarded by competitive tender. However, in December 1992 the ITC announced its decision not to award a licence. It had received only one bid and was not satisfied that the applicant would be able to maintain its proposed service throughout the period of the licence.

In mid-September 1994 the ITC announced that it was again inviting applications for the licence, the closing date for which is 1 May 1995. Earlier, in July 1994, the Government announced new

frequency allocations for Channel 5 and for up to 12 digital terrestrial television services.

Local Television

The Broadcasting Act 1990 makes provision for the further development of local television services. Local delivery licences are awarded by competitive tender and there is no quality threshold. ITC licence-holders can supply national and local television channels using both cable and microwave transmission systems. Services delivered could be aimed at communities such as ethnic minorities.

The Radio Authority

Independent local radio (ILR) is based on principles similar to those of ITV (see p. 466). The programme companies operate under licence to the Radio Authority and are financed mainly by advertising revenue. Licences for existing operators expire between 1994 and 1996.

The Radio Authority, which took over responsibility for independent radio from the IBA in 1991, is required to ensure that licensed services, taken as a whole, are of a high quality and offer a range of programmes calculated to appeal to a variety of tastes and interests.

The Authority awards national radio licences by competitive tender to the highest bidder. The licence for the first independent national radio service (INR1) was awarded to Classic FM in 1991. The station, which broadcasts mainly classical music, together with news and information, began operating in September 1992. The licence for the second independent national service (INR2) was awarded in 1992 to Virgin 1215. This station began broadcasting in April 1993, playing broad-based rock music. Talk Radio UK was awarded the licence for the third independent national service (INR3) in June 1994. The service must be speech-based and will begin in early 1995.

In the course of the 1990s more local radio stations will come on the air, some of which could be neighbourhood and 'community of interest' stations. Areas to be covered will initially be those not adequately served by independent local radio. Local radio licences are not allocated by competitive tender; the success of licence applications is in part determined by the extent to which applicants meet the needs and interests of the people living in the area and whether they have the necessary financial resources to sustain programme plans for the eight-year licence period.

Some of the locations have been selected with small-scale 'community radio' in mind. As part of its brief to develop a wide range of radio services, the Authority aims to establish a number of more specialist stations.

The Radio Authority also issues restricted service licences. These are issued on demand (subject to certain conditions and frequency availability), usually for a maximum of 28 days. They enable local events—such as sports events, arts festivals and conferences— to be covered by a temporary radio service in a limited area, for example, part of a city or town or an arena.

TELETEXT, CABLE AND SATELLITE SERVICES

Teletext

The BBC and independent television each operate a teletext service, offering constantly updated information on a variety of subjects, including news, sport, travel, weather conditions and entertainment. The teletext system allows the television signal to carry additional information which can be selected and displayed as 'pages' of text and graphics on receivers equipped with the necessary decoders. Both the BBC and Channels 3 and 4 have a subtitling facility for certain programmes for people with hearing difficulties. These services are available whenever the transmitters are on the air. Around 50 per cent of households in Britain have teletext sets.

Licences

The Broadcasting Act 1990 introduced a new regulatory system for licensing spare capacity within the lines of the television signal. This allows more varied use of the capacity—data transfer, for instance—but the position of teletext and subtitling on commercial television is safeguarded.

At the end of 1991 the ITC advertised three teletext licences—a single public service licence for teletext on Channels 3 and 4 (and S4C) and two separate licences for additional commercial services to subscription or closed user groups, using three lines of spare capacity on each channel. These ten-year licences are awarded by competitive tender, with applicants having to satisfy certain statutory requirements before their cash bid can be considered. The ITC awarded the main teletext licence to Teletext Ltd, which replaced Oracle in January 1993, and awarded one of the additional commercial service licences on Channel 3 to the only bidder, Data Broadcasting International. The other additional commercial service licence on Channel 4/S4C was re-advertised in June 1994.

Channel 3 and Channel 4 are required to offer subtitling services for at least 50 per cent of their programmes by 1998.

Cable Services

Cable services are delivered to consumers through underground cables and are paid for by subscription. The franchising of cable systems and the licensing of cable television services are carried out by the Cable and Satellite Division of the ITC, while the Radio Authority issues cable radio licences.

'Broadband cable', the cable systems currently being designed and built, can carry between 30 and 45 television channels, including terrestrial broadcasts, satellite television, and channels delivered to cable operators by video. Cable systems usually carry a local channel. Interactive services such as home shopping, home banking, security and alarm services, electronic mail and remote meter readings are also possible. Franchises have already been granted covering areas which include two-thirds of all homes and nearly all urban areas in Britain— around 14.5 million households in total. In April 1994, 66 broadband cable franchises were in operation in Britain, eight of which had been set up within the previous year. Regulation is as light as possible to encourage the development of a wide range of services, and flexible enough to adapt to new technology. The ITC is continuing the Cable Authority's practice of awarding only one broadband cable franchise in each area so that the new franchisee is protected from direct competition in the early stages. At present nearly 3 million homes are able to receive broadband cable services and there are almost 650,000 subscribers.

ITC licences are required for systems capable of serving more than 1,000 homes. They are awarded for each area on the basis of competitive tendering. Systems extending beyond a single building and up to 1,000 homes require only an individual licence from OFTEL (see p. 302). Cable investment must be privately financed.

Direct Broadcasting by Satellite

Direct broadcasting by satellite (DBS), by which television is transmitted directly by satellite into people's homes, has been available throughout Britain since 1989. The signals from satellite broadcasting are received through specially designed aerials or 'dishes'.

Several British-based satellite television channels have been set up to supply programmes to cable operators and viewers with dishes in Britain and, in some cases, throughout Europe. While some offer general entertainment, others concentrate on specific areas of interest, such as sport, music and children's programmes.

Licences are granted, on a non-competitive basis, to programme services which are likely to meet consumer protection standards and are run by suitably qualified people.

The largest satellite programmer is BSkyB (British Sky Broadcasting), which provides nine channels devoted to light entertainment, news, feature films, sport and home shopping transmitted from the Astra satellite.

Other satellite channels available to British viewers include Eurosport (sport), CNN (news), MTV (pop videos), and TV Asia (for Asian viewers). The choice available to viewers is expanding steadily.

BBC International Television (see p. 472) and Thames TV (one of the former ITV franchisees) operate a joint entertainment satellite channel—UK Gold—on the Astra satellite. Programmes include drama, soaps, comedy, children's television and quizzes.

OTHER ASPECTS

Educational Broadcasting

Both the BBC and Channel 4 broadcast educational programmes for schools and Continuing Education programmes for adults. Broadcasts to schools deal with all subjects of the National Curriculum (see p. 418), while programmes for adults cover many areas of learning and vocational training. Books, pamphlets, filmstrips, computer software, and audio and video cassettes, are produced to supplement the programmes. Around 90 per cent of primary and secondary schools in Britain use schools television. The ITC has a duty to ensure that schools programmes are presented on independent television.

During 1993 the BBC broadcast 181 hours of radio and 687 hours of television on behalf of the Open University (see p. 428).

Advertising and Sponsorship

The BBC may not obtain revenue or any consideration in kind from the broadcasting of advertisements or from commercial sponsorship of programmes. The policy of the BBC is to avoid giving publicity to any firm or organised interest except when this is necessary in providing effective and informative programmes. It does, however, cover sponsored sporting and artistic events.

Advertising and sponsorship are allowed on independent television and radio subject to controls. The ITC and the Radio Authority operate codes of advertising standards and programme sponsorship.

Advertisements on independent television and radio are broadcast between programmes as well as in breaks during programmes. Advertisers are not allowed to influence programme content. Advertisements must be distinct and separate from programmes. The time given to them must not be so great as to detract from the value of the programmes as a medium of information, education or entertainment. Television advertising is limited to an average of seven minutes an hour during the day and seven and a half minutes in the peak evening viewing period. Advertising is prohibited in broadcasts of religious services and in broadcasts to schools. The service provided by Teletext Ltd (see p. 468) carries advertisements.

The ITC and the Radio Authority's codes governing standards and practice in advertising give regulations on the forms of advertisement which are prohibited, alongside rules and guidance on scheduling and creative matters.

> Prohibited advertising includes political advertising, betting and advertisements for cigarettes and cigarette tobacco and—on television only—cigars and pipe tobacco. Advertisements for the last two are permitted on radio.

The Radio Authority, ITV and Channel 4 are permitted to screen religious advertisements, provided they comply with the guidelines issued by the ITC and the Radio Authority.

Both the ITC and the Radio Authority can impose severe penalties on any television or radio company failing to comply with their codes.

Sponsorship in Independent Broadcasting

In Britain sponsorship is a relatively new way of helping to finance commercial broadcasting, although the practice has long been established in other countries. In return for their financial contribution, sponsors receive a credit associating them with a particular programme.

The ITC's Code of Programme Sponsorship and the Radio Authority's Advertising and Sponsorship Code aim to ensure that sponsors do not exert influence on the editorial content of programmes and that sponsorships are made clear to viewers. News and current affairs programmes may not be sponsored. Potential sponsors for other categories of programme may be debarred if their involvement could constrain the editorial independence of the programme maker in any way. References to sponsors or their products

must be confined to the beginning and end of a programme and around commercial breaks; they must not appear in the programme itself. All commercial radio programmes other than news bulletins may be sponsored.

Government Publicity

Government publicity material to support non-political campaigns may be broadcast on independent television and radio. This is paid for on a normal commercial basis. The Central Office of Information (COI) produces short public service items, concerning health, safety and welfare, for free transmission by the BBC and independent television and radio. All government advertisements and public service information films are subtitled via electronic text to support the deaf community.

Broadcasting Standards

The independence enjoyed by the broadcasting authorities carries with it certain obligations over programme content. Programmes must display, as far as possible, a proper balance and wide range of subject matter, impartiality in matters of controversy and accuracy in news coverage, and must not offend against good taste. Broadcasters must also comply with legislation relating to obscenity and incitement to racial hatred.

The BBC, the ITC and the Radio Authority apply codes providing guidance on violence and standards of taste and decency in television programmes, particularly during hours when children are likely to be viewing.

The BBC opened its own Programme Complaints Unit in early 1994 to investigate serious complaints about BBC television or radio programmes.

Broadcasting Standards Council

The Broadcasting Standards Council (BSC) was set up by the Government in 1988 to act as a focus for public concern about the portrayal of violence and sex, and about standards of taste and decency. Its remit covers television and radio programmes and broadcast advertisements, and includes monitoring programmes broadcast into Britain from abroad.

Under the Broadcasting Act 1990 the Council was granted statutory powers requiring the codes of practice of the BBC and other broadcasting regulatory bodies to reflect the BSC's own code. The BSC monitors programmes, examines complaints from the public and undertakes research. In 1993–94 the Council received 2,390 complaints, of which 1,711 fell within its remit. It has published the results of several public attitude surveys.

Broadcasting Complaints Commission

The Broadcasting Complaints Commission, an independent statutory body, deals with complaints of unfair treatment in broadcast programmes and of unwarranted infringement of privacy in programmes or in their preparation. In 1993–94 it received 1,049 complaints, 156 of which fell within its jurisdiction.

The White Paper on the future of the BBC (see p. 464) proposed that the Broadcasting Standards Council and the Broadcasting Complaints Commission be merged in order to simplify the system of broadcasting regulation.

Parliamentary and Political Broadcasting

The proceedings of both Houses of Parliament may be broadcast on television and radio, either live, or more usually in recorded and edited form on news and current affairs programmes.

The BBC and the commercial services provide time on radio and television for an annual series of party political broadcasts. Party election broadcasts are arranged following the announcement of a general election. In addition, the Government may make ministerial broadcasts on radio and television, with opposition parties also being allotted broadcast time.

Audience Research

Both the BBC and the independent sector are required to keep themselves informed on the state of public opinion about the programmes and advertising that they broadcast. This is done through the continuous measurement of the size and composition of audiences and their opinions of programmes. For television, this work is undertaken through BARB (the Broadcasters' Audience Research Board), owned jointly by the BBC and the ITV Network Centre. For radio, joint research is undertaken for BBC radio and for commercial radio by RAJAR (Radio Joint Audience Research).

Both the BBC and the independent sector conduct regular surveys of audience opinion on television and radio services. Public opinion is further assessed by the BBC and ITC through the work of their advisory committees, councils and panels. Regular public meetings are also held to debate services, and consideration is given to letters and telephone calls from listeners and viewers.

Training

The BBC provides some non-financial technical assistance, particularly in training the staff of overseas broadcasting organisations. The Government finances overseas students on broadcasting training courses at the BBC, the British Council and the Thomson Foundation; the Foundation also conducts courses overseas in broadcast journalism, media management, radio and television production, and technology.

INTERNATIONAL SERVICES

The BBC

In May 1994 the Corporation announced a new organisational structure—BBC Worldwide—for the development of its international and commercial strategy. It focuses the activities into three separate divisions—BBC World Service, BBC International Television and BBC Publishing—operating across six distinct regions of the world: Europe, the Americas, Africa and the Middle East, South Asia, Asia-Pacific; and the former Soviet Union and South West Asia.

BBC World Service

The BBC World Service broadcasts radio services into each of the six world regions, using English and 38 other languages. Programmes in Azeri and Uzbek are also planned. Programme output amounts to 1,426 hours a week. News bulletins, current affairs programmes, political commentaries and topical magazine programmes form the main part of the output. These are supplemented by a sports service, music, drama and general entertainment. Regular listeners are estimated to number 130 million.

BBC World Service news bulletins and other programmes are re-broadcast by about 900 radio and cable stations in almost 100 countries, most receiving the programmes by satellite. Two World Service departments also specialise in supplying radio material for re-broadcast. *BBC Transcription* sells BBC radio programmes to over 750 overseas radio stations in 132 countries, while *BBC Topical Tapes* airmails about 200 tapes of original programmes to subscribers in over 50 countries each week.

BBC English specialises in teaching the English language worldwide. Lessons are broadcast by radio with explanations in 39 languages, including English, and re-broadcast by many radio stations. BBC English television programmes are also shown in more than 100 countries. A range of printed, audio and video material accompanies these programmes.

Another part of the World Service, *BBC Monitoring*, listens to and reports on foreign broadcasts, providing a daily flow of significant news and comment from overseas to the BBC and the Government. This information is also sold to the press, businesses, academic staff and public bodies.

BBC International Television

This division is responsible for programme sales and co-productions, non-news channel sales, BBC World Service Television and joint ventures with other companies.

World Service Television (WSTV) was set up in 1991 to establish a worldwide television service. The company is wholly self-funding, receiving no revenue from either the TV licence fees or from the Government. In addition to established satellite services in Europe, Asia, Africa and Canada, in mid-1994 WSTV launched its core news and information channel into Japan and began what will become a 24-hour Arabic language channel for the Middle East and North Africa. The English language news and information channel is expected to become available in the United States in 1995.

The BBC and Pearson plc, two of the largest organisations in the international media market, signed an agreement in May 1994 to develop satellite-delivered television services in chosen markets around the world. The first product of this alliance is a joint venture providing two pan-European, satellite-delivered BBC television channels—one for entertainment (funded by subscription) and the other for news and information (funded by advertising). The channels are expected to be launched before the end of 1994.

BBC Publishing

BBC Publishing produces and distributes consumer products—books, audio tapes, videos, magazines, merchandising, multimedia and interactive developments—for the British and international markets.

COI Overseas Radio and Television Services

The Central Office of Information, which provides publicity material and other information services on behalf of government departments and other public agencies, produces radio programmes for overseas. Recorded material is sent to radio stations all over the world. COI television services also make available material such as documentary and magazine programmes.

News Agencies

Reuters Television, the largest international television news agency in the world, supplies news pictures to over 200 broadcasters and their networks in 84 countries. Reuters Television is a wholly-owned subsidiary of Reuters (see p. 479) and uses 120 Reuters bureaux and a global satellite network to gather and distribute its material.

WTN (Worldwide Television News), owned by ITN, ABC (the American Broadcasting Corporation) and Channel 9 in Australia, supplies news and a wide range of television services to about 1,000 broadcasters in 93 countries, as well as to governments and international corporations. It also produces British Satellite News, an international satellite news service, for the Foreign & Commonwealth Office. The service, under FCO editorial control, transmits programmes five days a week. These are distributed, mainly by satellite, free to television stations throughout Eastern Europe, the Middle East and Southern Africa for use in news bulletins.

WTN and Reuters both provide services through the Eurovision network (see below) and by satellite.

International Relations

European Agreements

In 1991 Britain implemented two important European agreements on cross-border broadcasting: the European Community Directive on Broadcasting and the Council of Europe Convention on Transfrontier Television. Under these, countries have to remove restrictions on the retransmission of programmes originating from other participating countries. They must also ensure that their own broadcasters observe certain minimum standards on advertising, sponsorship, taste and decency and the portrayal of sex and violence on television.

European Broadcasting Union

The BBC and the Radio Authority are members of the European Broadcasting Union, which manages Eurovision, the international network of television news and programme exchange. The Union is responsible for co-ordinating the exchange of programmes and news over the Eurovision network and intercontinental satellite links. It

also maintains a technical monitoring station where frequency measurements and other observations on broadcasting stations are carried out. The Union provides a forum linking the major public services and national broadcasters of Western Europe and other parts of the world, and co-ordinates joint operations in radio and television.

International Telecommunications Union

The BBC takes part in the work of the International Telecommunications Union, the United Nations agency responsible for regulating and controlling all international telecommunications services, including radio and television. The Union also allocates and registers all radio frequencies, and promotes and co-ordinates the international study of technical problems in broadcasting.

Other International Bodies

The BBC is an associate member of the Asia-Pacific Broadcasting Union and also belongs to the Commonwealth Broadcasting Association, which meets every two years to discuss public service broadcasting issues.

TECHNICAL DEVELOPMENTS

The introduction of computer-based digital production equipment for both television and radio is one of the most significant technical advances affecting the broadcasting industry in Britain. It allows programmes to be made more quickly and more effectively with the sound and vision information being held and manipulated on computer disc storage units. A significant proportion of programmes produced by the BBC and independent companies are edited on this type of equipment.

Other recent advances include:
- the introduction of 'all-digital' studios (including digital video recorders and control desks) at both the BBC and independent companies;
- the introduction of digital transmission links, mainly based on optical fibre technology, between studios and from studios to the transmitters;

- the use of miniature cameras and transmitters;
- the increased use of remote controlled cameras in studios and at remote locations; and
- an increasing use by radio broadcasters of digital sound links using 'dial-up' ISDN lines.

The BBC and the ITC also undertake long-term research into broadcast technology. The key topics under investigation include:

- the transmission of digital radio (DAB) from terrestrial transmitters and by satellite;
- digital television transmission;
- widescreen and high definition television (HDTV);
- surround sound for use with HDTV and digital television; and
- audio descriptive systems for delivering additional television sound channels that can be used to describe the programme for people with impaired sight.

The Press

Six out of ten adults regularly read a national newspaper. A higher proportion—nine out of ten—regularly read a paid-for regional or local newspaper.

National papers have an average total circulation of over 14 million on weekdays and about 16 million on Sundays, although the total readership is considerably greater. Men are more likely to read newspapers than women, and more people in the 45–64 age group read a daily newspaper than in any other age group.

There are about 120 daily (Monday to Saturday) and Sunday newspapers, about 1,300 weekly paid-for and free newspapers (including business, sporting and religious newspapers), and over 6,600 periodical publications.

Several newspapers have had very long and distinguished histories. The *Observer*, for example, first published in 1791, is the oldest national Sunday newspaper in the world, and

The Times, Britain's oldest daily national newspaper, began publication in 1785. The weekly *Berrow's Worcester Journal* claims to be the world's oldest newspaper in continuous circulation, having been established in 1690.

The press caters for a range of political views, interests and levels of education. Newspapers are almost always financially independent of any political party. Where they express pronounced views and show obvious political leanings in their editorial comments, these derive from proprietorial and other non-party influences. Nevertheless, during General Election campaigns many newspapers recommend their readers to vote for a particular political party. Even newspapers which adopt strong political views in their editorial columns include feature and other types of articles by authors of different political persuasions.

In order to preserve their character and traditions, some newspapers and periodicals are governed by trustee-type arrangements. Others have management arrangements to ensure their editors' authority and independence.

In recent years working practices throughout the newspaper industry have undergone major changes in response to the challenges posed by computer-based technology and the need to contain costs. Newsprint, about three-quarters of which is imported, forms about a quarter of average national newspaper costs; labour represents over half. In addition to sales, many newspapers and periodicals earn considerable amounts from their advertising. Total yearly spending of around £5,100 million on press advertising makes the press by far the largest advertising medium in Britain. Unlike most of its European counterparts the British press receives no subsidies and relatively few tax and postal concessions.

New Printing Technology

Publishers have been able to reduce production costs in recent years by using advanced computer systems for editing and production processes. The 'single keying' system, for example, allows journalists and advertising staff to input copy directly into a computer terminal, and then to transfer it electronically into columns of type. Many newspapers arrange page layouts on screen and output full pages to photographic paper bromides or film which are then used to make plates for the printing press. A number of newspapers still output columns in bromide format from the computerised typesetting operation; these are then pasted up into pages before being sent to the camera room for negatives to be produced from which the plates are made.

News International, publisher of three daily and two Sunday papers, has at its London Docklands headquarters more than 500 computer terminals, one of the largest systems installed at one time anywhere in the world. The *Financial Times* runs its printing plant in Docklands with about 170 production workers, compared with the 600 formerly employed in the City of London. Associated Newspapers, at its Docklands plant, is the only newspaper company to use flexography, an advanced printing process. Most other newspapers print by offset lithography, a method whereby the printed image is transferred, or offset, from the printing plate to a rubber blanket (cylinder) and then on to the paper. A number of the national newspapers print their regional and northern editions on regional newspaper presses.

There has been a tendency within Britain's regional and local press in recent years for weekly newspapers to close ageing press plants and contract out the printing of their titles to larger groups. Many of these groups have invested heavily in state-of-the-art full colour printing plants to meet their own requirements and those of a growing number of contract customers.

NATIONAL AND REGIONAL TITLES

Newspaper Ownership

Ownership of the national, London and regional daily newspapers lies in the hands of a number of large press publishing groups. There are also over 260 independent regional and local newspaper publishers.

Although most enterprises are organised as limited liability companies, individual and partner proprietorship survives. The large national newspaper and periodical publishers are major corporations; many are involved in the whole field of publishing and communications. Some have shares in independent television and radio companies, while others have industrial and commercial interests.

The law provides safeguards against the risks inherent in undue concentration of ownership. Government consent is needed to transfer a newspaper or newspaper assets to a proprietor whose newspapers have an average daily circulation amounting, with that of the newspaper to be taken over, to 500,000 or more copies. Except in certain limited cases, consent may be given only after the President of the Board of Trade has referred the matter to the Monopolies and Mergers Commission and received its report.

Under the Broadcasting Act 1990 (see p. 462) no proprietor of a national newspaper or local newspaper is allowed more than a 20 per cent interest in direct broadcasting by satellite channels, independent television Channels 3 and 5, and national and local radio within its circulation area. A local newspaper can own a local radio station if the station does not serve an area overlapping that served by the newspaper. These rules are under review by the Government in the light of the technological advances and developments in the international media market.

The National Press

The national press consists of 11 morning daily papers and nine Sunday papers (see Table 29.1). Formerly they were produced in or near Fleet Street in central London with, in some cases, northern editions being printed in Manchester. All the national papers have now moved their editorial and printing facilities to other parts of London or away from the capital altogether; some use contract printing. The *Independent*, for example, is printed in Bradford, Northampton and Portsmouth. Scottish editions of the *Sun*, *Today*, the *News of the World* and the *Sunday Times* (Scottish Section) are printed in Glasgow.

Table 29.1: National Newspapers

Title and foundation date	Controlled by	Circulation[a] average February–July 1994
National dailies		
'Populars'		
Daily Mirror (1903)	Mirror Group Newspapers (1986) plc	2,497,076
Daily Star (1978)	United Newspapers	671,373
The Sun (1964)	News International plc	4,101,988
'Mid market'		
Daily Mail (1896)	Associated Newspapers Ltd	1,796,795
Daily Express (1900)	United Newspapers	1,358,246
Today (1986)	News International plc	595,468
'Qualities'		
Financial Times (1888)	Pearson	296,634
The Daily Telegraph (1855)	The Telegraph plc	1,013,860
The Guardian (1821)	Guardian Media Group plc	400,856
The Independent (1986)	Mirror Group consortium[b]	275,447
The Times (1785)	News International plc	507,894
National Sundays		
'Populars'		
News of the World (1843)	News International plc	4,769,105
Sunday Mirror (1963)	Mirror Group Newspapers (1986) plc	2,560,234
The People (1881)	Mirror Group Newspapers (1986) plc	2,006,393
'Mid market'		
The Mail on Sunday (1982)	Associated Newspapers Ltd	1,972,012
Sunday Express (1918)	United Newspapers	1,544,404
'Qualities'		
Sunday Telegraph (1961)	The Telegraph plc	633,112
The Independent on Sunday (1990)	Mirror Group consortium[b]	327,689
The Observer (1791)	Guardian Media Group plc	495,483
The Sunday Times (1822)	News International plc	1,205,457

[a]Circulation figures are those of the Audit Bureau of circulations (consisting of publishers, advertisers and advertising agencies) and are certified average daily or weekly net sales for the period.

[b]The consortium comprises Mirror Group Newspapers (1986) plc, Promotora de Informaciones and Espresso International Holding.

In order to improve distribution and sales overseas, editions of the *Financial Times* are printed in Frankfurt, Roubaix (northern France), New Jersey and Tokyo, while the *Guardian* prints an international edition in Frankfurt. The *European*, a weekly English–language international newspaper, is printed in Britain, France, Germany and Hungary.

National newspapers are often described as either 'quality', 'popular' or 'mid-market' papers on the basis of differences in style and content. Five dailies and four Sundays are usually described as 'quality' newspapers, which are directed at readers who want full information on a wide range of public matters. Popular newspapers appeal to people wanting news of a more entertaining character, presented more concisely. 'Mid-market' publications cover the intermediate market. Quality papers are normally broadsheet (large-sheet) in format and mid-market and popular papers tabloid (small-sheet).

Many newspapers are printed in colour and most produce colour supplements as part of the Saturday or Sunday paper, with articles on travel, food and wine, and other leisure topics.

The leading Scottish papers, *The Scotsman* and the *Herald*, have considerable circulations outside Scotland.

There is a growing market for news and information in the electronic media, and quality papers such as the *Financial Times* provide material for use on databases and videotext services.

Regional Newspapers

There are about 100 morning, evening and Sunday newspapers and some 1,300 weekly paid-for and free distribution newspapers, publishing mainly regional and local news.

England

Of the morning papers the *Yorkshire Post* (Leeds), the *Northern Echo* (Darlington) and the *Eastern Daily Press* (Norwich), each has a circulation of approximately 81,000, and two provincial Sunday papers—the *Sunday Mercury* (Birmingham) and the *Sunday Sun*

(Newcastle upon Tyne)—sell 146,500 and 124,200 copies respectively. Circulation figures of evening papers start at about 10,000 and most are in the 20,000 to 100,000 range. Those with much larger sales include the *Manchester Evening News* (210,600), Wolverhampton's *Express and Star* (215,300) and the *Birmingham Evening Mail* (200,400). Paid-for weekly papers have a mainly local appeal and most have circulations in the 5,000 to 60,000 range.

London has one paid-for evening paper, the *Evening Standard*, with a circulation of 475,000. It covers national and international news as well as local affairs. A number of evening papers are published in the outer metropolitan area. Local weeklies include papers for every district in Greater London, which are often local editions of individual papers.

Wales

Wales has one daily morning newspaper, the *Western Mail*, with a circulation of 68,500, and *Wales on Sunday*, with a circulation of 61,700. Both are published in Cardiff. Evening papers published in Wales are the *South Wales Echo*, Cardiff; the *South Wales Argus*, Newport; the *South Wales Evening Post*, Swansea; and the *Evening Leader*, Wrexham. Circulations range from 32,000 to 77,000. North Wales is served by the *Daily Post*, published in Liverpool, and the *Liverpool Echo*.

The weekly press (83 publications) includes English-language papers, some of which carry articles in Welsh; bilingual papers; and Welsh-language papers. Welsh community newspapers receive an annual grant as part of the Government's wider financial support for the Welsh language.

Scotland

Scotland has six morning, five evening and three Sunday newspapers. Local weekly newspapers number 118. The daily morning papers, with circulations of between 52,000 and 751,000, are *The Scotsman* (published in Edinburgh); the *Herald*, published in Glasgow; the *Daily Record* (sister paper of the *Daily Mirror*); the Scottish *Daily Express*; the Scottish edition of the *Sun*; the *Dundee Courier and Advertiser*; the *Aberdeen Press and Journal*; and the *Paisley Daily Express*. The daily evening papers have circulations in the range of 20,000 to 145,000 and include the *Evening News* of Edinburgh, Glasgow's *Evening Times*, Dundee's *Evening Telegraph*, Aberdeen's *Evening Express* and the Greenock *Telegraph*.

The Sunday papers are the *Sunday Mail*, the *Sunday Post* and a quality broadsheet paper, *Scotland on Sunday*. The national *Sunday Express* has a Scottish edition (printed in Manchester) and the *Observer* and the *Sunday Times* carry Scottish supplements.

Northern Ireland

Northern Ireland has two morning newspapers, one evening and two Sunday papers, all published in Belfast, with circulations ranging from 43,000 to 133,000. They are the *News Letter* (unionist), the *Irish News* (nationalist), the evening *Belfast Telegraph*, *Sunday Life* and *Sunday World* (Northern Ireland edition).

There are about 50 weeklies. Newspapers from the Irish Republic, as well as the British national press, are widely read in Northern Ireland.

Free Distribution Newspapers

More than 750 free distribution newspapers, mostly weekly and financed by advertising, are published in Britain; over half are produced by established newspaper publishers. They have enjoyed rapid growth in recent years and now have an estimated total weekly circulation of about 31 million. A free evening title for London, *Tonight*, was launched in July 1994.

Ethnic Minority Publications

Many newspapers and magazines in Britain are produced by members of ethnic minorities. Most are published weekly, fortnightly or monthly. A Chinese newspaper, *Sing Tao*, the Urdu *Daily Jang* (see below) and the Arabic *Al-Arab*, however, are dailies.

The *Asian Times* is an English language weekly for people of Asian descent; the *Sikh Courier* is produced quarterly. Afro-Caribbean newspapers include the *Gleaner* and *West Indian Digest*. The *Voice* and *Caribbean Times*, both weeklies, are aimed at the black population in general. The *Weekly Journal*, the first 'quality' broadsheet aimed at Britain's black community, was launched in 1992. Leading ethnic language newspapers include the Urdu *Daily Jang*, an offshoot of the largest circulation paper in Pakistan, and the weekly *Gujarat Samachar*, a Gujarati tabloid. Publications also appear in Bengali, Hindi and Punjabi.

Many provincial papers print special editions for their local populations. The *Leicester Mercury*, for example, publishes a daily Asian edition, incorporating news from the South Asian sub-continent.

THE PERIODICAL PRESS

The 6,600 periodical publications are classified as 'consumer general interest', 'special interest' and 'business-to-business'. There are also several hundred 'house magazines' produced by businesses or public services for their employees and/or clients. Directories and similar publications number more than 2,000. The 'alternative' press comprises a large number of titles, many of them devoted to radical politics, community matters, religion, the occult, science or ecology.

Consumer general and specialist periodicals comprise magazines for a wide range of interests. These include women's magazines; publications for children; religious periodicals; fiction magazines; magazines dealing with sport, motoring, gardening, youth interests and music; humour; retirement; and computer magazines. Learned societies, trade unions, regiments, universities and other organisations also produce publications.

Weekly periodicals with the highest sales are those which carry full details of the forthcoming week's television and radio programmes, including the satellite schedules. *What's on TV* has a circulation figure of 1.6 million, followed by the

Radio Times with 1.5 million and *TV Times* with 1 million.

Woman's Weekly, Woman's Own, Woman, Weekly News (which sells mainly in Scotland), *Woman's Realm, My Weekly* and *Me* have circulations in the 340,000 to 800,000 range. In recent years several women's magazines from overseas have achieved large circulations: *Prima* and *Best*, for instance, each sell over 500,000 copies, while *Bella* and *Hello!* are also widely read. *Smash Hits*, with a circulation of 346,600, is a fortnightly magazine dealing with pop music and teenage lifestyles. *Viz*, a cartoon comic aimed at young adults, sells 734,000 copies. Of monthly magazines, *Reader's Digest* has the highest circulation (1.7 million).

The leading journals of opinion include *The Economist*, an independent conservative publication covering a wide range of topics. The *New Statesman and Society* reviews social issues, politics, literature and the arts from an independent socialist point of view, and the *Spectator* covers similar subjects from an independent conservative standpoint.

New Scientist reports on science and technology in terms that the non-specialist reader can understand. *Private Eye*, a satirical fortnightly, also covers public affairs. Weekly 'listings' magazines, such as *Time Out*, provide details of cultural and other events in London and other large cities.

Literary and political journals, and those specialising in international and Commonwealth affairs, appear monthly or quarterly, and generally appeal to a more academic readership. Many of the business, scientific and professional journals, whose publication ranges from twice weekly to quarterly, have a considerable circulation overseas.

NEWS AGENCIES

The principal news agencies in Britain are Reuters, based in London, the Press Association and Extel Financial Ltd/AFP-Extel News Ltd.

Reuters

Reuters is a publicly owned company, employing over 11,000 staff in 80 countries.

It has more than 1,300 staff journalists and photographers. The company serves subscribers in 150 countries, including financial institutions; commodities houses; traders in currencies, equities and bonds; major corporations; government agencies; news agencies; newspapers; and radio and television stations.

Reuters has developed the world's largest private leased communications network to transmit its services. It provides the media with a wide range of news, news pictures and graphics. Services for business clients comprise constantly updated financial news, historical information, facilities for computerised trading, and the supply of communications and other equipment for financial dealing rooms. Information is distributed through video terminals and teleprinters. Reuters wholly owns Reuters Television, a television news agency (see p. 472).

The Press Association

The Press Association operates through three companies—PA News, PA Sport and PA Data Design—as the national news agency for Britain and the Irish Republic. It offers newspapers and broadcasters a comprehensive range of news and information services.

PA News provides editorial and photographic coverage of the nation's news to the media via satellite, and supplies the news and sports pages broadcast by Teletext on ITV and Channel 4. It also offers an on-line news and sport information service—NewsFile—as well as extensive news cuttings and picture libraries.

PA Sport distributes full coverage of national sport, complemented by a fast results service. PA Data Design creates camera-ready complete pages of sports results, share prices, racecards, TV listings and weather reports for printing by newspapers.

Extel Financial Ltd/AFP-Extel News Ltd

This agency, a joint venture of Agence France-Presse and Extel Financial Ltd, supplies information and services to financial and business communities throughout the world. Based in London, and now part of the Financial Times Group, Extel Financial has a network of offices in Europe, the United States and in the Asia Pacific region. Data is collected from all the world's major stock exchanges, companies and the international press. The company is a major source of reference material on companies and securities, and supplies up-to-the-minute business and company news.

Other Agencies

News services are also provided by Associated Press and United Press International, which are British subsidiaries of United States news agencies. A number of other agencies and news services have offices in London, and there are minor agencies in other cities. Syndication of features is not as common in Britain as in some countries, but a few agencies specialise in this type of work.

PRESS INSTITUTIONS

Trade associations include the Newspaper Publishers Association, whose members publish national newspapers, and the Newspaper Society, which represents regional and local newspapers in England, Wales and Northern Ireland. The Scottish Daily Newspaper Society represents the interests of daily and Sunday newspapers in Scotland; the Scottish Newspaper Publishers' Association acts on behalf of the owners of weekly newspapers in Scotland; and Associated Northern Ireland Newspapers is made up of proprietors of weekly newspapers in Northern Ireland. The membership of the Periodical Publishers Association includes most independent publishers of business, professional and consumer journals.

Organisations representing journalists are the National Union of Journalists, with nearly 25,000 members, and the Chartered Institute of Journalists, with about 1,500 members. The main printing union is the Graphical, Paper and Media Union, with a membership of around 270,000.

The Foreign Press Association was formed in 1888 to help the correspondents of overseas newspapers in their work by arranging press conferences, tours, briefings, and other services and facilities.

The Guild of Editors is the officially recognised professional body for newspaper editors. It has approximately 420 members and exists to defend press freedom and to promote high editorial standards. The British Association of Industrial Editors is the professional organisation for editors of house journals. The Association of British Editors represents the whole range of media, including radio, television, newspapers and magazines.

TRAINING AND EDUCATION

The National Council for the Training of Journalists (NCTJ), which represents many regional newspaper publishers, sets and conducts examinations, and organises short training courses for journalists.

The two main methods of entry into newspaper journalism are selection for a one-year NCTJ pre-entry course at a college of further or higher education or direct recruitment by a regional or local newspaper. Both types of entrant take part in 'on-the-job' training. Block-release courses, preceded by a period of distance learning, are provided for those who have not attended a pre-entry course. Similar courses exist for press photographers.

The first undergraduate courses in journalism in Britain started in 1991 at City University, London, at the University of Central Lancashire and at the London College of Printing, which also provides GCE (General Certificate of Education) Advanced (A) level courses in journalism. Postgraduate courses in journalism are available at the University of Wales College of Cardiff; City University, London; the London College of Printing; Strathclyde University/Glasgow Caledonian University; and the Universities of Central Lancashire and Bournemouth.

Courses for regional newspapers in such subjects as newspaper sales, advertising, and management are provided by the Newspaper Society's training service. Some newspaper publishers carry out journalist training independently of the NCTJ, awarding their own certificates or diplomas. New National Vocational Qualifications (see p. 425) are now available in newspaper journalism.

Specialist training courses for journalists and broadcasters from developing countries and from Eastern Europe are offered by the Thomson Foundation in Cardiff. The Foundation runs training courses overseas and provides consultants to assist newspapers and news agencies in editorial advertising as well as broadcast management. It runs an international journalism training centre in collaboration with Xinhua News Agency in Beijing.

Newspapers in Education, a worldwide scheme using newspapers to improve standards of literacy among young people, is run in Britain by the Newspaper Society. The scheme involves using newspapers in schools for teaching a wide range of subjects at all levels of education. Launched in Birmingham in 1984, the scheme has over 600 projects operated by regional newspapers in partnership with local schools.

Through its charitable trust, the Reuter Foundation, Reuters offers assistance to overseas journalists to study and train in Britain and other parts of the world. The Foundation awards fellowships to journalists from developing nations to spend up to one year at Oxford University. It also runs shorter practical training programmes in London for journalists from Eastern and Central Europe.

The Periodicals Training Council is the official training organisation in periodical publishing. It offers a range of short courses covering management, editorial work, advertisement sales and circulation sales. It has special responsibility for editorial training and administers an editorial training scheme for those already in employment.

PRESS CONDUCT AND LAW

There is no state control or censorship of the newspaper and periodical press, although newspaper proprietors, editors and journalists are subject to the law in the same way as any other citizen.

Readers' representatives have been appointed by most national papers to handle complaints. They also help to guarantee standards of accuracy, fairness and good behaviour on the part of journalists.

The Press Complaints Commission

The Press Complaints Commission, a non-statutory body, was established in 1991, following recommendations in a report on privacy and related matters by a government-appointed independent committee.

The Commission was set up by the newspaper and periodical industry in a final attempt to make self-regulation of the press work properly. It is funded by PRESSBOF (the Press Standards Board of Finance), which was set up in 1990 to co-ordinate and promote self-regulation within the industry. These measures were prompted by growing criticism of press standards, with allegations of unjustified invasion of privacy and inaccurate and biased reporting, among other abuses, resulting in calls for government regulation of the press.

The Commission's membership is drawn from newspaper and magazine editors and from people outside the industry. It deals with complaints by members of the public about the contents and conduct of newspapers and magazines, and advises editors and journalists. It operates a code of practice agreed by editors governing respect for privacy, opportunity to reply, corrections, journalists' behaviour, references to race and religion, payments to criminals for articles, protection of confidential sources and other matters. The Commission publishes regular reports of its findings.

In January 1993, a review of press self-regulation arrangements was published. The Government is reluctant to introduce, as the review recommended, a statutory complaints tribunal, but is considering possible legislative steps to deal with intrusion into personal privacy.

The industry and the Press Complaints Commission have reinforced voluntary regulation through:

- measures to increase the number of independent members of the Commission to ensure a lay majority;

- a strengthening of the code of practice;

- the setting up of a helpline service for members of the public who fear the code of practice has been, or is about to be, breached; and

- the appointment of a Privacy Commissioner with special powers to investigate urgent complaints about privacy.

Advertising Practice

Advertising in all non-broadcast media, such as newspapers, magazines, posters, sales promotions, cinema and direct mail, is regulated by the Advertising Standards Authority, an independent body funded by a levy on display advertising expenditure. The Authority aims to promote and enforce the highest standards of advertising in the interests of the public through its supervision of the British Codes of Advertising and Sales Promotion Practice.

The Codes' basic principles are to ensure that advertisements:

- are legal, decent, honest and truthful;

- are prepared with a sense of responsibility to the consumer and society; and

- conform to the principles of fair competition as generally accepted in business.

The Authority monitors advertisements to ensure their compliance with the Codes and investigates any complaints received.

The advertising industry has agreed to abide by the Codes and to support them with effective sanctions. Free and confidential pre–publication advice is offered to assist publishers, agencies and advertisers. The Authority's main sanction is the recommendation that advertisements considered to be in breach of the Code should not be published. This is normally sufficient to ensure that an advertisement is withdrawn or amended. The Authority also publishes monthly reports on the results of its investigations.

The Authority is recognised by the Office of Fair Trading as the established means of controlling non-broadcast advertising. The Authority can refer misleading advertisements to the Director General of Fair Trading, who has the power to seek an injunction to prevent their publication.

The Press and the Law

The press generally has the same freedom as the individual to comment on matters of public interest. No laws governing the content of the press are in operation, but certain statutes include sections which apply to the press.

There are laws governing:

- the extent of newspaper ownership in television and radio companies (see p. 475);

- the transfer of newspaper assets (see p. 475); and

- the right of press representatives to be supplied with agendas and reports for meetings of local authorities and reasonable facilities for taking notes and telephoning reports.

There is a legal requirement to reproduce 'the printer's imprint' (the printer's name and address) on all publications, including newspapers. Publishers are legally obliged to deposit copies of newspapers and other publications at the British Library (see p. 459).

Publication of advertisements is governed by wide-ranging legislation, including public health, financial services and fraud legislation. Legal restrictions are imposed on certain types of prize competition; copyrights come under various copyright laws.

Laws on contempt of court, official secrets and defamation are also relevant to the press. A newspaper may not publish comments on the conduct of judicial proceedings which are likely to prejudice the reputation of the courts for fairness before or during the actual proceedings, nor may it publish before or during a trial anything which might influence the result. The unauthorised acquisition and publication of official information in such areas as defence and international relations are offences under the Official Secrets Acts 1911 to 1989, where unauthorised disclosure would be harmful. However, these are restrictions on publication—that is, on dissemination to the public by any means—not just through the printed press.

Most legal proceedings against the press are libel actions brought by private individuals. In such cases, the editor, proprietor, publishers, printer and distributor of the newspaper, as well as the author, may all be held responsible.

Defence Advisory Notices

Government officials and representatives of the media form the Defence, Press and Broadcasting Advisory Committee, which has agreed that in some circumstances the publication of certain categories of information might endanger national security. Details of these categories are contained in Defence Advisory Notices (D Notices) circulated to the media, whose members are asked to seek advice from the Secretary of the Committee, a retired senior military officer, before publishing information in these areas. Compliance with any advice offered by the Secretary is expected but there is no legal force behind it and the final decision on whether to publish rests with the editor, producer or publisher concerned.

The Notices were published for the first time in July 1993 to promote a better understanding of the system and to contribute to greater openness in government (see p. 68).

Further Reading

The Future of the BBC: Serving the Nation, Competing World-wide. Cm 2621. HMSO, 1994.
Broadcasting. Aspects of Britain series, HMSO, 1993.

30 Sport and Active Recreation

There is widespread participation in sport in Britain, with the most popular activities ranging from swimming to snooker. Internationally, British sportsmen and women compete in about 70 different sports, and in 1994 British teams took part in a number of major championships, including the Commonwealth Games, the European Athletics Championships and the Winter Olympics. Britain has more than 80 world champions in over 30 sports.

PARTICIPATION

Improvements in facilities and growing awareness of the importance of regular exercise for good health have contributed to increasing levels of participation in sport.

It is estimated that 29 million people over the age of 16 regularly take part in sport or exercise. The *1990 General Household Survey* found that almost two-thirds of those interviewed had taken part in at least one sporting activity during the previous four weeks. The most popular participation sports or activities are walking (including rambling and hiking), swimming, snooker/pool, keep fit/yoga and cycling.

Women and Sport

A major effort was made in the 1980s to narrow the gap between men's and women's participation in sport and active recreation. This resulted in an increase between 1987 and 1990 of about 1 million in the number of women taking part in sport, including traditionally male-dominated sports, such as football, rugby and snooker.

During the 1990s emphasis has switched to encouraging women to adopt leadership roles, such as coaches, officials and administrators. Projects to promote coaching opportunities have been established by the Sports Councils (see p. 487) in partnership with the National Coaching Foundation (see p. 489) and the Women's Sports Foundation (WSF). Additional ways of encouraging women to become involved in sport at all levels and in all roles were outlined by the Sports Council in November 1993 in a policy document on women and sport.

The WSF is a voluntary organisation promoting the interests of women and girls in sport and active recreation. With Sports Council funding, the WSF encourages the establishment of women's sports groups throughout Britain and organises a wide range of events and activities. In 1986 it initiated the Sportswomen of the Year Awards and in 1992 it launched an annual nationwide awards scheme for girls and young women between the ages of 11 and 19.

In May 1994 an international conference on Women and Sport was held in Brighton. The event, organised by the Sports Council and the British Olympic Association, aimed to:

● discuss the best ways of bringing about change at national and international level; and

● agree international strategies for the development of women and sport.

Ethnic Minorities

The Sports Councils are encouraging local authorities and governing bodies to become more sensitive to the needs of minority groups in their communities. For example, in Yorkshire a network of contacts has been created within the black communities to involve ethnic minorities in cricket. The project is now being extended to some other sports.

Many sports, such as athletics, boxing, football, rugby union and rugby league, have already been successful in attracting significant numbers of participants from the ethnic minorities.

Young People

Special programmes of activity for young people are run by the governing bodies of individual sports. In addition, the four Sports Councils organise local and national initiatives to encourage more young people to take part in sport (see p. 487). In 1993 the Sports Council launched a new policy document—*Young People and Sport*—which provides practical advice to governing bodies, sports clubs, local authorities and schools on how to help young people take part in and enjoy sport.

The Sports Council is developing a national programme for sport and young people, which aims to develop sport at a local level for young people between the ages of 5 and 18. It is due to be launched later in 1994.

In Northern Ireland a report on the development of sporting opportunities for young people was launched in 1993.

Sport for People with Disabilities

The governing bodies of sport are increasingly taking responsibility for both able-bodied participants and those with disabilities. Close liaison takes place between individual sports and the Sports Council, which provides advice to governing bodies on encouraging the integration of people with disabilities.

The key organisations for people with disabilities are the British Sports Association for the Disabled (BSAD), the United Kingdom Sports Association for People with Learning Disability (UKSAPLD), the British Paralympic Association (BPA—see p. 489) and a range of bodies concerned with individual disabilities and single sports. These include the Riding for the Disabled Association, which caters for some 25,000 riders.

The BSAD is a national body working across all the disabilities. It organises regional and national championships in a wide range of sports and also runs training courses, coaching courses and development days. The Scottish Sports Association for the Disabled, the Federation of Sports Associations for the Disabled (Wales) and Disability Action (Northern Ireland) have similar co-ordinating roles.

The UKSAPLD is a co-ordinating body with a membership of over 20 national organisations. The Association promotes and develops opportunities in sport and recreation for people with learning disability throughout Britain. It is also responsible, in partnership with the BPA, for the training and preparation of the Great Britain team in the Paralympics.

There are six national disability sports organisations concerned with individual disabilities. These organisations provide coaching and help to organise national competitions in conjunction with the national governing bodies of sport and the BSAD. They comprise:

● the British Amputee Sports Association;

- British Blind Sport;
- the British Deaf Sports Council;
- the British Wheelchair Sports Foundation;
- Cerebral Palsy Sport; and
- the British Les Autres Sports Association, which caters for those whose disabilities are not covered by other organisations.

SPORT IN SCHOOLS

All schools (except those solely for infants) are expected to have a playing field or the use of one, and most secondary schools have a gymnasium. Some have other amenities such as swimming pools, sports halls and halls designed for dance and movement.

National Curriculum

The Government believes that all young children should have the opportunity to learn basic sports skills. It has therefore made physical education (PE), which includes sport, a compulsory subject in the National Curriculum (see p. 418) for all pupils aged 5 to 16 in state-maintained schools in England and Wales. Pupils will also be required from autumn 1994 to have been taught to swim at least 25 metres by the age of 11.

In Scotland the Secretary of State for Scotland has issued National Guidelines which contain programmes of study and attainment targets for physical activity for pupils aged 5 to 14.

Partnerships with the Local Community

The Government is encouraging stronger links between schools and the wider community to ensure that children have access to the sports amenities which clubs and associations can make available outside school hours.

In Scotland an initiative aimed at strengthening the links between schools, clubs and the community was launched by the Scottish Sports Council in 1991. 'Team Sport Scotland' seeks to promote the development of school-aged team sport and has been supported in its first three years through Scottish Office assistance of over £400,000. In 1993 more than 5,000 youngsters took part in Team Sport festivals, and 4,250 coaches, teachers and leaders benefited from coaching courses in the nine sports covered by the initiative.

In 1991 the Government launched a new guide—*A Sporting Double: School and Community*—to encourage and assist the sharing of school facilities with the local community. The Education Act 1993 includes new provisions to allow school governors to enter into agreements for the joint management of school premises for community purposes.

TELEVISED SPORT

Most of the major sporting events throughout the year, such as the Wimbledon lawn tennis championships and the Open Golf Championship, receive extensive television coverage and are watched by millions of viewers. The biggest television audiences for a single event in 1993 were for:

1 Horse racing: the Grand National (16.5 million viewers);

2 Boxing: Chris Eubank v. Nigel Benn (16.4 million);

3 World Cup football: Holland v. England (14.1 million);

4 Boxing: Frank Bruno v. Hank Williams (14.0 million); and

5 FA (Football Association) Cup Final replay: Arsenal v. Sheffield Wednesday (13.4 million).

> The biggest ever audience for a sporting event shown on one channel was achieved in February 1994, when some 23 million viewers watched Jayne Torvill and Christopher Dean take part in the ice dance competition at the Winter Olympics (see p. 500).

Following the introduction of direct broadcasting by satellite (DBS) and the greater availability of cable, the amount of televised coverage has increased substantially.

Important sporting occasions ('listed events'), such as the Olympic Games, may not be shown exclusively by DBS or cable and must be made generally available to television viewers.

On terrestrial television the sports which receive the most coverage are football, horse racing, snooker and cricket.

ORGANISATION AND ADMINISTRATION

Responsibility for government policy on sport and active recreation in England rests with the Secretary of State for National Heritage. The Secretaries of State for Wales, Scotland and Northern Ireland are responsible for sport in their countries.

Responsibility for the organisation and promotion of sport is largely decentralised, and many sport and recreation facilities are provided by local authorities. The main mechanism by which the Government directly channels financial assistance to sport is through the Sports Councils.

Sports Councils

The Sports Councils, appointed and directly funded by the Government, are the Government's principal advisers on sporting matters. The Government works closely with them in implementing its sports policies.

There are four Councils:

- the Sports Council—for general matters affecting Great Britain and specifically English matters;

- the Sports Council for Wales;

- the Scottish Sports Council; and

- the Sports Council for Northern Ireland.

The Councils make grants for sports development, coaching and administration to the governing bodies of sports and other national organisations, and administer the National Sports Centres (see p. 490). Grants and loans are also made to voluntary organisations, local authorities and commercial organisations to help them provide sports facilities. For 1994–95 the Councils have been allocated government funds of approximately £67 million.

Facilities receiving support from the Sports Councils include sports halls, indoor swimming pools, intensive-use pitches, indoor tennis halls and school facilities.

In 1992–93 the Sports Council contributed more than £1 million towards the construction of sports halls in England. Twenty-four were completed during the year and a further 14 were under construction. Other recent support includes a grant of £1.5 million towards the development of a National Hockey Stadium at Milton Keynes. In Scotland a number of national, regional and demonstration projects were completed in 1993 with support from the Scottish Sports Council. These include the opening of a national water skiing centre at Town Loch near Dunfermline.

The Sports Council for Wales provided some £350,000 in grants for capital purposes in 1992–93. In Northern Ireland the Department of Education transferred its capital grants role to the Sports Council for Northern Ireland in April 1994.

Development of Sport

Strategies for the development of sport have been drawn up by the four Sports Councils. The aims are broadly to ensure that:

- all young people have the opportunity to acquire basic sports skills;

- everyone has the opportunity to take part in the sports or active recreation of their choice; and

- everyone with the interest and the ability has the opportunity to improve their standard of performance in sport and fulfil their potential.

Much of the Sports Councils' budget is directed at increasing participation by the general public. The Councils are concentrating in particular on raising participation rates among young inner city dwellers and people with disabilities.

Restructuring

In July 1994 the Government announced that the Sports Council covering Great Britain and English matters would be replaced during 1995–96 by two new bodies: the United Kingdom Sports Council (UKSC) and the English Sports Council. The UKSC would have ten members: an independent chairman; the chairmen of the four other sports councils; representatives of the British Olympic Association, of amateur non-Olympic sport and of professional sport; and two independent members, one from a professional and one from an amateur sporting background.

The UKSC would represent Britain and seek to increase its influence in international sport, with a co-ordinating role for bringing major international events to Britain. It would not have a supervisory role, but instead would oversee areas where the Government considers that there is a need for a policy covering the whole of Britain. These include doping control, sports science, sports medicine and coaching. The Government would be inviting the UKSC to consult and then introduce proposals for the establishment of an effective confederation of non-governmental sports interests in Britain.

The Government's intention is that the new English Sports Council would have a sharper focus and concentrate its resources on an increased programme of direct support to sporting governing bodies, to help the 'grass roots' of sport, and on services in support of sporting excellence, such as the National Sports Centres in England. The new council would be expected to give greater support to the pursuit of high standards of sporting achievement, concentrating a greater proportion of its funding on fewer sports than at present. Governing bodies would be required to prepare plans with specific targets for the development of their sports, from the grass roots to the highest competitive levels.

Local Authorities

Local authorities are the main providers of basic sport and recreation facilities for the local community. In England local authorities manage over 1,500 indoor centres, largely built in the last 20 years, as well as numerous outdoor amenities. The facilities include parks, lakes, playing fields, sports halls, tennis courts, golf courses, swimming pools, gymnasiums and sports centres catering for a wide range of activities.

There has been a rapid growth in the provision of artificial pitches—largely for hockey—and a similar increase in the number of leisure pools, which offer wave machines, waterfalls, jacuzzis and other leisure equipment. Gross annual expenditure by local authorities on sport and recreation amounts to over £1,000 million in England alone.

National Sports Associations

The Central Council of Physical Recreation (CCPR) is the largest sport and recreation federation in the world. It comprises 202 British bodies and 66 English associations, most of which are governing bodies. Similar associations in Scotland, Wales and Northern Ireland are the Scottish Sports Association, the Welsh Sports Association and the Northern Ireland Council of Physical Recreation (NICPR). Their primary aim is to represent the interests of their members to the appropriate national and local authorities, including the Sports Councils, from which they receive funding. Award schemes run by the associations include the CCPR's Community Sports Leaders Award scheme and the NICPR's Service to Sport Awards.

In 1985 the CCPR set up the Institute of Sports Sponsorship (ISS). Comprising some 80 British companies involved in the sponsorship of sport, the ISS aims to develop sponsorship at local, national and international level.

Sports Governing Bodies

Individual sports are run by over 400 independent governing bodies, whose functions include drawing up rules, holding events, regulating membership, selecting and training national teams. Governing bodies receiving grant in aid from the Sports Council are required to produce four-year development plans for their sports. There are also organisations representing people who take part in more informal physical recreation, such as walking and cycling. The majority of the sports clubs in Britain belong to the appropriate governing body.

Sports Clubs

A wide variety of recreational facilities are provided by local sports clubs. Some cater for indoor recreation, but more common are those providing sports grounds, particularly for cricket, football, rugby, hockey, tennis and golf. There are approximately 150,000 sports clubs in Britain, with about 6.5 million members. Many clubs linked to business firms cater for sporting activities. Commercial facilities include tenpin bowling centres, ice and roller-skating rinks, squash courts, golf courses and driving ranges, riding stables, marinas and, increasingly, fitness centres. In all, the private sector owns and runs some 500 major sports facilities.

Countryside Bodies

The Countryside Commission (for England), the Countryside Council for Wales and Scottish Natural Heritage are responsible for conserving and improving the natural beauty of the countryside, and for encouraging the provision of facilities for open-air recreation. The three bodies assist in the provision or improvement of recreational parks, country parks and picnic sites and the opening up of rights of way and National Trails.

In Northern Ireland the Ulster Countryside Committee advises the Department of the Environment on the preservation of amenities and the designation of 'areas of outstanding natural beauty'.

British Waterways

British Waterways is a publicly owned body responsible for managing and developing much of Great Britain's inland waterways. Many leisure and recreational pursuits, such as angling and various types of sailing and boating, are enjoyed on waterways and reservoirs. British Waterways, which is responsible for approximately 2,000 miles (3,220 km) of canals and water navigations, actively promotes water safety and organises community activities.

National Coaching Foundation

The National Coaching Foundation (NCF) works closely with national governing bodies of sport, local authorities, and higher and further education. Supported by the Sports Councils, it provides a comprehensive range of coach education and coaching development services for coaches in all sports. The NCF network has 15 national coaching centres in Britain.

The NCF also runs Champion Coaching, a scheme which provides after-school coaching in 16 sports throughout Britain for those aged 11 to 14. In 1993–94 there were 65 projects, with about 50,000 children and 6,000 coaches participating.

British Olympic Association

The British Olympic Association (BOA) is the National Olympic Committee for Britain and comprises representatives of the 33 governing bodies of Olympic sports. Its primary function is to organise the participation of British teams in the Olympic Games, but it is also responsible for nominating British cities for staging the Olympics.

The BOA determines the size of British Olympic teams and sets standards for selection, raises funds and makes all necessary arrangements. It also makes important contributions in the fields of coaching, drug testing and control, and sports medicine. The Association's British Olympic Medical Centre at Northwick Park Hospital in north London supplies a medical back-up service for competitors before and during the Olympic Games.

The BOA is supported by sponsorship and by donations from the private sector and the public.

British Paralympic Association

Britain's participation in the Paralympics is organised by the BPA, which liaises closely with the BOA. The BPA assists in the preparation and training of Paralympic and other international teams, and advises the Sports Council on the distribution of grants for all international disabled sports events.

National Playing Fields Association

The National Playing Fields Association (NPFA) is a registered charity which aims to ensure that there are adequate playing fields and playspace available for use by the community. There are affiliated associations in the English and Welsh counties and independent organisations in Scotland and Northern Ireland.

A major study of England's recreational land was completed in 1993 as part of a strategy to safeguard playing fields. The £500,000 project, funded by the Department of National Heritage, was commissioned by the Sports Council, the NPFA and the CCPR. The Register of Recreational Land is the first comprehensive record of England's sports pitches and their facilities. It reveals that England has over 73,000 pitches on about 24,000 sites, about half of which are owned by education authorities. The Register will be used in future sports planning and management and will be regularly updated.

Commonwealth Games Bid by Manchester

Manchester has been selected as England's candidate for the Commonwealth Games of 2002. A number of the facilities are already under construction, including an indoor arena. Britain's first indoor velodrome—the National Cycling Centre—was opened in September 1994. Both facilities were assisted by government grants of £35 million and £8 million respectively and had originally been planned as part of Manchester's ultimately unsuccessful bid to stage the 2000 Olympic Games. Manchester is seeking additional public and private sector support to build a £187 million stadium.

The Commonwealth Games Federation will decide the host of the 2002 event in November 1995. Britain last staged the Games in 1986, when they were hosted by Edinburgh.

NATIONAL SPORTS CENTRES

The four Sports Councils operate a total of 12 National Sports Centres, which provide world-class facilities for training and competition at the highest level. First priority at the Centres is given to the governing bodies of sport for national squad training and for the training of coaches. However, the Centres also make their facilities available to top sportsmen and women for individual training and to the local community. All of the Centres provide residential facilities.

England

In England the Sports Council operates four major National Centres and a minor National Centre for climbers at Harrison's Rocks in Kent. A fifth major National Sports Centre— the National Cycling Centre—was opened in Manchester in 1994 (see above).

Crystal Palace in London is a leading competition venue for a wide range of sports and a major training centre for national squads, clubs, schools and serious enthusiasts. Its facilities are used by over 20 separate governing bodies of sport, and the Centre is a regional centre of excellence for athletics, netball, weightlifting and swimming. Crystal Palace stadium is Britain's major international athletics venue, with capacity for 17,000 spectators. Other facilities include an Olympic-size swimming pool and a Sports Injury Centre.

Bisham Abbey in Berkshire caters for a number of sports, including tennis, football, hockey, weightlifting, squash, rugby and golf. The England football, rugby and hockey squads all train at the Centre. Bisham Abbey has long-standing partnerships with the British Amateur Weightlifters Association and the Lawn Tennis Association, which has helped to develop the Abbey as the National Tennis Training Centre.

Lilleshall National Sports Centre in Shropshire offers extensive sports facilities, which are used by a variety of national teams. Facilities include a world-class gymnastic training centre, regularly used by the British gymnastic squads, and extensive playing fields for football and hockey. The Football Association uses Lilleshall as its base for major coaching activities and has established a training school there.

The National Watersports Centre at

Holme Pierrepont in Nottinghamshire is one of the most comprehensive water sports centres in the world, with facilities for rowing, canoeing, water skiing, powerboating, ski-racing, angling and sailing. Its main feature is a 2,000-metre regatta course.

Wales

The Sports Council for Wales runs two National Sports Centres: the Welsh Institute of Sport and the National Watersports Centre. A further Centre—Plas y Brenin—is run by the Sports Council.

The Welsh Institute of Sport in Cardiff is the country's premier venue for top-level training and for competition in a large number of sports. Facilities include a world-standard gymnastics hall, a sports science laboratory and a sports injury clinic.

The National Watersports Centre at Plas Menai in north Wales is primarily a centre of excellence for sailing and canoeing, with an extensive range of activities including dinghy and catamaran sailing, offshore cruising and powerboat training.

Plas y Brenin National Mountain Centre, situated in Snowdonia National Park in north Wales, offers a variety of courses in rock climbing, mountaineering, sea and river canoeing, orienteering, skiing and most other mountain-based activities.

Scotland

Scotland has three National Sports Centres, which are operated by the Scottish Sports Council.

The National Outdoor Training Centre at Glenmore Lodge near Aviemore caters for a wide range of activities, including hill walking, rock climbing, mountaineering, kayaking, skiing and canoeing. Its main purpose is to provide top-quality training for those who intend to lead or instruct others in outdoor activities. The Centre recently underwent a £1.6 million refurbishment.

The Inverclyde National Sports Training Centre at Largs has a large number of facilities, including a gymnastics hall, a purpose-built golf training facility and a laboratory for fitness assessment. The

Centre also acts as an important competition venue for major national and international championships. Facilities were improved during 1993 with the assistance of major investment from the Scottish Sports Council.

The Cumbrae National Water Sports Training Centre on the island of Great Cumbrae in the Firth of Clyde offers an extensive range of courses catering for all levels of ability. The Centre has a comprehensive range of modern craft for a wide variety of sailing activities, as well as sub-aqua diving equipment.

Northern Ireland

The Northern Ireland Centre for Outdoor Activities at Tollymore in County Down, run by the Sports Council for Northern Ireland, offers courses in mountaineering, rock climbing, canoeing and outdoor adventure. Also available are leadership and instructor courses leading to nationally recognised qualifications.

A new Northern Ireland Sports Centre is being built at Upper Malone, Belfast, with the assistance of a £1 million grant from the Foundation for Sport and the Arts (see p. 492). The Centre's first facilities (synthetic pitches) are expected to be ready in autumn 1994.

SPONSORSHIP AND OTHER FUNDING

Sport is a major industry in Britain. In addition to professional sportsmen and women, over 450,000 people are employed in the provision of sports clothing, publicity, ground and club maintenance and other activities connected with sport. In total an estimated £9,750 million is spent on sport annually in Britain. The private sector makes a substantial investment in sports sponsorship, contributing over £250 million a year. This involves more than 2,000 British companies.

Sponsorship may take the form of financing specific events, or of grants to individual sports organisations or sportsmen and women. Investment includes sponsorship of cricket and football leagues, sporting events such as horse races, and of individual performers. Motor sport and football receive the largest amounts of private sponsorship.

Sponsorship of sport is encouraged by a number of bodies, including:

- the Institute of Sports Sponsorship (ISS—see p. 488);

- the Sports Sponsorship Advisory Service, administered by the CCPR and funded by the Sports Council, which has helped sporting bodies to raise over £1 million in England over the last three years;

- the Scottish Sports Council's Sponsorship Advisory Service, which has raised almost £3 million directly for Scottish sport over the last ten years; and

- the Sports Council for Wales's Sponsorship Advisory Service, which generated about £158,000 for Welsh sport in 1992–93.

Successive governments have negotiated voluntary agreements with the tobacco industry to regulate tobacco companies' sponsorship of sport.

Business Sponsorship Incentive Scheme

In 1992 the Government launched the Business Sponsorship Incentive Scheme, known as Sportsmatch. The purpose of the scheme is to increase the amount of business sponsorship going into 'grass roots' sport and physical recreation. The scheme offers matching funding for new sponsorships and extension of existing sponsorships. In England funding is subject to a minimum of £1,000 and a maximum of £75,000; in Scotland and Wales the minimum is £500 and in Wales the maximum is £25,000. Government funds for the scheme total £4.1 million in 1994–95. Priority is given for projects involving groups such as the young, disabled people, ethnic minorities and for projects in deprived areas.

In England the ISS runs the scheme on behalf of the Department of National Heritage. In Scotland and Wales the scheme is administered by the appropriate Sports Council. Northern Ireland has its own sports sponsorship incentive scheme, which is currently being reviewed.

Sports Aid Foundation

The Sports Aid Foundation raises and distributes funds from industry, commerce and private sponsors in order to assist the training of talented individuals. Grants are awarded on the recommendation of the appropriate governing bodies of sport to British competitors who need help preparing for Olympic, World and European championships. The Scottish and Welsh Sports Aid Foundations and the Ulster Sports and Recreation Trust have similar functions.

Foundation for Sport and the Arts

The Foundation for Sport and the Arts was set up by the football pools promoters in 1991 to channel funds into sport and the arts. The pools promoters are providing the Foundation with some £43.5 million a year. A further £21.8 million a year is received as a result of the 2.5 per cent reduction in pool betting duty in the 1990 Budget. About £43.5 million a year is available for sport.

The Foundation works closely with the Sports Councils and other sports bodies, and makes numerous grants to sports clubs and sporting organisations.

Recent assistance includes:

- a grant of £36,000 to the Lodge Moor Spinal Unit Sports Club in Sheffield to provide two racing sail yachts and a sailing yacht for cruises; and

- £75,000 to the Sports Council for Northern Ireland Trust to assist with the refurbishment of the National Sports Centre at Tollymore (see p. 491).

Horserace Betting Levy

Most betting in Britain takes place on horse racing and greyhound racing. Bets may be made at racecourses and greyhound tracks, or through over 9,000 licensed off-course betting offices, which take about 90 per cent of the money staked. A form of pool betting—totalisator betting—is organised on racecourses by the Horserace Totalisator Board (the Tote). Racecourse bets may also be placed with independent on-course bookmakers.

Bookmakers and the Tote contribute an annual levy—a fixed proportion of their turnover—to the Horserace Betting Levy Board. The amount of levy payable is decided by the racing and bookmaking industries or, in cases where agreement cannot be achieved, by the Home Secretary. The Levy Board promotes the improvement of horse breeds, advancement of veterinary science and the improvement of horse racing.

In 1991–92 the total money staked in all forms of gambling, excluding gaming machines, was estimated at £24,594 million.

National Lottery

The National Lottery is expected to generate substantial additional funds for sport when it comes into operation in November 1994. In accordance with the National Lottery etc. Act 1993, the Lottery will be run by a private sector company which was chosen through a competitive tendering process by the regulator, the Director General of the National Lottery.

> Camelot Group plc has been selected to operate the National Lottery. It estimates that the annual turnover could rise to a peak of £5,500 million, with £1,600 million being available for distribution to good causes.

The net proceeds will be equally divided between charities, the arts, sport, heritage and projects to mark the millennium. Independent bodies have been given the responsibility for distributing these funds within each sector. For sport the national Sports Councils will make the funding decisions, in accordance with directions issued by the Secretary of State for National Heritage.

SPORTS MEDICINE AND SCIENCE

Sports Medicine

The National Sports Medicine Institute was set up by the Sports Council in 1991 to provide clinical services aimed at assessing and improving fitness as well as treating and preventing sports injuries. Based at St Bartholomew's Hospital, London, its facilities include a physiology laboratory and an information centre.

Work is in progress to develop a network of regional centres to provide both clinical and educational services, which will be linked with new support services at the National Sports Centres. The Sports Council is allocating £575,000 towards sports medicine in 1994–95. In Scotland a network of about 30 sports medicine centres has been created.

Sports Injuries

The adult population of England and Wales experience 19 million sports injuries a year, according to a report published by the Sports Council in 1993. Based on research undertaken at Sheffield University Medical School, *Injuries in Sport and Exercise* aims to identify for the first time the extent of sports injuries in Britain and some of the possible causes. The Sports Council plans to use the research to improve sports medicine services. The report reveals that:

- three-quarters of sports injuries are suffered by men;
- half of the injuries occur in the age group 16 to 25; and
- the largest number of injuries occur in association football—however, the sport with the highest risk rate is rugby (one injury for every 20 playing occasions).

Sports Science

The development of sports science support services for the national governing bodies of sport is being promoted by the Sports Councils, in collaboration with the BOA and the NCF, in an effort to raise the standards of performance of national squads. Some 34 sports governing bodies receive financial support. In 1994–95 the Sports Council is contributing £672,000 in support of sports science studies. The Sports Council for Wales received £250,000 from the Welsh Office in 1992–93 to establish a sports science service at the Welsh Institute of Sport (see p. 491).

Drug Abuse in Sport

The Sports Council introduced a new independent drug testing regime in 1988. This provides for random testing in and out of competition by independent sampling officers, and the publication of adverse findings. The Council also funds an international laboratory, accredited by the International Olympic Committee, at King's College, London University, which carries out analysis and research into methods of detection for new drugs which unfairly aid performance.

The Sports Council has intensified its drugs-testing programme, with greater emphasis being placed on out-of-competition tests. There were 47 positive reports in 1993–94, compared with 58 in 1992–93. Anabolic agents continue to be the substance most regularly discovered. Funding in Britain by the four Sports Councils for the programme exceeded £910,000 in 1993–94.

The Sports Council for Northern Ireland launched a Schools' Education Pack in 1993, aimed at 9- to 16-year-olds, as part of its campaign against drug abuse in sport.

International Action

In 1990 the Council of Europe developed an Anti-doping Convention to tackle the problem of drug abuse in sport. Its main aim is to provide an international framework within which national anti-doping campaigns can work effectively. Britain has fully implemented the provisions of the convention.

The Fourth Permanent World Conference on Anti-doping in Sport took place in London in 1993. The conference was organised by the Sports Council in association with the IOC Medical Commission and brought together more than 200 experts on drugs in sport from 60 countries. The conference examined anti-doping developments throughout the world, why competitors take drugs and how they obtain them, and the views of the next generation of competitors on drug abuse.

SPECTATOR SAFETY

Safety at sports grounds is governed by legislation. The main instrument of control is a safety certificate which is issued by the relevant local authority. When determining the conditions of a safety certificate, the local authority is expected to comply with the *Guide to Safety at Sports Grounds*. This was revised in 1990 to include the relevant safety recommendations of the Taylor Report on the Hillsborough stadium disaster in Sheffield in 1989, which resulted in the death of 96 spectators.

The Taylor Report

The Taylor Report, published in 1990, contained 76 recommendations for promoting better and safer conditions at all sports grounds. Its major recommendation was that standing accommodation should be eliminated at all grounds designated under the Safety of Sports Grounds Act 1975. The Government accepted the report but limited the all-seating requirement to football in view of the particular problems of safety and crowd control in that sport. It set a timetable for all-seater football stadiums.

Following a review of the policy in 1992, the timetable was modified. Clubs in the Second and Third Divisions of the Football League are permitted to keep some standing accommodation, providing that the terracing is safe. In England and Wales the all-seater policy is being enforced through licences issued by the Football Licensing Authority. Conditions in these licences require Premier League and First Division clubs to have all-seater grounds by a specified date; in the majority of cases this is 1 August 1994.

In Scotland the all-seating policy is being implemented through a voluntary agreement under the direction of the Scottish football authorities.

The Football Trust

The Football Trust was founded in 1990 by the football pools companies, and provides grant aid to help football clubs at all levels. Its income is about £37 million a year and it is funded partly by the pools companies from their spot-the-ball competition and partly from a 2.5 per cent reduction in pool betting duty. This concession was announced in the 1990 Budget and was originally for five years. By 1995 the concession will have provided over £100 million to football on the understanding that the money is used to assist clubs in the Premier League, the Football League and the Scottish Football League to finance projects to improve the comfort and safety of spectators in line with the Taylor Report recommendations.

The Government has agreed to extend the concession for a further five years from March 1995 in order to help clubs in the lower divisions of the Football League and the Scottish Football League to meet the safe terracing requirements.

Crowd Control

The Government has worked closely with the police, football authorities and the governments of other European countries to implement crowd control measures.

Legislation has made it an offence in England and Wales to throw objects at football matches, run onto the playing area or chant indecent or racist abuse. There are also controls on the sale and possession of alcohol at football grounds and on transport to and from grounds.

Courts in England and Wales have the power to prohibit convicted football hooligans from attending football matches. They also have powers to impose restriction orders on convicted football hooligans to prevent them travelling abroad to attend specified matches. The National Criminal Intelligence Service Football Unit co-ordinates police intelligence about football hooligans and liaises with overseas police forces.

A TO Z OF POPULAR SPORTS

Some of the major sports in Britain are described below. Additional information on these and other sports not covered here can be found in *A Digest of Sports Statistics for the UK*, published by the Sports Council.

Angling

One of the most popular countryside sports is angling, of which there are three main types: coarse, game and sea.

Angling is an overwhelmingly male sport, with an estimated ten times as many male as female participants among Britain's 4 million anglers. Many fish for salmon and trout, particularly in the rivers and lochs of Scotland and in Wales. In England and Wales the most widely practised form of angling is for coarse fish. Separate organisations represent game, coarse and sea fishing clubs in England, Wales, Scotland and Northern Ireland.

The National Federation of Anglers in England organises national championships for coarse fishing and enters a team in the world angling championships.

Athletics

Athletics is governed in Britain by the British Athletic Federation (BAF), which is affiliated to the International Amateur Athletic Federation. The BAF is responsible for the selection of British teams for international events, and also administers coaching schemes. For the Olympic Games and the World and European championships one team represents Britain.

Athletics is attracting increasing numbers of participants. In recent years there has been a significant growth in mass participation events, such as marathons and half marathons. The London Marathon, which takes place every spring, regularly attracts over 25,000 runners.

Recent successes at international level include two gold medals at the 1993 World Indoor Athletics Championships in Toronto, Canada—Yvonne Murray in the 3,000 metres and Tom McKean in the 800 metres—and three gold medals at the 1993 World Athletics Championships in Stuttgart. Britain's gold medallists were Linford Christie in the 100 metres, Colin Jackson in the 110 metres hurdles (in a new world record) and Sally Gunnell in the 400 metres hurdles, also in a world record. Britain won a total of ten medals in Stuttgart and finished fourth in the overall medals table. Britain's men's team was second in the World Cup, held at Crystal Palace in September 1994.

Badminton

Badminton is organised by the Badminton Association of England and the Scottish, Welsh and Irish (Ulster branch) Badminton Unions. Around 5 million people play badminton in Britain and there are over 5,000 clubs. Most clubs do not own their own facilities but hire courts from local authority sports centres, schools and churches. Badminton was introduced into the Olympics in 1992.

In 1994 the world's major team event—the Thomas and Uber Cup—held its preliminary rounds in Glasgow.

Basketball

In Britain over 750,000 people participate in basketball. The English Basket Ball Association is the governing body in England, and there are similar associations in Wales, Scotland and Northern Ireland. All the associations are represented on the British and Irish Basketball Federation, which acts as the co-ordinating body for Britain and the Irish Republic.

The leading clubs play in the National Basketball Leagues. Mini-basketball and micro-basketball are versions of the game which have been developed for players under the age of 13.

Wheelchair basketball is played under the same rules, with a few basic adaptations, and on the same court as the running game. Over 30 teams play in the National League.

Bowls

The two main forms of bowls are lawn (flat green and crown green) and indoor bowls. The game is increasingly enjoyed by adults of all ages. In recent years the most notable increases have been in the number of women taking part. Bowls is also popular among people with disabilities.

About 4,000 lawn bowling clubs are affiliated to the English, Scottish, Welsh and Irish (Northern Ireland Region) Bowling Associations, which, together with Women's Bowling Associations for the four countries, play to the rules of the International Bowling Board. The British Crown Green Bowling Association is the governing body of crown green bowls and the indoor game in England is administered by the English Indoor Bowling Association. Similar associations exist for Scotland, Wales and Northern Ireland and there are separate women's associations in each country.

In 1993 Richard Corsie won the world indoor singles championships for the third time in five years.

Boxing

Boxing in Britain is both amateur and professional, and in both strict medical regulations are observed.

All amateur boxing in England is controlled by the Amateur Boxing Association of England. There are separate associations in Scotland and Wales, and boxing in Northern Ireland is controlled by the Irish Boxing Association. The associations organise amateur boxing championships as well as training courses for referees, coaches and others. The wearing of headguards is now compulsory in all British amateur competitions.

Professional boxing is controlled by the British Boxing Board of Control. The Board appoints inspectors, medical officers and representatives to ensure that regulations are observed and to guard against overmatching and exploitation. Britain currently has three world champions: Chris Eubank (World Boxing Organisation—WBO—super-middleweight champion), Nigel Benn (World Boxing Council super-middleweight) and Steve Robinson (WBO featherweight).

Cricket

The Marylebone Cricket Club (MCC), which frames the laws of the game, and the Test and County Cricket Board (TCCB), which represents first-class cricket, are both based at Lord's cricket ground in north London, the administrative centre of the world game. Men's cricket in Britain is governed by the Cricket Council, consisting of representatives of the TCCB, the National Cricket Association (NCA—representing club and junior cricket), the Minor Counties Association, the Scottish Cricket Union, the Irish Cricket Union and the MCC.

Following an inquiry in 1993–94 into the organisation of cricket, the Griffiths Working Party recommended the setting up of a single body to guide the development of the game at both professional and amateur level. This would replace the Cricket Council, the TCCB and the NCA.

Cricket is played in schools, colleges and universities, and amateur teams play weekly games in cities, towns and villages from late April to the end of September. Throughout Britain there is a network of league cricket, minor counties and club games.

The main competition in professional cricket is the Britannic Assurance County Championship, played by 18 first-class county teams in four-day matches. There are also three one-day competitions: the Benson and Hedges Cup, the National Westminster Trophy and the AXA Equity & Law Sunday League.

Every year there is a series of five-day Cornhill Insurance Test matches played between England and one or more touring teams from Australia, India, New Zealand, Pakistan, South Africa, Sri Lanka or the West Indies. A team representing England usually tours one or more of these countries in the British winter. A World Cup competition takes place every four years.

The governing body of cricket for women and girls is the Women's Cricket Association. Women's cricket clubs have regular local fixtures and there are regular county matches as well as an area championship. Test match series and a World Cup competition are also played. In 1993 England won the Women's World Cup for the second time.

Cycling

Cycling, one of Britain's fastest growing outdoor activities, includes road and track racing, time-trialling, cyclo-cross (cross country racing), touring and bicycle moto-cross (BMX). All-terrain or mountain bikes have grown significantly in popularity.

The British Cycling Federation has 17,360 members and is the governing body for cycling as a sport. The Cyclists' Touring Club (CTC), with 40,000 members, is the representative body for recreational and urban cycling. The Scottish Cyclists' Union controls the sport in Scotland, with control in Wales resting with the Welsh Cycling Union. In Northern Ireland the sport is controlled by the Ulster Cycling Federation and the Northern Ireland Cycling Federation.

In the last two years two British cyclists—Chris Boardman and Graeme Obree—have broken the one-hour world record; in 1993 Chris Boardman became the first man to break through 52 km. Graeme Obree also broke a world record when winning the world 4,000 metres pursuit title at Hamar, Norway, in 1993.

Major cycling events taking place each year in Britain include the Kelloggs Tour of Britain and the CTC rally at York. In July 1994 Britain hosted two stages of the Tour de France, which were based in Dover and Portsmouth and attracted large numbers of spectators.

Equestrianism

Equestrian activities include recreational riding, endurance riding, carriage driving, one- and three-day eventing and show jumping. The arts of riding and driving are promoted by the British Horse Society, which is concerned with the welfare of horses, road safety, riding rights of way and training. It runs the British Equestrian Centre at Stoneleigh in Warwickshire. With some 60,000 members, the Society is the parent body of the Pony Club and the Riding Club movements, which hold rallies, meetings and competitions culminating in annual national championships.

Leading horse trials, comprising dressage, cross-country and show jumping, are held every year at a number of locations, including Badminton (Avon) and Gatcombe Park (Gloucestershire).

Show jumping is regulated and promoted by the British Show Jumping Association. The major show jumping events each year include the Royal International Horse Show at Hickstead (West Sussex) and the Horse of the Year Show at Wembley in London.

The authority responsible for equestrian competitions (other than racing) at international and Olympic level is the British Equestrian Federation, which co-ordinates the activities of the British Horse Society and the British Show Jumping Association.

In July 1994 the British team of Charlotte Bathe, Karen Dixon, Kristina Gifford and Mary Thomson won the three-day event team title at the World Equestrian Games in The Hague. Karen Dixon won a bronze medal in the individual competition.

Football

Association football is controlled by separate football associations in England, Wales, Scotland and Northern Ireland. In England 340 clubs are affiliated to the English Football Association (FA) and more than 42,000 clubs through regional or district associations. The FA, founded in 1863, and the Football League, founded in 1888, were both the first of their kind in the world.

In England and Wales a major change occurred in 1992 when a new FA Premier League was started, comprising 22 clubs. The remaining 70 full-time professional clubs play in three main divisions run by the Football League. Three Welsh clubs play in the Football League, while the National League of Wales contains 20 semi-professional clubs. In Scotland the Scottish Football League has been increased for 1994–95 to 40 clubs, equally divided into four divisions. In Northern Ireland, 16 semi-professional clubs play in the Irish Football League. During the season, which lasts from August until May, over 2,000 English League matches are played.

The major annual knock-out competitions are the FA Challenge Cup and the Coca-Cola Cup (the League Cup) in England, the Tennents Scottish Cup, the Coca-Cola Cup (the Scottish League Cup), the Irish Cup and the Welsh FA Cup.

England is to host the European Championships finals in 1996.

Golf

The Royal and Ancient Golf Club (R & A), situated at St Andrews in Scotland, is the ruling authority of the sport for most of the world. The Golfing Union of Ireland and parallel unions in Wales, Scotland and England are the national governing bodies for men's amateur golf. These bodies co-operate with the R & A and are represented on the Council of National Golf Unions, which is the British co-ordinating body responsible for handicapping and organising international matches. Women's amateur golf is governed by the Ladies' Golf Union.

Club professional golf is governed by the Professional Golfers' Association (PGA) and the Women's PGA. For tournament professionals the governing bodies are the PGA European Tour and the Women Professional Golfers' European Tour Ltd.

The main event of the British golfing year is the Open Championship, one of the world's leading tournaments. Other important events include the Walker Cup and Curtis Cup matches for amateurs, played between Great Britain and Ireland and the United States, and the Ryder Cup match for professionals, played between Europe and the United States.

There are about 1,900 golf courses in Britain. Among the many famous courses, where the British Open Championship is held, are Turnberry (which hosted the 1994 Open), Muirfield, St Andrews, Troon, Royal Birkdale, Royal Lytham St Annes and Royal St George's (at Sandwich). Three of the top 20 players in the men's world rankings are British: Nick Faldo, Ian Woosnam and Colin Montgomerie.

Greyhound Racing

Greyhound racing is one of Britain's most popular spectator sports and takes place at 37 major tracks. Meetings are usually held three times a week at each track, with at least ten races a meeting. The main event of the year is the Greyhound Derby, run in June at Wimbledon Stadium, London. There are also about 50 mainly small tracks which operate independently. Like the major tracks, they are licensed by local authorities.

The rules for the sport are drawn up by the National Greyhound Racing Club, the sport's judicial and administrative body. The representative body is the British Greyhound Racing Board.

Gymnastics

Gymnastics is divided into four main disciplines: artistic (or Olympic) gymnastics, rhythmic gymnastics, sports acrobatics and general gymnastics. Both men and women compete in artistic gymnastics, although the apparatus used differs. Rhythmic gymnastics is for women only and consists of routines performed to music with ribbon, balls, clubs, hoop and rope. Sports acrobatics is gymnastics with people rather than apparatus. General gymnastics is non-competitive and is available to all age groups and to people with special needs.

The governing body for the sport is the British Amateur Gymnastics Association (BAGA). Over the past decade the number of clubs affiliated to the BAGA has nearly doubled. The sport is particularly popular with schoolchildren and young adults, and it is estimated that between 3 and 4 million schoolchildren take part in some form of gymnastics every day.

At the 1993 World Gymnastics Championships in Birmingham Neil Thomas became the first British medallist ever in world-class gymnastics when he won the silver medal in the floor exercise.

Highland Games

Scottish Highland Games cover a wide range of athletic competitions in addition to activities such as dancing and piping competitions. The main events include running, cycling, throwing the hammer, tossing the caber and putting the shot.

Over 70 gatherings of various kinds take place throughout Scotland, the most famous of which include the annual Braemar Gathering and the Argyllshire and Cowal Gatherings.

The Scottish Games Association is the official governing body responsible for athletic sports and games at Highland and Border events in Scotland.

Hockey

The modern game of hockey was started by the Hockey Association (of England), which acts as the governing body for men's hockey. Parallel associations serve in Wales and Ireland. In Scotland an association covers both men's and women's hockey.

Levels of sponsorship and participation have increased in recent years following British success at the 1988 and 1992 Olympics. Cup competitions and leagues exist at national, divisional or district, and club levels, both indoors (six-a-side) and outdoors, and there are regular international matches.

The controlling body of women's hockey in England is the All England Women's Hockey Association; separate associations regulate the sport in Scotland, Wales and Ireland. League, county, club and school championships for both outdoor and indoor hockey are played annually in England. Regular international matches are also played.

Traditionally hockey has been played on grass pitches, but recently there has been an increase in the use of artificial pitches, which allow a faster, more free-flowing game. All major competitions are now played on an artificial surface.

Horse Racing

Horse racing takes two forms—flat racing, and National Hunt (steeplechasing and hurdle racing). The main flat race season runs from late March to early November, but following the introduction of all-weather racing in 1989 flat race meetings now take place throughout the year. The Derby, run at Epsom, is the outstanding event in the flat racing calendar. Other classic races are: the Two Thousand Guineas and the One Thousand Guineas, both run at Newmarket; the Oaks (Epsom); and the St Leger (Doncaster). Floodlit racing was introduced in December 1993 at Wolverhampton all-weather racecourse. Britain has 59 racecourses and about 12,000 horses currently in training.

The National Hunt season runs from late July/early August to early June, but in 1995 for the first time there will be some meetings in the period from early

June to late July. The most important meeting is the National Hunt Festival held at Cheltenham in March, which features the Gold Cup and the Champion Hurdle. The Grand National, run at Aintree, near Liverpool, is the world's best-known steeplechase and dates from 1839. In 1994 Richard Dunwoody became only the fourth National Hunt jockey to ride over 1,000 winners in Britain.

In 1993 the British Horseracing Board was established as the governing authority for racing in Britain. Its responsibilities include the fixture list, race programmes, the financing of racing administration, relations with the Government and the betting industry, and central marketing. The Jockey Club, as the regulatory authority, remains responsible for licensing, discipline and security.

Ice Skating

Ice skating takes three main forms: figure skating (solo and pairs), ice dancing and speed-skating (indoor and outdoor). The governing body is the National Ice Skating Association of United Kingdom Ltd.

Participation in ice skating is concentrated among the under-25s, and is one of the few sports that attracts more female than male participants as individuals. There are over 70 rinks in Britain; almost half have opened since 1985.

British couples have won the world ice dance championship 17 times. Jayne Torvill and Christopher Dean, who won four consecutive world championships between 1981 and 1984, returned to amateur competition for a short time in 1994 following a rule change regarding professional status. The couple won a gold medal at the European Championships in Copenhagen and a bronze medal at the 1994 Winter Olympics in Lillehammer, Norway. A bronze was also won by Nicky Gooch in the indoor speed skating, making it Britain's best performance at a Winter Olympics since 1948.

Judo

Judo, an individual combat sport derived from the ancient Japanese art of ju-jitsu, is popular not only as a competitive sport and self-defence technique, but also as a means of general fitness training. An internationally recognised grading system is in operation through the sport's governing body, the British Judo Association.

In the 1992 Olympics women's judo was included for the first time, and Britain won a total of four medals in the women's and men's events. Britain has won medals for judo at every Olympic Games since 1972.

At the 1993 World Judo Championships Nicola Fairbrother won a gold medal in the lightweight category.

Keep Fit

Various forms of movement and exercise activities are practised in Britain. In March 1994 the Sports Council launched the Exercise Association of England, as an impartial advisory authority for the organisations involved in these activities. The Keep Fit Association, one of the largest governing bodies in England, receives funding from the Sports Council to promote physical fitness and a positive attitude to health in England. Its national certificated training scheme for keep fit teachers is recognised by local education authorities throughout Britain. Autonomous associations serve Scotland, Wales and Northern Ireland.

Martial Arts

A broad range of martial arts, mainly derived from Japan, the People's Republic of China, Taiwan, Hong Kong and Korea, has been introduced into Britain during the 20th century. There are recognised governing bodies responsible for their own activities in karate, ju-jitsu, aikido, Chinese martial arts, kendo, taekwondo and tang soo do. The most popular martial art is karate, with over 100,000 participants.

Following a review of martial arts organisations undertaken in 1990, the Sports Council has set up an Advisory Group on Martial Arts to provide a forum for discussing martial arts issues.

Motor-car Sports

The main four-wheeled motor sports include motor racing, autocross, rallycross, rallying and karting. In motor racing the Grand Prix Formula 1 World Championship is the major form of the sport.

The governing body for four-wheeled motor sport in Britain is the RAC (Royal Automobile Club) Motor Sports Association. The Association issues licences for a variety of motoring competitions and organises the Network Q RAC Rally, an event in the contest for the World Rally Championship, and the British Grand Prix, which is held at Silverstone as part of the Formula 1 World Championship.

In 1993 Nigel Mansell became the first person to win the IndyCar World Series Championship in his debut year and the only driver to win the Formula 1 world championship and IndyCar titles in successive years. By October 1994 Damon Hill had recorded eight Grand Prix victories in his first two full seasons of Formula 1 racing.

British car constructors, including Lotus, McLaren and Williams, have enjoyed outstanding success in Grand Prix racing and many other forms of racing, and Britain has had seven world champion motor racing drivers.

Motor-cycle Sports

Motor-cycle sports include road racing, moto-cross, grass track, speedway, trials, drag racing and sprint. It is estimated that there are between 40,000 and 50,000 competitive motor cyclists in Britain.

The governing bodies of the sport are the Auto-Cycle Union in England and Wales, the Scottish Auto-Cycle Union and Motor Cycle Union of Ireland (in Northern Ireland). The major events of the year include the Isle of Man TT races and the British Road Race Grand Prix. The Auto-Cycle Union provides off-road training by approved instructors for riders of all ages.

Mountaineering

All forms of mountaineering, which includes mountain walking and rock-climbing, are growing in popularity. A recent survey estimated that there were 700,000 climbers in Britain. The representative body is the British Mountaineering Council (BMC), which works closely with the Mountaineering Councils of Scotland and Ireland. The main areas of work include access and conservation. There are over 300 mountaineering and climbing clubs in Britain, and four National Centres for mountaineering activities run by the Sports Councils (see pp. 490–1).

British mountaineers have played a leading role in the exploration of the world's great mountain ranges. The best-known is Chris Bonington, who has climbed Everest and led many other successful expeditions. Some of the world's hardest rock climbs are found on cliffs in Britain, and leading British climbers, such as Jerry Moffat and Ben Moon, have set new standards of difficulty on cliffs overseas. The BMC sends a team to international competitions on artificial climbing walls, and the first world champion in this relatively new sport was Simon Nadin in 1989.

Netball

More than 60,000 adults play netball regularly in England and a further 1 million participants play in schools. The sport is played almost exclusively by women and girls both indoors and outdoors.

The All England Netball Association is the governing body in England. Scotland, Wales and Northern Ireland have their own governing bodies. The number of clubs affiliated to the All England Association has more than doubled in recent years.

The 1995 World Netball Championships are to be held at the National Indoor Arena in Birmingham.

Rowing

Rowing is taught in many schools, universities and rowing clubs throughout Britain. The main types of boats are single, pairs and double sculls, fours and eights. The governing body in England is the Amateur Rowing Association; similar bodies regulate the sport in Scotland, Wales and Northern Ireland.

The University Boat Race, between eight-oared crews from Oxford and Cambridge, has been rowed on the Thames almost every spring since 1836. The Head of the River Race, also on the Thames, is the largest assembly of racing craft in the world, with more than 420 eights racing in procession. At the Henley Regatta in Oxfordshire crews from all over the world compete each July in various kinds of race over a straight course of 1 mile 550 yards (about 2.1 km).

At the World Rowing Championships in September 1994 Britain won three gold medals: the coxless pairs (Steven Redgrave and Matthew Pinsent), lightweight single sculls (Peter Haining), and the men's lightweight eights.

Rugby Football

The amateur sport of rugby union football (a 15-a-side game) has been played in Britain since the first half of the 19th century. It is played under the auspices of the Rugby Football Union in England and parallel bodies in Wales, Scotland and Ireland (for the Irish Republic and Northern Ireland).

The Five Nations Championship between England, Scotland, Wales, Ireland and France is contested each year, and in 1994 was won by Wales. Overseas tours are undertaken by the national sides and by the British Lions, a team representing Great Britain and Ireland. Tours are also made to Britain by teams representing the major rugby-playing nations. There are important domestic competitions such as the divisional and county championships in England and the league and national club knock-out competitions in England and Wales.

The Rugby World Cup is held every four years and in 1991 England were runners-up in the final at Twickenham. In April 1994 England won the Women's World Cup.

Tournaments of seven-a-side rugby union take place, the most famous being the Middlesex Sevens, held every year at Twickenham. An inaugural World Cup

Sevens, held in Edinburgh in 1993, was won by England. Youngsters aged six and upwards are often introduced to the game through mini rugby, which is played on smaller pitches and involves a minimum of physical contact.

Rugby league (a 13-a-side game) has its own distinct set of rules, but has kept many of the features of the union game. However, unlike rugby union, which is played nationally, it is concentrated in the north of England, although an amateur version of the game is played throughout the country.

The governing body of the professional game is the Rugby Football League, which sends touring teams representing Great Britain to Australia, New Zealand and Papua New Guinea; annual matches are also played against France. The Challenge Cup Final, the major club match of the season, is played at Wembley Stadium in London. There are two divisions of the League, each with 16 teams. The amateur game is governed by the British Amateur Rugby League Association.

Skiing

Skiing takes place in Scotland from December to May and also at several English locations when there is sufficient snow. The five established winter sports areas in Scotland are Cairngorm, Glencoe, Glenshee, the Lecht and Nevis Range, all of which have a full range of ski-lifts, prepared ski runs and professional instructors.

There are over 115 artificial or dry ski-slopes located throughout Britain, and it is estimated that 1.5 million people in Britain take part in the sport. The sport's governing body is the British Ski Federation.

Snooker and Billiards

Snooker has greatly increased in popularity in recent years and become a major spectator sport as a result of extensive television coverage of the professional tournaments. It is estimated that between 7 and 8 million people now play the game.

British players have an outstanding record in snooker and have dominated the major professional championships. The main tournament is the annual Embassy World Professional Championship, held in Sheffield. In the 1980s Steve Davis won the world title six times and in 1994 Stephen Hendry became world champion for the fourth time.

The controlling body for the non-professional game in England is the English Association for Snooker and Billiards. Scotland, Wales and Northern Ireland have separate associations. The World Professional Billiards and Snooker Association is responsible for professional players, organises all world-ranking professional events and holds the copyright for the rules.

A growing number of women play snooker and billiards. Their representative body is the World Ladies' Billiards and Snooker Association, with around 250 members. A women's world snooker championship is played every year in London. The Embassy World Professional Championship was opened to women in 1992.

Squash

The governing body for squash in England is the Squash Rackets Association; there are separate governing bodies in Wales, Scotland and Northern Ireland. The British Open Championships is one of the major world events in the sport.

The number of players in Britain is estimated at over 2 million, of whom more than 500,000 compete regularly in inter-club league competitions. There are nearly 9,000 squash courts in England. The main providers of facilities are member clubs, commercial organisations and local authorities.

Swimming

Swimming is enjoyed by millions of people with a wide range of abilities from all age groups. All forms of competitive swimming are governed by the Amateur Swimming Association (ASA) in England and by similar associations in Scotland and Wales. These three associations combine to form the Amateur Swimming Federation of Great Britain, which acts as the co-ordinating body for the selection of Great Britain teams and

the organisation of international competitions. Northern Ireland forms part of the Irish Amateur Swimming Association. Instruction and coaching are provided by qualified teachers and coaches who hold certificates awarded mainly by the ASA.

Britain won eight medals at the inaugural World Short Course Championships in Palma, Mallorca, in December 1993 and finished fourth in the overall medals table. Gold medals were won by Nick Gillingham in the 200 metres breaststroke, Karen Pickering in the 200 metres freestyle and Mark Foster in the 50 metres freestyle.

Table Tennis

Table tennis is played by a broad range of adults, with men far outnumbering women. The sport is particularly popular in schools and youth clubs, and is also a major recreational and competitive sport for people with disabilities.

The governing body in England is the English Table Tennis Association. There are separate governing bodies in Scotland, Wales and Northern Ireland.

Tennis

The controlling body for tennis in Great Britain is the Lawn Tennis Association (LTA), to which the Welsh and Scottish LTAs are affiliated. The equivalent body covering Northern Ireland is Tennis Ireland (which covers the whole of Ireland).

The main tournament is the annual Wimbledon fortnight, one of the four tennis 'Grand Slam' tournaments. This draws large crowds to the All England Club, and the tournament is covered extensively on television. Prize money has increased dramatically over the last decade and totalled £5.7 million in 1994. Since 1981 the All England Club has donated over £100 million to the LTA.

There are national and county championships and national competitions for boys' and girls' schools. Short tennis has been introduced to encourage children aged five and over to take part in the sport. The game uses a court of similar size to a badminton court and is played in over 3,000 schools and in leisure centres. In all, about 3 million people play tennis in Britain. There has been a big increase in the number of indoor courts in the last decade.

Tenpin Bowling

It is estimated that about 4.8 million people take part in tenpin bowling every year in Britain. There are over 200 national tournaments and an annual National Championship.

Britain has over 200 indoor bowling centres, the first having opened in 1960. More than 30,000 people belong to the sport's governing body, the British Tenpin Bowling Association.

Volleyball

Volleyball is played both indoors and outdoors, and is particularly popular among schoolchildren and college students. Minivolley is a version of the game adapted for children under 13.

The English Volleyball Association and parallel associations in Scotland, Wales and Northern Ireland act as the sport's governing bodies. The British Volleyball Federation meets regularly to discuss interests of common concern and to draw up policies.

Yachting

Yachting comprises sailing, powerboating and windsurfing on both inland and offshore waters. Offshore racing takes place between one-design classes or under handicap, which provides level racing for boats of different size and shape. The most well-known ocean races include the Whitbread Round The World Yacht Race and the Fastnet Race.

Powerboat racing has two main forms: inland circuit racing and offshore racing. Events take place at many locations, including Liverpool and Cardiff docks.

The Royal Yachting Association is the governing body for all yachting in Britain. It is estimated that about 3 million people participate in the sport.

Further Reading

Sport and Leisure. Aspects of Britain series, HMSO, 1994.
A Digest of Sports Statistics for the UK. The Sports Council. £25.

Appendices
and Index

Government Departments and Agencies

An outline of the principal functions of the main government departments and executive agencies (see p. 64) is given below.

Cabinet ministries are indicated by an asterisk. Executive agencies for which the Secretaries of State for Northern Ireland, Scotland or Wales are responsible appear in italics. Executive agencies are normally listed under the relevant department, although in some cases they are included within the description of the departments' responsibilities.

The work of many of the departments and agencies listed below covers Britain as a whole. Where this is not the case, the following abbreviations are used:

- (GB) for functions covering England, Wales and Scotland;
- (E,W & NI) for those covering England, Wales and Northern Ireland;
- (E & W) for those covering England and Wales; and
- (E) for those concerned with England only.

The principal address and telephone number of each department are given. For details of the addresses of executive agencies see the Civil Service Year Book.

The Cabinet Office and the responsibilities of the Office of Public Service and Science—OPSS—are described on p. 63.

Cabinet Office (Office of Public Service and Science)
70 Whitehall, London SW1A 2AS
Tel: 0171 271 1234

Executive Agencies

Chessington Computer Centre
Civil Service College
Civil Service Occupational Health Service
Recruitment and Assessment Services Agency

Two further agencies report to the Chancellor of the Duchy of Lancaster but are departments in their own right rather than part of OPSS. They are:

Central Office of Information (see p. 512)
HMSO (Her Majesty's Stationery Office—see p. 512)

Economic Affairs

*Ministry of Agriculture, Fisheries and Food
Whitehall Place, London SW1A 2HH
Tel: 0171 270 3000
Policies for agriculture, horticulture, fisheries and food; responsibilities for related environmental and rural issues (E); food policies.

Executive Agencies

ADAS (Agricultural Development and Advisory Service)
Central Science Laboratory
Central Veterinary Laboratory
Intervention Board
Pesticides Safety Directorate
Veterinary Medicines Directorate

*Department of Employment
Caxton House, Tothill Street, London
SW1H 9NF Tel: 0171 273 3000
Employment policy; training policy, youth
education and business start-up; vocational
qualifications; health and safety at work;
industrial relations; equal opportunities;
co-ordinating government policy on issues
of particular concern to women; statistics
on labour and industrial matters (GB); the
Careers Service (E); international representation
on employment and training matters.

Executive Agency

Employment Service

*Department of Trade and Industry
Ashdown House, 123 Victoria Street, London
SW1E 6RB Tel: 0171 215 5000
Industrial and commercial affairs; promotion of
new enterprise and competition; information
about new business methods and opportunities;
investor protection and consumer affairs.
Specific responsibilities include innovation
policy; regional industrial policy and inward
investment promotion; small businesses;
management best practice and business/education
links; deregulation; international trade policy;
commercial relations and export promotion;
competition policy; company law;
insolvency; radio regulation; patents and
copyright protection (GB); the development of
new sources of energy and the Government's
relations with the energy industries.

Executive Agencies
Accounts Services Agency
Companies House
Insolvency Service
Laboratory of the Government Chemist
NEL (National Engineering Laboratory)
National Physical Laboratory
National Weights and Measures Laboratory
Patent Office
Radiocommunications Agency

*Department of Transport
2 Marsham Street, London SW1P 3EB
Tel: 0171 276 3000

Land, sea and air transport; domestic and
international civil aviation; international
transport agreements; shipping and the ports
industry; marine pollution; regulation of
drivers and vehicles (including road safety);
regulation of the road haulage industry;
transport and the environment. Motorways
and trunk roads; oversight of local authority
transport (E). Sponsorship of London
Transport (E), British Rail (GB) and the
Civil Aviation Authority.

Executive Agencies
Coastguard Agency
Driver and Vehicle Licensing Agency
Driving Standards Agency
Highways Agency
Marine Safety Agency
Transport Research Laboratory
Vehicle Certification Agency
Vehicle Inspectorate

*HM Treasury
Parliament Street, London SW1P 3AG
Tel: 0171 270 3000
Oversight of tax and monetary policy;
planning and control of public spending;
international financial relations; supervision
of the financial system; and responsibility for
a range of Civil Service management issues.

HM Customs and Excise
New King's Beam House, 22 Upper Ground,
London SE1 9PJ Tel: 0171 620 1313
Collecting and accounting for Customs and
Excise revenues, including value added tax;
agency functions, including controlling
certain imports and exports and compiling
trade statistics.

**ECGD (Export Credits Guarantee
Department)**
2 Exchange Tower, Harbour Exchange
Square, London E14 9GS Tel: 0171 512 7000
Provision of insurance for project
exporters against the risk of not being paid
for goods and services; access to bank finance
for exports; insurance cover for new

investment overseas; reinsurance to private sector insurance companies offering export credit insurance.

Board of Inland Revenue
Somerset House, London WC2R 1LB
Tel: 0171 438 6622
Administration and collection of direct taxes; valuation of property (GB).

Executive Agency

Valuation Office

PAYMASTER: Office of HM Paymaster General
Sutherland House, Russell Way, Crawley, West Sussex RH10 1UH Tel: 01293 560999
An executive agency providing banking services for government departments other than the Boards of Inland Revenue and Customs and Excise, and the administration and payment of public service pensions.

Central Statistical Office
Great George Street, London SW1P 3AQ
Tel: 0171 270 3000
Preparing and interpreting key economic statistics needed for government policies; collecting and publishing business statistics; publishing annual and monthly statistical digests.

REGULATORY BODIES

The Office of Electricity Regulation (OFFER)
Hagley House, Hagley Road, Birmingham B16 8QG Tel: 0121 456 2100
Regulating and monitoring the electricity supply industry; promoting competition in the generation and supply of electricity; ensuring that companies comply with the licences under which they operate; protecting customers' interests (GB).

Office of Gas Supply (OFGAS)
Stockley House, 130 Wilton Road, London SW1V 1LQ Tel: 0171 828 0898
Regulating and monitoring British Gas to ensure value for money for customers, and

granting authorisations to other suppliers of gas through pipes; enabling development of competition in the industrial market.

Office of the National Lottery (OFLOT)
PO Box 4465, London SW1Y 5XL
Tel: 0171 240 4624
Responsible for the grant, variation and enforcement of licences to run the National Lottery and promote lotteries as part of it.

Office for Standards in Education (OFSTED)
Elizabeth House, York Road, London SE1 7PH Tel: 0171 925 6800
Monitoring standards in English schools; regulating the work of independent registered schools inspectors (E).

Office of Telecommunications (OFTEL)
50 Ludgate Hill, London EC4M 7JJ
Tel: 0171 634 8700
Monitoring telecommunications operators' licences; enforcing competition legislation; representing users' interests.

Office of Water Services (OFWAT)
Centre City Tower, 7 Hill Street, Birmingham B5 4UA Tel: 0121 625 1300
Monitoring the activities of companies appointed as water and sewerage undertakers (E & W); regulating of prices and representing customers' interests.

Legal Affairs

*The Lord Chancellor's Department
Trevelyan House, 30 Great Peter Street, London SW1P 2BY Tel: 0171 210 8500
Administration of the Supreme Court (Court of Appeal, High Court and Crown Court), the county courts, ministerial responsibility for the locally administered

magistrates' courts (E & W), together
with certain tribunals and the Council on
Tribunals, and the Official Solicitor's
Department.

All work relating to judicial and quasi-
judicial appointments (see p. 104). Overall
responsibility for civil and criminal legal aid,
for the Law Commission and for the
promotion of general reforms in the civil
law. Lead responsibility for private
international law. The Legal Services
Ombudsman and the Advisory Committee
on Legal Education and Conduct are
independent of the Department but report
to the Lord Chancellor. The Lord
Chancellor also has responsibility for the
Northern Ireland Court Service; national
archives (maintained by the Public Record
Office—see below) and the Public Trust
Office. Except for the Northern Ireland
Court Service, the Lord Chancellor's remit
covers England and Wales only.

Executive Agencies

HM Land Registry
Public Record Office
Public Trust Office

Crown Prosecution Service
50 Ludgate Hill, London EC4M 7EX
Tel: 0171 273 8000
An independent organisation responsible for
the prosecution of criminal cases resulting
from police investigations, headed by the
Director of Public Prosecutions and
accountable to Parliament through the
Attorney General, superintending minister
for the service (E & W).

Legal Secretariat to the Law Officers
Attorney General's Chambers, 9
Buckingham Gate, London SW1E 6JP
Tel: 0171 828 7155
Supporting the Law Officers of the Crown
(Attorney General and Solicitor General) in
their functions as the Government's
principal legal advisers (E, W & NI).

The Attorney General, who is also
Attorney General for Northern Ireland, is
the Minister responsible for the Treasury
Solicitor's Department (see below), and has

a statutory duty to superintend the Crown
Prosecution Service (see above), the
Serious Fraud Office (see below), and the
Director of Public Prosecutions for
Northern Ireland.

Parliamentary Counsel
36 Whitehall, London SW1A 2AY
Tel: 0171 210 6633
Drafting of government Bills (except those
relating exclusively to Scotland); advising
departments on parliamentary procedure
(E, W & NI).

**HM Procurator General and Treasury
Solicitor's Department**
Queen Anne's Chambers, 28 Broadway,
London SW1H 9JS Tel: 0171 210 3000
Provision of a legal service for a large number
of government departments. Duties include
instructing Parliamentary Counsel on Bills
and drafting subordinate legislation;
providing litigation and, through an executive
agency, conveyancing services; and giving
general advice on interpreting and applying
the law (E & W).

Executive Agency

The Government Property Lawyers

**Lord Advocate's Department and Crown
Office** (see p. 514)

Serious Fraud Office
Elm House, 10–16 Elm Street, London
WC1X 0BJ Tel: 0171 239 7272
Investigating and prosecuting serious and
complex fraud under the superintendence of
the Attorney General (E, W & NI).

External Affairs and Defence

*Ministry of Defence
Main Building, Whitehall, London SW1A
2HB Tel: 0171 218 9000
Defence policy and control and
administration of the armed services.

Defence Agencies

Army Base Repair Organisation
Chemical and Biological Defence Establishment
Defence Accounts Agency
Defence Analytical Services Agency
Defence Animal Centre
Defence Operational Analysis Centre
Defence Postal and Courier Services Agency
Defence Research Agency
Duke of York's Royal Military School
Hydrographic Office
Meteorological Office
Military Survey
Naval Aircraft Repair Organisation
Queen Victoria School
RAF Support Command's Maintenance
   Group Defence Agency
RAF Training Group
Service Children's Schools (North West Europe)

Foreign & Commonwealth Office

King Charles Street, London SW1A 2AH
Tel: 0171 270 3000
Conduct of Britain's overseas relations, including advising on policy, negotiating with overseas governments and conducting business in international organisations, promoting British exports and trade generally; administering aid (see below). Presenting British ideas, policies and objectives to the people of overseas countries; administering the remaining dependent territories; and protecting British interests abroad, including the welfare of British citizens.

Executive Agency

Wilton Park Conference Centre

*Overseas Development Administration

94 Victoria Street, London SW1E 5JL
Tel: 0171 917 7000
Responsibility for Britain's overseas aid to developing countries, for global environmental assistance, and also for the joint administration, with the Foreign & Commonwealth Office, of assistance to Eastern Europe and the countries of the former Soviet Union. Responsibility for overseas superannuation.

Executive Agency

Natural Resources Institute

Social Affairs, the Environment and Culture

*Department for Education

Sanctuary Buildings, Great Smith Street, London SW1P 3BT Tel: 0171 925 5000
Formulates and promotes policies for education (E); responsibility for the Government's relations with universities (GB).

Executive Agency

Teachers' Pensions Agency

*Department of the Environment

2 Marsham Street, London SW1P 3EB
Tel: 0171 276 0900
Policies for local government finance and structure; land use planning; housing; construction industry; energy efficiency; environmental protection; water industry and the British Waterways Board; urban and rural regeneration; countryside and wildlife protection (E); and the management of the Government estate, through Property Holdings (GB).

Executive Agencies

Building Research Establishment
The Buying Agency
Planning Inspectorate
Queen Elizabeth II Conference Centre
The Security Facilities Executive

The Ordnance Survey (see p. 512) is not part of the Department of the Environment, but reports to the Secretary of State for the Environment.

*Department of Health

Richmond House, 79 Whitehall, London SW1A 2NS Tel: 0171 210 3000
National Health Service; personal social services provided by local authorities; and certain aspects of public health, including hygiene (E).

Executive Agencies

Medicines Control Agency
Medical Devices Agency
NHS Estates
NHS Pensions Agency

Home Office

50 Queen Anne's Gate, London SW1H 9AT
Tel: 0171 273 3000
Administration of justice; criminal law;
treatment of offenders, including probation and
the prison service; the police; crime prevention;
fire service and emergency planning; licensing
laws; regulation of firearms and dangerous
drugs; electoral matters and local legislation (E
& W). Gaming (GB). Passports, immigration
and nationality; race relations; royal matters.
Responsibilities relating to the Channel Islands
and the Isle of Man.

Executive Agencies

Fire Service College
Forensic Science Service
HM Prison Service
United Kingdom Passport Agency

*Department of National Heritage

2-4 Cockspur Street, London SW1Y 5DH
Tel: 0171 211 6000.
The arts; public libraries; national museums
and galleries; tourism; sport; heritage—
including listing and scheduling buildings, and
royal parks and palaces (E);
broadcasting; press regulation; film industry;
export licensing of antiques; the National Lottery.

Executive Agencies

Historic Royal Palaces Agency
Royal Parks Agency

*Social Security Department

Richmond House, 79 Whitehall, London
SW1A 2NS Tel: 0171 210 3000
The social security system (GB).

Executive Agencies

Benefits Agency
Child Support Agency
Contributions Agency

Information Technology Services Agency
Resettlement Agency
War Pensions Agency

Central Office of Information

Hercules Road, London SE1 7DU
Tel: 0171 928 2345
An executive agency procuring publicity
material and other information services on
behalf of government departments and
publicly funded organisations.

HMSO (Her Majesty's Stationery Office)

St Crispins, Duke Street, Norwich NR3 1PD
and Sovereign House, Botolph Street,
Norwich NR3 1DN Tel: 01603 622211
An executive agency providing stationery,
office machinery and furniture, printing and
related services to Parliament, government
departments and other public bodies.
Publishing and selling government documents.

Ordnance Survey

Romsey Road, Maybush, Southampton SO16
4GU Tel: 01703 792000
An executive agency providing official
surveying, mapping and associated scientific
work covering Great Britain and some
overseas countries.

Office of Population Censuses and Surveys

St Catherine's House, 10 Kingsway, London
WC2B 6JP Tel: 0171 242 0262
A department responsible for
administration of the marriage laws and local
registration of births, marriages and deaths;
provision of population estimates and
projections and statistics on health and other
demographic matters; Census of Population
(E & W). Surveys for other government
departments and public bodies (GB).

Northern Ireland

Northern Ireland Office

Stormont, Belfast BT4 3ST
Tel: 01232 520700
Whitehall, London SW1A 2AZ
Tel: 0171 210 3000

Department of Agriculture for Northern Ireland
Development of agricultural, forestry and fishing industries; veterinary, scientific and development services; food and farming policy; and rural development.

Department of Economic Development for Northern Ireland
Promotion of inward investment and development of larger home industry; promotion of enterprise and small business; development of tourism; training and employment through the *Training and Employment Agency;* promotion of industrially relevant research and development; energy; minerals; company regulation; consumer protection; health and safety at work; industrial relations; and equal opportunity in employment.

Department of Education for Northern Ireland
Control of the five education and library boards and education from nursery to further and higher education; youth services; sport and recreation; the arts and culture (including libraries); and the development of community relations within and between schools.

Department of the Environment for Northern Ireland
Environmental protection; housing; planning; roads; transport and traffic management; vehicle licensing and taxation (including the *Driver and Vehicle Testing Agency*); harbours, water and sewage; *Ordnance Survey of Northern Ireland;* maintenance of public records; certain controls over local government; and the *Rate Collection Agency.*

Department of Finance and Personnel
Control of public expenditure; liaison with HM Treasury and the Northern Ireland Office on financial matters, economic and social research and analysis; EC co-ordination charities; *Valuation and Lands Agency;* policies for equal opportunities and personnel management; and management and control of the Northern Ireland Civil Service.

Department of Health and Social Services for Northern Ireland
Health and personal social services and social legislation. Responsibility for the *Northern Ireland Child Support Agency.* The *Social Security Agency (Northern Ireland)* has responsibility for the administration of all social security benefits and the collection of National Insurance contributions.

Scotland

*The Scottish Office
St Andrew's House, Edinburgh EH1 3DG
Tel: 0131 556 8400
Dover House, Whitehall, London SW1A 2AU
Tel: 0171 270 3000
The Scottish Office's responsibilities are discharged principally through its five departments (which include six executive agencies). There are also four smaller departments: the *Registers of Scotland* and the *Scottish Record Office*; the General Register Office for Scotland and the Scottish Courts Administration, which is also responsible to the Lord Advocate for certain legal functions.

Scottish Office Agriculture and Fisheries Department
Promotion and regulation of the agricultural and fishing industries; safeguarding public, plant and animal health welfare; enforcement of fisheries laws and regulations through the *Scottish Fisheries Protection Agency.*

Scottish Office Education Department
Education; student awards (through the *Student Awards Agency for Scotland*); the arts, libraries, museums and galleries, Gaelic language; sport and recreation.

Scottish Office Environment Department
Environment, including environmental protection, nature conservation and the countryside; land-use planning; water supplies and sewerage; local government, including finance; housing; building control; protection and presentation to the public of historic buildings and ancient monuments through *Historic Scotland.*

Scottish Office Home and Health Department

Central administration of law and order (includes police service, criminal justice, legal aid and the *Scottish Prison Service*); National Health Service; fire, home defence and civil emergency services; social work services.

Scottish Office Industry Department

Industrial and regional economic development matters; co-ordination of Scottish Office European interests; employment; training; energy; tourism; urban regeneration; new towns; roads and certain transport functions, particularly in the Highlands and Islands.

Central Services

Services to the five Scottish departments. These include the Office of the Solicitor to the Secretary of State, The Scottish Office Information Directorate, Finance, Personnel, Management and Office Management Divisions.

Lord Advocate's Department

Fielden House, 10 Great College Street, London SW1P 3SL Tel: 0171 276 3000 Provision of legal advice to the Government on issues affecting Scotland; responsibility for drafting government primary legislation relating to Scotland and adapting for Scotland other primary legislation. Provision of advice in matters of parliamentary procedure affecting Scotland.

Crown Office

25 Chambers Street, Edinburgh EH1 12A Tel: 0131 226 2626 Control of all prosecutions in Scotland.

These are directly responsible to the Law Officers and are not part of The Scottish Office.

Wales

*Welsh Office

Cathays Park, Cardiff CF1 3NQ Tel: 01222 825111 Gwydyr House, Whitehall, London SW1A 2ER Tel: 0171 270 3000 Many aspects of Welsh affairs, including health, community care and personal social services; education, except for terms and conditions of service, student awards and the University of Wales; Welsh language and culture; agriculture and fisheries; forestry; local government; housing; water and sewerage; environmental protection; sport; land use, including town and country planning; countryside and nature conservation; new towns; and ancient monuments and historic buildings (through *CADW:Welsh Historic Monuments*).

The Department's responsibilities also include roads; tourism; enterprise and training; selective financial assistance to industry; the Urban Programme and urban investment grants in Wales; the operation of the European Regional Development Fund in Wales and other European Union matters; women's issues; non-departmental public bodies; civil emergencies; all financial aspects of these matters, including Welsh revenue support grant; and oversight responsibilities for economic affairs and regional planning in Wales.

Britain's Economy: Statistical Annex

All the following statistics, apart from some relating to the labour market and retail sales, cover England, Wales, Scotland and Northern Ireland. Some figures may be subject to revision at a later stage.

Gross Domestic Product (GDP)

£ million

	1986	1991	1992	1993
GDP at market prices[a]	384,843	575,321	597,121	630,023
GDP at factor cost[b]	328,272	495,900	516,027	546,120
GDP at factor cost at 1990 prices	424,214	468,913	466,564	475,889
Value indices at current prices —GDP at factor cost (1990 = 100)	68.5	103.6	107.8	114.0
Percentage change since previous year	*+6.5*	*+3.6*	*+4.1*	*+5.8*
Volume indices at 1990 prices—GDP at factor cost	88.6	97.9	97.4	99.4

[a] Market prices are the prices people pay for goods and services.
[b] Factor cost is the cost of goods and services before adding taxes and subtracting subsidies.

Output

	1986	1991	1992	1993
Output of production[a] industries (1990 = 100)	90.1	96.1	95.9	97.9
Output per person employed (1990 = 100)				
Whole economy	96.3	100.4	102.6	105.9
Percentage change since previous year	*–*	*+0.4*	*+2.2*	*+3.2*
Manufacturing	84.6	101.2	105.8	109.8
Percentage change since previous year	*–*	*+1.2*	*+4.5*	*+3.8*

[a] Consists of the mining and quarrying, manufacturing and electricity, gas and water supply industries.

Labour Market[a]

Thousands

	1988	1991	1992	1993	June 1994
Employees in employment	22,266	22,220	21,851	21,493	21,397
Self-employed	3,204	3,383	3,196	3,166	3,266
Unemployment	2,273	2,286	2,765	2,901	2,643
Percentage of workforce	8.0	8.0	9.7	10.3	9.4
Percentage increase in earnings on previous year	n.a.	+8.0	+6.1	+3.4	+3.5

[a] Figures for employees in employment and self-employment are for June each year and are seasonally adjusted. Other figures are annual averages, except for June 1994. The figures for unemployment are seasonally adjusted, while those for earnings are not seasonally adjusted and are for Great Britain.
n.a. = not available.

Retail Sales in Great Britain

	1989	1991	1992	1993
Volume index (average 1990 prices) 1990 =100	99.3	98.9	99.5	103.0
Percentage change since previous year	–	*-1.1*	*+0.6*	*+3.5*
Value in current prices (1990 = 100)	93.5	104.7	108.5	114.7
Percentage change since previous year	–	*+4.7*	*+3.6*	*+5.7*

Prices

(Jan 1987 = 100)	1990	1991	1992	1993	June 1994
Retail Prices Index (RPI)	126.1	133.5	138.5	140.7	144.7
Percentage change since previous year	*+9.5*	*+5.9*	*+3.7*	*+1.6*	*+2.6*
RPI excluding mortgage interest payments	122.1	130.3	136.4	140.5	144.4
Percentage change since previous year	*+8.1*	*+6.7*	*+4.7*	*+3.0*	*+2.4*

Sources

The following Central Statistical Office publications:
United Kingdom National Accounts 1994 Edition
Monthly Digest of Statistics
CSO press notices
Department of Employment *Employment Gazette*

Recent Legislation

The public Acts of Parliament passed since autumn 1993 are listed below. Fourteen Acts were introduced by Private Members; these are indicated by asterisks. All are available from HMSO.

1993

Cardiff Bay Barrage Act 1993. Ch 42. £7.
Consolidated Fund (No 3) Act 1993.
  Ch 52. 65p.
Crofters (Scotland) Act 1993. Ch 44. £8.45.
European Economic Area Act 1993.
  Ch 51. £1.50.
European Parliamentary Elections Act 1993.
  Ch 41. £1.50.
Health Service Commissioners Act 1993.
  Ch 46. £4.30.
*Noise and Statutory Nuisance Act 1993.
  Ch 40. £4.30.
Pension Schemes Act 1993. Ch 48. £16.45.
Pension Schemes (Northern Ireland) Act 1993.
  Ch 49. £15.10.
Probation Service Act 1993. Ch 47. £4.30.
Railways Act 1993. Ch 43. £18.
Scottish Land Court Act 1993. Ch 45. £1.90.
Statute Law (Repeals) Act 1993.
  Ch 50. £8.45.

1994

*Antarctic Act 1994. Ch 15. £3.30.
Appropriation Act 1994. Ch 24. £7.
*Chiropractors Act 1994. Ch 17. £7.
Coal Industry Act 1994. Ch 21. £15.10.
Consolidated Fund Act 1994. Ch 4. 65p.
Education Act 1994. Ch 30. £4.85.
Finance Act 1994. Ch 9. £30.50.
*Firearms (Amendment) Act 1994. Ch 31. 65p.
*Inshore Fishing (Scotland) Act 1994.
  Ch 27. £1.10.

Insolvency Act 1994. Ch 7. £1.90.
*Insolvency (No 2) Act 1994. Ch 12. £1.90.
Intelligence Services Act 1994. Ch 13. £3.80.
*Land Drainage Act 1994. Ch 25. £1.90.
Local Government (Wales) Act 1994.
  Ch 19. £15.10.
*Mental Health (Amendment) Act 1994.
  Ch 6. 65p.
*Merchant Shipping (Salvage and Pollution)
  Act 1994. Ch 28. £4.30.
*New Towns (Amendment) Act 1994.
  Ch 5. 65p.
Non-Domestic Rating Act 1994. Ch 3. £1.50.
*Parliamentary Commissioner Act 1994.
  Ch 14. 65p.
Police and Magistrates' Courts Act 1994.
  Ch 29. £11.
*Race Relations (Remedies) Act 1994.
  Ch 10. £1.10.
*Road Traffic Regulation (Special Events) Act
  1994. Ch 11. £1.90.
Social Security (Contributions) Act 1994.
  Ch 1. 65p.
Social Security (Incapacity for Work) Act
  1994. Ch 18. £6.30.
*State Hospitals (Scotland) Act 1994.
  Ch 16. 65p.
Statutory Sick Pay Act 1994. Ch 2. £1.10.
Sunday Trading Act 1994. Ch 20. £4.30.
Trade Marks Act 1994. Ch 26. £8.40.
Transport Police (Jurisdiction) Act 1994.
  Ch 8. £1.10.
Value Added Tax Act 1994. Ch 23. £16.40.
Vehicle Excise and Registration Act 1994.
  Ch 22. £9.25.

The Citizen's Charter Initiative

A detailed account of the Citizen's Charter initiative is given on pp. 66–8. The publications which launched the initiative and the most recent follow-up report are:

- *The Citizen's Charter. Raising the Standard.* Cm 1599. HMSO, 1991, £8.50. (See p. 66.)
- *The Citizens' Charter for Northern Ireland.* HMSO, 1992, £8.50.
- *The Citizen's Charter Second Report*: 1994. Cm 2540. HMSO, 1994, £12.50. (See p. 66.)

A White Paper on Open Government was published in July 1993—see p. 68. (*Open Government*. Cm 2290. HMSO, £11.)

INDIVIDUAL CHARTERS

The 40 Charters for individual public services, published as part of the Citizen's Charter initiative, with the name of the department or organisation responsible in brackets,[1] are:

Benefits Agency Customer Charter (Benefits Agency)

Charter for Further Education—see p. 423 (Department for Education)

Charter for Higher Education—see p. 423 (Department for Education)

Child Support Agency Charter (Child Support Agency)

Contributors' Charter (Contributions Agency)

Council Tenant's Charter (Department of the Environment)

Courts Charter—see p. 90 (Lord Chancellor's Department, Home Office, Crown Prosecution Service)

Employers' Charter (Contributions Agency)

Jobseeker's Charter—see p. 182 (Employment Service)

London Bus Passenger's Charter (London Buses Ltd)

London Underground Customer Charter—see p. 294 (London Underground Ltd)

Parent's Charter (Department for Education)

Passenger's Charter—see p. 292 (British Rail)

Patient's Charter—see p. 370 (Department of Health)

Redundancy Payments Service Charter (Department of Employment)

Road Users' Charter—see p. 286 (Department of Transport)

Taxpayer's Charter—see p. 162 (Inland Revenue)

Taxpayer's Charter (HM Customs and Excise)

Travellers' Charter (HM Customs and Excise)

Northern Ireland

Bus Passenger's Charter (Ulsterbus)

Charter for Patients and Clients (Northern Ireland Office—Department of Health and Social Services)

Social Security Agency Charter (Northern Ireland Social Security Agency)

Child Support Agency Charter (Northern Ireland Child Support Agency)

Council Tenant's Charter (Northern Ireland Housing Executive)

Courts Charter (Northern Ireland Court Service)

---

[1] The addresses and telephone numbers of government departments are given on pp. 507–14.

Parent's Charter (Northern Ireland Office—Department of Education)

Railway Passenger's Charter (Northern Ireland Railways)

RUC Charter (Royal Ulster Constabulary)

Training and Employment Agency Customer's Charter (Training and Employment Agency, Northern Ireland)

Scotland

Charter for Further Education (see p. 423)

Charter for Higher Education (see p. 423)

Justice Charter (see p. 90)

Parent's Charter

Patient's Charter

Council Tenant's Charter

(All published by The Scottish Office)

Wales

Charter for Further Education (see p. 423)

Charter for Higher Education (see p. 423)

Council Tenant's Charter

Parent's Charter

Patient's Charter

(All published by the Welsh Office in English and Welsh)

Further Information

Information about the charters, including telephone numbers and addresses, can be obtained by calling 01345 223242 (all calls are charged at local rates). The service is available 24 hours a day. For copies of the guide to the Charter Mark awards (see p. 67), ring 0171 270 6304.

Obituaries

Sir Harold Acton, CBE
Historian and aesthete
Born 1904, died February 1994

The Rt Rev Lord Blanch, PC
Archbishop of York, 1975–83
Born 1918, died June 1994

Anthony Burgess
Novelist and critic
Born 1917, died November 1993

Sir Matt Busby, CBE
Football manager
Born 1909, died January 1994

Elias Canetti
Nobel Prize for Literature, 1981
Born 1905, died August 1994

John Curry, OBE
Ice skater and actor
Born 1949, died April 1994

Roy Castle, OBE
Comedian, musician, dancer
Born 1932, died September 1994

Lord Delfont
Theatrical impresario
Born 1909, died September 1994

Alec Dickson, CBE
Founder of Voluntary Service Overseas and
Community Service Volunteers
Born 1914, died September 1994

Lord Farrer-Brown, CBE
First director of the Nuffield Foundation,
Born 1904, died April 1994

Professor Dorothy Hodgkin, OM, FRS
Nobel Prize for Chemistry, 1964
Born 1910, died July 1994

The Earl of Inchcape
Chairman of P&O, 1973–83
Born 1917, died March 1994

Brian Johnston, CBE, MC
Broadcaster and cricket commentator
Born 1912, died January 1994

Sir Wylie McKissock, OBE
Pioneer in neurosurgery
Born 1906, died October 1994

Professor Sir Karl Popper, CH, FRS
Philosopher
Born 1902, died September 1994

Dennis Potter
Television playwright, author and journalist
Born 1935, died June 1994

Brian Redhead
Broadcaster and journalist
Born 1929, died January 1994

Lord Shackleton, KG, OBE, FRS, PC
Leader of the House of Lords and Lord
Privy Seal, 1965–70
Born 1911, died September 1994

John Smith, PC, QC, MP
Leader of the Labour Party and of the
Opposition, 1992–94
Born 1938, died May 1994

Professor Richard Synge, FRS
Nobel Prize for Chemistry, 1952
Born 1914, died August 1994

Jessica Tandy
Stage and film actress
Born 1909, died September 1994

Air Commodore Frederick 'Tommy' Thompson, CBE, DSO, DFC, AFC
Battle of Britain pilot and later AOC Military
Air Traffic Operations
Born 1914, died July 1994

Lord Thorneycroft, CH (formerly Peter
Thorneycroft)
Conservative MP and Government Minister
Born 1909, died June 1994

Billy Wright, CBE
England football captain 90 times
Born 1924, died September 1994

Principal Abbreviations

ACAS: Advisory, Conciliation and Arbitration Service

BBC: British Broadcasting Corporation

BR: British Rail

BT: British Telecommunications plc

CAA: Civil Aviation Authority

CAP: Common Agricultural Policy

CBI: Confederation of British Industry

CCW: Countryside Council for Wales

CO_2: carbon dioxide

CPS: Crown Prosecution Service

DFE: Department for Education

DTI: Department of Trade and Industry

EC: European Community

ECGD: Export Credits Guarantee Department

EFTA: European Free Trade Association

ESAs: Environmentally Sensitive Areas

EU: European Union

FCO: Foreign & Commonwealth Office

GATT: General Agreement on Tariffs and Trade

GDP: gross domestic product

GNP: gross national product

GPs: general practitioners

HMIP: Her Majesty's Inspectorate of Pollution

HMSO: Her Majesty's Stationery Office

HSE: Health and Safety Executive

IPC: integrated pollution control

ITC: Independent Television Commission

ITV: independent television

LEAs: local education authorities

LECs: Local Enterprise Companies

LT: London Transport

MAFF: Ministry of Agriculture, Fisheries and Food

MFA: Multi-Fibre Arrangement

MP: Member of Parliament

NATO: North Atlantic Treaty Organisation

NHS: National Health Service

NO_x: oxides of nitrogen

NRA: National Rivers Authority

ODA: Overseas Development Administration

OECD: Organisation for Economic Co-operation and Development

OPSS: Office of Public Service and Science

plc: public limited company

PSBR: public sector borrowing requirement

RAF: Royal Air Force

R & D: research and development

RPI: Retail Prices Index

SIB: Securities and Investments Board

SNH: Scottish Natural Heritage

SO_2: sulphur dioxide

TECs: Training and Enterprise Councils

TUC: Trades Union Congress

TWh: terawatt hours

UKCS: United Kingdom Continental Shelf

UN: United Nations

VAT: value added tax

WEU: Western European Union

Index

Acknowledgments for photographs

Cover: COI Pictures; **Natural History** (photographs in colour sections listed top to bottom and left to right): COI Pictures; **Multi-cultural Britain:** COI Pictures; Scottish Dancing—PA Photo Library; **Industrial Heritage:** COI Pictures, Wales Tourist Board; **Environmental Design:** BBC Photo Library, COI Pictures; **Rural Development:** Department of Agriculture for Northern Ireland; Rural Development Commission/Gary-John Norman; The Scottish Highland Photo Library/Edward Garner; Development Board for Rural Wales/Steve Benbow; **Computer Technology:** COI Pictures; **Overseas Trade:** COI Pictures; **Channel Tunnel:** QA Photos, stamps—COI Pictures; **World War II Remembered:** COI Pictures, PA Photo Library; **Astronomy:** Royal Greenwich Observatory; **Archaeology:** COI Pictures/Ann Katrin-Purkis, COI Pictures; **Housing:** Countryside Properties plc; Soho Housing Association Ltd; **Education:** COI Pictures, Department for Education (three pictures); **Medicine:** COI Pictures; **Religion:** COI Pictures; **Food and Drink:** COI Pictures, Tŷ Nant Spring Water Limited; **Women in Sport:** Kit Houghton, COI Pictures; **Royal Heritage:** Her Majesty Queen Elizabeth II, Crown Copyright/P. Gates; **Film and Animation:** COI Pictures, Aardman Animations; **Visual Arts:** COI Pictures.

Main railway passenger routes

Electrified major lines

Other major lines

Other routes

Channel Tunnel

Inverness

Aberdeen

Dundee

Perth

Stirling

Glasgow

Edinburgh

Berwick

Newcastle upon Tyne

Londonderry

Larne

Carlisle

Belfast

Darlington

Middlesbrough

Scarborough

Harrogate

York

Hull

Bradford

Leeds

Blackpool

Preston

Manchester

Doncaster

Grimsby

Liverpool

Sheffield

Holyhead

Nottingham

Crewe

Derby

King's Lynn

Stafford

Norwich

Shrewsbury

Leicester

Peterborough

Birmingham

Coventry

Ipswich

Worcester

Cambridge

Harwich

Hereford

Colchester

Fishguard

Gloucester

Oxford

London

Margate

Swansea

Newport

Swindon

Ashford

Dover

Cardiff

Bristol

Bath

Reading

Folkestone

Gatwick

Salisbury

Hastings

Taunton

Southampton

Portsmouth

Brighton

Eastbourne

Bournemouth

Exeter

Weymouth

Newton Abbot

Plymouth

Penzance

0 20 40 60 80 100 km

0 20 40 60 miles